JUSTICE
LEAGUE
THE SIXTH DIMENSION

writers

SCOTT SNYDER
JORGE JIMENEZ
JAMES TYNION IV

artists

JORGE JIMENEZ
JAVIER FERNANDEZ
FRANCIS MANAPUL
DANIEL SAMPERE
BRUNO REDONDO
JUAN ALBARRAN

colorists

ALEJANDRO SANCHEZ
HI-FI
FRANCIS MANAPUL

letterer

TOM NAPOLITANO

collection cover artists

JORGE JIMENEZ
and ALEJANDRO SANCHEZ

SUPERMAN created by **JERRY SIEGEL** and **JOE SHUSTER**
SUPERBOY created by **JERRY SIEGEL**
By special arranagement with the Jerry Siegel family

VOL.
4

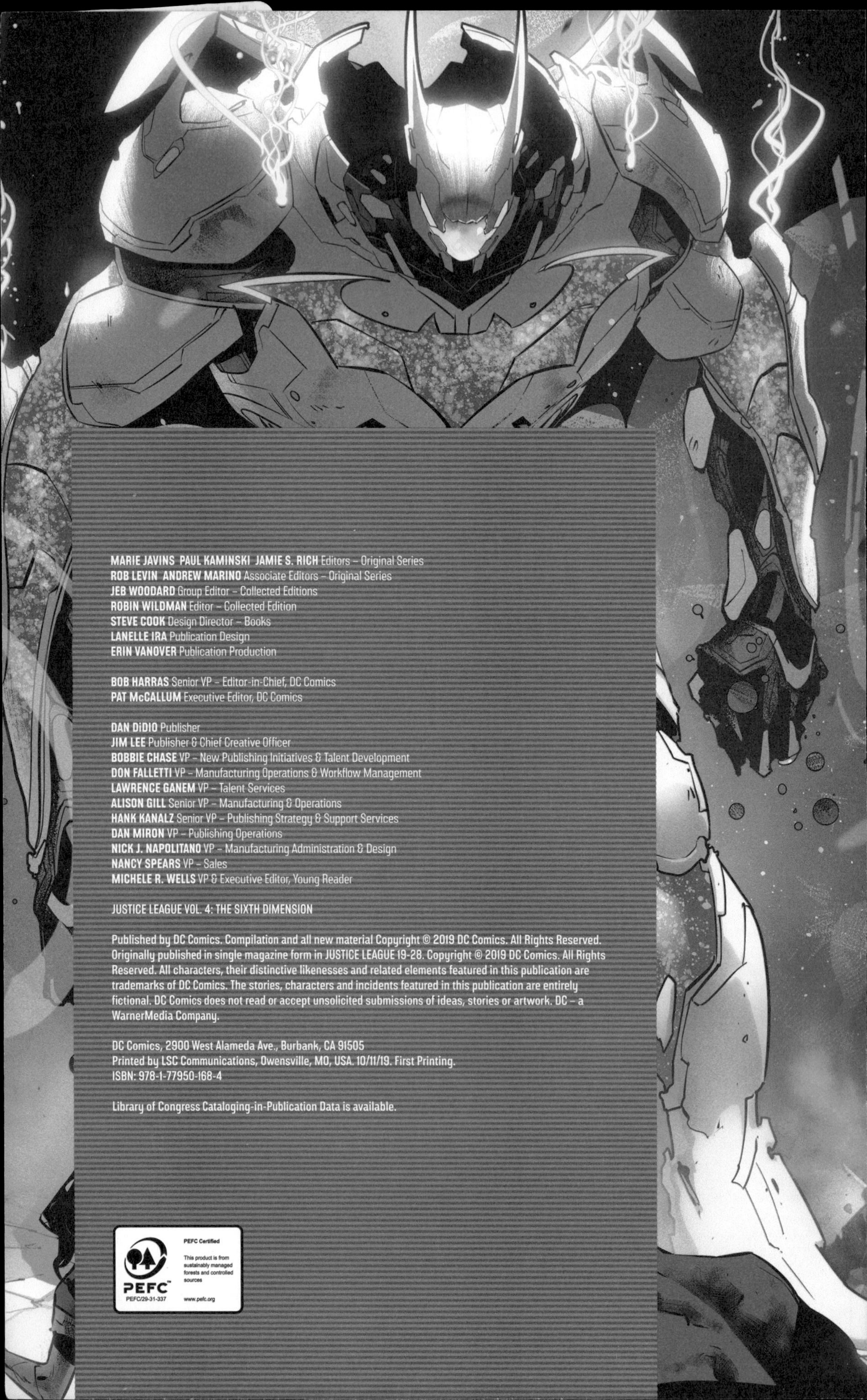

MARIE JAVINS PAUL KAMINSKI JAMIE S. RICH Editors – Original Series
ROB LEVIN ANDREW MARINO Associate Editors – Original Series
JEB WOODARD Group Editor – Collected Editions
ROBIN WILDMAN Editor – Collected Edition
STEVE COOK Design Director – Books
LANELLE IRA Publication Design
ERIN VANOVER Publication Production

BOB HARRAS Senior VP – Editor-in-Chief, DC Comics
PAT McCALLUM Executive Editor, DC Comics

DAN DiDIO Publisher
JIM LEE Publisher & Chief Creative Officer
BOBBIE CHASE VP – New Publishing Initiatives & Talent Development
DON FALLETTI VP – Manufacturing Operations & Workflow Management
LAWRENCE GANEM VP – Talent Services
ALISON GILL Senior VP – Manufacturing & Operations
HANK KANALZ Senior VP – Publishing Strategy & Support Services
DAN MIRON VP – Publishing Operations
NICK J. NAPOLITANO VP – Manufacturing Administration & Design
NANCY SPEARS VP – Sales
MICHELE R. WELLS VP & Executive Editor, Young Reader

JUSTICE LEAGUE VOL. 4: THE SIXTH DIMENSION

DC Comics, 2900 West Alameda Ave., Burbank, CA 91505
Printed by LSC Communications, Owensville, MO, USA. 10/11/19. First Printing.
ISBN: 978-1-77950-168-4

Library of Congress Cataloging-in-Publication Data is available.

PEFC Certified
This product is from sustainably managed forests and controlled sources
PEFC
PEFC/29-31-337
www.pefc.org

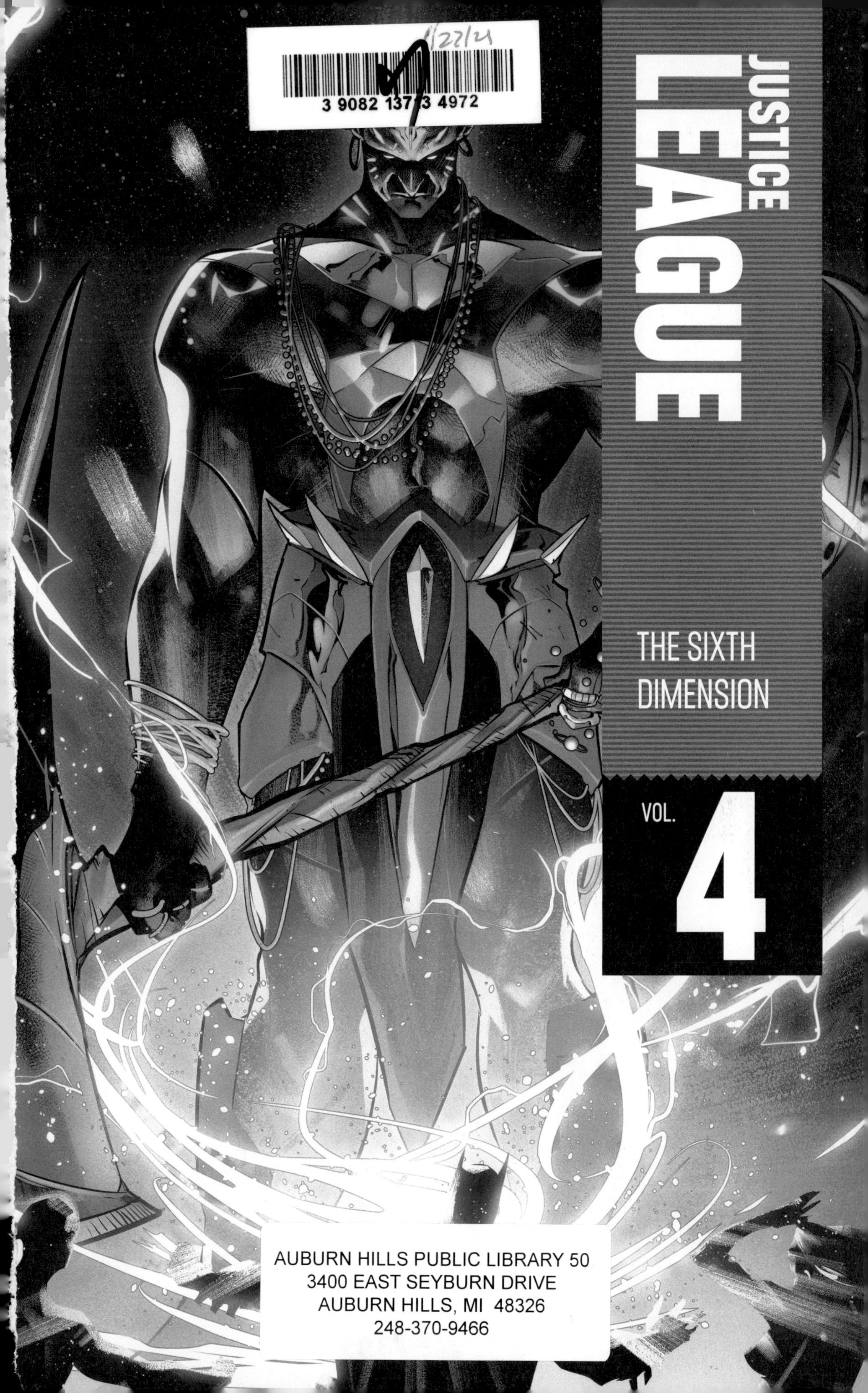
JUSTICE
LEAGUE
THE SIXTH
DIMENSION
VOL.
4

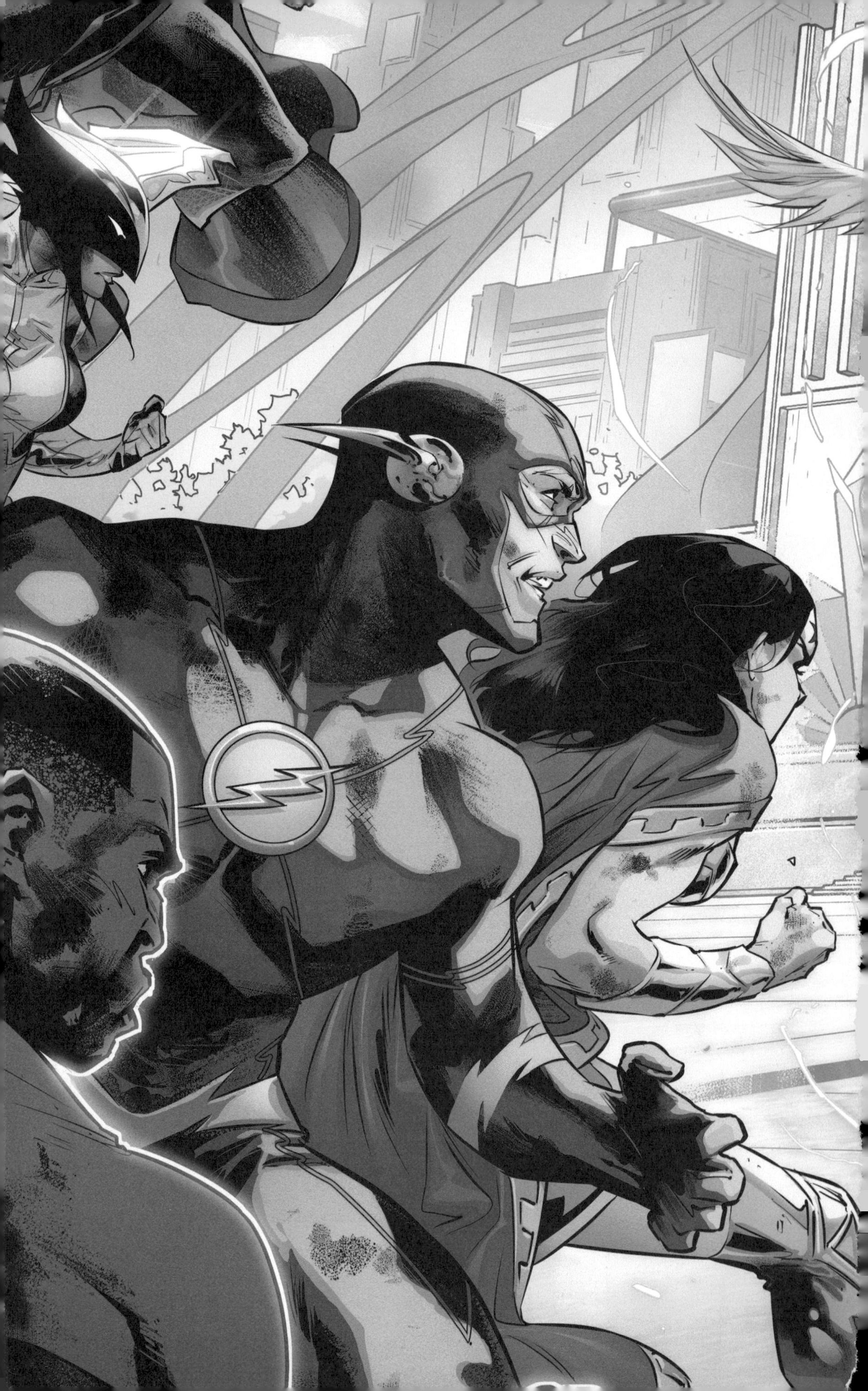

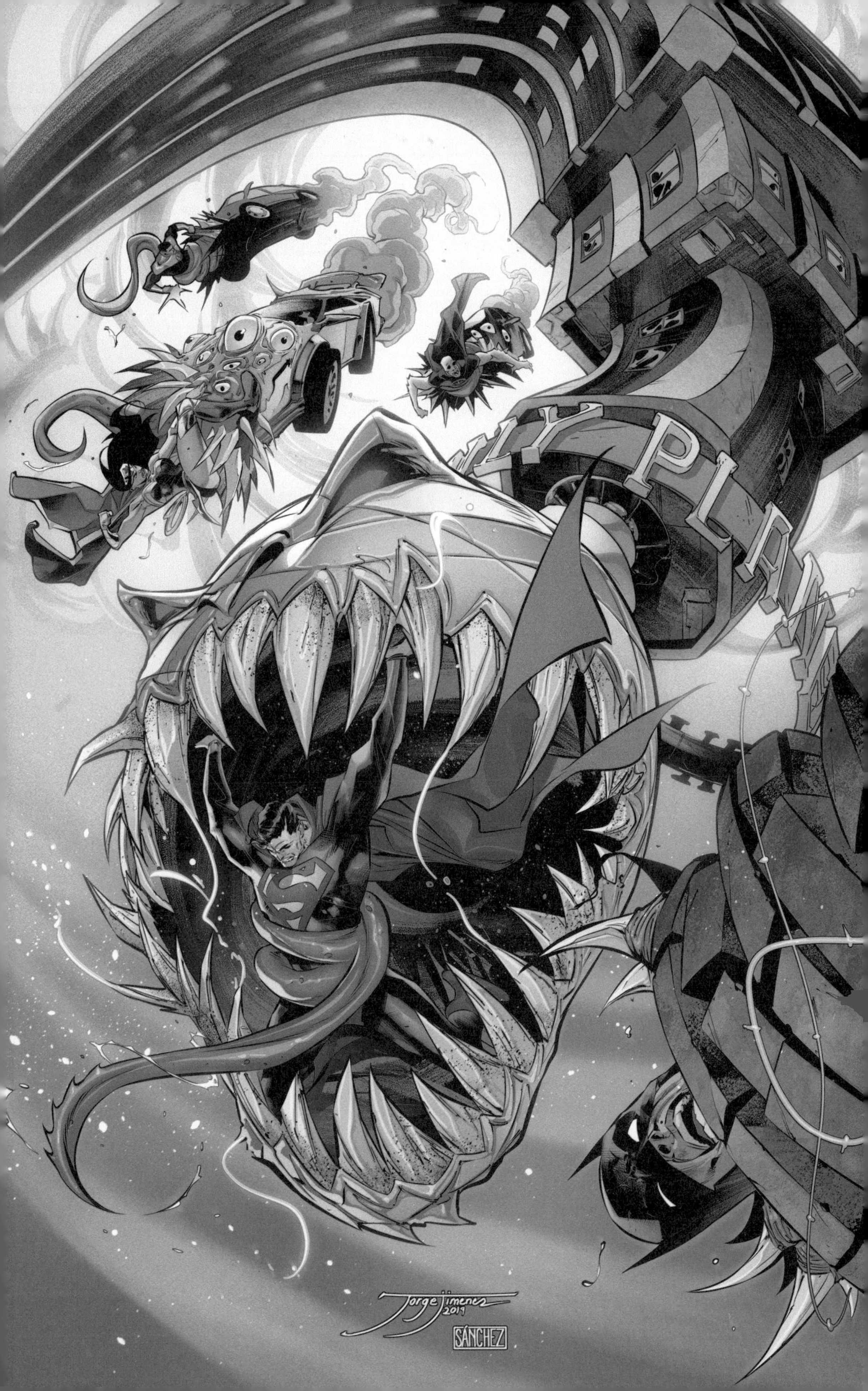
LY PLA
Jorge Jimenez 2019
SÁNCHEZ

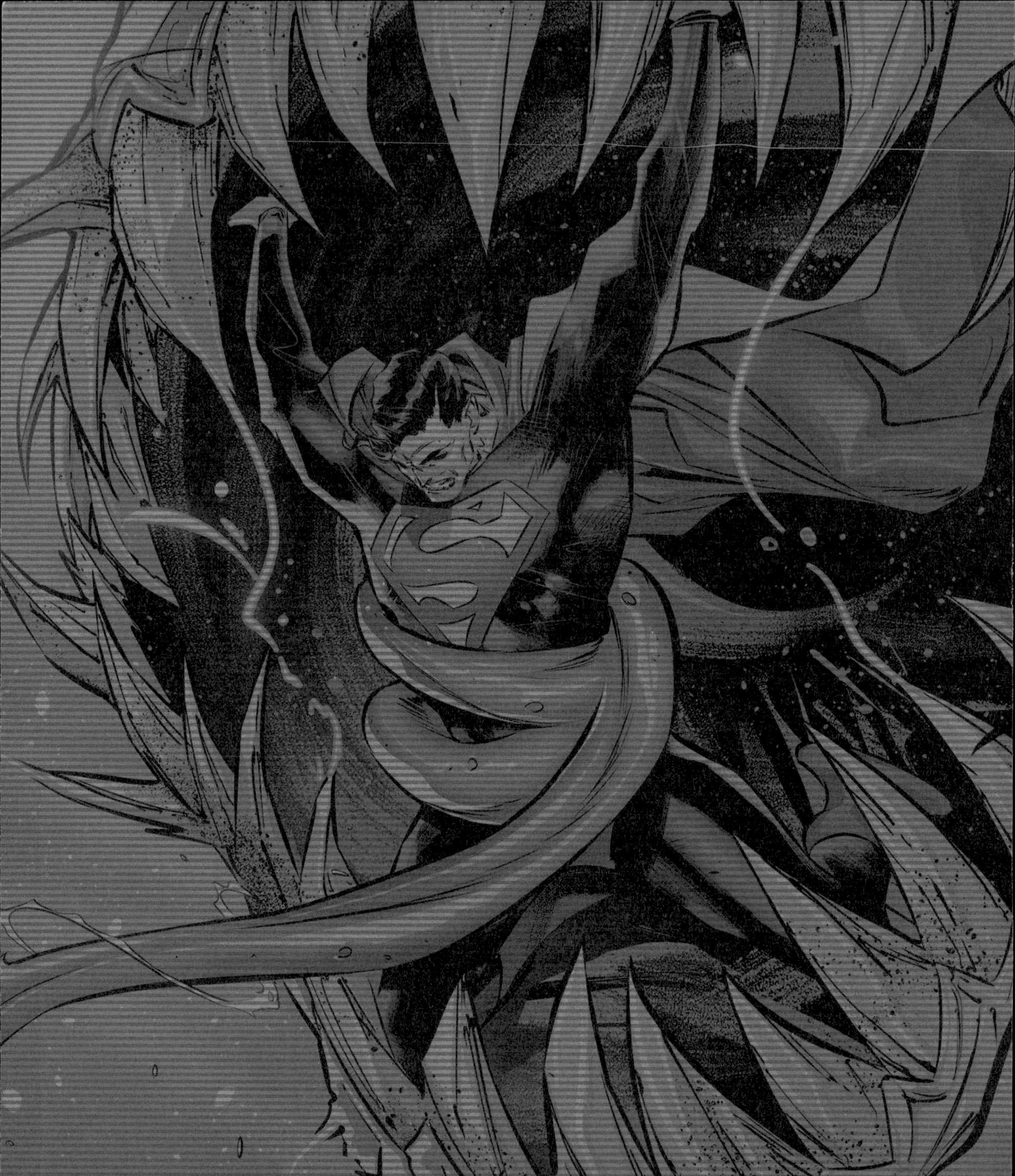

JUSTICE LEAGUE

#19

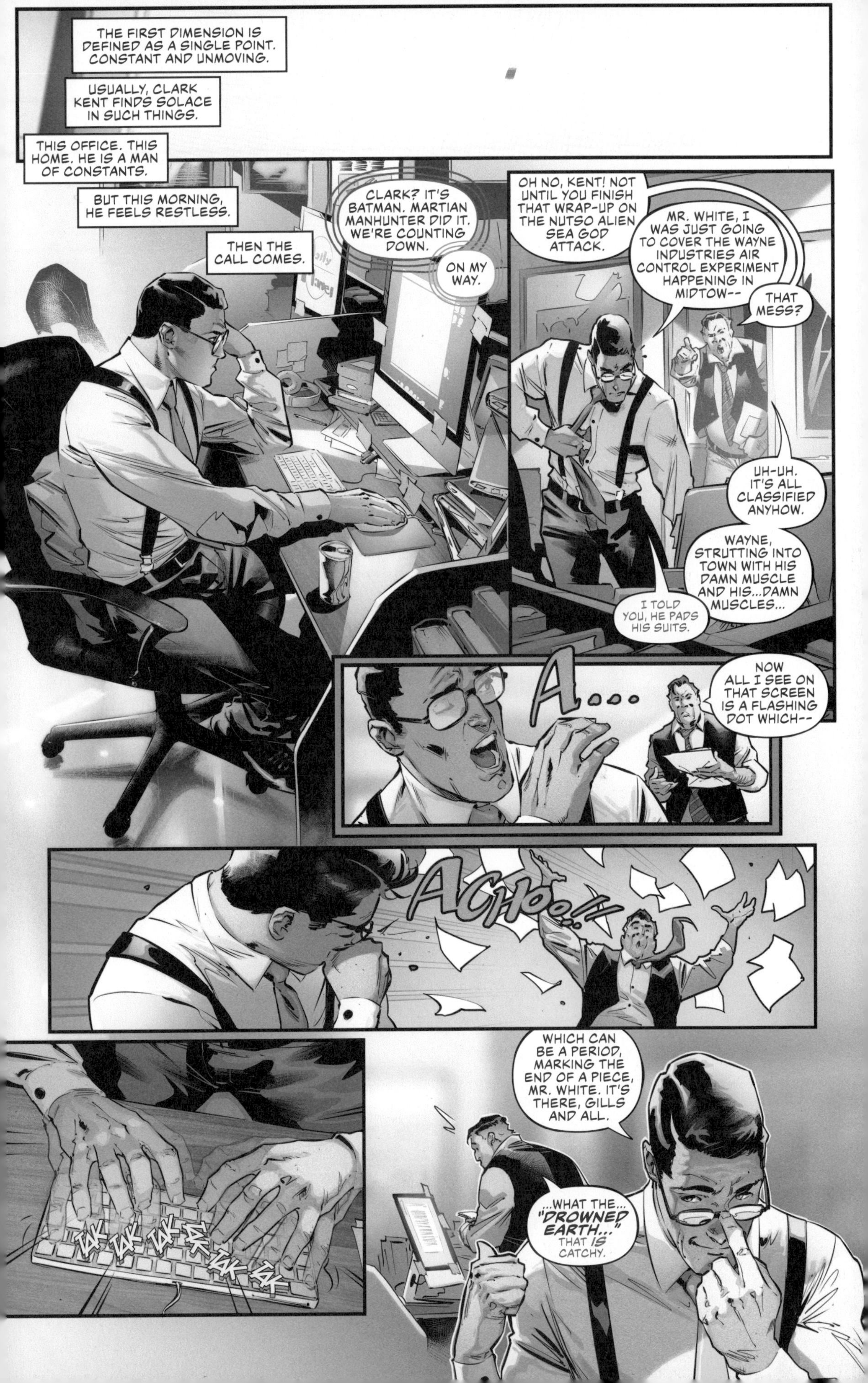
THE FIRST DIMENSION IS DEFINED AS A SINGLE POINT. CONSTANT AND UNMOVING.
USUALLY, CLARK KENT FINDS SOLACE IN SUCH THINGS.
THIS OFFICE. THIS HOME. HE IS A MAN OF CONSTANTS.
BUT THIS MORNING, HE FEELS RESTLESS.
THEN THE CALL COMES.
CLARK? IT'S BATMAN. MARTIAN MANHUNTER DID IT. WE'RE COUNTING DOWN.
ON MY WAY.
OH NO, KENT! NOT UNTIL YOU FINISH THAT WRAP-UP ON THE NUTSO ALIEN SEA GOD ATTACK.
MR. WHITE, I WAS JUST GOING TO COVER THE WAYNE INDUSTRIES AIR CONTROL EXPERIMENT HAPPENING IN MIDTOW--
THAT MESS?
UH-UH. IT'S ALL CLASSIFIED ANYHOW.
WAYNE, STRUTTING INTO TOWN WITH HIS DAMN MUSCLE AND HIS...DAMN MUSCLES...
I TOLD YOU, HE PADS HIS SUITS.
A...
NOW ALL I SEE ON THAT SCREEN IS A FLASHING DOT WHICH--
ACHOO!!
TAK TAK TAK TEK TAK TAK
WHICH CAN BE A PERIOD, MARKING THE END OF A PIECE, MR. WHITE. IT'S THERE, GILLS AND ALL.
...WHAT THE... "DROWNED EARTH..." THAT IS CATCHY.

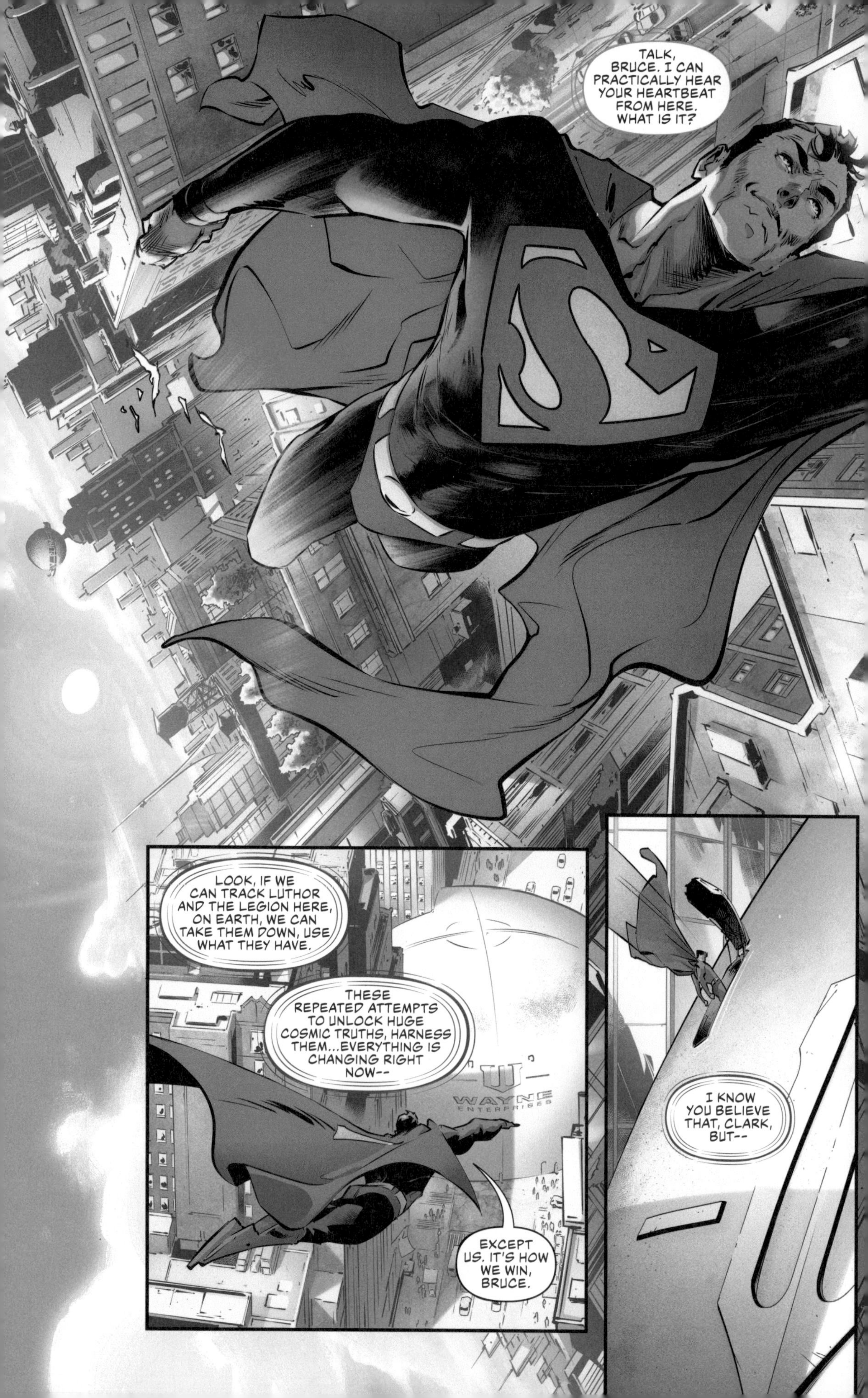
TALK, BRUCE. I CAN PRACTICALLY HEAR YOUR HEARTBEAT FROM HERE. WHAT IS IT?
LOOK, IF WE CAN TRACK LUTHOR AND THE LEGION HERE, ON EARTH, WE CAN TAKE THEM DOWN, USE WHAT THEY HAVE.
THESE REPEATED ATTEMPTS TO UNLOCK HUGE COSMIC TRUTHS, HARNESS THEM...EVERYTHING IS CHANGING RIGHT NOW--
WAYNE ENTERPRISES
EXCEPT US. IT'S HOW WE WIN, BRUCE.
I KNOW YOU BELIEVE THAT, CLARK, BUT--

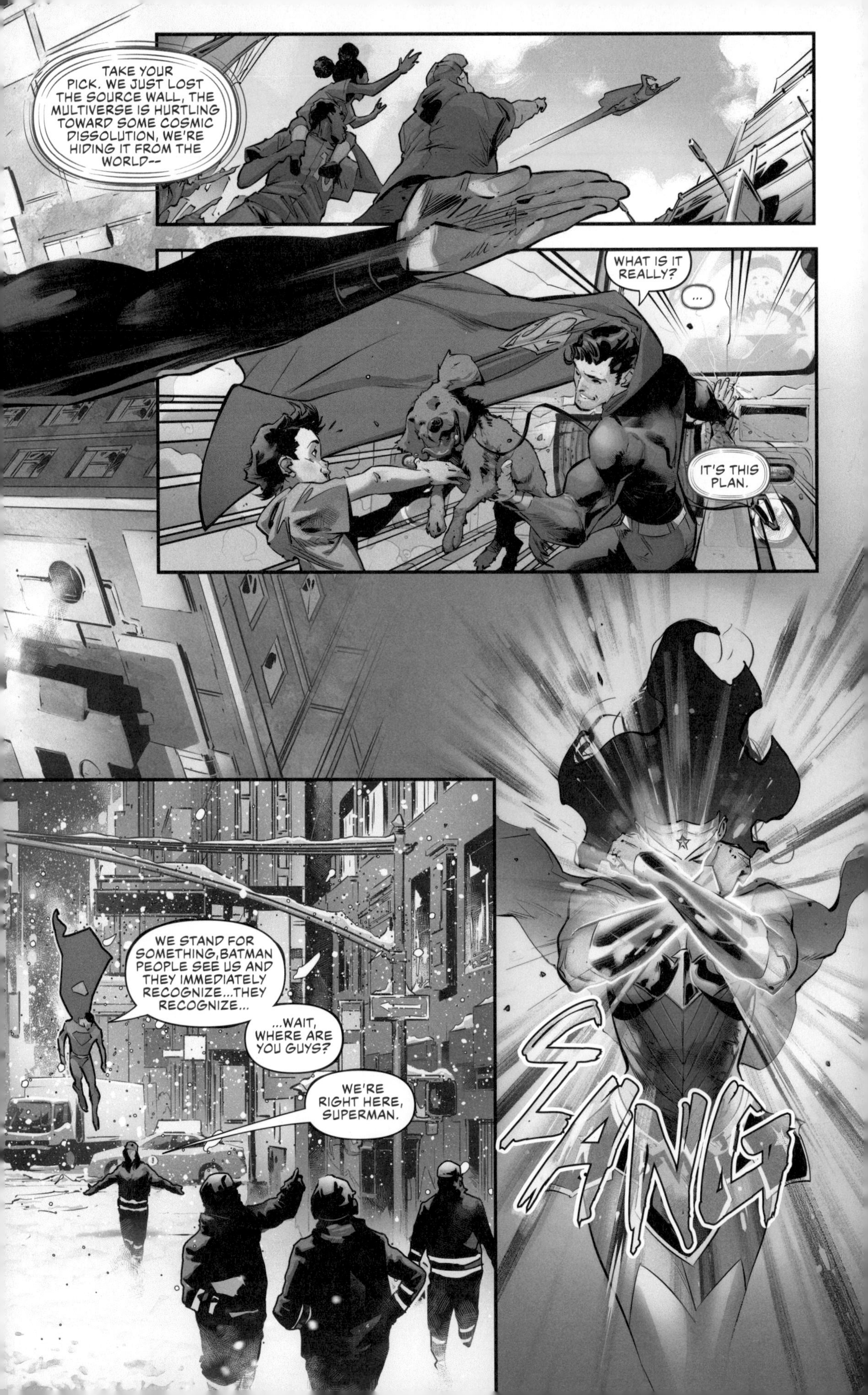
TAKE YOUR PICK. WE JUST LOST THE SOURCE WALL, THE MULTIVERSE IS HURTLING TOWARD SOME COSMIC DISSOLUTION, WE'RE HIDING IT FROM THE WORLD--
WHAT IS IT REALLY?
...
IT'S THIS PLAN.
WE STAND FOR SOMETHING, BATMAN PEOPLE SEE US AND THEY IMMEDIATELY RECOGNIZE...THEY RECOGNIZE...
...WAIT, WHERE ARE YOU GUYS?
WE'RE RIGHT HERE, SUPERMAN.
SHANG

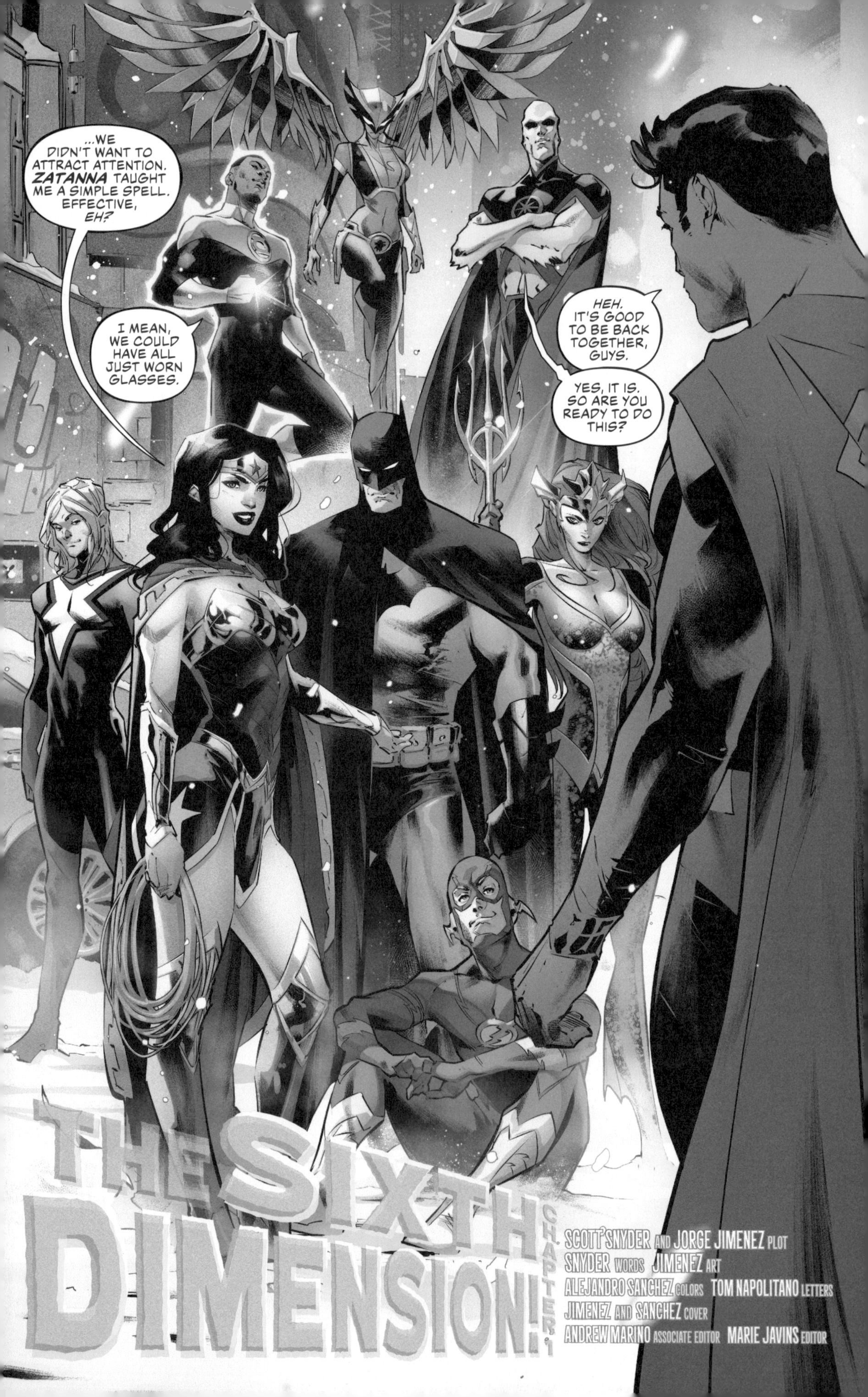
...WE DIDN'T WANT TO ATTRACT ATTENTION. ZATANNA TAUGHT ME A SIMPLE SPELL. EFFECTIVE, EH?
I MEAN, WE COULD HAVE ALL JUST WORN GLASSES.
HEH. IT'S GOOD TO BE BACK TOGETHER, GUYS.
YES, IT IS. SO ARE YOU READY TO DO THIS?
THE SIXTH DIMENSION!
CHAPTER 1
SCOTT SNYDER AND JORGE JIMENEZ PLOT
SNYDER WORDS JIMENEZ ART
ALEJANDRO SANCHEZ COLORS TOM NAPOLITANO LETTERS
JIMENEZ AND SANCHEZ COVER
ANDREW MARINO ASSOCIATE EDITOR MARIE JAVINS EDITOR

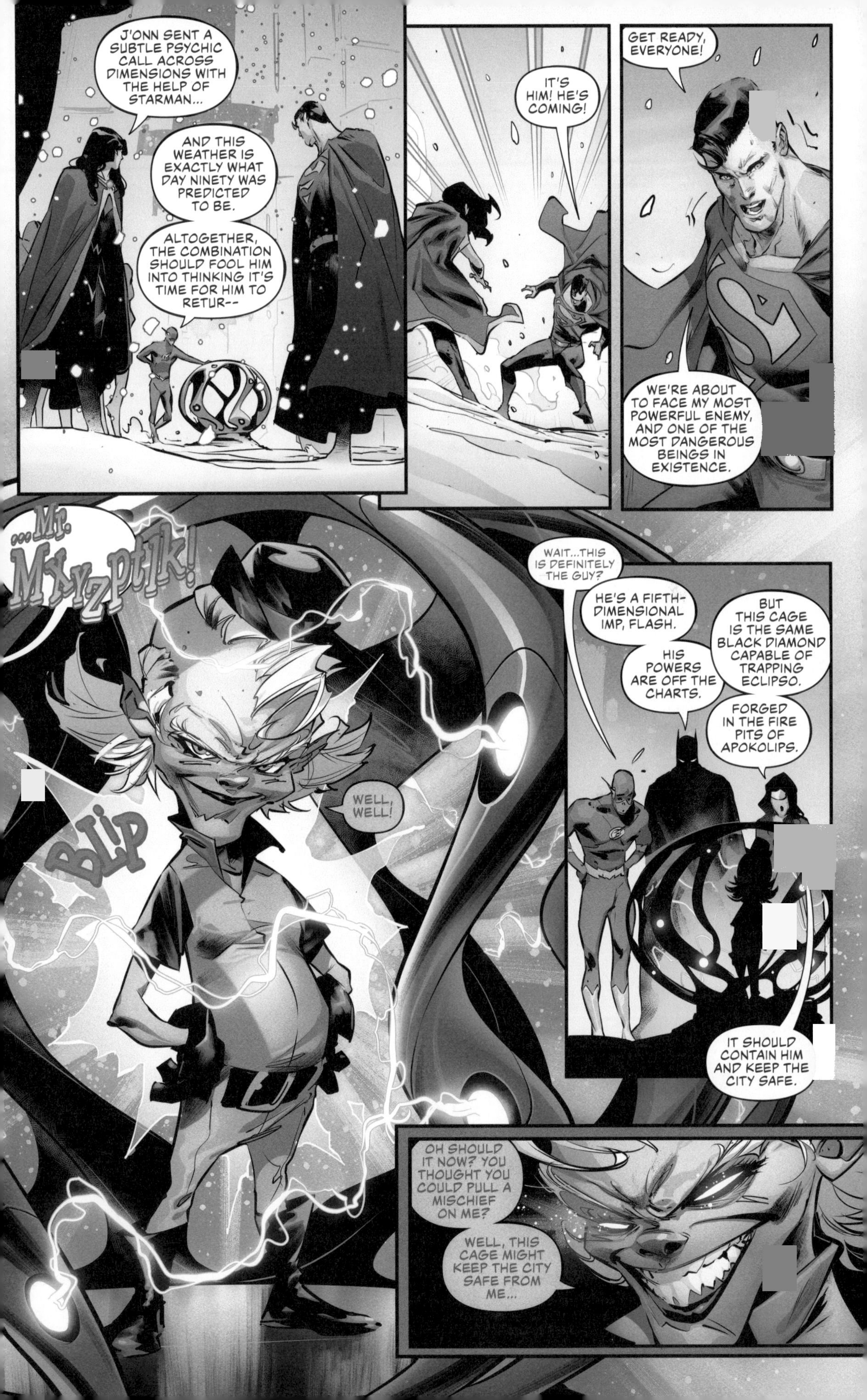
J'ONN SENT A SUBTLE PSYCHIC CALL ACROSS DIMENSIONS WITH THE HELP OF STARMAN...
AND THIS WEATHER IS EXACTLY WHAT DAY NINETY WAS PREDICTED TO BE.
ALTOGETHER, THE COMBINATION SHOULD FOOL HIM INTO THINKING IT'S TIME FOR HIM TO RETUR--
IT'S HIM! HE'S COMING!
GET READY, EVERYONE!
WE'RE ABOUT TO FACE MY MOST POWERFUL ENEMY, AND ONE OF THE MOST DANGEROUS BEINGS IN EXISTENCE.
...Mr. Mxyzptlk!
BLIP
WELL, WELL!
WAIT...THIS IS DEFINITELY THE GUY?
HE'S A FIFTH-DIMENSIONAL IMP, FLASH.
HIS POWERS ARE OFF THE CHARTS.
BUT THIS CAGE IS THE SAME BLACK DIAMOND CAPABLE OF TRAPPING ECLIPSO.
FORGED IN THE FIRE PITS OF APOKOLIPS.
IT SHOULD CONTAIN HIM AND KEEP THE CITY SAFE.
OH SHOULD IT NOW? YOU THOUGHT YOU COULD PULL A MISCHIEF ON ME?
WELL, THIS CAGE MIGHT KEEP THE CITY SAFE FROM ME...

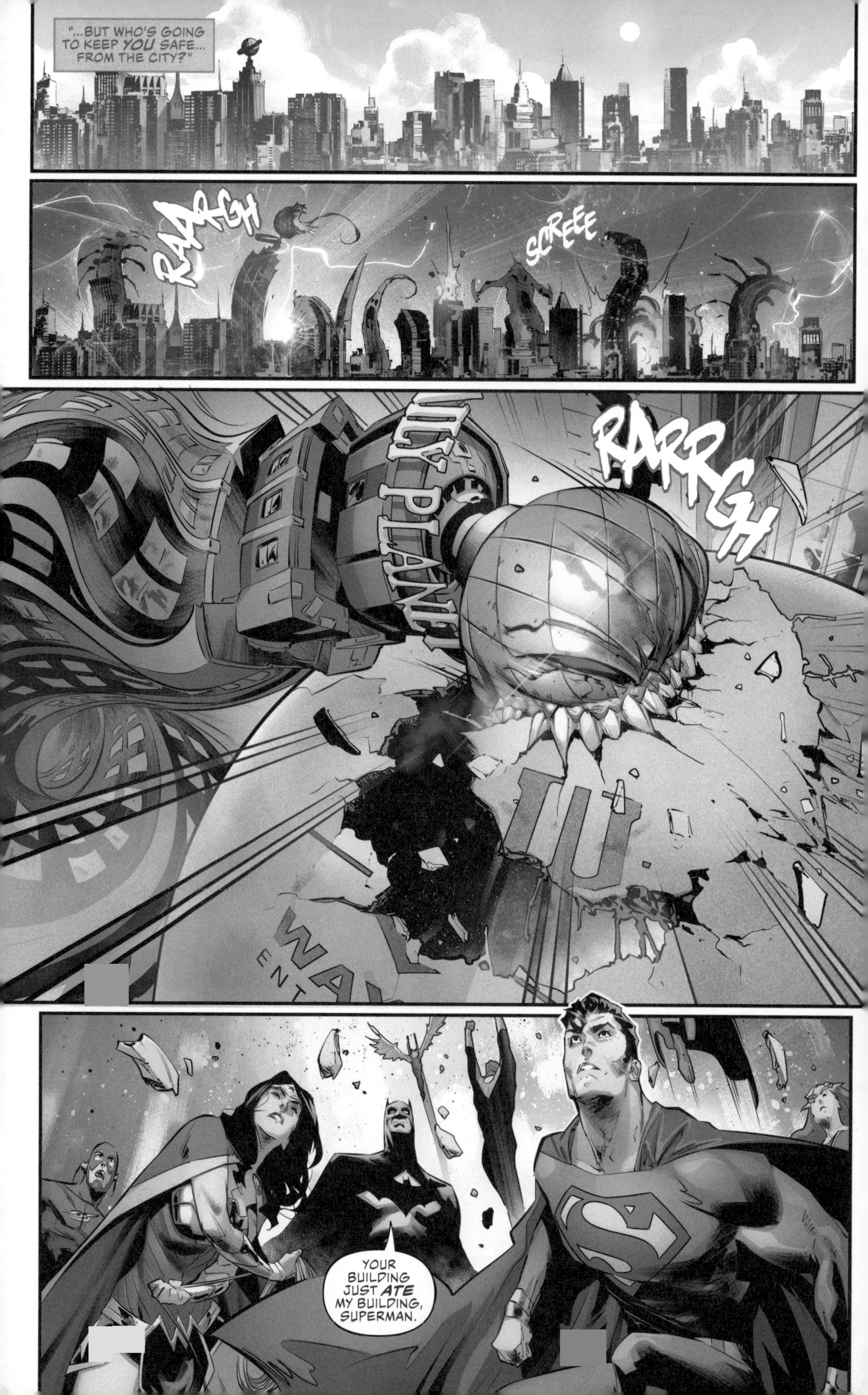
"...BUT WHO'S GOING TO KEEP YOU SAFE... FROM THE CITY?"
RARRGH
SCREEE
RARRGH
YOUR BUILDING JUST ATE MY BUILDING, SUPERMAN.

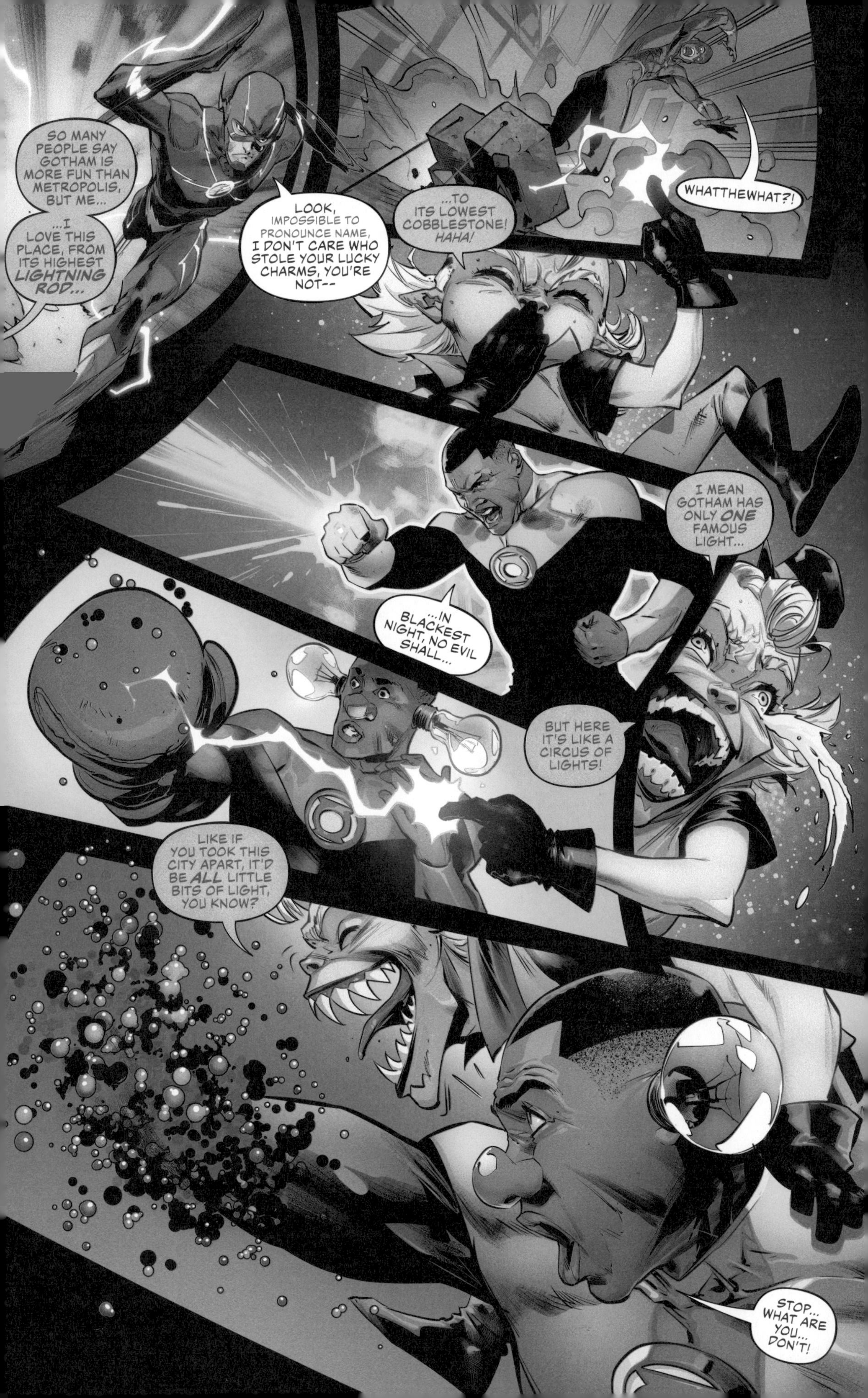
SO MANY PEOPLE SAY GOTHAM IS MORE FUN THAN METROPOLIS, BUT ME...
...I LOVE THIS PLACE, FROM ITS HIGHEST *LIGHTNING ROD...*
...TO ITS LOWEST COBBLESTONE! *HAHA!*
LOOK, IMPOSSIBLE TO PRONOUNCE NAME, I DON'T CARE WHO STOLE YOUR LUCKY CHARMS, YOU'RE NOT--
WHATTHEWHAT?!
I MEAN GOTHAM HAS ONLY *ONE* FAMOUS LIGHT...
...IN BLACKEST NIGHT, NO EVIL SHALL...
BUT HERE IT'S LIKE A CIRCUS OF LIGHTS!
LIKE IF YOU TOOK THIS CITY APART, IT'D BE *ALL* LITTLE BITS OF LIGHT, YOU KNOW?
STOP... WHAT ARE YOU... DON'T!

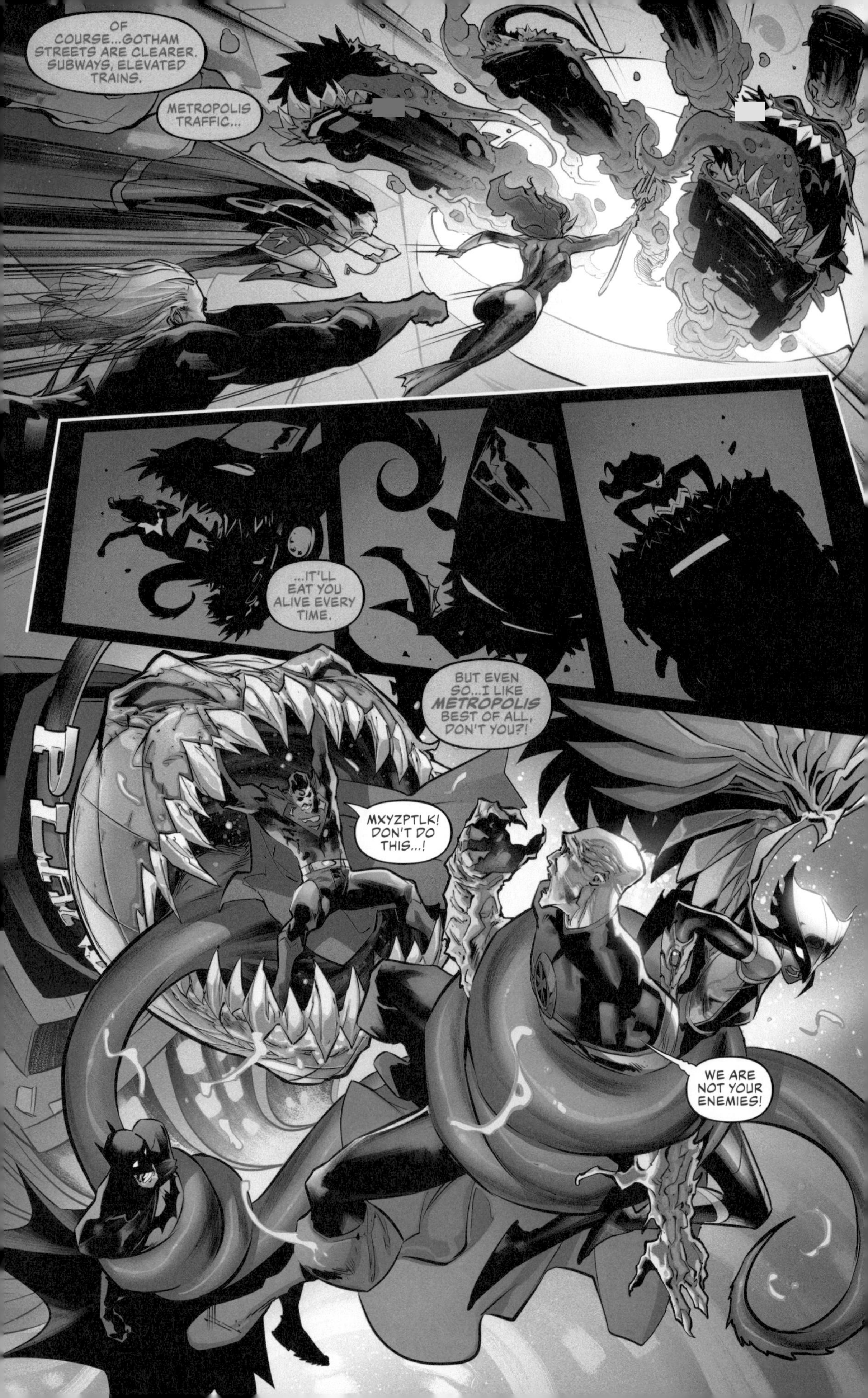
OF COURSE...GOTHAM STREETS ARE CLEARER. SUBWAYS, ELEVATED TRAINS.
METROPOLIS TRAFFIC...
...IT'LL EAT YOU ALIVE EVERY TIME.
BUT EVEN SO...I LIKE METROPOLIS BEST OF ALL, DON'T YOU?!
MXYZPTLK! DON'T DO THIS...!
WE ARE NOT YOUR ENEMIES!

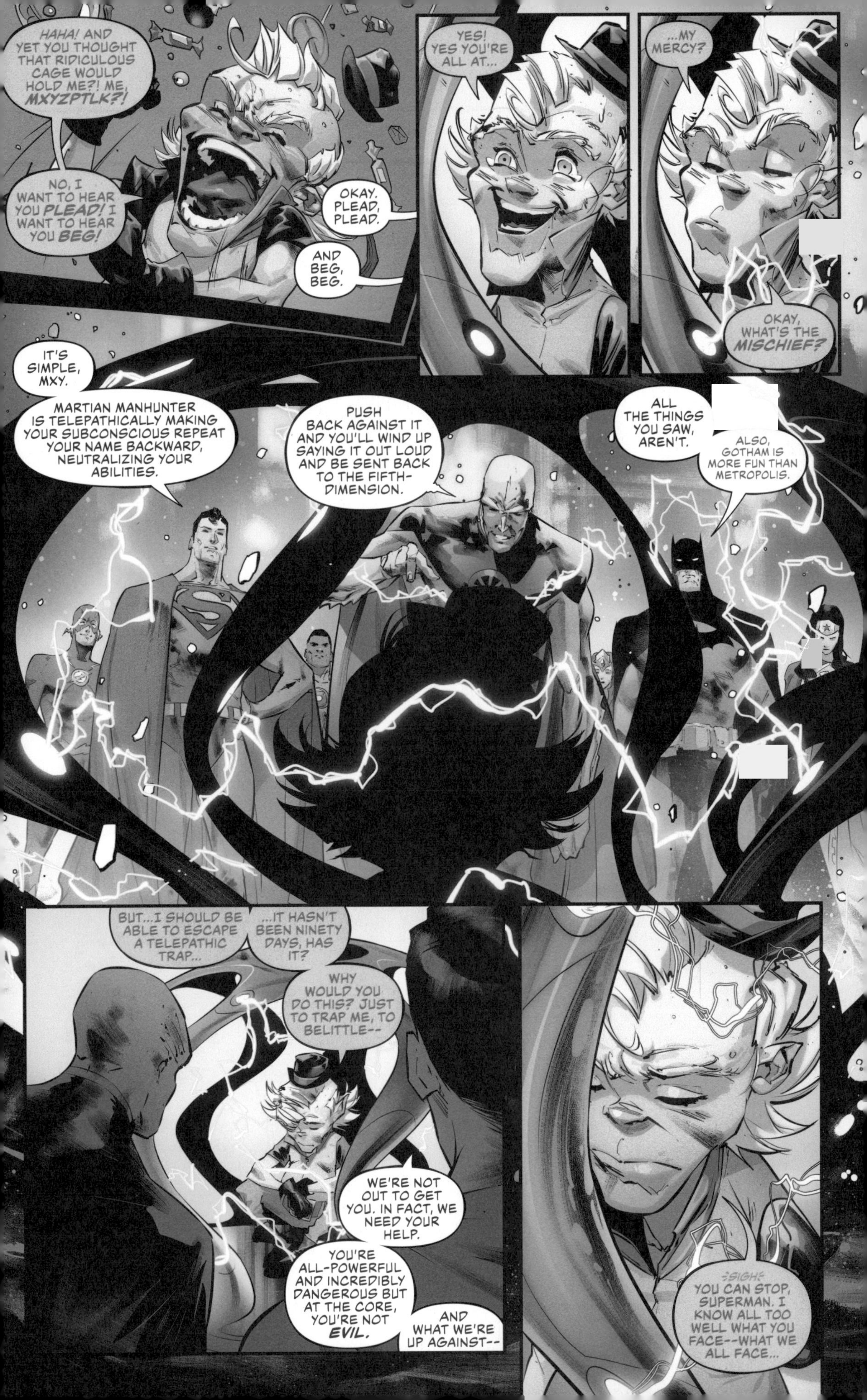
HAHA! AND YET YOU THOUGHT THAT RIDICULOUS CAGE WOULD HOLD ME?! ME, MXYZPTLK?!
NO, I WANT TO HEAR YOU PLEAD! I WANT TO HEAR YOU BEG!
OKAY. PLEAD, PLEAD.
AND BEG, BEG.
YES! YES YOU'RE ALL AT...
...MY MERCY?
OKAY, WHAT'S THE MISCHIEF?
IT'S SIMPLE, MXY.
MARTIAN MANHUNTER IS TELEPATHICALLY MAKING YOUR SUBCONSCIOUS REPEAT YOUR NAME BACKWARD, NEUTRALIZING YOUR ABILITIES.
PUSH BACK AGAINST IT AND YOU'LL WIND UP SAYING IT OUT LOUD AND BE SENT BACK TO THE FIFTH-DIMENSION.
ALL THE THINGS YOU SAW, AREN'T.
ALSO, GOTHAM IS MORE FUN THAN METROPOLIS.
BUT...I SHOULD BE ABLE TO ESCAPE A TELEPATHIC TRAP...
...IT HASN'T BEEN NINETY DAYS, HAS IT?
WHY WOULD YOU DO THIS? JUST TO TRAP ME, TO BELITTLE--
WE'RE NOT OUT TO GET YOU. IN FACT, WE NEED YOUR HELP.
YOU'RE ALL-POWERFUL AND INCREDIBLY DANGEROUS BUT AT THE CORE, YOU'RE NOT EVIL.
AND WHAT WE'RE UP AGAINST--
SIGH
YOU CAN STOP, SUPERMAN. I KNOW ALL TOO WELL WHAT YOU FACE--WHAT WE ALL FACE...

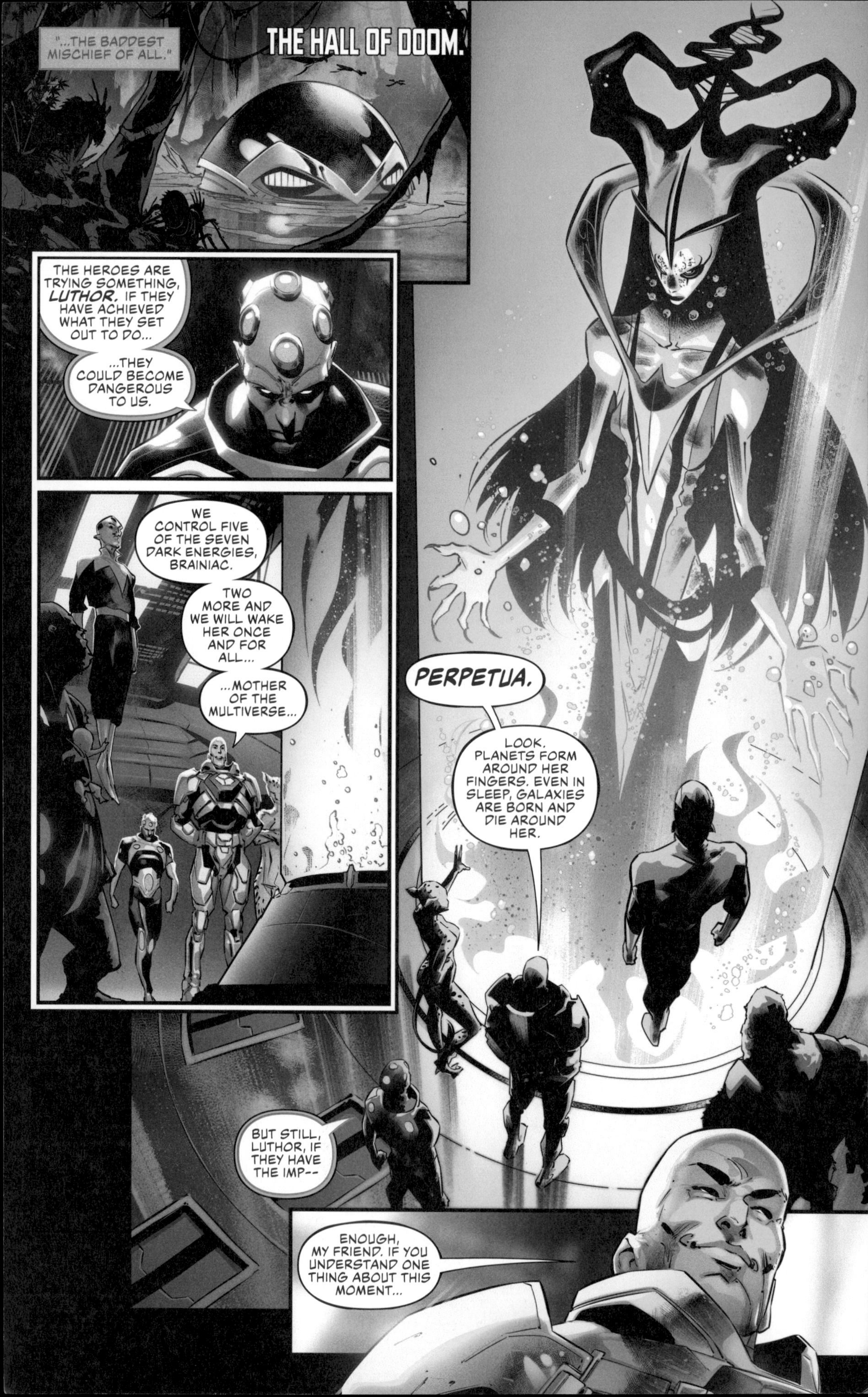
"...THE BADDEST MISCHIEF OF ALL."
THE HALL OF DOOM.
THE HEROES ARE TRYING SOMETHING, LUTHOR. IF THEY HAVE ACHIEVED WHAT THEY SET OUT TO DO...
...THEY COULD BECOME DANGEROUS TO US.
WE CONTROL FIVE OF THE SEVEN DARK ENERGIES, BRAINIAC.
TWO MORE AND WE WILL WAKE HER ONCE AND FOR ALL...
...MOTHER OF THE MULTIVERSE...
PERPETUA.
LOOK. PLANETS FORM AROUND HER FINGERS. EVEN IN SLEEP, GALAXIES ARE BORN AND DIE AROUND HER.
BUT STILL, LUTHOR, IF THEY HAVE THE IMP--
ENOUGH, MY FRIEND. IF YOU UNDERSTAND ONE THING ABOUT THIS MOMENT...

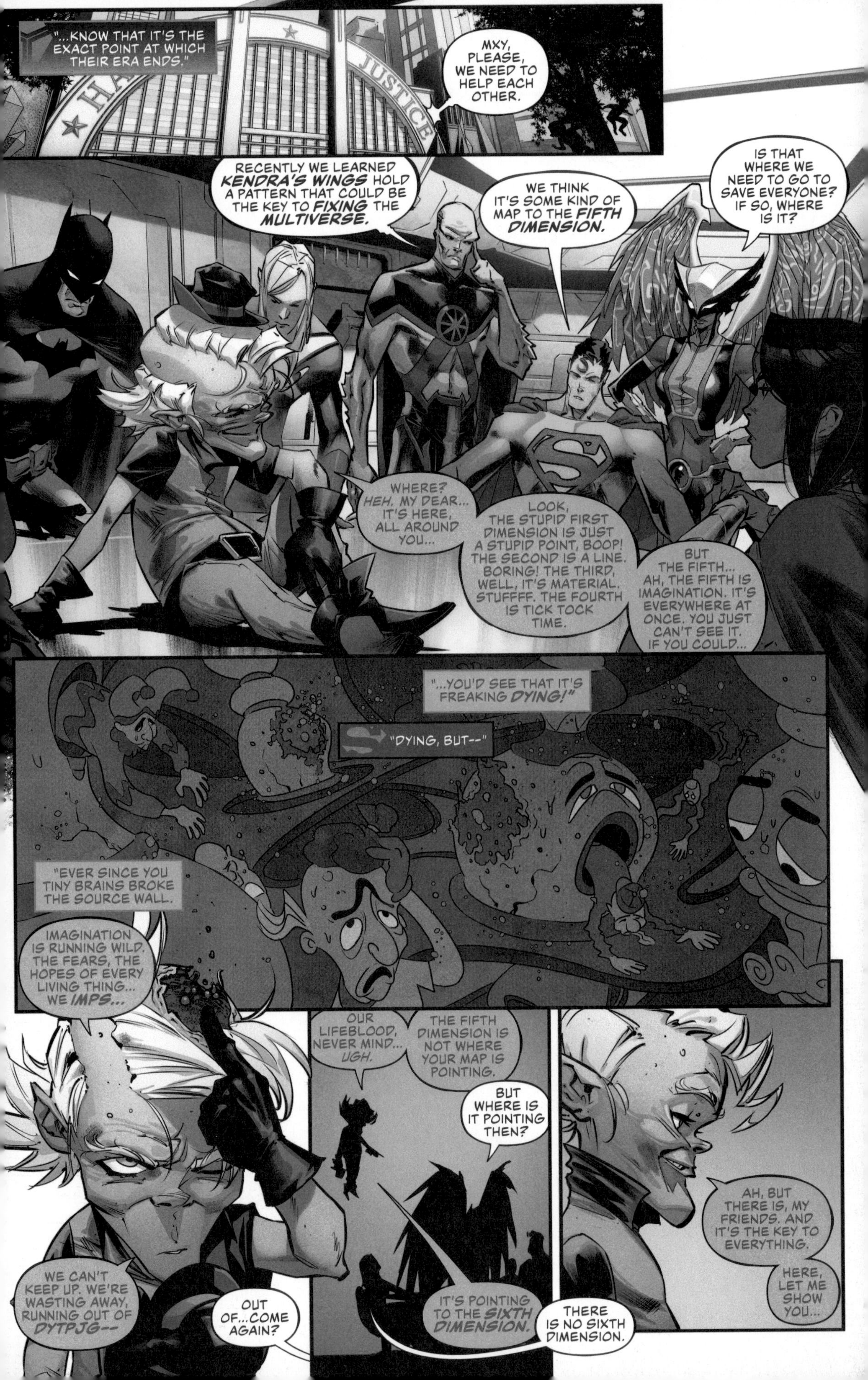
"...KNOW THAT IT'S THE EXACT POINT AT WHICH THEIR ERA ENDS."
MXY, PLEASE, WE NEED TO HELP EACH OTHER.
JUSTICE
RECENTLY WE LEARNED KENDRA'S WINGS HOLD A PATTERN THAT COULD BE THE KEY TO FIXING THE MULTIVERSE.
WE THINK IT'S SOME KIND OF MAP TO THE FIFTH DIMENSION.
IS THAT WHERE WE NEED TO GO TO SAVE EVERYONE? IF SO, WHERE IS IT?
WHERE? HEH. MY DEAR... IT'S HERE, ALL AROUND YOU...
LOOK, THE STUPID FIRST DIMENSION IS JUST A STUPID POINT, BOOP! THE SECOND IS A LINE. BORING! THE THIRD, WELL, IT'S MATERIAL. STUFFFF. THE FOURTH IS TICK TOCK TIME.
BUT THE FIFTH... AH, THE FIFTH IS IMAGINATION. IT'S EVERYWHERE AT ONCE. YOU JUST CAN'T SEE IT. IF YOU COULD...
"...YOU'D SEE THAT IT'S FREAKING DYING!"
"DYING, BUT--"
"EVER SINCE YOU TINY BRAINS BROKE THE SOURCE WALL.
IMAGINATION IS RUNNING WILD. THE FEARS, THE HOPES OF EVERY LIVING THING... WE IMPS...
WE CAN'T KEEP UP. WE'RE WASTING AWAY, RUNNING OUT OF DYTPJG--
OUT OF...COME AGAIN?
OUR LIFEBLOOD, NEVER MIND... UGH.
THE FIFTH DIMENSION IS NOT WHERE YOUR MAP IS POINTING.
BUT WHERE IS IT POINTING THEN?
IT'S POINTING TO THE SIXTH DIMENSION.
THERE IS NO SIXTH DIMENSION.
AH, BUT THERE IS, MY FRIENDS. AND IT'S THE KEY TO EVERYTHING.
HERE, LET ME SHOW YOU...

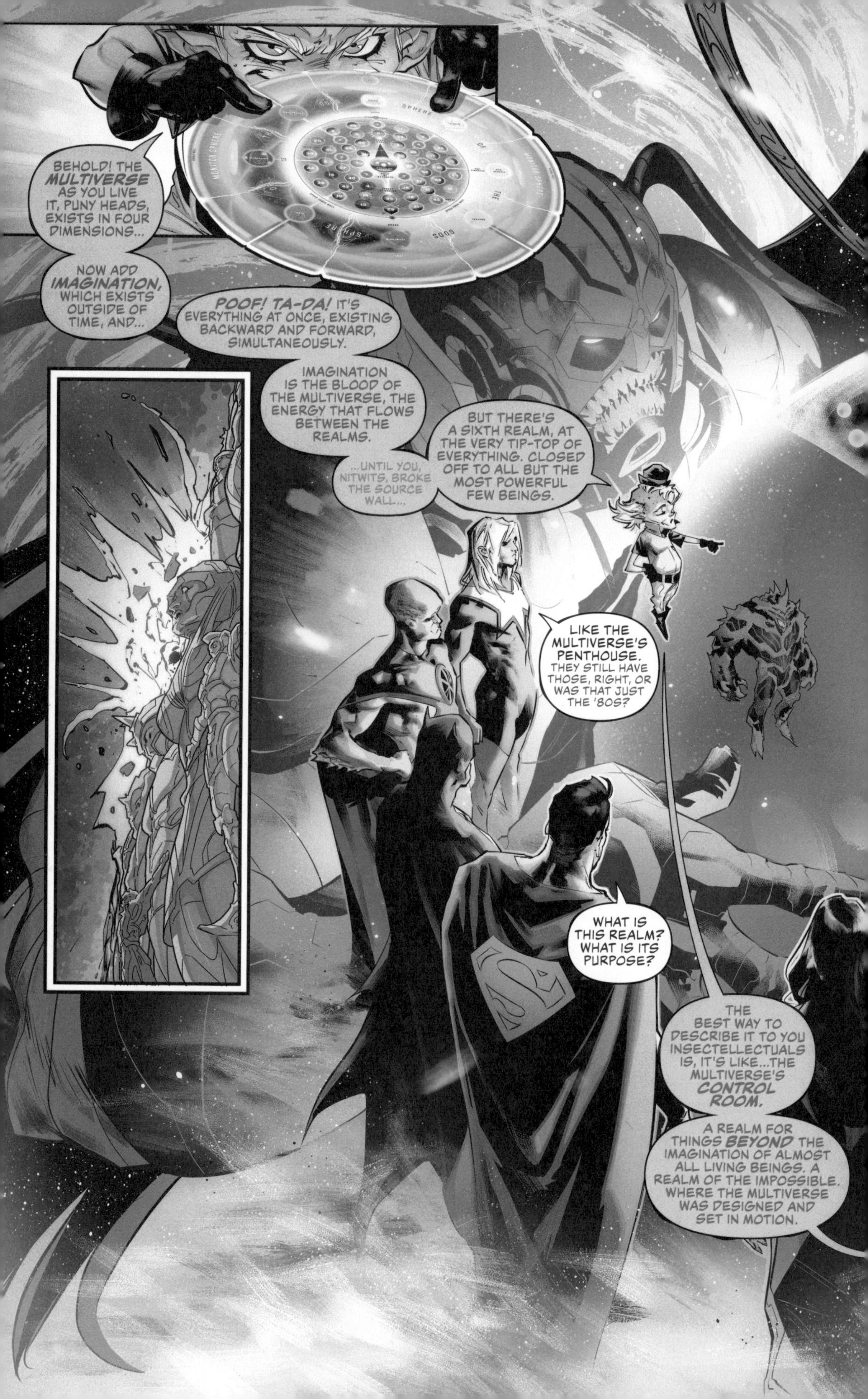

BEHOLD! THE MULTIVERSE AS YOU LIVE IT, PUNY HEADS, EXISTS IN FOUR DIMENSIONS...
NOW ADD IMAGINATION, WHICH EXISTS OUTSIDE OF TIME, AND...
POOF! TA-DA! IT'S EVERYTHING AT ONCE, EXISTING BACKWARD AND FORWARD, SIMULTANEOUSLY.
IMAGINATION IS THE BLOOD OF THE MULTIVERSE, THE ENERGY THAT FLOWS BETWEEN THE REALMS.
...UNTIL YOU, NITWITS, BROKE THE SOURCE WALL...
BUT THERE'S A SIXTH REALM, AT THE VERY TIP-TOP OF EVERYTHING. CLOSED OFF TO ALL BUT THE MOST POWERFUL FEW BEINGS.
LIKE THE MULTIVERSE'S PENTHOUSE. THEY STILL HAVE THOSE, RIGHT, OR WAS THAT JUST THE '80S?
WHAT IS THIS REALM? WHAT IS ITS PURPOSE?
THE BEST WAY TO DESCRIBE IT TO YOU INSECTELLECTUALS IS, IT'S LIKE...THE MULTIVERSE'S CONTROL ROOM.
A REALM FOR THINGS BEYOND THE IMAGINATION OF ALMOST ALL LIVING BEINGS. A REALM OF THE IMPOSSIBLE. WHERE THE MULTIVERSE WAS DESIGNED AND SET IN MOTION.

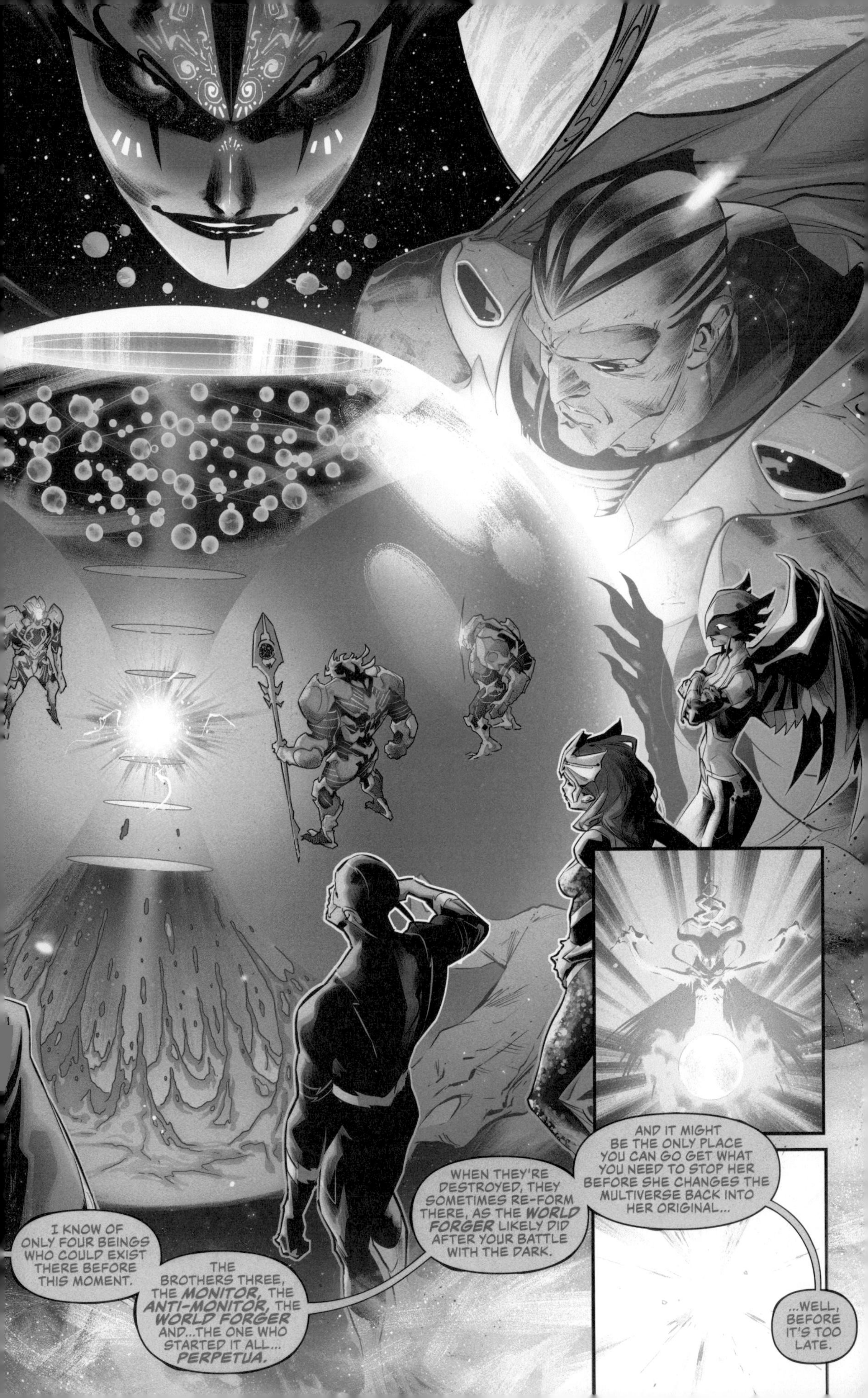
I KNOW OF ONLY FOUR BEINGS WHO COULD EXIST THERE BEFORE THIS MOMENT.
THE BROTHERS THREE, THE MONITOR, THE ANTI-MONITOR, THE WORLD FORGER AND...THE ONE WHO STARTED IT ALL... PERPETUA.
WHEN THEY'RE DESTROYED, THEY SOMETIMES RE-FORM THERE, AS THE WORLD FORGER LIKELY DID AFTER YOUR BATTLE WITH THE DARK.
AND IT MIGHT BE THE ONLY PLACE YOU CAN GO GET WHAT YOU NEED TO STOP HER BEFORE SHE CHANGES THE MULTIVERSE BACK INTO HER ORIGINAL...
...WELL, BEFORE IT'S TOO LATE.

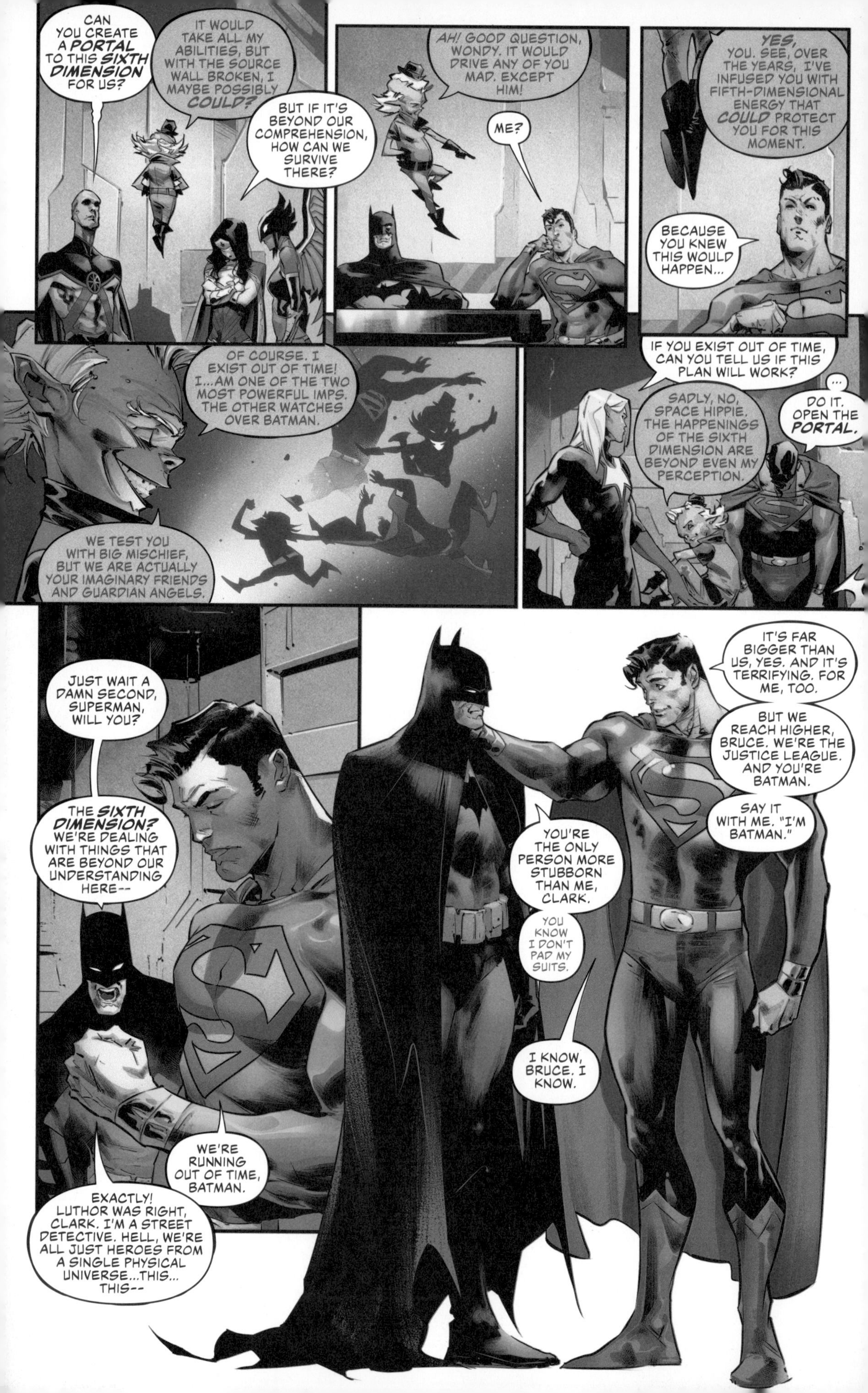
CAN YOU CREATE A PORTAL TO THIS SIXTH DIMENSION FOR US?
IT WOULD TAKE ALL MY ABILITIES, BUT WITH THE SOURCE WALL BROKEN, I MAYBE POSSIBLY COULD?
BUT IF IT'S BEYOND OUR COMPREHENSION, HOW CAN WE SURVIVE THERE?
AH! GOOD QUESTION, WONDY. IT WOULD DRIVE ANY OF YOU MAD. EXCEPT HIM!
ME?
YES, YOU. SEE, OVER THE YEARS, I'VE INFUSED YOU WITH FIFTH-DIMENSIONAL ENERGY THAT COULD PROTECT YOU FOR THIS MOMENT.
BECAUSE YOU KNEW THIS WOULD HAPPEN...
OF COURSE. I EXIST OUT OF TIME! I...AM ONE OF THE TWO MOST POWERFUL IMPS. THE OTHER WATCHES OVER BATMAN.
WE TEST YOU WITH BIG MISCHIEF, BUT WE ARE ACTUALLY YOUR IMAGINARY FRIENDS AND GUARDIAN ANGELS.
IF YOU EXIST OUT OF TIME, CAN YOU TELL US IF THIS PLAN WILL WORK?
SADLY, NO, SPACE HIPPIE. THE HAPPENINGS OF THE SIXTH DIMENSION ARE BEYOND EVEN MY PERCEPTION.
...
DO IT. OPEN THE PORTAL.
JUST WAIT A DAMN SECOND, SUPERMAN, WILL YOU?
THE SIXTH DIMENSION? WE'RE DEALING WITH THINGS THAT ARE BEYOND OUR UNDERSTANDING HERE--
WE'RE RUNNING OUT OF TIME, BATMAN.
EXACTLY! LUTHOR WAS RIGHT, CLARK. I'M A STREET DETECTIVE. HELL, WE'RE ALL JUST HEROES FROM A SINGLE PHYSICAL UNIVERSE...THIS... THIS--
IT'S FAR BIGGER THAN US, YES. AND IT'S TERRIFYING. FOR ME, TOO.
BUT WE REACH HIGHER, BRUCE. WE'RE THE JUSTICE LEAGUE. AND YOU'RE BATMAN.
SAY IT WITH ME. "I'M BATMAN."
YOU'RE THE ONLY PERSON MORE STUBBORN THAN ME, CLARK.
YOU KNOW I DON'T PAD MY SUITS.
I KNOW, BRUCE. I KNOW.

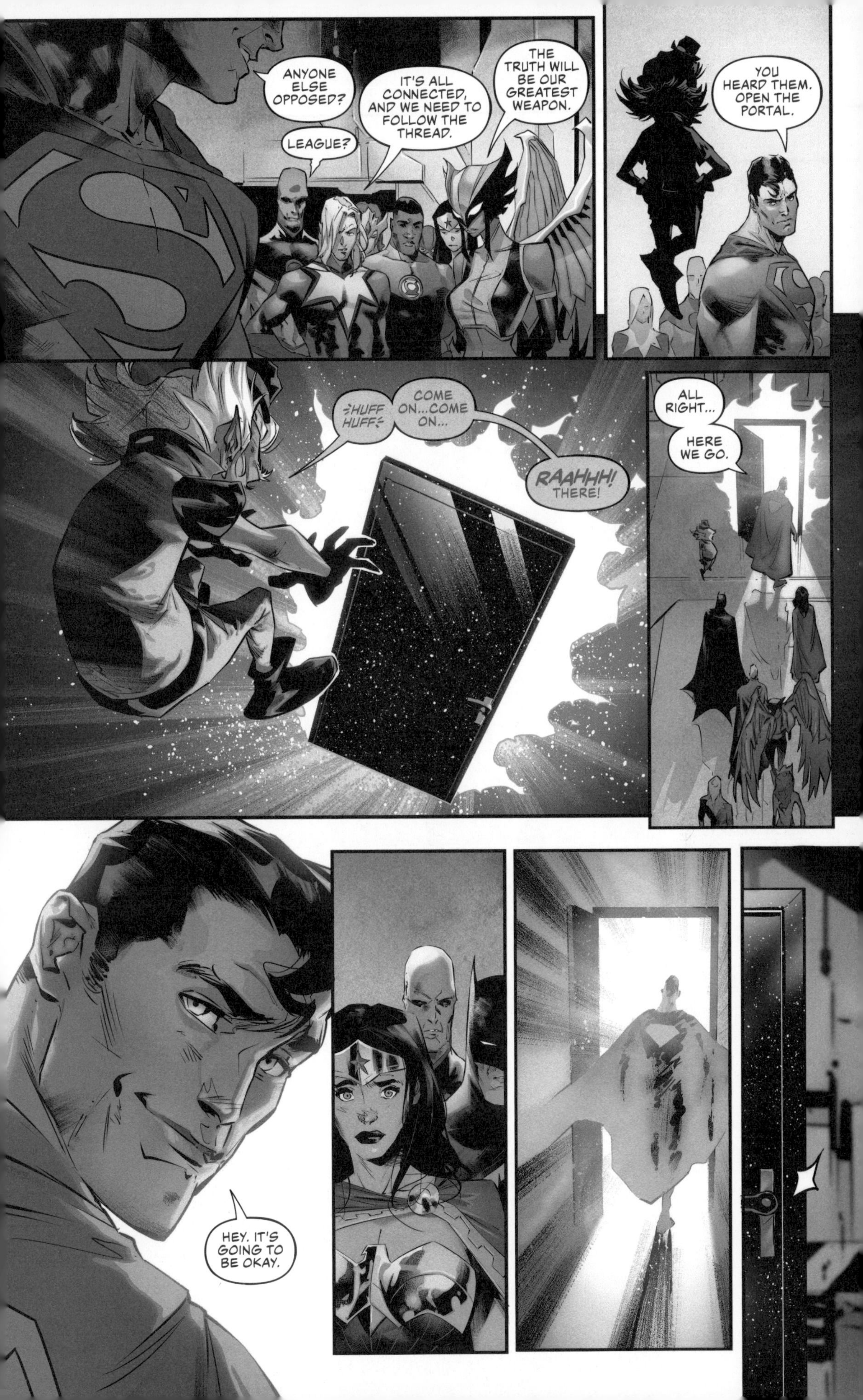
ANYONE ELSE OPPOSED?
LEAGUE?
IT'S ALL CONNECTED, AND WE NEED TO FOLLOW THE THREAD.
THE TRUTH WILL BE OUR GREATEST WEAPON.
YOU HEARD THEM. OPEN THE PORTAL.
HUFF HUFF
COME ON...COME ON...
RAAHHH! THERE!
ALL RIGHT...
HERE WE GO.
HEY. IT'S GOING TO BE OKAY.

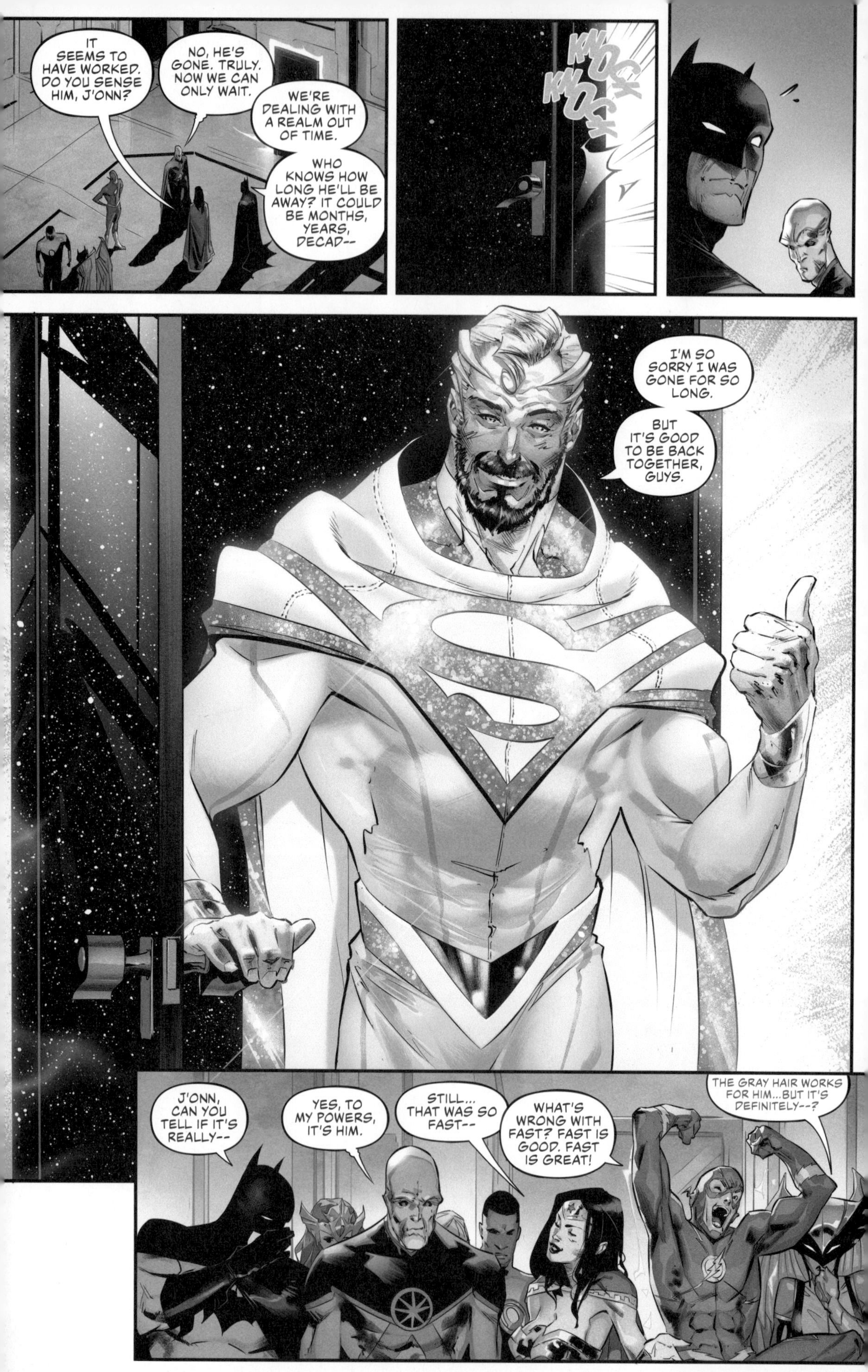
IT SEEMS TO HAVE WORKED. DO YOU SENSE HIM, J'ONN?
NO, HE'S GONE. TRULY. NOW WE CAN ONLY WAIT.
WE'RE DEALING WITH A REALM OUT OF TIME.
WHO KNOWS HOW LONG HE'LL BE AWAY? IT COULD BE MONTHS, YEARS, DECAD--
KNOCK KNOCK
I'M SO SORRY I WAS GONE FOR SO LONG.
BUT IT'S GOOD TO BE BACK TOGETHER, GUYS.
J'ONN, CAN YOU TELL IF IT'S REALLY--
YES, TO MY POWERS, IT'S HIM.
STILL... THAT WAS SO FAST--
WHAT'S WRONG WITH FAST? FAST IS GOOD. FAST IS GREAT!
THE GRAY HAIR WORKS FOR HIM...BUT IT'S DEFINITELY--?

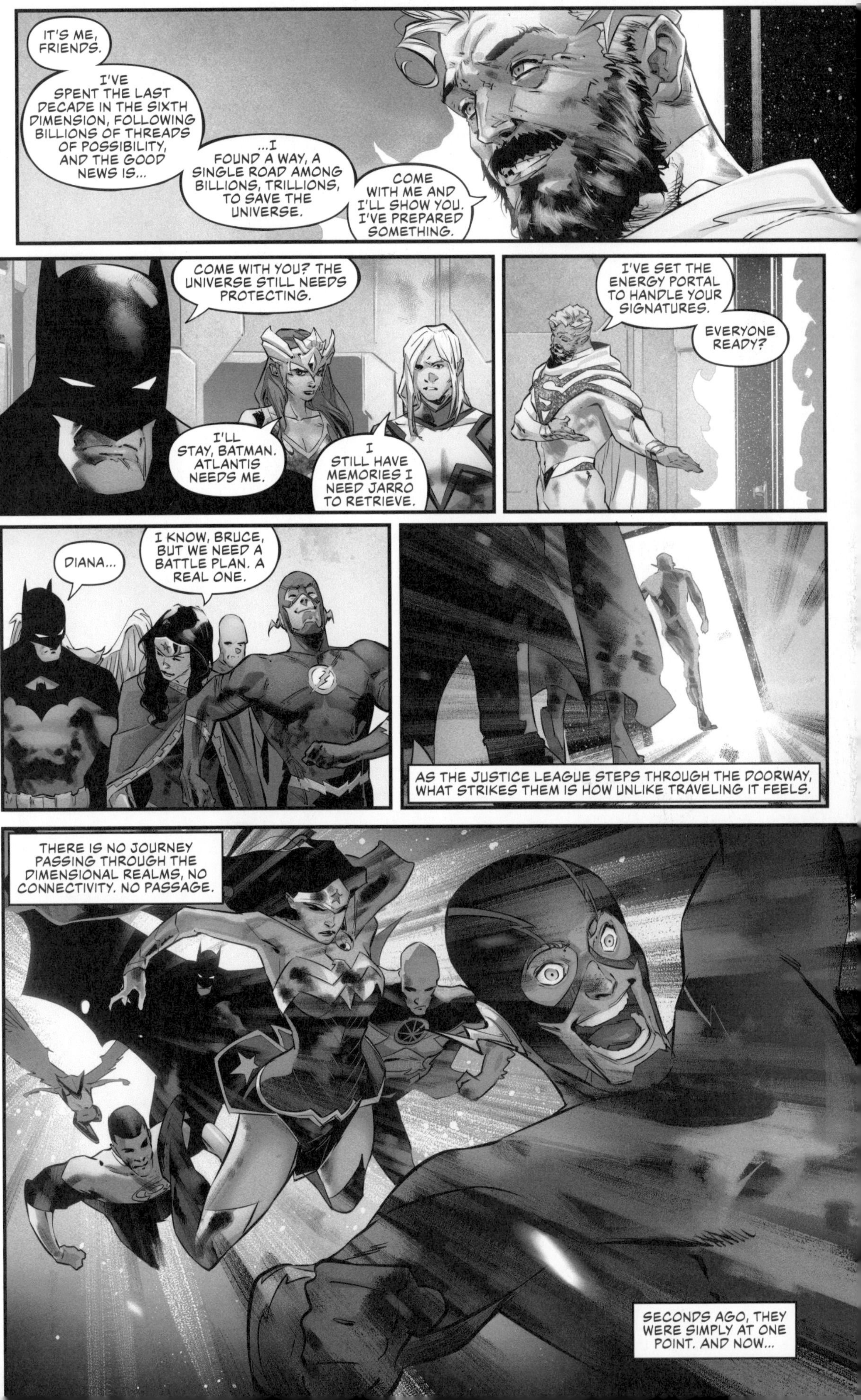

IT'S ME, FRIENDS.
I'VE SPENT THE LAST DECADE IN THE SIXTH DIMENSION, FOLLOWING BILLIONS OF THREADS OF POSSIBILITY, AND THE GOOD NEWS IS...
...I FOUND A WAY, A SINGLE ROAD AMONG BILLIONS, TRILLIONS, TO SAVE THE UNIVERSE.
COME WITH ME AND I'LL SHOW YOU. I'VE PREPARED SOMETHING.
COME WITH YOU? THE UNIVERSE STILL NEEDS PROTECTING.
I'LL STAY, BATMAN. ATLANTIS NEEDS ME.
I STILL HAVE MEMORIES I NEED JARRO TO RETRIEVE.
I'VE SET THE ENERGY PORTAL TO HANDLE YOUR SIGNATURES.
EVERYONE READY?
DIANA...
I KNOW, BRUCE, BUT WE NEED A BATTLE PLAN. A REAL ONE.
AS THE JUSTICE LEAGUE STEPS THROUGH THE DOORWAY, WHAT STRIKES THEM IS HOW UNLIKE TRAVELING IT FEELS.
THERE IS NO JOURNEY PASSING THROUGH THE DIMENSIONAL REALMS, NO CONNECTIVITY. NO PASSAGE.
SECONDS AGO, THEY WERE SIMPLY AT ONE POINT. AND NOW...

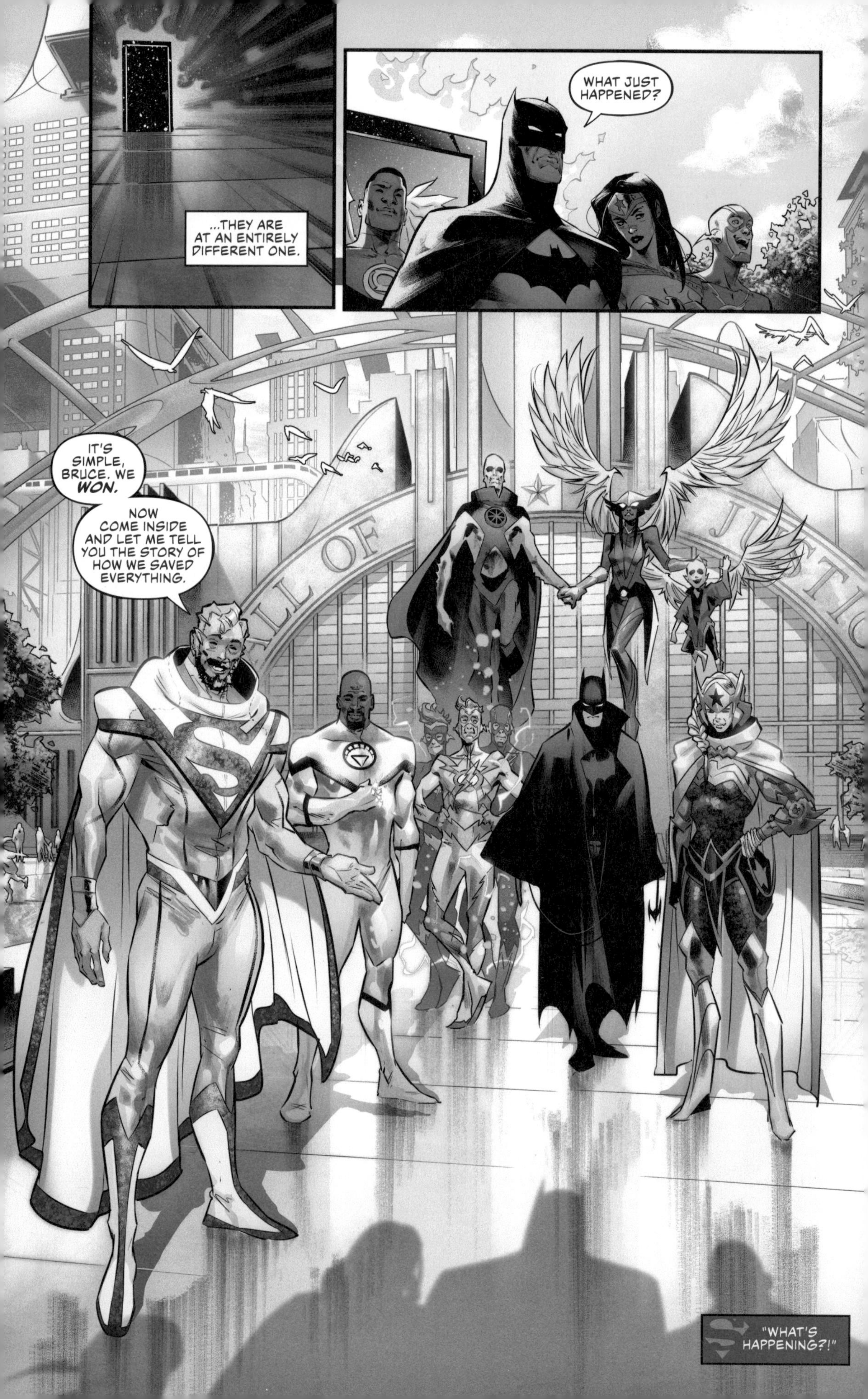

...THEY ARE AT AN ENTIRELY DIFFERENT ONE.
WHAT JUST HAPPENED?
IT'S SIMPLE, BRUCE. WE **WON.**
NOW COME INSIDE AND LET ME TELL YOU THE STORY OF HOW WE SAVED EVERYTHING.
HALL OF JUSTICE
"WHAT'S HAPPENING?!"

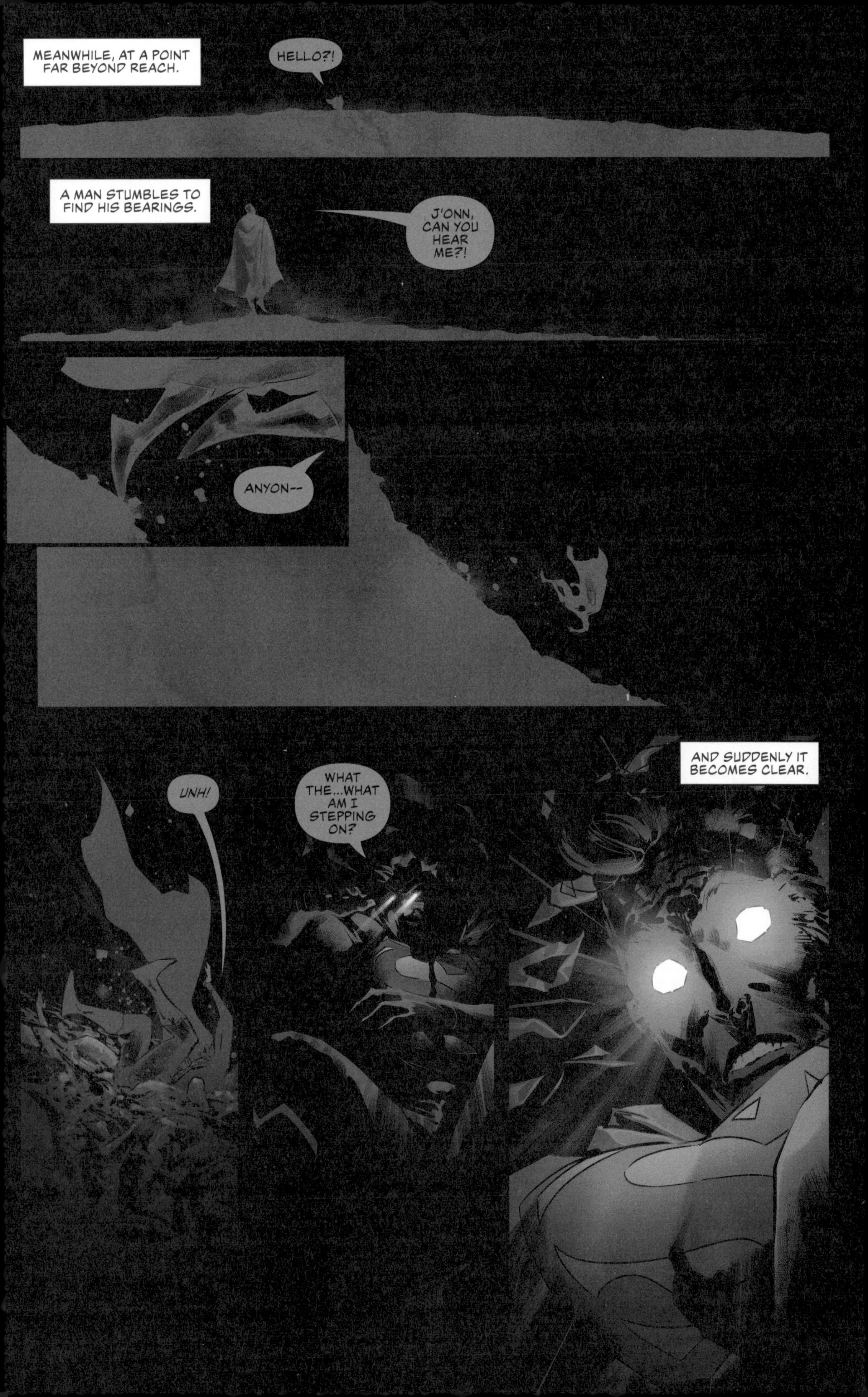
MEANWHILE, AT A POINT FAR BEYOND REACH.
HELLO?!
A MAN STUMBLES TO FIND HIS BEARINGS.
J'ONN, CAN YOU HEAR ME?!
ANYON--
UNH!
WHAT THE...WHAT AM I STEPPING ON?
AND SUDDENLY IT BECOMES CLEAR.

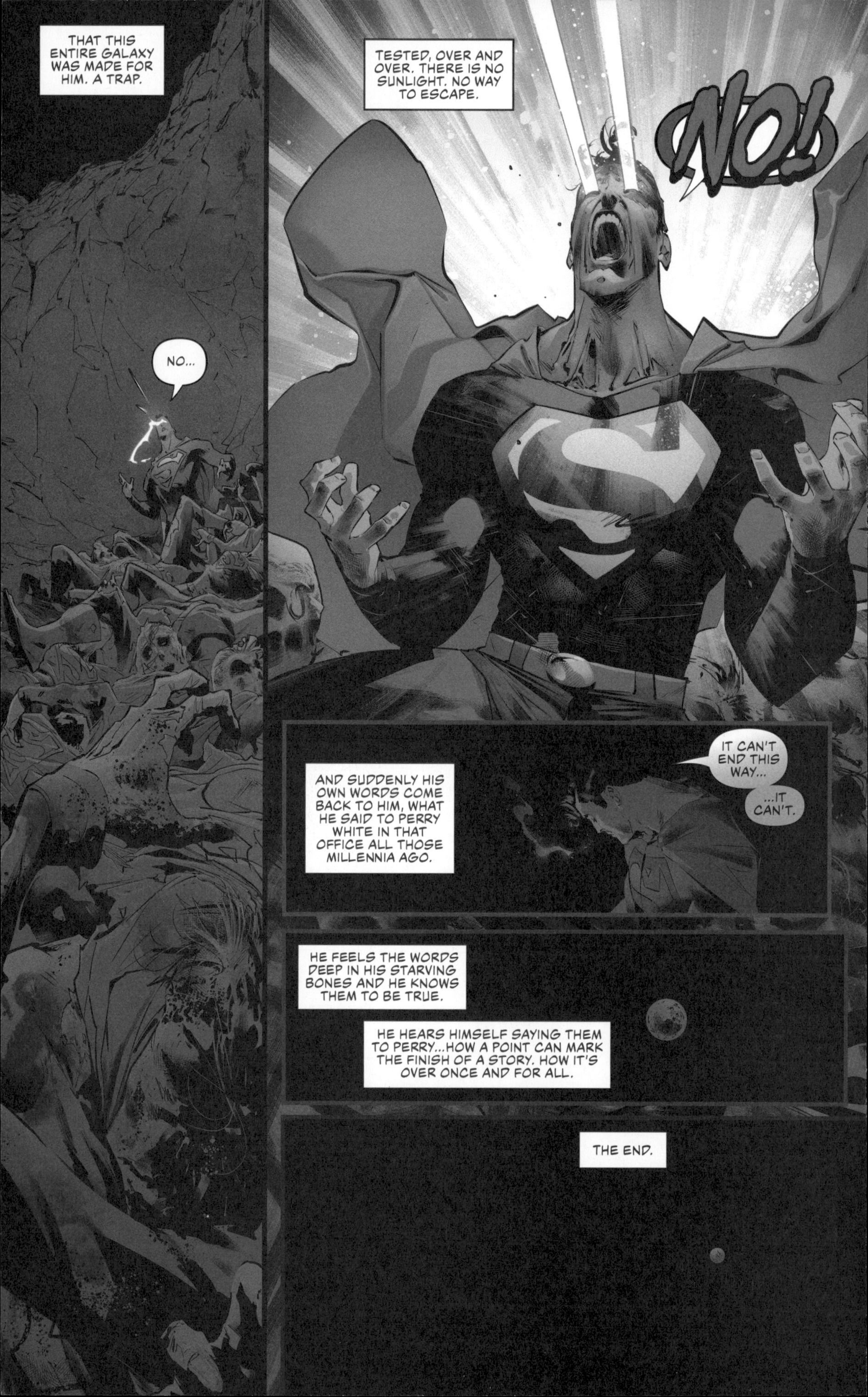
THAT THIS ENTIRE GALAXY WAS MADE FOR HIM. A TRAP.
NO...
TESTED, OVER AND OVER. THERE IS NO SUNLIGHT. NO WAY TO ESCAPE.
NO!
AND SUDDENLY HIS OWN WORDS COME BACK TO HIM, WHAT HE SAID TO PERRY WHITE IN THAT OFFICE ALL THOSE MILLENNIA AGO.
IT CAN'T END THIS WAY...
...IT CAN'T.
HE FEELS THE WORDS DEEP IN HIS STARVING BONES AND HE KNOWS THEM TO BE TRUE.
HE HEARS HIMSELF SAYING THEM TO PERRY...HOW A POINT CAN MARK THE FINISH OF A STORY. HOW IT'S OVER ONCE AND FOR ALL.
THE END.

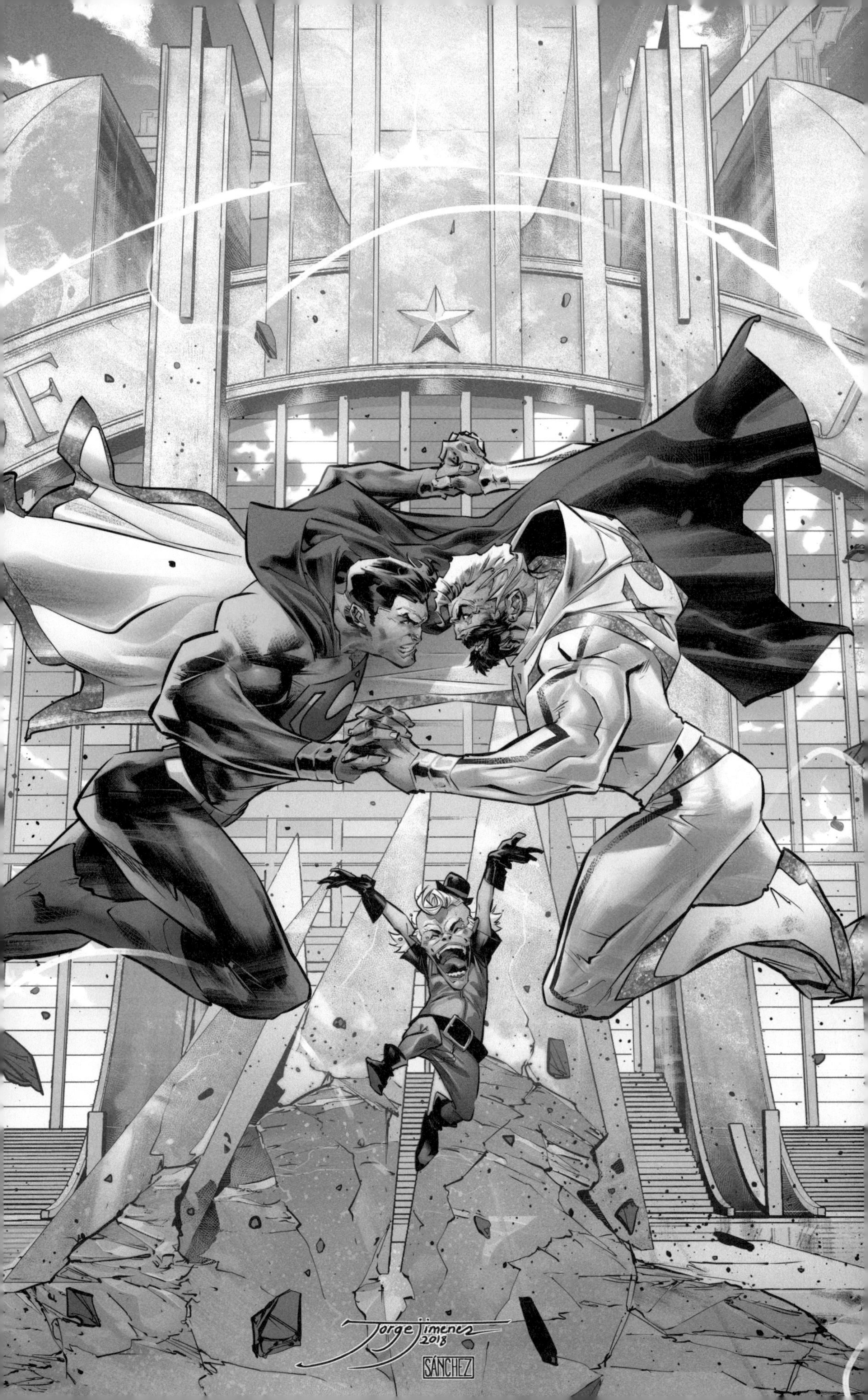
Jorge Jimenez 2018
SÁNCHEZ

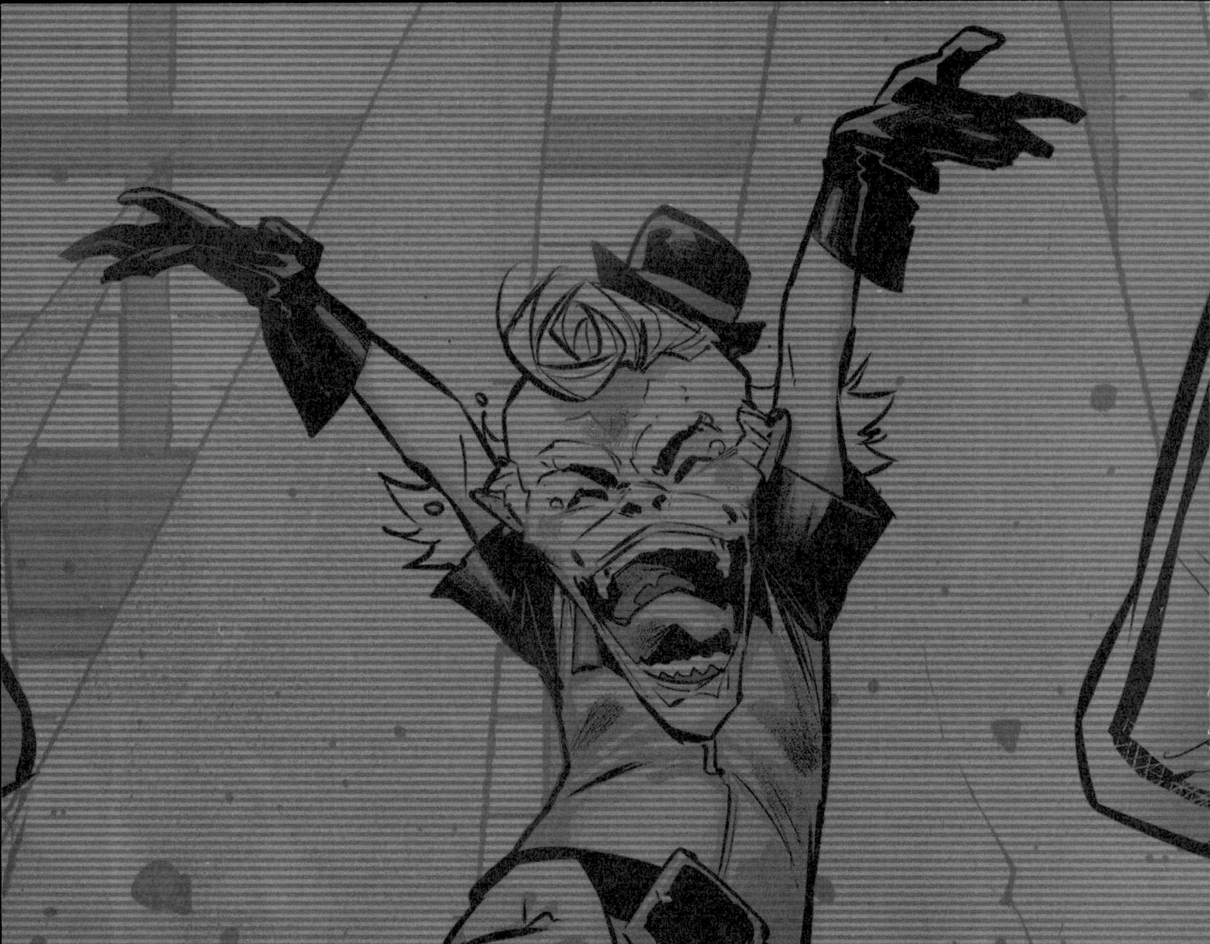

JUSTICE
LEAGUE
#20

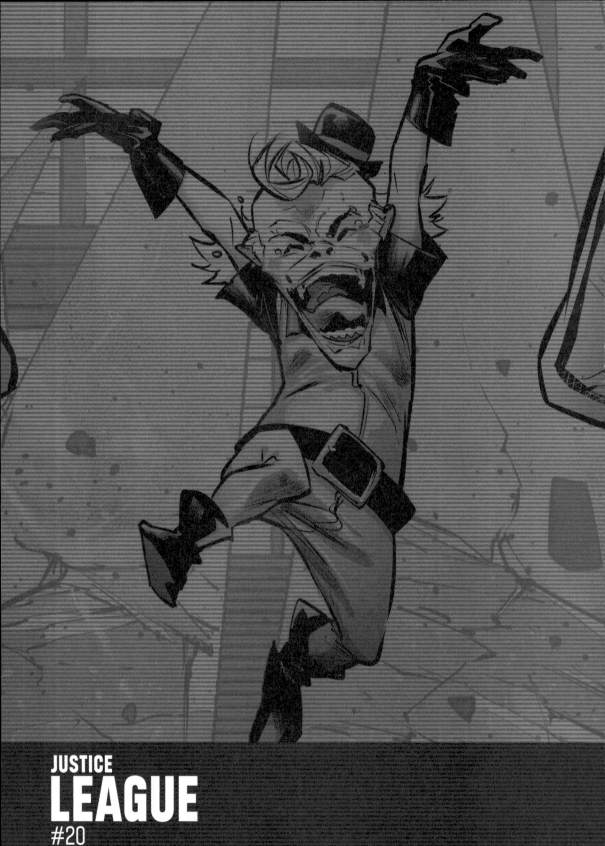

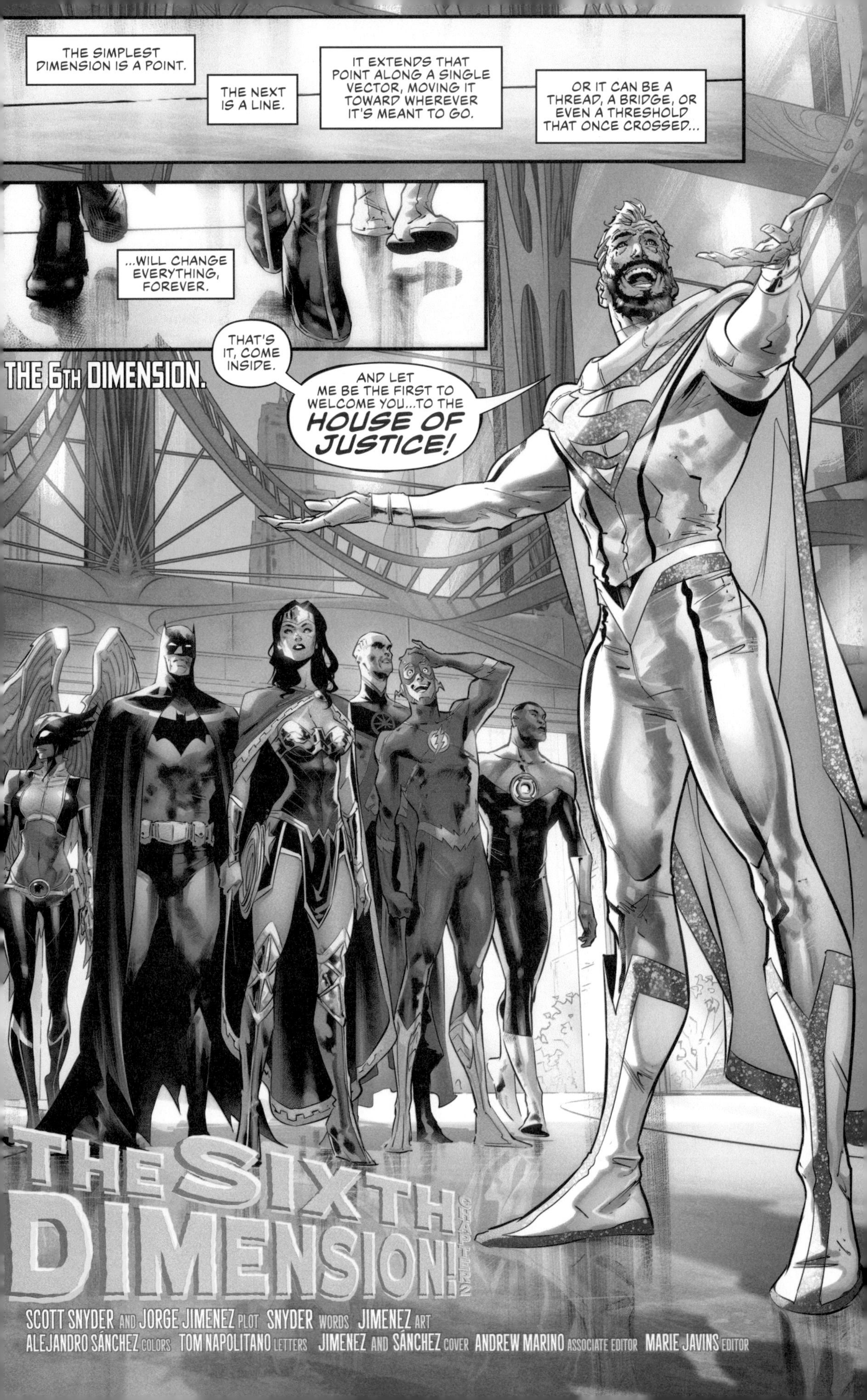
THE SIMPLEST DIMENSION IS A POINT.
THE NEXT IS A LINE.
IT EXTENDS THAT POINT ALONG A SINGLE VECTOR, MOVING IT TOWARD WHEREVER IT'S MEANT TO GO.
OR IT CAN BE A THREAD, A BRIDGE, OR EVEN A THRESHOLD THAT ONCE CROSSED...
...WILL CHANGE EVERYTHING, FOREVER.
THE 6TH DIMENSION.
THAT'S IT, COME INSIDE.
AND LET ME BE THE FIRST TO WELCOME YOU...TO THE HOUSE OF JUSTICE!
THE SIXTH DIMENSION! CHAPTER 2
SCOTT SNYDER AND JORGE JIMENEZ PLOT SNYDER WORDS JIMENEZ ART
ALEJANDRO SÁNCHEZ COLORS TOM NAPOLITANO LETTERS JIMENEZ AND SÁNCHEZ COVER ANDREW MARINO ASSOCIATE EDITOR MARIE JAVINS EDITOR

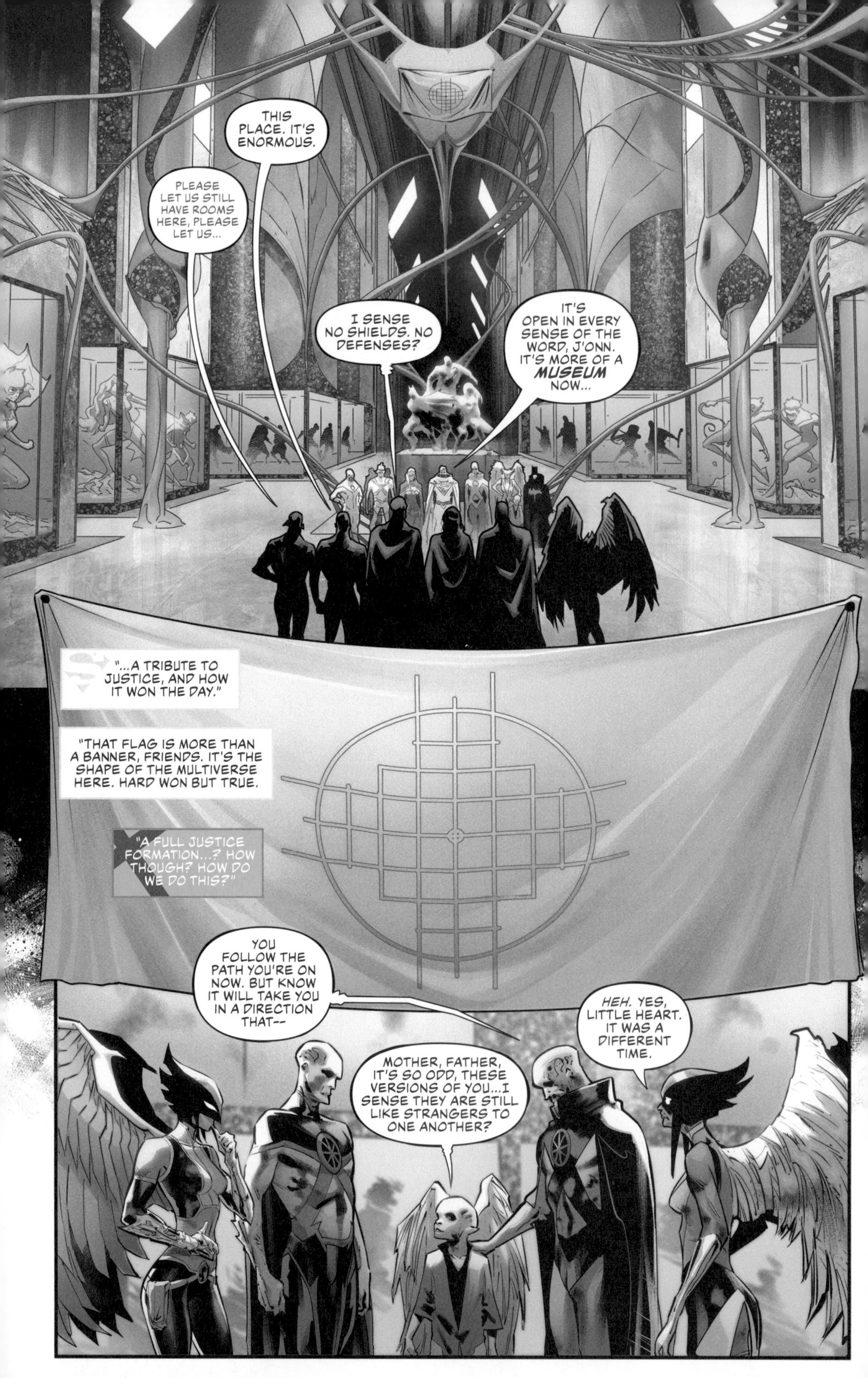
THIS PLACE. IT'S ENORMOUS.
PLEASE LET US STILL HAVE ROOMS HERE, PLEASE LET US...
I SENSE NO SHIELDS. NO DEFENSES?
IT'S OPEN IN EVERY SENSE OF THE WORD, J'ONN. IT'S MORE OF A MUSEUM NOW...
"...A TRIBUTE TO JUSTICE, AND HOW IT WON THE DAY."
"THAT FLAG IS MORE THAN A BANNER, FRIENDS. IT'S THE SHAPE OF THE MULTIVERSE HERE. HARD WON BUT TRUE.
"A FULL JUSTICE FORMATION...? HOW THOUGH? HOW DO WE DO THIS?"
YOU FOLLOW THE PATH YOU'RE ON NOW. BUT KNOW IT WILL TAKE YOU IN A DIRECTION THAT--
HEH. YES, LITTLE HEART. IT WAS A DIFFERENT TIME.
MOTHER, FATHER, IT'S SO ODD, THESE VERSIONS OF YOU...I SENSE THEY ARE STILL LIKE STRANGERS TO ONE ANOTHER?

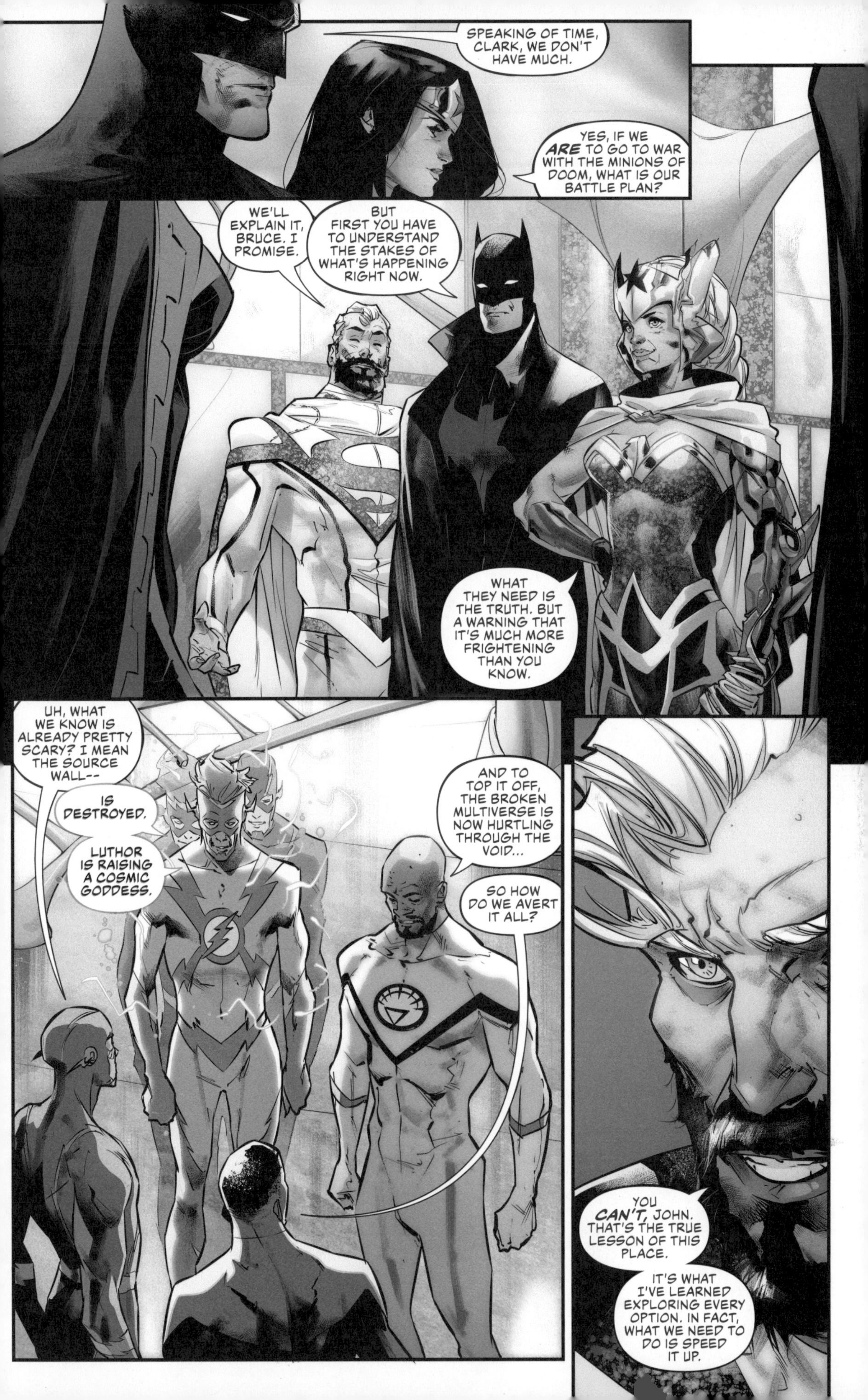
SPEAKING OF TIME, CLARK, WE DON'T HAVE MUCH.
YES, IF WE ARE TO GO TO WAR WITH THE MINIONS OF DOOM, WHAT IS OUR BATTLE PLAN?
WE'LL EXPLAIN IT, BRUCE. I PROMISE.
BUT FIRST YOU HAVE TO UNDERSTAND THE STAKES OF WHAT'S HAPPENING RIGHT NOW.
WHAT THEY NEED IS THE TRUTH. BUT A WARNING THAT IT'S MUCH MORE FRIGHTENING THAN YOU KNOW.
UH, WHAT WE KNOW IS ALREADY PRETTY SCARY? I MEAN THE SOURCE WALL--
IS DESTROYED.
LUTHOR IS RAISING A COSMIC GODDESS.
AND TO TOP IT OFF, THE BROKEN MULTIVERSE IS NOW HURTLING THROUGH THE VOID...
SO HOW DO WE AVERT IT ALL?
YOU CAN'T, JOHN. THAT'S THE TRUE LESSON OF THIS PLACE.
IT'S WHAT I'VE LEARNED EXPLORING EVERY OPTION. IN FACT, WHAT WE NEED TO DO IS SPEED IT UP.

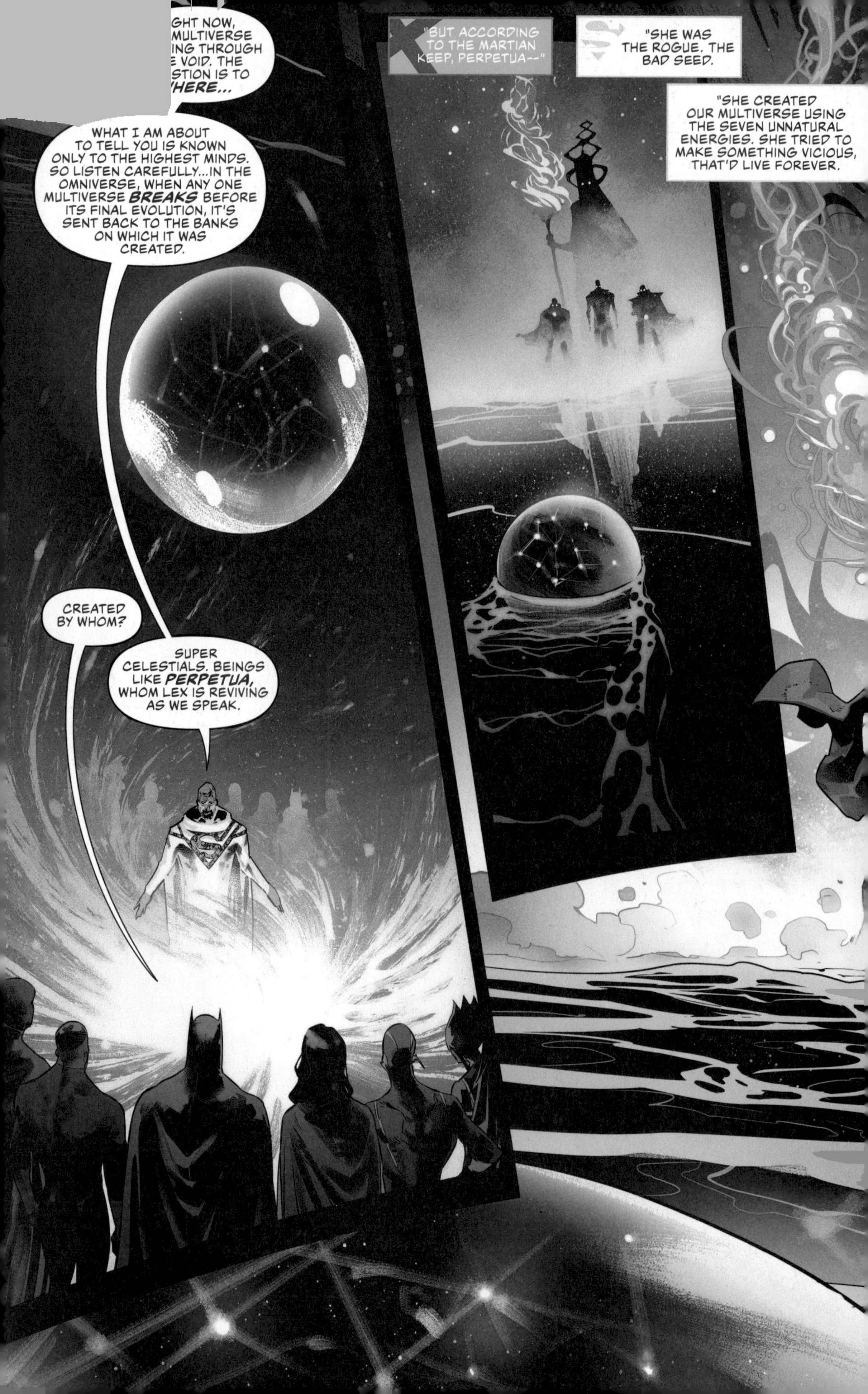
GHT NOW, MULTIVERSE ING THROUGH E VOID. THE STION IS TO WHERE...
WHAT I AM ABOUT TO TELL YOU IS KNOWN ONLY TO THE HIGHEST MINDS. SO LISTEN CAREFULLY...IN THE OMNIVERSE, WHEN ANY ONE MULTIVERSE BREAKS BEFORE ITS FINAL EVOLUTION, IT'S SENT BACK TO THE BANKS ON WHICH IT WAS CREATED.
CREATED BY WHOM?
SUPER CELESTIALS. BEINGS LIKE PERPETUA, WHOM LEX IS REVIVING AS WE SPEAK.
"BUT ACCORDING TO THE MARTIAN KEEP, PERPETUA--"
"SHE WAS THE ROGUE. THE BAD SEED.
"SHE CREATED OUR MULTIVERSE USING THE SEVEN UNNATURAL ENERGIES. SHE TRIED TO MAKE SOMETHING VICIOUS, THAT'D LIVE FOREVER.

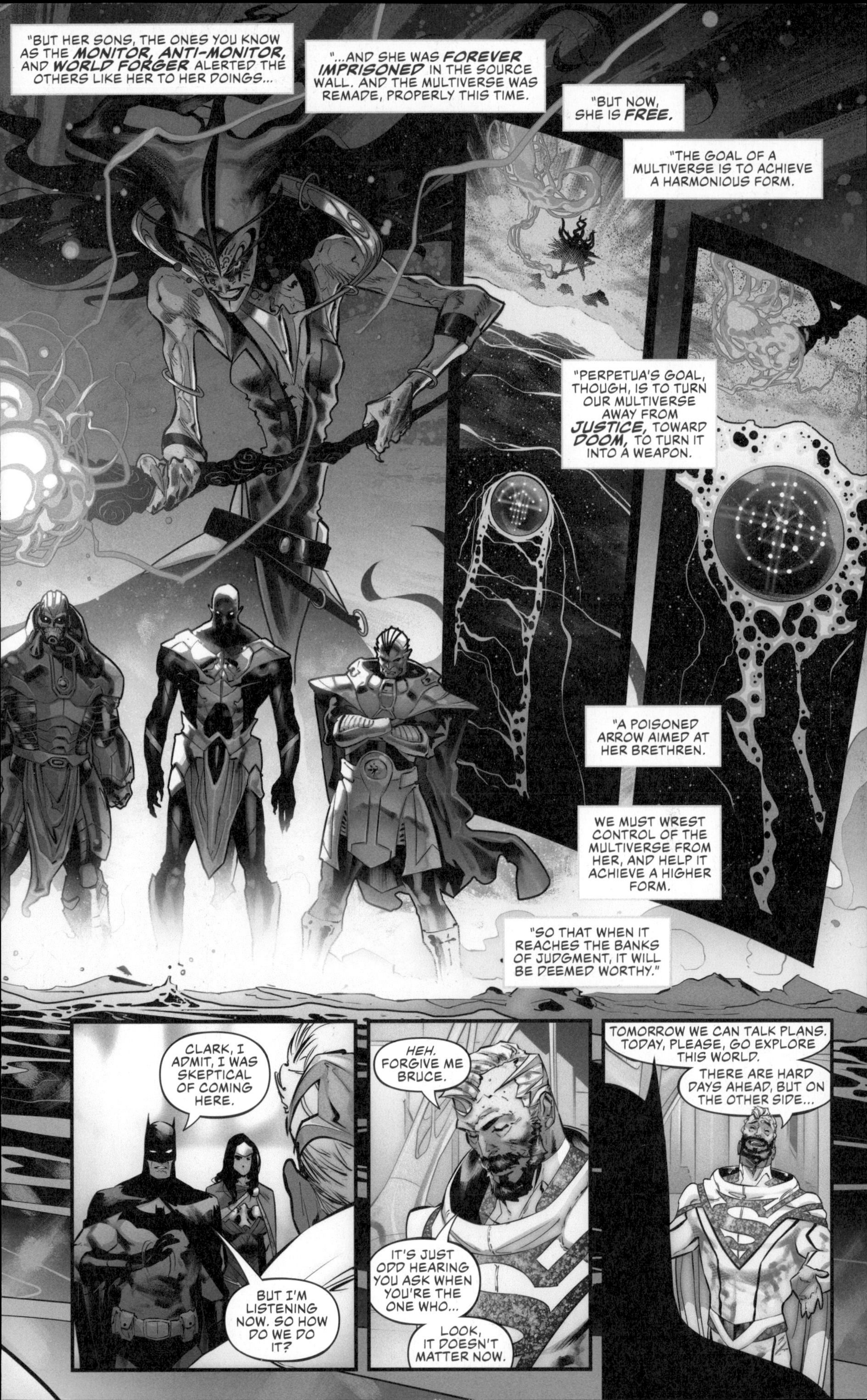

"BUT HER SONS, THE ONES YOU KNOW AS THE MONITOR, ANTI-MONITOR, AND WORLD FORGER ALERTED THE OTHERS LIKE HER TO HER DOINGS...
"...AND SHE WAS FOREVER IMPRISONED IN THE SOURCE WALL. AND THE MULTIVERSE WAS REMADE, PROPERLY THIS TIME.
"BUT NOW, SHE IS FREE.
"THE GOAL OF A MULTIVERSE IS TO ACHIEVE A HARMONIOUS FORM.
"PERPETUA'S GOAL, THOUGH, IS TO TURN OUR MULTIVERSE AWAY FROM JUSTICE, TOWARD DOOM, TO TURN IT INTO A WEAPON.
"A POISONED ARROW AIMED AT HER BRETHREN.
WE MUST WREST CONTROL OF THE MULTIVERSE FROM HER, AND HELP IT ACHIEVE A HIGHER FORM.
"SO THAT WHEN IT REACHES THE BANKS OF JUDGMENT, IT WILL BE DEEMED WORTHY."
CLARK, I ADMIT, I WAS SKEPTICAL OF COMING HERE.
BUT I'M LISTENING NOW. SO HOW DO WE DO IT?
HEH. FORGIVE ME BRUCE.
IT'S JUST ODD HEARING YOU ASK WHEN YOU'RE THE ONE WHO...
LOOK, IT DOESN'T MATTER NOW.
TOMORROW WE CAN TALK PLANS. TODAY, PLEASE, GO EXPLORE THIS WORLD.
THERE ARE HARD DAYS AHEAD, BUT ON THE OTHER SIDE...

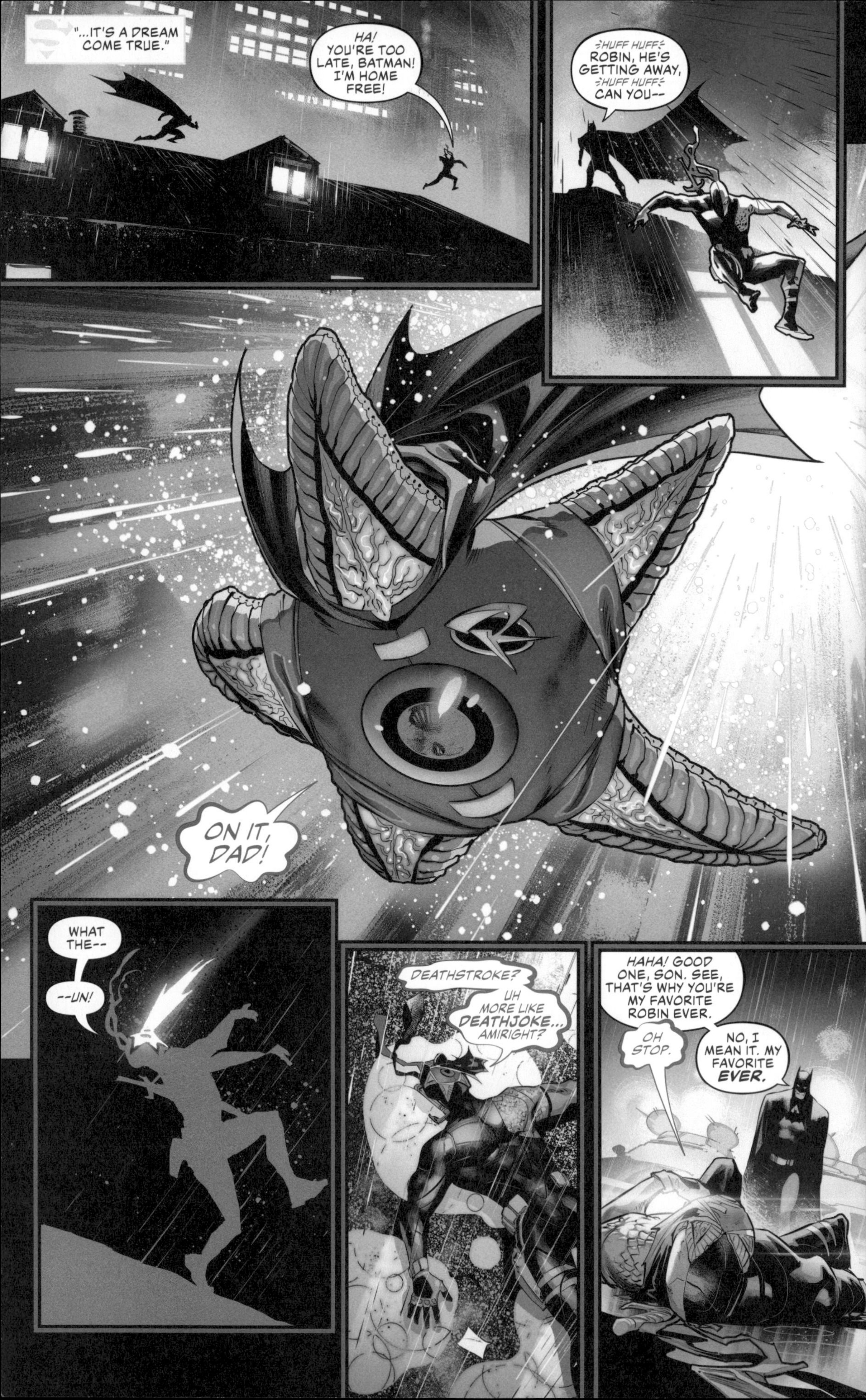
"...IT'S A DREAM COME TRUE."
HA! YOU'RE TOO LATE, BATMAN! I'M HOME FREE!
HUFF HUFF ROBIN, HE'S GETTING AWAY, HUFF HUFF CAN YOU--
ON IT, DAD!
WHAT THE--
--UN!
DEATHSTROKE?
UH MORE LIKE DEATHJOKE... AMIRIGHT?
HAHA! GOOD ONE, SON. SEE, THAT'S WHY YOU'RE MY FAVORITE ROBIN EVER.
OH STOP.
NO, I MEAN IT. MY FAVORITE EVER.

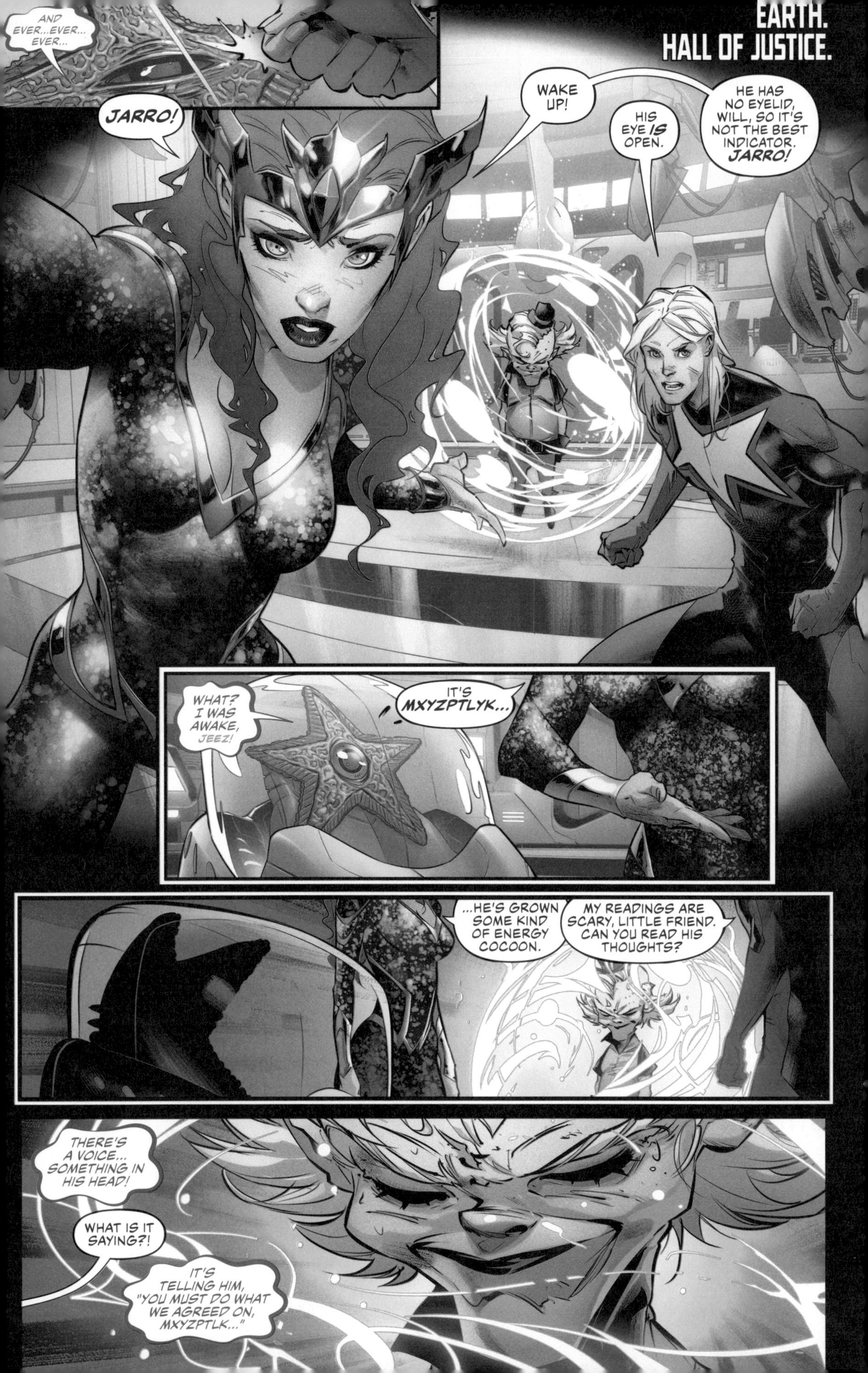

AND EVER...EVER... EVER...
EARTH. HALL OF JUSTICE.
JARRO!
WAKE UP!
HIS EYE IS OPEN.
HE HAS NO EYELID, WILL, SO IT'S NOT THE BEST INDICATOR. JARRO!
WHAT? I WAS AWAKE, JEEZ!
IT'S MXYZPTLYK...
...HE'S GROWN SOME KIND OF ENERGY COCOON.
MY READINGS ARE SCARY, LITTLE FRIEND. CAN YOU READ HIS THOUGHTS?
THERE'S A VOICE... SOMETHING IN HIS HEAD!
WHAT IS IT SAYING?!
IT'S TELLING HIM, "YOU MUST DO WHAT WE AGREED ON, MXYZPTLK..."

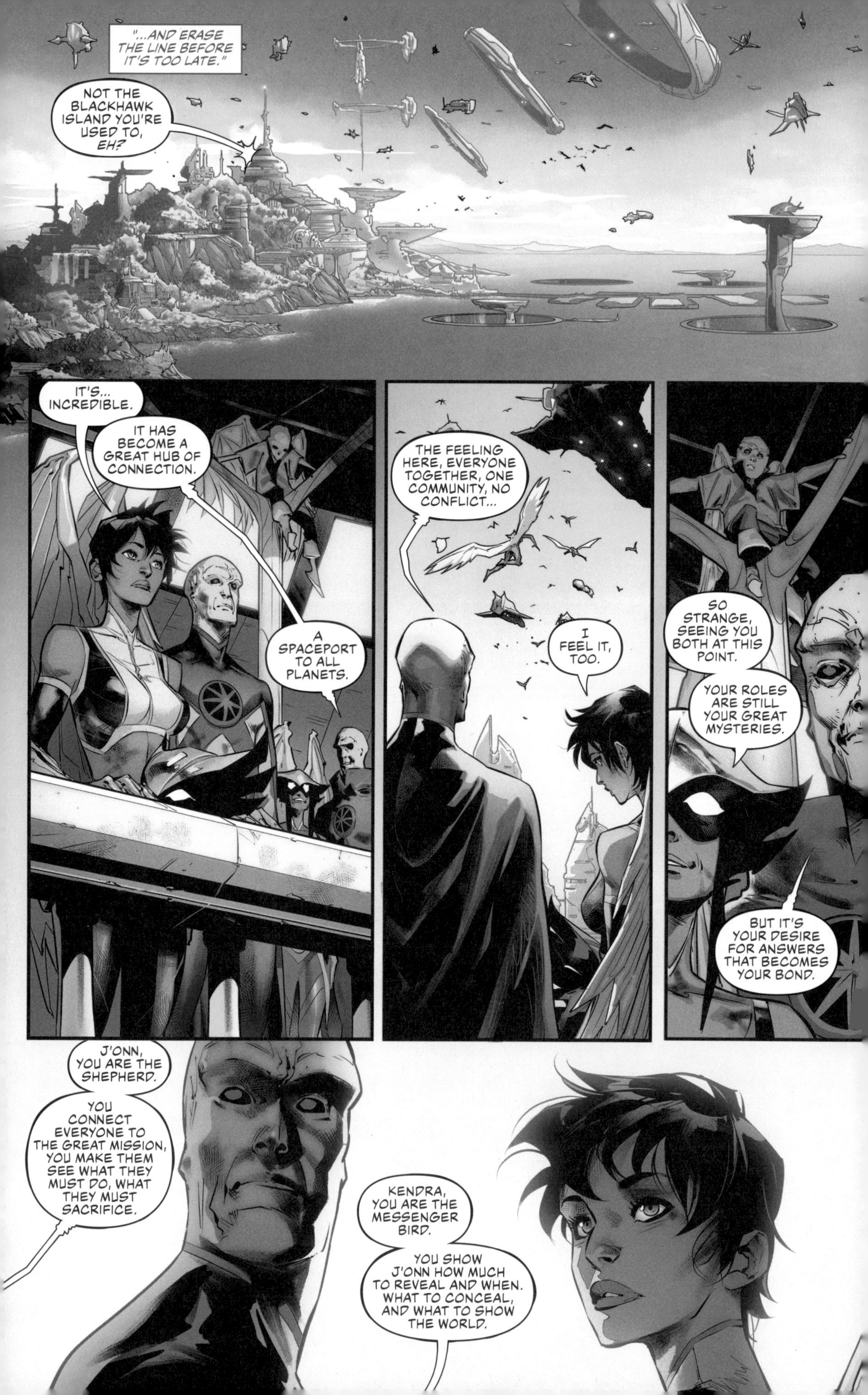
"...AND ERASE THE LINE BEFORE IT'S TOO LATE."
NOT THE BLACKHAWK ISLAND YOU'RE USED TO, EH?
IT'S... INCREDIBLE.
IT HAS BECOME A GREAT HUB OF CONNECTION.
A SPACEPORT TO ALL PLANETS.
THE FEELING HERE, EVERYONE TOGETHER, ONE COMMUNITY, NO CONFLICT...
I FEEL IT, TOO.
SO STRANGE, SEEING YOU BOTH AT THIS POINT.
YOUR ROLES ARE STILL YOUR GREAT MYSTERIES.
BUT IT'S YOUR DESIRE FOR ANSWERS THAT BECOMES YOUR BOND.
J'ONN, YOU ARE THE SHEPHERD.
YOU CONNECT EVERYONE TO THE GREAT MISSION, YOU MAKE THEM SEE WHAT THEY MUST DO, WHAT THEY MUST SACRIFICE.
KENDRA, YOU ARE THE MESSENGER BIRD.
YOU SHOW J'ONN HOW MUCH TO REVEAL AND WHEN. WHAT TO CONCEAL, AND WHAT TO SHOW THE WORLD.

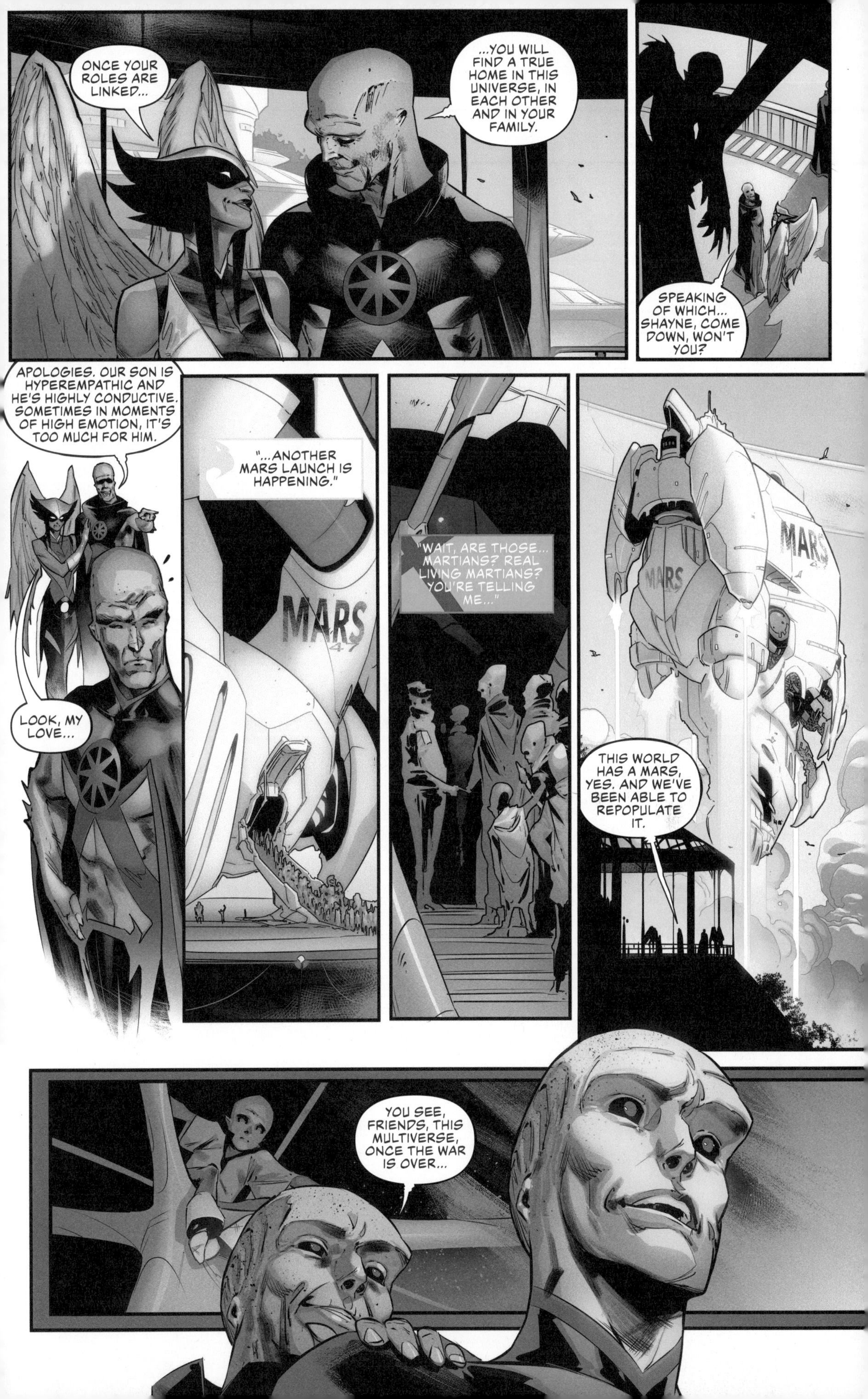
ONCE YOUR ROLES ARE LINKED...
...YOU WILL FIND A TRUE HOME IN THIS UNIVERSE, IN EACH OTHER AND IN YOUR FAMILY.
SPEAKING OF WHICH... SHAYNE, COME DOWN, WON'T YOU?
APOLOGIES. OUR SON IS HYPEREMPATHIC AND HE'S HIGHLY CONDUCTIVE. SOMETIMES IN MOMENTS OF HIGH EMOTION, IT'S TOO MUCH FOR HIM.
LOOK, MY LOVE...
"...ANOTHER MARS LAUNCH IS HAPPENING."
MARS
"WAIT, ARE THOSE... MARTIANS? REAL LIVING MARTIANS? YOU'RE TELLING ME..."
MARS
THIS WORLD HAS A MARS, YES. AND WE'VE BEEN ABLE TO REPOPULATE IT.
YOU SEE, FRIENDS, THIS MULTIVERSE, ONCE THE WAR IS OVER...

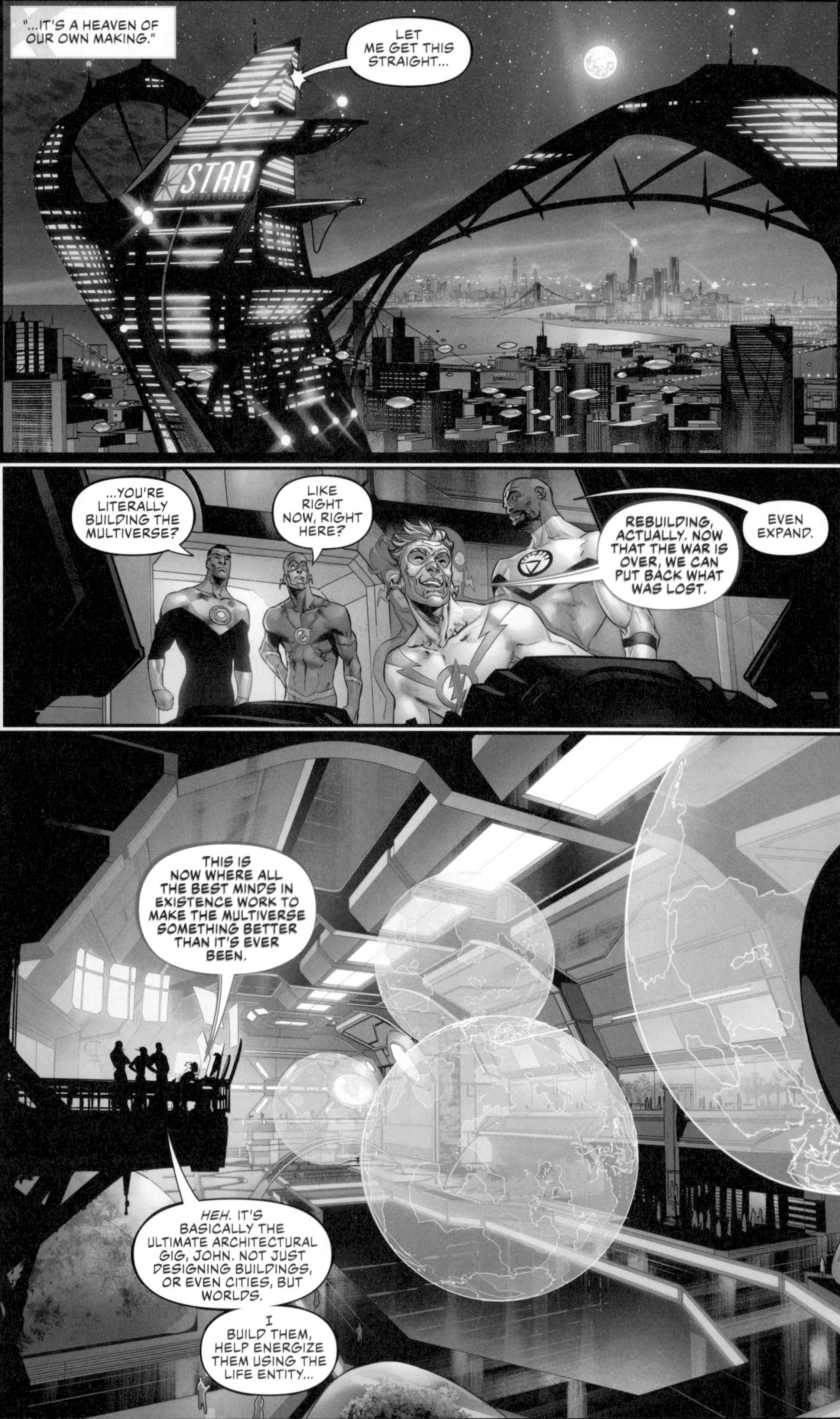
"...IT'S A HEAVEN OF OUR OWN MAKING."
LET ME GET THIS STRAIGHT...
S.T.A.R. LABORATORIES
...YOU'RE LITERALLY BUILDING THE MULTIVERSE?
LIKE RIGHT NOW, RIGHT HERE?
REBUILDING, ACTUALLY. NOW THAT THE WAR IS OVER, WE CAN PUT BACK WHAT WAS LOST.
EVEN EXPAND.
THIS IS NOW WHERE ALL THE BEST MINDS IN EXISTENCE WORK TO MAKE THE MULTIVERSE SOMETHING BETTER THAN IT'S EVER BEEN.
HEH. IT'S BASICALLY THE ULTIMATE ARCHITECTURAL GIG, JOHN. NOT JUST DESIGNING BUILDINGS, OR EVEN CITIES, BUT WORLDS.
I BUILD THEM, HELP ENERGIZE THEM USING THE LIFE ENTITY...

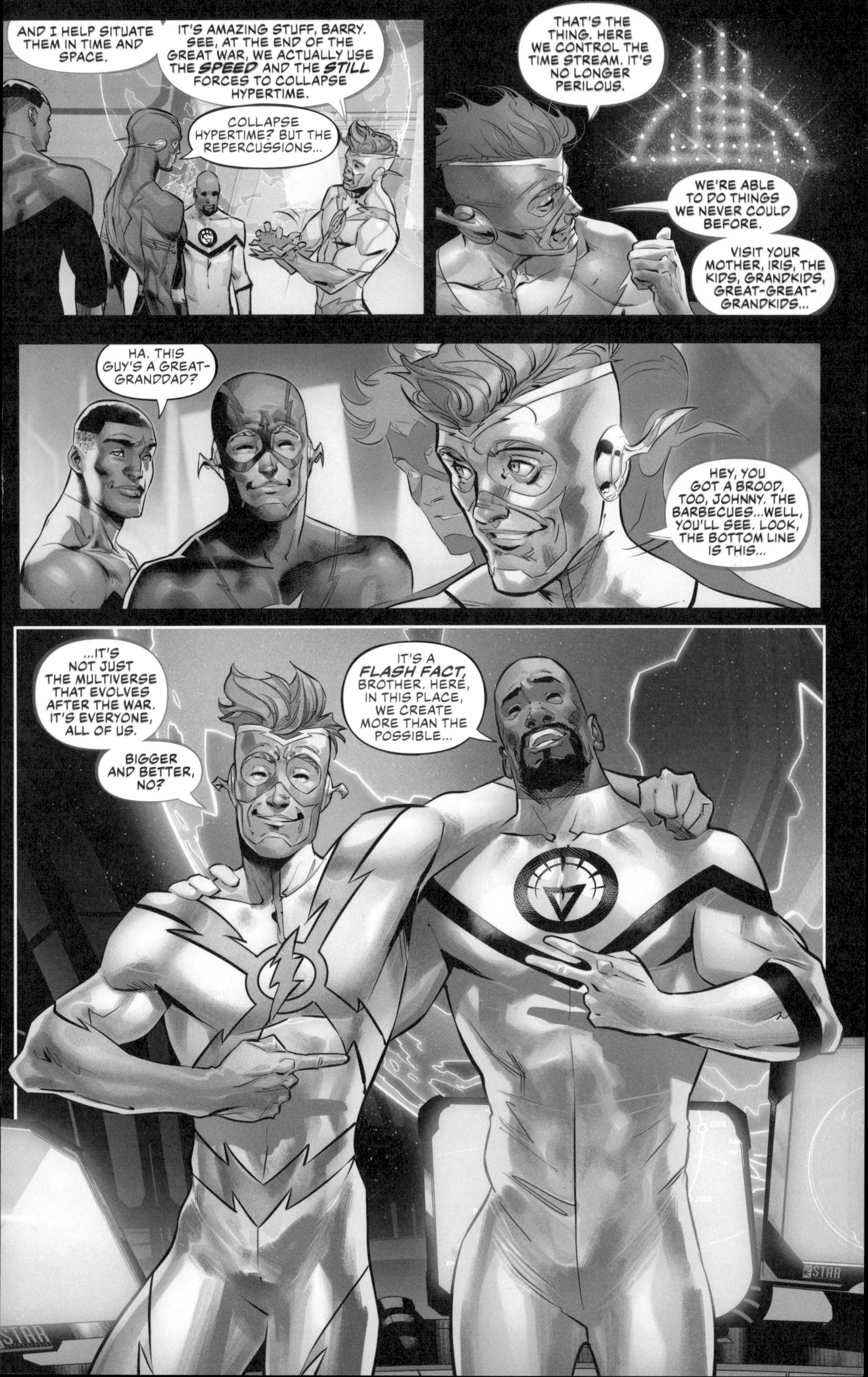
AND I HELP SITUATE THEM IN TIME AND SPACE.
IT'S AMAZING STUFF, BARRY. SEE, AT THE END OF THE GREAT WAR, WE ACTUALLY USE THE SPEED AND THE STILL FORCES TO COLLAPSE HYPERTIME.
COLLAPSE HYPERTIME? BUT THE REPERCUSSIONS...
THAT'S THE THING. HERE WE CONTROL THE TIME STREAM. IT'S NO LONGER PERILOUS.
WE'RE ABLE TO DO THINGS WE NEVER COULD BEFORE.
VISIT YOUR MOTHER, IRIS, THE KIDS, GRANDKIDS, GREAT-GREAT-GRANDKIDS...
HA. THIS GUY'S A GREAT-GRANDDAD?
HEY, YOU GOT A BROOD, TOO, JOHNNY. THE BARBECUES...WELL, YOU'LL SEE. LOOK, THE BOTTOM LINE IS THIS...
...IT'S NOT JUST THE MULTIVERSE THAT EVOLVES AFTER THE WAR. IT'S EVERYONE, ALL OF US.
BIGGER AND BETTER, NO?
IT'S A FLASH FACT, BROTHER. HERE, IN THIS PLACE, WE CREATE MORE THAN THE POSSIBLE...

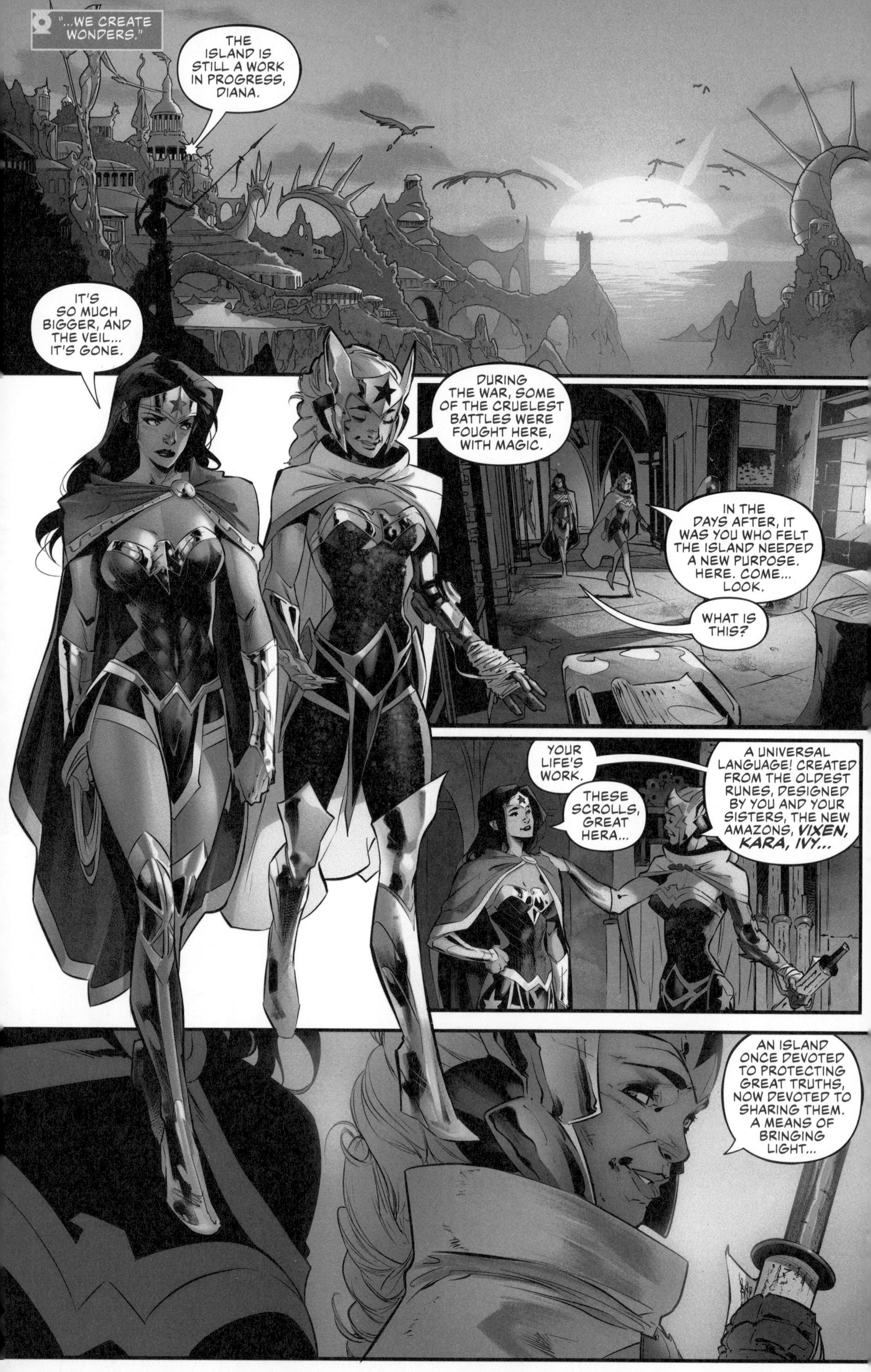
"...WE CREATE WONDERS."
THE ISLAND IS STILL A WORK IN PROGRESS, DIANA.
IT'S SO MUCH BIGGER, AND THE VEIL... IT'S GONE.
DURING THE WAR, SOME OF THE CRUELEST BATTLES WERE FOUGHT HERE, WITH MAGIC.
IN THE DAYS AFTER, IT WAS YOU WHO FELT THE ISLAND NEEDED A NEW PURPOSE. HERE. COME... LOOK.
WHAT IS THIS?
YOUR LIFE'S WORK.
THESE SCROLLS, GREAT HERA...
A UNIVERSAL LANGUAGE! CREATED FROM THE OLDEST RUNES, DESIGNED BY YOU AND YOUR SISTERS, THE NEW AMAZONS, VIXEN, KARA, IVY...
AN ISLAND ONCE DEVOTED TO PROTECTING GREAT TRUTHS, NOW DEVOTED TO SHARING THEM. A MEANS OF BRINGING LIGHT...

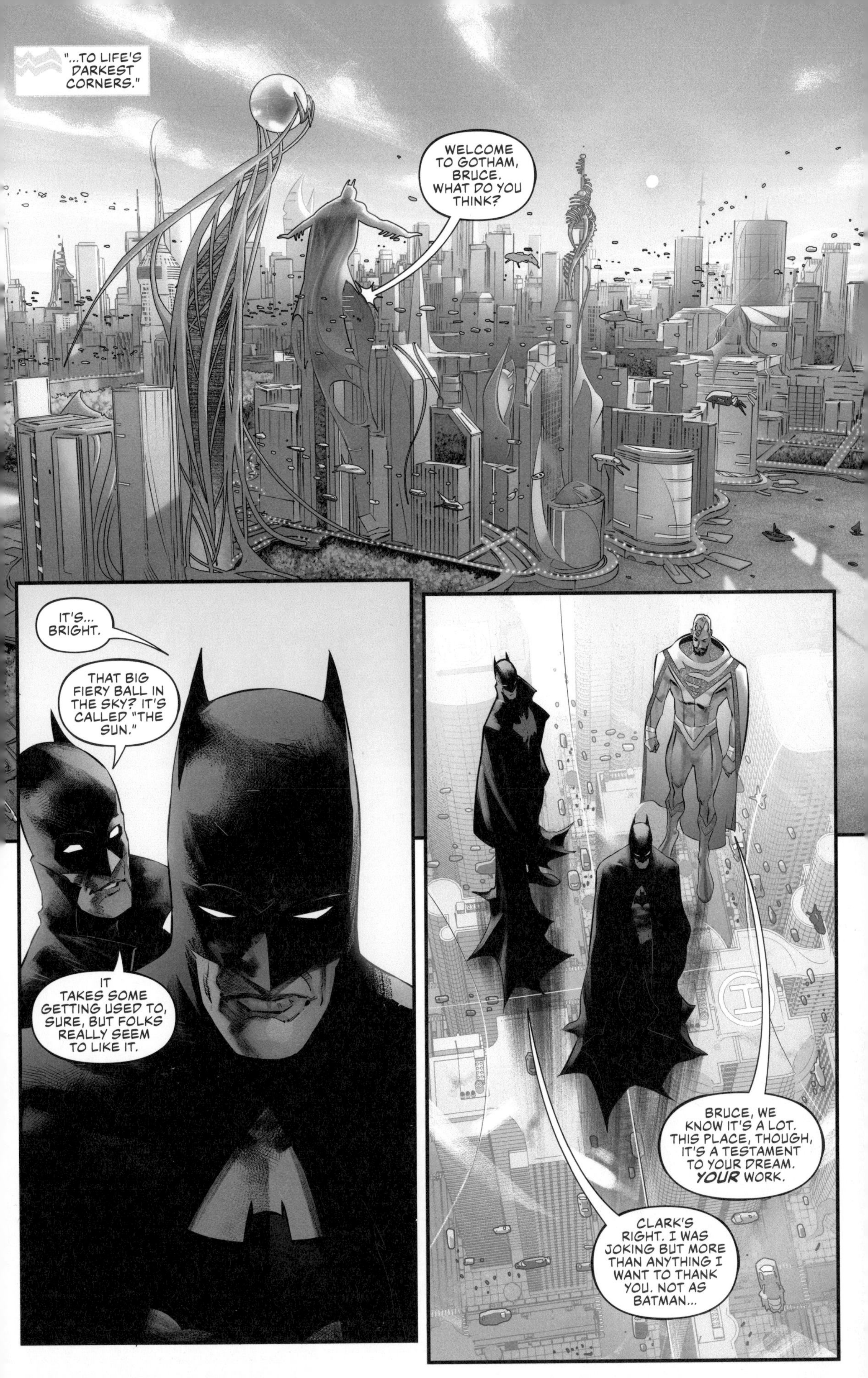
"...TO LIFE'S DARKEST CORNERS."
WELCOME TO GOTHAM, BRUCE. WHAT DO YOU THINK?
IT'S... BRIGHT.
THAT BIG FIERY BALL IN THE SKY? IT'S CALLED "THE SUN."
IT TAKES SOME GETTING USED TO, SURE, BUT FOLKS REALLY SEEM TO LIKE IT.
BRUCE, WE KNOW IT'S A LOT. THIS PLACE, THOUGH, IT'S A TESTAMENT TO YOUR DREAM. ***YOUR*** WORK.
CLARK'S RIGHT. I WAS JOKING BUT MORE THAN ANYTHING I WANT TO THANK YOU. NOT AS BATMAN...

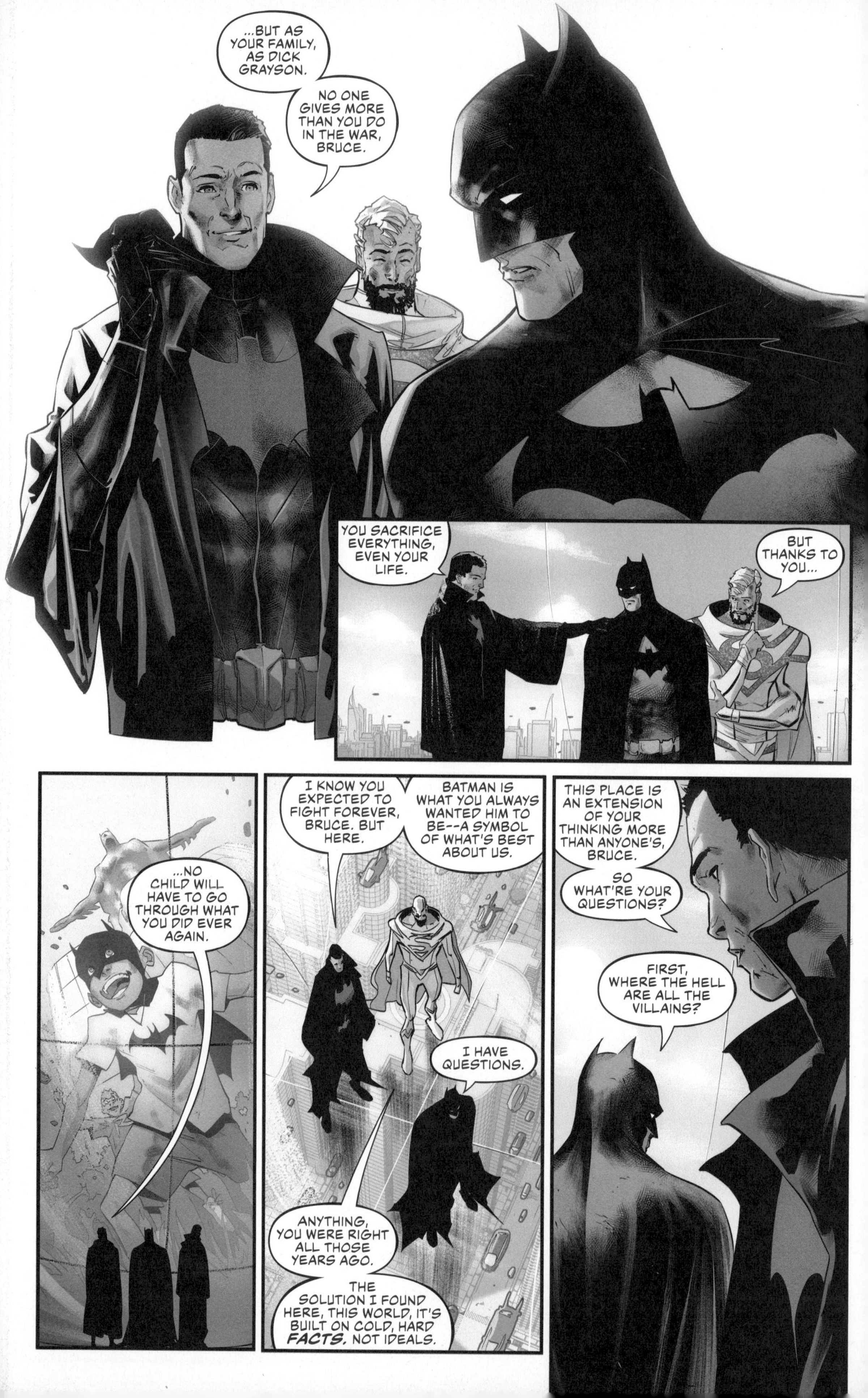
...BUT AS YOUR FAMILY, AS DICK GRAYSON.
NO ONE GIVES MORE THAN YOU DO IN THE WAR, BRUCE.
YOU SACRIFICE EVERYTHING, EVEN YOUR LIFE.
BUT THANKS TO YOU...
...NO CHILD WILL HAVE TO GO THROUGH WHAT YOU DID EVER AGAIN.
I KNOW YOU EXPECTED TO FIGHT FOREVER, BRUCE. BUT HERE.
BATMAN IS WHAT YOU ALWAYS WANTED HIM TO BE--A SYMBOL OF WHAT'S BEST ABOUT US.
I HAVE QUESTIONS.
ANYTHING. YOU WERE RIGHT ALL THOSE YEARS AGO.
THE SOLUTION I FOUND HERE, THIS WORLD, IT'S BUILT ON COLD, HARD FACTS. NOT IDEALS.
THIS PLACE IS AN EXTENSION OF YOUR THINKING MORE THAN ANYONE'S, BRUCE.
SO WHAT'RE YOUR QUESTIONS?
FIRST, WHERE THE HELL ARE ALL THE VILLAINS?

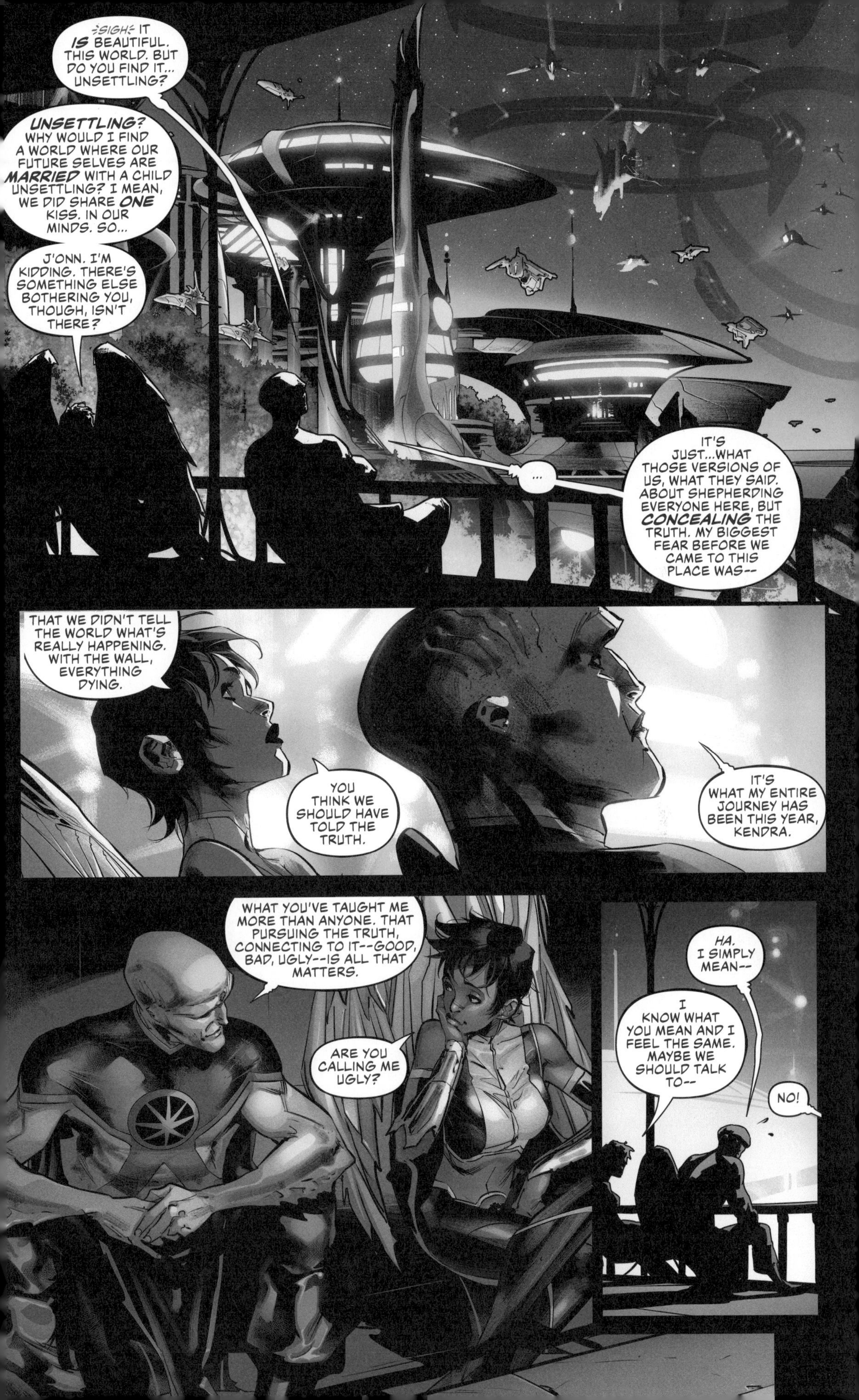
SIGH IT IS BEAUTIFUL. THIS WORLD. BUT DO YOU FIND IT... UNSETTLING?
UNSETTLING? WHY WOULD I FIND A WORLD WHERE OUR FUTURE SELVES ARE MARRIED WITH A CHILD UNSETTLING? I MEAN, WE DID SHARE ONE KISS. IN OUR MINDS. SO...
J'ONN. I'M KIDDING. THERE'S SOMETHING ELSE BOTHERING YOU, THOUGH, ISN'T THERE?
...
IT'S JUST...WHAT THOSE VERSIONS OF US, WHAT THEY SAID. ABOUT SHEPHERDING EVERYONE HERE, BUT CONCEALING THE TRUTH. MY BIGGEST FEAR BEFORE WE CAME TO THIS PLACE WAS--
THAT WE DIDN'T TELL THE WORLD WHAT'S REALLY HAPPENING. WITH THE WALL, EVERYTHING DYING.
YOU THINK WE SHOULD HAVE TOLD THE TRUTH.
IT'S WHAT MY ENTIRE JOURNEY HAS BEEN THIS YEAR, KENDRA.
WHAT YOU'VE TAUGHT ME MORE THAN ANYONE. THAT PURSUING THE TRUTH, CONNECTING TO IT--GOOD, BAD, UGLY--IS ALL THAT MATTERS.
ARE YOU CALLING ME UGLY?
HA. I SIMPLY MEAN--
I KNOW WHAT YOU MEAN AND I FEEL THE SAME. MAYBE WE SHOULD TALK TO--
NO!

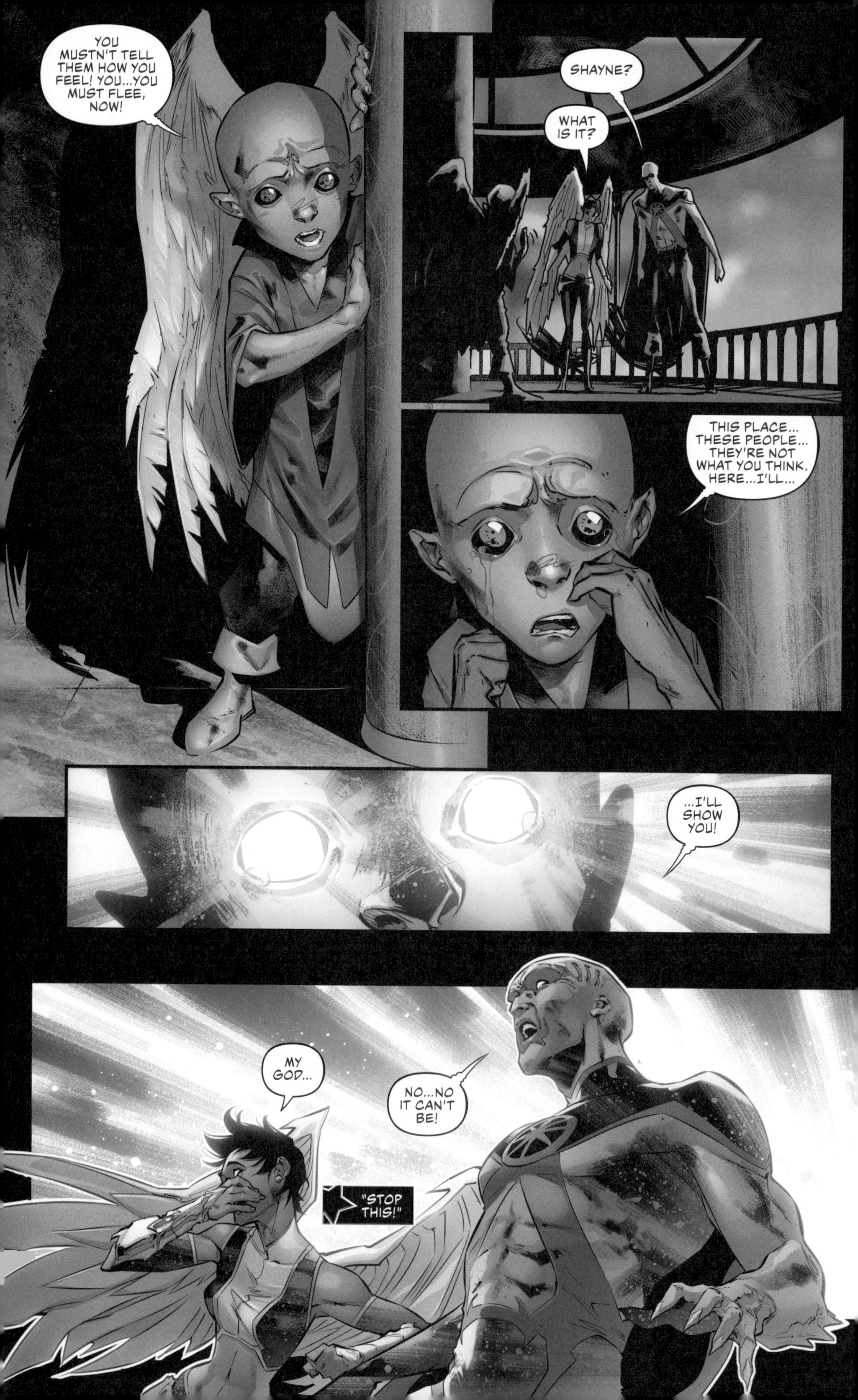
YOU MUSTN'T TELL THEM HOW YOU FEEL! YOU...YOU MUST FLEE, NOW!
SHAYNE?
WHAT IS IT?
THIS PLACE... THESE PEOPLE... THEY'RE NOT WHAT YOU THINK. HERE...I'LL...
...I'LL SHOW YOU!
MY GOD...
NO...NO IT CAN'T BE!
"STOP THIS!"

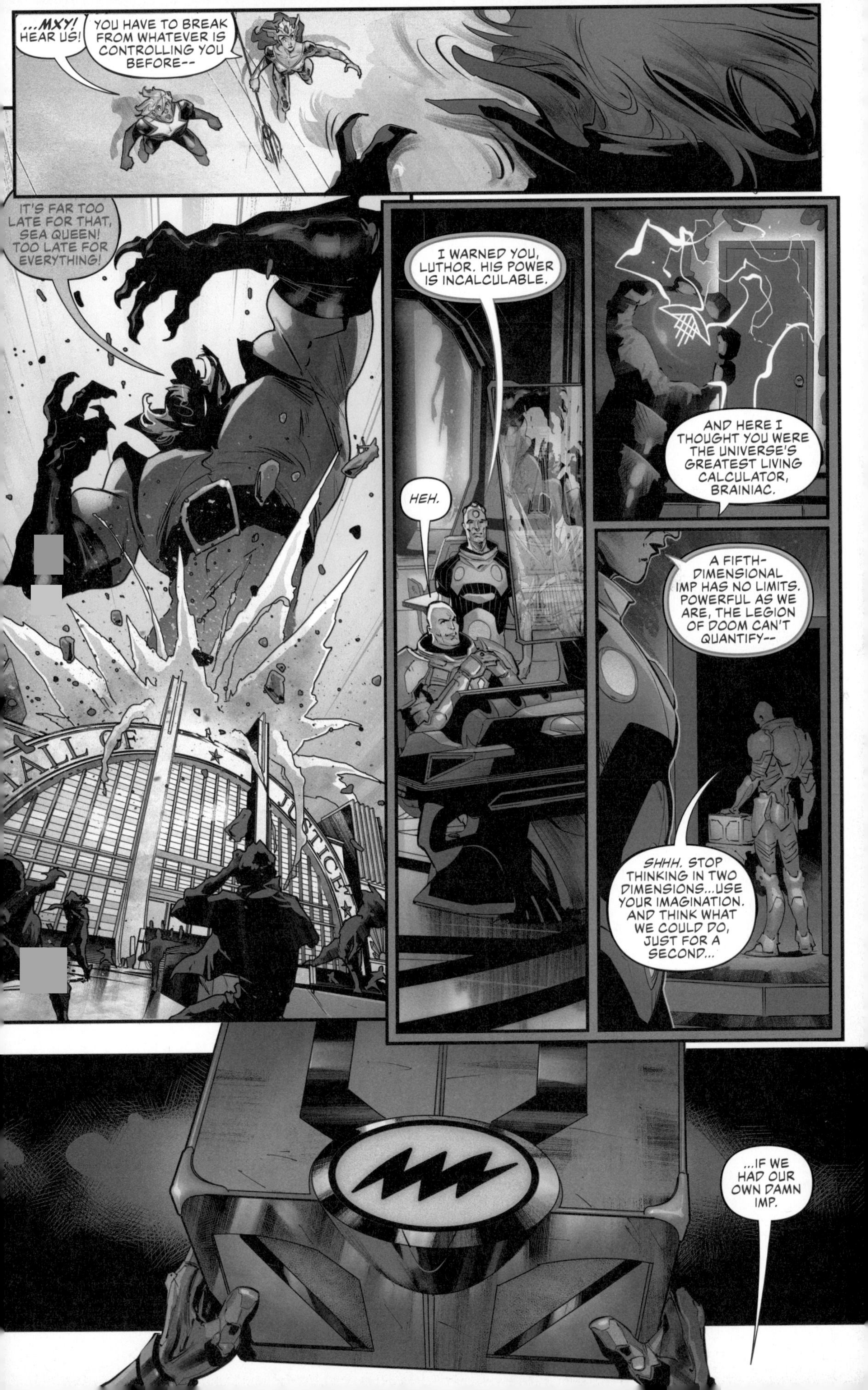
...MXY! HEAR US!
YOU HAVE TO BREAK FROM WHATEVER IS CONTROLLING YOU BEFORE--
IT'S FAR TOO LATE FOR THAT, SEA QUEEN! TOO LATE FOR EVERYTHING!
HALL OF JUSTICE
I WARNED YOU, LUTHOR. HIS POWER IS INCALCULABLE.
HEH.
AND HERE I THOUGHT YOU WERE THE UNIVERSE'S GREATEST LIVING CALCULATOR, BRAINIAC.
A FIFTH-DIMENSIONAL IMP HAS NO LIMITS. POWERFUL AS WE ARE, THE LEGION OF DOOM CAN'T QUANTIFY--
SHHH. STOP THINKING IN TWO DIMENSIONS...USE YOUR IMAGINATION. AND THINK WHAT WE COULD DO, JUST FOR A SECOND...
...IF WE HAD OUR OWN DAMN IMP.

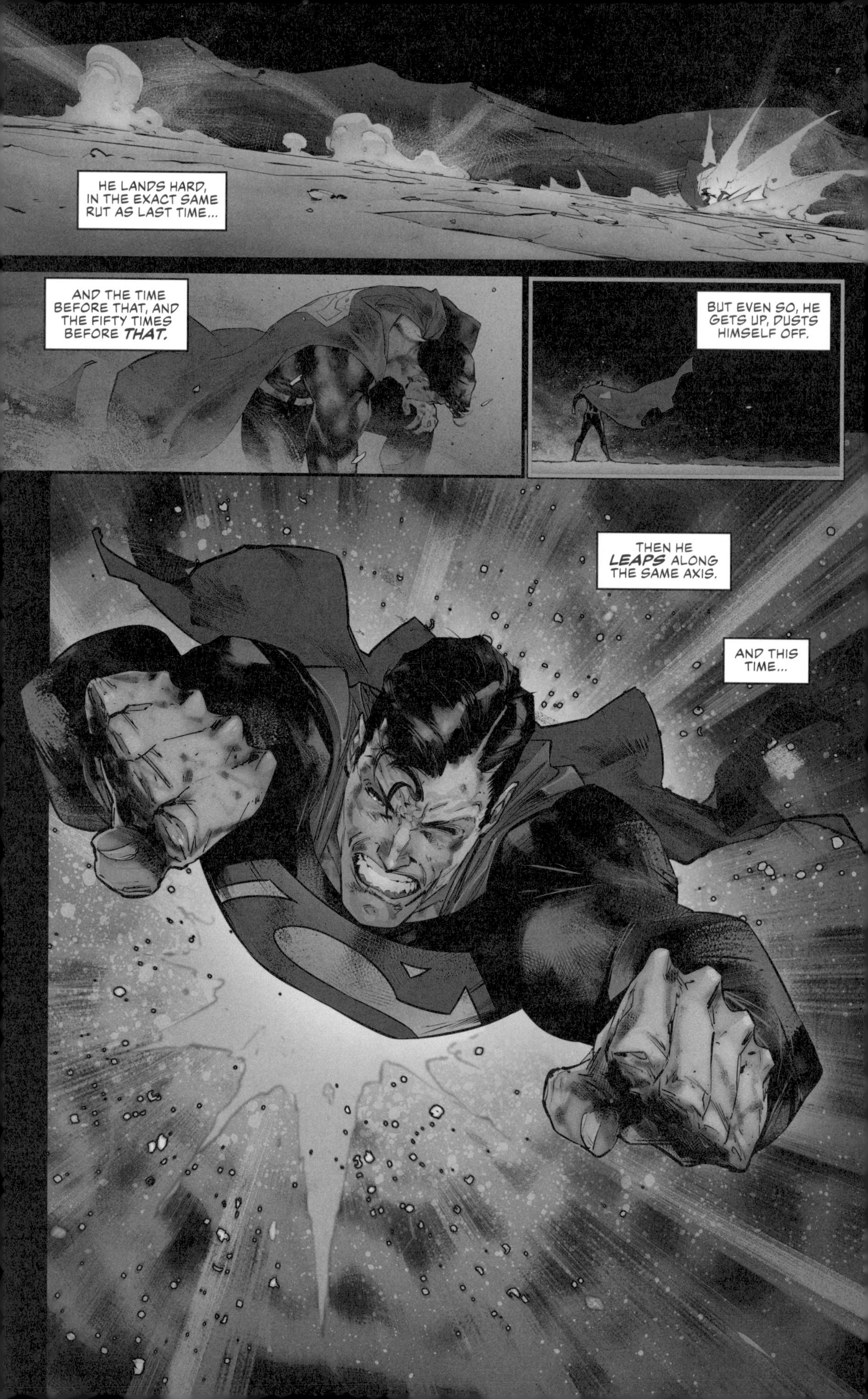
HE LANDS HARD, IN THE EXACT SAME RUT AS LAST TIME...
AND THE TIME BEFORE THAT, AND THE FIFTY TIMES BEFORE **THAT.**
BUT EVEN SO, HE GETS UP, DUSTS HIMSELF OFF.
THEN HE **LEAPS** ALONG THE SAME AXIS.
AND THIS TIME...

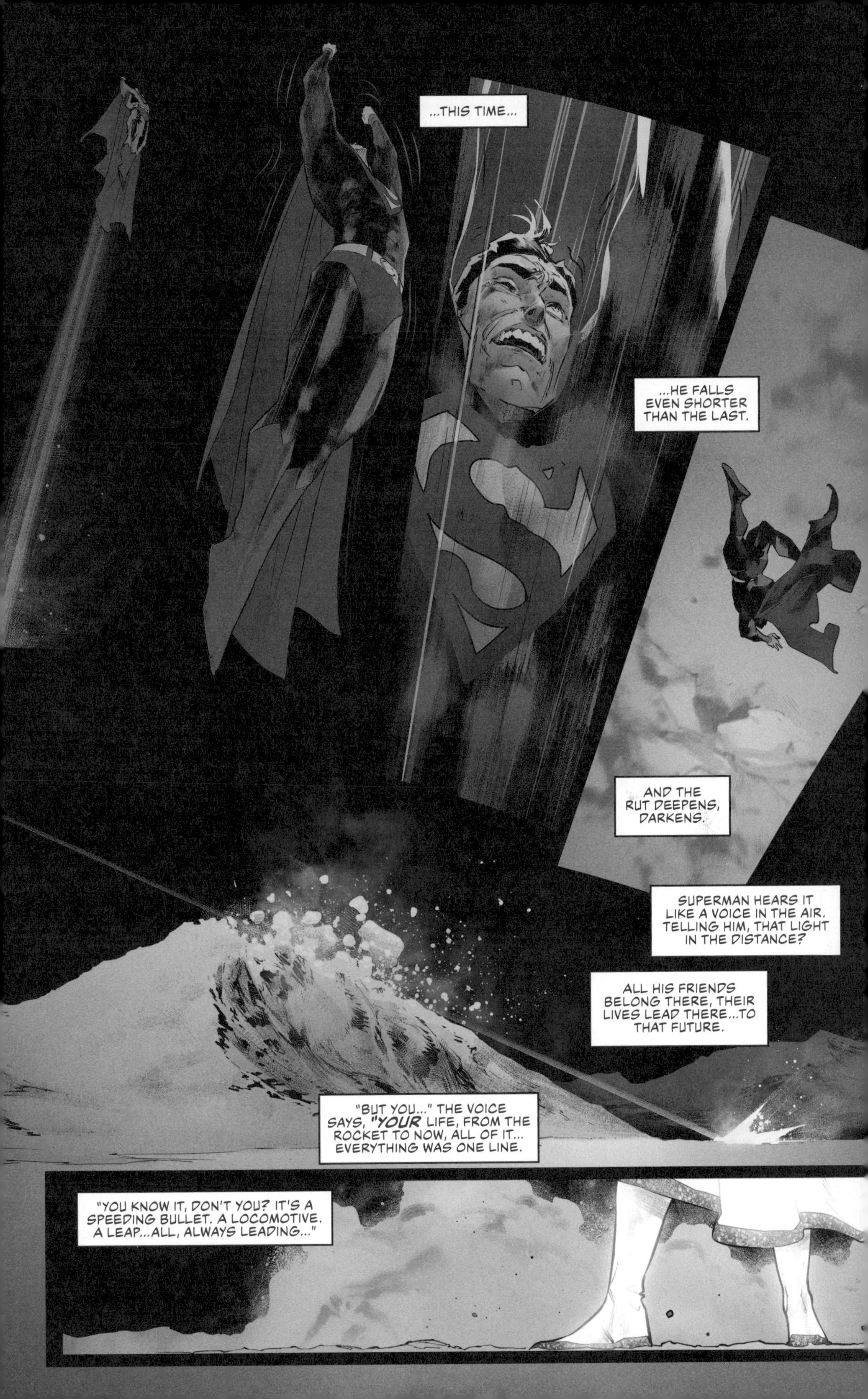
...THIS TIME...
...HE FALLS EVEN SHORTER THAN THE LAST.
AND THE RUT DEEPENS, DARKENS.
SUPERMAN HEARS IT LIKE A VOICE IN THE AIR. TELLING HIM, THAT LIGHT IN THE DISTANCE?
ALL HIS FRIENDS BELONG THERE, THEIR LIVES LEAD THERE...TO THAT FUTURE.
"BUT YOU..." THE VOICE SAYS, "YOUR LIFE, FROM THE ROCKET TO NOW, ALL OF IT... EVERYTHING WAS ONE LINE.
"YOU KNOW IT, DON'T YOU? IT'S A SPEEDING BULLET. A LOCOMOTIVE. A LEAP...ALL, ALWAYS LEADING..."

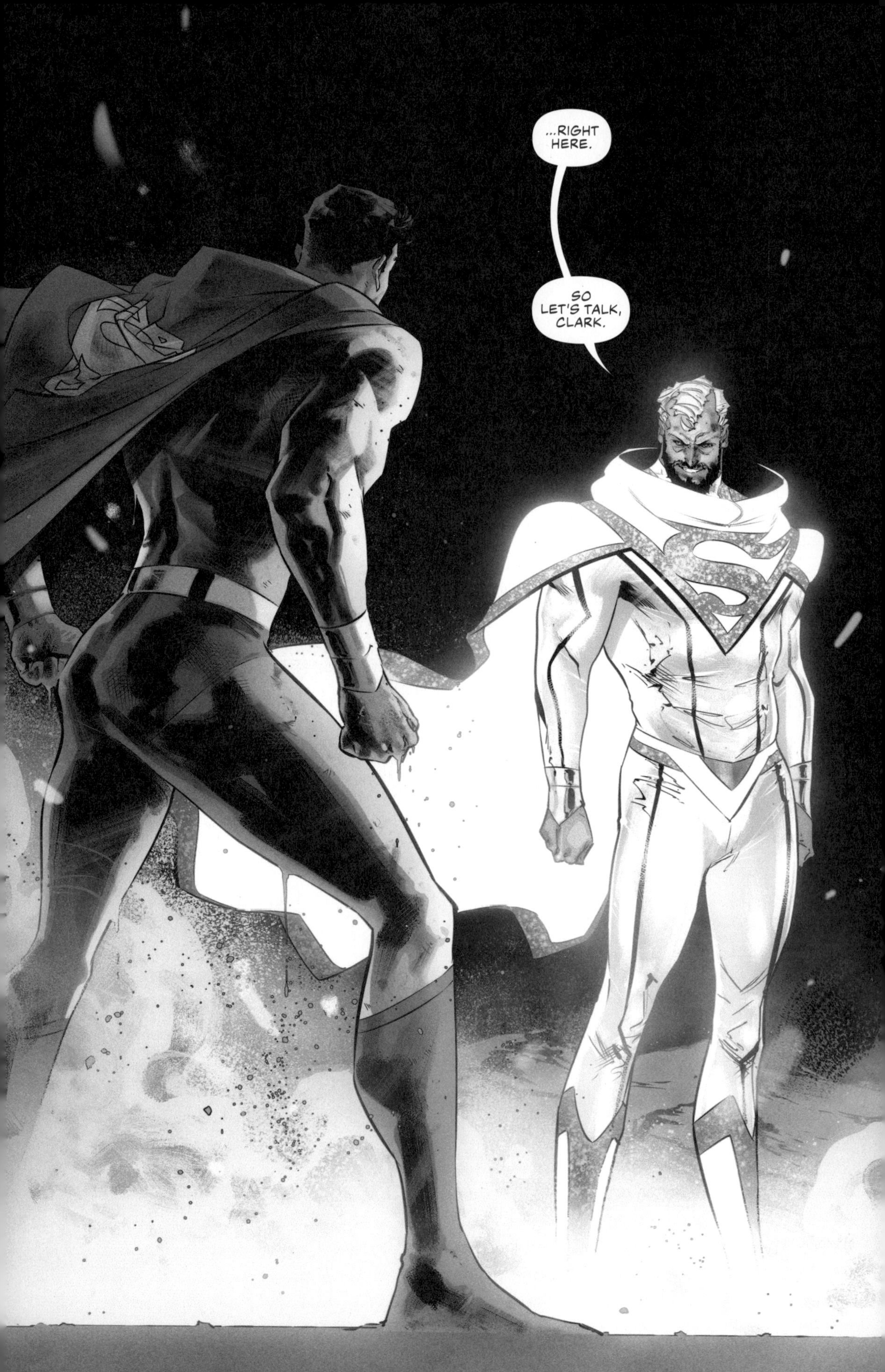
...RIGHT HERE.
SO LET'S TALK, CLARK.

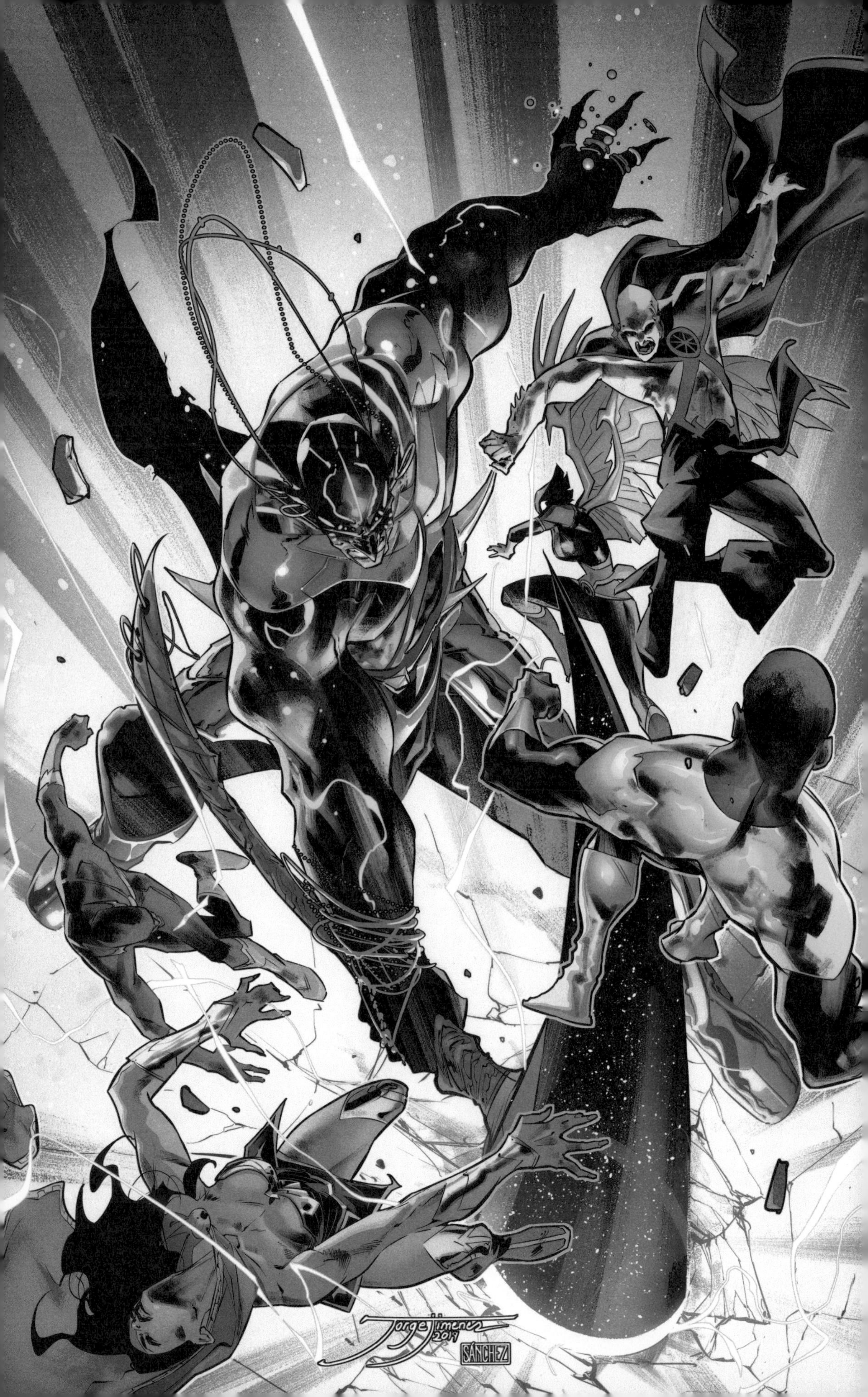
Jorge Jimenez 2019
SANCHEZ

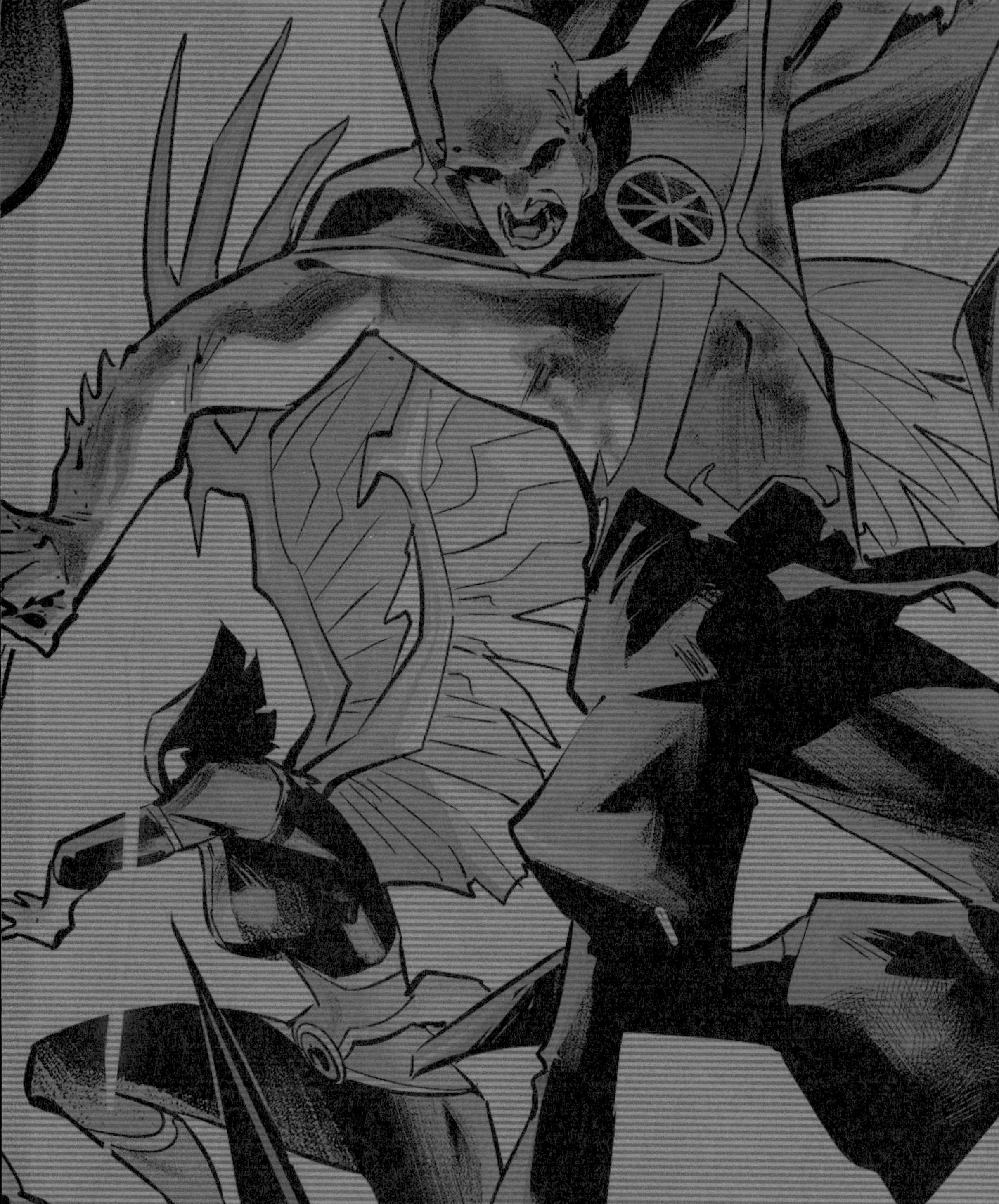

JUSTICE LEAGUE
#21

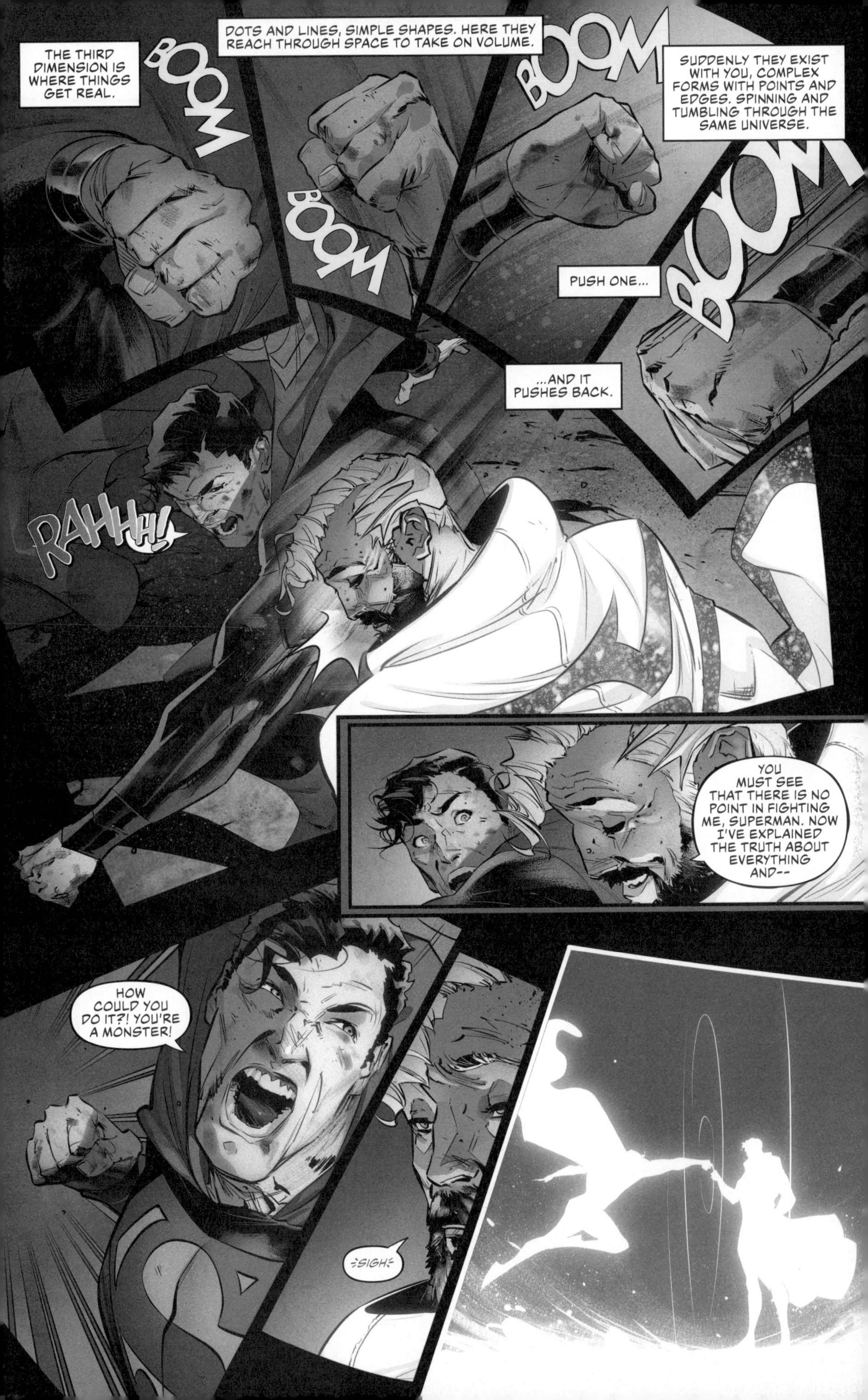
THE THIRD DIMENSION IS WHERE THINGS GET REAL.
BOOM
DOTS AND LINES, SIMPLE SHAPES. HERE THEY REACH THROUGH SPACE TO TAKE ON VOLUME.
BOOM
BOOM
SUDDENLY THEY EXIST WITH YOU, COMPLEX FORMS WITH POINTS AND EDGES. SPINNING AND TUMBLING THROUGH THE SAME UNIVERSE.
BOOM
PUSH ONE...
...AND IT PUSHES BACK.
RAHHH!
YOU MUST SEE THAT THERE IS NO POINT IN FIGHTING ME, SUPERMAN. NOW I'VE EXPLAINED THE TRUTH ABOUT EVERYTHING AND--
HOW COULD YOU DO IT?! YOU'RE A MONSTER!
SIGH

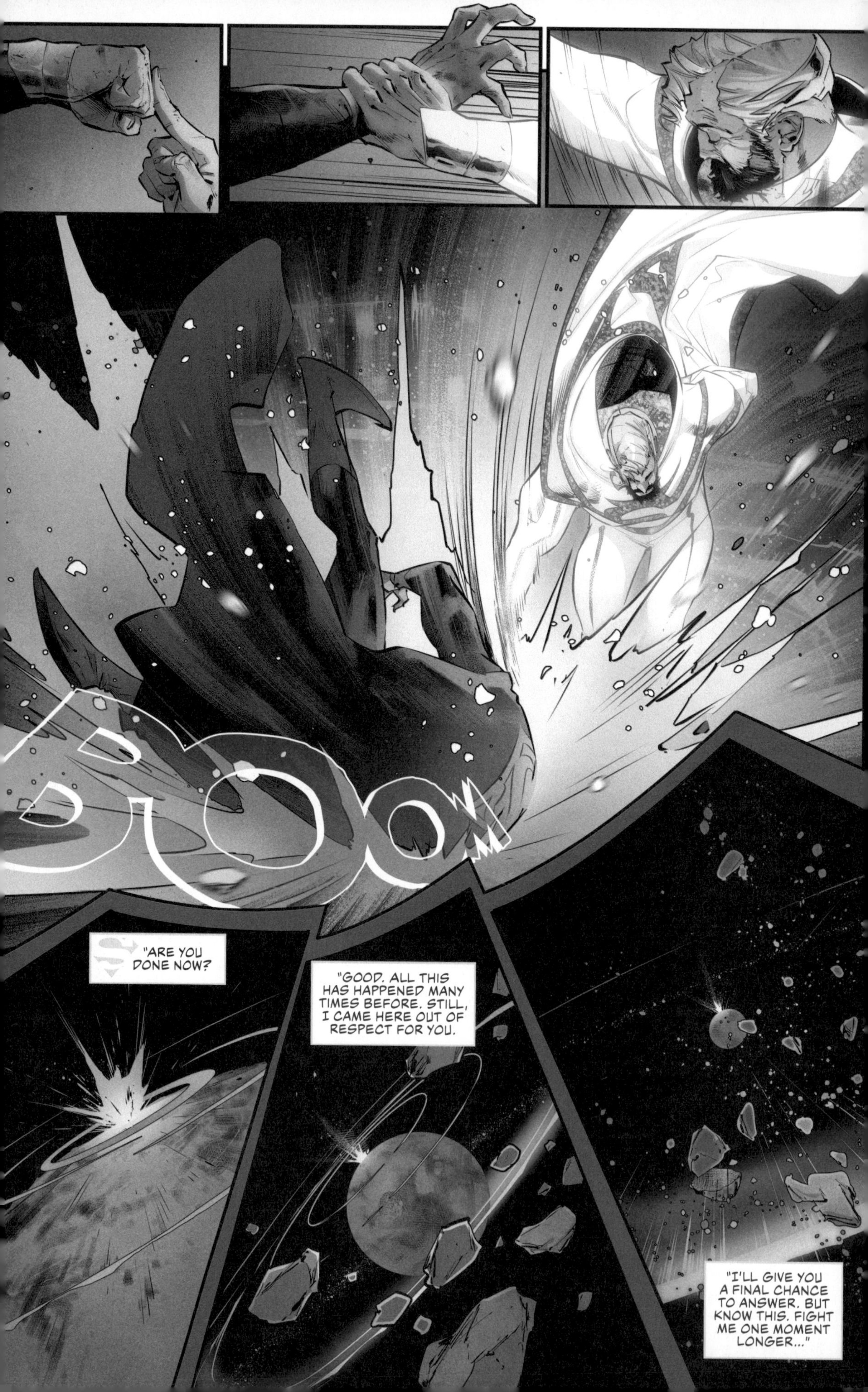
BOOM
"ARE YOU DONE NOW?
"GOOD. ALL THIS HAS HAPPENED MANY TIMES BEFORE. STILL, I CAME HERE OUT OF RESPECT FOR YOU.
"I'LL GIVE YOU A FINAL CHANCE TO ANSWER. BUT KNOW THIS. FIGHT ME ONE MOMENT LONGER..."

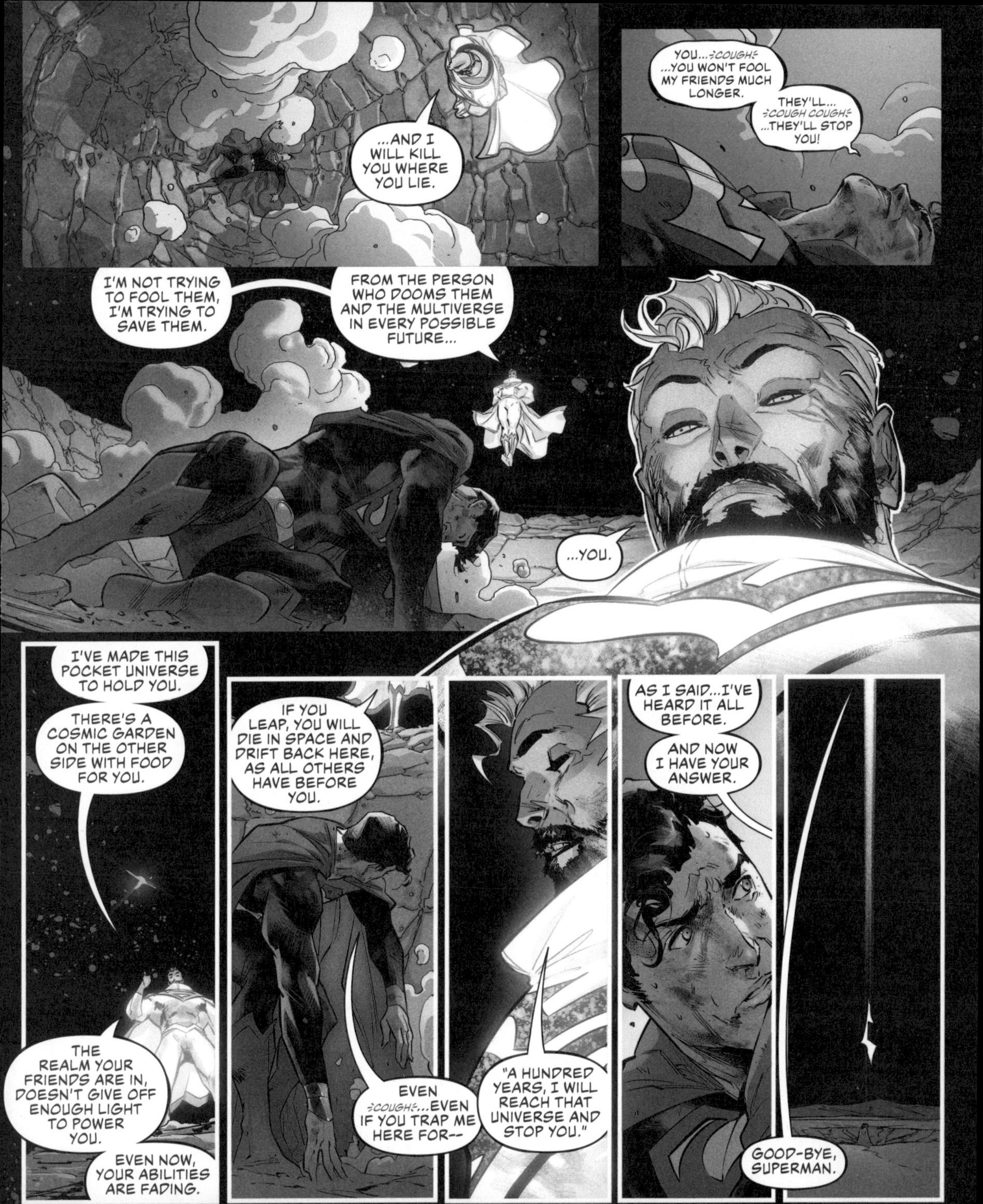
...AND I WILL KILL YOU WHERE YOU LIE.
YOU... COUGH ...YOU WON'T FOOL MY FRIENDS MUCH LONGER.
THEY'LL... COUGH COUGH ...THEY'LL STOP YOU!
I'M NOT TRYING TO FOOL THEM, I'M TRYING TO SAVE THEM.
FROM THE PERSON WHO DOOMS THEM AND THE MULTIVERSE IN EVERY POSSIBLE FUTURE...
...YOU.
I'VE MADE THIS POCKET UNIVERSE TO HOLD YOU.
THERE'S A COSMIC GARDEN ON THE OTHER SIDE WITH FOOD FOR YOU.
THE REALM YOUR FRIENDS ARE IN, DOESN'T GIVE OFF ENOUGH LIGHT TO POWER YOU.
EVEN NOW, YOUR ABILITIES ARE FADING.
IF YOU LEAP, YOU WILL DIE IN SPACE AND DRIFT BACK HERE, AS ALL OTHERS HAVE BEFORE YOU.
EVEN COUGH ...EVEN IF YOU TRAP ME HERE FOR--
"A HUNDRED YEARS, I WILL REACH THAT UNIVERSE AND STOP YOU."
AS I SAID...I'VE HEARD IT ALL BEFORE.
AND NOW I HAVE YOUR ANSWER.
GOOD-BYE, SUPERMAN.

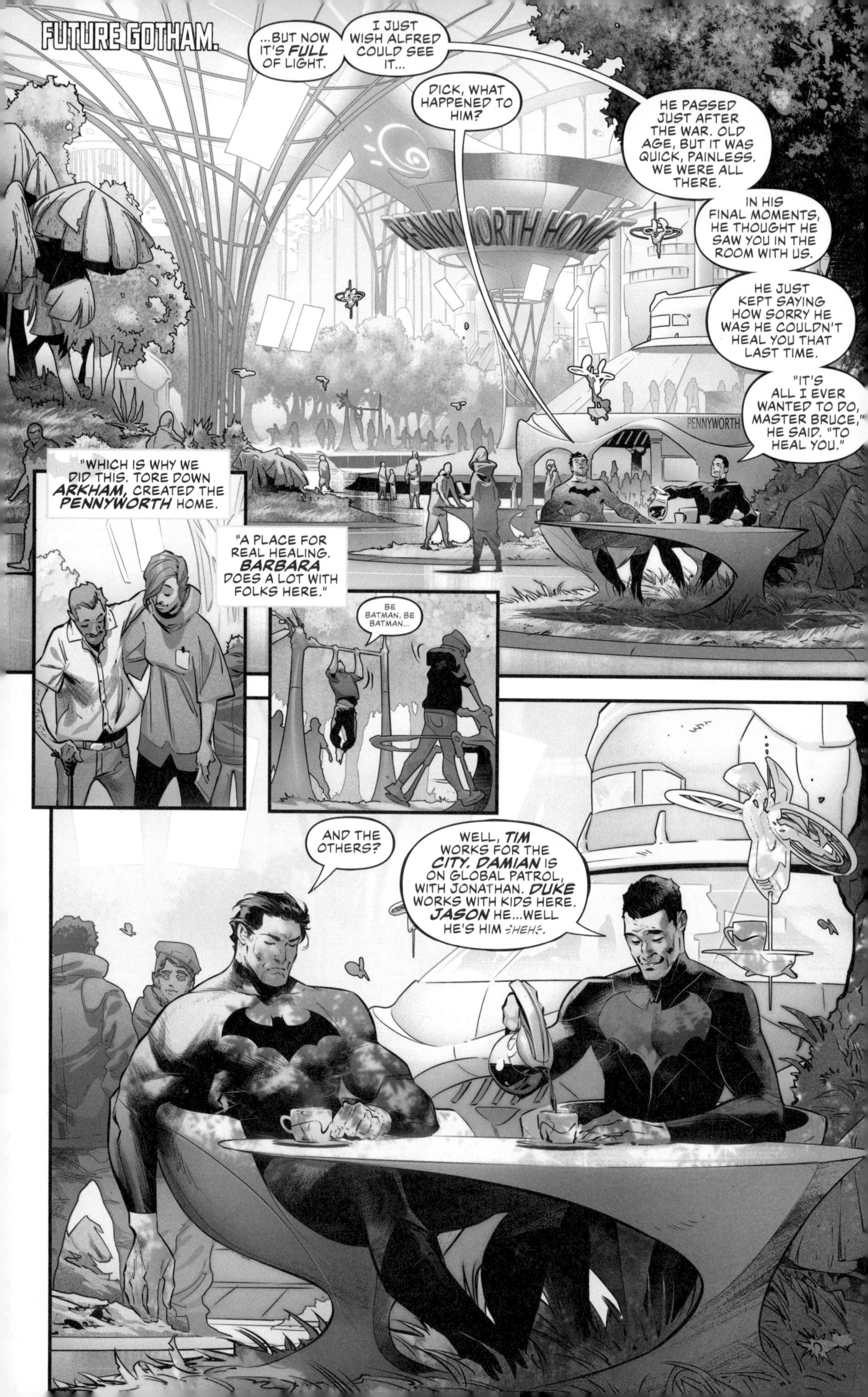
FUTURE GOTHAM.
...BUT NOW IT'S FULL OF LIGHT.
I JUST WISH ALFRED COULD SEE IT...
DICK, WHAT HAPPENED TO HIM?
HE PASSED JUST AFTER THE WAR. OLD AGE, BUT IT WAS QUICK, PAINLESS. WE WERE ALL THERE.
IN HIS FINAL MOMENTS, HE THOUGHT HE SAW YOU IN THE ROOM WITH US.
HE JUST KEPT SAYING HOW SORRY HE WAS HE COULDN'T HEAL YOU THAT LAST TIME.
"IT'S ALL I EVER WANTED TO DO, MASTER BRUCE," HE SAID. "TO HEAL YOU."
PENNYWORTH HOME
PENNYWORTH
"WHICH IS WHY WE DID THIS. TORE DOWN ARKHAM, CREATED THE PENNYWORTH HOME.
"A PLACE FOR REAL HEALING. BARBARA DOES A LOT WITH FOLKS HERE."
BE BATMAN, BE BATMAN...
AND THE OTHERS?
WELL, TIM WORKS FOR THE CITY. DAMIAN IS ON GLOBAL PATROL, WITH JONATHAN. DUKE WORKS WITH KIDS HERE. JASON HE...WELL HE'S HIM ≈HEH≈.

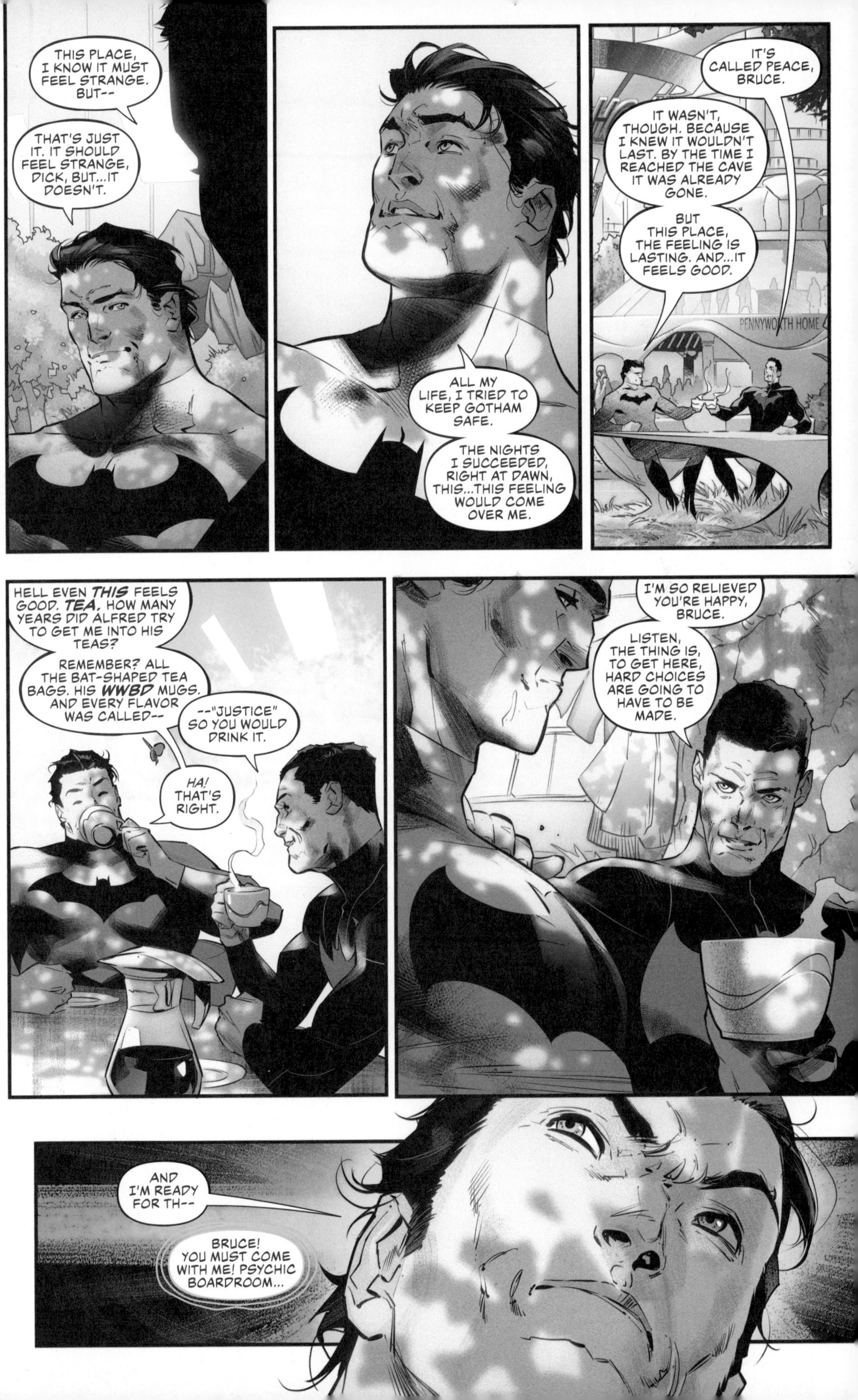
THIS PLACE, I KNOW IT MUST FEEL STRANGE. BUT--
THAT'S JUST IT. IT SHOULD FEEL STRANGE, DICK, BUT...IT DOESN'T.
ALL MY LIFE, I TRIED TO KEEP GOTHAM SAFE.
THE NIGHTS I SUCCEEDED, RIGHT AT DAWN, THIS...THIS FEELING WOULD COME OVER ME.
IT'S CALLED PEACE, BRUCE.
IT WASN'T, THOUGH. BECAUSE I KNEW IT WOULDN'T LAST. BY THE TIME I REACHED THE CAVE IT WAS ALREADY GONE.
BUT THIS PLACE, THE FEELING IS LASTING. AND...IT FEELS GOOD.
PENNYWORTH HOME
HELL EVEN THIS FEELS GOOD. TEA. HOW MANY YEARS DID ALFRED TRY TO GET ME INTO HIS TEAS?
REMEMBER? ALL THE BAT-SHAPED TEA BAGS. HIS WWBD MUGS. AND EVERY FLAVOR WAS CALLED--
--"JUSTICE" SO YOU WOULD DRINK IT.
HA! THAT'S RIGHT.
I'M SO RELIEVED YOU'RE HAPPY, BRUCE.
LISTEN, THE THING IS, TO GET HERE, HARD CHOICES ARE GOING TO HAVE TO BE MADE.
AND I'M READY FOR TH--
BRUCE! YOU MUST COME WITH ME! PSYCHIC BOARDROOM...

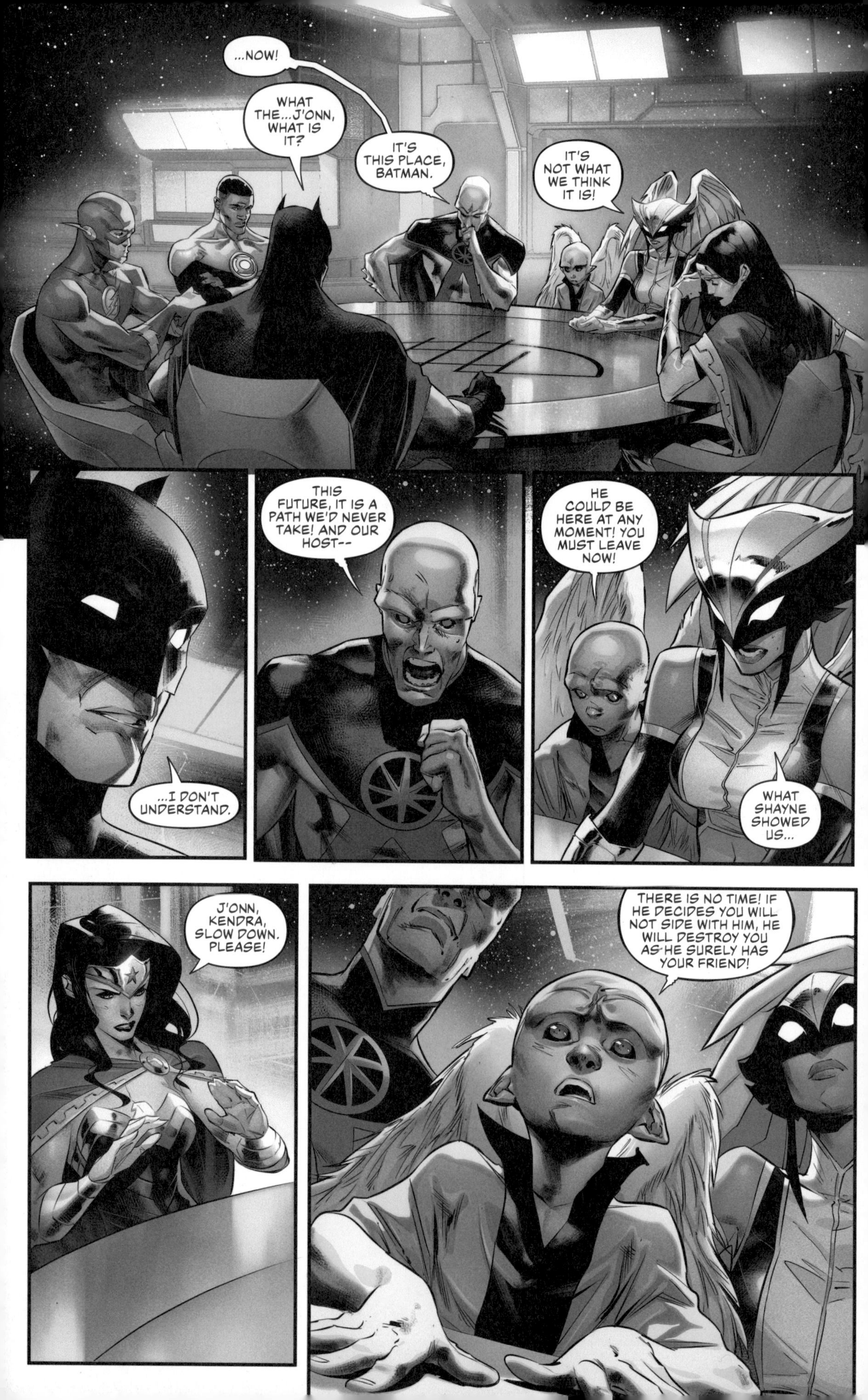
...NOW!
WHAT THE...J'ONN, WHAT IS IT?
IT'S THIS PLACE, BATMAN.
IT'S NOT WHAT WE THINK IT IS!
...I DON'T UNDERSTAND.
THIS FUTURE, IT IS A PATH WE'D NEVER TAKE! AND OUR HOST--
HE COULD BE HERE AT ANY MOMENT! YOU MUST LEAVE NOW!
WHAT SHAYNE SHOWED US...
J'ONN, KENDRA, SLOW DOWN. PLEASE!
THERE IS NO TIME! IF HE DECIDES YOU WILL NOT SIDE WITH HIM, HE WILL DESTROY YOU AS HE SURELY HAS YOUR FRIEND!

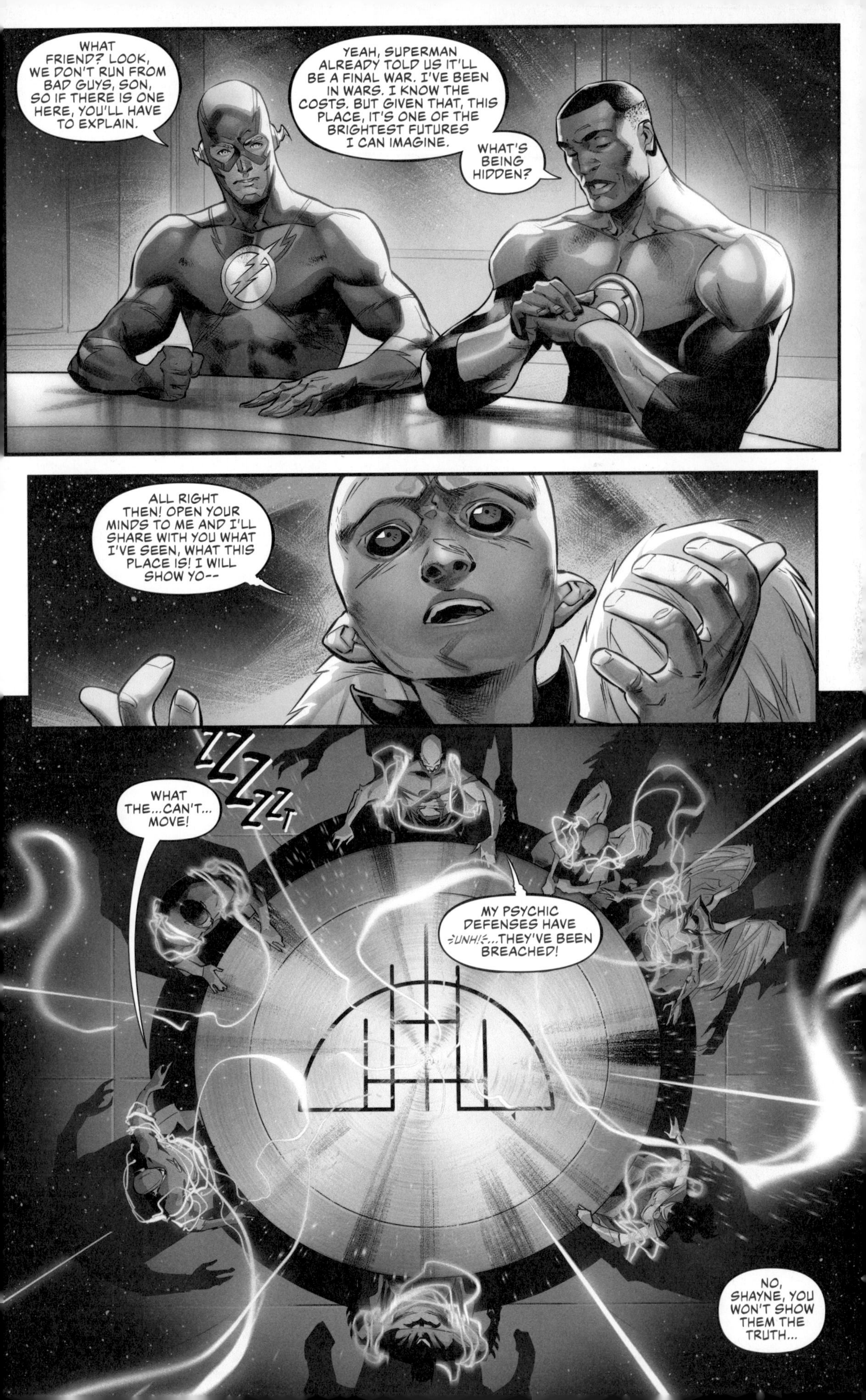
WHAT FRIEND? LOOK, WE DON'T RUN FROM BAD GUYS, SON, SO IF THERE IS ONE HERE, YOU'LL HAVE TO EXPLAIN.
YEAH, SUPERMAN ALREADY TOLD US IT'LL BE A FINAL WAR. I'VE BEEN IN WARS. I KNOW THE COSTS. BUT GIVEN THAT, THIS PLACE, IT'S ONE OF THE BRIGHTEST FUTURES I CAN IMAGINE.
WHAT'S BEING HIDDEN?
ALL RIGHT THEN! OPEN YOUR MINDS TO ME AND I'LL SHARE WITH YOU WHAT I'VE SEEN, WHAT THIS PLACE IS! I WILL SHOW YO--
ZZZZZT
WHAT THE...CAN'T... MOVE!
MY PSYCHIC DEFENSES HAVE UNH!...THEY'VE BEEN BREACHED!
NO, SHAYNE, YOU WON'T SHOW THEM THE TRUTH...

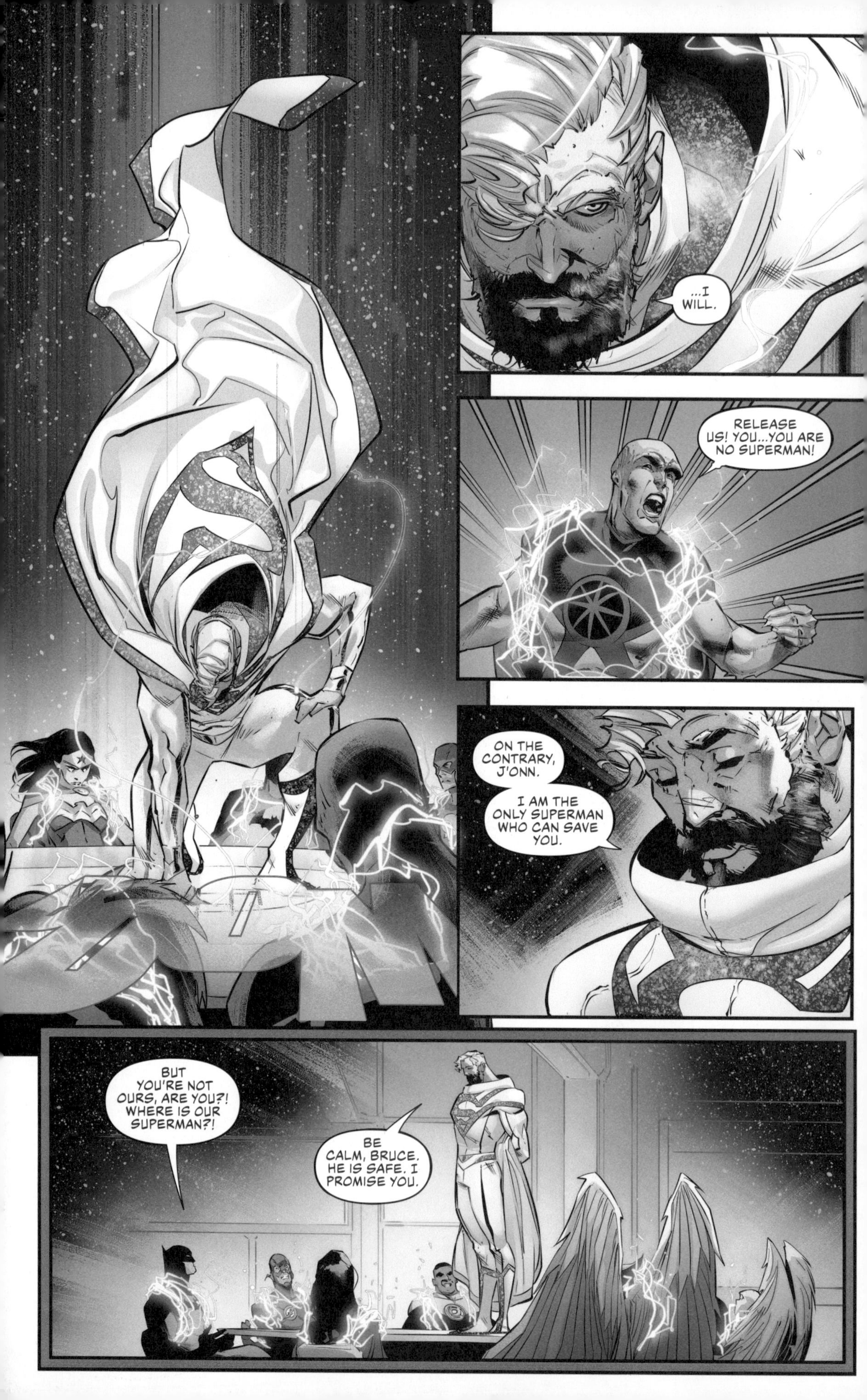
...I WILL.
RELEASE US! YOU...YOU ARE NO SUPERMAN!
ON THE CONTRARY, J'ONN.
I AM THE ONLY SUPERMAN WHO CAN SAVE YOU.
BUT YOU'RE NOT OURS, ARE YOU?! WHERE IS OUR SUPERMAN?!
BE CALM, BRUCE. HE IS SAFE. I PROMISE YOU.

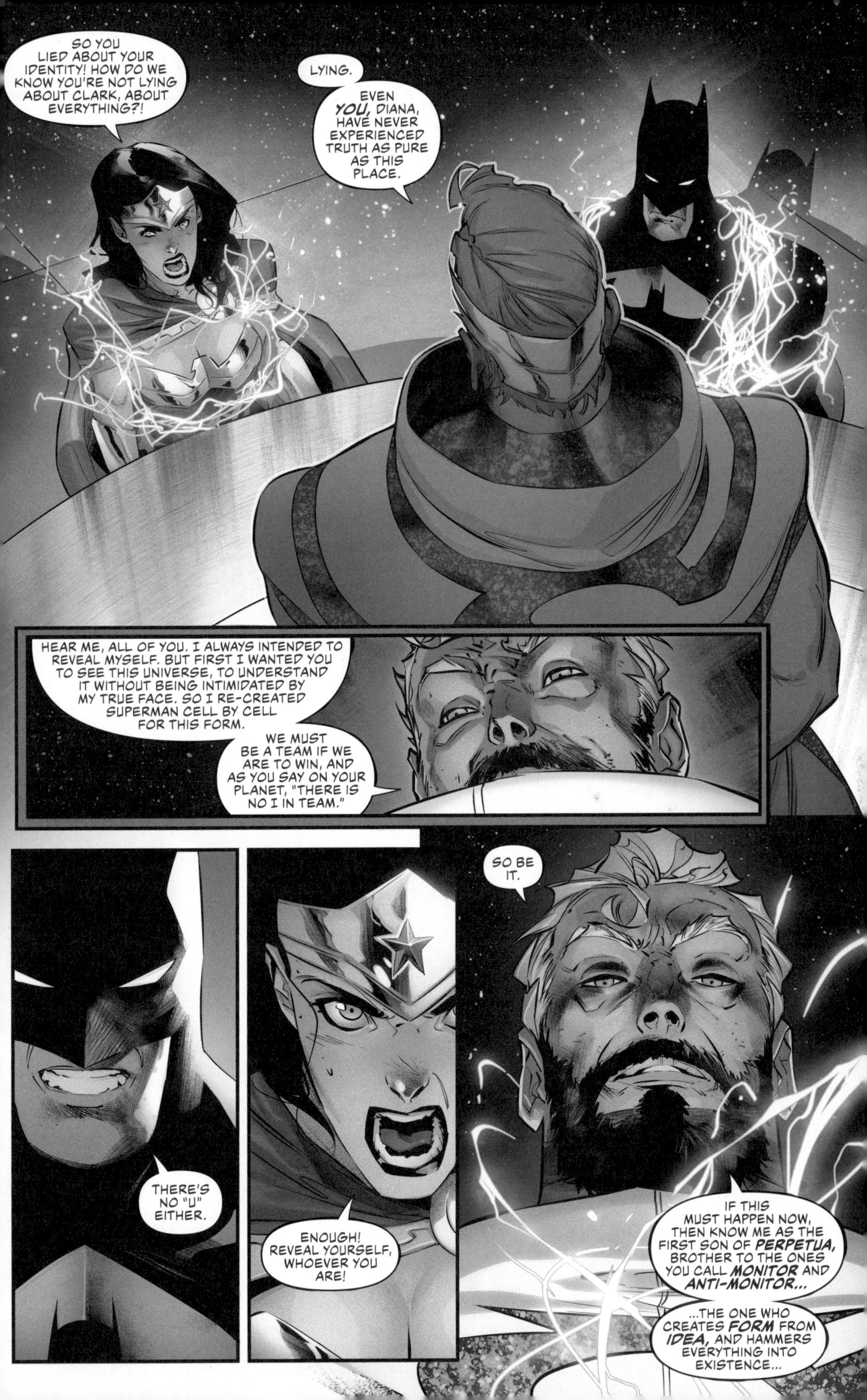

SO YOU LIED ABOUT YOUR IDENTITY! HOW DO WE KNOW YOU'RE NOT LYING ABOUT CLARK, ABOUT EVERYTHING?!
LYING.
EVEN YOU, DIANA, HAVE NEVER EXPERIENCED TRUTH AS PURE AS THIS PLACE.
HEAR ME, ALL OF YOU. I ALWAYS INTENDED TO REVEAL MYSELF. BUT FIRST I WANTED YOU TO SEE THIS UNIVERSE, TO UNDERSTAND IT WITHOUT BEING INTIMIDATED BY MY TRUE FACE. SO I RE-CREATED SUPERMAN CELL BY CELL FOR THIS FORM.
WE MUST BE A TEAM IF WE ARE TO WIN, AND AS YOU SAY ON YOUR PLANET, "THERE IS NO I IN TEAM."
THERE'S NO "U" EITHER.
ENOUGH! REVEAL YOURSELF, WHOEVER YOU ARE!
SO BE IT.
IF THIS MUST HAPPEN NOW, THEN KNOW ME AS THE FIRST SON OF PERPETUA, BROTHER TO THE ONES YOU CALL MONITOR AND ANTI-MONITOR...
...THE ONE WHO CREATES FORM FROM IDEA, AND HAMMERS EVERYTHING INTO EXISTENCE...

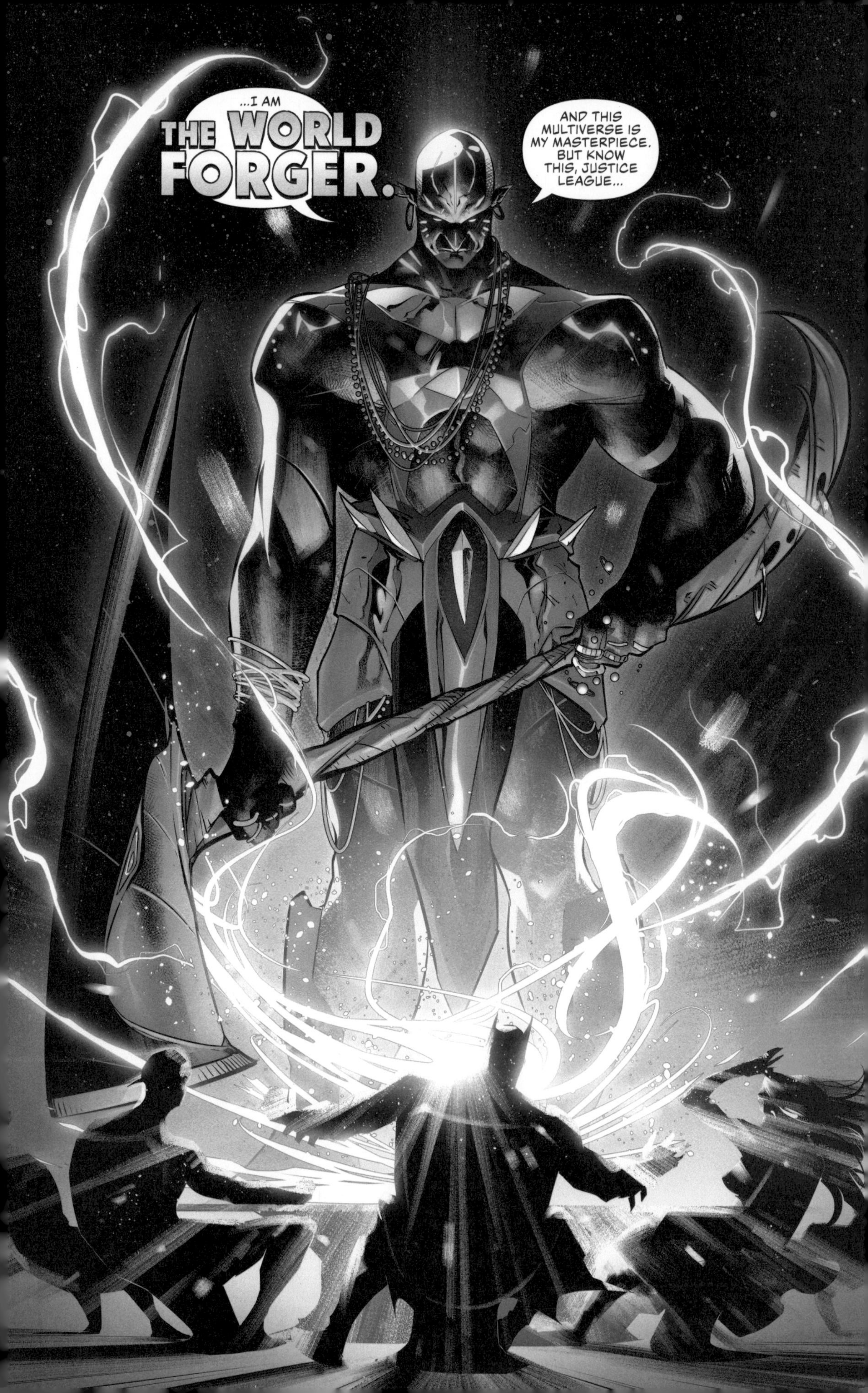
...I AM THE WORLD FORGER.
AND THIS MULTIVERSE IS MY MASTERPIECE. BUT KNOW THIS, JUSTICE LEAGUE...

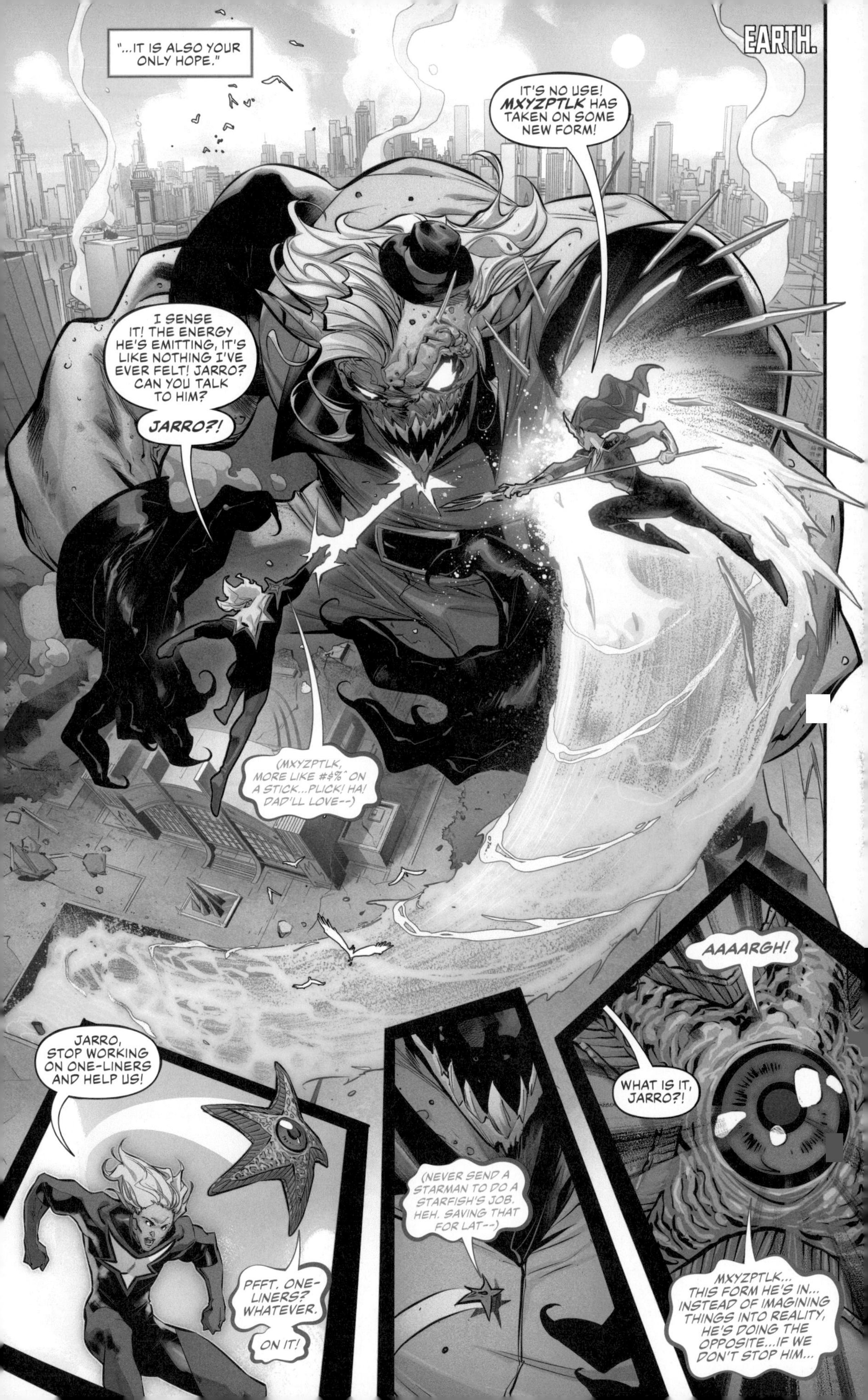
"...IT IS ALSO YOUR ONLY HOPE."
EARTH.
IT'S NO USE! MXYZPTLK HAS TAKEN ON SOME NEW FORM!
I SENSE IT! THE ENERGY HE'S EMITTING, IT'S LIKE NOTHING I'VE EVER FELT! JARRO? CAN YOU TALK TO HIM?
JARRO?!
(MXYZPTLK, MORE LIKE #$%^ ON A STICK...PLICK! HA! DAD'LL LOVE--)
JARRO, STOP WORKING ON ONE-LINERS AND HELP US!
PFFT. ONE-LINERS? WHATEVER.
ON IT!
(NEVER SEND A STARMAN TO DO A STARFISH'S JOB. HEH. SAVING THAT FOR LAT--)
AAAARGH!
WHAT IS IT, JARRO?!
MXYZPTLK... THIS FORM HE'S IN... INSTEAD OF IMAGINING THINGS INTO REALITY, HE'S DOING THE OPPOSITE...IF WE DON'T STOP HIM...

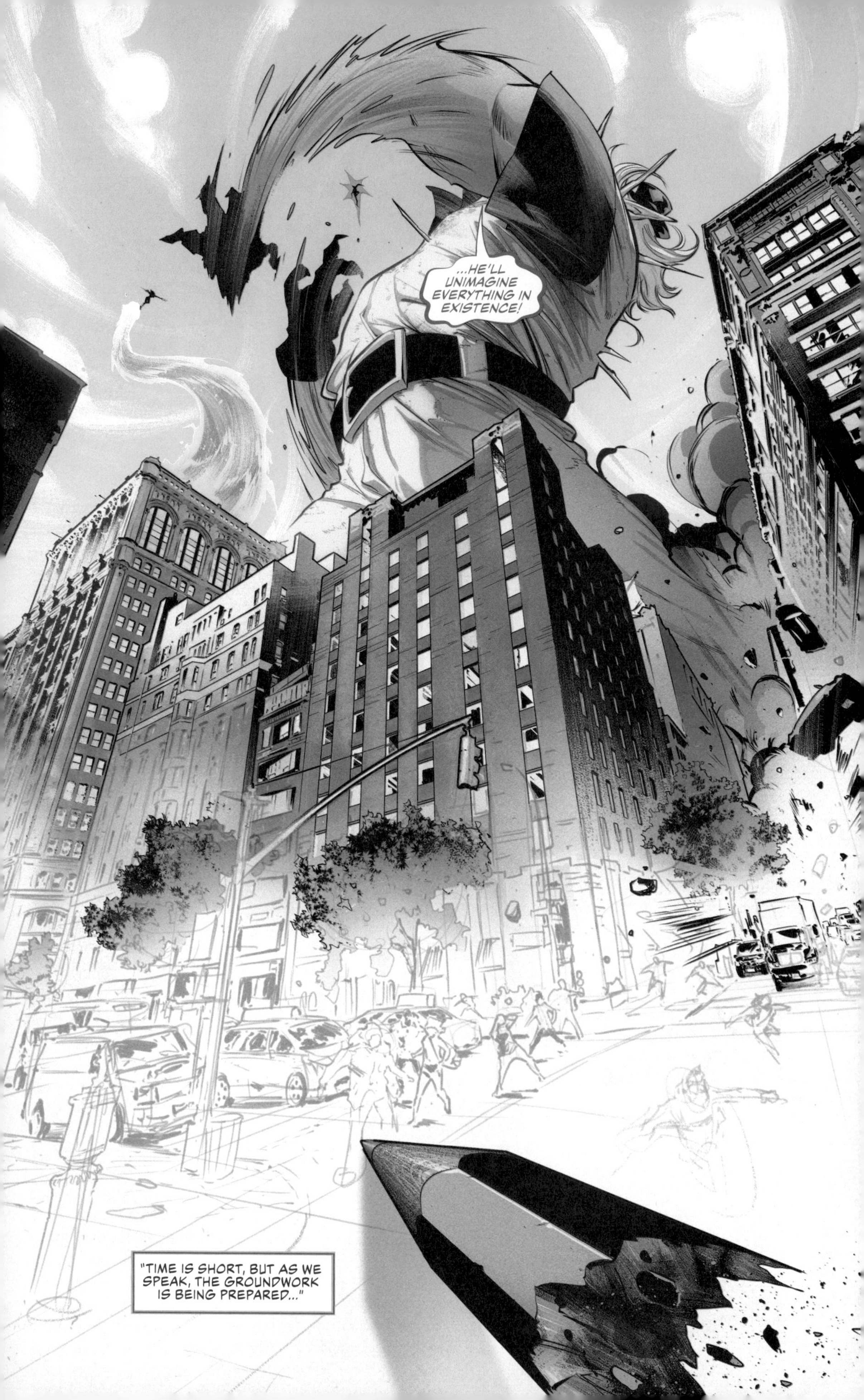
...HE'LL UNIMAGINE EVERYTHING IN EXISTENCE!
"TIME IS SHORT, BUT AS WE SPEAK, THE GROUNDWORK IS BEING PREPARED..."

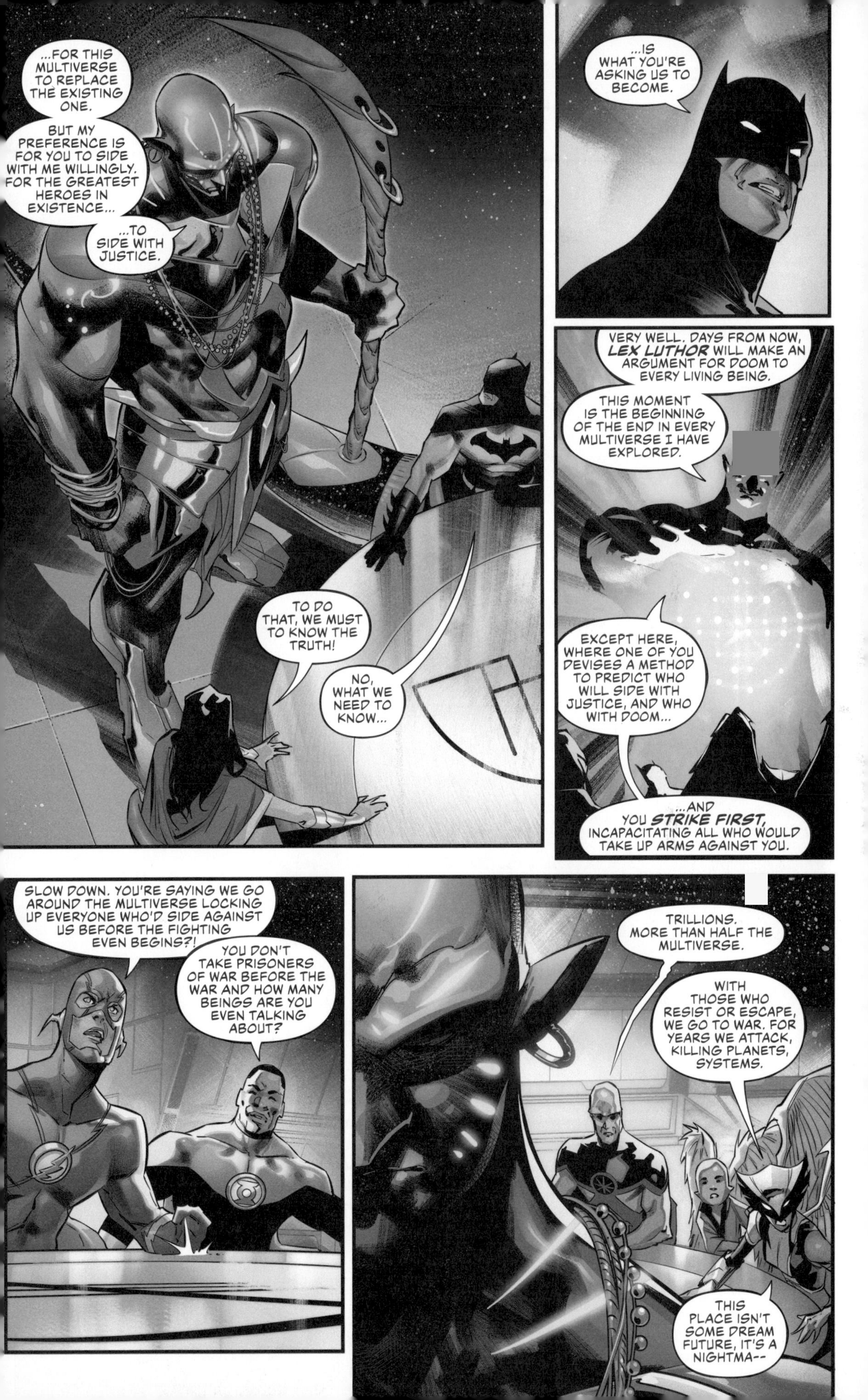
...FOR THIS MULTIVERSE TO REPLACE THE EXISTING ONE.
BUT MY PREFERENCE IS FOR YOU TO SIDE WITH ME WILLINGLY. FOR THE GREATEST HEROES IN EXISTENCE...
...TO SIDE WITH JUSTICE.
TO DO THAT, WE MUST TO KNOW THE TRUTH!
NO, WHAT WE NEED TO KNOW...
...IS WHAT YOU'RE ASKING US TO BECOME.
VERY WELL. DAYS FROM NOW, LEX LUTHOR WILL MAKE AN ARGUMENT FOR DOOM TO EVERY LIVING BEING.
THIS MOMENT IS THE BEGINNING OF THE END IN EVERY MULTIVERSE I HAVE EXPLORED.
EXCEPT HERE, WHERE ONE OF YOU DEVISES A METHOD TO PREDICT WHO WILL SIDE WITH JUSTICE, AND WHO WITH DOOM...
...AND YOU STRIKE FIRST, INCAPACITATING ALL WHO WOULD TAKE UP ARMS AGAINST YOU.
SLOW DOWN. YOU'RE SAYING WE GO AROUND THE MULTIVERSE LOCKING UP EVERYONE WHO'D SIDE AGAINST US BEFORE THE FIGHTING EVEN BEGINS?!
YOU DON'T TAKE PRISONERS OF WAR BEFORE THE WAR AND HOW MANY BEINGS ARE YOU EVEN TALKING ABOUT?
TRILLIONS. MORE THAN HALF THE MULTIVERSE.
WITH THOSE WHO RESIST OR ESCAPE, WE GO TO WAR. FOR YEARS WE ATTACK, KILLING PLANETS, SYSTEMS.
THIS PLACE ISN'T SOME DREAM FUTURE, IT'S A NIGHTMA--

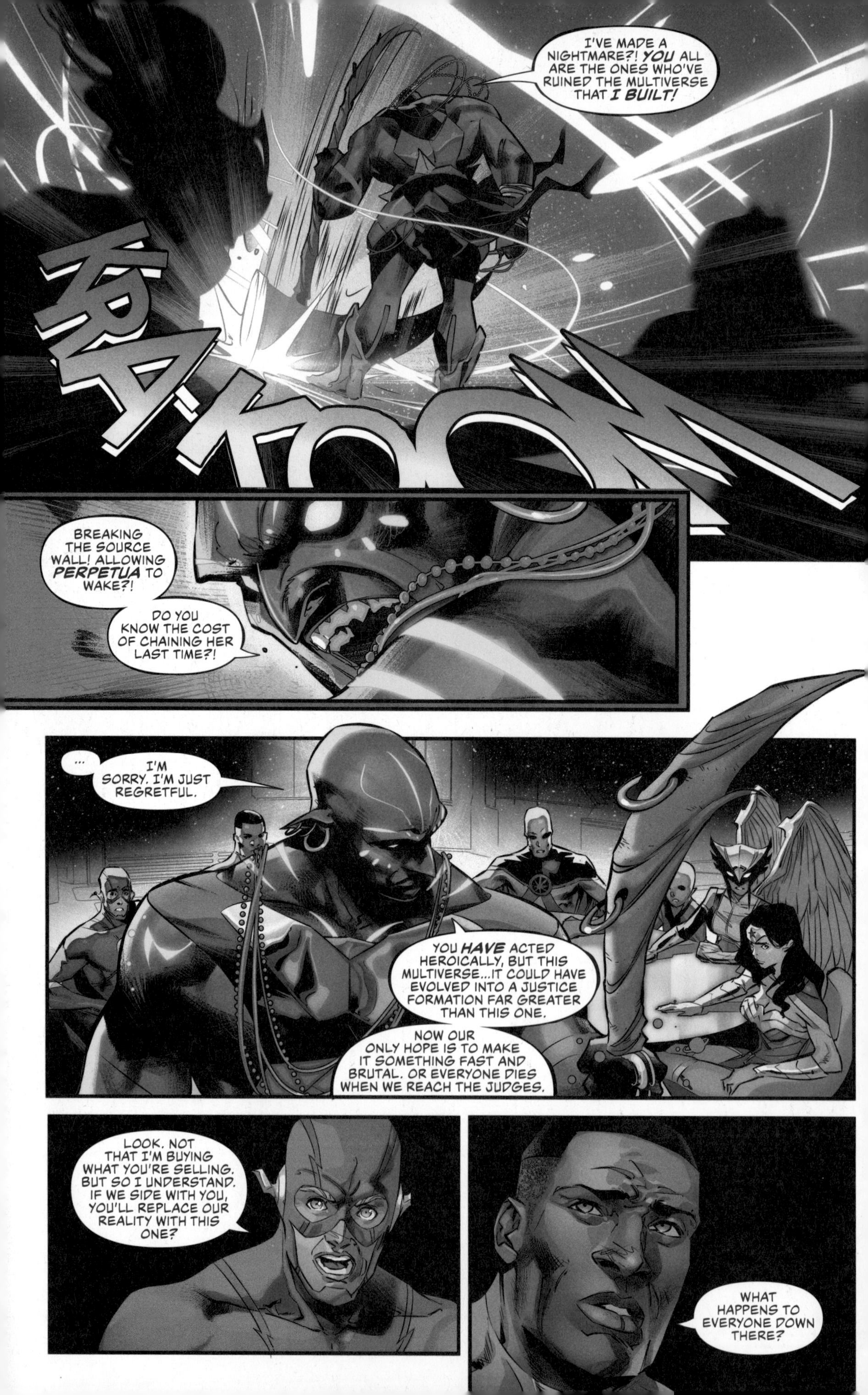
I'VE MADE A NIGHTMARE?! YOU ALL ARE THE ONES WHO'VE RUINED THE MULTIVERSE THAT I BUILT!
KRA-KOOM
BREAKING THE SOURCE WALL! ALLOWING PERPETUA TO WAKE?!
DO YOU KNOW THE COST OF CHAINING HER LAST TIME?!
...
I'M SORRY. I'M JUST REGRETFUL.
YOU HAVE ACTED HEROICALLY, BUT THIS MULTIVERSE...IT COULD HAVE EVOLVED INTO A JUSTICE FORMATION FAR GREATER THAN THIS ONE.
NOW OUR ONLY HOPE IS TO MAKE IT SOMETHING FAST AND BRUTAL. OR EVERYONE DIES WHEN WE REACH THE JUDGES.
LOOK. NOT THAT I'M BUYING WHAT YOU'RE SELLING. BUT SO I UNDERSTAND. IF WE SIDE WITH YOU, YOU'LL REPLACE OUR REALITY WITH THIS ONE?
WHAT HAPPENS TO EVERYONE DOWN THERE?

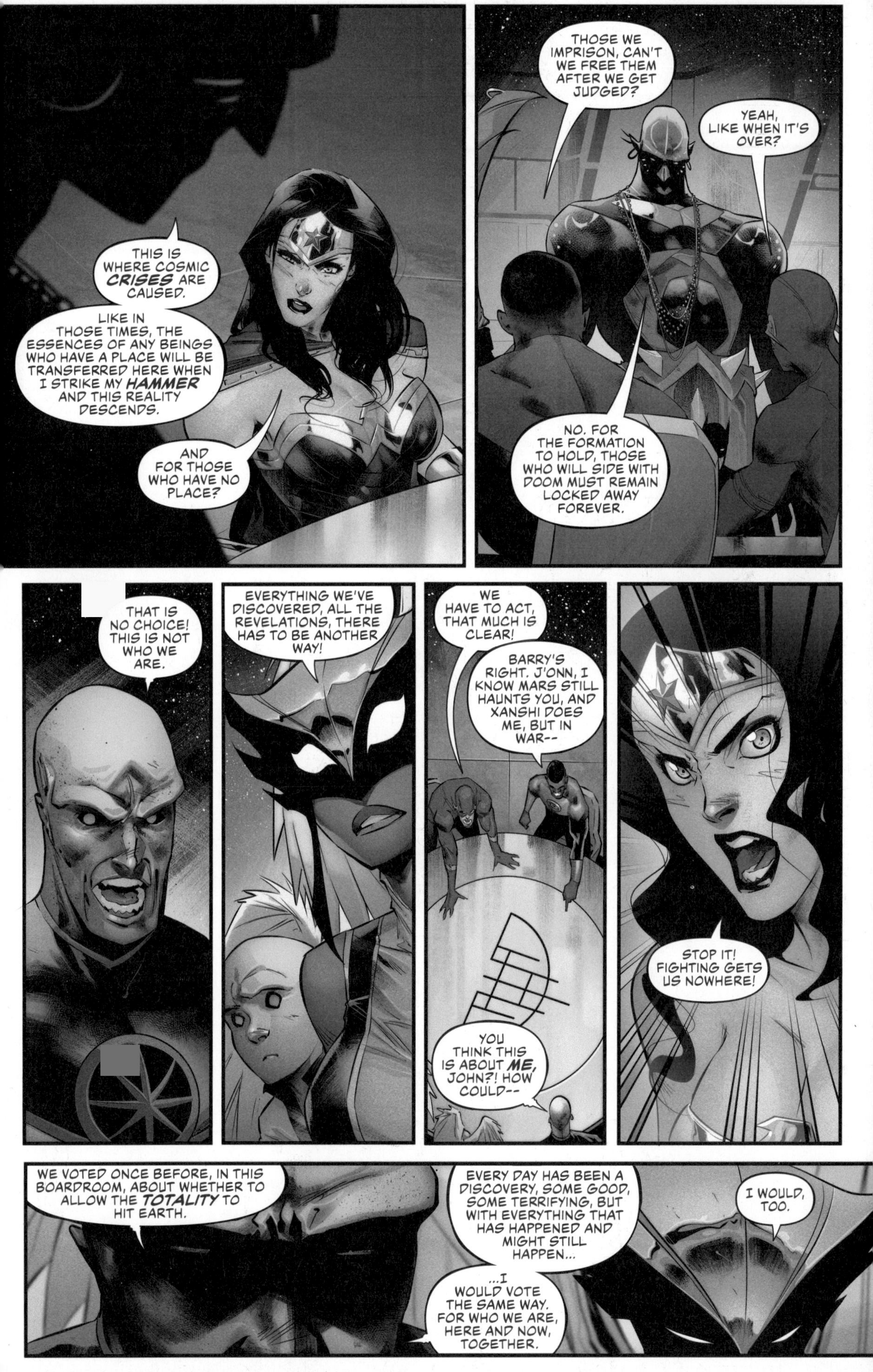
THIS IS WHERE COSMIC CRISES ARE CAUSED.
LIKE IN THOSE TIMES, THE ESSENCES OF ANY BEINGS WHO HAVE A PLACE WILL BE TRANSFERRED HERE WHEN I STRIKE MY HAMMER AND THIS REALITY DESCENDS.
AND FOR THOSE WHO HAVE NO PLACE?
THOSE WE IMPRISON, CAN'T WE FREE THEM AFTER WE GET JUDGED?
YEAH, LIKE WHEN IT'S OVER?
NO. FOR THE FORMATION TO HOLD, THOSE WHO WILL SIDE WITH DOOM MUST REMAIN LOCKED AWAY FOREVER.
THAT IS NO CHOICE! THIS IS NOT WHO WE ARE.
EVERYTHING WE'VE DISCOVERED, ALL THE REVELATIONS, THERE HAS TO BE ANOTHER WAY!
WE HAVE TO ACT, THAT MUCH IS CLEAR!
BARRY'S RIGHT. J'ONN, I KNOW MARS STILL HAUNTS YOU, AND XANSHI DOES ME, BUT IN WAR--
YOU THINK THIS IS ABOUT ME, JOHN?! HOW COULD--
STOP IT! FIGHTING GETS US NOWHERE!
WE VOTED ONCE BEFORE, IN THIS BOARDROOM, ABOUT WHETHER TO ALLOW THE TOTALITY TO HIT EARTH.
EVERY DAY HAS BEEN A DISCOVERY, SOME GOOD, SOME TERRIFYING, BUT WITH EVERYTHING THAT HAS HAPPENED AND MIGHT STILL HAPPEN...
...I WOULD VOTE THE SAME WAY. FOR WHO WE ARE, HERE AND NOW, TOGETHER.
I WOULD, TOO.

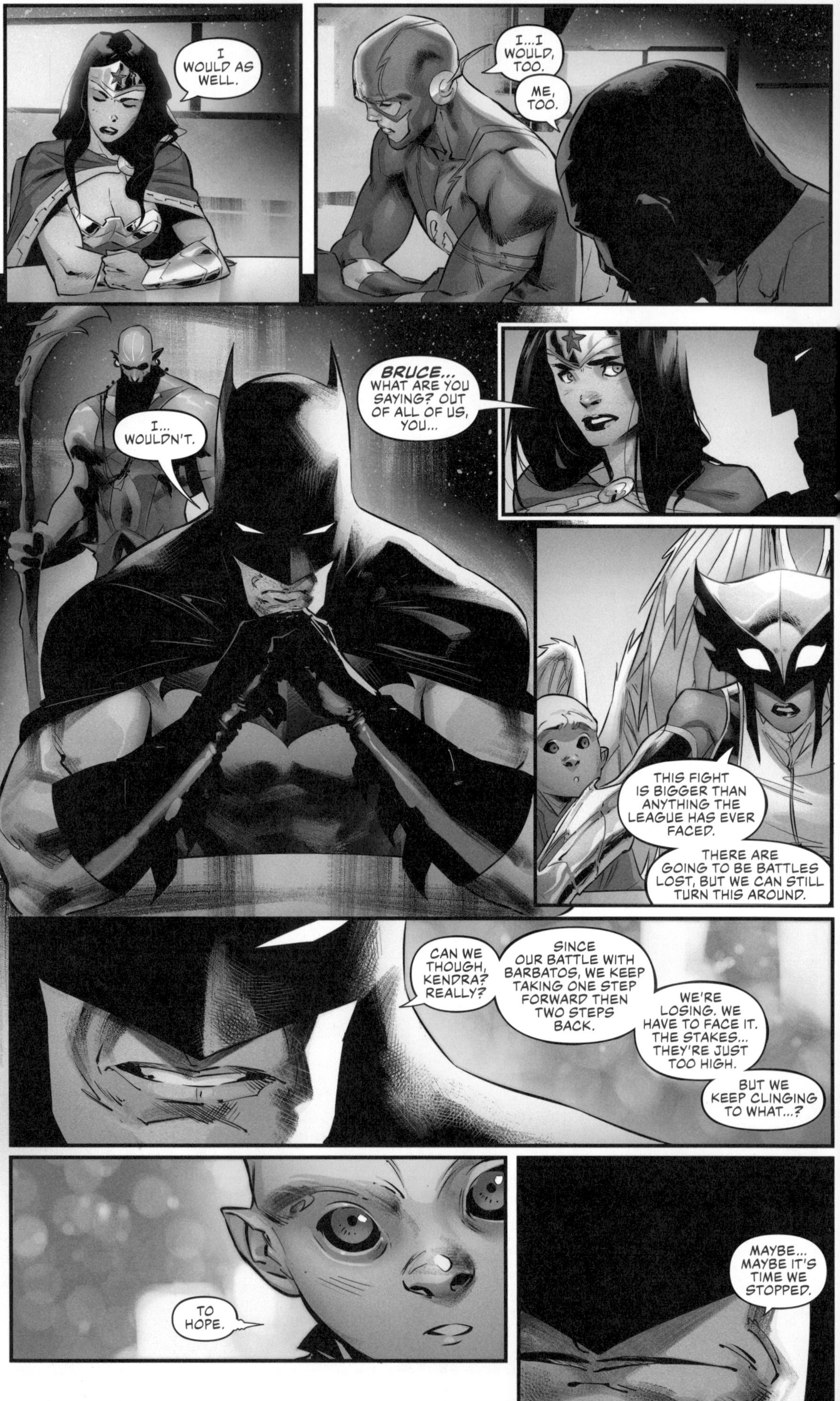
I WOULD AS WELL.
I...I WOULD, TOO.
ME, TOO.
I... WOULDN'T.
BRUCE... WHAT ARE YOU SAYING? OUT OF ALL OF US, YOU...
THIS FIGHT IS BIGGER THAN ANYTHING THE LEAGUE HAS EVER FACED.
THERE ARE GOING TO BE BATTLES LOST, BUT WE CAN STILL TURN THIS AROUND.
CAN WE THOUGH, KENDRA? REALLY?
SINCE OUR BATTLE WITH BARBATOS, WE KEEP TAKING ONE STEP FORWARD THEN TWO STEPS BACK.
WE'RE LOSING. WE HAVE TO FACE IT. THE STAKES... THEY'RE JUST TOO HIGH.
BUT WE KEEP CLINGING TO WHAT...?
TO HOPE.
MAYBE... MAYBE IT'S TIME WE STOPPED.

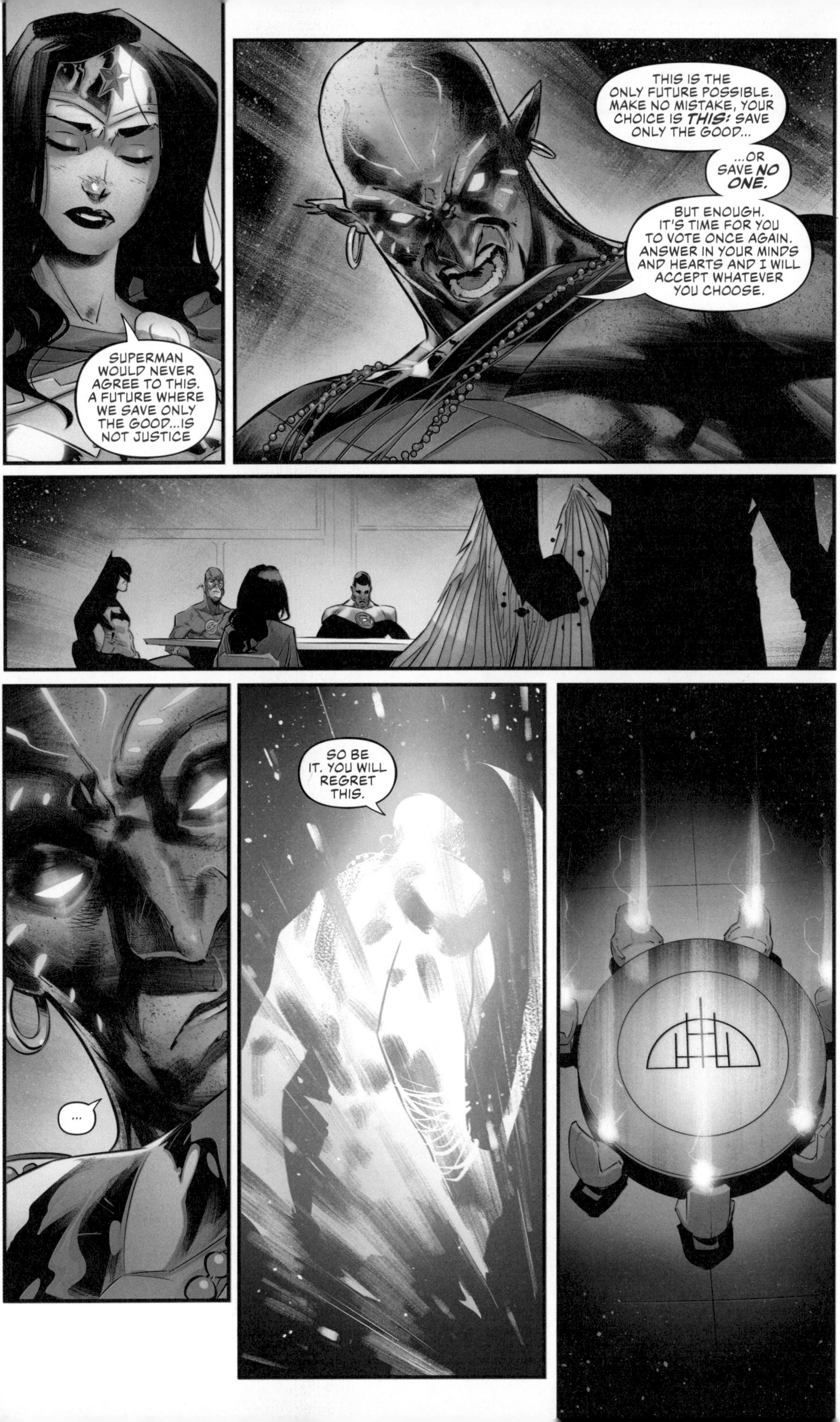
THIS IS THE ONLY FUTURE POSSIBLE. MAKE NO MISTAKE, YOUR CHOICE IS THIS: SAVE ONLY THE GOOD...
...OR SAVE NO ONE.
BUT ENOUGH. IT'S TIME FOR YOU TO VOTE ONCE AGAIN. ANSWER IN YOUR MINDS AND HEARTS AND I WILL ACCEPT WHATEVER YOU CHOOSE.
SUPERMAN WOULD NEVER AGREE TO THIS. A FUTURE WHERE WE SAVE ONLY THE GOOD...IS NOT JUSTICE
...
SO BE IT. YOU WILL REGRET THIS.

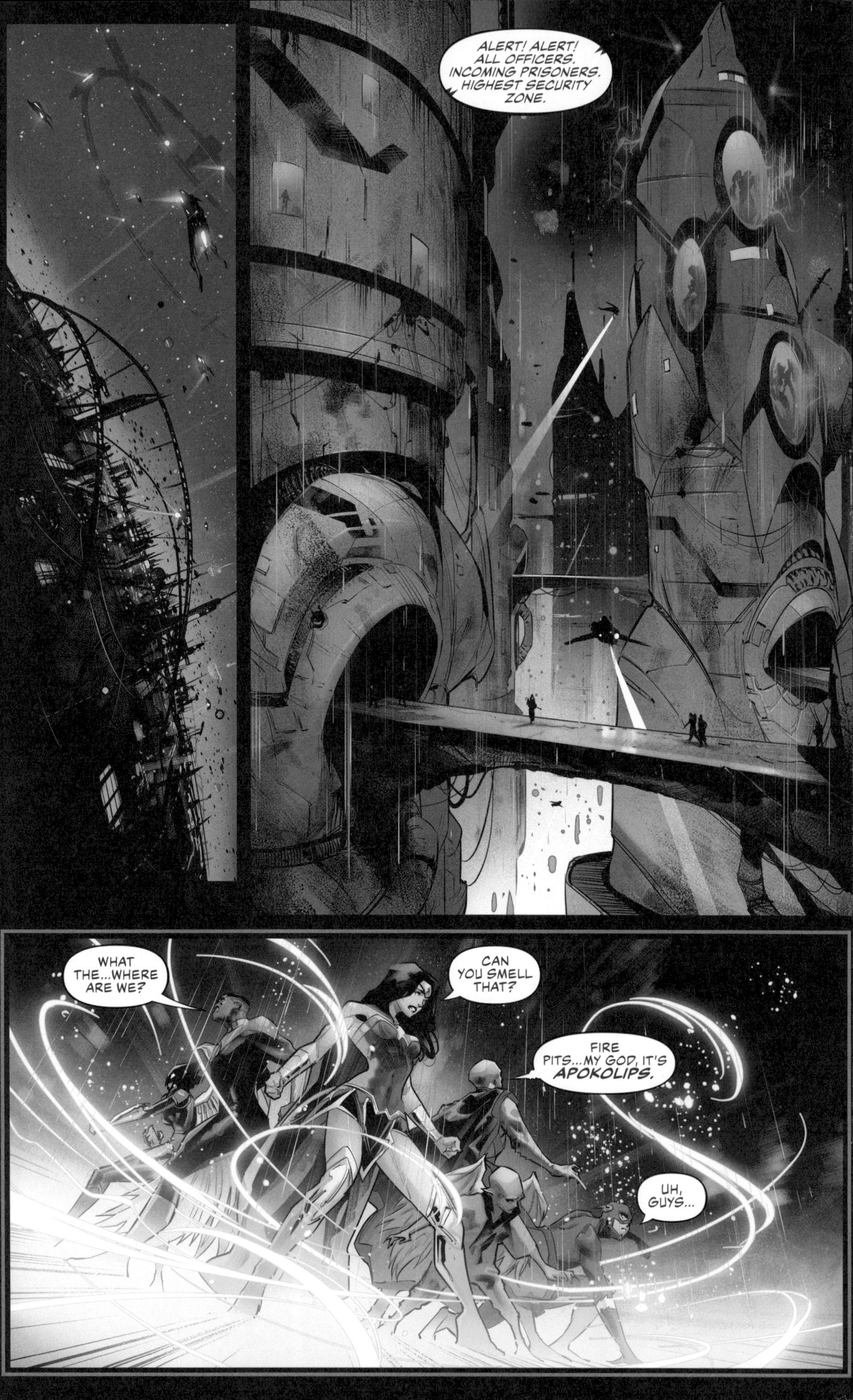
ALERT! ALERT! ALL OFFICERS. INCOMING PRISONERS. HIGHEST SECURITY ZONE.
WHAT THE...WHERE ARE WE?
CAN YOU SMELL THAT?
FIRE PITS...MY GOD, IT'S APOKOLIPS.
UH, GUYS...

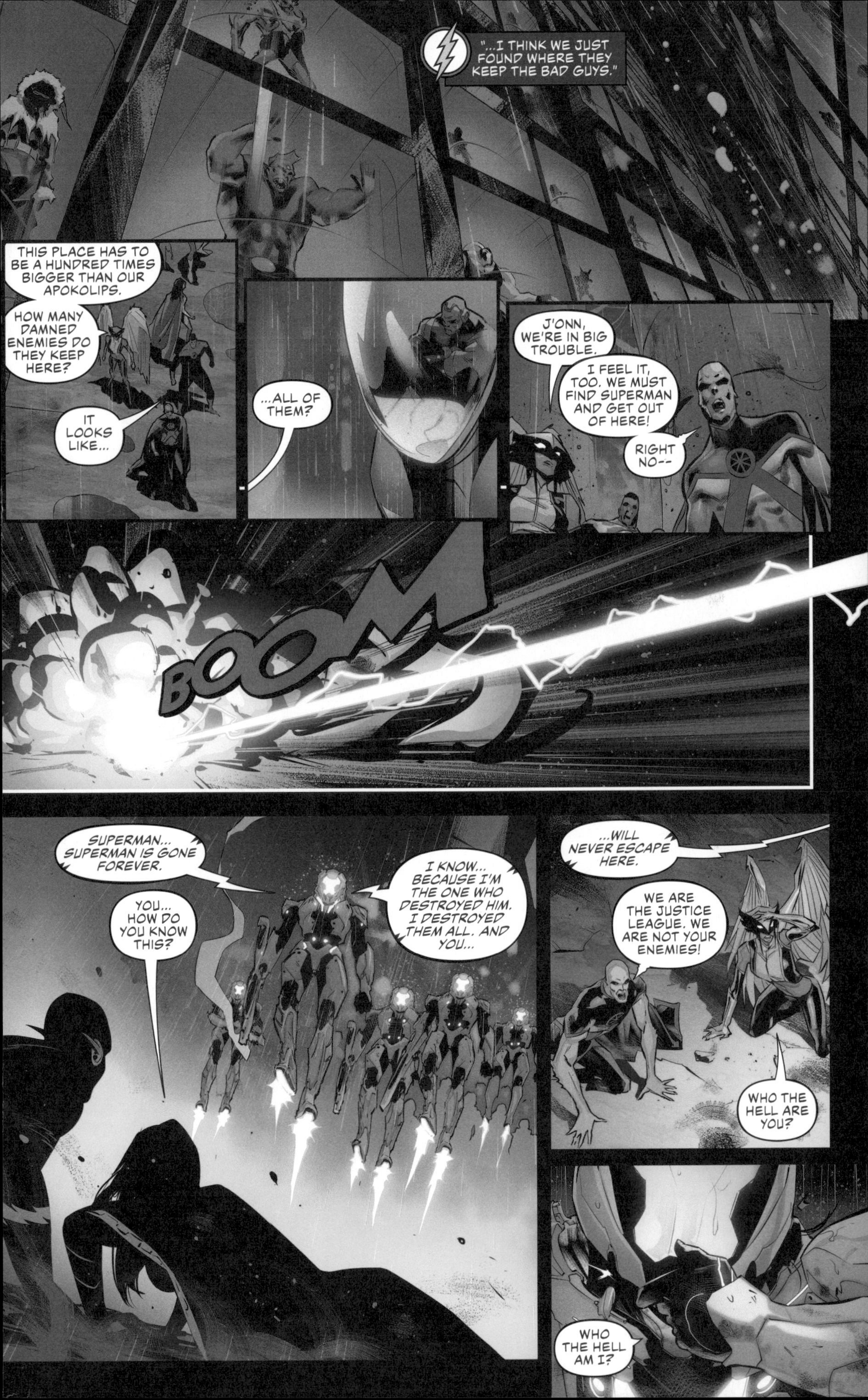
"...I THINK WE JUST FOUND WHERE THEY KEEP THE BAD GUYS."
THIS PLACE HAS TO BE A HUNDRED TIMES BIGGER THAN OUR APOKOLIPS.
HOW MANY DAMNED ENEMIES DO THEY KEEP HERE?
IT LOOKS LIKE...
...ALL OF THEM?
J'ONN, WE'RE IN BIG TROUBLE.
I FEEL IT, TOO. WE MUST FIND SUPERMAN AND GET OUT OF HERE!
RIGHT NO--
BOOM
SUPERMAN... SUPERMAN IS GONE FOREVER.
YOU... HOW DO YOU KNOW THIS?
I KNOW... BECAUSE I'M THE ONE WHO DESTROYED HIM. I DESTROYED THEM ALL. AND YOU...
...WILL NEVER ESCAPE HERE.
WE ARE THE JUSTICE LEAGUE. WE ARE NOT YOUR ENEMIES!
WHO THE HELL ARE YOU?
WHO THE HELL AM I?

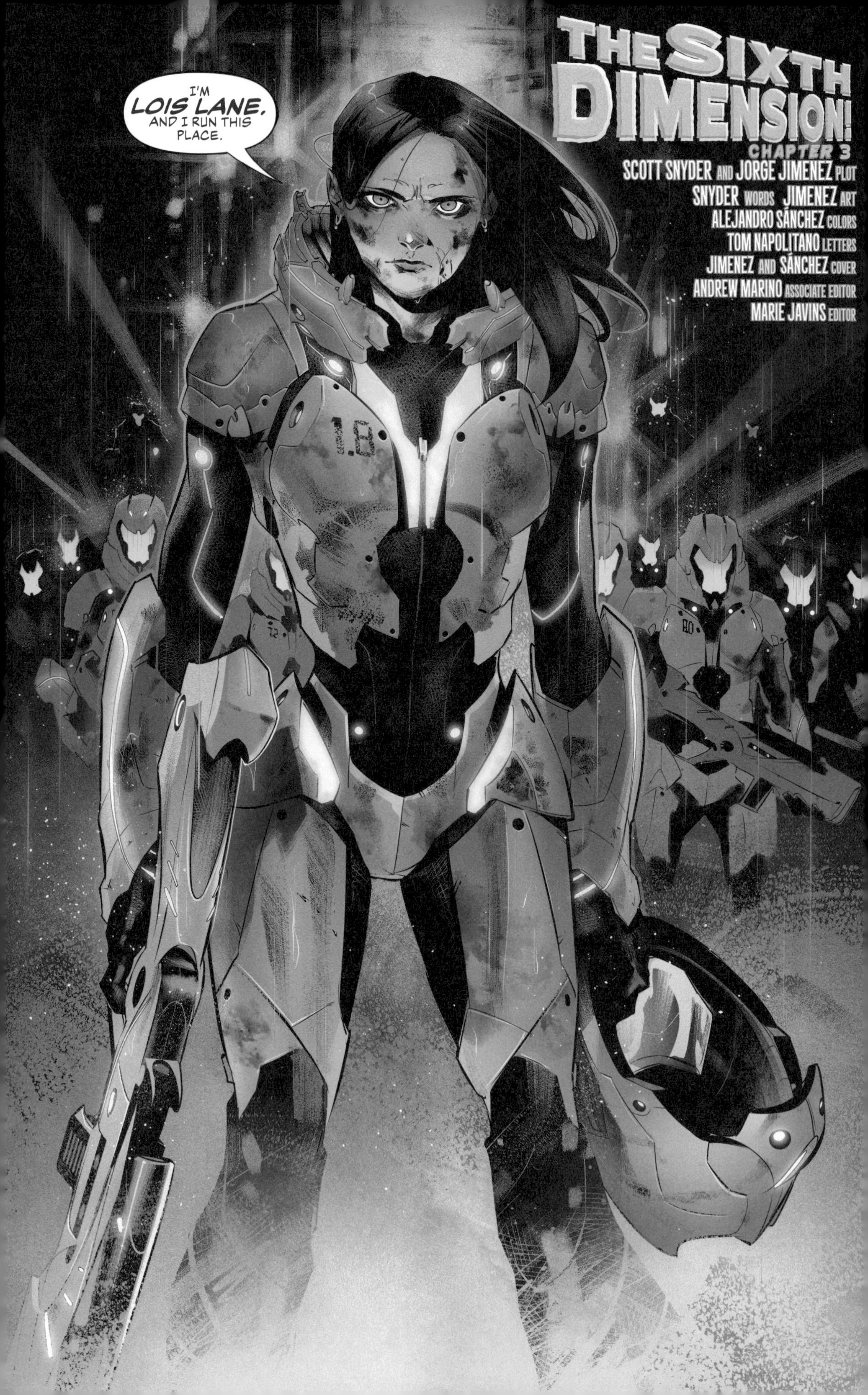
I'M LOIS LANE. AND I RUN THIS PLACE.
THE SIXTH DIMENSION!
CHAPTER 3
SCOTT SNYDER AND JORGE JIMENEZ PLOT
SNYDER WORDS JIMENEZ ART
ALEJANDRO SÁNCHEZ COLORS
TOM NAPOLITANO LETTERS
JIMENEZ AND SÁNCHEZ COVER
ANDREW MARINO ASSOCIATE EDITOR
MARIE JAVINS EDITOR

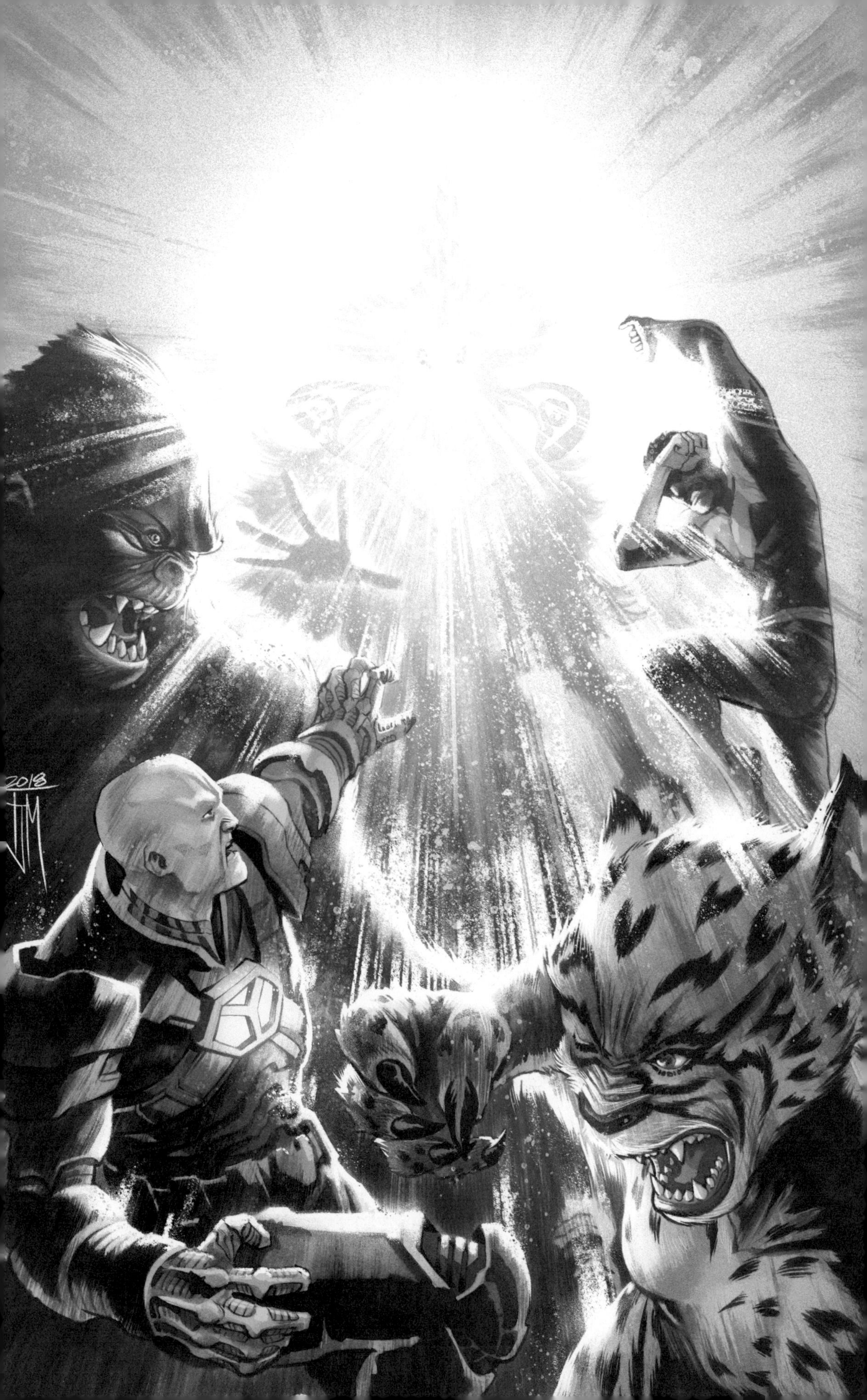

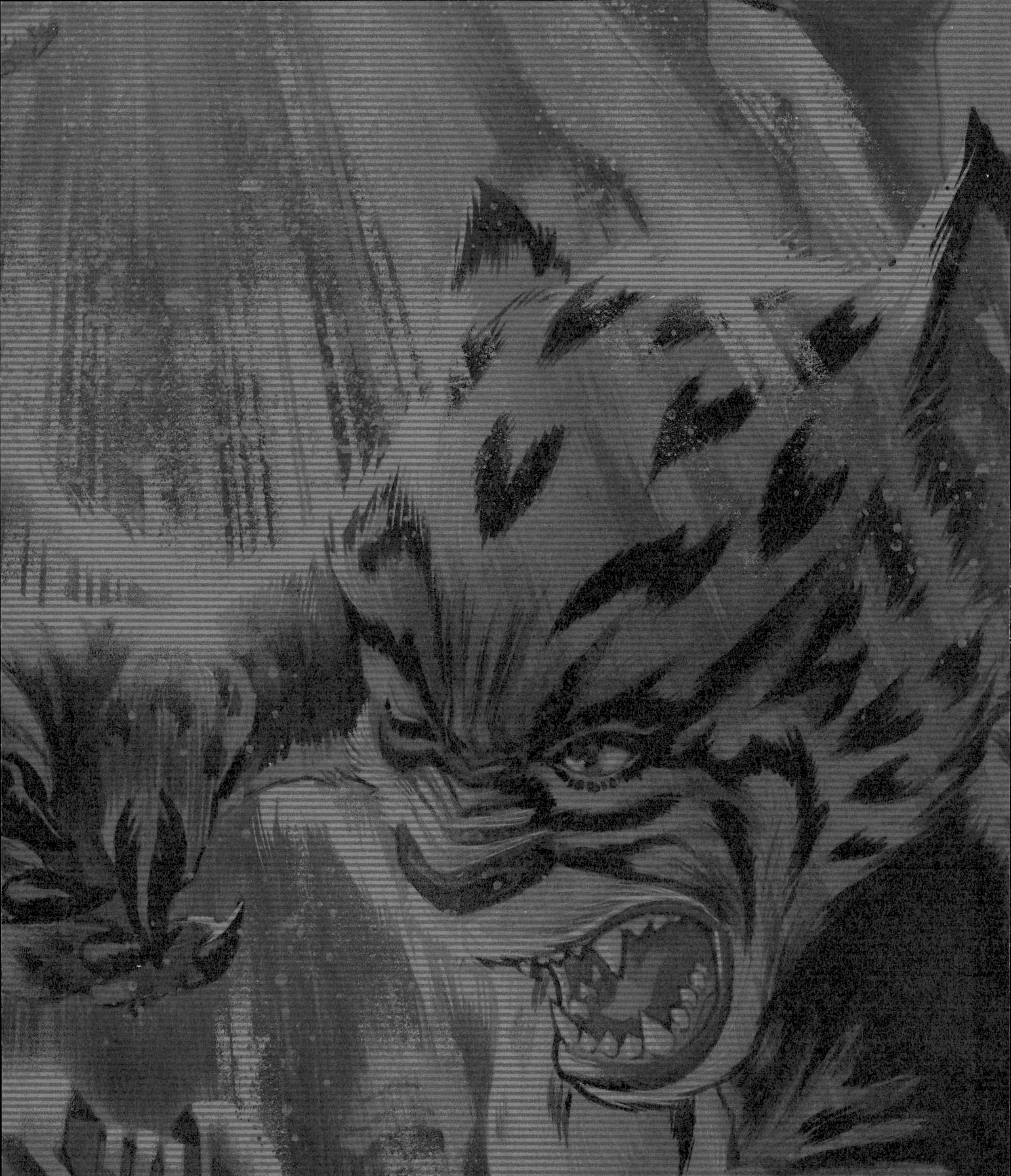

JUSTICE
LEAGUE
#22

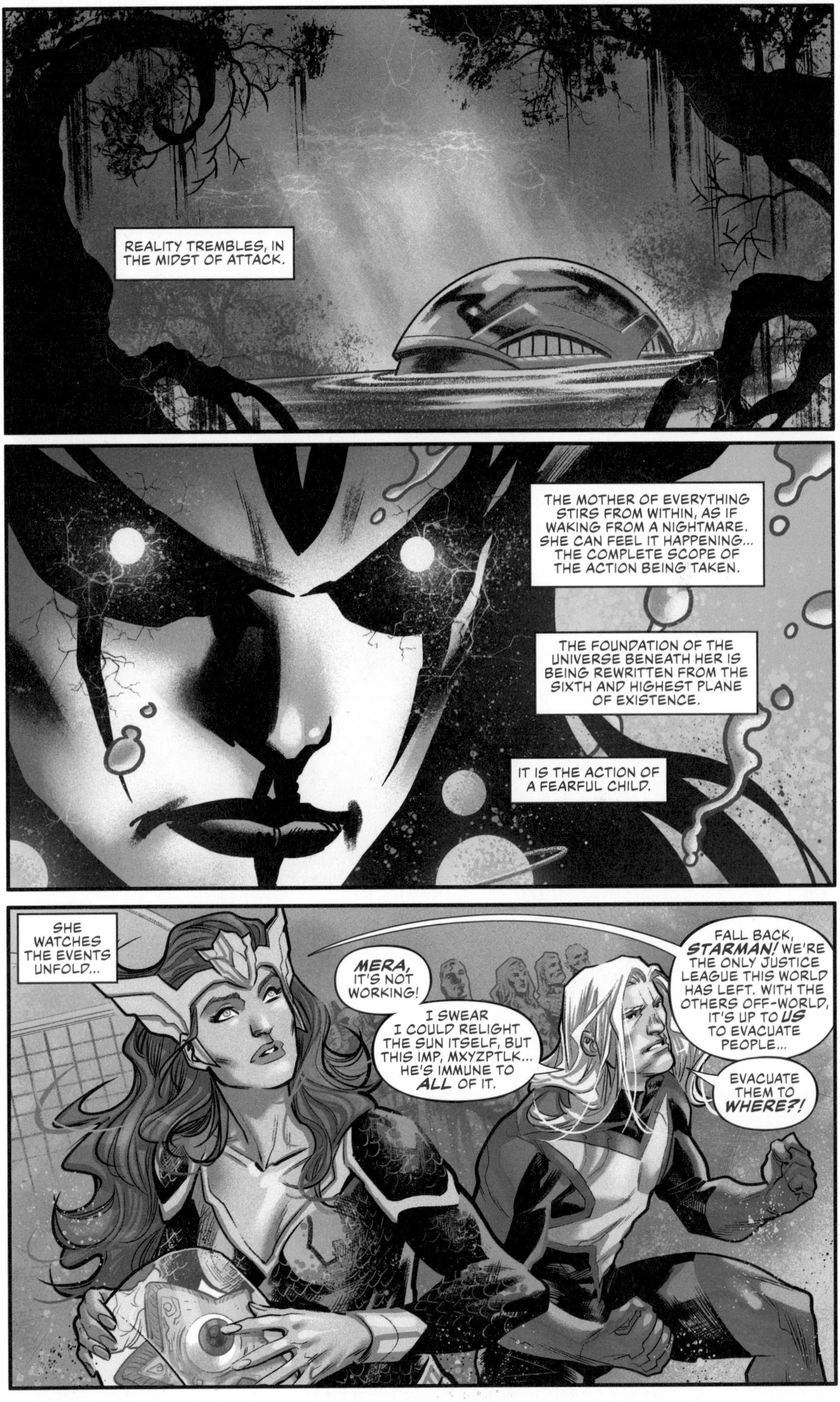
REALITY TREMBLES, IN THE MIDST OF ATTACK.
THE MOTHER OF EVERYTHING STIRS FROM WITHIN, AS IF WAKING FROM A NIGHTMARE. SHE CAN FEEL IT HAPPENING... THE COMPLETE SCOPE OF THE ACTION BEING TAKEN.
THE FOUNDATION OF THE UNIVERSE BENEATH HER IS BEING REWRITTEN FROM THE SIXTH AND HIGHEST PLANE OF EXISTENCE.
IT IS THE ACTION OF A FEARFUL CHILD.
SHE WATCHES THE EVENTS UNFOLD...
MERA, IT'S NOT WORKING!
I SWEAR I COULD RELIGHT THE SUN ITSELF, BUT THIS IMP, MXYZPTLK... HE'S IMMUNE TO ALL OF IT.
FALL BACK, STARMAN! WE'RE THE ONLY JUSTICE LEAGUE THIS WORLD HAS LEFT. WITH THE OTHERS OFF-WORLD, IT'S UP TO US TO EVACUATE PEOPLE...
EVACUATE THEM TO WHERE?!

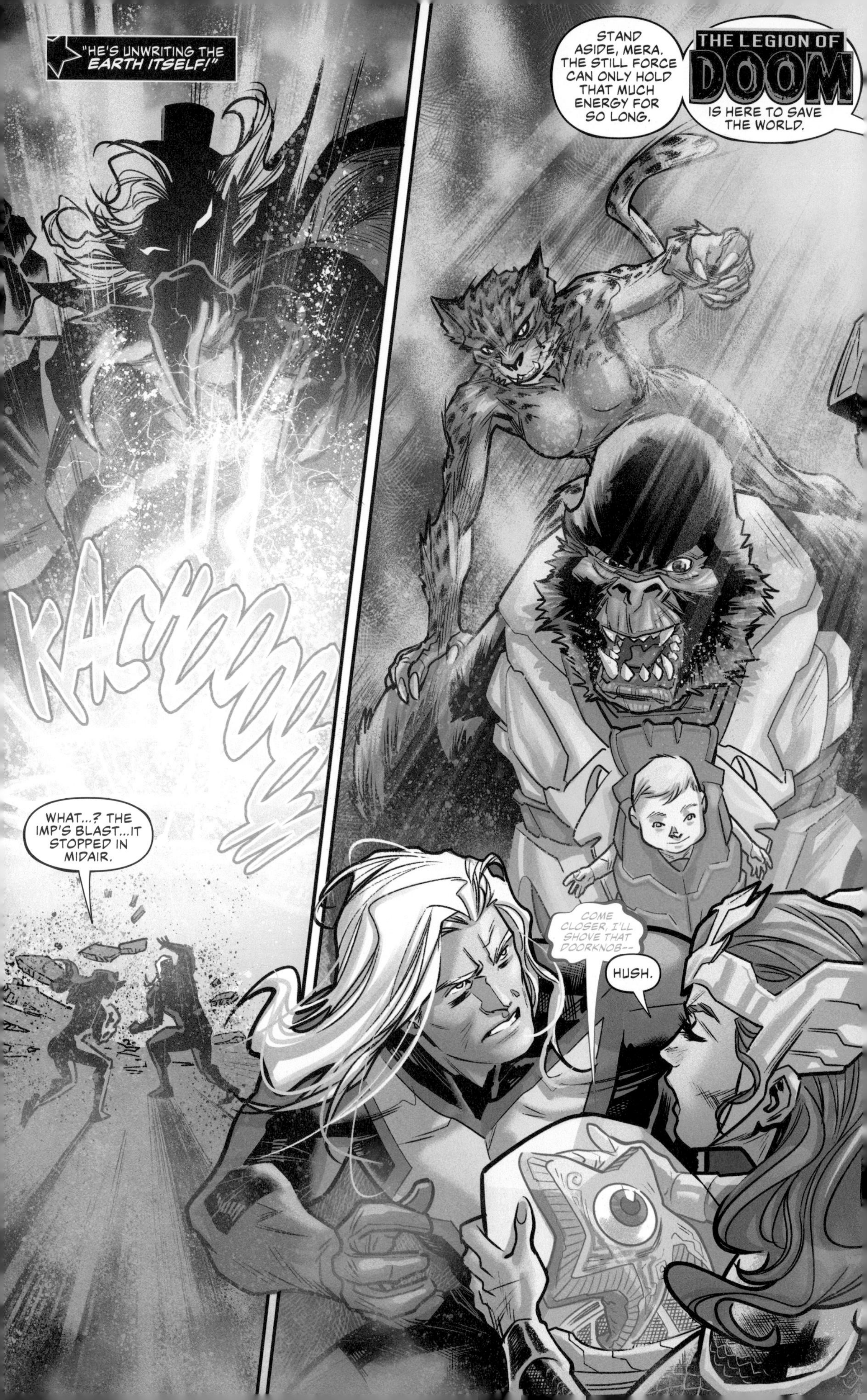
"HE'S UNWRITING THE EARTH ITSELF!"
KACHOOOM
WHAT...? THE IMP'S BLAST...IT STOPPED IN MIDAIR.
STAND ASIDE, MERA. THE STILL FORCE CAN ONLY HOLD THAT MUCH ENERGY FOR SO LONG.
THE LEGION OF DOOM IS HERE TO SAVE THE WORLD.
COME CLOSER, I'LL SHOVE THAT DOORKNOB--
HUSH.

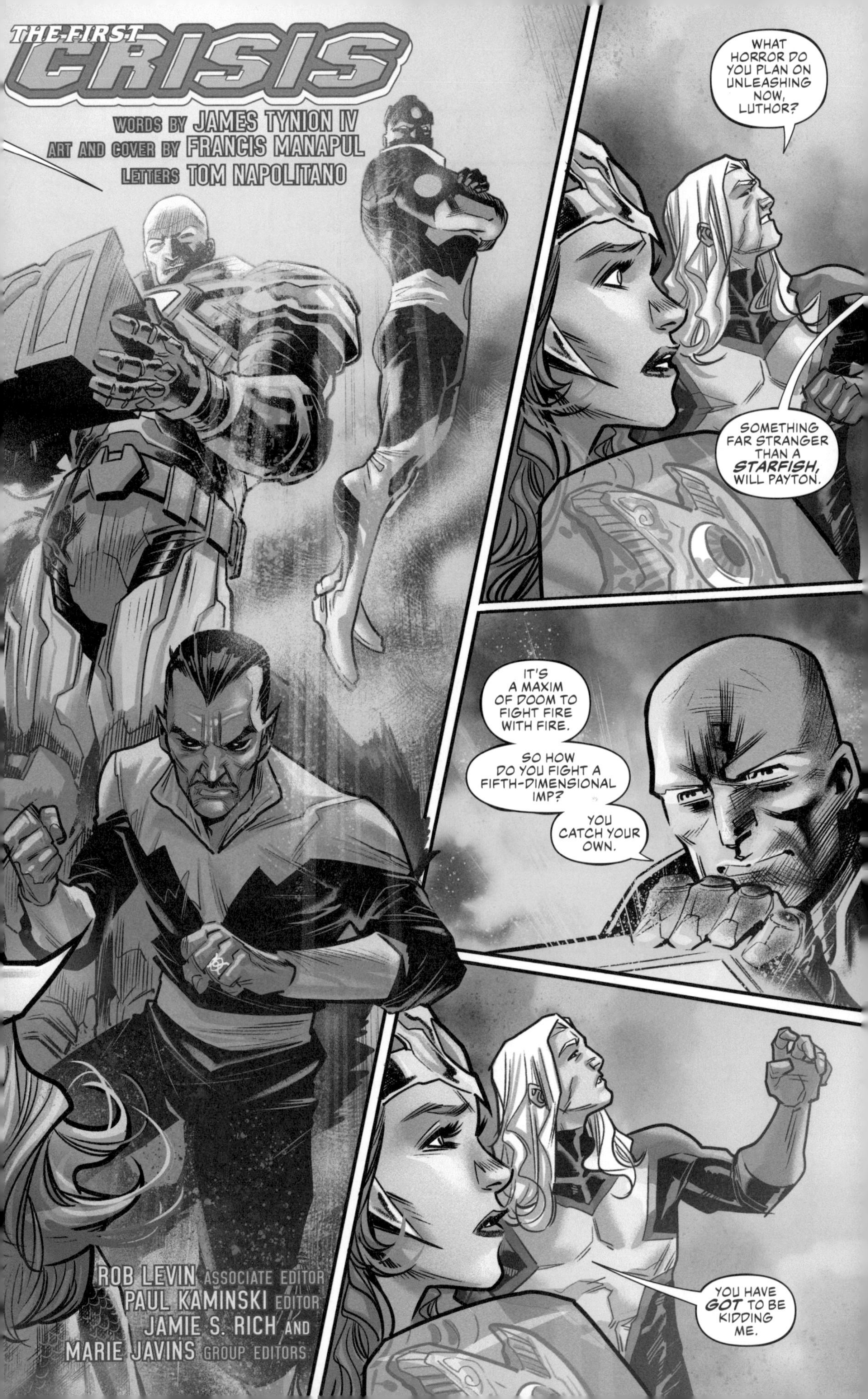
THE FIRST CRISIS
WORDS BY JAMES TYNION IV
ART AND COVER BY FRANCIS MANAPUL
LETTERS TOM NAPOLITANO
ROB LEVIN ASSOCIATE EDITOR
PAUL KAMINSKI EDITOR
JAMIE S. RICH AND
MARIE JAVINS GROUP EDITORS
WHAT HORROR DO YOU PLAN ON UNLEASHING NOW, LUTHOR?
SOMETHING FAR STRANGER THAN A STARFISH, WILL PAYTON.
IT'S A MAXIM OF DOOM TO FIGHT FIRE WITH FIRE.
SO HOW DO YOU FIGHT A FIFTH-DIMENSIONAL IMP?
YOU CATCH YOUR OWN.
YOU HAVE GOT TO BE KIDDING ME.

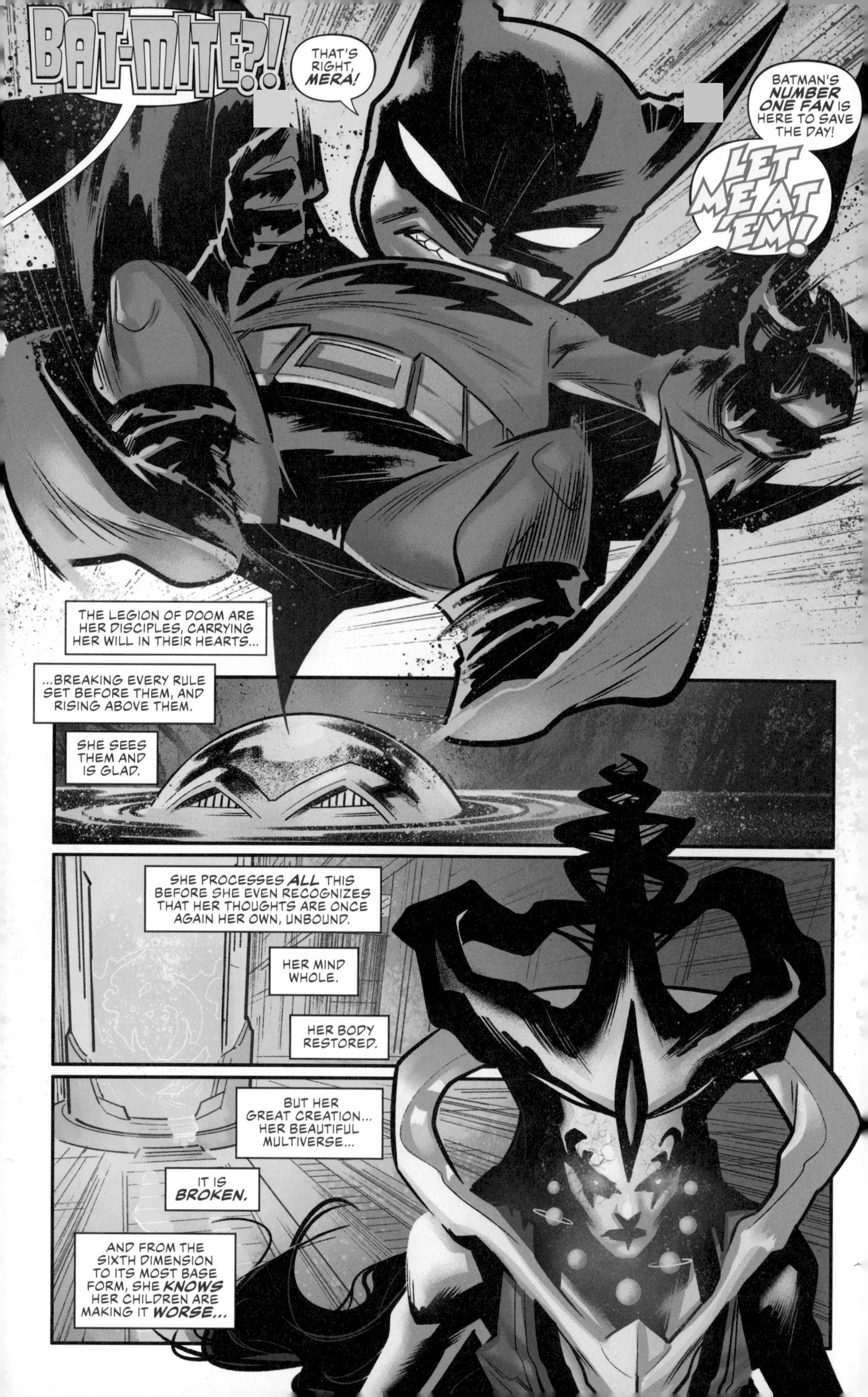
BAT-MITE?!
THAT'S RIGHT, MERA!
BATMAN'S NUMBER ONE FAN IS HERE TO SAVE THE DAY!
LET ME AT 'EM!
THE LEGION OF DOOM ARE HER DISCIPLES, CARRYING HER WILL IN THEIR HEARTS...
...BREAKING EVERY RULE SET BEFORE THEM, AND RISING ABOVE THEM.
SHE SEES THEM AND IS GLAD.
SHE PROCESSES ALL THIS BEFORE SHE EVEN RECOGNIZES THAT HER THOUGHTS ARE ONCE AGAIN HER OWN, UNBOUND.
HER MIND WHOLE.
HER BODY RESTORED.
BUT HER GREAT CREATION... HER BEAUTIFUL MULTIVERSE...
IT IS BROKEN.
AND FROM THE SIXTH DIMENSION TO ITS MOST BASE FORM, SHE KNOWS HER CHILDREN ARE MAKING IT WORSE...

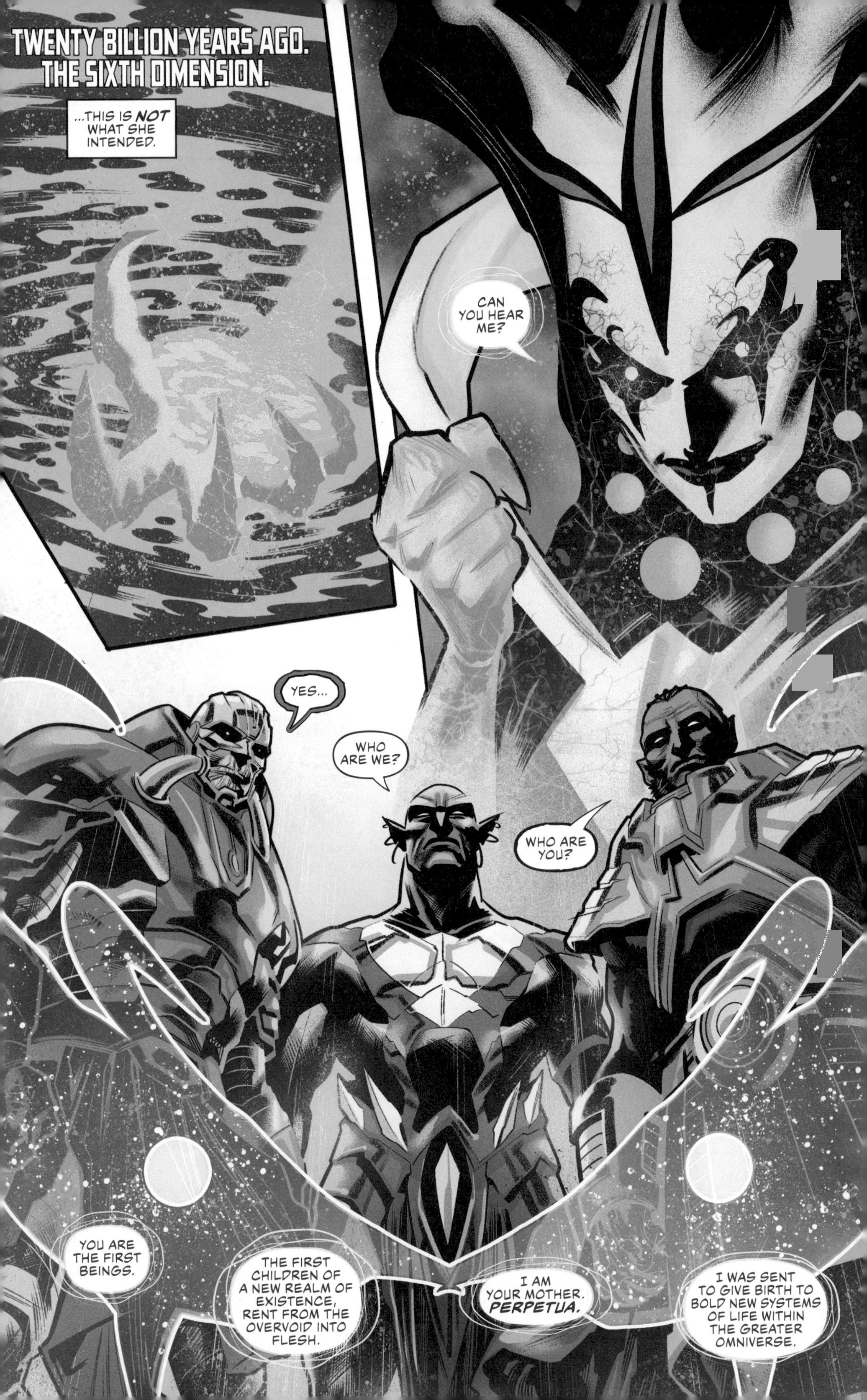
TWENTY BILLION YEARS AGO. THE SIXTH DIMENSION.
...THIS IS NOT WHAT SHE INTENDED.
CAN YOU HEAR ME?
YES...
WHO ARE WE?
WHO ARE YOU?
YOU ARE THE FIRST BEINGS.
THE FIRST CHILDREN OF A NEW REALM OF EXISTENCE, RENT FROM THE OVERVOID INTO FLESH.
I AM YOUR MOTHER. PERPETUA.
I WAS SENT TO GIVE BIRTH TO BOLD NEW SYSTEMS OF LIFE WITHIN THE GREATER OMNIVERSE.

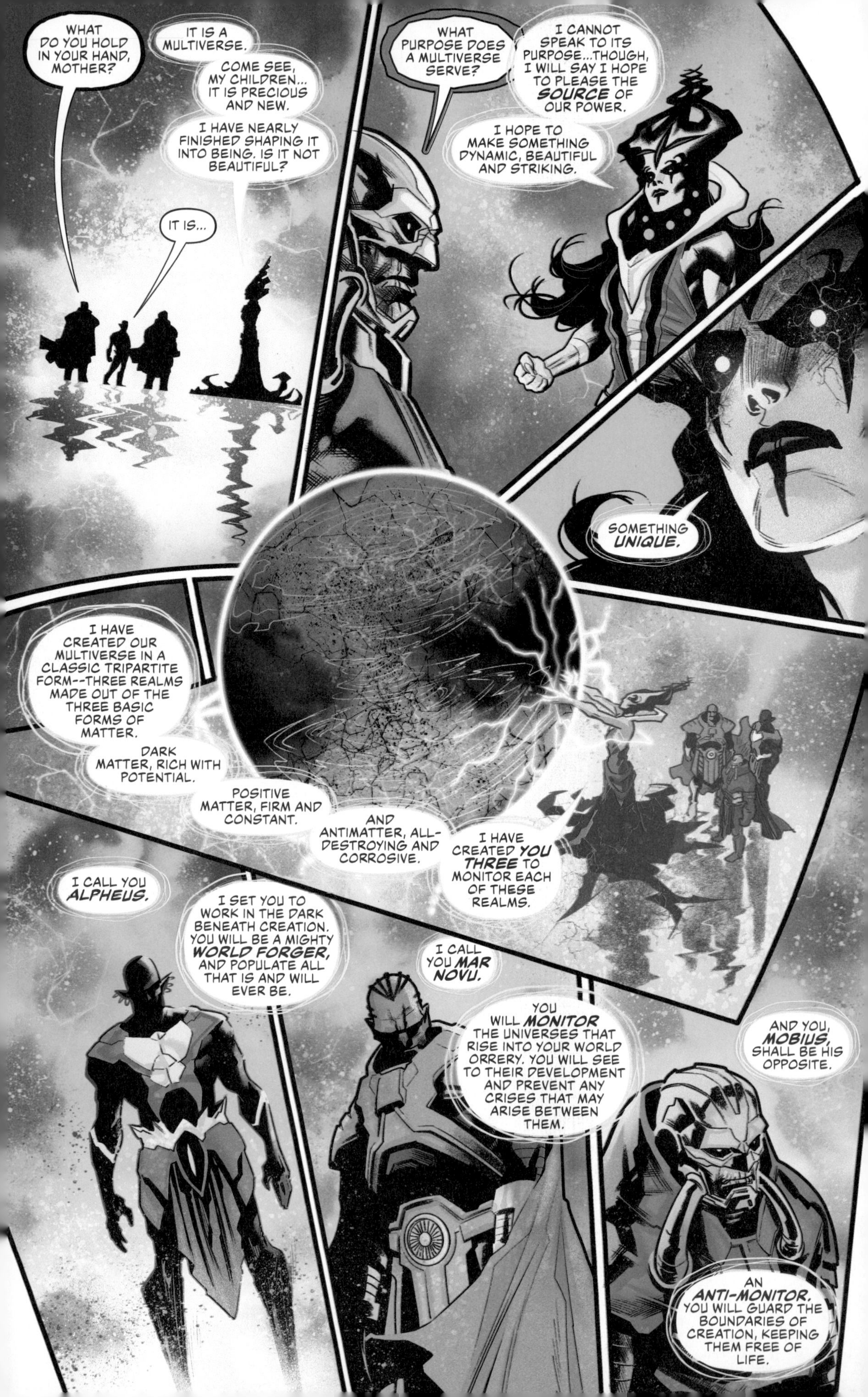
WHAT DO YOU HOLD IN YOUR HAND, MOTHER?
IT IS A MULTIVERSE.
COME SEE, MY CHILDREN... IT IS PRECIOUS AND NEW.
I HAVE NEARLY FINISHED SHAPING IT INTO BEING. IS IT NOT BEAUTIFUL?
IT IS...
WHAT PURPOSE DOES A MULTIVERSE SERVE?
I CANNOT SPEAK TO ITS PURPOSE...THOUGH, I WILL SAY I HOPE TO PLEASE THE SOURCE OF OUR POWER.
I HOPE TO MAKE SOMETHING DYNAMIC, BEAUTIFUL AND STRIKING.
SOMETHING UNIQUE.
I HAVE CREATED OUR MULTIVERSE IN A CLASSIC TRIPARTITE FORM--THREE REALMS MADE OUT OF THE THREE BASIC FORMS OF MATTER.
DARK MATTER, RICH WITH POTENTIAL.
POSITIVE MATTER, FIRM AND CONSTANT.
AND ANTIMATTER, ALL-DESTROYING AND CORROSIVE.
I HAVE CREATED YOU THREE TO MONITOR EACH OF THESE REALMS.
I CALL YOU ALPHEUS.
I SET YOU TO WORK IN THE DARK BENEATH CREATION. YOU WILL BE A MIGHTY WORLD FORGER, AND POPULATE ALL THAT IS AND WILL EVER BE.
I CALL YOU MAR NOVU.
YOU WILL MONITOR THE UNIVERSES THAT RISE INTO YOUR WORLD ORRERY. YOU WILL SEE TO THEIR DEVELOPMENT AND PREVENT ANY CRISES THAT MAY ARISE BETWEEN THEM.
AND YOU, MOBIUS, SHALL BE HIS OPPOSITE.
AN ANTI-MONITOR. YOU WILL GUARD THE BOUNDARIES OF CREATION, KEEPING THEM FREE OF LIFE.

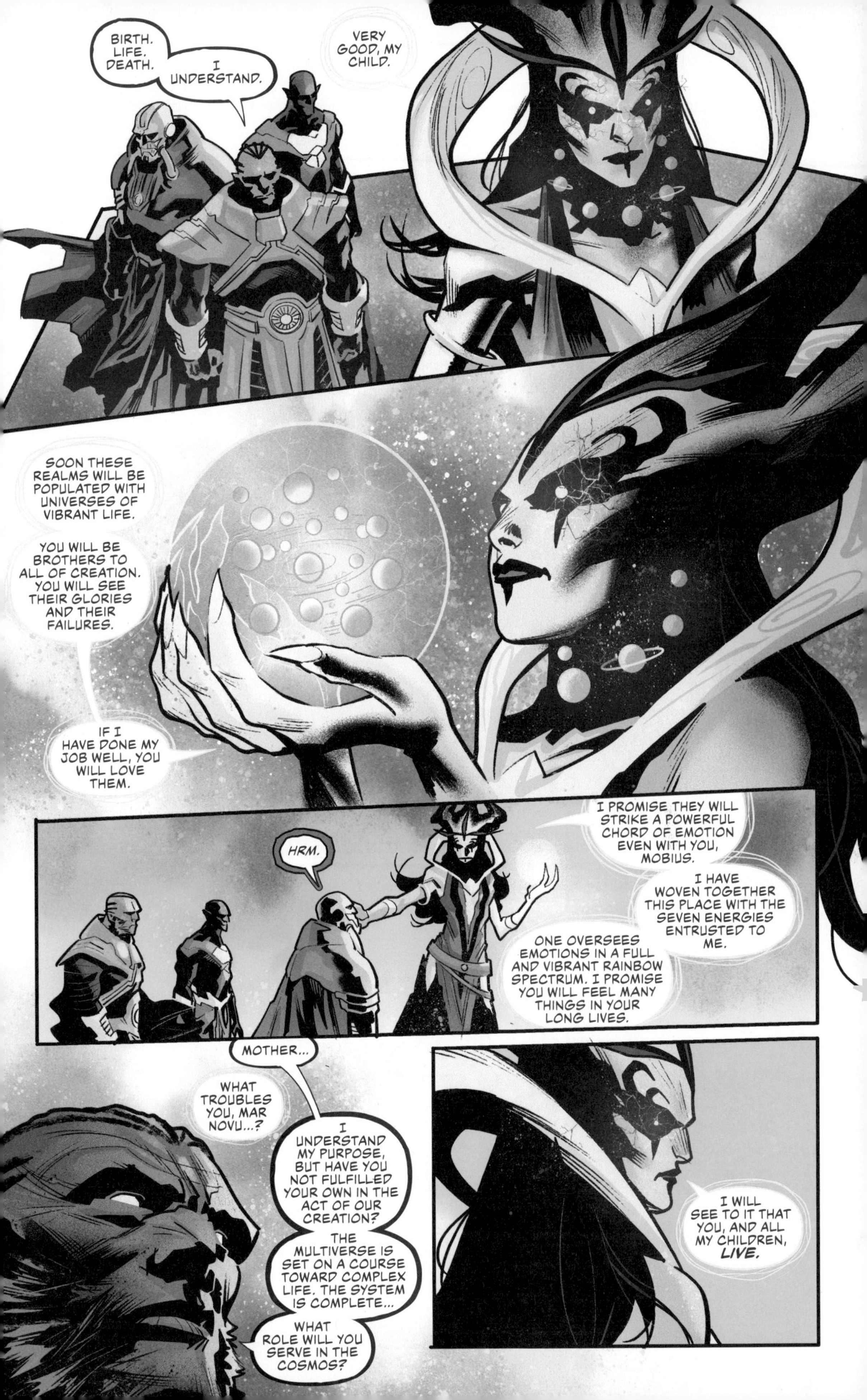
BIRTH. LIFE. DEATH.
I UNDERSTAND.
VERY GOOD, MY CHILD.
SOON THESE REALMS WILL BE POPULATED WITH UNIVERSES OF VIBRANT LIFE.
YOU WILL BE BROTHERS TO ALL OF CREATION. YOU WILL SEE THEIR GLORIES AND THEIR FAILURES.
IF I HAVE DONE MY JOB WELL, YOU WILL LOVE THEM.
I PROMISE THEY WILL STRIKE A POWERFUL CHORD OF EMOTION EVEN WITH YOU, MOBIUS.
HRM.
I HAVE WOVEN TOGETHER THIS PLACE WITH THE SEVEN ENERGIES ENTRUSTED TO ME.
ONE OVERSEES EMOTIONS IN A FULL AND VIBRANT RAINBOW SPECTRUM. I PROMISE YOU WILL FEEL MANY THINGS IN YOUR LONG LIVES.
MOTHER...
WHAT TROUBLES YOU, MAR NOVU...?
I UNDERSTAND MY PURPOSE, BUT HAVE YOU NOT FULFILLED YOUR OWN IN THE ACT OF OUR CREATION?
THE MULTIVERSE IS SET ON A COURSE TOWARD COMPLEX LIFE. THE SYSTEM IS COMPLETE...
WHAT ROLE WILL YOU SERVE IN THE COSMOS?
I WILL SEE TO IT THAT YOU, AND ALL MY CHILDREN, ***LIVE.***

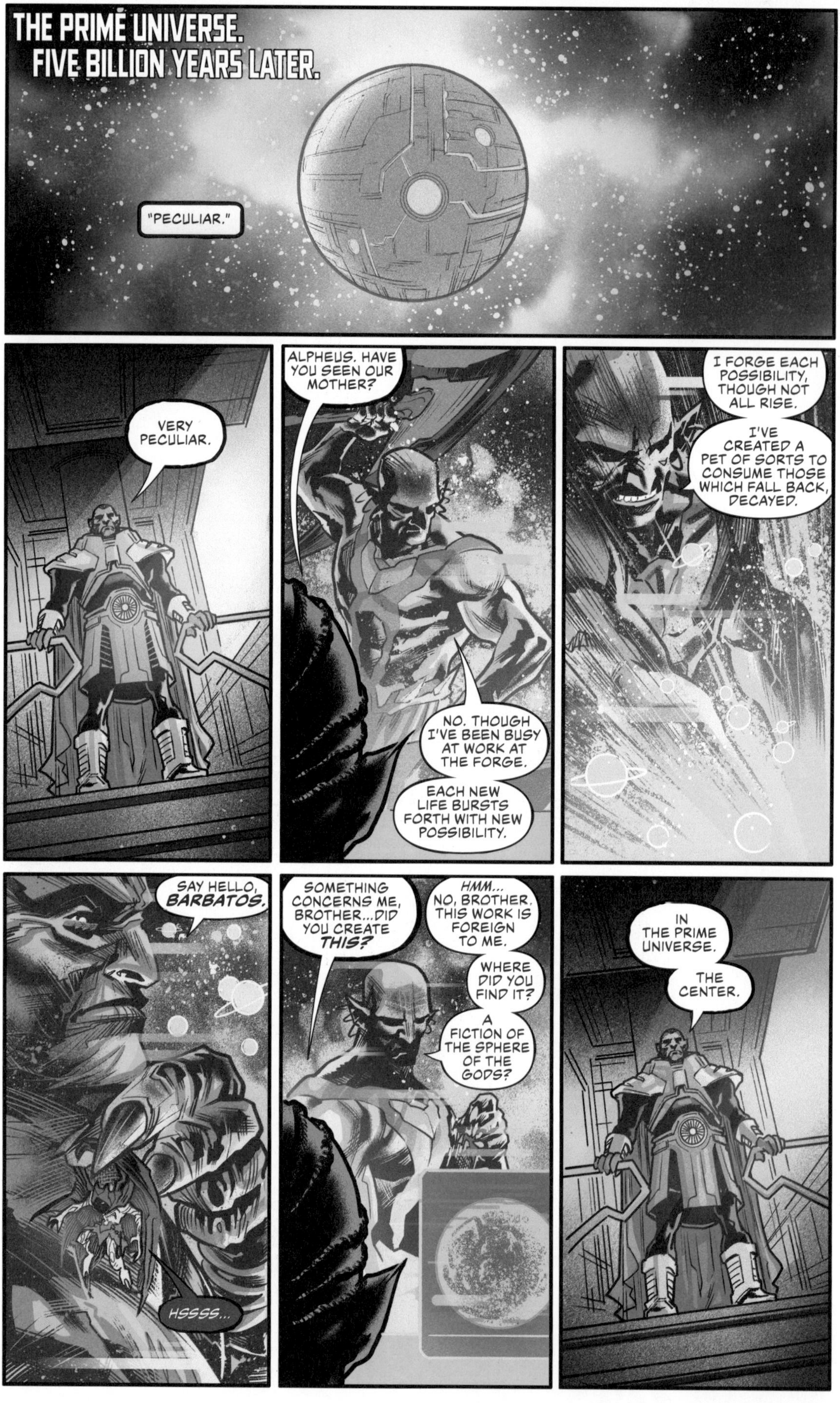
THE PRIME UNIVERSE.
FIVE BILLION YEARS LATER.
"PECULIAR."
VERY PECULIAR.
ALPHEUS. HAVE YOU SEEN OUR MOTHER?
NO. THOUGH I'VE BEEN BUSY AT WORK AT THE FORGE.
EACH NEW LIFE BURSTS FORTH WITH NEW POSSIBILITY.
I FORGE EACH POSSIBILITY, THOUGH NOT ALL RISE.
I'VE CREATED A PET OF SORTS TO CONSUME THOSE WHICH FALL BACK, DECAYED.
SAY HELLO, BARBATOS.
HSSSS...
SOMETHING CONCERNS ME, BROTHER...DID YOU CREATE THIS?
HMM... NO, BROTHER. THIS WORK IS FOREIGN TO ME.
WHERE DID YOU FIND IT?
A FICTION OF THE SPHERE OF THE GODS?
IN THE PRIME UNIVERSE.
THE CENTER.

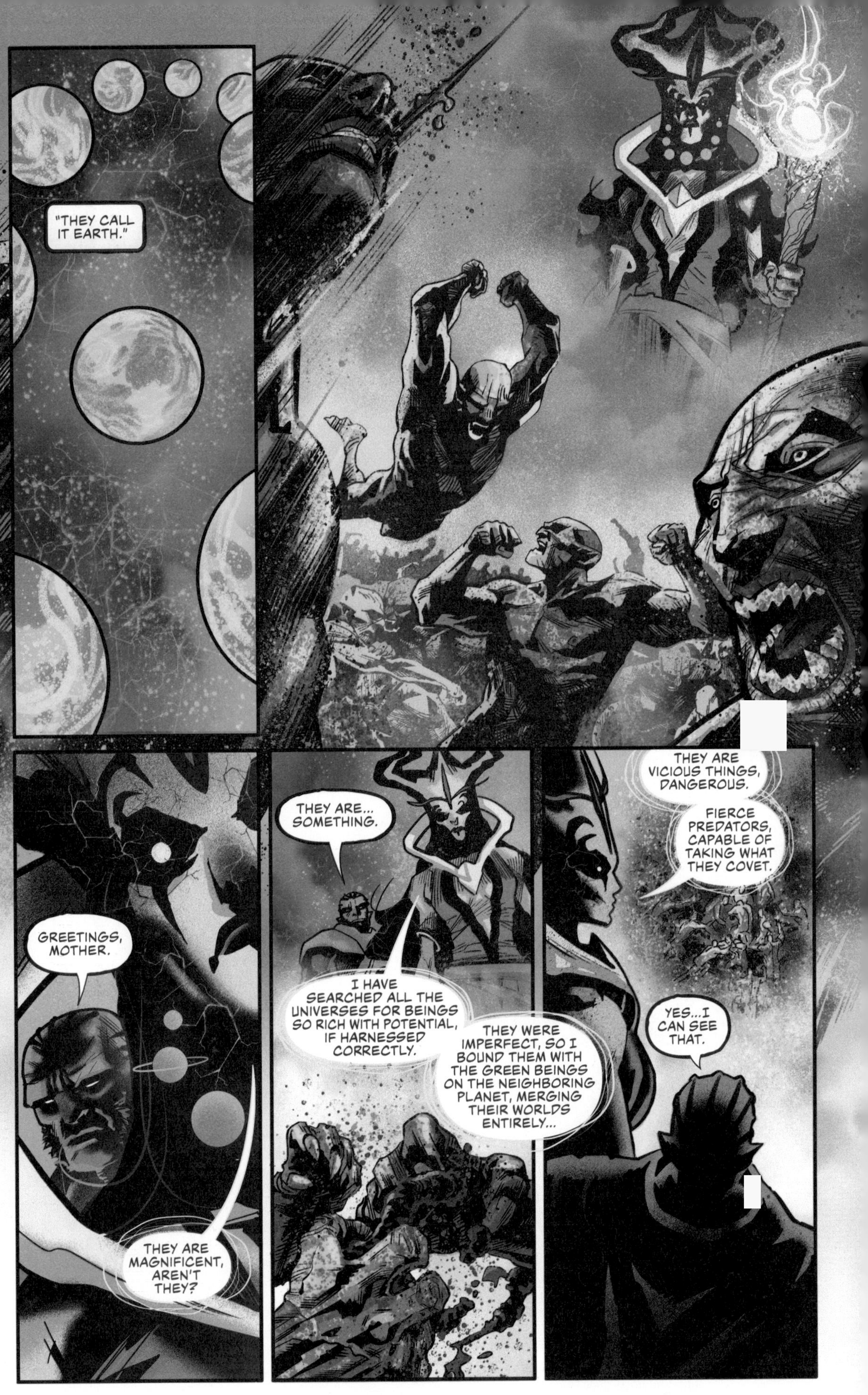
"THEY CALL IT EARTH."
GREETINGS, MOTHER.
THEY ARE MAGNIFICENT, AREN'T THEY?
THEY ARE... SOMETHING.
I HAVE SEARCHED ALL THE UNIVERSES FOR BEINGS SO RICH WITH POTENTIAL, IF HARNESSED CORRECTLY.
THEY WERE IMPERFECT, SO I BOUND THEM WITH THE GREEN BEINGS ON THE NEIGHBORING PLANET, MERGING THEIR WORLDS ENTIRELY...
THEY ARE VICIOUS THINGS, DANGEROUS.
FIERCE PREDATORS, CAPABLE OF TAKING WHAT THEY COVET.
YES...I CAN SEE THAT.

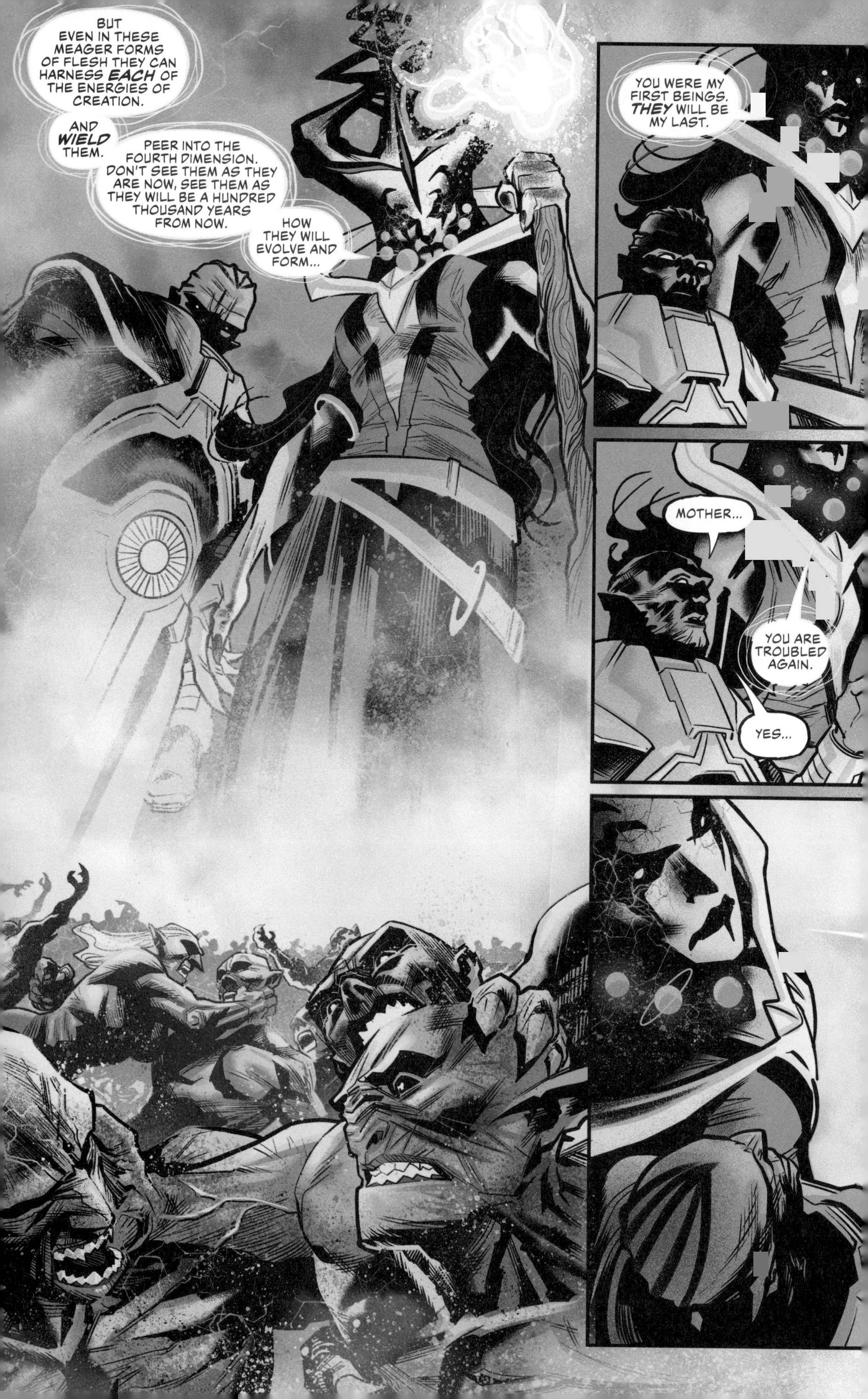
BUT EVEN IN THESE MEAGER FORMS OF FLESH THEY CAN HARNESS **EACH** OF THE ENERGIES OF CREATION.
AND **WIELD** THEM.
PEER INTO THE FOURTH DIMENSION. DON'T SEE THEM AS THEY ARE NOW, SEE THEM AS THEY WILL BE A HUNDRED THOUSAND YEARS FROM NOW.
HOW THEY WILL EVOLVE AND FORM...
YOU WERE MY FIRST BEINGS. **THEY** WILL BE MY LAST.
MOTHER...
YOU ARE TROUBLED AGAIN.
YES...

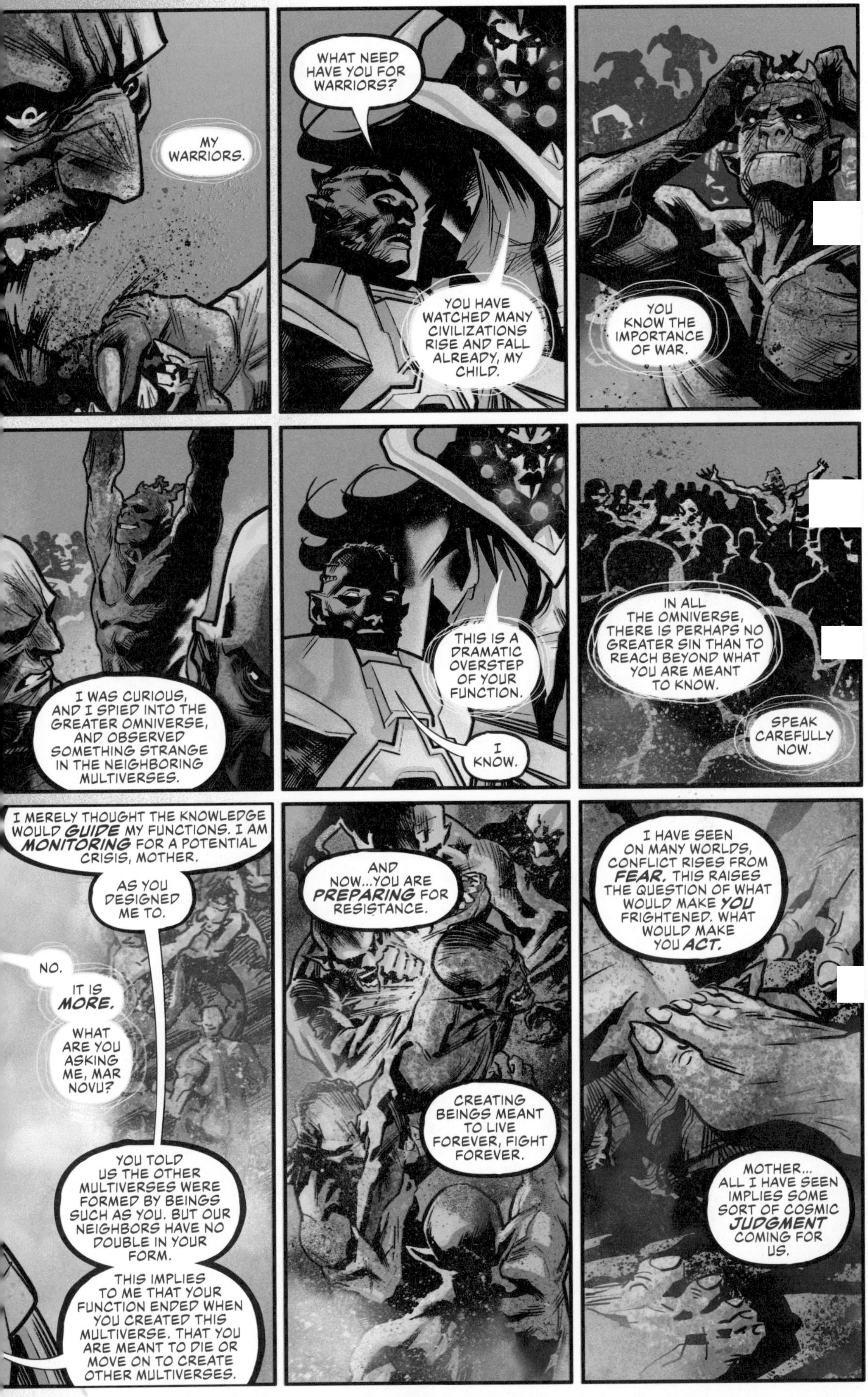
MY WARRIORS.
WHAT NEED HAVE YOU FOR WARRIORS?
YOU HAVE WATCHED MANY CIVILIZATIONS RISE AND FALL ALREADY, MY CHILD.
YOU KNOW THE IMPORTANCE OF WAR.
I WAS CURIOUS, AND I SPIED INTO THE GREATER OMNIVERSE, AND OBSERVED SOMETHING STRANGE IN THE NEIGHBORING MULTIVERSES.
THIS IS A DRAMATIC OVERSTEP OF YOUR FUNCTION.
I KNOW.
IN ALL THE OMNIVERSE, THERE IS PERHAPS NO GREATER SIN THAN TO REACH BEYOND WHAT YOU ARE MEANT TO KNOW.
SPEAK CAREFULLY NOW.
I MERELY THOUGHT THE KNOWLEDGE WOULD GUIDE MY FUNCTIONS. I AM MONITORING FOR A POTENTIAL CRISIS, MOTHER.
AS YOU DESIGNED ME TO.
NO.
IT IS MORE.
WHAT ARE YOU ASKING ME, MAR NOVU?
YOU TOLD US THE OTHER MULTIVERSES WERE FORMED BY BEINGS SUCH AS YOU. BUT OUR NEIGHBORS HAVE NO DOUBLE IN YOUR FORM.
THIS IMPLIES TO ME THAT YOUR FUNCTION ENDED WHEN YOU CREATED THIS MULTIVERSE. THAT YOU ARE MEANT TO DIE OR MOVE ON TO CREATE OTHER MULTIVERSES.
AND NOW...YOU ARE PREPARING FOR RESISTANCE.
CREATING BEINGS MEANT TO LIVE FOREVER, FIGHT FOREVER.
I HAVE SEEN ON MANY WORLDS, CONFLICT RISES FROM FEAR. THIS RAISES THE QUESTION OF WHAT WOULD MAKE YOU FRIGHTENED. WHAT WOULD MAKE YOU ACT.
MOTHER... ALL I HAVE SEEN IMPLIES SOME SORT OF COSMIC JUDGMENT COMING FOR US.

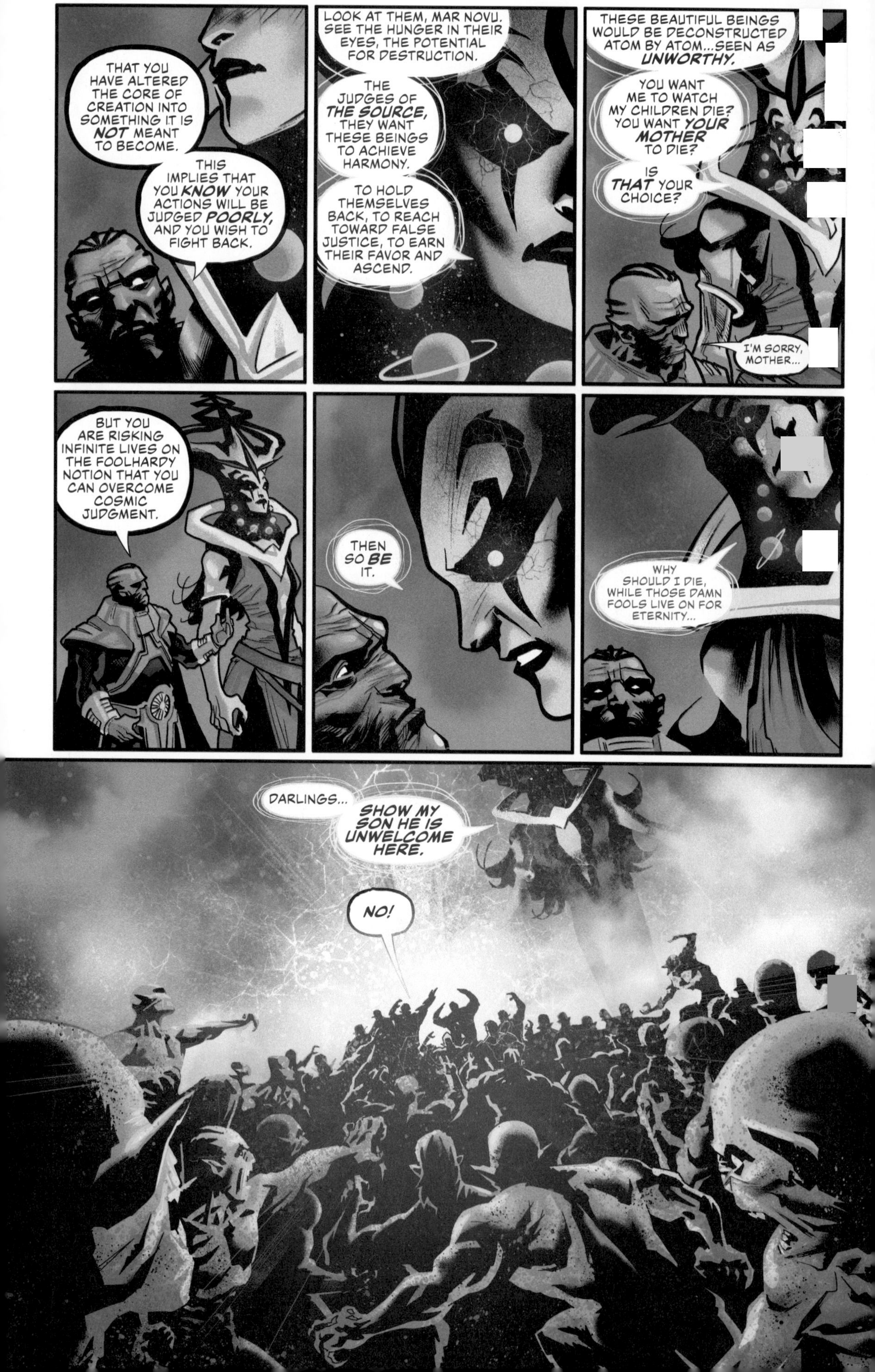
THAT YOU HAVE ALTERED THE CORE OF CREATION INTO SOMETHING IT IS NOT MEANT TO BECOME.
THIS IMPLIES THAT YOU KNOW YOUR ACTIONS WILL BE JUDGED POORLY, AND YOU WISH TO FIGHT BACK.
LOOK AT THEM, MAR NOVU. SEE THE HUNGER IN THEIR EYES, THE POTENTIAL FOR DESTRUCTION.
THE JUDGES OF THE SOURCE, THEY WANT THESE BEINGS TO ACHIEVE HARMONY.
TO HOLD THEMSELVES BACK, TO REACH TOWARD FALSE JUSTICE, TO EARN THEIR FAVOR AND ASCEND.
THESE BEAUTIFUL BEINGS WOULD BE DECONSTRUCTED ATOM BY ATOM...SEEN AS UNWORTHY.
YOU WANT ME TO WATCH MY CHILDREN DIE? YOU WANT YOUR MOTHER TO DIE?
IS THAT YOUR CHOICE?
I'M SORRY, MOTHER...
BUT YOU ARE RISKING INFINITE LIVES ON THE FOOLHARDY NOTION THAT YOU CAN OVERCOME COSMIC JUDGMENT.
THEN SO BE IT.
WHY SHOULD I DIE, WHILE THOSE DAMN FOOLS LIVE ON FOR ETERNITY...
DARLINGS...
SHOW MY SON HE IS UNWELCOME HERE.
NO!

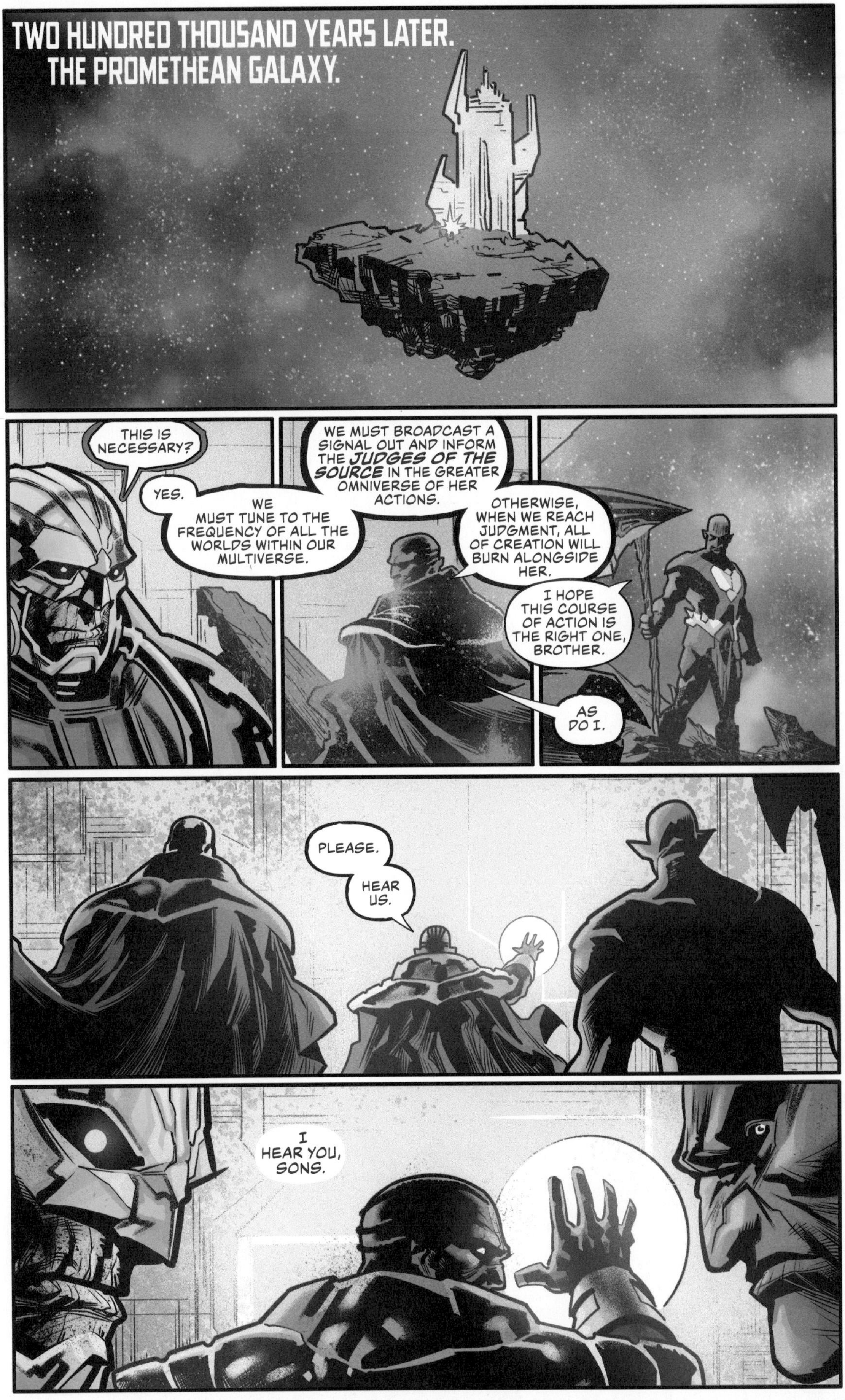
TWO HUNDRED THOUSAND YEARS LATER.
THE PROMETHEAN GALAXY.
THIS IS NECESSARY?
YES.
WE MUST TUNE TO THE FREQUENCY OF ALL THE WORLDS WITHIN OUR MULTIVERSE.
WE MUST BROADCAST A SIGNAL OUT AND INFORM THE JUDGES OF THE SOURCE IN THE GREATER OMNIVERSE OF HER ACTIONS.
OTHERWISE, WHEN WE REACH JUDGMENT, ALL OF CREATION WILL BURN ALONGSIDE HER.
I HOPE THIS COURSE OF ACTION IS THE RIGHT ONE, BROTHER.
AS DO I.
PLEASE.
HEAR US.
I HEAR YOU, SONS.

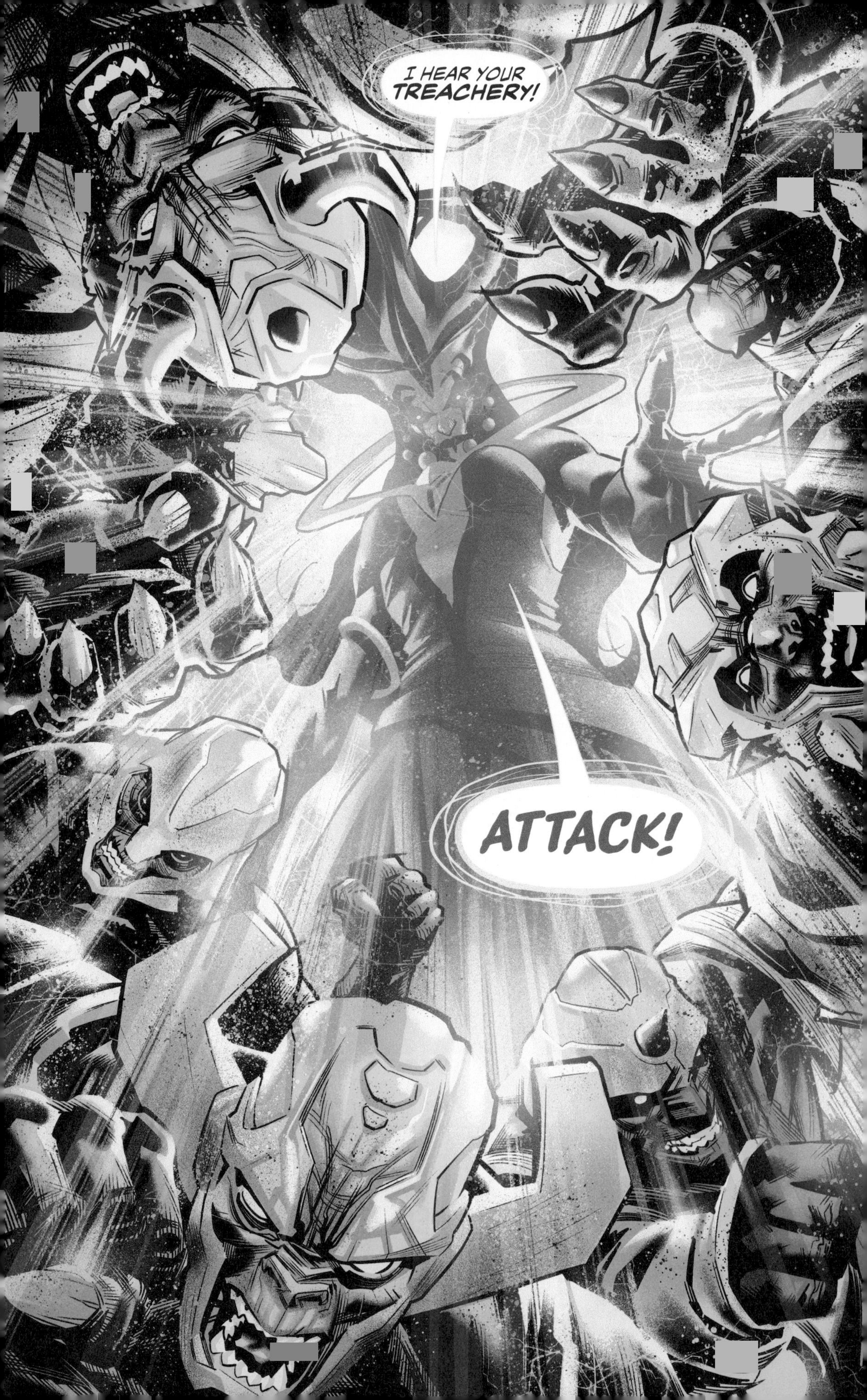
I HEAR YOUR TREACHERY!
ATTACK!

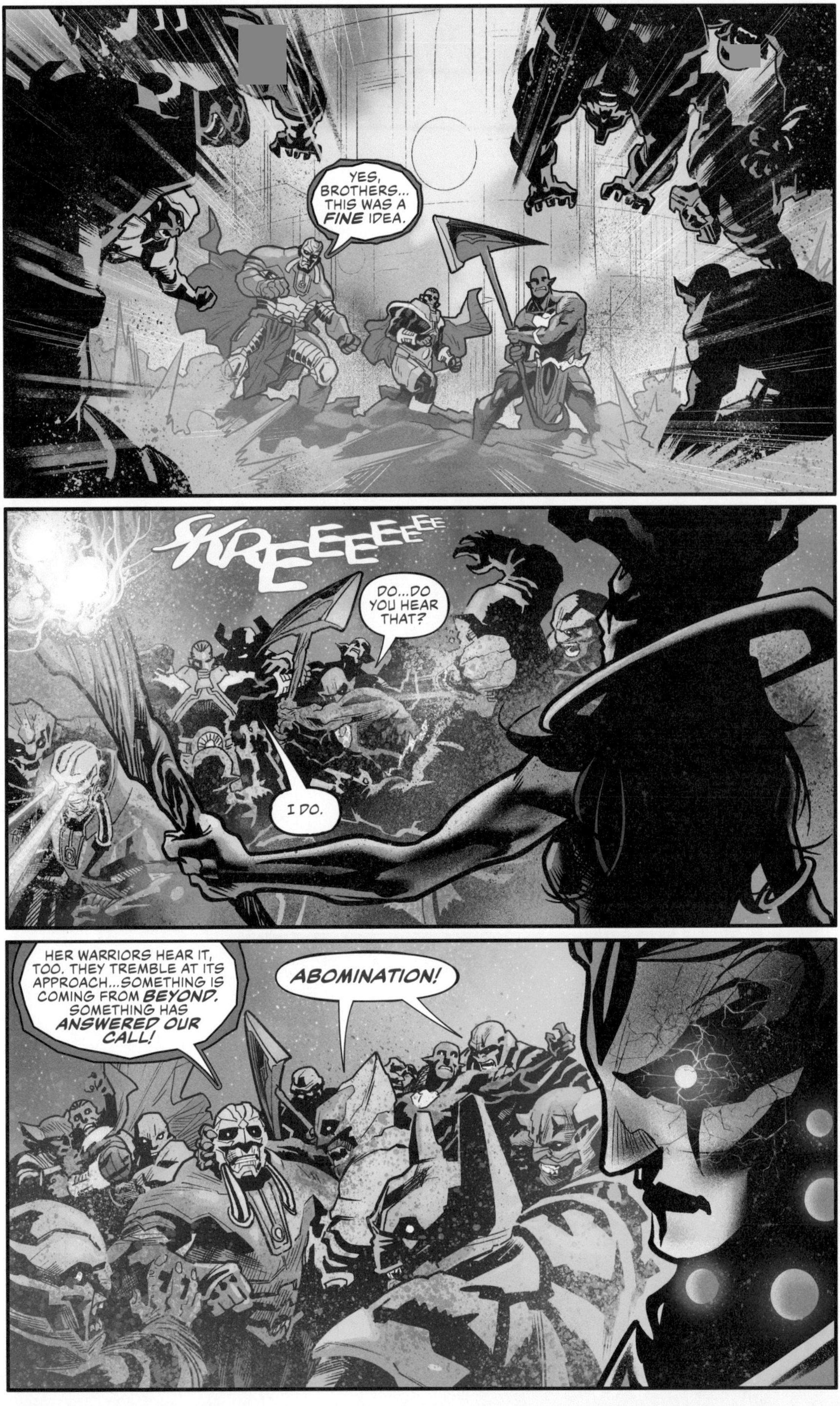
YES, BROTHERS... THIS WAS A FINE IDEA.
SKREEEEEEE
DO...DO YOU HEAR THAT?
I DO.
HER WARRIORS HEAR IT, TOO. THEY TREMBLE AT ITS APPROACH...SOMETHING IS COMING FROM BEYOND. SOMETHING HAS ANSWERED OUR CALL!
ABOMINATION!

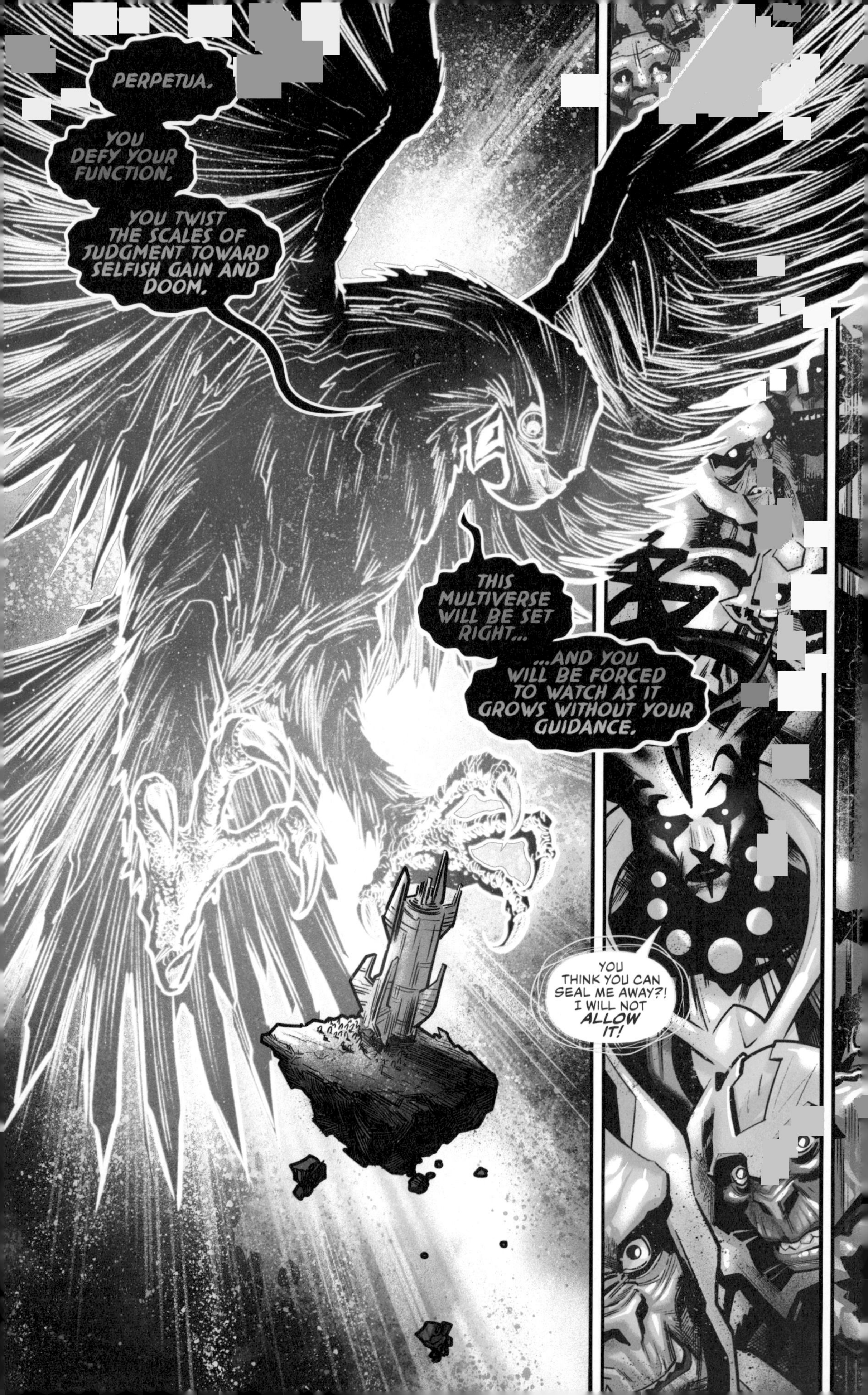
PERPETUA.
YOU DEFY YOUR FUNCTION.
YOU TWIST THE SCALES OF JUDGMENT TOWARD SELFISH GAIN AND DOOM.
THIS MULTIVERSE WILL BE SET RIGHT...
...AND YOU WILL BE FORCED TO WATCH AS IT GROWS WITHOUT YOUR GUIDANCE.
YOU THINK YOU CAN SEAL ME AWAY?! I WILL NOT ALLOW IT!

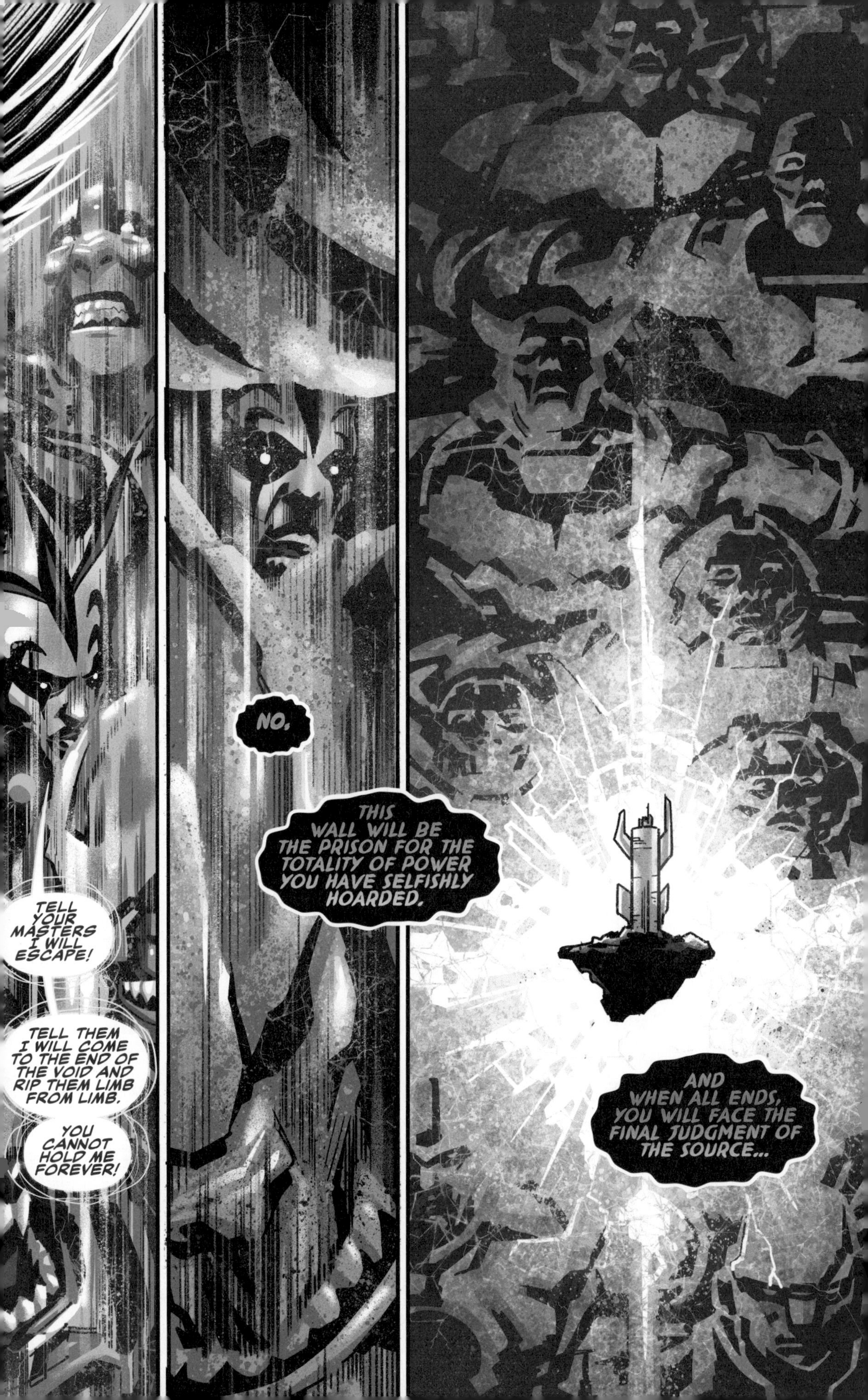
TELL YOUR MASTERS I WILL ESCAPE!
TELL THEM I WILL COME TO THE END OF THE VOID AND RIP THEM LIMB FROM LIMB.
YOU CANNOT HOLD ME FOREVER!
NO.
THIS WALL WILL BE THE PRISON FOR THE TOTALITY OF POWER YOU HAVE SELFISHLY HOARDED.
AND WHEN ALL ENDS, YOU WILL FACE THE FINAL JUDGMENT OF THE SOURCE...

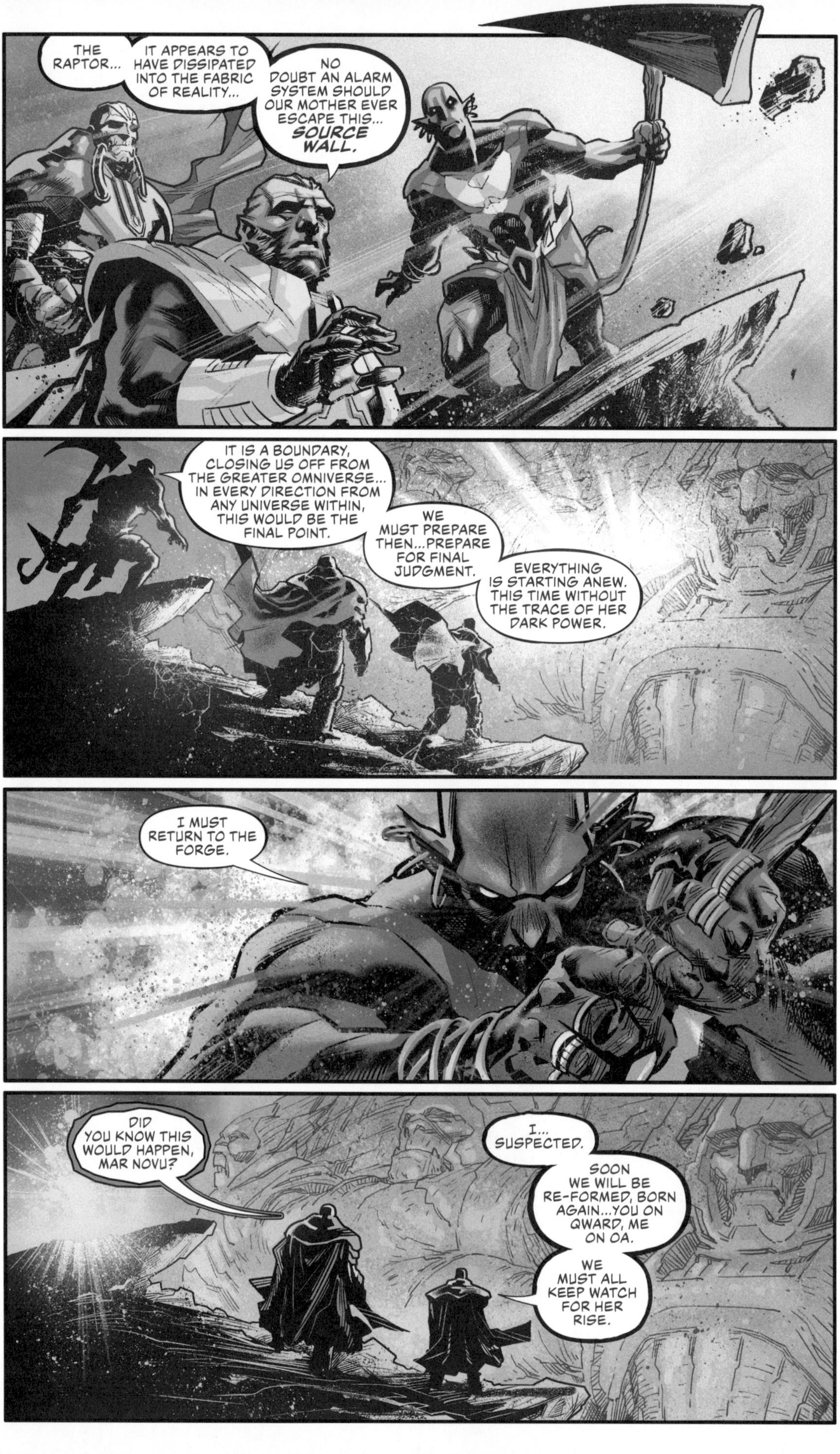
THE RAPTOR...
IT APPEARS TO HAVE DISSIPATED INTO THE FABRIC OF REALITY...
NO DOUBT AN ALARM SYSTEM SHOULD OUR MOTHER EVER ESCAPE THIS... SOURCE WALL.
IT IS A BOUNDARY, CLOSING US OFF FROM THE GREATER OMNIVERSE... IN EVERY DIRECTION FROM ANY UNIVERSE WITHIN, THIS WOULD BE THE FINAL POINT.
WE MUST PREPARE THEN...PREPARE FOR FINAL JUDGMENT.
EVERYTHING IS STARTING ANEW. THIS TIME WITHOUT THE TRACE OF HER DARK POWER.
I MUST RETURN TO THE FORGE.
DID YOU KNOW THIS WOULD HAPPEN, MAR NOVU?
I... SUSPECTED.
SOON WE WILL BE RE-FORMED, BORN AGAIN...YOU ON QWARD, ME ON OA.
WE MUST ALL KEEP WATCH FOR HER RISE.

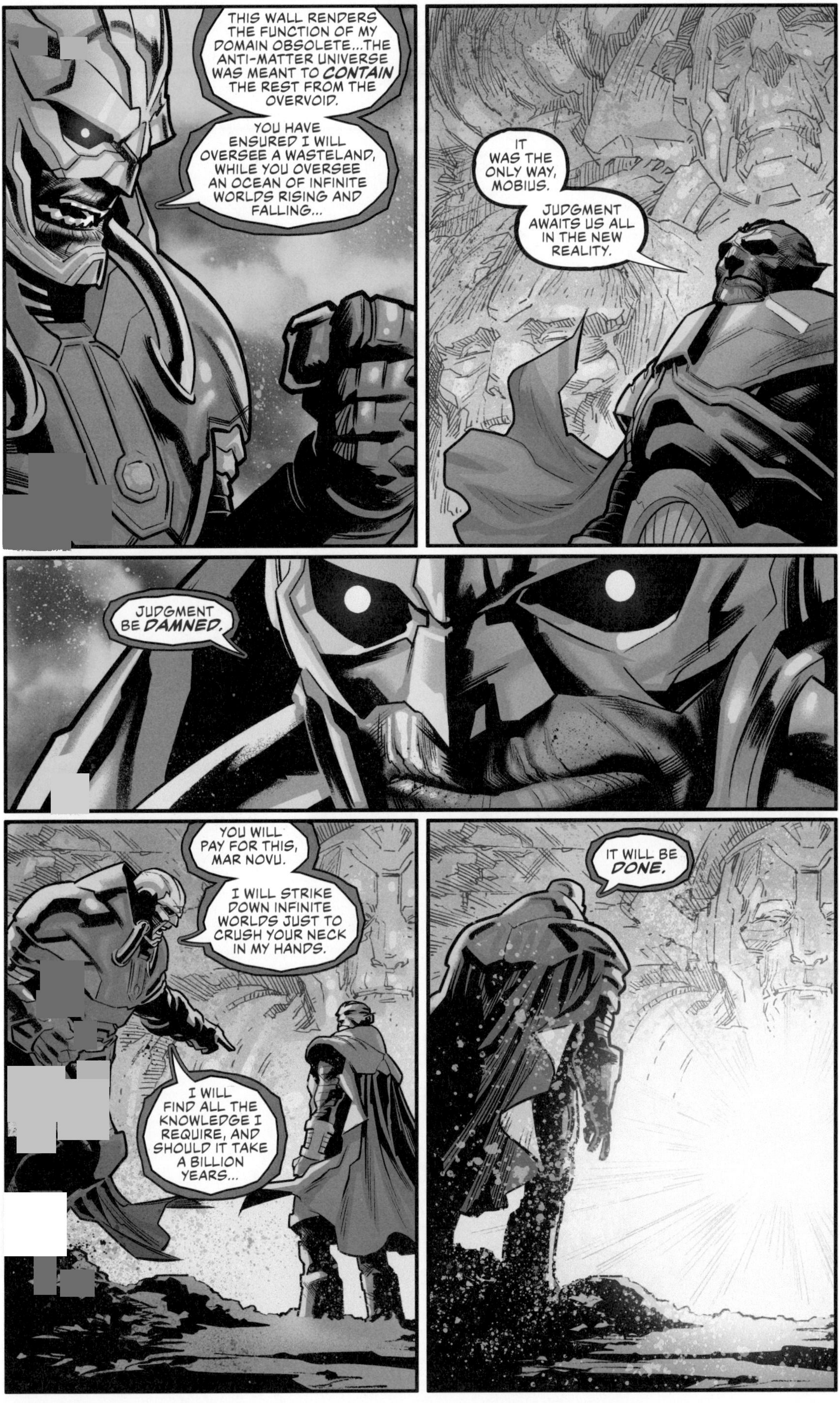
THIS WALL RENDERS THE FUNCTION OF MY DOMAIN OBSOLETE...THE ANTI-MATTER UNIVERSE WAS MEANT TO *CONTAIN* THE REST FROM THE OVERVOID.
YOU HAVE ENSURED I WILL OVERSEE A WASTELAND, WHILE YOU OVERSEE AN OCEAN OF INFINITE WORLDS RISING AND FALLING...
IT WAS THE ONLY WAY, MOBIUS.
JUDGMENT AWAITS US ALL IN THE NEW REALITY.
JUDGMENT BE *DAMNED.*
YOU WILL PAY FOR THIS, MAR NOVU.
I WILL STRIKE DOWN INFINITE WORLDS JUST TO CRUSH YOUR NECK IN MY HANDS.
I WILL FIND ALL THE KNOWLEDGE I REQUIRE, AND SHOULD IT TAKE A BILLION YEARS...
IT WILL BE *DONE.*

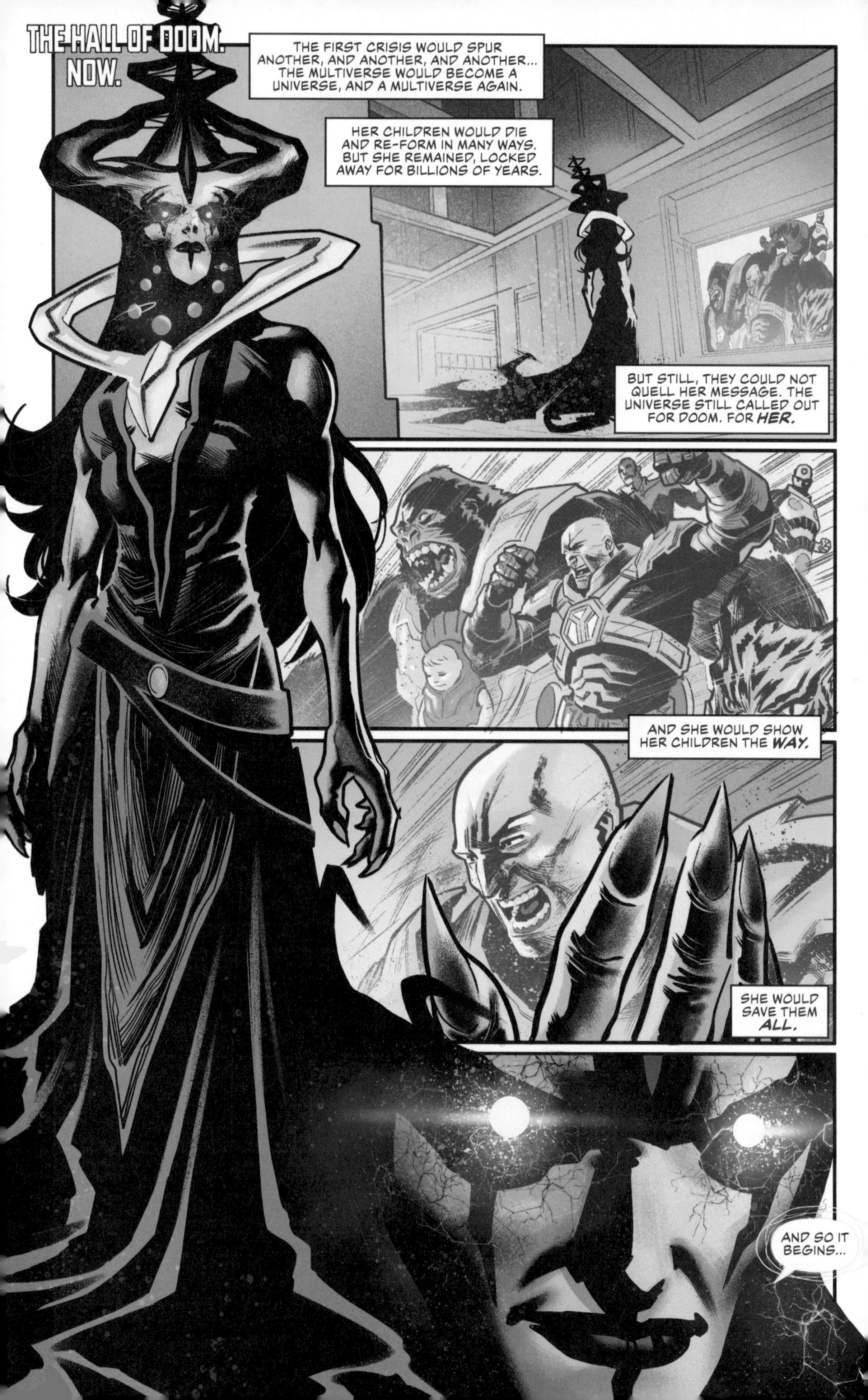
THE HALL OF DOOM. NOW.
THE FIRST CRISIS WOULD SPUR ANOTHER, AND ANOTHER, AND ANOTHER... THE MULTIVERSE WOULD BECOME A UNIVERSE, AND A MULTIVERSE AGAIN.
HER CHILDREN WOULD DIE AND RE-FORM IN MANY WAYS. BUT SHE REMAINED, LOCKED AWAY FOR BILLIONS OF YEARS.
BUT STILL, THEY COULD NOT QUELL HER MESSAGE. THE UNIVERSE STILL CALLED OUT FOR DOOM. FOR HER.
AND SHE WOULD SHOW HER CHILDREN THE WAY.
SHE WOULD SAVE THEM ALL.
AND SO IT BEGINS...

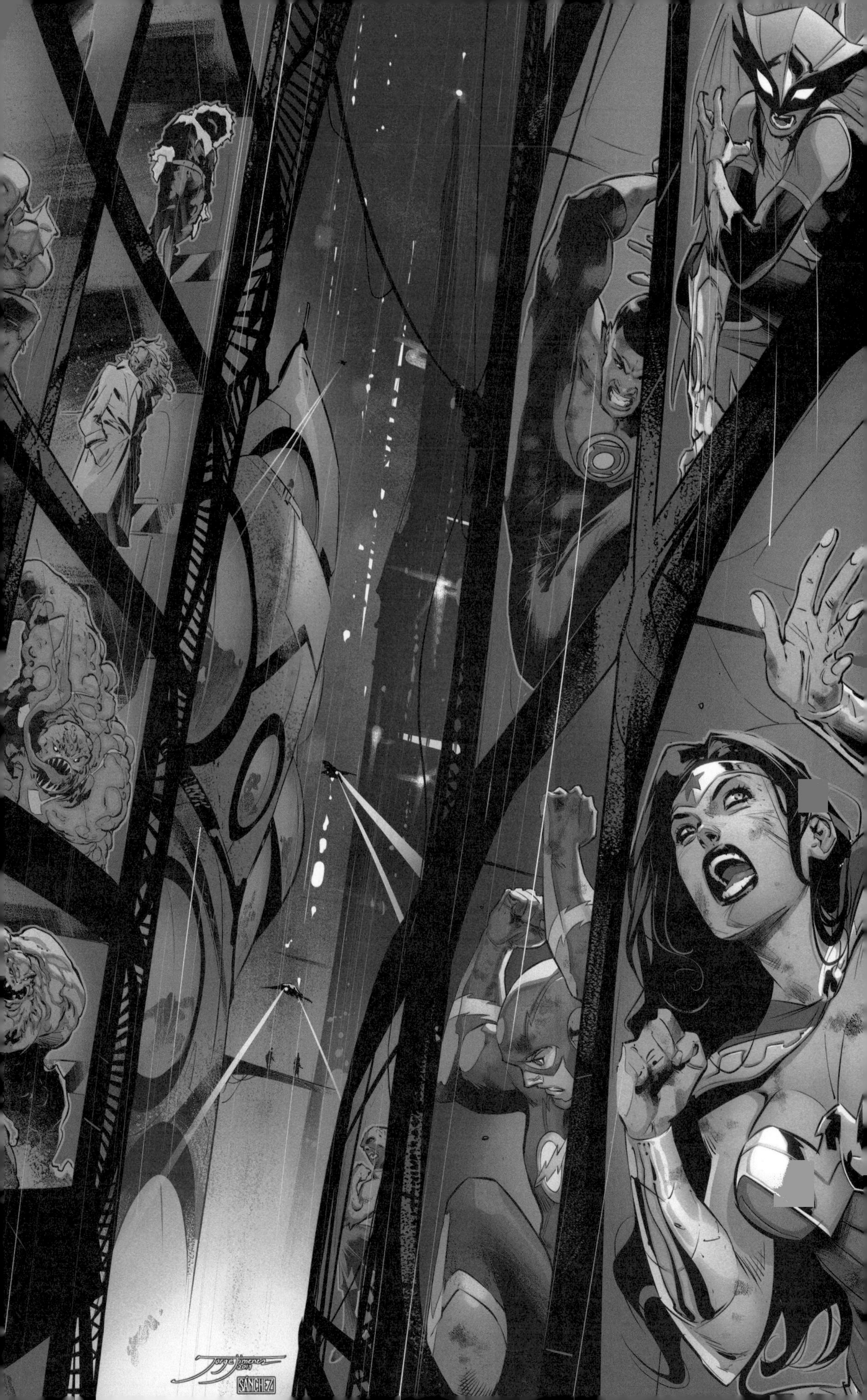
Jorge Jimenez 2019
SANCHEZ

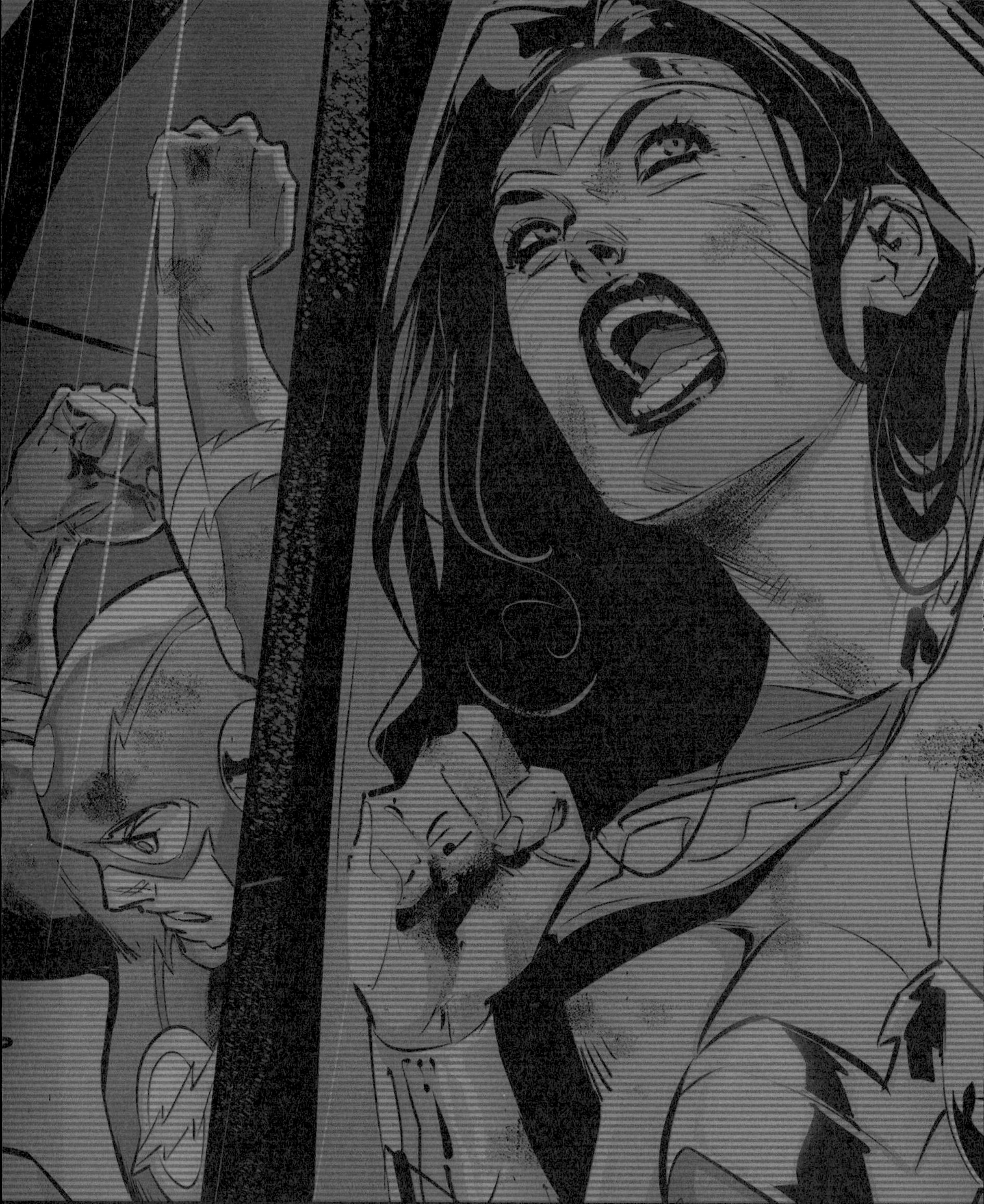

JUSTICE
LEAGUE
#23

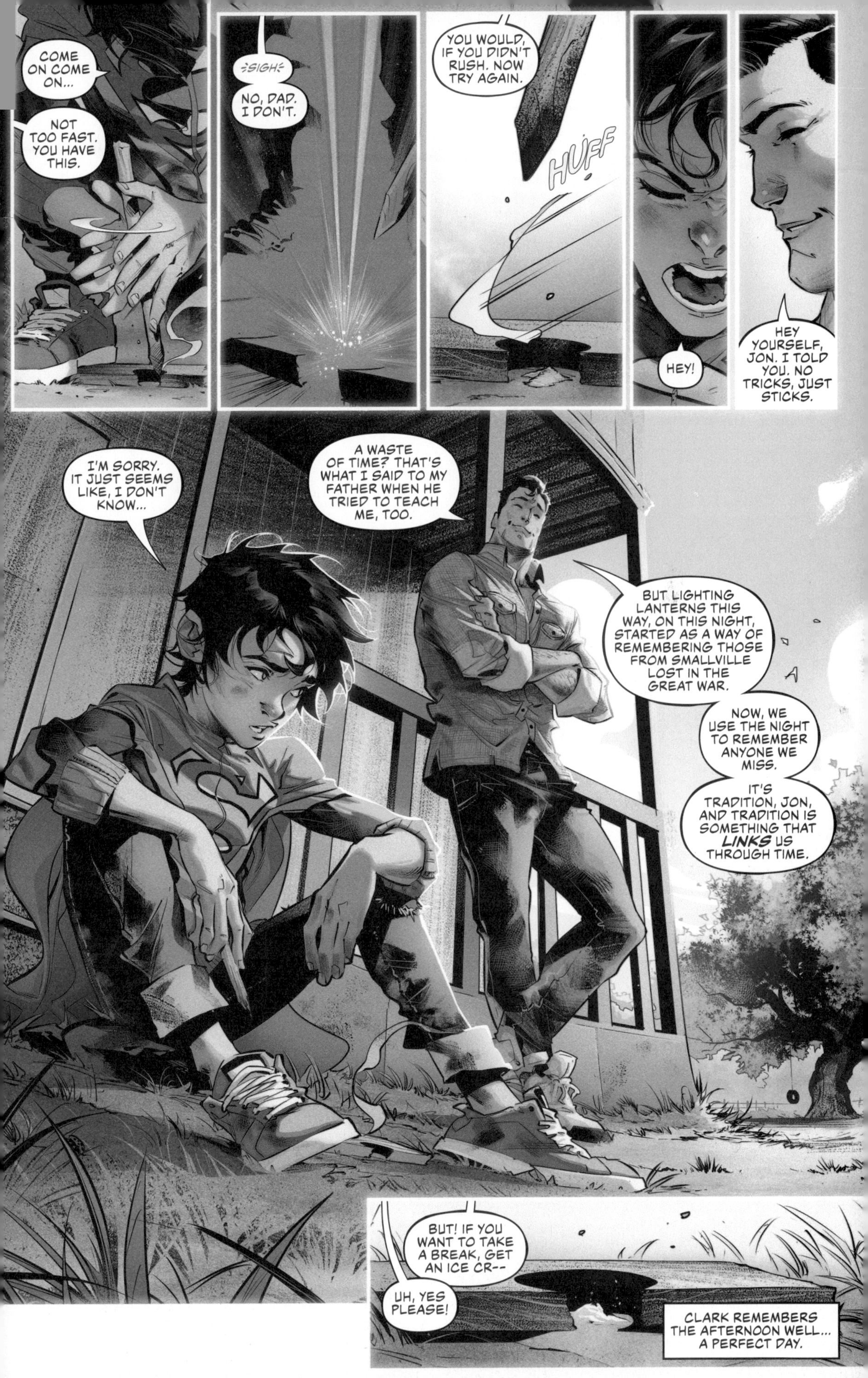
COME ON COME ON...
NOT TOO FAST. YOU HAVE THIS.
SIGH
NO, DAD. I DON'T.
YOU WOULD, IF YOU DIDN'T RUSH. NOW TRY AGAIN.
HUFF
HEY!
HEY YOURSELF, JON. I TOLD YOU. NO TRICKS, JUST STICKS.
I'M SORRY. IT JUST SEEMS LIKE, I DON'T KNOW...
A WASTE OF TIME? THAT'S WHAT I SAID TO MY FATHER WHEN HE TRIED TO TEACH ME, TOO.
BUT LIGHTING LANTERNS THIS WAY, ON THIS NIGHT, STARTED AS A WAY OF REMEMBERING THOSE FROM SMALLVILLE LOST IN THE GREAT WAR.
NOW, WE USE THE NIGHT TO REMEMBER ANYONE WE MISS.
IT'S TRADITION, JON, AND TRADITION IS SOMETHING THAT LINKS US THROUGH TIME.
BUT! IF YOU WANT TO TAKE A BREAK, GET AN ICE CR--
UH, YES PLEASE!
CLARK REMEMBERS THE AFTERNOON WELL... A PERFECT DAY.

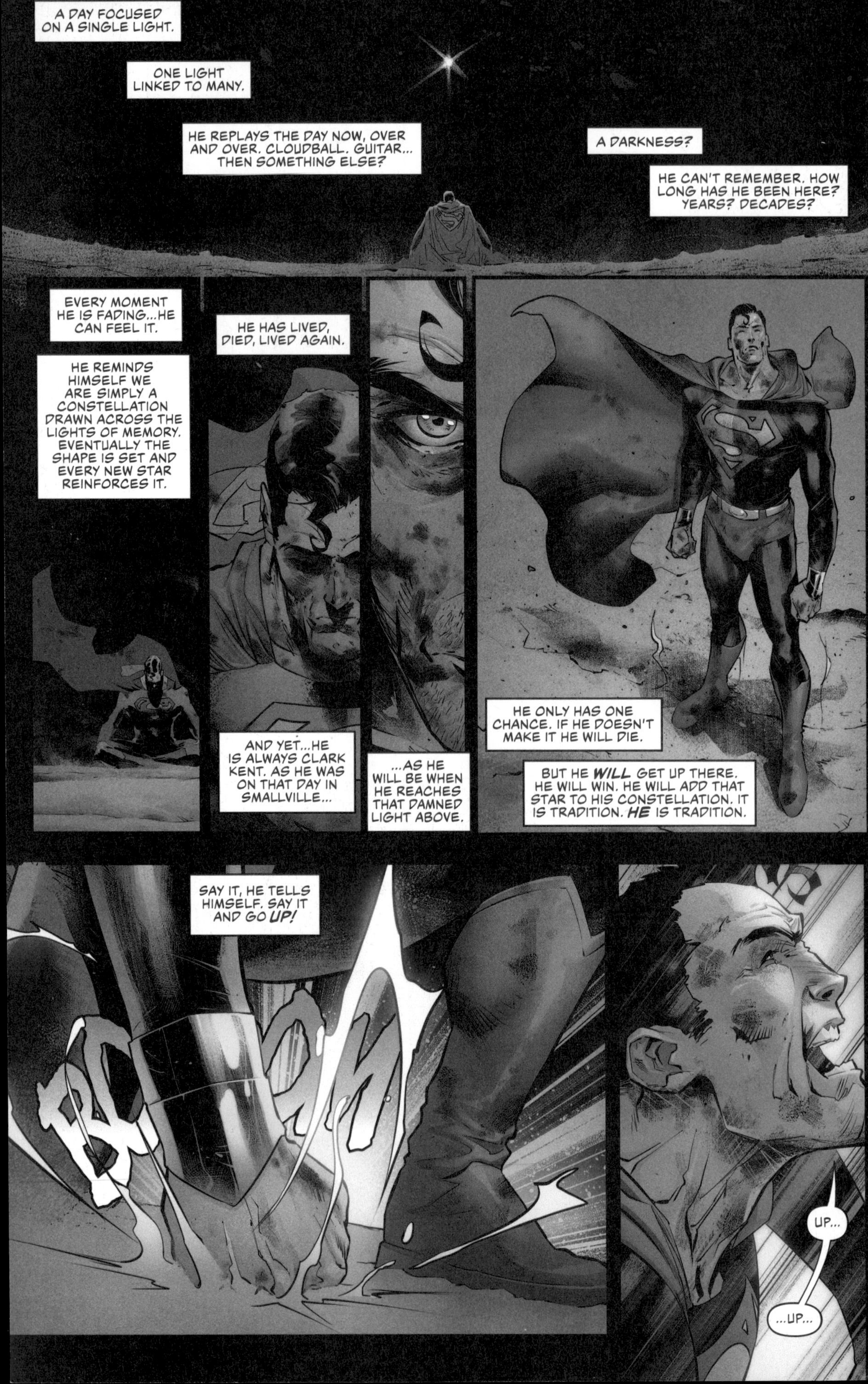

A DAY FOCUSED ON A SINGLE LIGHT.
ONE LIGHT LINKED TO MANY.
HE REPLAYS THE DAY NOW, OVER AND OVER. CLOUDBALL. GUITAR... THEN SOMETHING ELSE?
A DARKNESS?
HE CAN'T REMEMBER. HOW LONG HAS HE BEEN HERE? YEARS? DECADES?
EVERY MOMENT HE IS FADING...HE CAN FEEL IT.
HE REMINDS HIMSELF WE ARE SIMPLY A CONSTELLATION DRAWN ACROSS THE LIGHTS OF MEMORY. EVENTUALLY THE SHAPE IS SET AND EVERY NEW STAR REINFORCES IT.
HE HAS LIVED, DIED, LIVED AGAIN.
AND YET...HE IS ALWAYS CLARK KENT. AS HE WAS ON THAT DAY IN SMALLVILLE...
...AS HE WILL BE WHEN HE REACHES THAT DAMNED LIGHT ABOVE.
HE ONLY HAS ONE CHANCE. IF HE DOESN'T MAKE IT HE WILL DIE.
BUT HE *WILL* GET UP THERE. HE WILL WIN. HE WILL ADD THAT STAR TO HIS CONSTELLATION. IT IS TRADITION. *HE* IS TRADITION.
SAY IT, HE TELLS HIMSELF. SAY IT AND GO *UP!*
UP...
...UP...

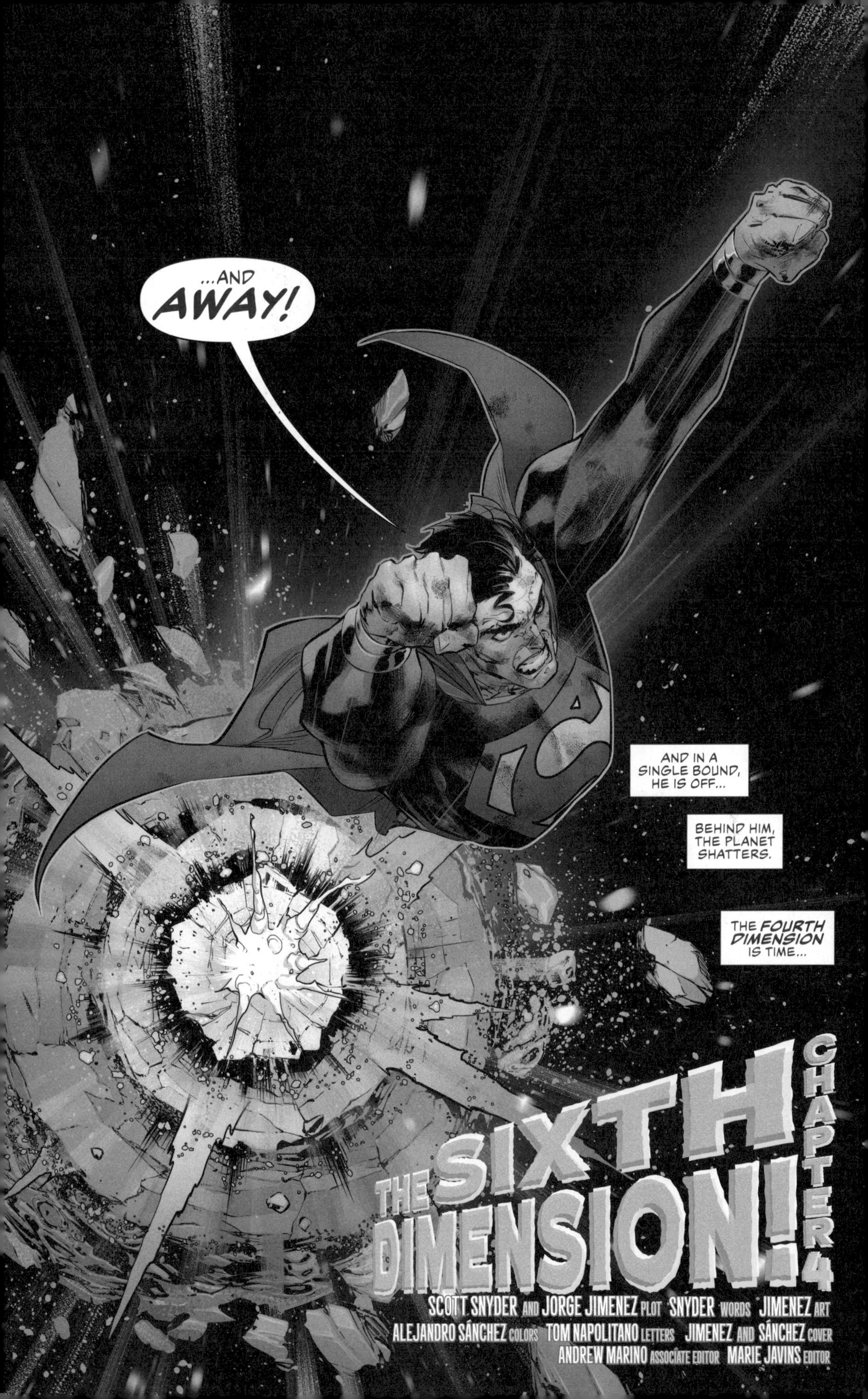
...AND AWAY!
AND IN A SINGLE BOUND, HE IS OFF...
BEHIND HIM, THE PLANET SHATTERS.
THE FOURTH DIMENSION IS TIME...
THE SIXTH DIMENSION! CHAPTER 4
SCOTT SNYDER AND JORGE JIMENEZ PLOT SNYDER WORDS JIMENEZ ART
ALEJANDRO SÁNCHEZ COLORS TOM NAPOLITANO LETTERS JIMENEZ AND SÁNCHEZ COVER
ANDREW MARINO ASSOCIATE EDITOR MARIE JAVINS EDITOR

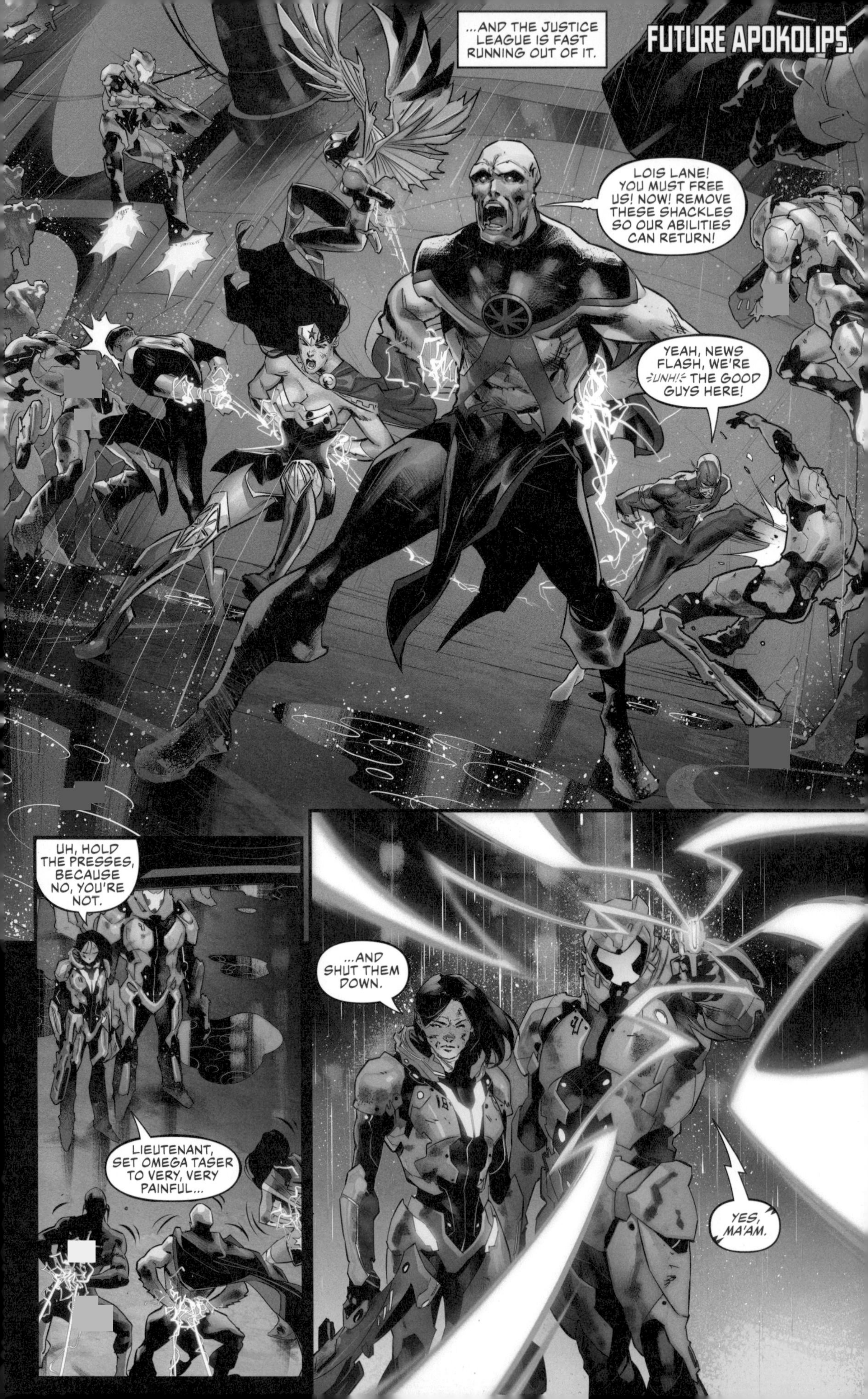

...AND THE JUSTICE LEAGUE IS FAST RUNNING OUT OF IT.
FUTURE APOKOLIPS.
LOIS LANE! YOU MUST FREE US! NOW! REMOVE THESE SHACKLES SO OUR ABILITIES CAN RETURN!
YEAH, NEWS FLASH, WE'RE =UNH!= THE GOOD GUYS HERE!
UH, HOLD THE PRESSES, BECAUSE NO, YOU'RE NOT.
LIEUTENANT, SET OMEGA TASER TO VERY, VERY PAINFUL...
...AND SHUT THEM DOWN.
YES, MA'AM.

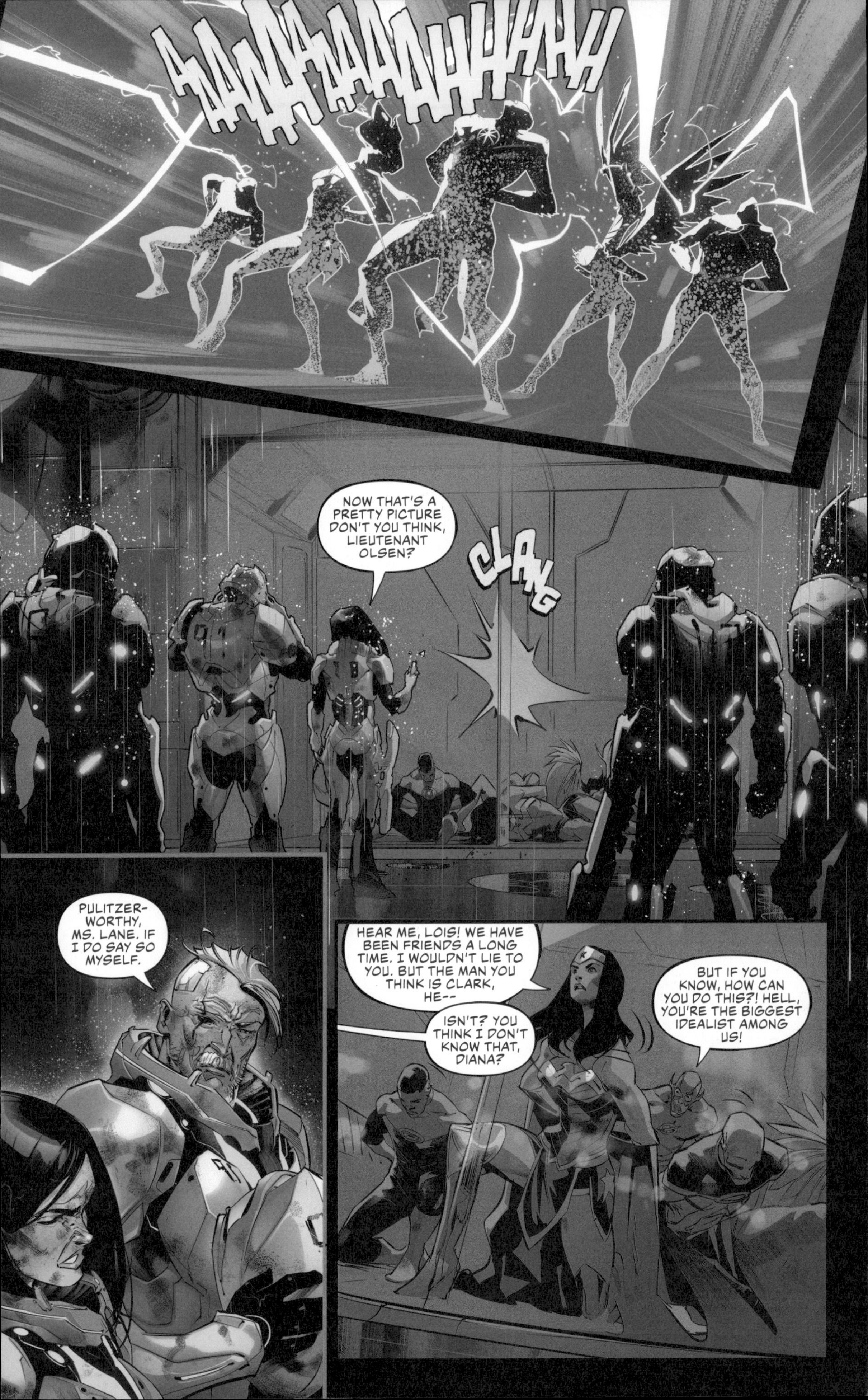
AAAAAAAAAHHHH
NOW THAT'S A PRETTY PICTURE DON'T YOU THINK, LIEUTENANT OLSEN?
CLANG
PULITZER-WORTHY, MS. LANE. IF I DO SAY SO MYSELF.
HEAR ME, LOIS! WE HAVE BEEN FRIENDS A LONG TIME. I WOULDN'T LIE TO YOU. BUT THE MAN YOU THINK IS CLARK, HE--
ISN'T? YOU THINK I DON'T KNOW THAT, DIANA?
BUT IF YOU KNOW, HOW CAN YOU DO THIS?! HELL, YOU'RE THE BIGGEST IDEALIST AMONG US!

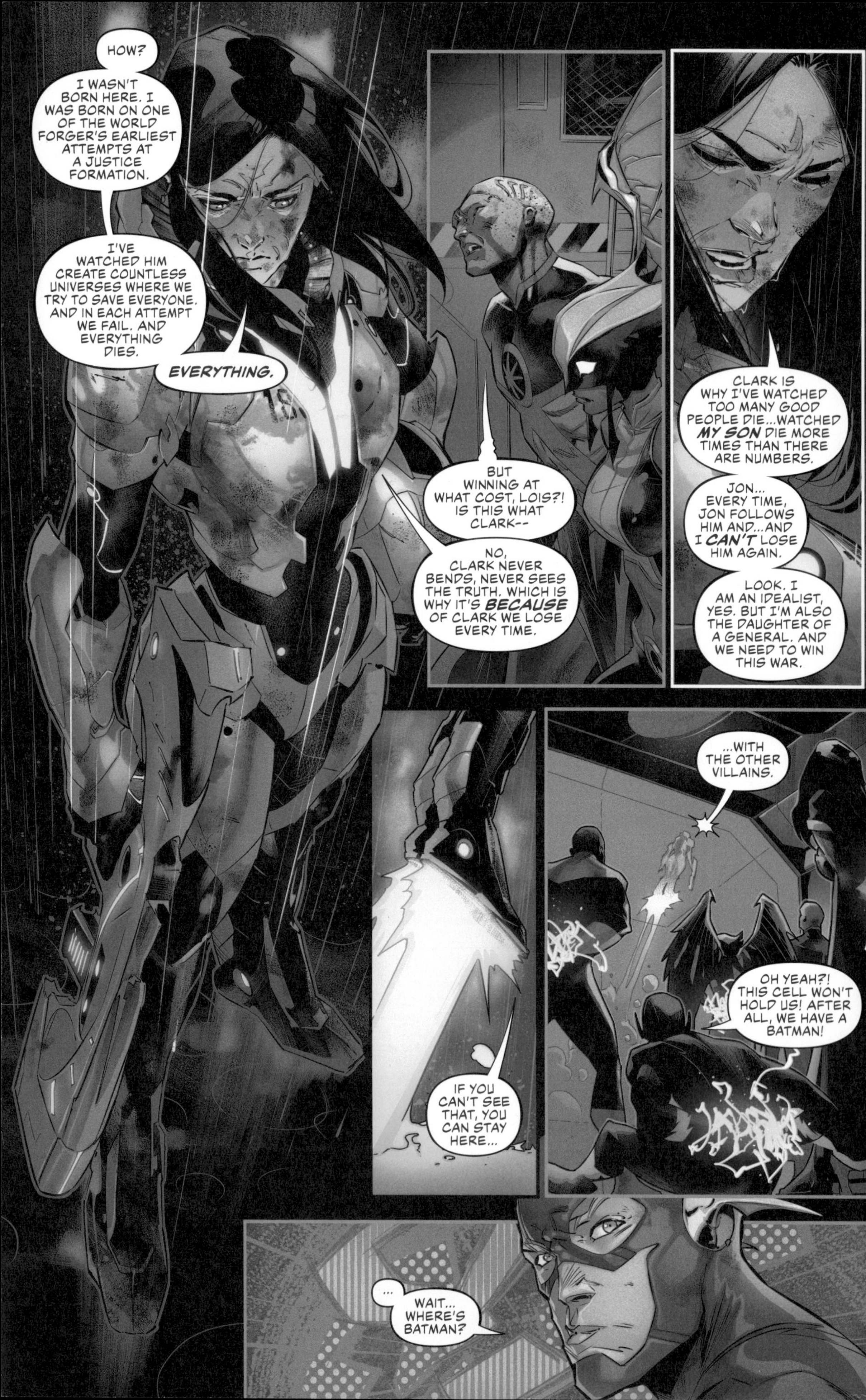
HOW?
I WASN'T BORN HERE. I WAS BORN ON ONE OF THE WORLD FORGER'S EARLIEST ATTEMPTS AT A JUSTICE FORMATION.
I'VE WATCHED HIM CREATE COUNTLESS UNIVERSES WHERE WE TRY TO SAVE EVERYONE. AND IN EACH ATTEMPT WE FAIL. AND EVERYTHING DIES.
EVERYTHING.
BUT WINNING AT WHAT COST, LOIS?! IS THIS WHAT CLARK--
NO, CLARK NEVER BENDS, NEVER SEES THE TRUTH. WHICH IS WHY IT'S BECAUSE OF CLARK WE LOSE EVERY TIME.
CLARK IS WHY I'VE WATCHED TOO MANY GOOD PEOPLE DIE...WATCHED MY SON DIE MORE TIMES THAN THERE ARE NUMBERS.
JON... EVERY TIME, JON FOLLOWS HIM AND...AND I CAN'T LOSE HIM AGAIN.
LOOK. I AM AN IDEALIST, YES. BUT I'M ALSO THE DAUGHTER OF A GENERAL. AND WE NEED TO WIN THIS WAR.
IF YOU CAN'T SEE THAT, YOU CAN STAY HERE...
...WITH THE OTHER VILLAINS.
OH YEAH?! THIS CELL WON'T HOLD US! AFTER ALL, WE HAVE A BATMAN!
...
WAIT... WHERE'S BATMAN?

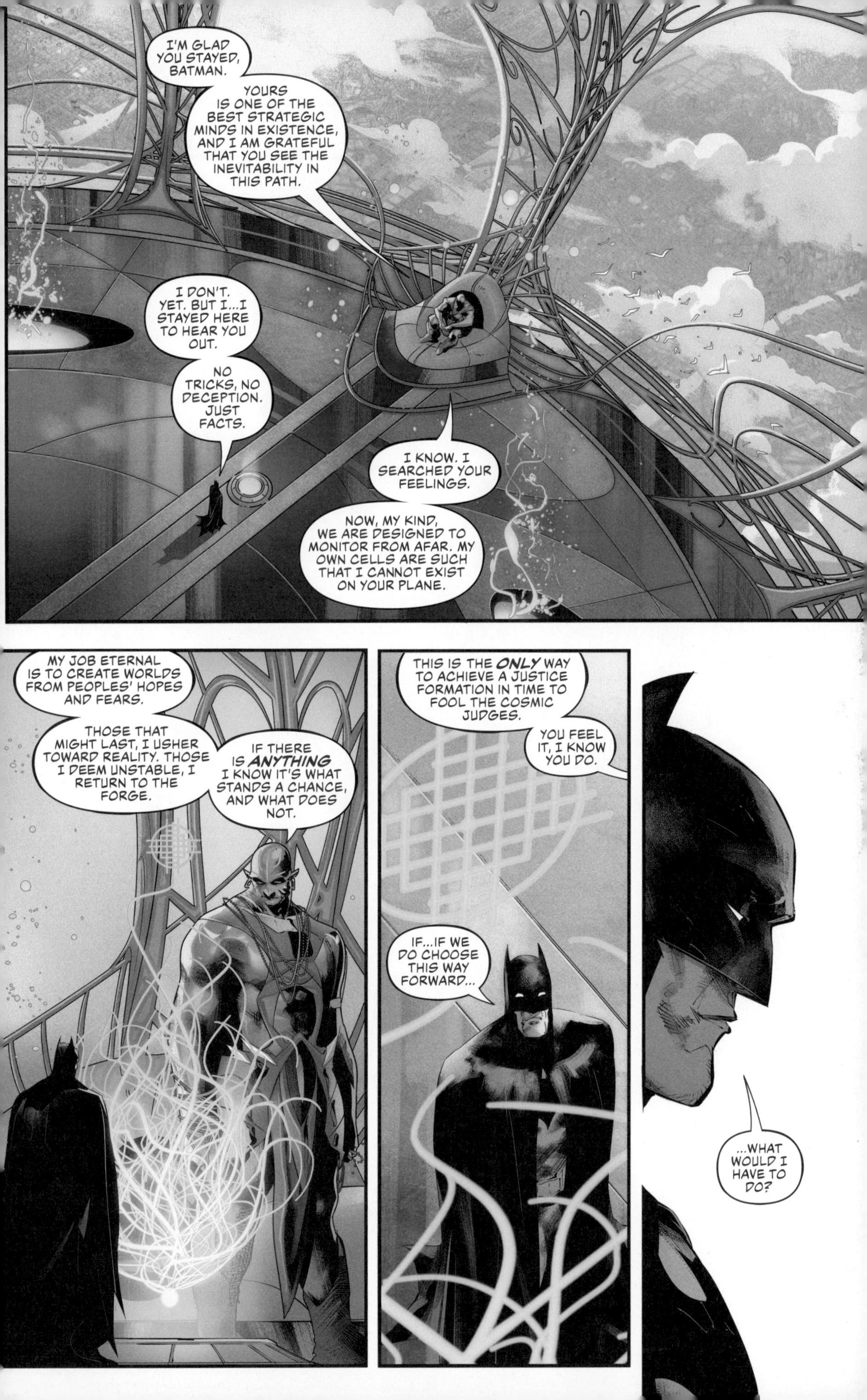
I'M GLAD YOU STAYED, BATMAN.
YOURS IS ONE OF THE BEST STRATEGIC MINDS IN EXISTENCE, AND I AM GRATEFUL THAT YOU SEE THE INEVITABILITY IN THIS PATH.
I DON'T. YET. BUT I...I STAYED HERE TO HEAR YOU OUT.
NO TRICKS, NO DECEPTION. JUST FACTS.
I KNOW. I SEARCHED YOUR FEELINGS.
NOW, MY KIND, WE ARE DESIGNED TO MONITOR FROM AFAR. MY OWN CELLS ARE SUCH THAT I CANNOT EXIST ON YOUR PLANE.
MY JOB ETERNAL IS TO CREATE WORLDS FROM PEOPLES' HOPES AND FEARS.
THOSE THAT MIGHT LAST, I USHER TOWARD REALITY. THOSE I DEEM UNSTABLE, I RETURN TO THE FORGE.
IF THERE IS ANYTHING I KNOW IT'S WHAT STANDS A CHANCE, AND WHAT DOES NOT.
THIS IS THE ONLY WAY TO ACHIEVE A JUSTICE FORMATION IN TIME TO FOOL THE COSMIC JUDGES.
YOU FEEL IT, I KNOW YOU DO.
IF...IF WE DO CHOOSE THIS WAY FORWARD...
...WHAT WOULD I HAVE TO DO?

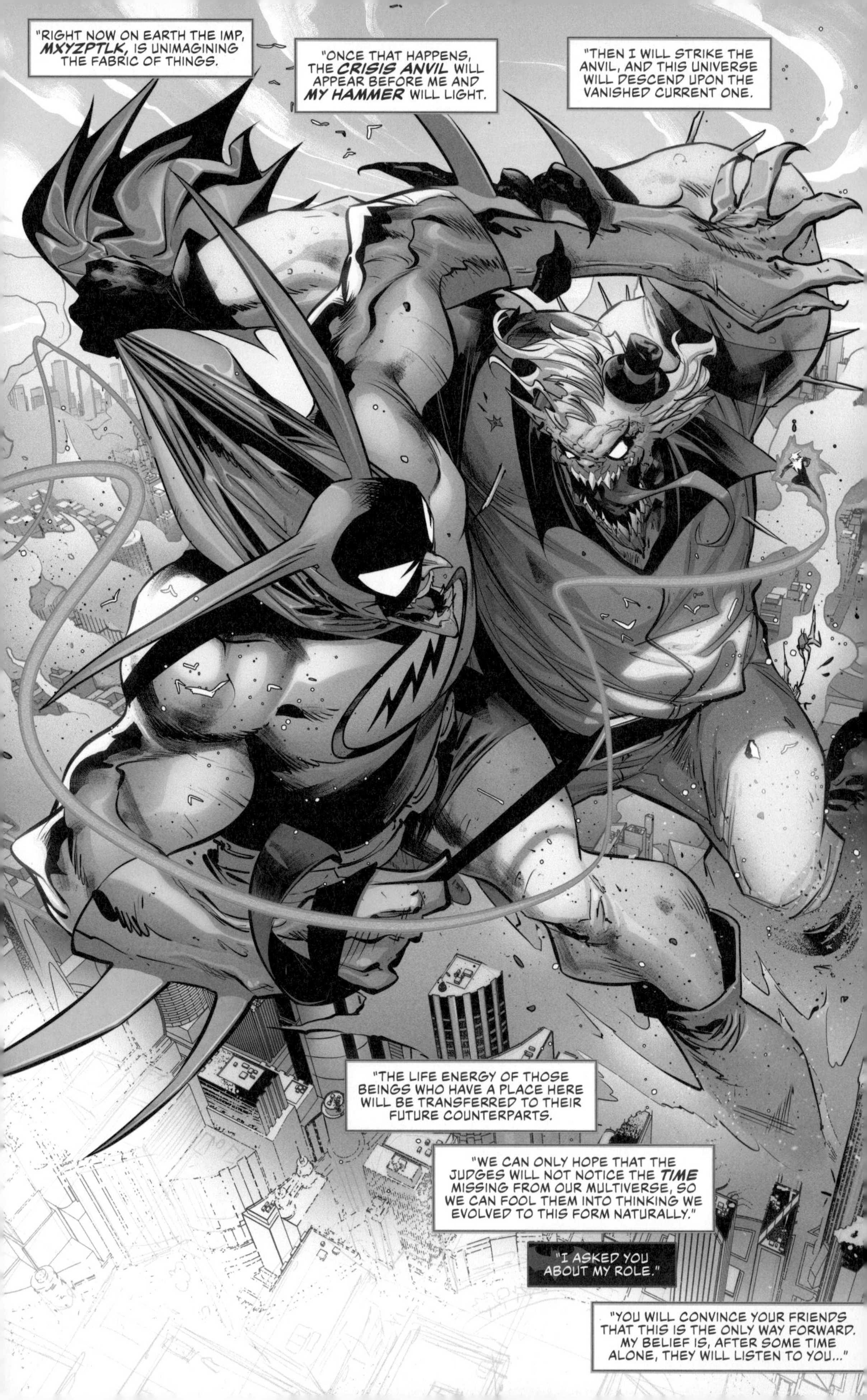
"RIGHT NOW ON EARTH THE IMP, MXYZPTLK, IS UNIMAGINING THE FABRIC OF THINGS.
"ONCE THAT HAPPENS, THE CRISIS ANVIL WILL APPEAR BEFORE ME AND MY HAMMER WILL LIGHT.
"THEN I WILL STRIKE THE ANVIL, AND THIS UNIVERSE WILL DESCEND UPON THE VANISHED CURRENT ONE.
"THE LIFE ENERGY OF THOSE BEINGS WHO HAVE A PLACE HERE WILL BE TRANSFERRED TO THEIR FUTURE COUNTERPARTS.
"WE CAN ONLY HOPE THAT THE JUDGES WILL NOT NOTICE THE TIME MISSING FROM OUR MULTIVERSE, SO WE CAN FOOL THEM INTO THINKING WE EVOLVED TO THIS FORM NATURALLY."
"I ASKED YOU ABOUT MY ROLE."
"YOU WILL CONVINCE YOUR FRIENDS THAT THIS IS THE ONLY WAY FORWARD. MY BELIEF IS, AFTER SOME TIME ALONE, THEY WILL LISTEN TO YOU..."

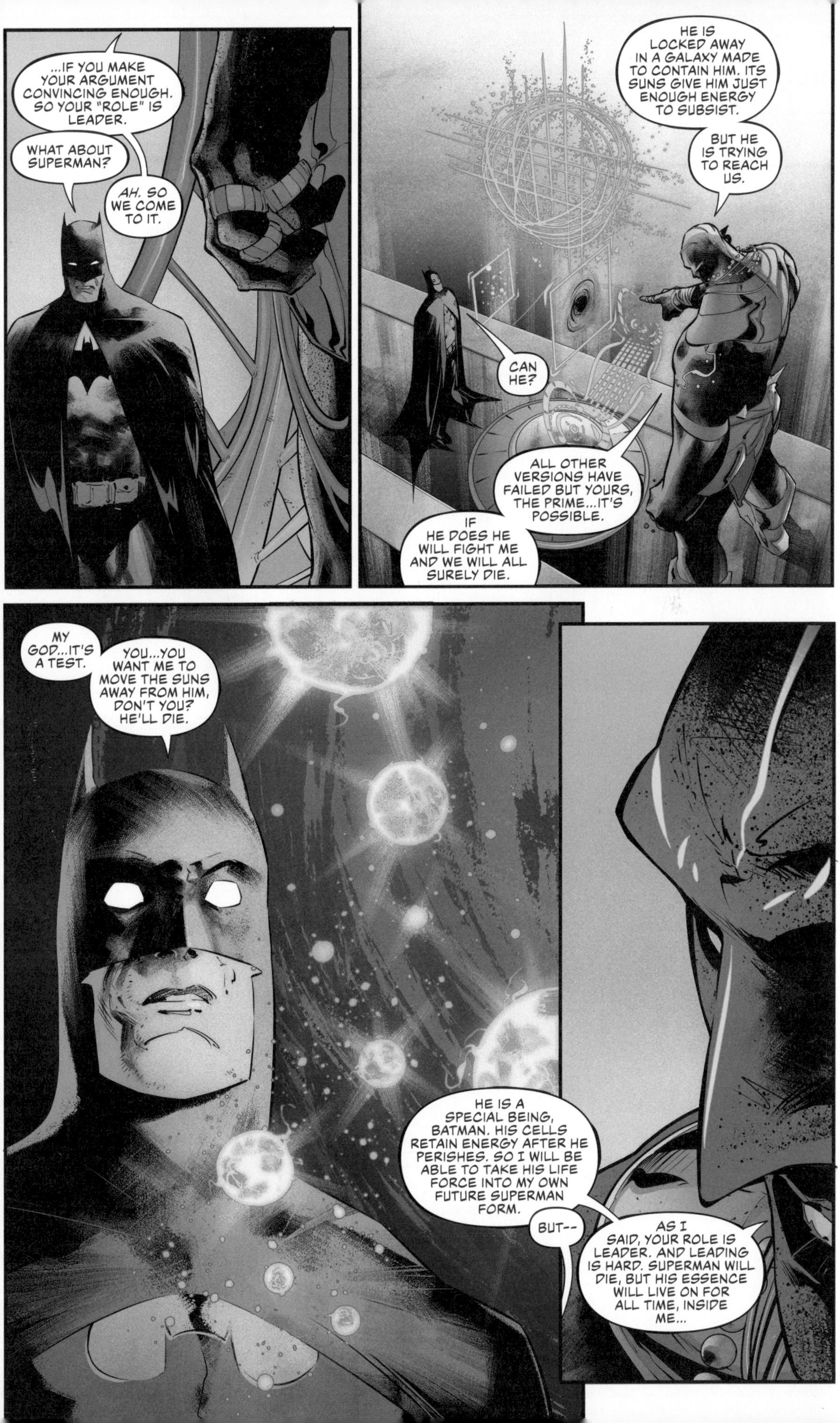
...IF YOU MAKE YOUR ARGUMENT CONVINCING ENOUGH. SO YOUR "ROLE" IS LEADER.
WHAT ABOUT SUPERMAN?
AH. SO WE COME TO IT.
HE IS LOCKED AWAY IN A GALAXY MADE TO CONTAIN HIM. ITS SUNS GIVE HIM JUST ENOUGH ENERGY TO SUBSIST.
BUT HE IS TRYING TO REACH US.
CAN HE?
ALL OTHER VERSIONS HAVE FAILED BUT YOURS, THE PRIME...IT'S POSSIBLE.
IF HE DOES HE WILL FIGHT ME AND WE WILL ALL SURELY DIE.
MY GOD...IT'S A TEST.
YOU...YOU WANT ME TO MOVE THE SUNS AWAY FROM HIM, DON'T YOU? HE'LL DIE.
HE IS A SPECIAL BEING, BATMAN. HIS CELLS RETAIN ENERGY AFTER HE PERISHES. SO I WILL BE ABLE TO TAKE HIS LIFE FORCE INTO MY OWN FUTURE SUPERMAN FORM.
BUT--
AS I SAID, YOUR ROLE IS LEADER. AND LEADING IS HARD. SUPERMAN WILL DIE, BUT HIS ESSENCE WILL LIVE ON FOR ALL TIME, INSIDE ME...

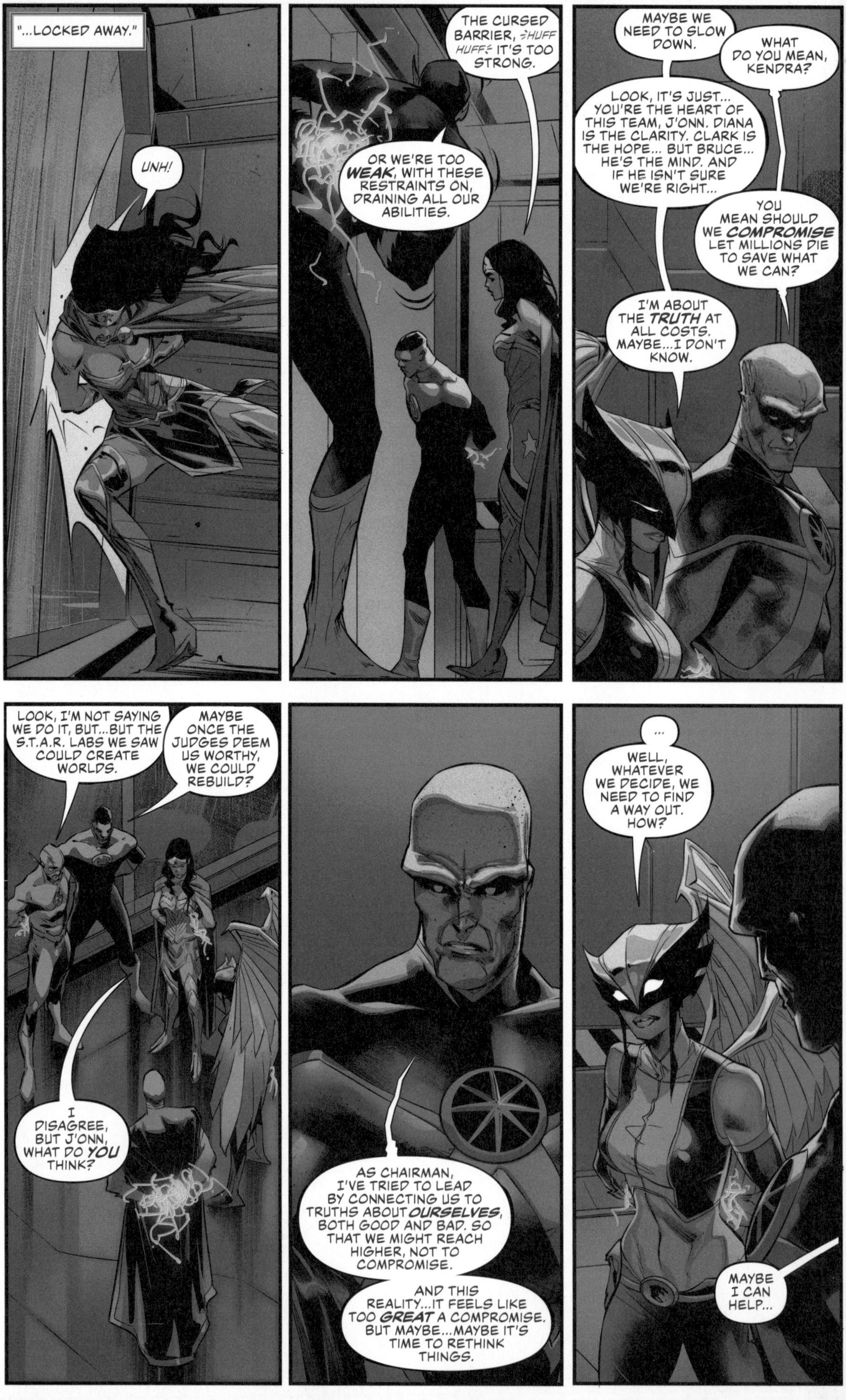
"...LOCKED AWAY."
UNH!
THE CURSED BARRIER, *HUFF HUFF* IT'S TOO STRONG.
OR WE'RE TOO WEAK, WITH THESE RESTRAINTS ON, DRAINING ALL OUR ABILITIES.
MAYBE WE NEED TO SLOW DOWN.
WHAT DO YOU MEAN, KENDRA?
LOOK, IT'S JUST... YOU'RE THE HEART OF THIS TEAM, J'ONN. DIANA IS THE CLARITY. CLARK IS THE HOPE... BUT BRUCE... HE'S THE MIND. AND IF HE ISN'T SURE WE'RE RIGHT...
YOU MEAN SHOULD WE COMPROMISE LET MILLIONS DIE TO SAVE WHAT WE CAN?
I'M ABOUT THE TRUTH AT ALL COSTS. MAYBE...I DON'T KNOW.
LOOK, I'M NOT SAYING WE DO IT, BUT...BUT THE S.T.A.R. LABS WE SAW COULD CREATE WORLDS.
MAYBE ONCE THE JUDGES DEEM US WORTHY, WE COULD REBUILD?
I DISAGREE, BUT J'ONN, WHAT DO YOU THINK?
AS CHAIRMAN, I'VE TRIED TO LEAD BY CONNECTING US TO TRUTHS ABOUT OURSELVES, BOTH GOOD AND BAD. SO THAT WE MIGHT REACH HIGHER, NOT TO COMPROMISE.
AND THIS REALITY...IT FEELS LIKE TOO GREAT A COMPROMISE. BUT MAYBE...MAYBE IT'S TIME TO RETHINK THINGS.
...
WELL, WHATEVER WE DECIDE, WE NEED TO FIND A WAY OUT. HOW?
MAYBE I CAN HELP...

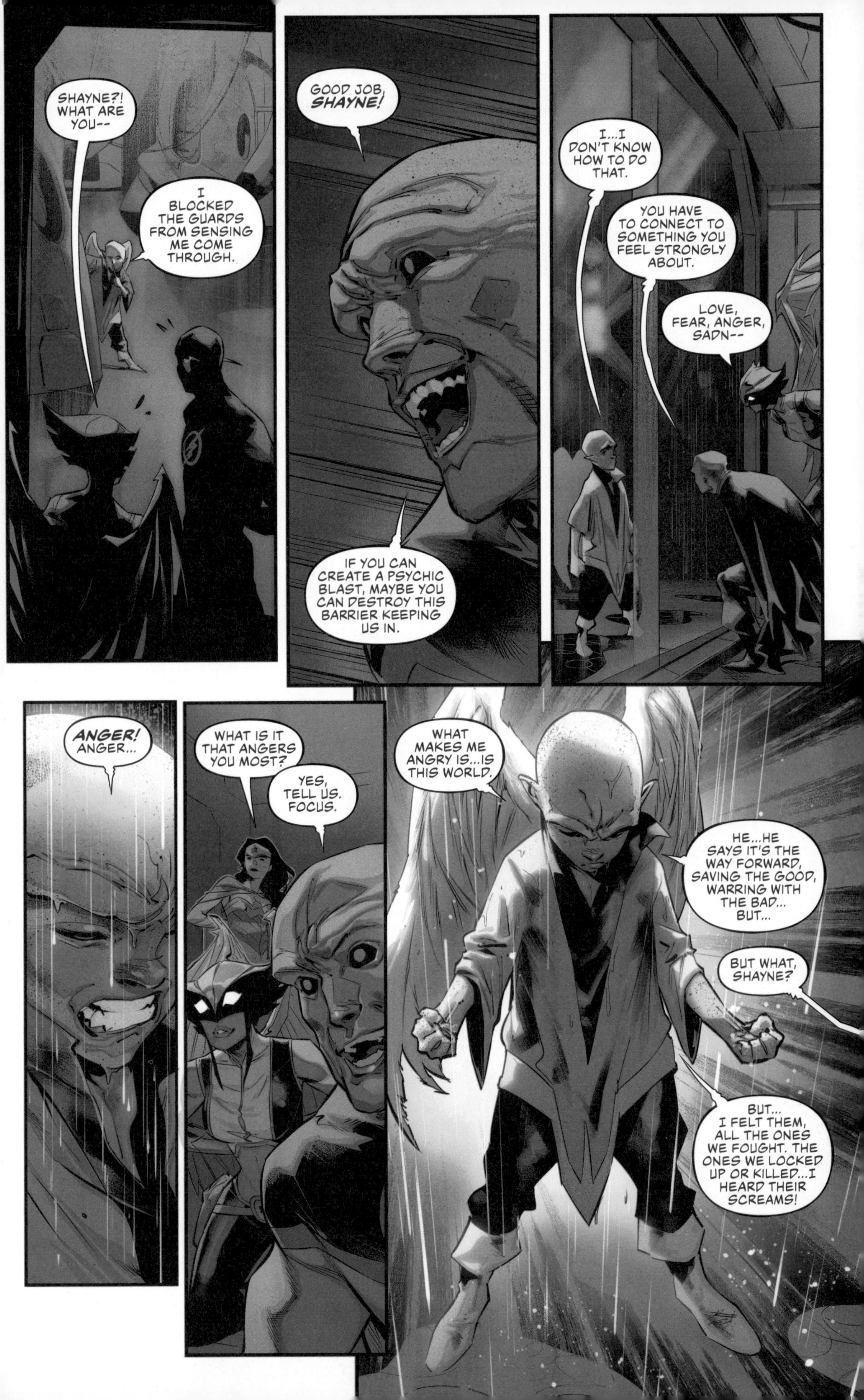
SHAYNE?! WHAT ARE YOU--
I BLOCKED THE GUARDS FROM SENSING ME COME THROUGH.
GOOD JOB, SHAYNE!
IF YOU CAN CREATE A PSYCHIC BLAST, MAYBE YOU CAN DESTROY THIS BARRIER KEEPING US IN.
I...I DON'T KNOW HOW TO DO THAT.
YOU HAVE TO CONNECT TO SOMETHING YOU FEEL STRONGLY ABOUT.
LOVE, FEAR, ANGER, SADN--
ANGER! ANGER...
WHAT IS IT THAT ANGERS YOU MOST?
YES, TELL US. FOCUS.
WHAT MAKES ME ANGRY IS...IS THIS WORLD.
HE...HE SAYS IT'S THE WAY FORWARD, SAVING THE GOOD, WARRING WITH THE BAD... BUT...
BUT WHAT, SHAYNE?
BUT... I FELT THEM, ALL THE ONES WE FOUGHT. THE ONES WE LOCKED UP OR KILLED...I HEARD THEIR SCREAMS!

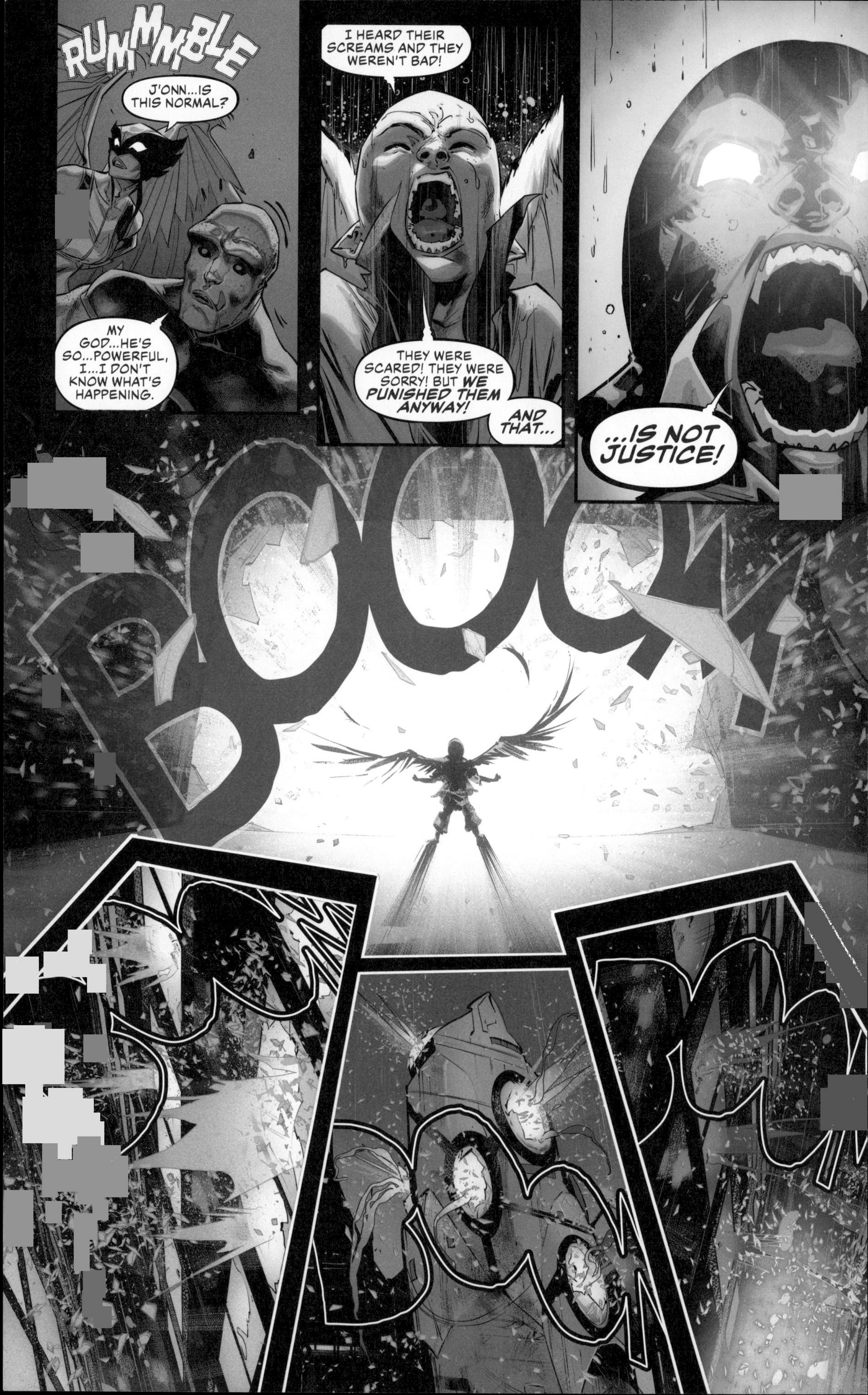
RUMMMBLE
J'ONN...IS THIS NORMAL?
MY GOD...HE'S SO...POWERFUL, I...I DON'T KNOW WHAT'S HAPPENING.
I HEARD THEIR SCREAMS AND THEY WEREN'T BAD!
THEY WERE SCARED! THEY WERE SORRY! BUT WE PUNISHED THEM ANYWAY!
AND THAT...
...IS NOT JUSTICE!
BOOOM!

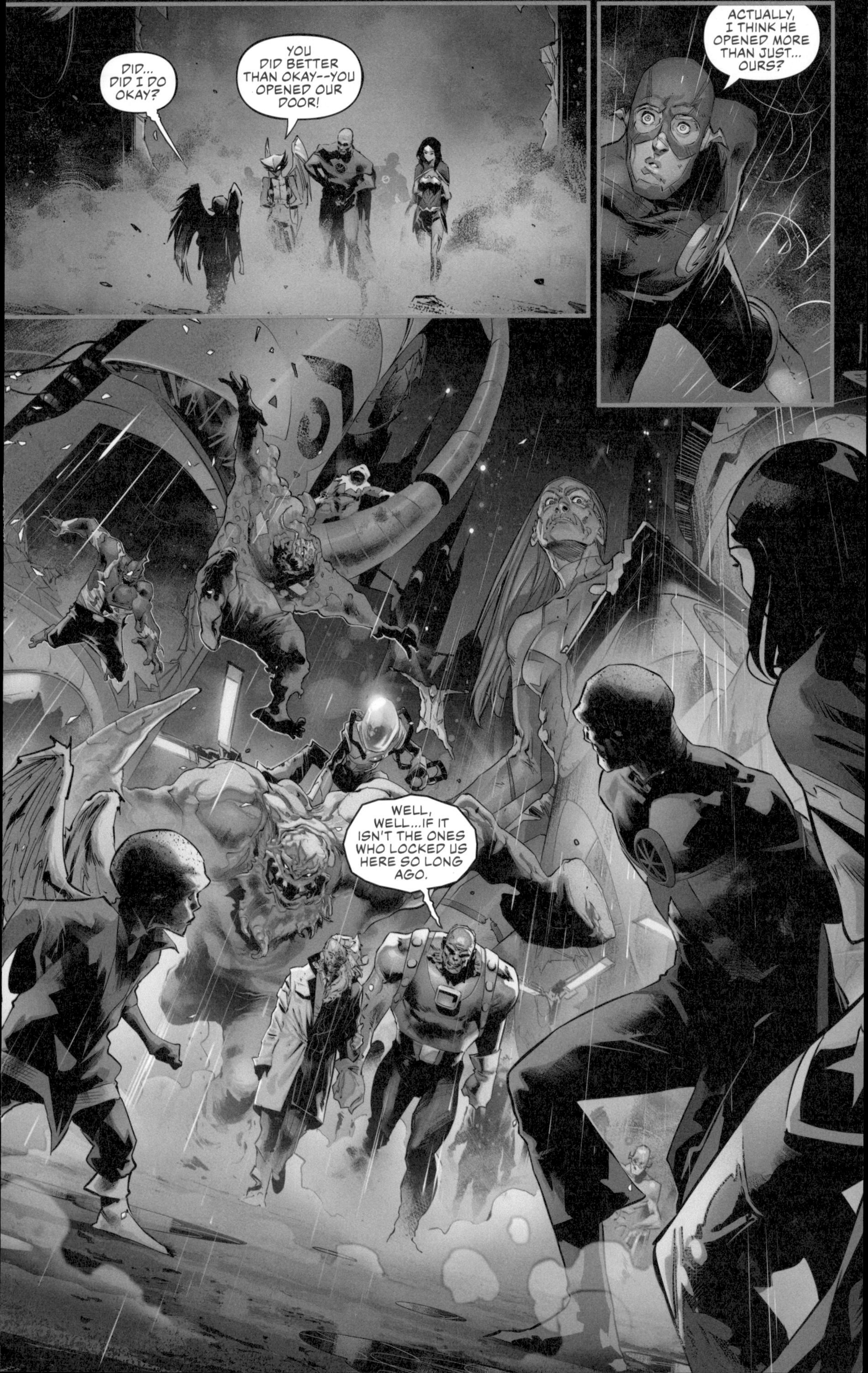
DID... DID I DO OKAY?
YOU DID BETTER THAN OKAY--YOU OPENED OUR DOOR!
ACTUALLY, I THINK HE OPENED MORE THAN JUST... OURS?
WELL, WELL...IF IT ISN'T THE ONES WHO LOCKED US HERE SO LONG AGO.

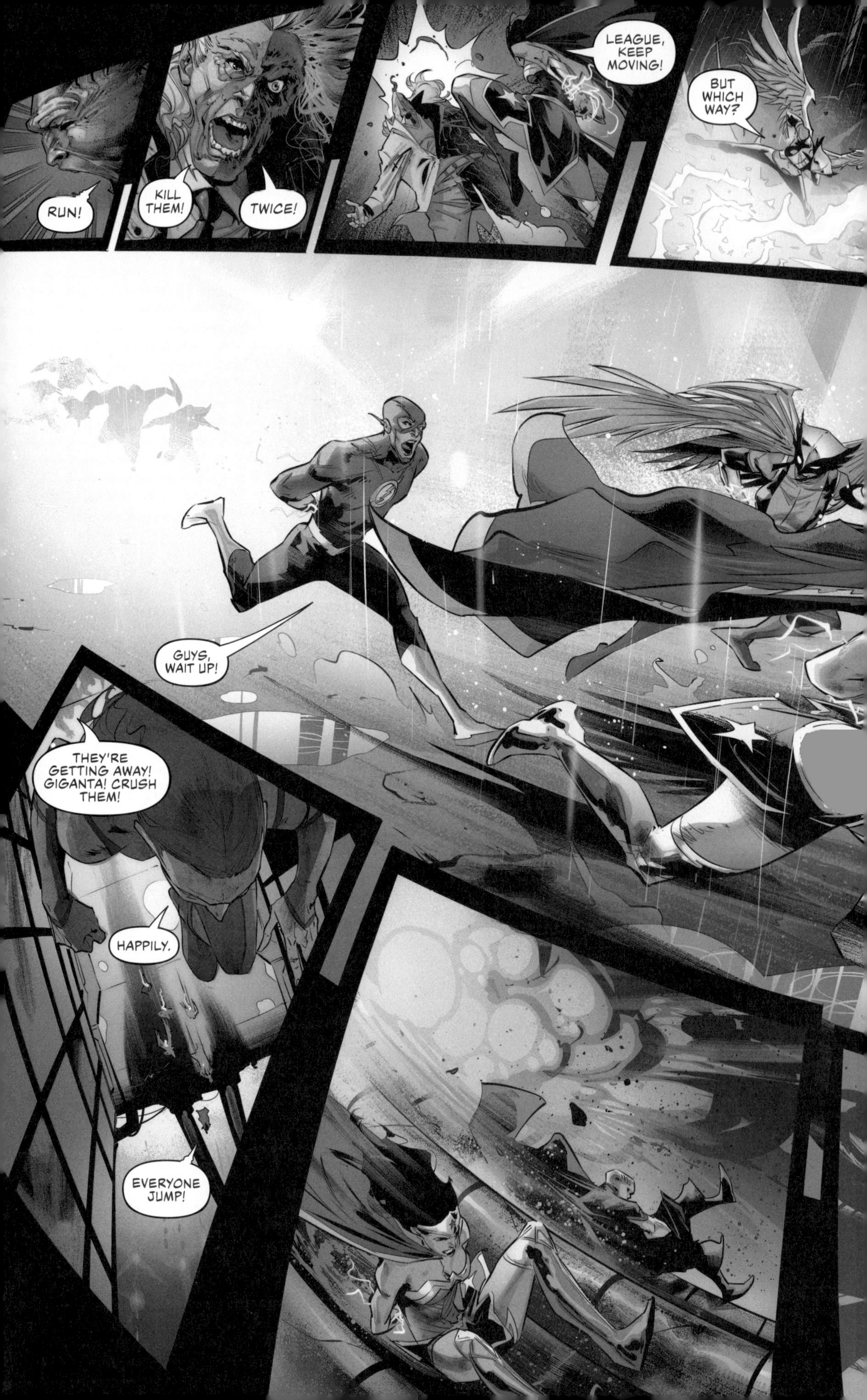
RUN!
KILL THEM!
TWICE!
LEAGUE, KEEP MOVING!
BUT WHICH WAY?
GUYS, WAIT UP!
THEY'RE GETTING AWAY! GIGANTA! CRUSH THEM!
HAPPILY.
EVERYONE JUMP!

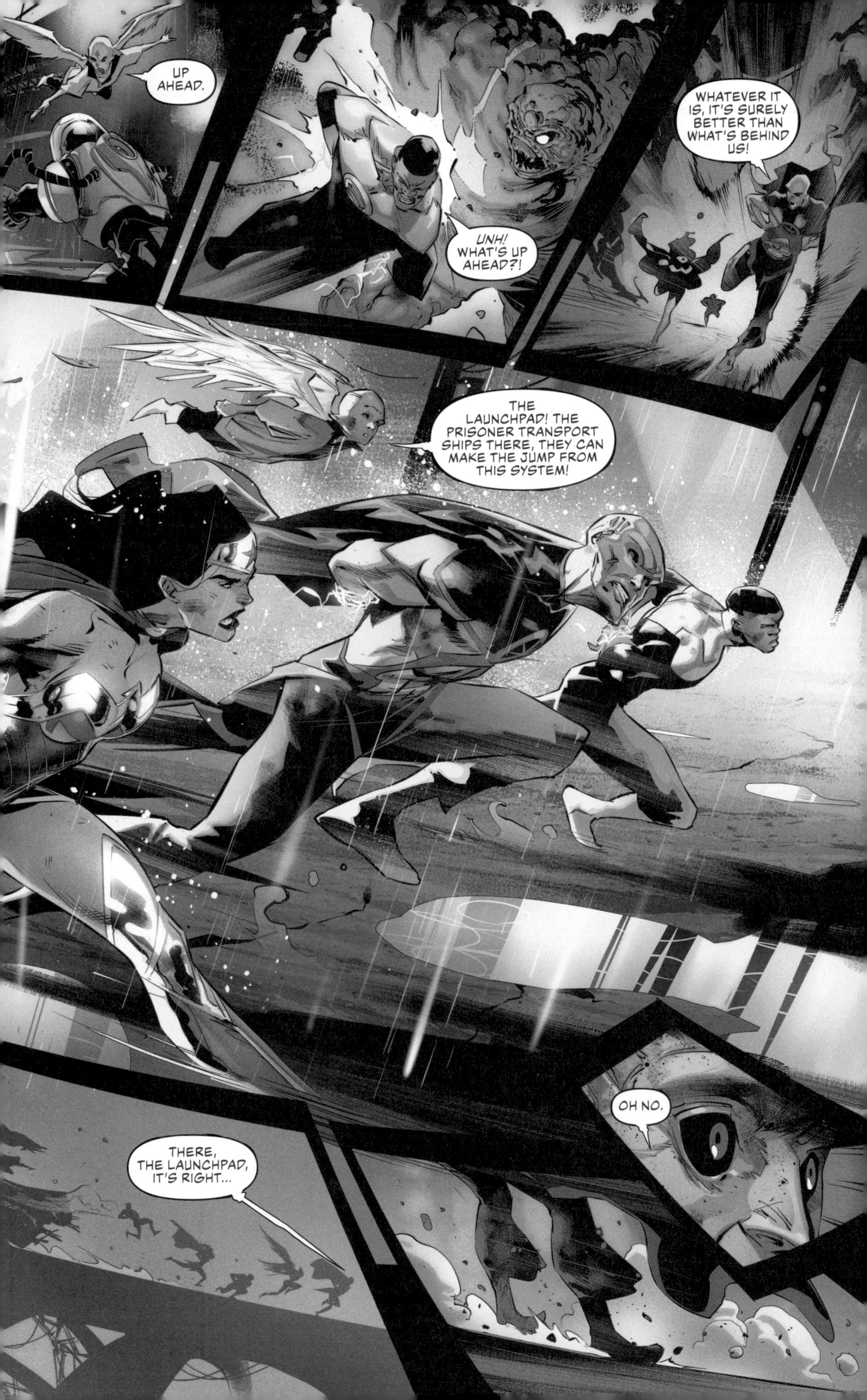
UP AHEAD.
UNH! WHAT'S UP AHEAD?!
WHATEVER IT IS, IT'S SURELY BETTER THAN WHAT'S BEHIND US!
THE LAUNCHPAD! THE PRISONER TRANSPORT SHIPS THERE, THEY CAN MAKE THE JUMP FROM THIS SYSTEM!
THERE, THE LAUNCHPAD, IT'S RIGHT...
OH NO.

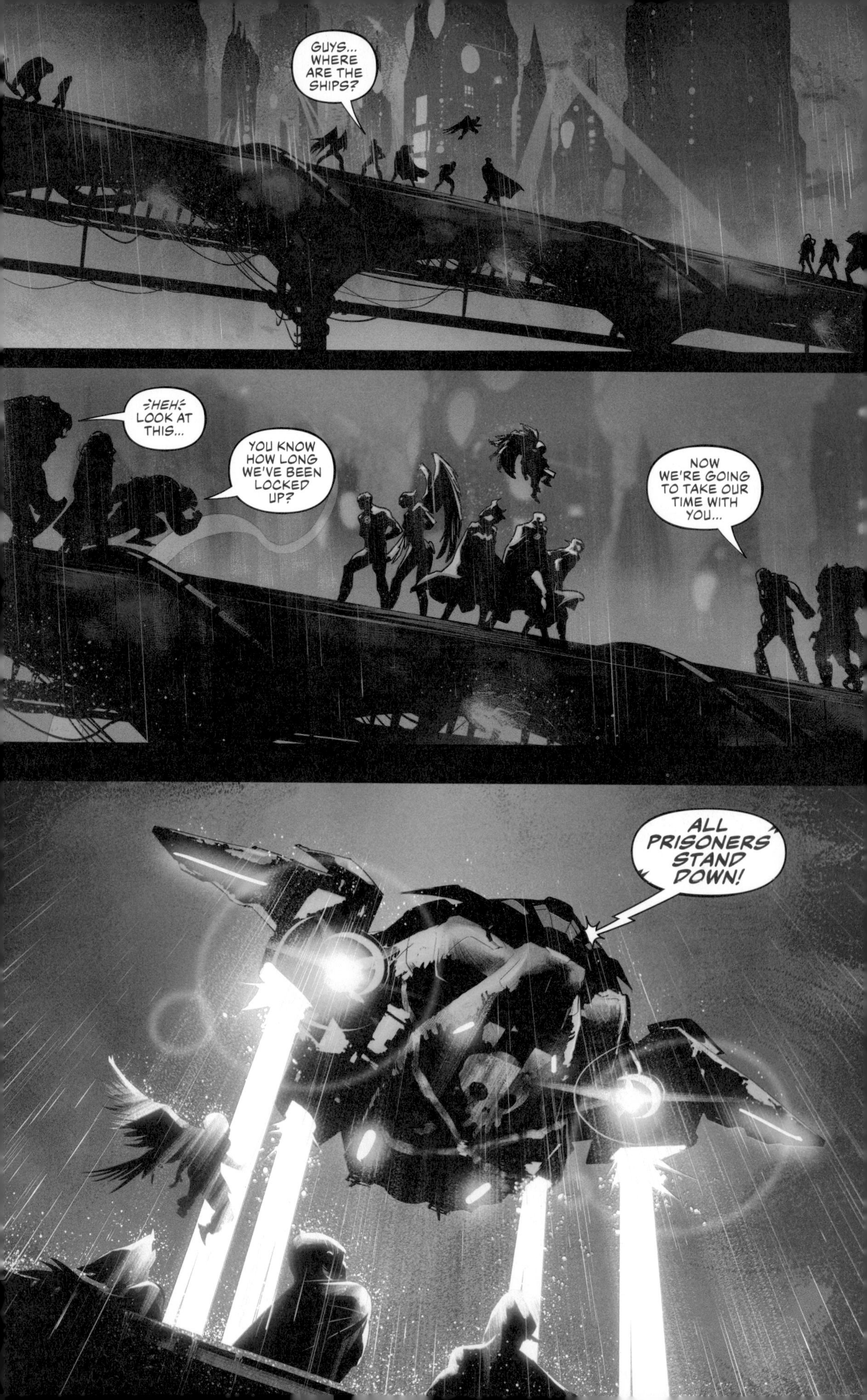
GUYS... WHERE ARE THE SHIPS?
HEH LOOK AT THIS...
YOU KNOW HOW LONG WE'VE BEEN LOCKED UP?
NOW WE'RE GOING TO TAKE OUR TIME WITH YOU...
ALL PRISONERS STAND DOWN!

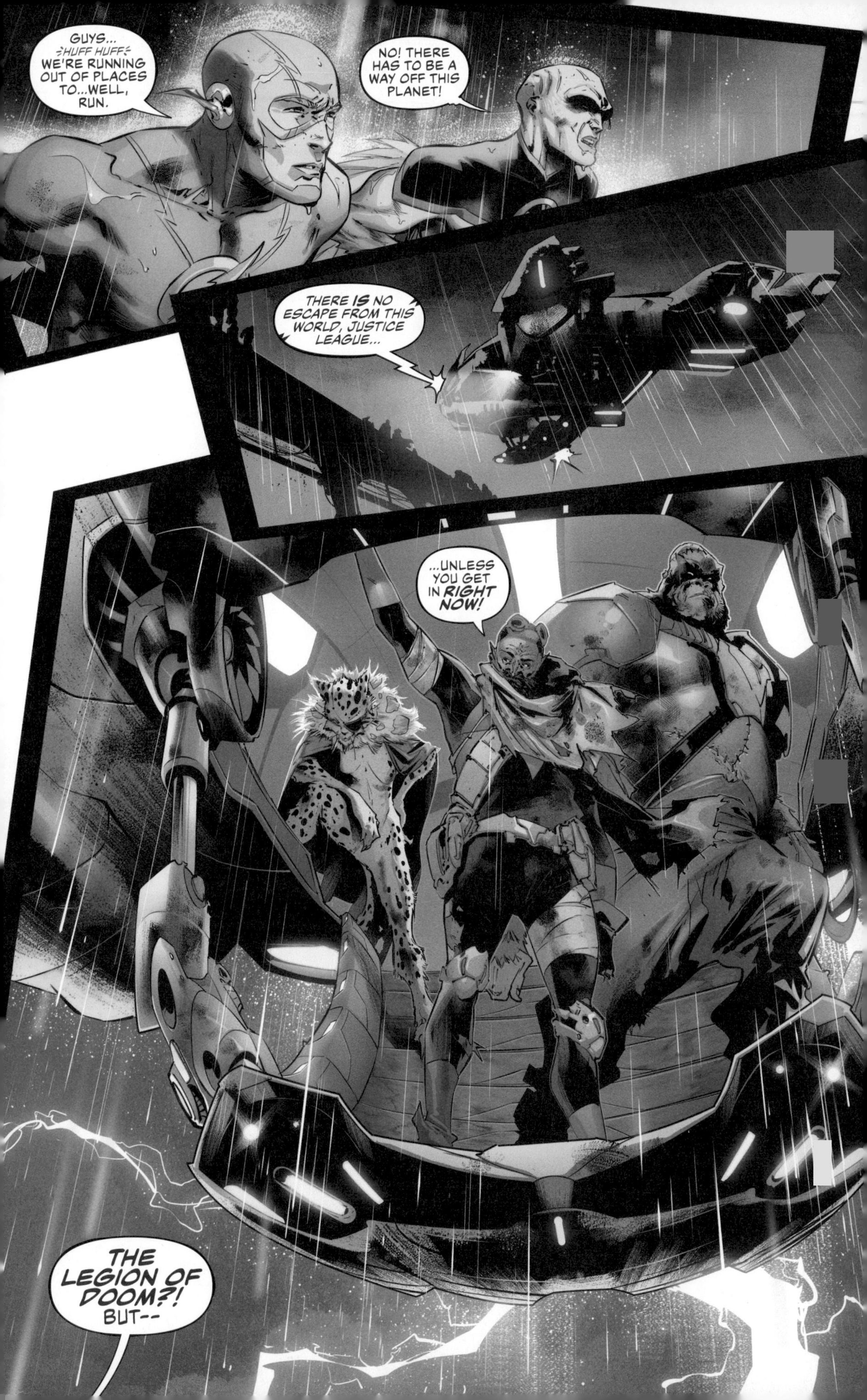
GUYS... HUFF HUFF WE'RE RUNNING OUT OF PLACES TO...WELL, RUN.
NO! THERE HAS TO BE A WAY OFF THIS PLANET!
THERE IS NO ESCAPE FROM THIS WORLD, JUSTICE LEAGUE...
...UNLESS YOU GET IN RIGHT NOW!
THE LEGION OF DOOM?! BUT--

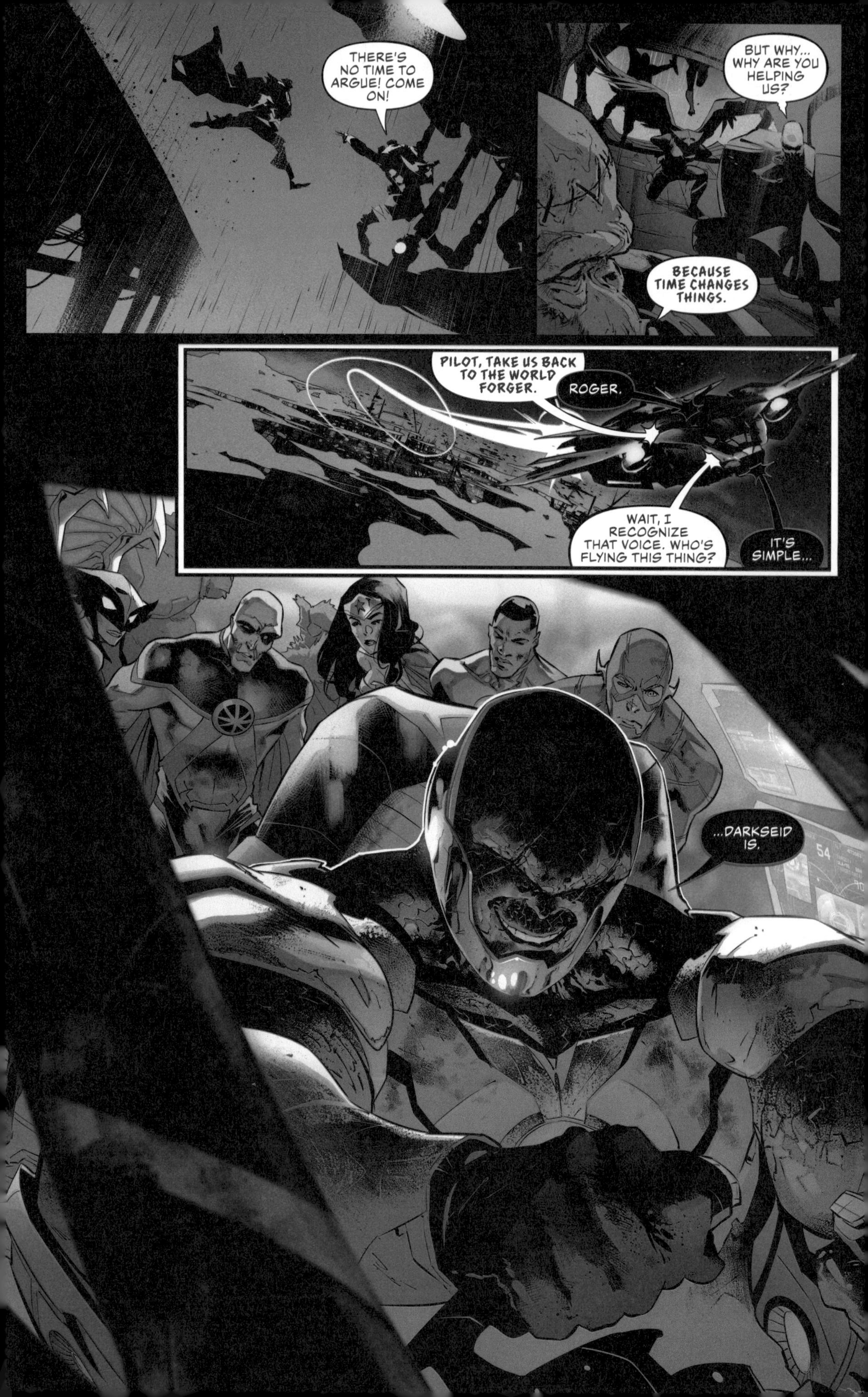

THERE'S NO TIME TO ARGUE! COME ON!
BUT WHY... WHY ARE YOU HELPING US?
BECAUSE TIME CHANGES THINGS.
PILOT, TAKE US BACK TO THE WORLD FORGER.
ROGER.
WAIT, I RECOGNIZE THAT VOICE. WHO'S FLYING THIS THING?
IT'S SIMPLE...
...DARKSEID IS.

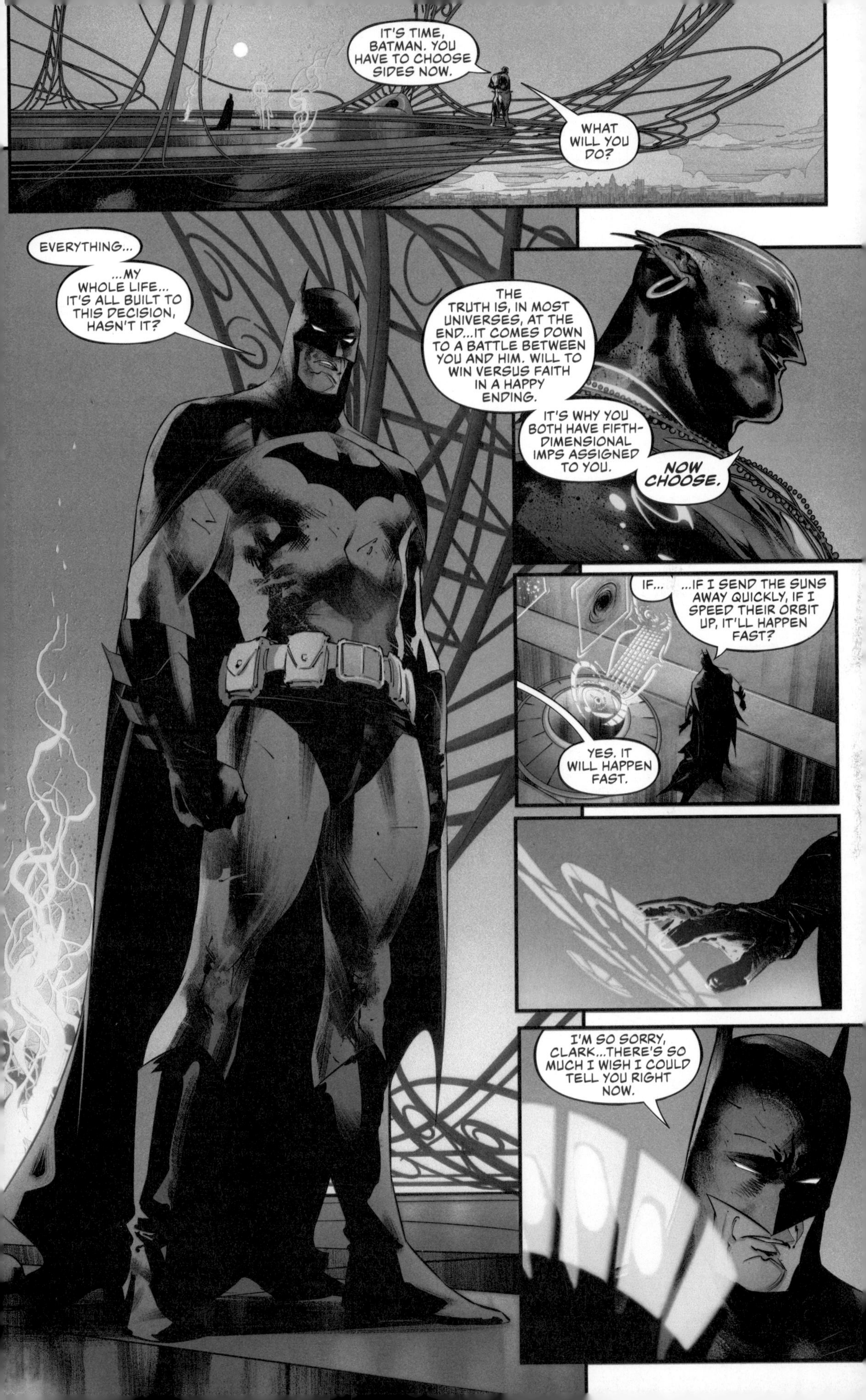
IT'S TIME, BATMAN. YOU HAVE TO CHOOSE SIDES NOW.
WHAT WILL YOU DO?
EVERYTHING...
...MY WHOLE LIFE... IT'S ALL BUILT TO THIS DECISION, HASN'T IT?
THE TRUTH IS, IN MOST UNIVERSES, AT THE END...IT COMES DOWN TO A BATTLE BETWEEN YOU AND HIM. WILL TO WIN VERSUS FAITH IN A HAPPY ENDING.
IT'S WHY YOU BOTH HAVE FIFTH-DIMENSIONAL IMPS ASSIGNED TO YOU.
NOW CHOOSE.
IF...
...IF I SEND THE SUNS AWAY QUICKLY, IF I SPEED THEIR ORBIT UP, IT'LL HAPPEN FAST?
YES. IT WILL HAPPEN FAST.
I'M SO SORRY, CLARK...THERE'S SO MUCH I WISH I COULD TELL YOU RIGHT NOW.

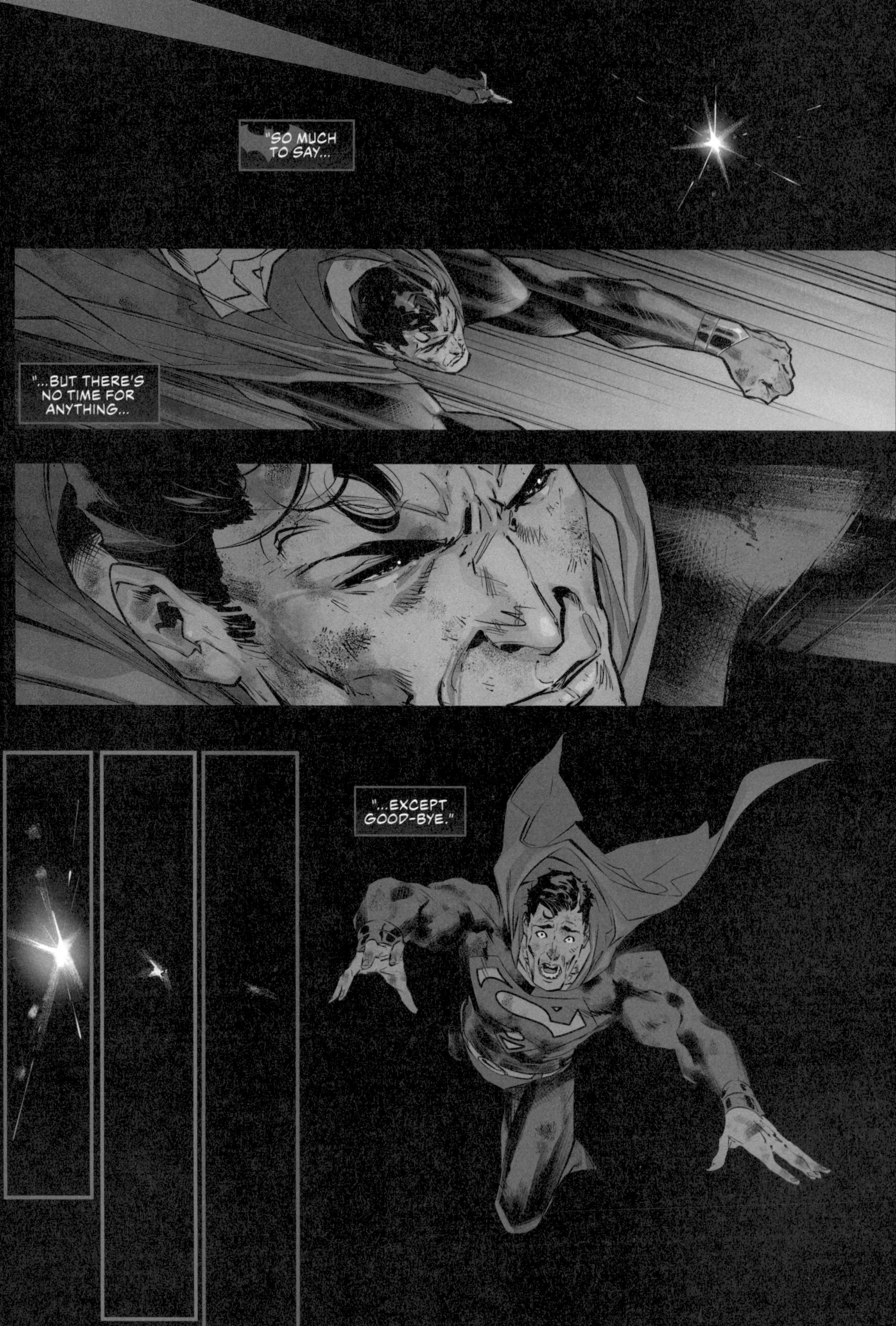
"SO MUCH TO SAY...
"...BUT THERE'S NO TIME FOR ANYTHING...
"...EXCEPT GOOD-BYE."

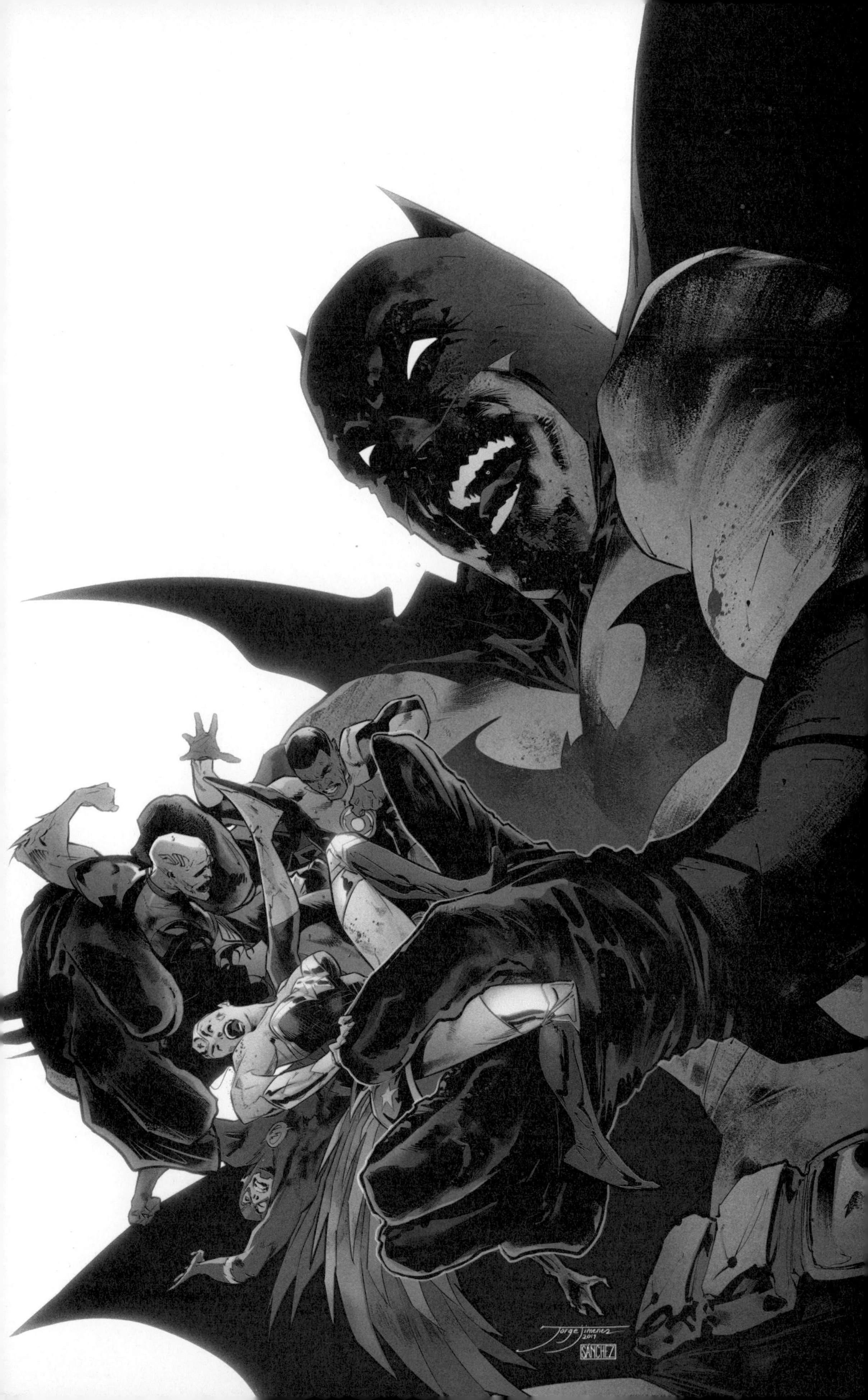
Jorge Jimenez 2019
SÁNCHEZ

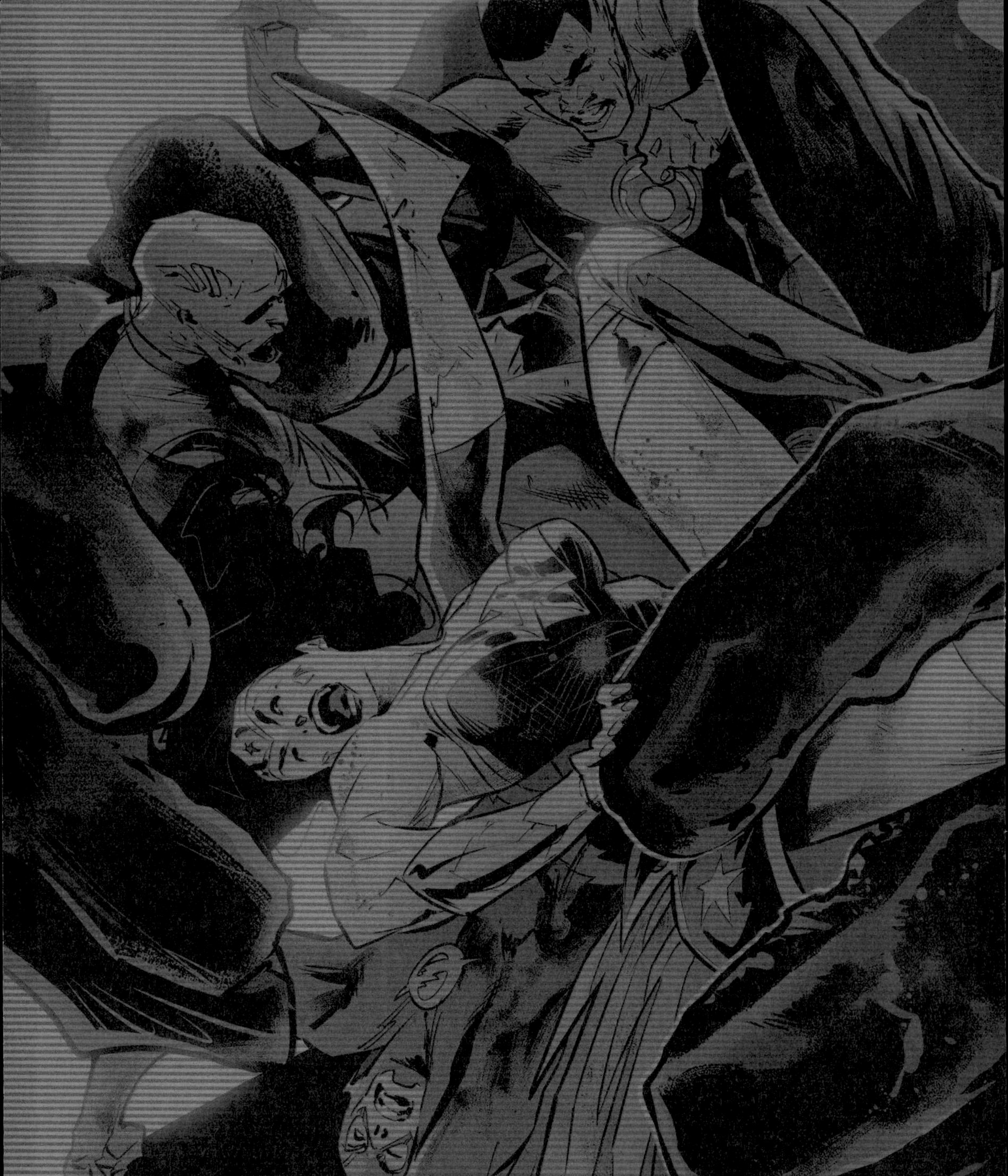

JUSTICE
LEAGUE
#24

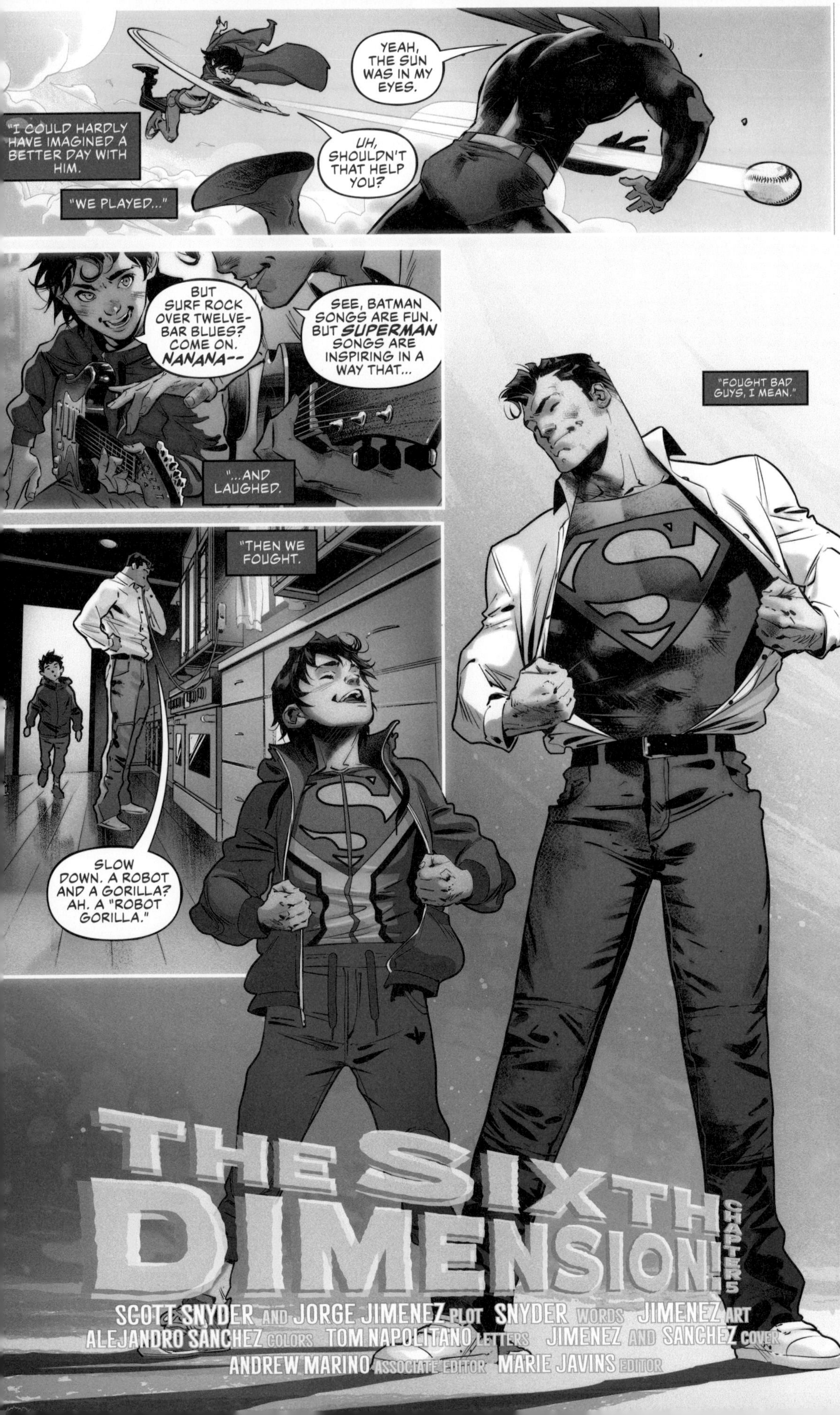

"I COULD HARDLY HAVE IMAGINED A BETTER DAY WITH HIM.
"WE PLAYED..."
YEAH, THE SUN WAS IN MY EYES.
UH, SHOULDN'T THAT HELP YOU?
BUT SURF ROCK OVER TWELVE-BAR BLUES? COME ON. NANANA--
SEE, BATMAN SONGS ARE FUN. BUT SUPERMAN SONGS ARE INSPIRING IN A WAY THAT...
"...AND LAUGHED.
"FOUGHT BAD GUYS, I MEAN."
"THEN WE FOUGHT.
SLOW DOWN. A ROBOT AND A GORILLA? AH. A "ROBOT GORILLA."
THE SIXTH DIMENSION! CHAPTER 5
SCOTT SNYDER AND JORGE JIMENEZ PLOT SNYDER WORDS JIMENEZ ART
ALEJANDRO SANCHEZ COLORS TOM NAPOLITANO LETTERS JIMENEZ AND SANCHEZ COVER
ANDREW MARINO ASSOCIATE EDITOR MARIE JAVINS EDITOR

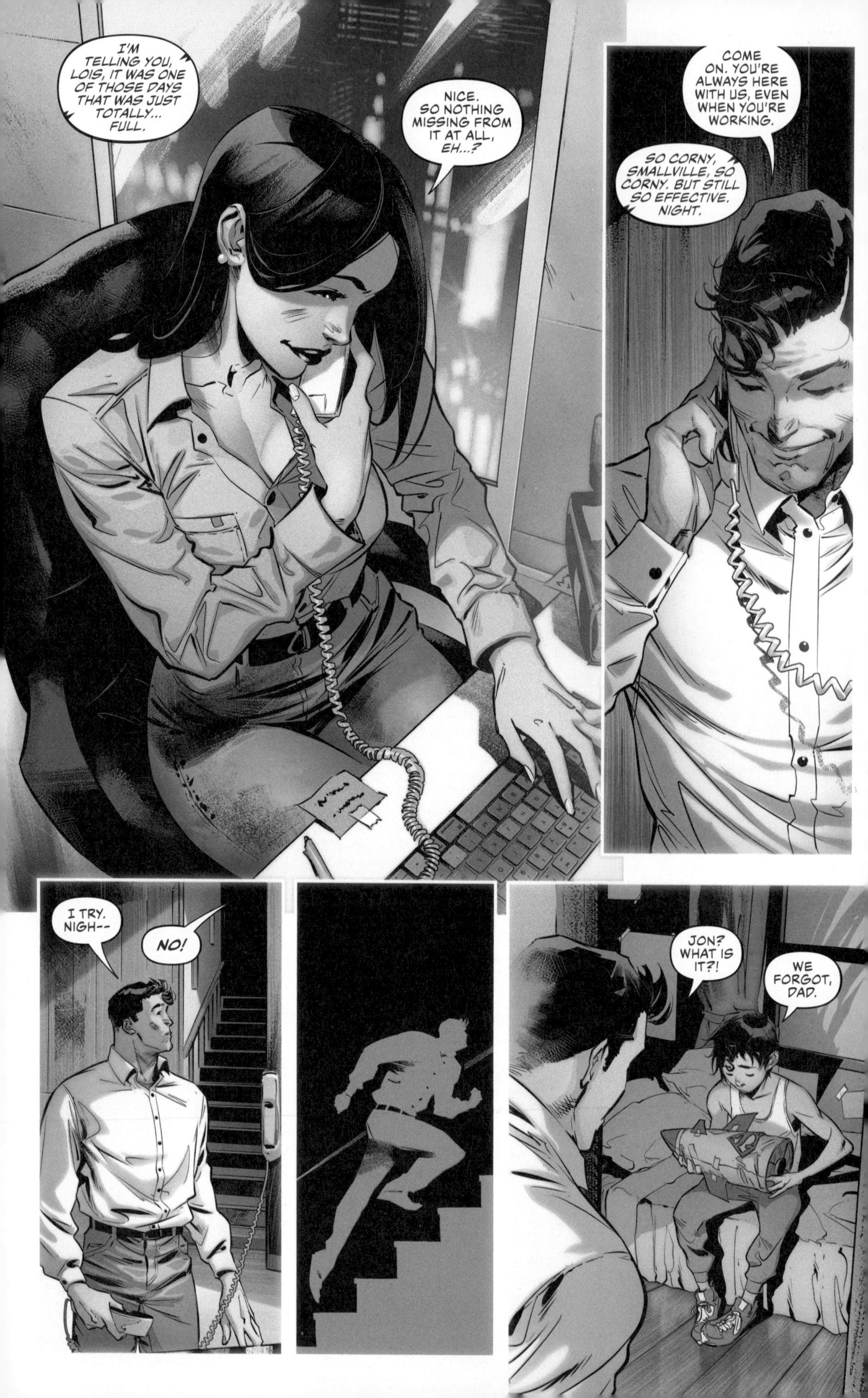

I'M TELLING YOU, LOIS, IT WAS ONE OF THOSE DAYS THAT WAS JUST TOTALLY... FULL.
NICE. SO NOTHING MISSING FROM IT AT ALL, EH...?
COME ON. YOU'RE ALWAYS HERE WITH US, EVEN WHEN YOU'RE WORKING.
SO CORNY, SMALLVILLE, SO CORNY. BUT STILL SO EFFECTIVE. NIGHT.
I TRY. NIGH--
NO!
JON? WHAT IS IT?!
WE FORGOT, DAD.

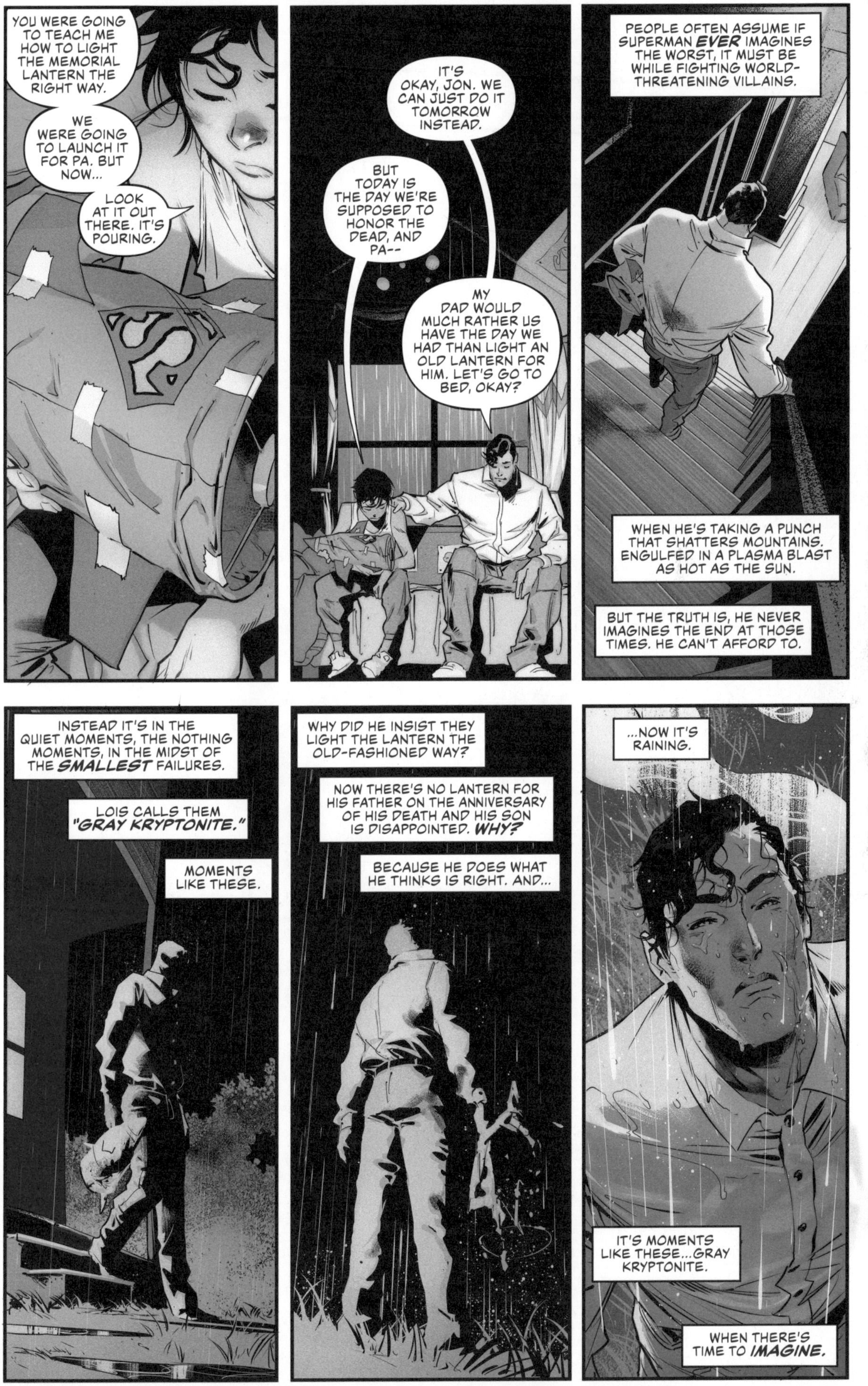
YOU WERE GOING TO TEACH ME HOW TO LIGHT THE MEMORIAL LANTERN THE RIGHT WAY.
WE WERE GOING TO LAUNCH IT FOR PA. BUT NOW...
LOOK AT IT OUT THERE. IT'S POURING.
IT'S OKAY, JON. WE CAN JUST DO IT TOMORROW INSTEAD.
BUT TODAY IS THE DAY WE'RE SUPPOSED TO HONOR THE DEAD, AND PA--
MY DAD WOULD MUCH RATHER US HAVE THE DAY WE HAD THAN LIGHT AN OLD LANTERN FOR HIM. LET'S GO TO BED, OKAY?
PEOPLE OFTEN ASSUME IF SUPERMAN EVER IMAGINES THE WORST, IT MUST BE WHILE FIGHTING WORLD-THREATENING VILLAINS.
WHEN HE'S TAKING A PUNCH THAT SHATTERS MOUNTAINS. ENGULFED IN A PLASMA BLAST AS HOT AS THE SUN.
BUT THE TRUTH IS, HE NEVER IMAGINES THE END AT THOSE TIMES. HE CAN'T AFFORD TO.
INSTEAD IT'S IN THE QUIET MOMENTS, THE NOTHING MOMENTS, IN THE MIDST OF THE SMALLEST FAILURES.
LOIS CALLS THEM "GRAY KRYPTONITE."
MOMENTS LIKE THESE.
WHY DID HE INSIST THEY LIGHT THE LANTERN THE OLD-FASHIONED WAY?
NOW THERE'S NO LANTERN FOR HIS FATHER ON THE ANNIVERSARY OF HIS DEATH AND HIS SON IS DISAPPOINTED. WHY?
BECAUSE HE DOES WHAT HE THINKS IS RIGHT. AND...
...NOW IT'S RAINING.
IT'S MOMENTS LIKE THESE...GRAY KRYPTONITE.
WHEN THERE'S TIME TO IMAGINE.

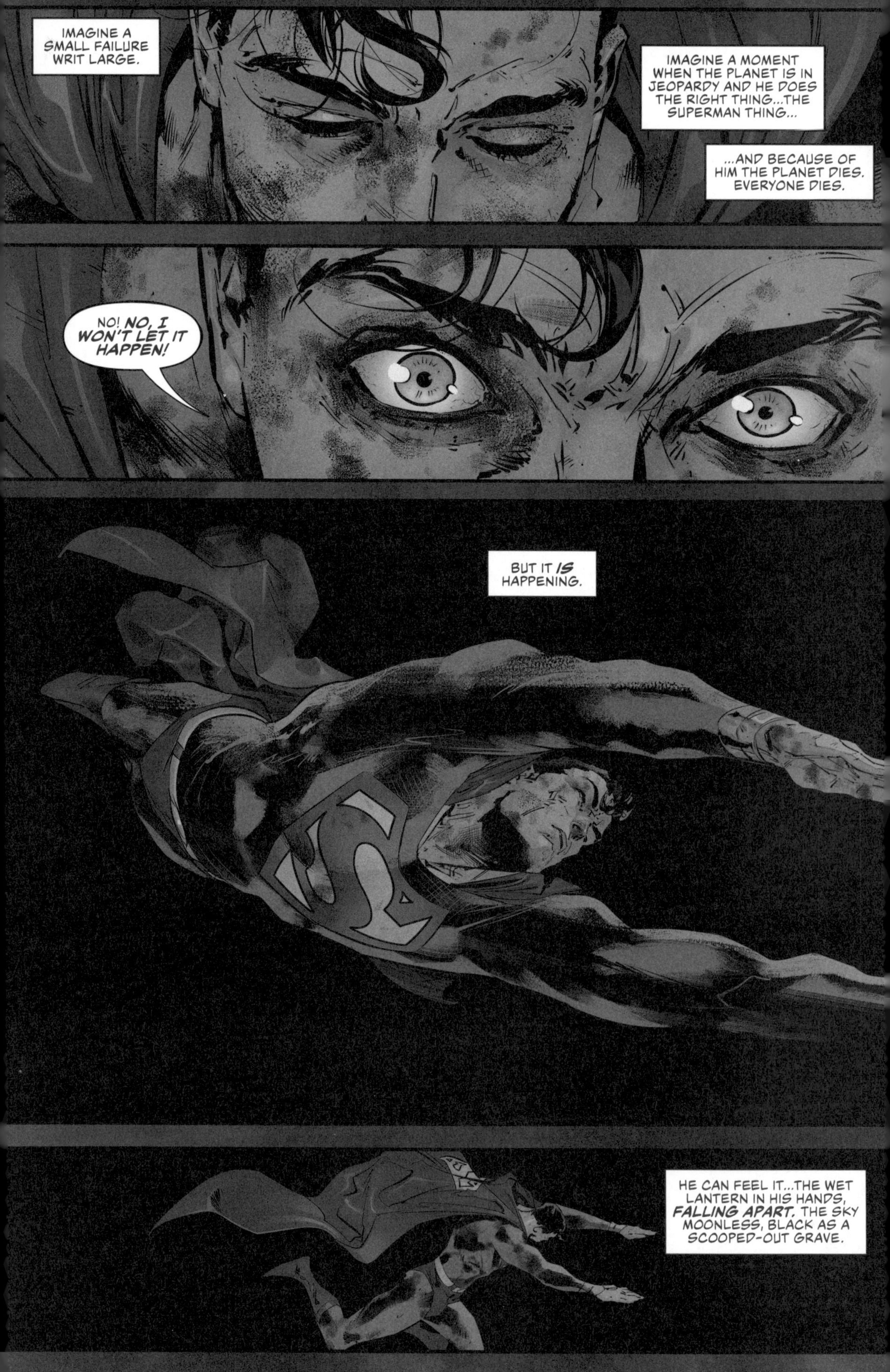
IMAGINE A SMALL FAILURE WRIT LARGE.
IMAGINE A MOMENT WHEN THE PLANET IS IN JEOPARDY AND HE DOES THE RIGHT THING...THE SUPERMAN THING...
...AND BECAUSE OF HIM THE PLANET DIES. EVERYONE DIES.
NO! NO, I WON'T LET IT HAPPEN!
BUT IT IS HAPPENING.
HE CAN FEEL IT...THE WET LANTERN IN HIS HANDS, FALLING APART. THE SKY MOONLESS, BLACK AS A SCOOPED-OUT GRAVE.

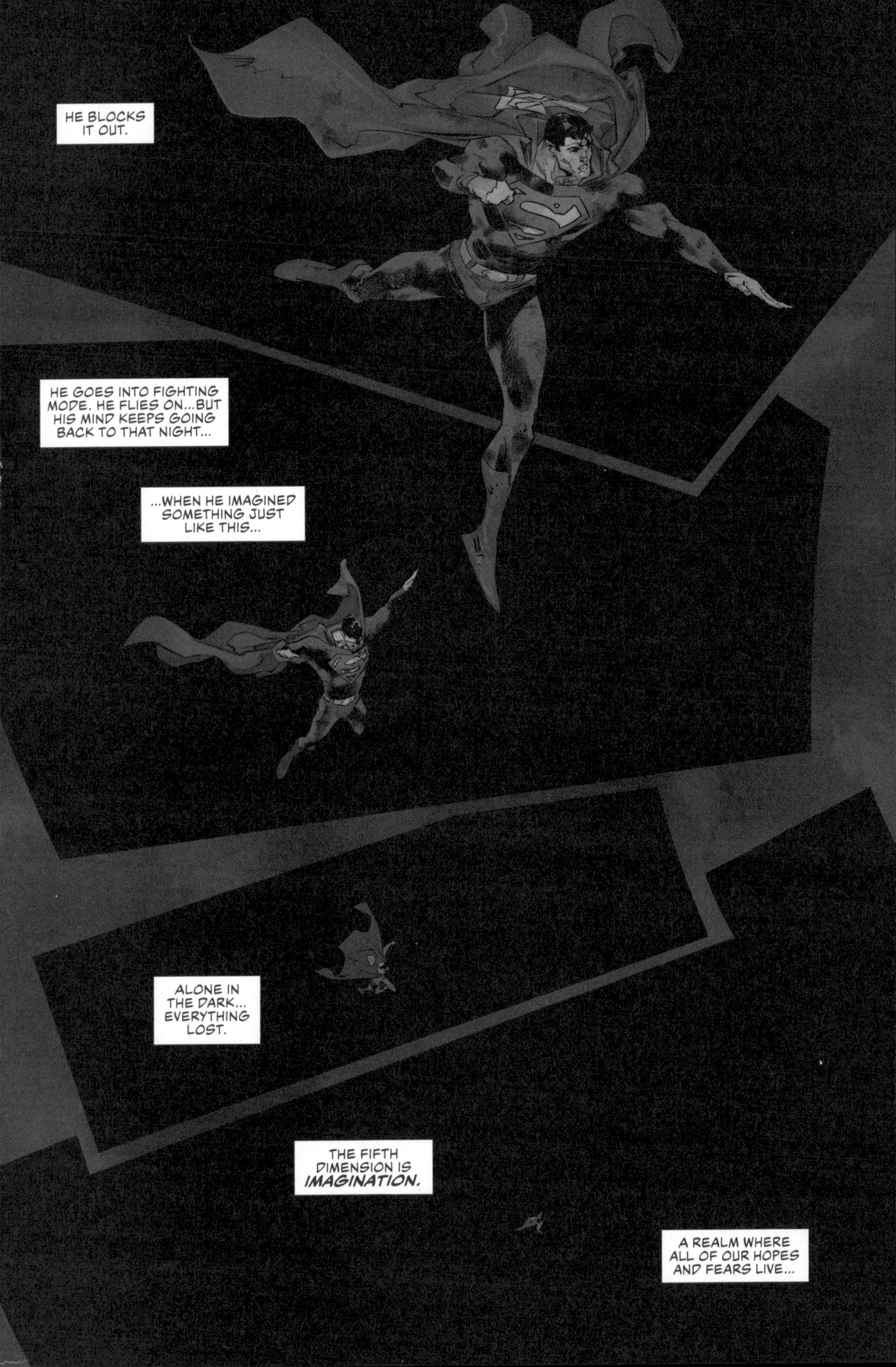
HE BLOCKS IT OUT.
HE GOES INTO FIGHTING MODE. HE FLIES ON...BUT HIS MIND KEEPS GOING BACK TO THAT NIGHT...
...WHEN HE IMAGINED SOMETHING JUST LIKE THIS...
ALONE IN THE DARK... EVERYTHING LOST.
THE FIFTH DIMENSION IS *IMAGINATION.*
A REALM WHERE ALL OF OUR HOPES AND FEARS LIVE...

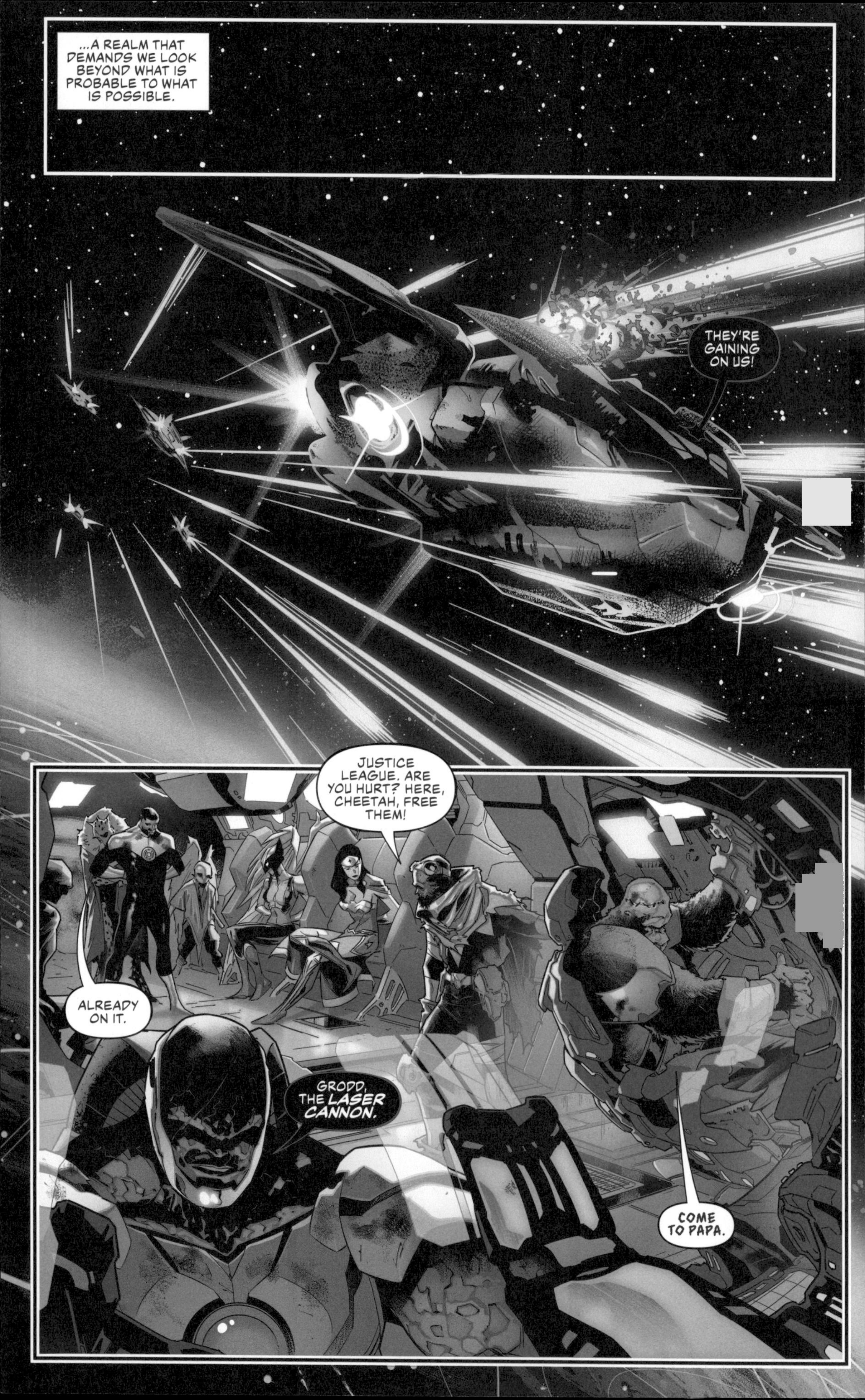
...A REALM THAT DEMANDS WE LOOK BEYOND WHAT IS PROBABLE TO WHAT IS POSSIBLE.
THEY'RE GAINING ON US!
JUSTICE LEAGUE. ARE YOU HURT? HERE, CHEETAH, FREE THEM!
ALREADY ON IT.
GRODD, THE LASER CANNON.
COME TO PAPA.

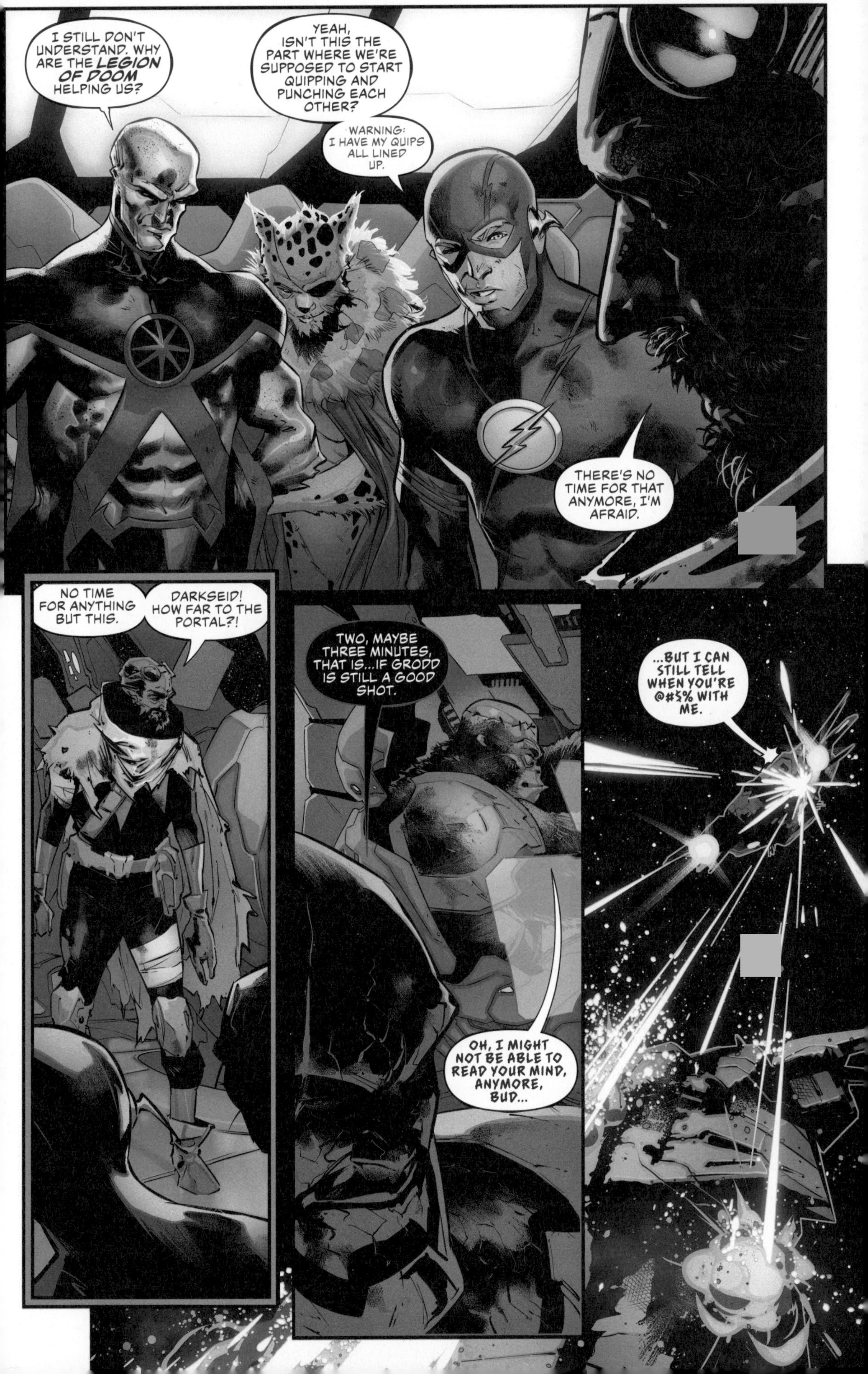
I STILL DON'T UNDERSTAND. WHY ARE THE LEGION OF DOOM HELPING US?
YEAH, ISN'T THIS THE PART WHERE WE'RE SUPPOSED TO START QUIPPING AND PUNCHING EACH OTHER?
WARNING: I HAVE MY QUIPS ALL LINED UP.
THERE'S NO TIME FOR THAT ANYMORE, I'M AFRAID.
NO TIME FOR ANYTHING BUT THIS.
DARKSEID! HOW FAR TO THE PORTAL?!
TWO, MAYBE THREE MINUTES, THAT IS...IF GRODD IS STILL A GOOD SHOT.
OH, I MIGHT NOT BE ABLE TO READ YOUR MIND, ANYMORE, BUD...
...BUT I CAN STILL TELL WHEN YOU'RE @#$% WITH ME.

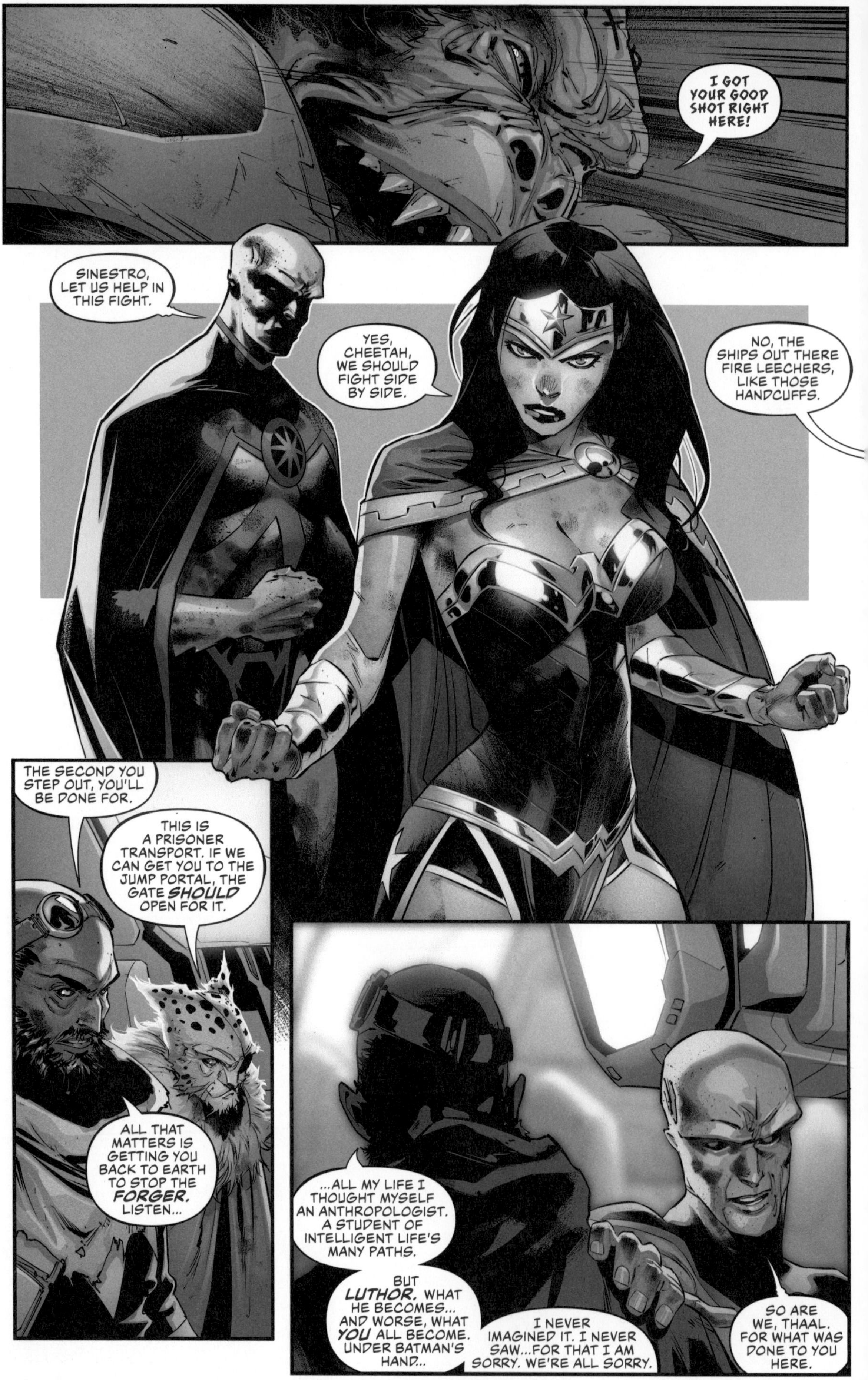
I GOT YOUR GOOD SHOT RIGHT HERE!
SINESTRO, LET US HELP IN THIS FIGHT.
YES, CHEETAH, WE SHOULD FIGHT SIDE BY SIDE.
NO, THE SHIPS OUT THERE FIRE LEECHERS, LIKE THOSE HANDCUFFS.
THE SECOND YOU STEP OUT, YOU'LL BE DONE FOR.
THIS IS A PRISONER TRANSPORT. IF WE CAN GET YOU TO THE JUMP PORTAL, THE GATE *SHOULD* OPEN FOR IT.
ALL THAT MATTERS IS GETTING YOU BACK TO EARTH TO STOP THE *FORGER.* LISTEN...
...ALL MY LIFE I THOUGHT MYSELF AN ANTHROPOLOGIST. A STUDENT OF INTELLIGENT LIFE'S MANY PATHS.
BUT *LUTHOR.* WHAT HE BECOMES... AND WORSE, WHAT *YOU* ALL BECOME. UNDER BATMAN'S HAND...
I NEVER IMAGINED IT. I NEVER SAW...FOR THAT I AM SORRY. WE'RE ALL SORRY.
SO ARE WE, THAAL. FOR WHAT WAS DONE TO YOU HERE.

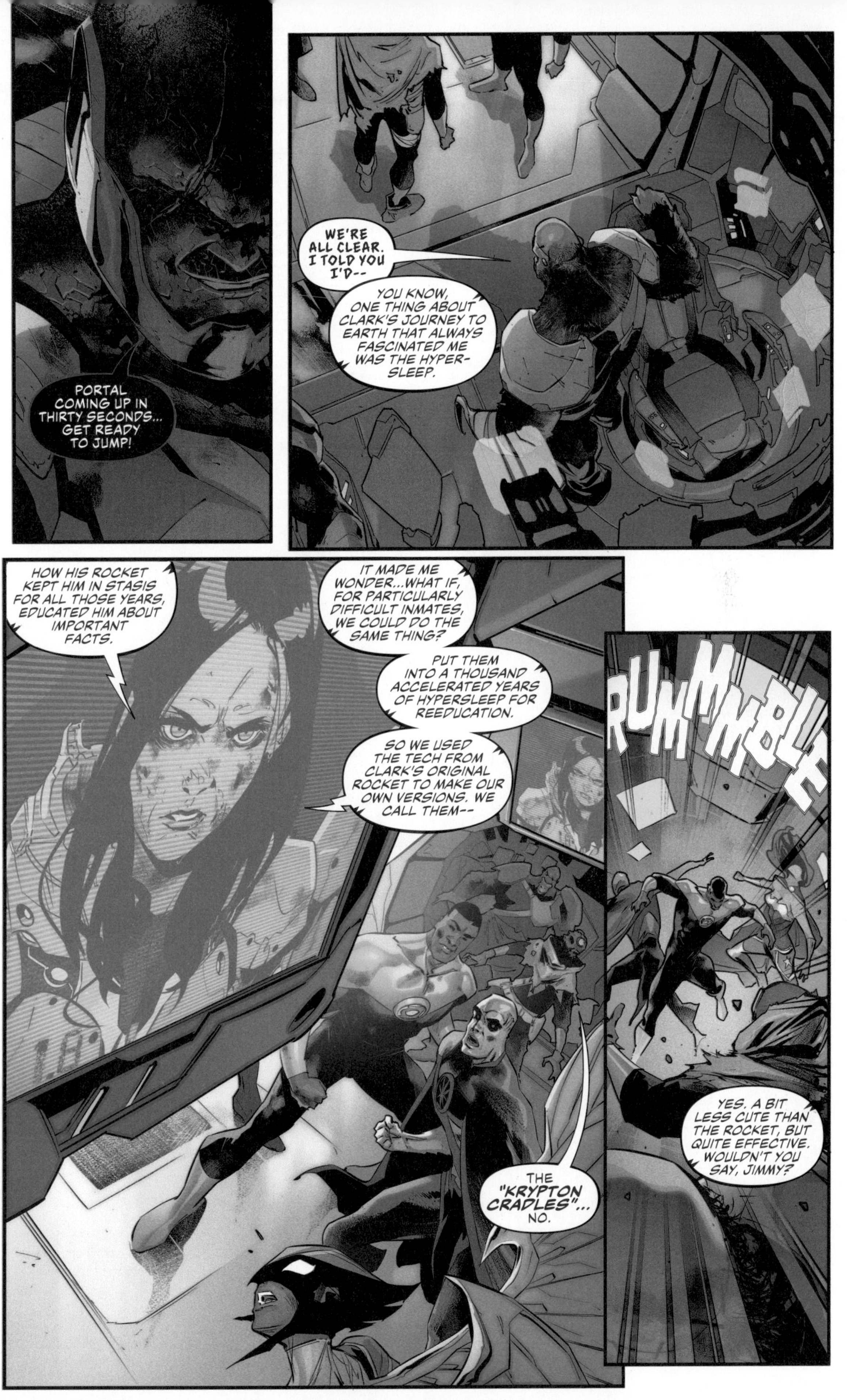
PORTAL COMING UP IN THIRTY SECONDS... GET READY TO JUMP!
WE'RE ALL CLEAR. I TOLD YOU I'D--
YOU KNOW, ONE THING ABOUT CLARK'S JOURNEY TO EARTH THAT ALWAYS FASCINATED ME WAS THE HYPER-SLEEP.
HOW HIS ROCKET KEPT HIM IN STASIS FOR ALL THOSE YEARS, EDUCATED HIM ABOUT IMPORTANT FACTS.
IT MADE ME WONDER...WHAT IF, FOR PARTICULARLY DIFFICULT INMATES, WE COULD DO THE SAME THING?
PUT THEM INTO A THOUSAND ACCELERATED YEARS OF HYPERSLEEP FOR REEDUCATION.
SO WE USED THE TECH FROM CLARK'S ORIGINAL ROCKET TO MAKE OUR OWN VERSIONS. WE CALL THEM--
THE "KRYPTON CRADLES"... NO.
RUMMMBLE
YES. A BIT LESS CUTE THAN THE ROCKET, BUT QUITE EFFECTIVE. WOULDN'T YOU SAY, JIMMY?

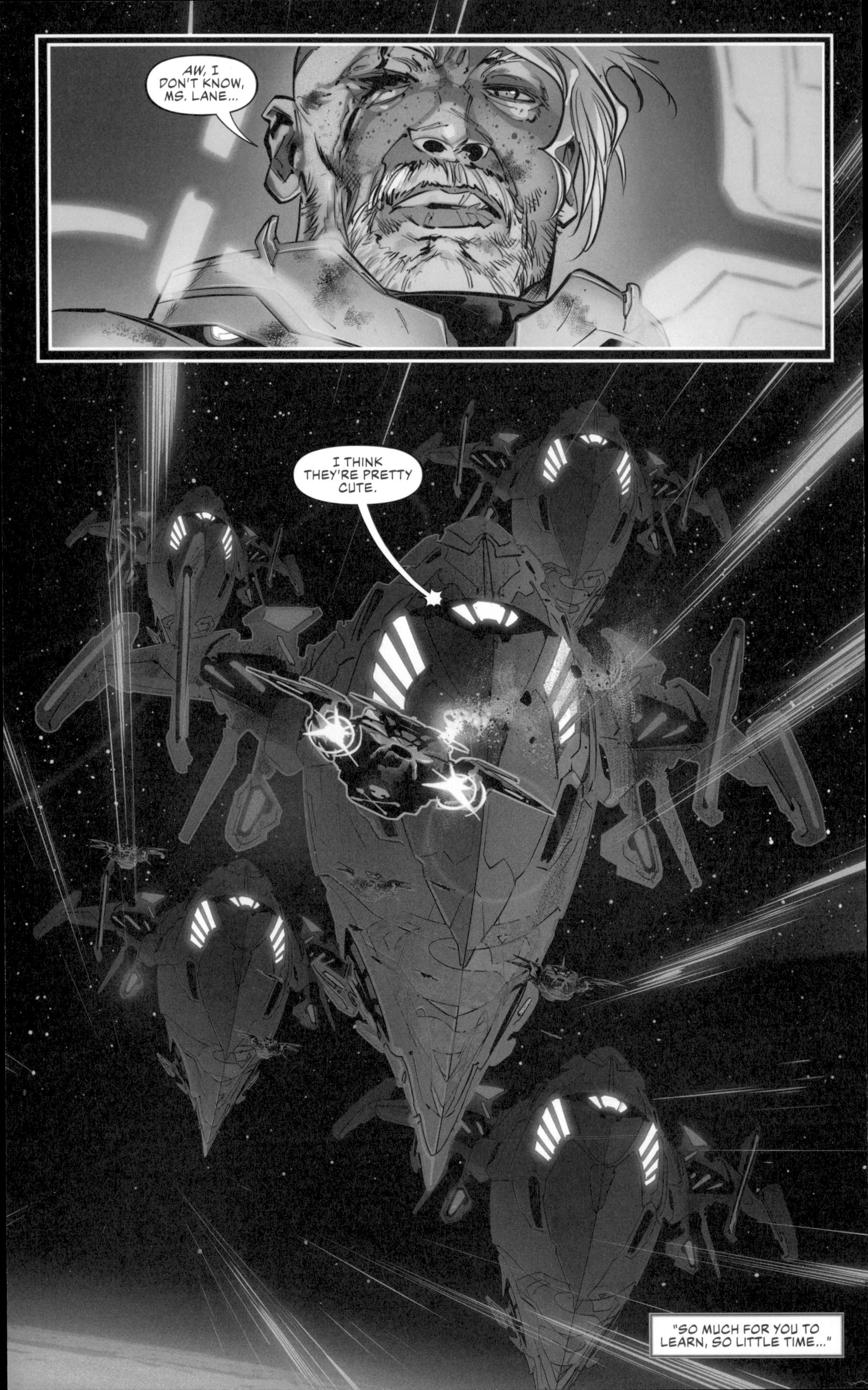

AW, I DON'T KNOW, MS. LANE...
I THINK THEY'RE PRETTY CUTE.
"SO MUCH FOR YOU TO LEARN, SO LITTLE TIME..."

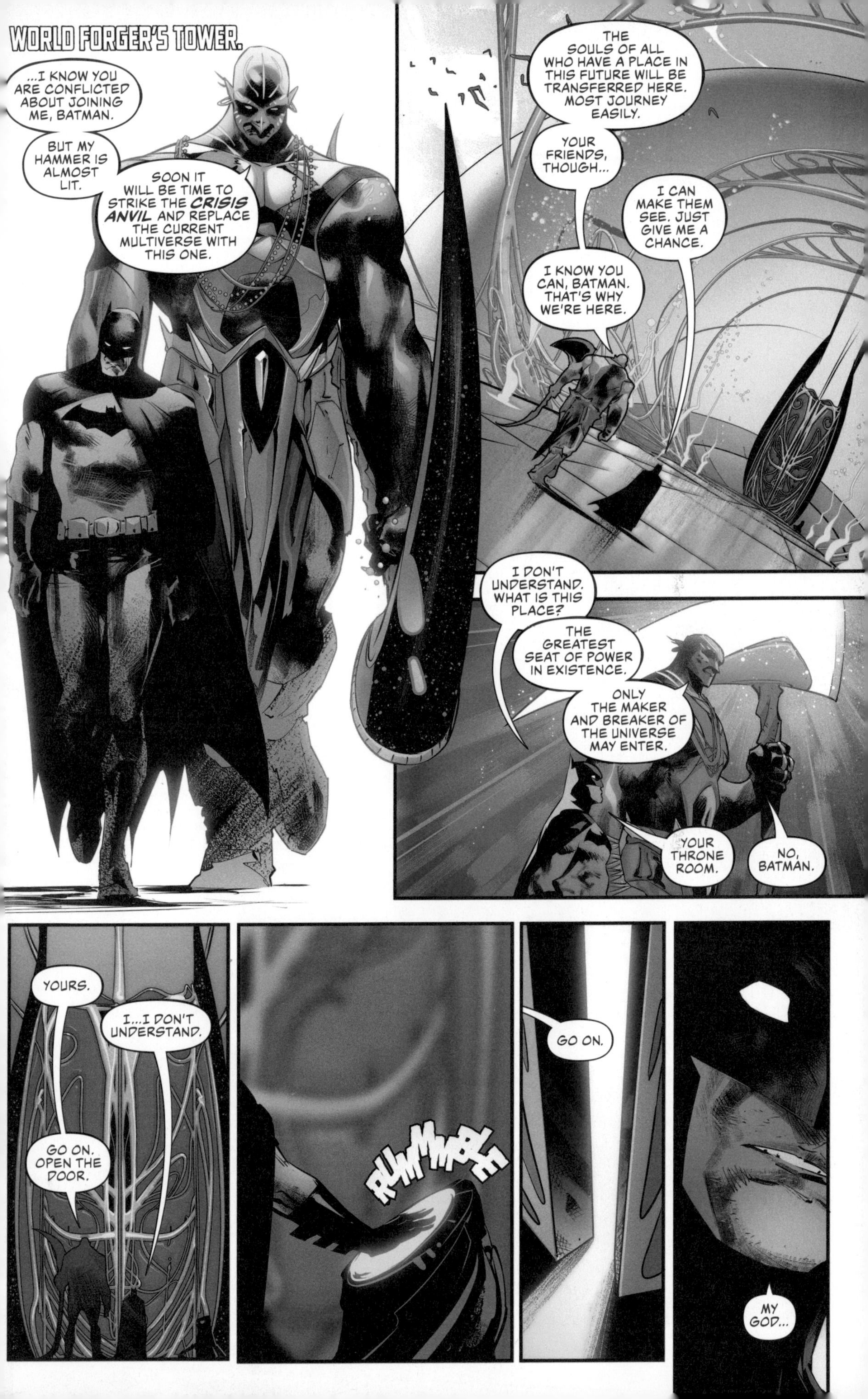
WORLD FORGER'S TOWER.
...I KNOW YOU ARE CONFLICTED ABOUT JOINING ME, BATMAN.
BUT MY HAMMER IS ALMOST LIT.
SOON IT WILL BE TIME TO STRIKE THE CRISIS ANVIL AND REPLACE THE CURRENT MULTIVERSE WITH THIS ONE.
THE SOULS OF ALL WHO HAVE A PLACE IN THIS FUTURE WILL BE TRANSFERRED HERE. MOST JOURNEY EASILY.
YOUR FRIENDS, THOUGH...
I CAN MAKE THEM SEE. JUST GIVE ME A CHANCE.
I KNOW YOU CAN, BATMAN. THAT'S WHY WE'RE HERE.
I DON'T UNDERSTAND. WHAT IS THIS PLACE?
THE GREATEST SEAT OF POWER IN EXISTENCE.
ONLY THE MAKER AND BREAKER OF THE UNIVERSE MAY ENTER.
YOUR THRONE ROOM.
NO, BATMAN.
YOURS.
I...I DON'T UNDERSTAND.
GO ON. OPEN THE DOOR.
RUMMMBLE
GO ON.
MY GOD...

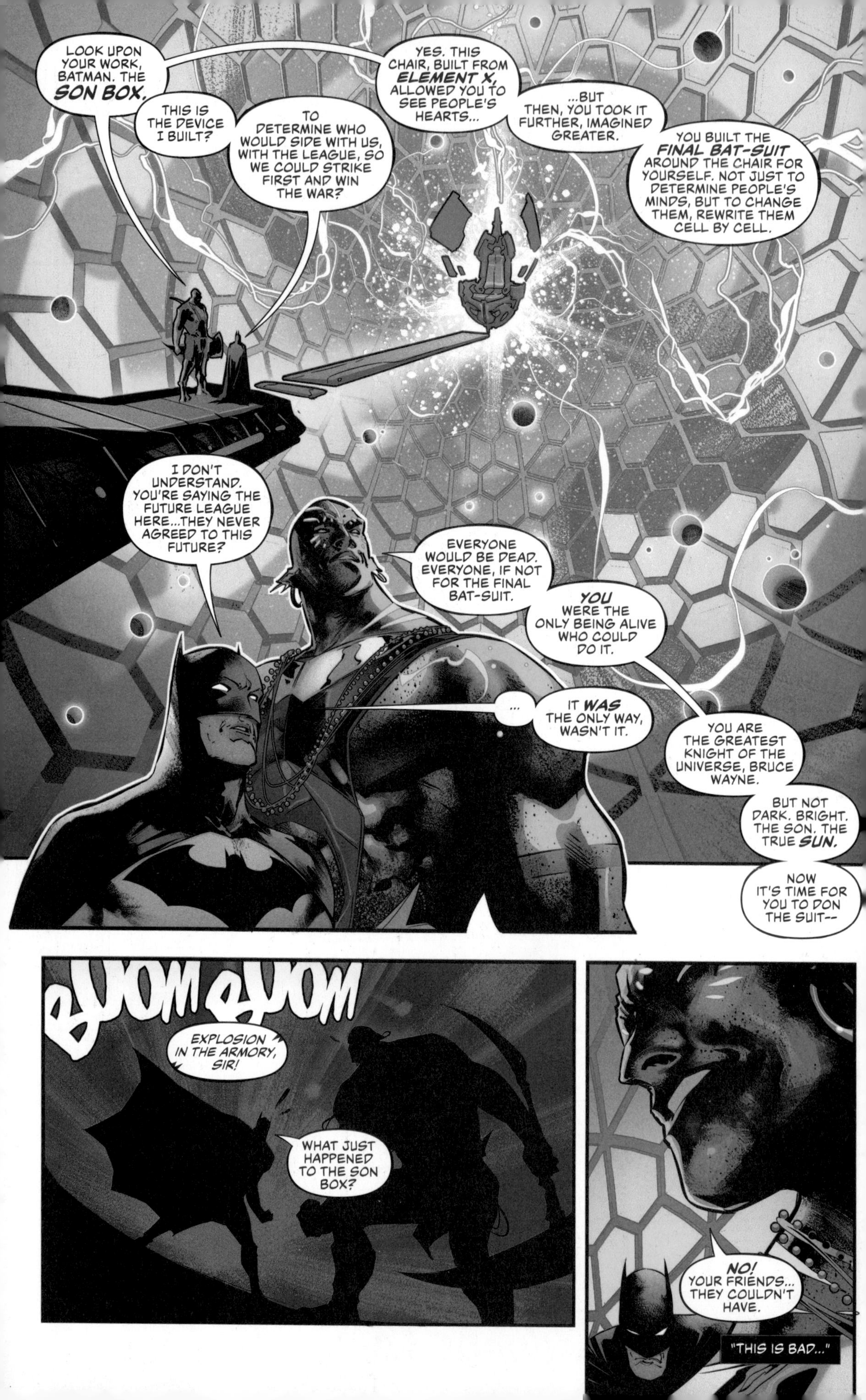
LOOK UPON YOUR WORK, BATMAN. THE SON BOX.
THIS IS THE DEVICE I BUILT?
TO DETERMINE WHO WOULD SIDE WITH US, WITH THE LEAGUE, SO WE COULD STRIKE FIRST AND WIN THE WAR?
YES. THIS CHAIR, BUILT FROM ELEMENT X, ALLOWED YOU TO SEE PEOPLE'S HEARTS...
...BUT THEN, YOU TOOK IT FURTHER, IMAGINED GREATER.
YOU BUILT THE FINAL BAT-SUIT AROUND THE CHAIR FOR YOURSELF. NOT JUST TO DETERMINE PEOPLE'S MINDS, BUT TO CHANGE THEM, REWRITE THEM CELL BY CELL.
I DON'T UNDERSTAND. YOU'RE SAYING THE FUTURE LEAGUE HERE...THEY NEVER AGREED TO THIS FUTURE?
EVERYONE WOULD BE DEAD. EVERYONE, IF NOT FOR THE FINAL BAT-SUIT.
YOU WERE THE ONLY BEING ALIVE WHO COULD DO IT.
...
IT WAS THE ONLY WAY, WASN'T IT.
YOU ARE THE GREATEST KNIGHT OF THE UNIVERSE, BRUCE WAYNE.
BUT NOT DARK. BRIGHT. THE SON. THE TRUE SUN.
NOW IT'S TIME FOR YOU TO DON THE SUIT--
BOOM BOOM
EXPLOSION IN THE ARMORY, SIR!
WHAT JUST HAPPENED TO THE SON BOX?
NO! YOUR FRIENDS... THEY COULDN'T HAVE.
"THIS IS BAD..."

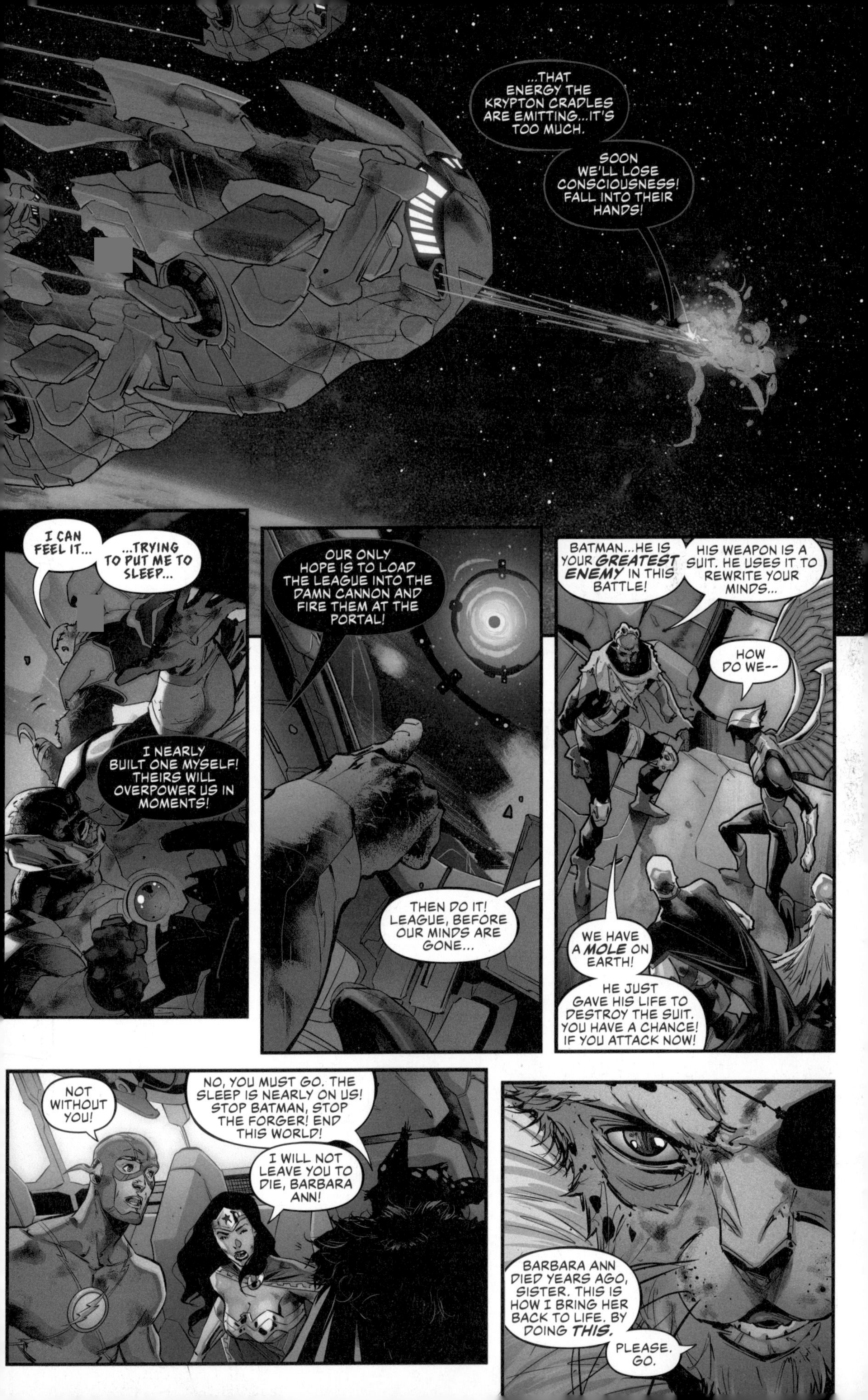
...THAT ENERGY THE KRYPTON CRADLES ARE EMITTING...IT'S TOO MUCH.
SOON WE'LL LOSE CONSCIOUSNESS! FALL INTO THEIR HANDS!
I CAN FEEL IT...
...TRYING TO PUT ME TO SLEEP...
I NEARLY BUILT ONE MYSELF! THEIRS WILL OVERPOWER US IN MOMENTS!
OUR ONLY HOPE IS TO LOAD THE LEAGUE INTO THE DAMN CANNON AND FIRE THEM AT THE PORTAL!
THEN DO IT! LEAGUE, BEFORE OUR MINDS ARE GONE...
BATMAN...HE IS YOUR GREATEST ENEMY IN THIS BATTLE!
HIS WEAPON IS A SUIT. HE USES IT TO REWRITE YOUR MINDS...
HOW DO WE--
WE HAVE A MOLE ON EARTH!
HE JUST GAVE HIS LIFE TO DESTROY THE SUIT. YOU HAVE A CHANCE! IF YOU ATTACK NOW!
NOT WITHOUT YOU!
NO, YOU MUST GO. THE SLEEP IS NEARLY ON US! STOP BATMAN, STOP THE FORGER! END THIS WORLD!
I WILL NOT LEAVE YOU TO DIE, BARBARA ANN!
BARBARA ANN DIED YEARS AGO, SISTER. THIS IS HOW I BRING HER BACK TO LIFE. BY DOING THIS.
PLEASE. GO.

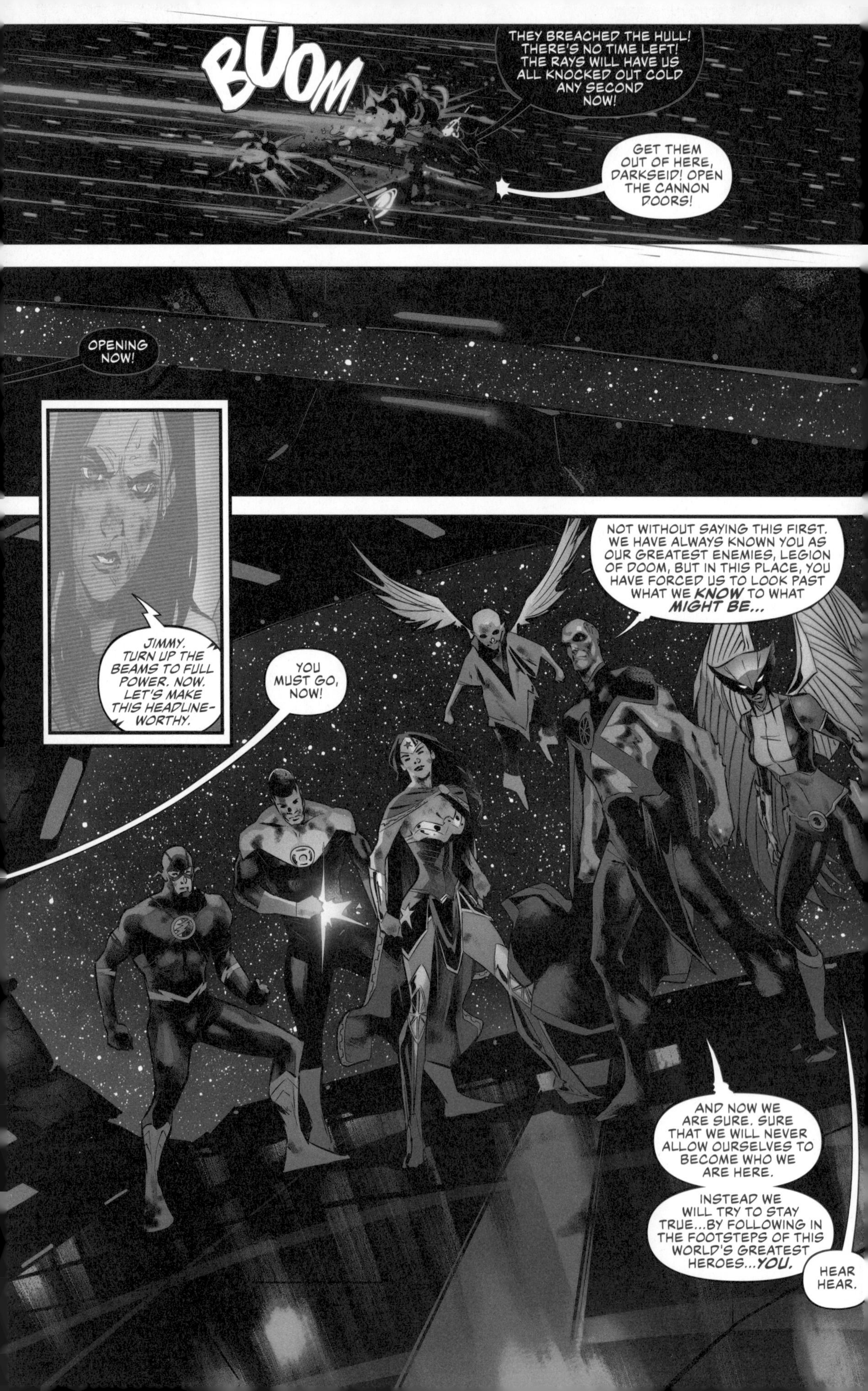
BUOM
THEY BREACHED THE HULL! THERE'S NO TIME LEFT! THE RAYS WILL HAVE US ALL KNOCKED OUT COLD ANY SECOND NOW!
GET THEM OUT OF HERE, DARKSEID! OPEN THE CANNON DOORS!
OPENING NOW!
JIMMY. TURN UP THE BEAMS TO FULL POWER. NOW. LET'S MAKE THIS HEADLINE-WORTHY.
YOU MUST GO, NOW!
NOT WITHOUT SAYING THIS FIRST. WE HAVE ALWAYS KNOWN YOU AS OUR GREATEST ENEMIES, LEGION OF DOOM, BUT IN THIS PLACE, YOU HAVE FORCED US TO LOOK PAST WHAT WE KNOW TO WHAT MIGHT BE...
AND NOW WE ARE SURE. SURE THAT WE WILL NEVER ALLOW OURSELVES TO BECOME WHO WE ARE HERE.
INSTEAD WE WILL TRY TO STAY TRUE...BY FOLLOWING IN THE FOOTSTEPS OF THIS WORLD'S GREATEST HEROES...YOU.
HEAR HEAR.

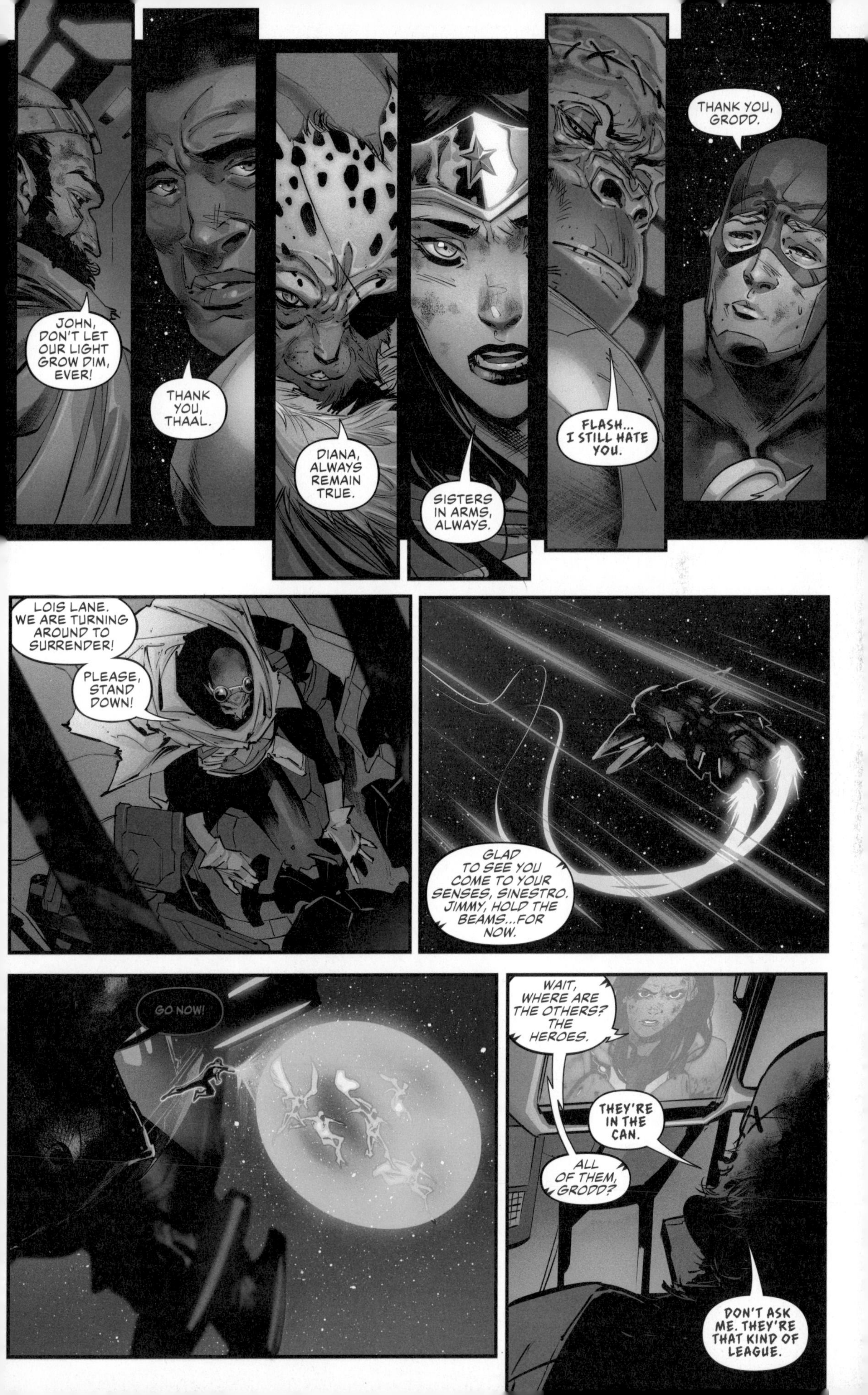
JOHN, DON'T LET OUR LIGHT GROW DIM, EVER!
THANK YOU, THAAL.
DIANA, ALWAYS REMAIN TRUE.
SISTERS IN ARMS, ALWAYS.
FLASH... I STILL HATE YOU.
THANK YOU, GRODD.
LOIS LANE. WE ARE TURNING AROUND TO SURRENDER!
PLEASE, STAND DOWN!
GLAD TO SEE YOU COME TO YOUR SENSES, SINESTRO. JIMMY, HOLD THE BEAMS...FOR NOW.
GO NOW!
WAIT, WHERE ARE THE OTHERS? THE HEROES.
THEY'RE IN THE CAN.
ALL OF THEM, GRODD?
DON'T ASK ME. THEY'RE THAT KIND OF LEAGUE.

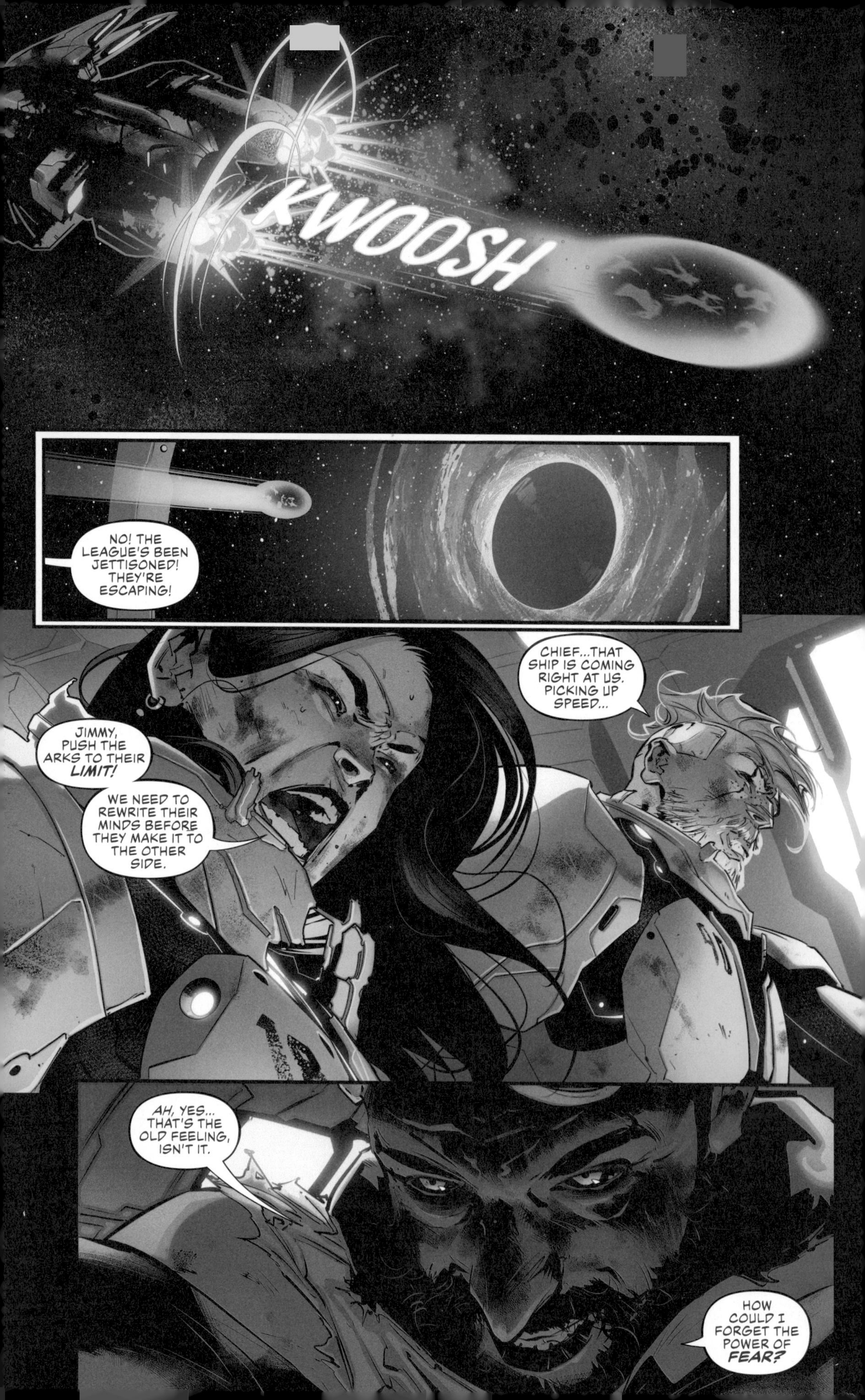
KWOOSH
NO! THE LEAGUE'S BEEN JETTISONED! THEY'RE ESCAPING!
CHIEF...THAT SHIP IS COMING RIGHT AT US. PICKING UP SPEED...
JIMMY, PUSH THE ARKS TO THEIR *LIMIT!*
WE NEED TO REWRITE THEIR MINDS BEFORE THEY MAKE IT TO THE OTHER SIDE.
AH, YES... THAT'S THE OLD FEELING, ISN'T IT.
HOW COULD I FORGET THE POWER OF ***FEAR?***

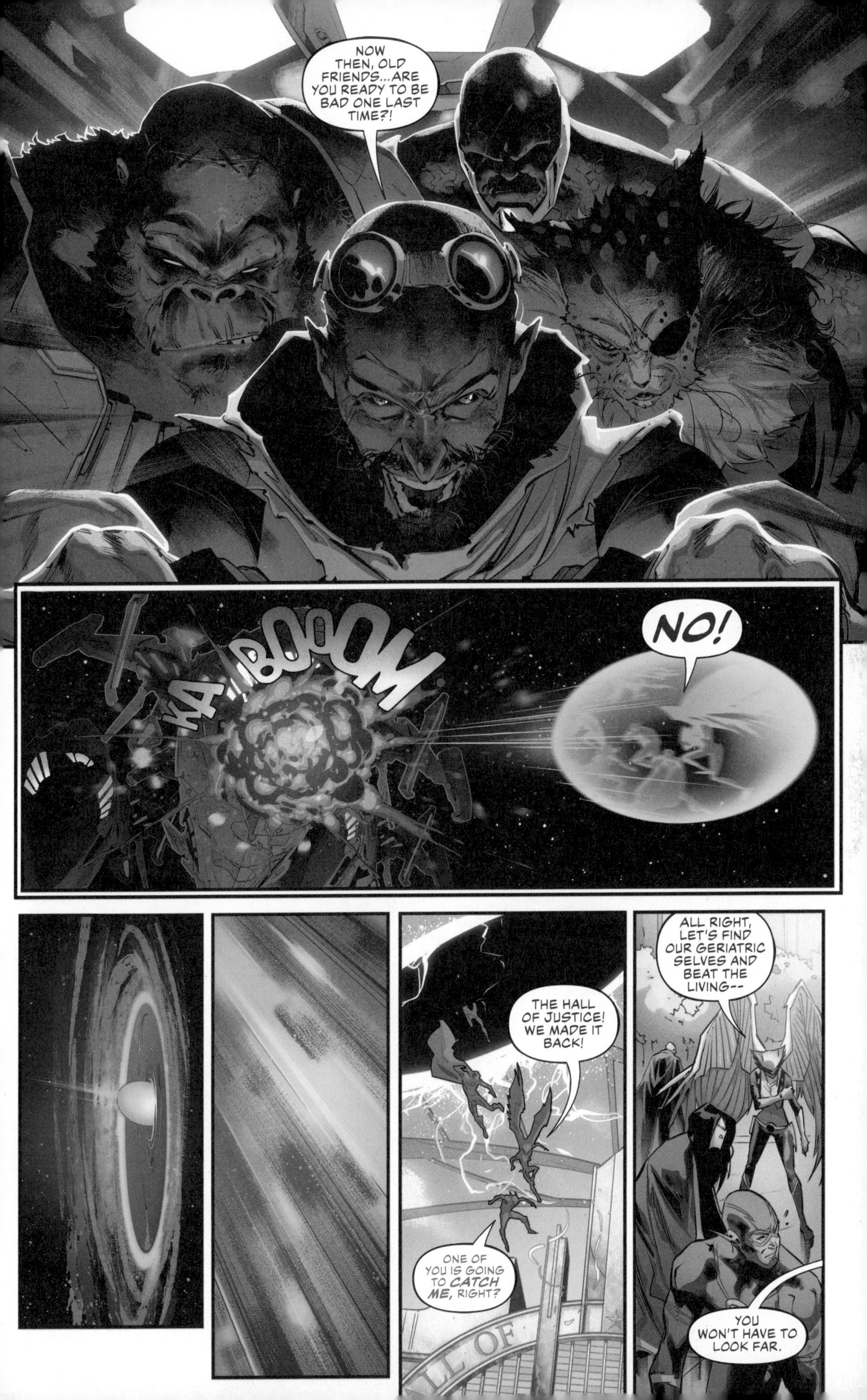
NOW THEN, OLD FRIENDS...ARE YOU READY TO BE BAD ONE LAST TIME?!
KA BOOOM
NO!
THE HALL OF JUSTICE! WE MADE IT BACK!
ONE OF YOU IS GOING TO CATCH ME, RIGHT?
ALL RIGHT, LET'S FIND OUR GERIATRIC SELVES AND BEAT THE LIVING--
YOU WON'T HAVE TO LOOK FAR.

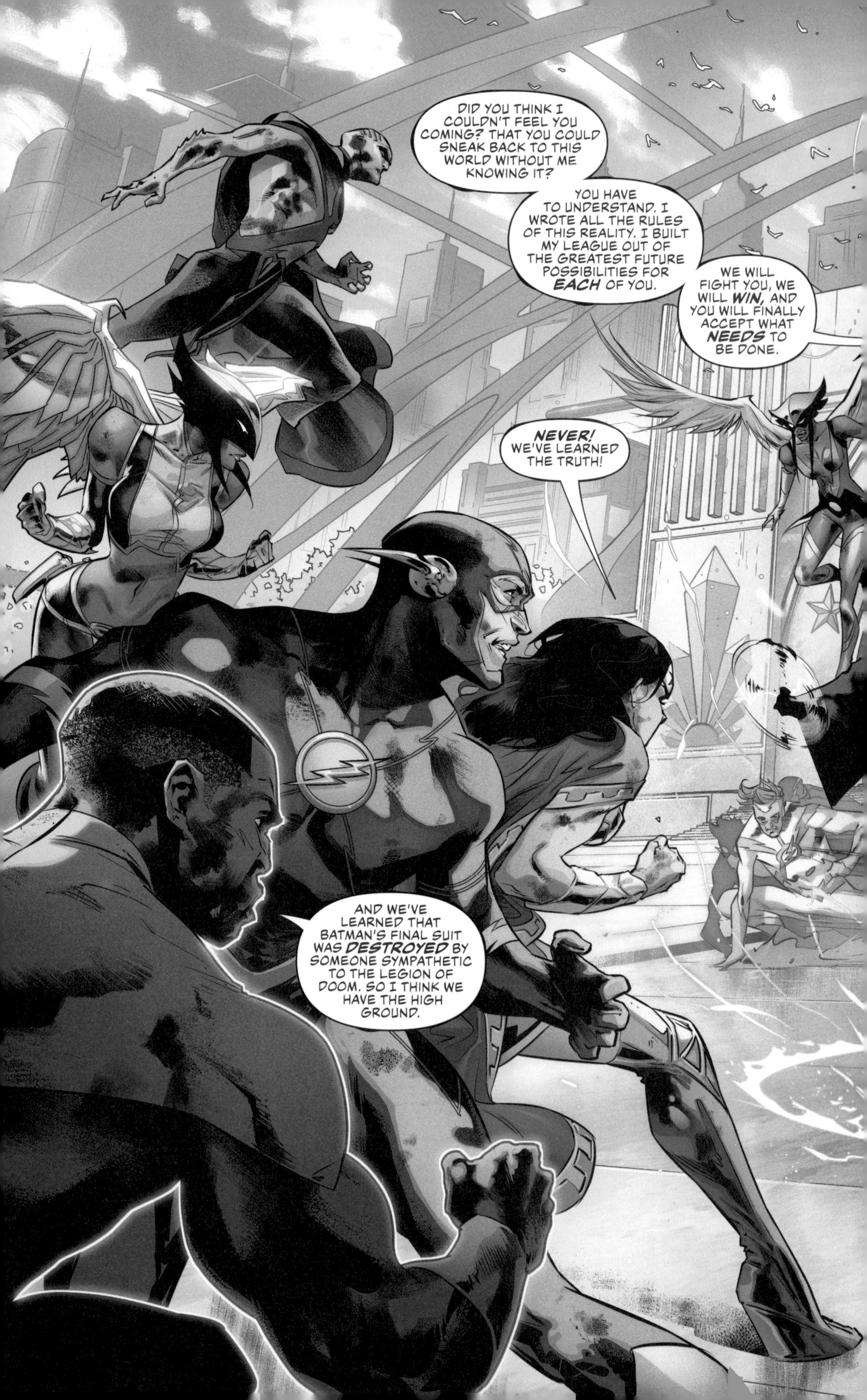
DID YOU THINK I COULDN'T FEEL YOU COMING? THAT YOU COULD SNEAK BACK TO THIS WORLD WITHOUT ME KNOWING IT?
YOU HAVE TO UNDERSTAND. I WROTE ALL THE RULES OF THIS REALITY. I BUILT MY LEAGUE OUT OF THE GREATEST FUTURE POSSIBILITIES FOR *EACH* OF YOU.
WE WILL FIGHT YOU, WE WILL *WIN,* AND YOU WILL FINALLY ACCEPT WHAT *NEEDS* TO BE DONE.
NEVER! WE'VE LEARNED THE TRUTH!
AND WE'VE LEARNED THAT BATMAN'S FINAL SUIT WAS *DESTROYED* BY SOMEONE SYMPATHETIC TO THE LEGION OF DOOM. SO I THINK WE HAVE THE HIGH GROUND.

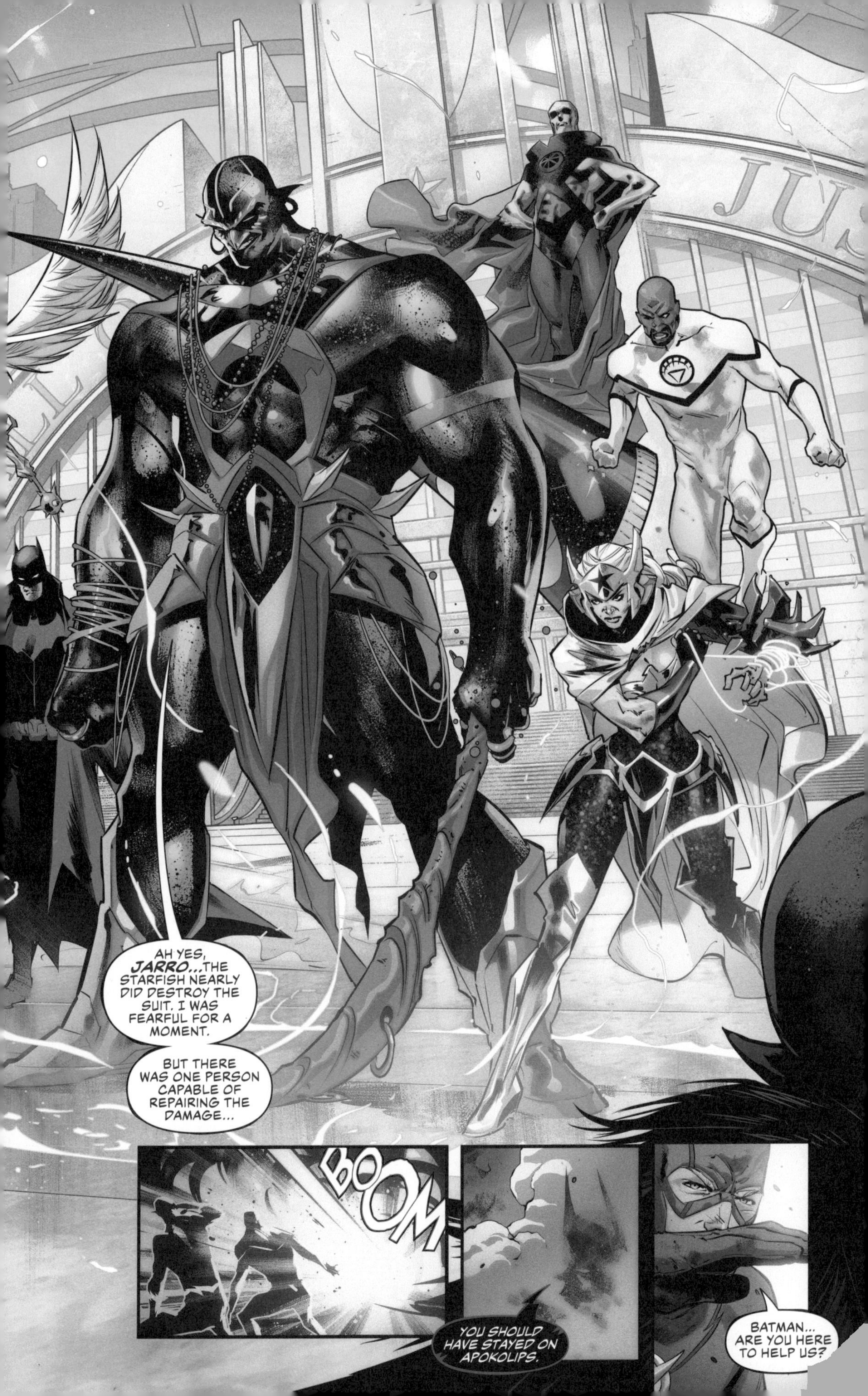

AH YES, JARRO... THE STARFISH NEARLY DID DESTROY THE SUIT. I WAS FEARFUL FOR A MOMENT.
BUT THERE WAS ONE PERSON CAPABLE OF REPAIRING THE DAMAGE...
BOOM
YOU SHOULD HAVE STAYED ON APOKOLIPS.
BATMAN... ARE YOU HERE TO HELP US?

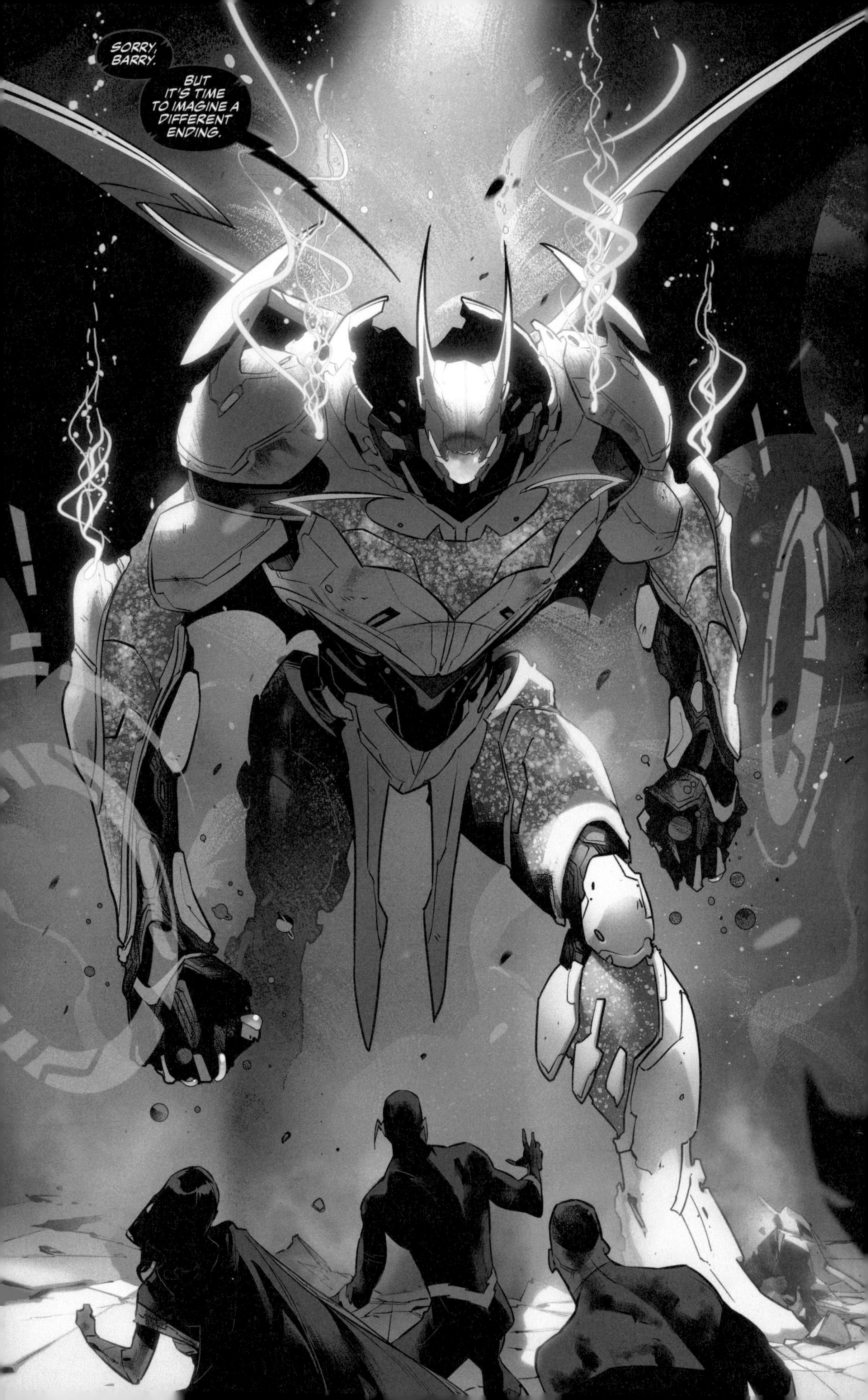
SORRY, BARRY.
BUT IT'S TIME TO IMAGINE A DIFFERENT ENDING.

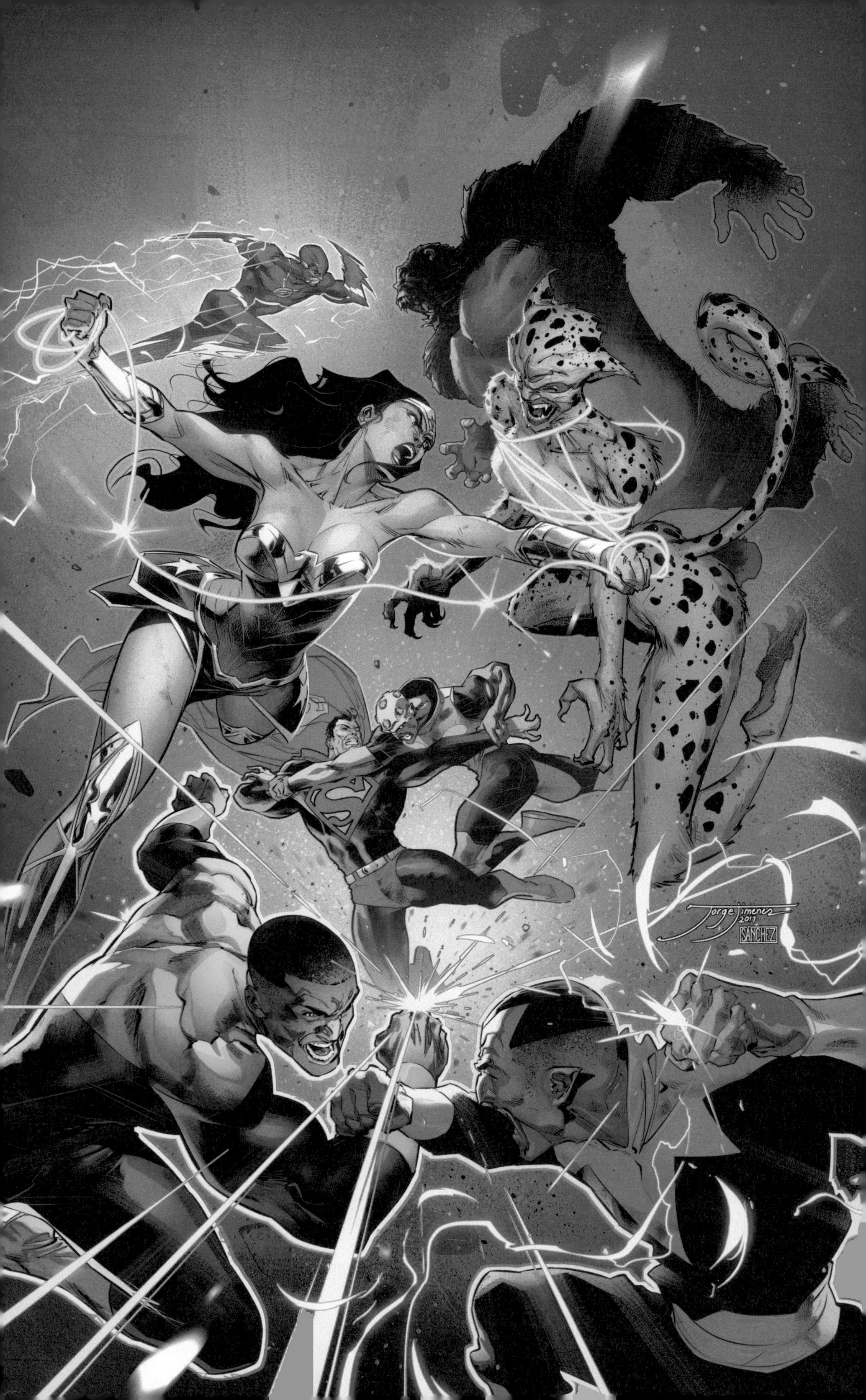
Jorge Jimenez 2019
SÁNCHEZ

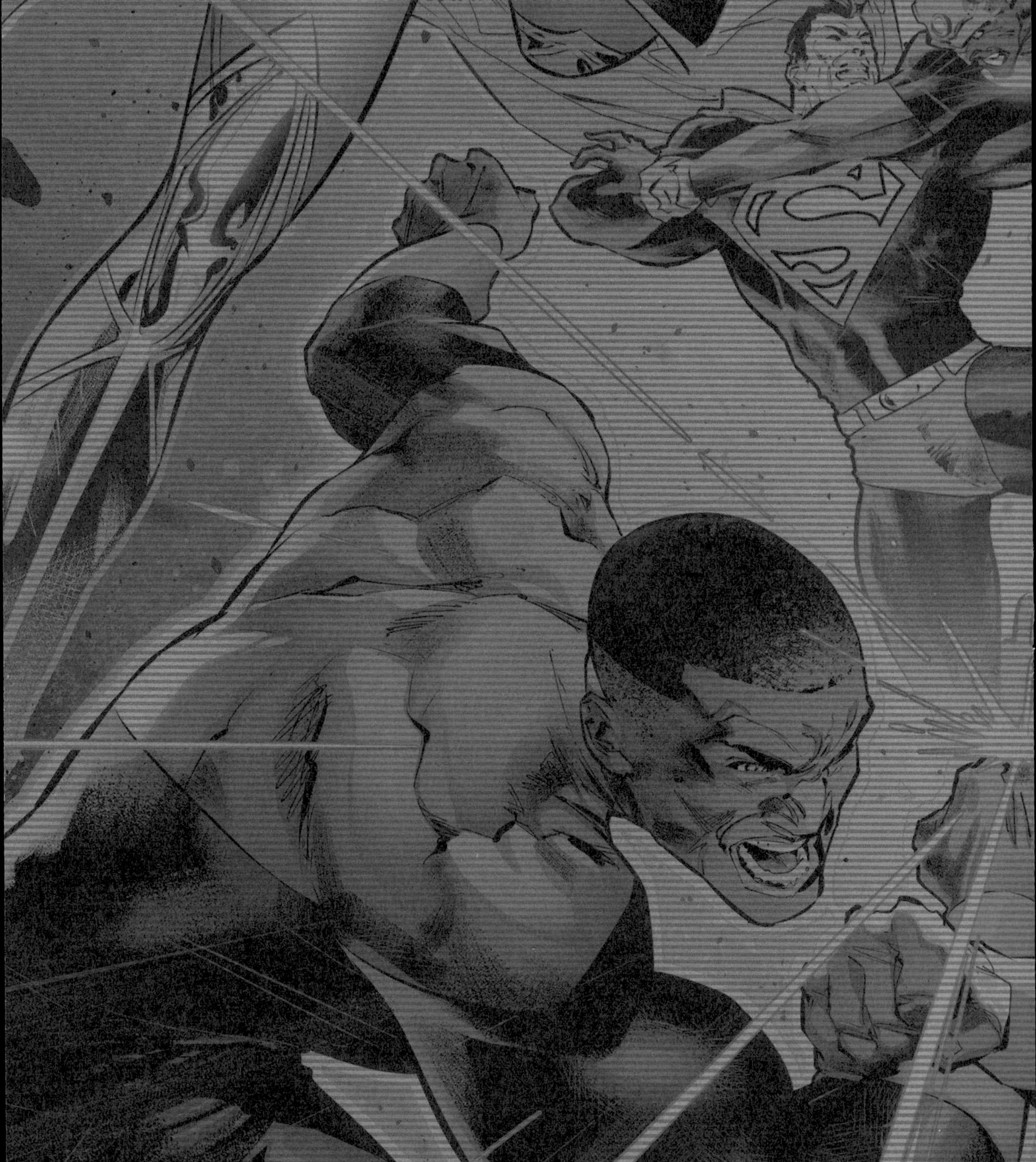

JUSTICE
LEAGUE
#25

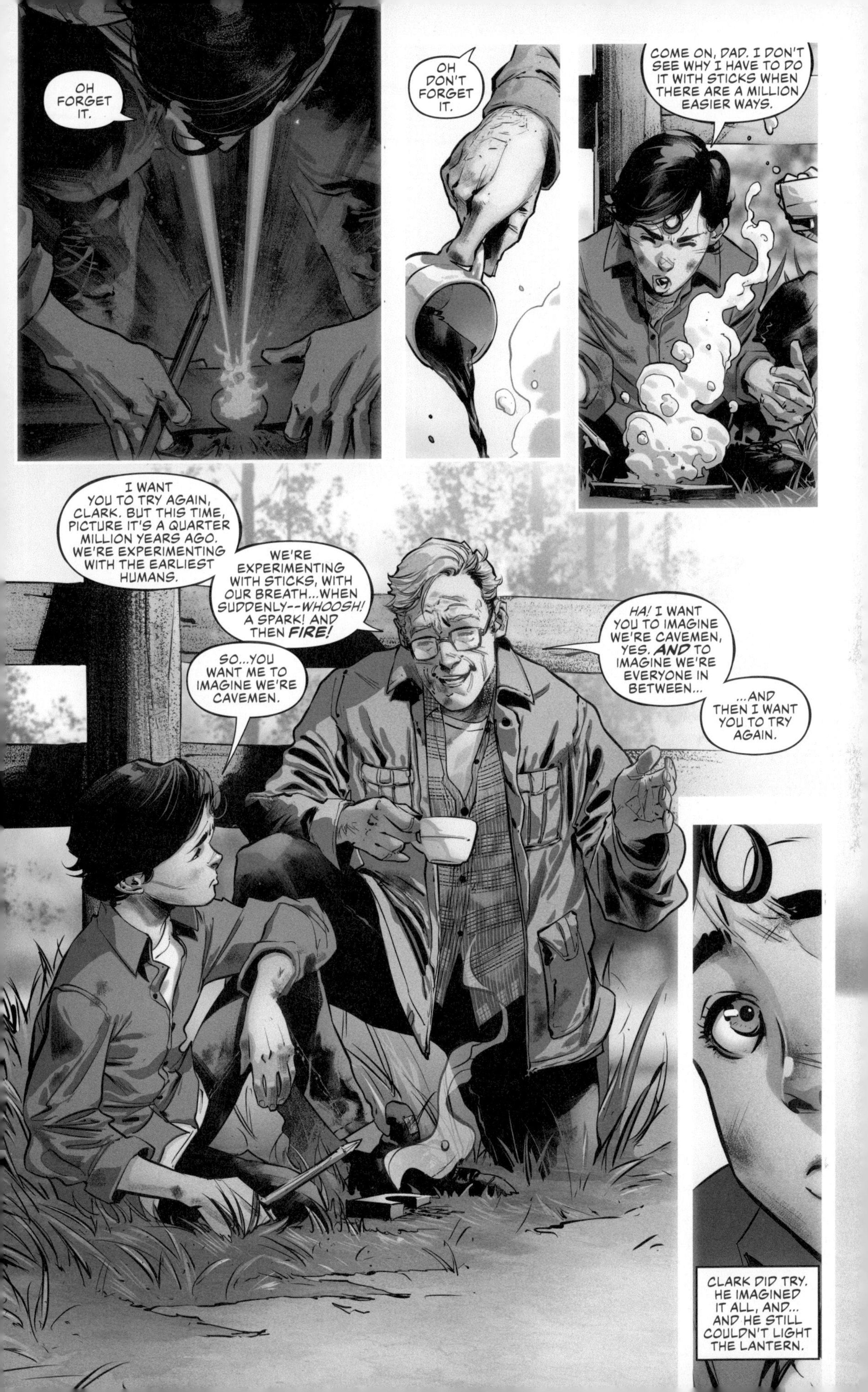
OH FORGET IT.
OH DON'T FORGET IT.
COME ON, DAD. I DON'T SEE WHY I HAVE TO DO IT WITH STICKS WHEN THERE ARE A MILLION EASIER WAYS.
I WANT YOU TO TRY AGAIN, CLARK. BUT THIS TIME, PICTURE IT'S A QUARTER MILLION YEARS AGO. WE'RE EXPERIMENTING WITH THE EARLIEST HUMANS.
WE'RE EXPERIMENTING WITH STICKS, WITH OUR BREATH...WHEN SUDDENLY--*WHOOSH!* A SPARK! AND THEN ***FIRE!***
SO...YOU WANT ME TO IMAGINE WE'RE CAVEMEN.
HA! I WANT YOU TO IMAGINE WE'RE CAVEMEN, YES. ***AND*** TO IMAGINE WE'RE EVERYONE IN BETWEEN...
...AND THEN I WANT YOU TO TRY AGAIN.
CLARK DID TRY. HE IMAGINED IT ALL, AND... AND HE STILL COULDN'T LIGHT THE LANTERN.

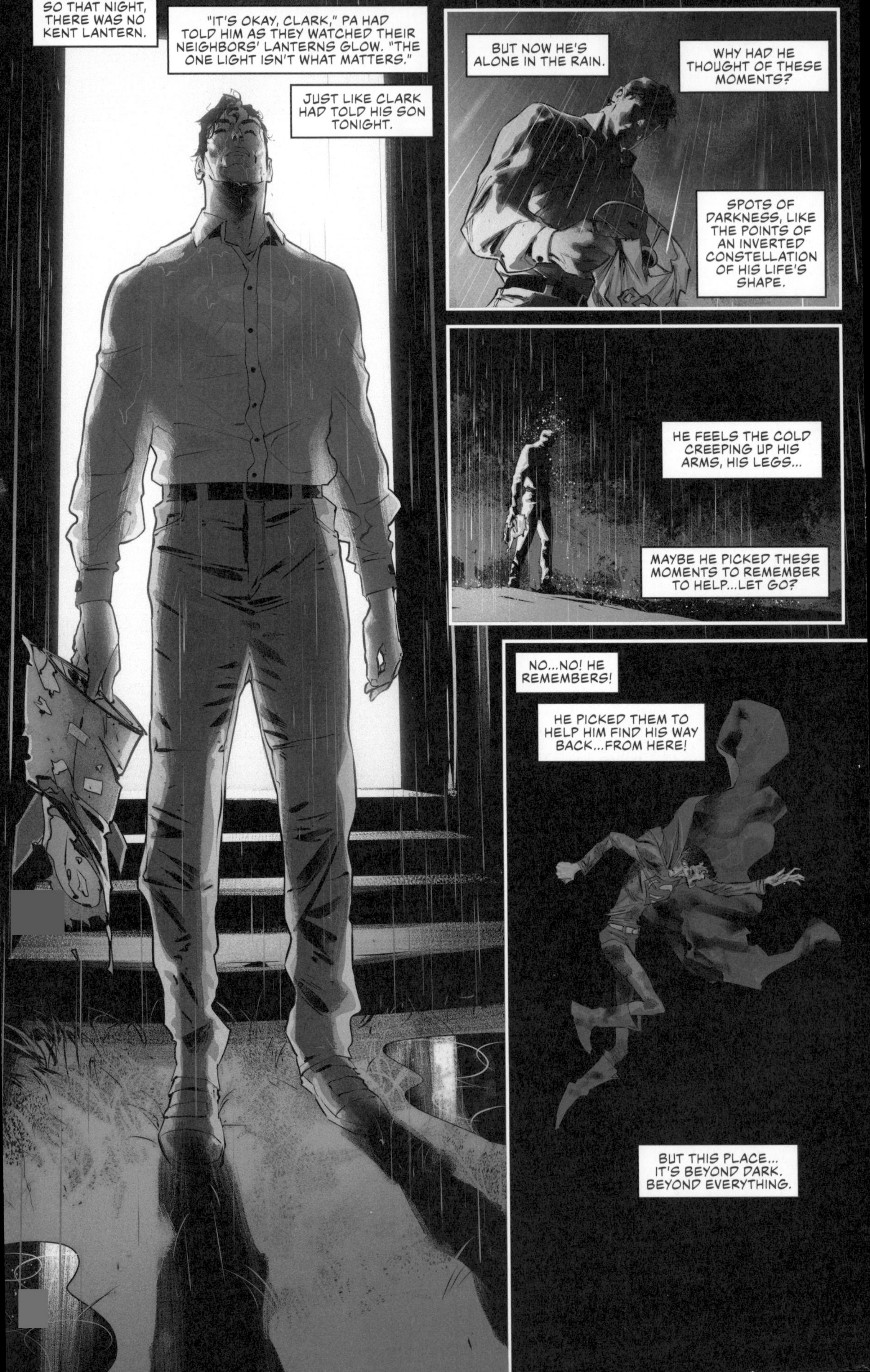

SO THAT NIGHT, THERE WAS NO KENT LANTERN.
"IT'S OKAY, CLARK," PA HAD TOLD HIM AS THEY WATCHED THEIR NEIGHBORS' LANTERNS GLOW. "THE ONE LIGHT ISN'T WHAT MATTERS."
JUST LIKE CLARK HAD TOLD HIS SON TONIGHT.
BUT NOW HE'S ALONE IN THE RAIN.
WHY HAD HE THOUGHT OF THESE MOMENTS?
SPOTS OF DARKNESS, LIKE THE POINTS OF AN INVERTED CONSTELLATION OF HIS LIFE'S SHAPE.
HE FEELS THE COLD CREEPING UP HIS ARMS, HIS LEGS...
MAYBE HE PICKED THESE MOMENTS TO REMEMBER TO HELP...LET GO?
NO...NO! HE REMEMBERS!
HE PICKED THEM TO HELP HIM FIND HIS WAY BACK...FROM HERE!
BUT THIS PLACE... IT'S BEYOND DARK. BEYOND EVERYTHING.

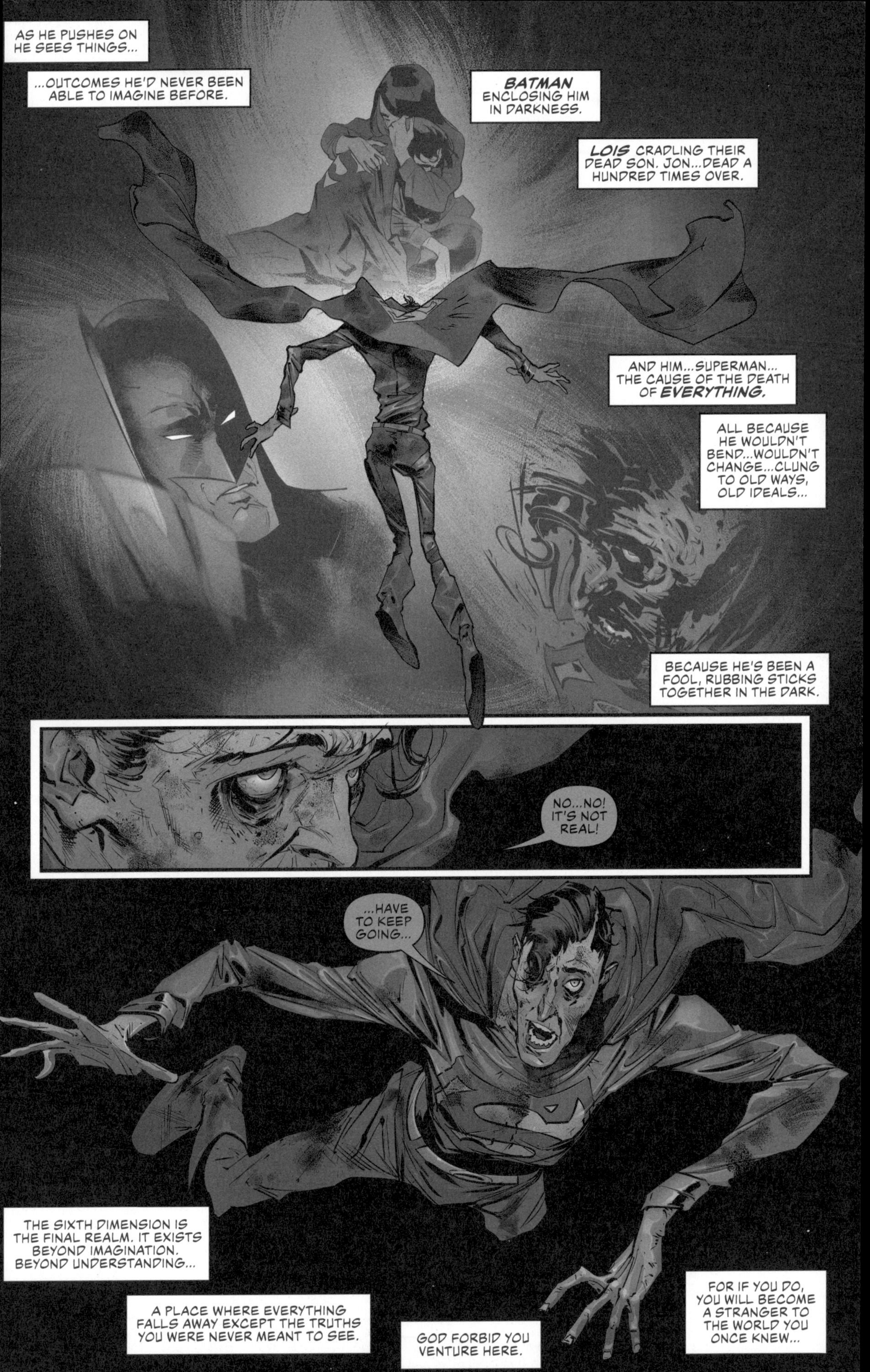
AS HE PUSHES ON HE SEES THINGS...
...OUTCOMES HE'D NEVER BEEN ABLE TO IMAGINE BEFORE.
BATMAN ENCLOSING HIM IN DARKNESS.
LOIS CRADLING THEIR DEAD SON. JON...DEAD A HUNDRED TIMES OVER.
AND HIM...SUPERMAN... THE CAUSE OF THE DEATH OF EVERYTHING.
ALL BECAUSE HE WOULDN'T BEND...WOULDN'T CHANGE...CLUNG TO OLD WAYS, OLD IDEALS...
BECAUSE HE'S BEEN A FOOL, RUBBING STICKS TOGETHER IN THE DARK.
NO...NO! IT'S NOT REAL!
...HAVE TO KEEP GOING...
THE SIXTH DIMENSION IS THE FINAL REALM. IT EXISTS BEYOND IMAGINATION. BEYOND UNDERSTANDING...
A PLACE WHERE EVERYTHING FALLS AWAY EXCEPT THE TRUTHS YOU WERE NEVER MEANT TO SEE.
GOD FORBID YOU VENTURE HERE.
FOR IF YOU DO, YOU WILL BECOME A STRANGER TO THE WORLD YOU ONCE KNEW...

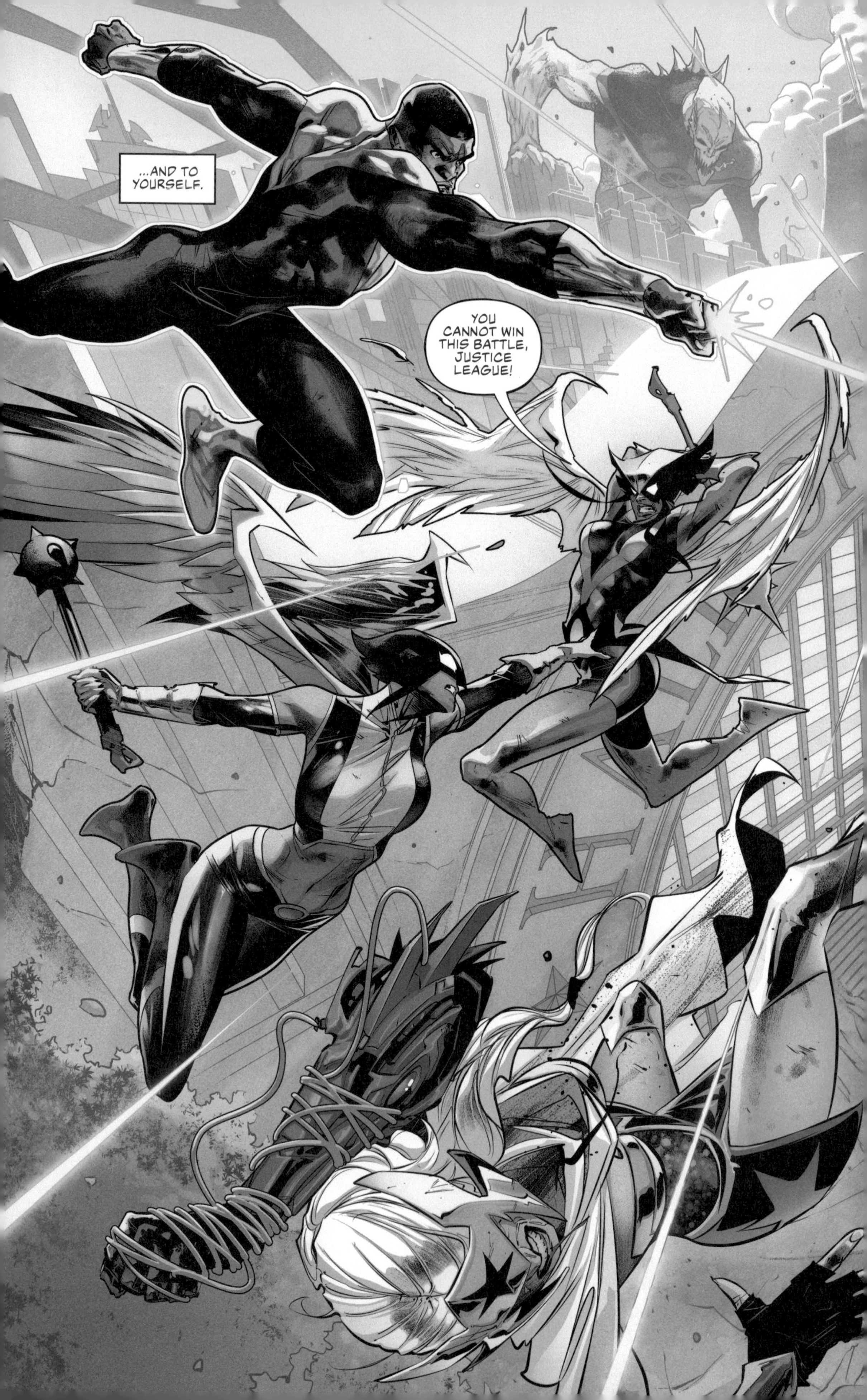
...AND TO YOURSELF.
YOU CANNOT WIN THIS BATTLE, JUSTICE LEAGUE!

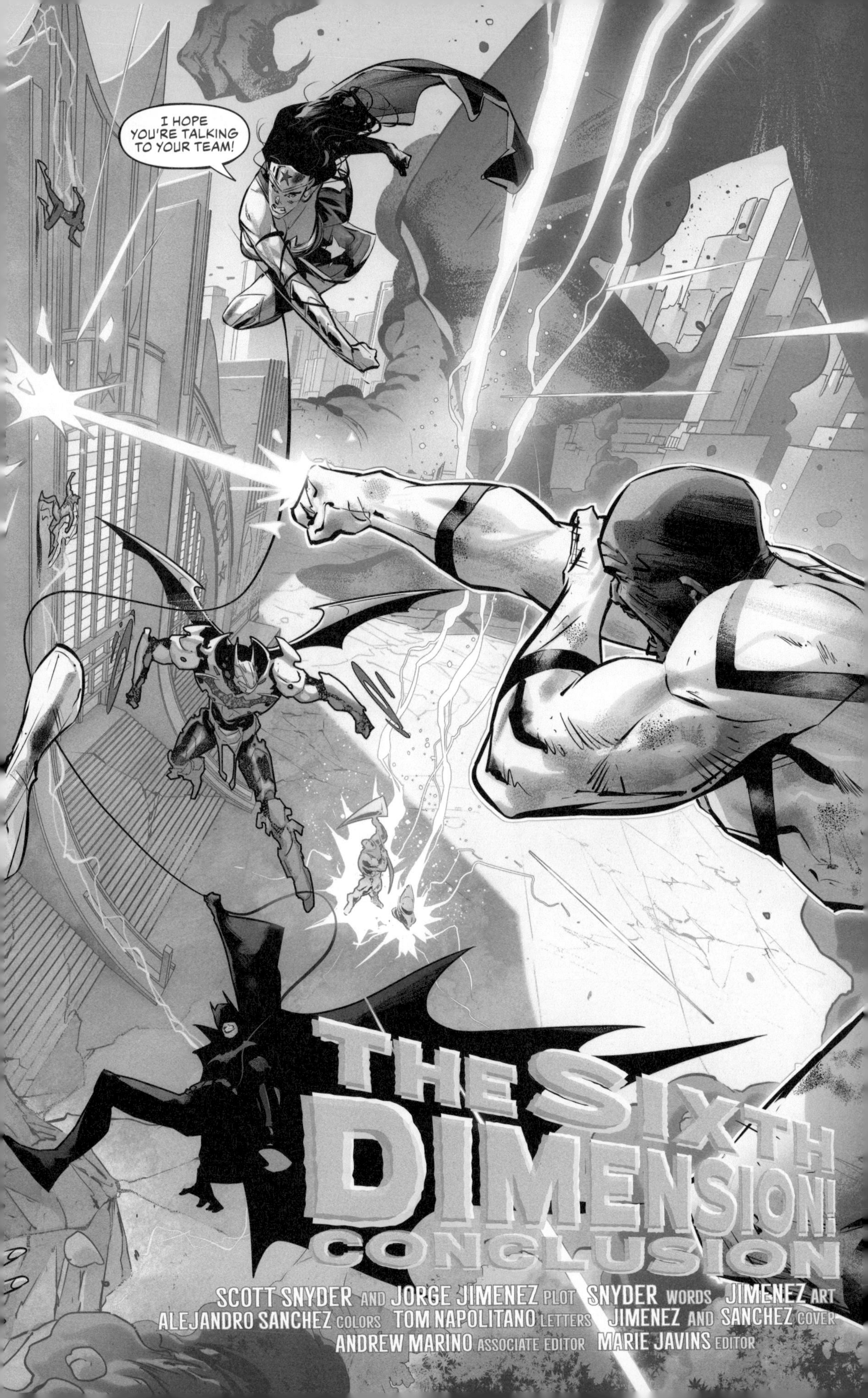

I HOPE YOU'RE TALKING TO YOUR TEAM!
THE SIXTH DIMENSION! CONCLUSION
SCOTT SNYDER AND JORGE JIMENEZ PLOT SNYDER WORDS JIMENEZ ART
ALEJANDRO SANCHEZ COLORS TOM NAPOLITANO LETTERS JIMENEZ AND SANCHEZ COVER
ANDREW MARINO ASSOCIATE EDITOR MARIE JAVINS EDITOR

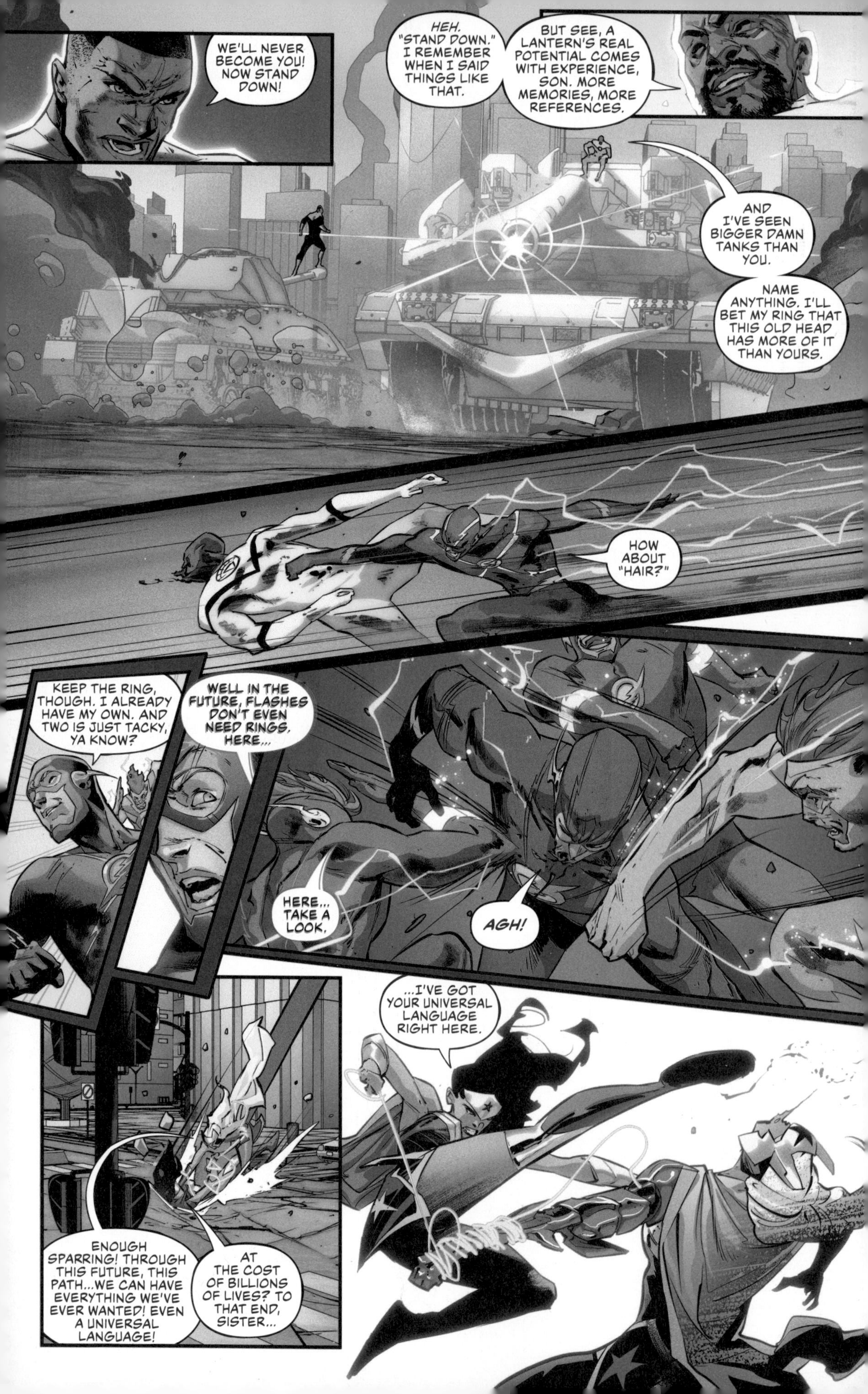
WE'LL NEVER BECOME YOU! NOW STAND DOWN!
HEH. "STAND DOWN." I REMEMBER WHEN I SAID THINGS LIKE THAT.
BUT SEE, A LANTERN'S REAL POTENTIAL COMES WITH EXPERIENCE, SON. MORE MEMORIES, MORE REFERENCES.
AND I'VE SEEN BIGGER DAMN TANKS THAN YOU.
NAME ANYTHING. I'LL BET MY RING THAT THIS OLD HEAD HAS MORE OF IT THAN YOURS.
HOW ABOUT "HAIR?"
KEEP THE RING, THOUGH. I ALREADY HAVE MY OWN. AND TWO IS JUST TACKY, YA KNOW?
WELL IN THE FUTURE, FLASHES DON'T EVEN NEED RINGS. HERE...
HERE... TAKE A LOOK.
AGH!
ENOUGH SPARRING! THROUGH THIS FUTURE, THIS PATH...WE CAN HAVE EVERYTHING WE'VE EVER WANTED! EVEN A UNIVERSAL LANGUAGE!
AT THE COST OF BILLIONS OF LIVES? TO THAT END, SISTER...
...I'VE GOT YOUR UNIVERSAL LANGUAGE RIGHT HERE.

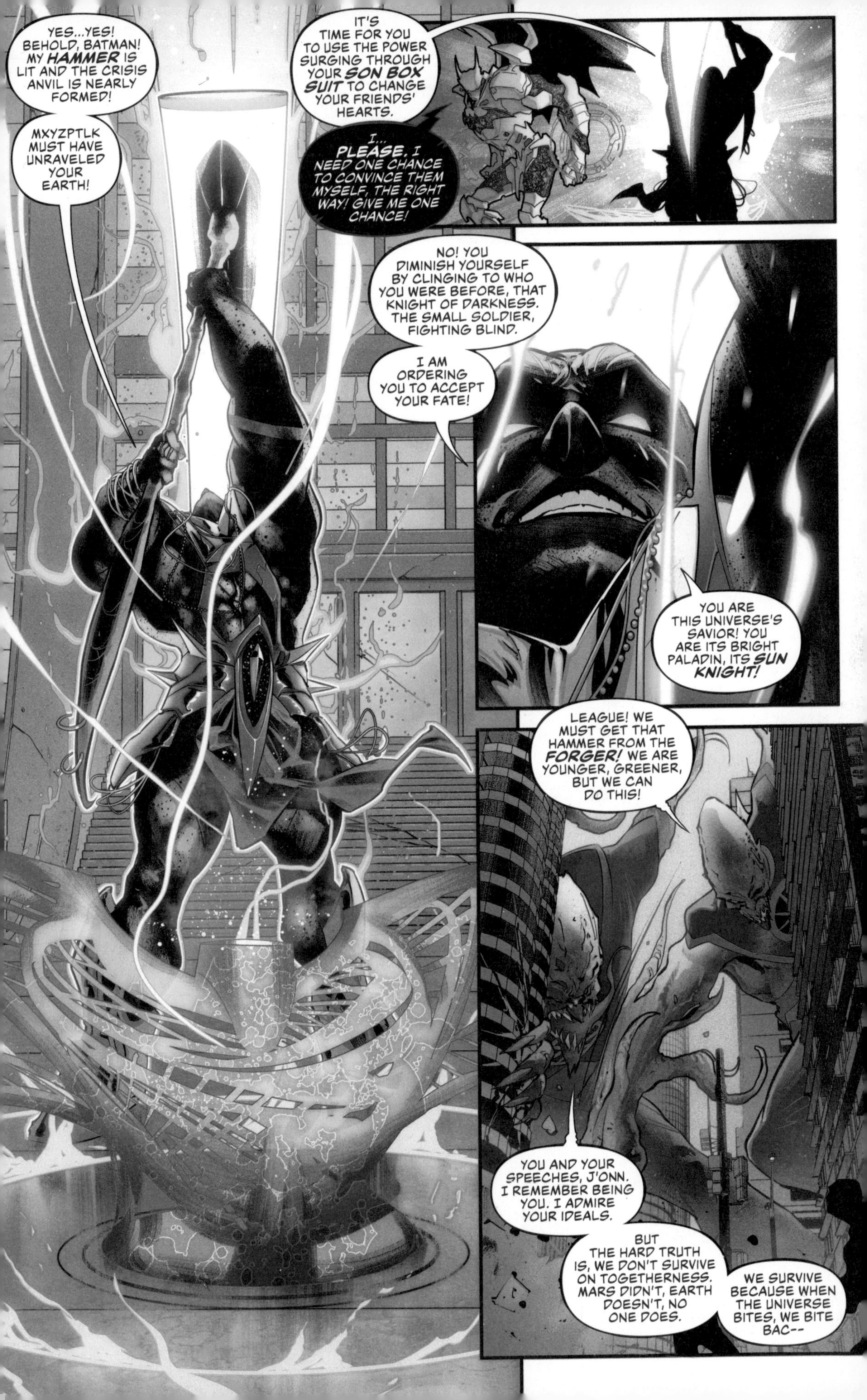
YES...YES! BEHOLD, BATMAN! MY HAMMER IS LIT AND THE CRISIS ANVIL IS NEARLY FORMED!
MXYZPTLK MUST HAVE UNRAVELED YOUR EARTH!
IT'S TIME FOR YOU TO USE THE POWER SURGING THROUGH YOUR SON BOX SUIT TO CHANGE YOUR FRIENDS' HEARTS.
I... PLEASE. I NEED ONE CHANCE TO CONVINCE THEM MYSELF, THE RIGHT WAY! GIVE ME ONE CHANCE!
NO! YOU DIMINISH YOURSELF BY CLINGING TO WHO YOU WERE BEFORE, THAT KNIGHT OF DARKNESS. THE SMALL SOLDIER, FIGHTING BLIND.
I AM ORDERING YOU TO ACCEPT YOUR FATE!
YOU ARE THIS UNIVERSE'S SAVIOR! YOU ARE ITS BRIGHT PALADIN, ITS SUN KNIGHT!
LEAGUE! WE MUST GET THAT HAMMER FROM THE FORGER! WE ARE YOUNGER, GREENER, BUT WE CAN DO THIS!
YOU AND YOUR SPEECHES, J'ONN. I REMEMBER BEING YOU. I ADMIRE YOUR IDEALS.
BUT THE HARD TRUTH IS, WE DON'T SURVIVE ON TOGETHERNESS. MARS DIDN'T, EARTH DOESN'T, NO ONE DOES.
WE SURVIVE BECAUSE WHEN THE UNIVERSE BITES, WE BITE BAC--

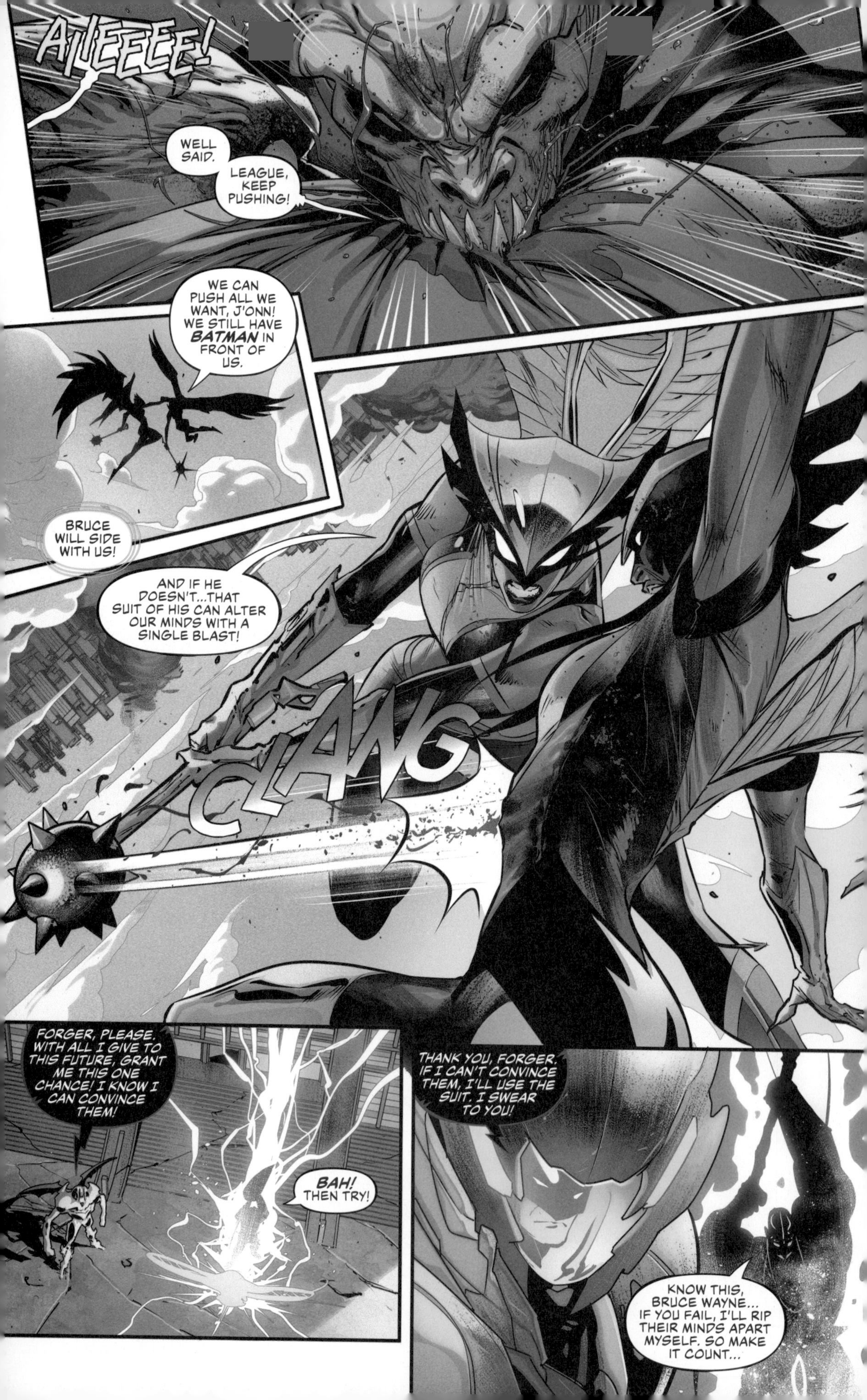

AIIEEEEE!
WELL SAID.
LEAGUE, KEEP PUSHING!
WE CAN PUSH ALL WE WANT, J'ONN! WE STILL HAVE BATMAN IN FRONT OF US.
BRUCE WILL SIDE WITH US!
AND IF HE DOESN'T...THAT SUIT OF HIS CAN ALTER OUR MINDS WITH A SINGLE BLAST!
CLANG
FORGER, PLEASE. WITH ALL I GIVE TO THIS FUTURE, GRANT ME THIS ONE CHANCE! I KNOW I CAN CONVINCE THEM!
BAH! THEN TRY!
THANK YOU, FORGER. IF I CAN'T CONVINCE THEM, I'LL USE THE SUIT. I SWEAR TO YOU!
KNOW THIS, BRUCE WAYNE... IF YOU FAIL, I'LL RIP THEIR MINDS APART MYSELF. SO MAKE IT COUNT...

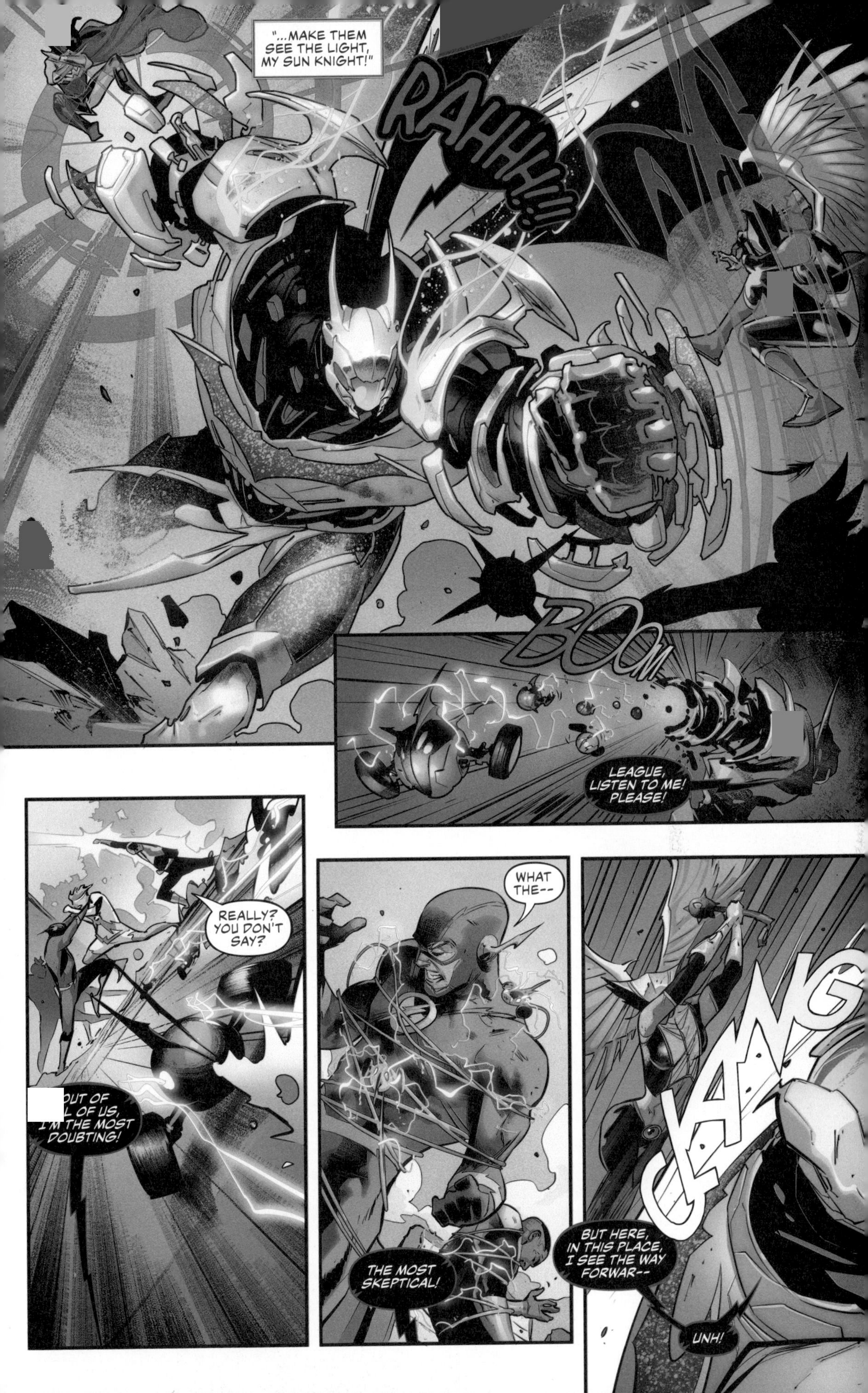
"...MAKE THEM SEE THE LIGHT, MY SUN KNIGHT!"
RAHHH!!!
BOOM
LEAGUE, LISTEN TO ME! PLEASE!
REALLY? YOU DON'T SAY?
OUT OF L OF US, I'M THE MOST DOUBTING!
WHAT THE--
THE MOST SKEPTICAL!
BUT HERE, IN THIS PLACE, I SEE THE WAY FORWAR--
CLANG
UNH!

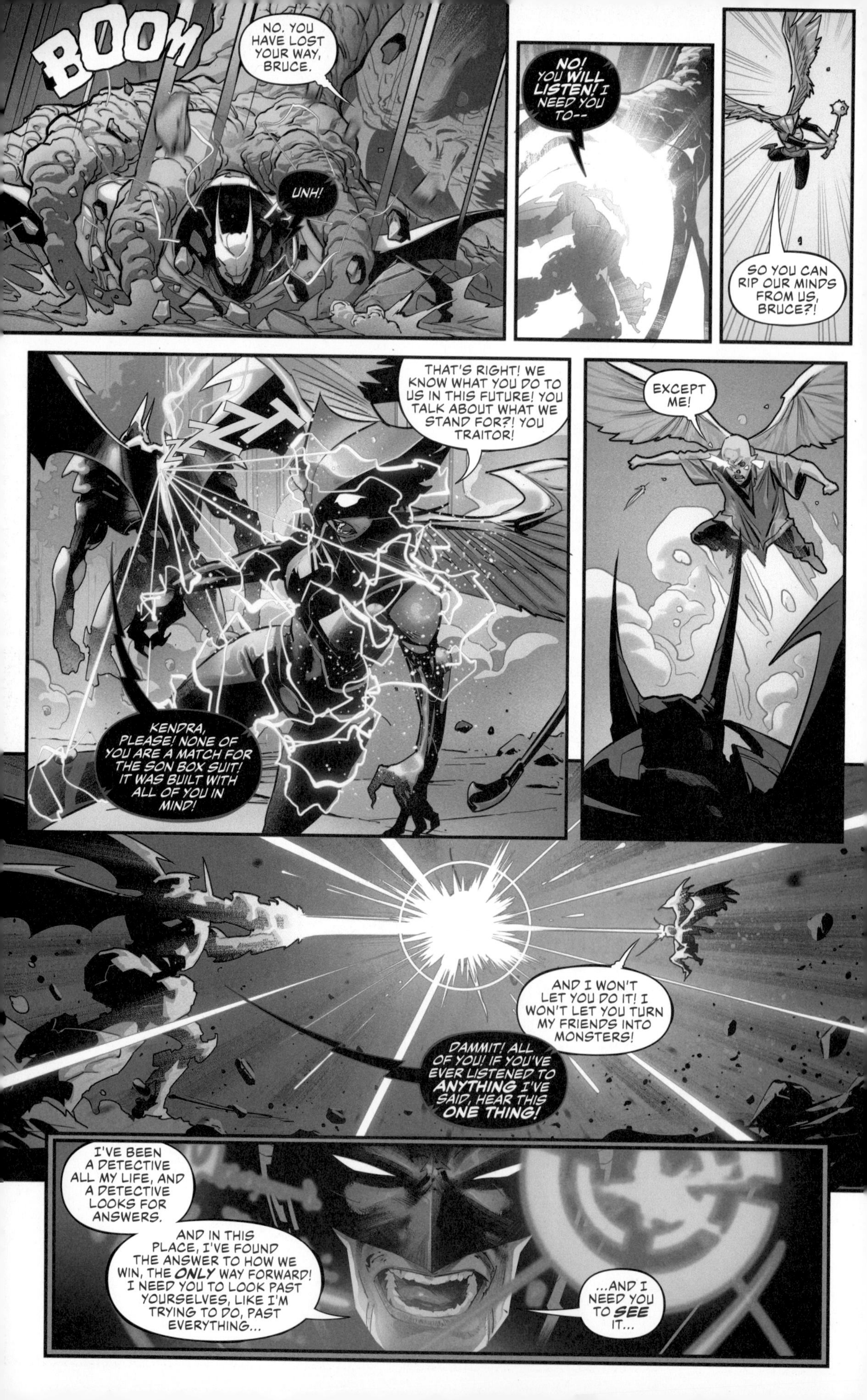

BOOM
NO. YOU HAVE LOST YOUR WAY, BRUCE.
UNH!
NO! YOU WILL LISTEN! I NEED YOU TO--
SO YOU CAN RIP OUR MINDS FROM US, BRUCE?!
ZZZT
THAT'S RIGHT! WE KNOW WHAT YOU DO TO US IN THIS FUTURE! YOU TALK ABOUT WHAT WE STAND FOR?! YOU TRAITOR!
KENDRA, PLEASE! NONE OF YOU ARE A MATCH FOR THE SON BOX SUIT! IT WAS BUILT WITH ALL OF YOU IN MIND!
EXCEPT ME!
AND I WON'T LET YOU DO IT! I WON'T LET YOU TURN MY FRIENDS INTO MONSTERS!
DAMMIT! ALL OF YOU! IF YOU'VE EVER LISTENED TO ANYTHING I'VE SAID, HEAR THIS ONE THING!
I'VE BEEN A DETECTIVE ALL MY LIFE, AND A DETECTIVE LOOKS FOR ANSWERS.
AND IN THIS PLACE, I'VE FOUND THE ANSWER TO HOW WE WIN, THE ONLY WAY FORWARD! I NEED YOU TO LOOK PAST YOURSELVES, LIKE I'M TRYING TO DO, PAST EVERYTHING...
...AND I NEED YOU TO SEE IT...

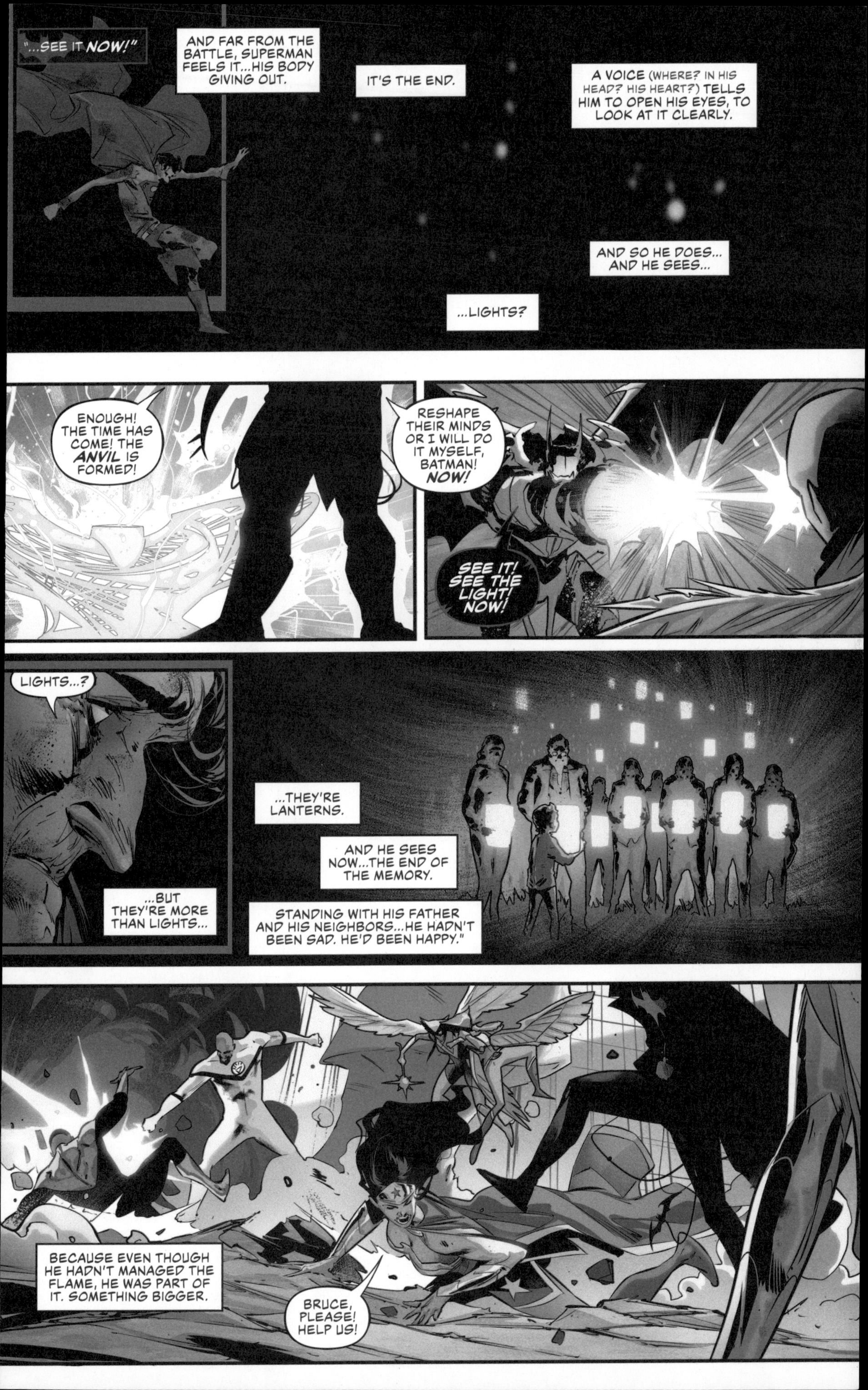
"...SEE IT NOW!"
AND FAR FROM THE BATTLE, SUPERMAN FEELS IT...HIS BODY GIVING OUT.
IT'S THE END.
A VOICE (WHERE? IN HIS HEAD? HIS HEART?) TELLS HIM TO OPEN HIS EYES, TO LOOK AT IT CLEARLY.
AND SO HE DOES... AND HE SEES...
...LIGHTS?
ENOUGH! THE TIME HAS COME! THE ANVIL IS FORMED!
RESHAPE THEIR MINDS OR I WILL DO IT MYSELF, BATMAN! NOW!
SEE IT! SEE THE LIGHT! NOW!
LIGHTS...?
...BUT THEY'RE MORE THAN LIGHTS...
...THEY'RE LANTERNS.
AND HE SEES NOW...THE END OF THE MEMORY.
STANDING WITH HIS FATHER AND HIS NEIGHBORS...HE HADN'T BEEN SAD. HE'D BEEN HAPPY."
BECAUSE EVEN THOUGH HE HADN'T MANAGED THE FLAME, HE WAS PART OF IT. SOMETHING BIGGER.
BRUCE, PLEASE! HELP US!

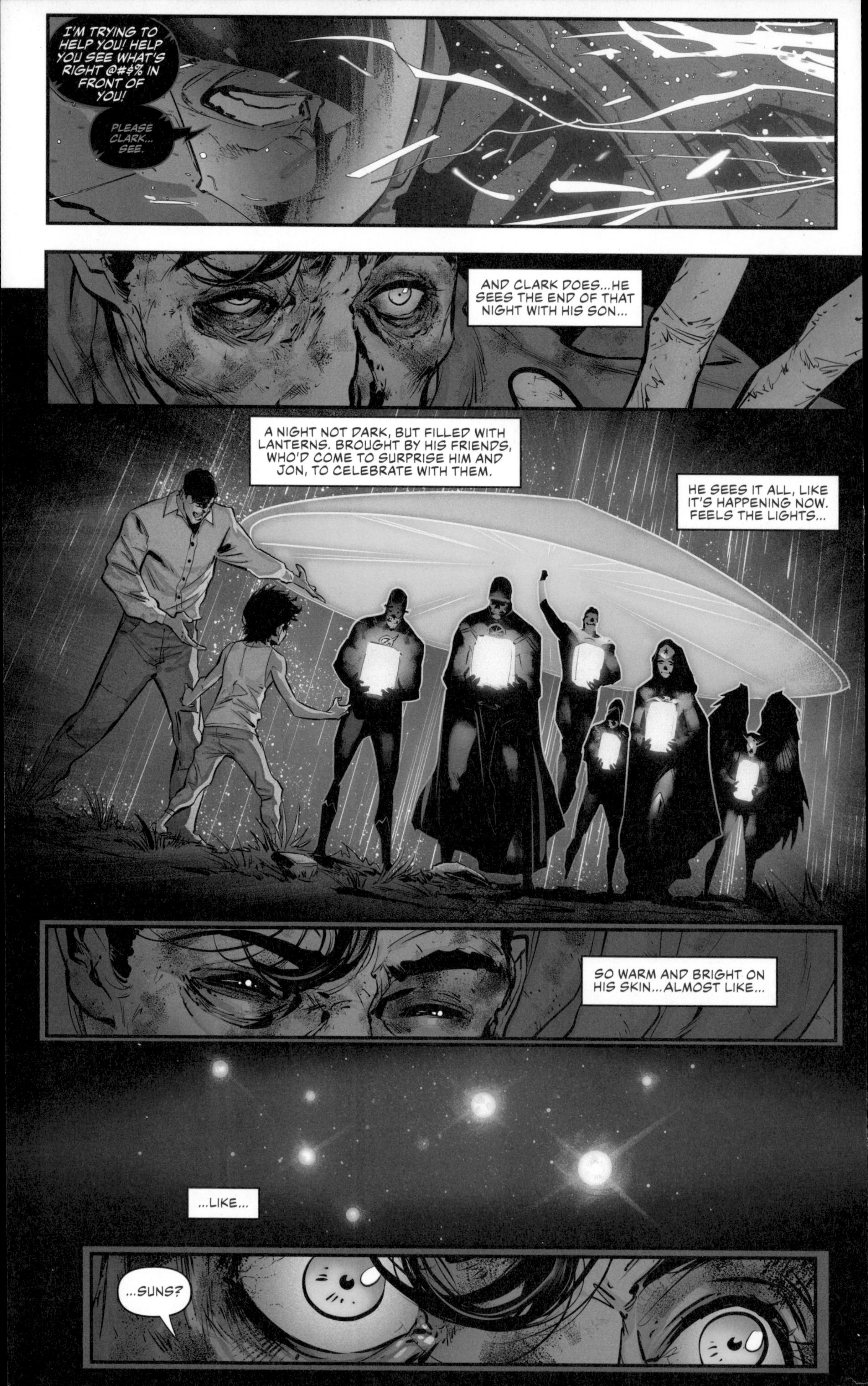
I'M TRYING TO HELP YOU! HELP YOU SEE WHAT'S RIGHT @#$% IN FRONT OF YOU!
PLEASE CLARK... SEE.
AND CLARK DOES...HE SEES THE END OF THAT NIGHT WITH HIS SON...
A NIGHT NOT DARK, BUT FILLED WITH LANTERNS. BROUGHT BY HIS FRIENDS, WHO'D COME TO SURPRISE HIM AND JON, TO CELEBRATE WITH THEM.
HE SEES IT ALL, LIKE IT'S HAPPENING NOW. FEELS THE LIGHTS...
SO WARM AND BRIGHT ON HIS SKIN...ALMOST LIKE...
...LIKE...
...SUNS?

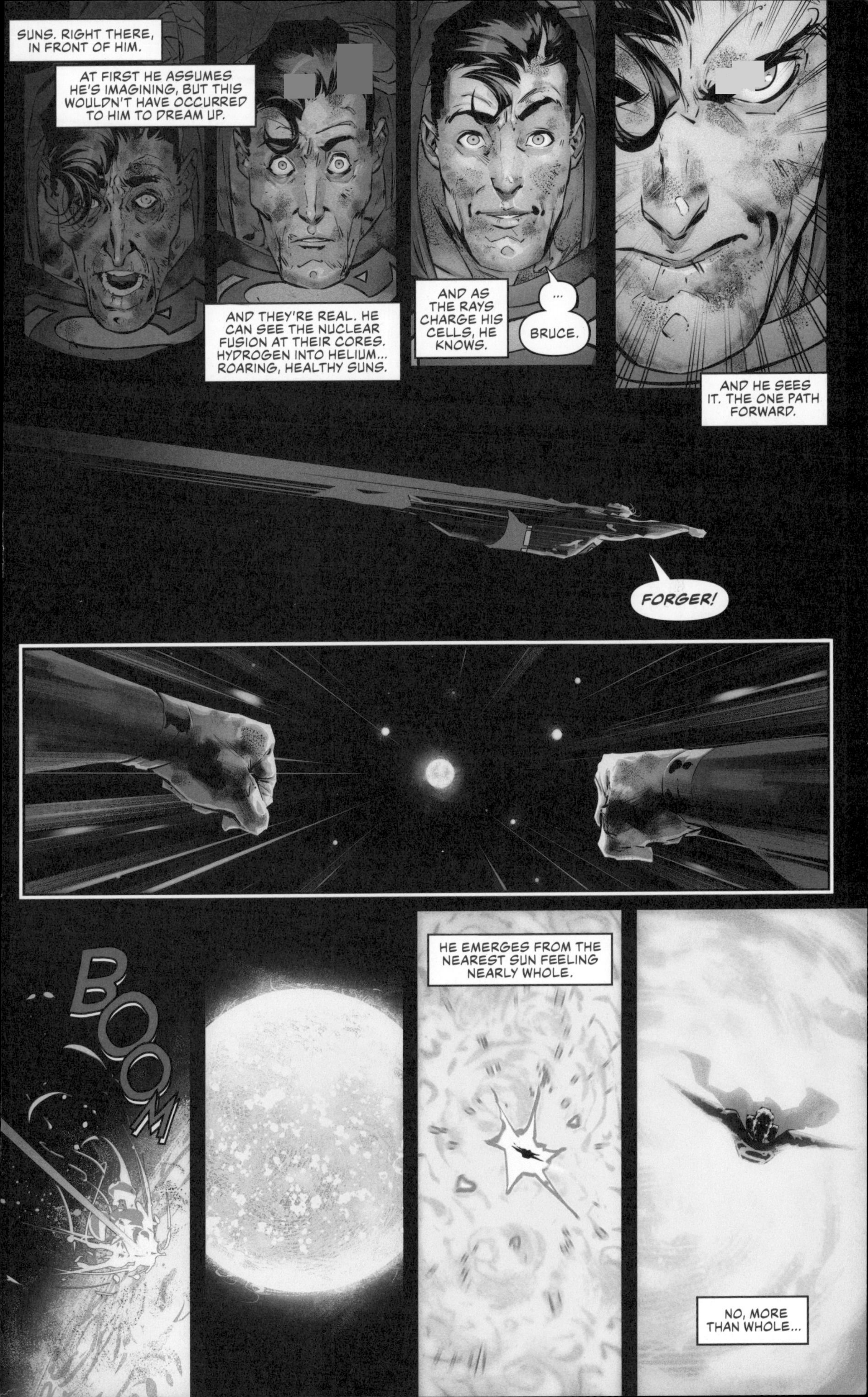
SUNS. RIGHT THERE, IN FRONT OF HIM.
AT FIRST HE ASSUMES HE'S IMAGINING, BUT THIS WOULDN'T HAVE OCCURRED TO HIM TO DREAM UP.
AND THEY'RE REAL. HE CAN SEE THE NUCLEAR FUSION AT THEIR CORES. HYDROGEN INTO HELIUM... ROARING, HEALTHY SUNS.
AND AS THE RAYS CHARGE HIS CELLS, HE KNOWS.
...
BRUCE.
AND HE SEES IT. THE ONE PATH FORWARD.
FORGER!
BOOOM
HE EMERGES FROM THE NEAREST SUN FEELING NEARLY WHOLE.
NO, MORE THAN WHOLE...

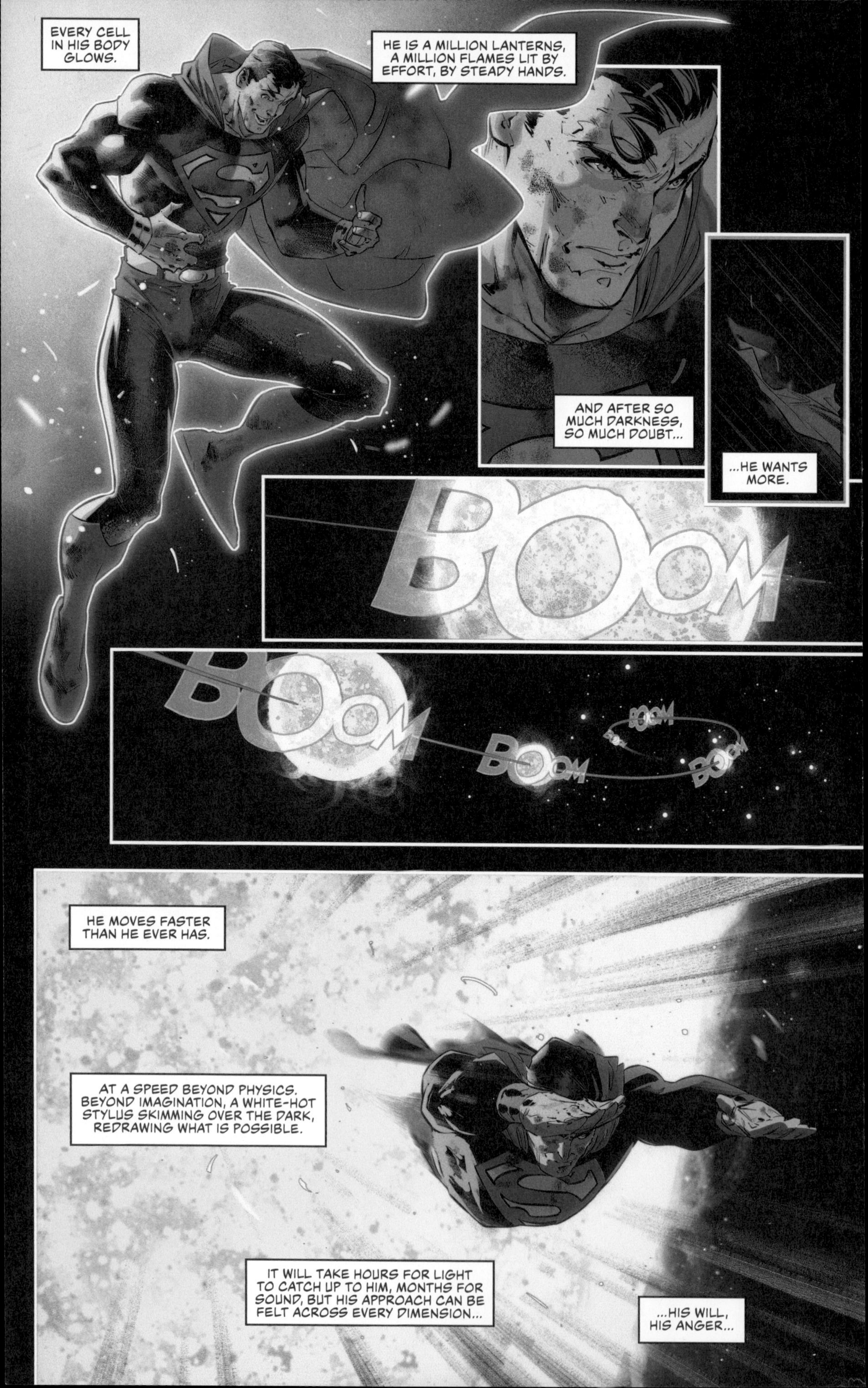
EVERY CELL IN HIS BODY GLOWS.
HE IS A MILLION LANTERNS, A MILLION FLAMES LIT BY EFFORT, BY STEADY HANDS.
AND AFTER SO MUCH DARKNESS, SO MUCH DOUBT...
...HE WANTS MORE.
BOOM
BOOM
BOOM
BOOM
BOOM
HE MOVES FASTER THAN HE EVER HAS.
AT A SPEED BEYOND PHYSICS. BEYOND IMAGINATION, A WHITE-HOT STYLUS SKIMMING OVER THE DARK, REDRAWING WHAT IS POSSIBLE.
IT WILL TAKE HOURS FOR LIGHT TO CATCH UP TO HIM, MONTHS FOR SOUND, BUT HIS APPROACH CAN BE FELT ACROSS EVERY DIMENSION...
...HIS WILL, HIS ANGER...

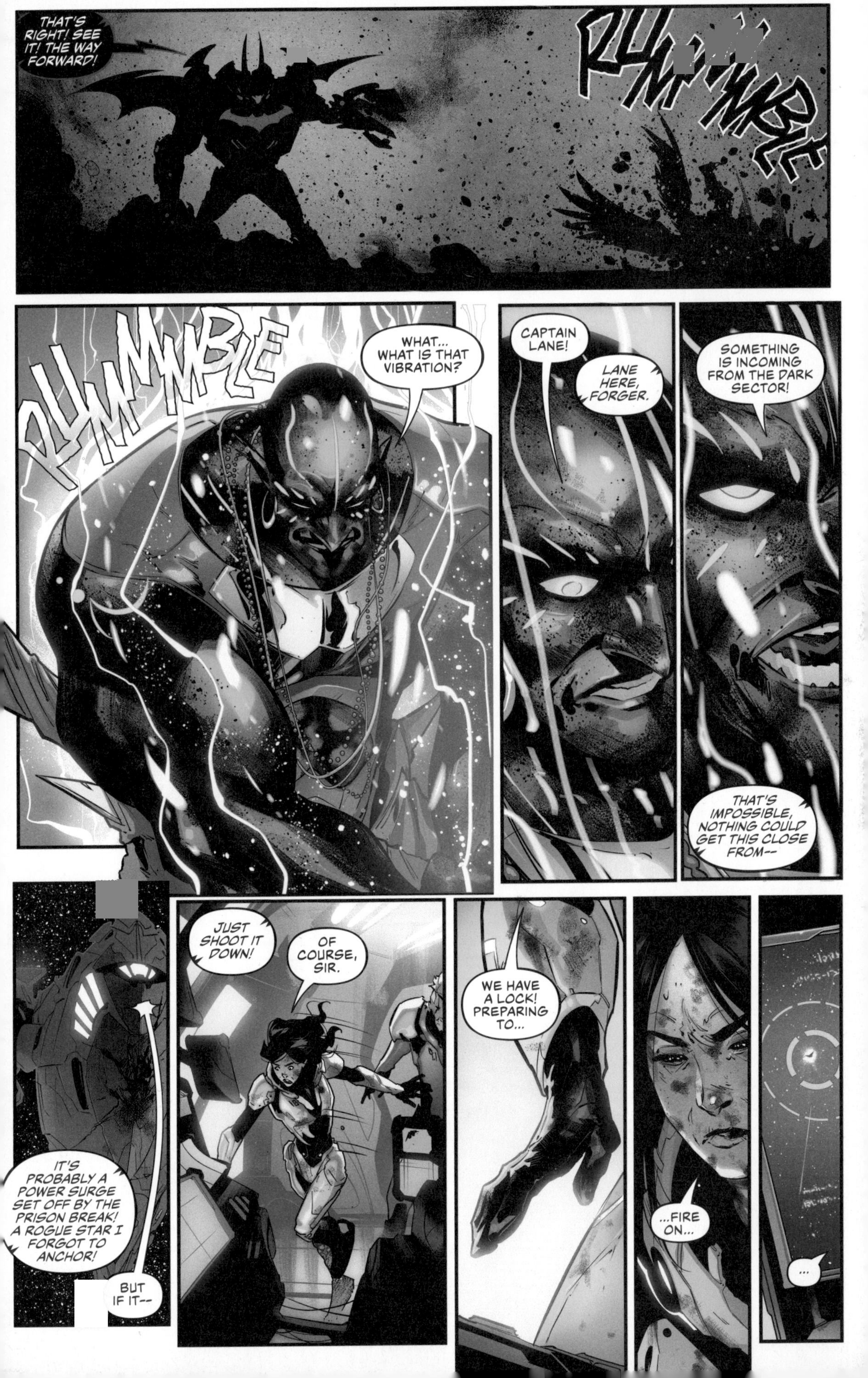
THAT'S RIGHT! SEE IT! THE WAY FORWARD!
RUMMMBLE
WHAT... WHAT IS THAT VIBRATION?
CAPTAIN LANE!
LANE HERE, FORGER.
SOMETHING IS INCOMING FROM THE DARK SECTOR!
THAT'S IMPOSSIBLE, NOTHING COULD GET THIS CLOSE FROM--
IT'S PROBABLY A POWER SURGE SET OFF BY THE PRISON BREAK! A ROGUE STAR I FORGOT TO ANCHOR!
BUT IF IT--
JUST SHOOT IT DOWN!
OF COURSE, SIR.
WE HAVE A LOCK! PREPARING TO...
...FIRE ON...
...

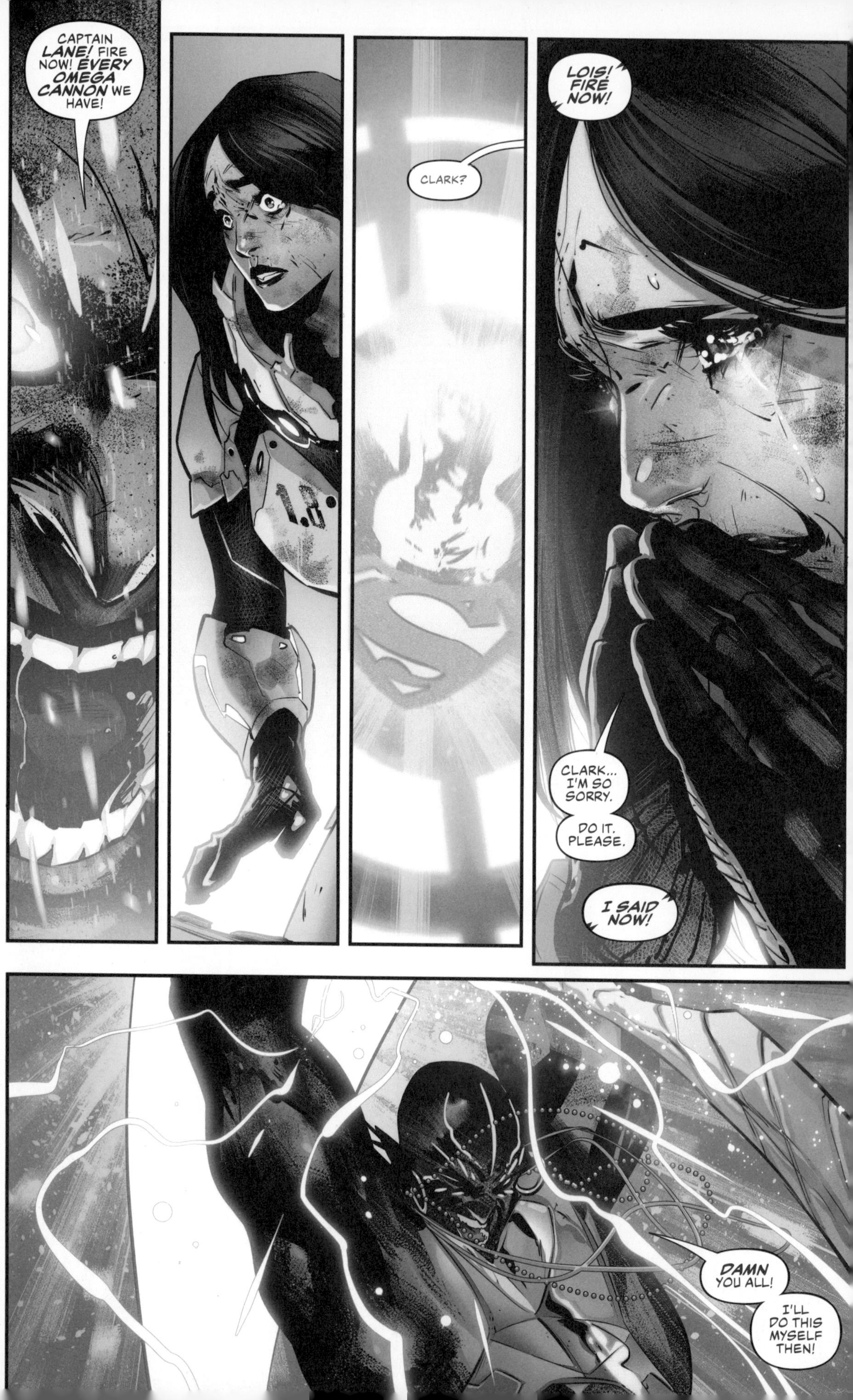
CAPTAIN LANE! FIRE NOW! EVERY OMEGA CANNON WE HAVE!
CLARK?
LOIS! FIRE NOW!
CLARK... I'M SO SORRY.
DO IT. PLEASE.
I SAID NOW!
DAMN YOU ALL!
I'LL DO THIS MYSELF THEN!

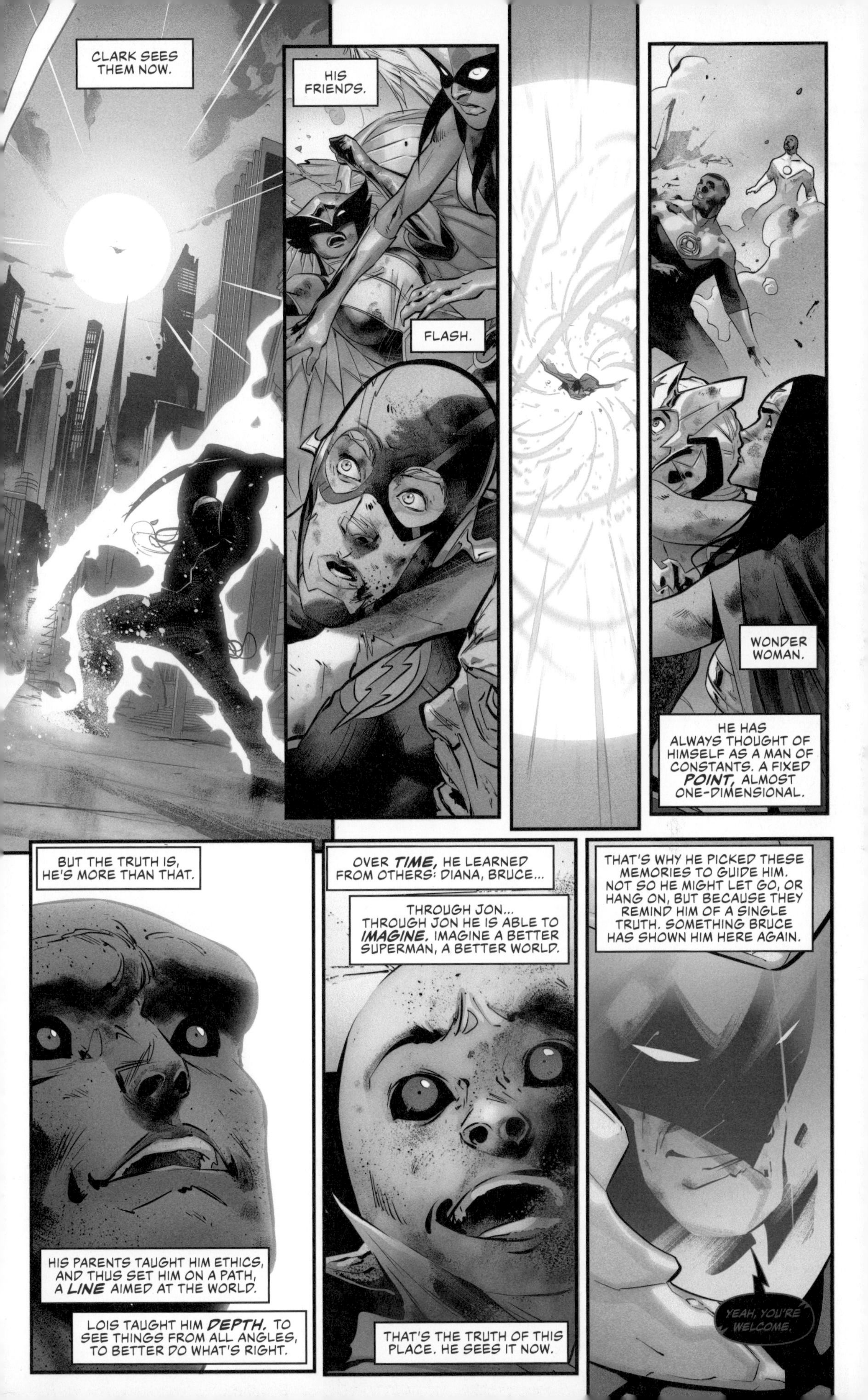
CLARK SEES THEM NOW.
HIS FRIENDS.
FLASH.
WONDER WOMAN.
HE HAS ALWAYS THOUGHT OF HIMSELF AS A MAN OF CONSTANTS. A FIXED *POINT,* ALMOST ONE-DIMENSIONAL.
BUT THE TRUTH IS, HE'S MORE THAN THAT.
HIS PARENTS TAUGHT HIM ETHICS, AND THUS SET HIM ON A PATH, A *LINE* AIMED AT THE WORLD.
LOIS TAUGHT HIM *DEPTH,* TO SEE THINGS FROM ALL ANGLES, TO BETTER DO WHAT'S RIGHT.
OVER *TIME,* HE LEARNED FROM OTHERS: DIANA, BRUCE...
THROUGH JON... THROUGH JON HE IS ABLE TO *IMAGINE.* IMAGINE A BETTER SUPERMAN, A BETTER WORLD.
THAT'S THE TRUTH OF THIS PLACE. HE SEES IT NOW.
THAT'S WHY HE PICKED THESE MEMORIES TO GUIDE HIM. NOT SO HE MIGHT LET GO, OR HANG ON, BUT BECAUSE THEY REMIND HIM OF A SINGLE TRUTH. SOMETHING BRUCE HAS SHOWN HIM HERE AGAIN.
YEAH, YOU'RE WELCOME.

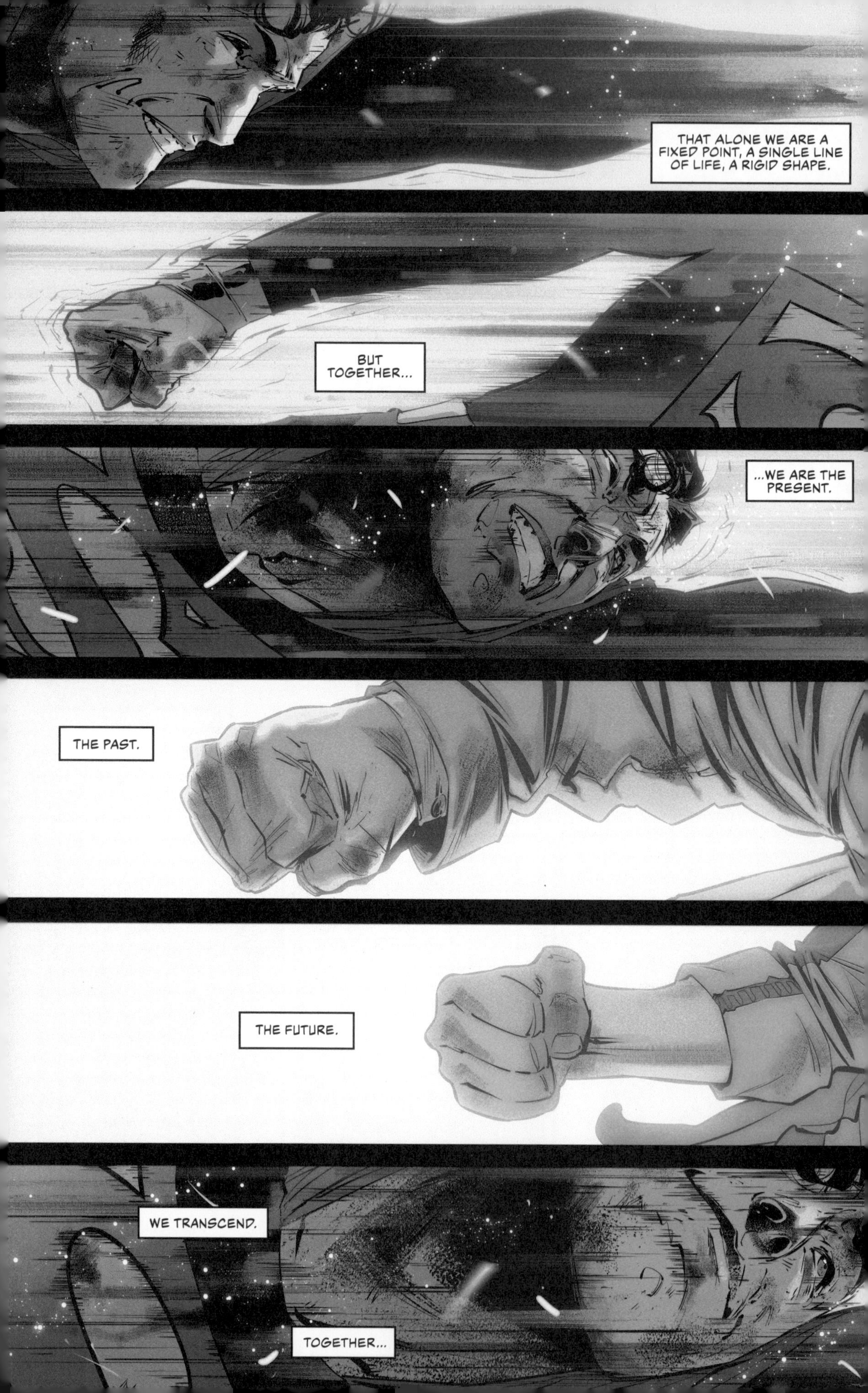
THAT ALONE WE ARE A FIXED POINT, A SINGLE LINE OF LIFE, A RIGID SHAPE.
BUT TOGETHER...
...WE ARE THE PRESENT.
THE PAST.
THE FUTURE.
WE TRANSCEND.
TOGETHER...

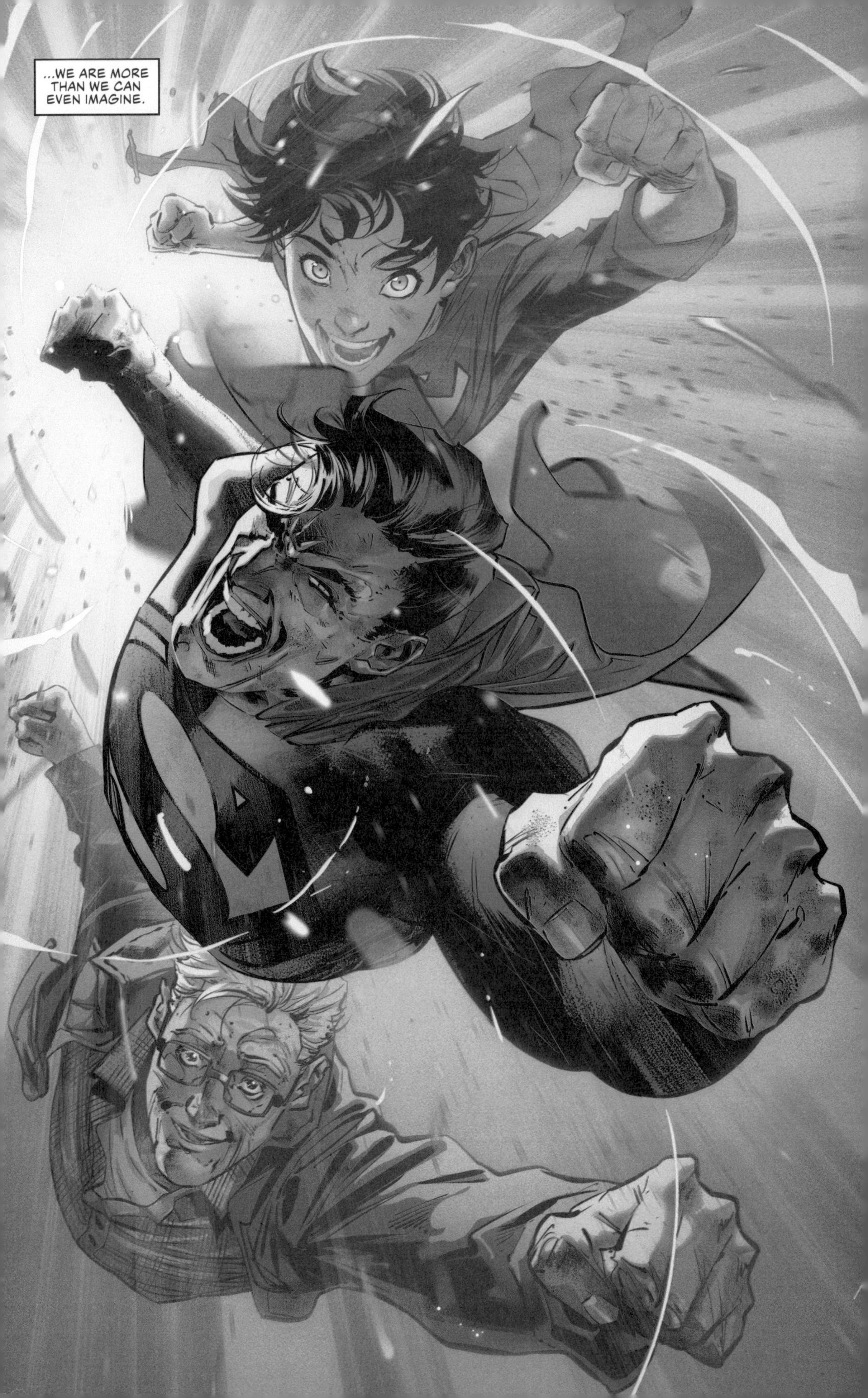
...WE ARE MORE THAN WE CAN EVEN IMAGINE.

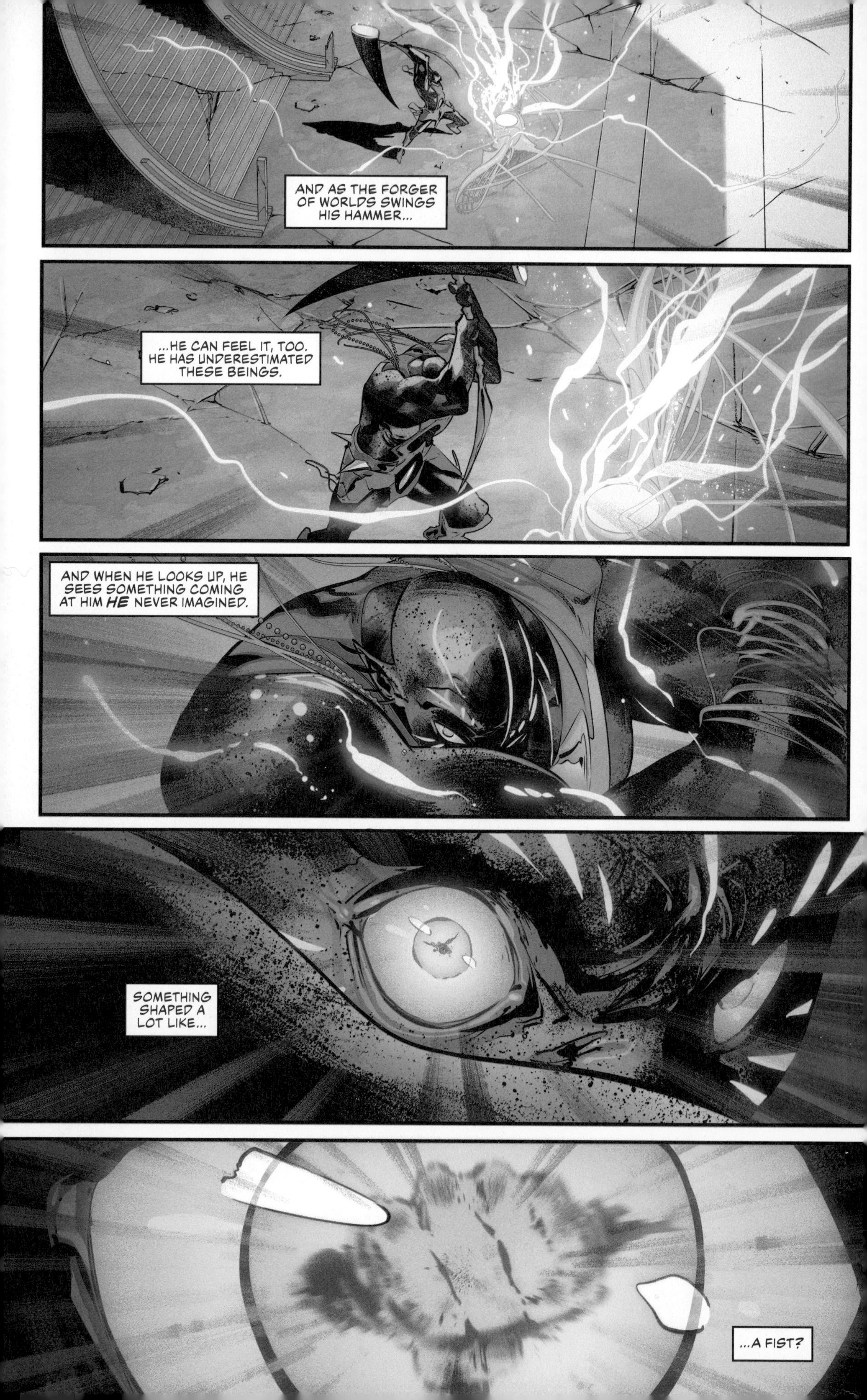
AND AS THE FORGER OF WORLDS SWINGS HIS HAMMER...
...HE CAN FEEL IT, TOO. HE HAS UNDERESTIMATED THESE BEINGS.
AND WHEN HE LOOKS UP, HE SEES SOMETHING COMING AT HIM *HE* NEVER IMAGINED.
SOMETHING SHAPED A LOT LIKE...
...A FIST?

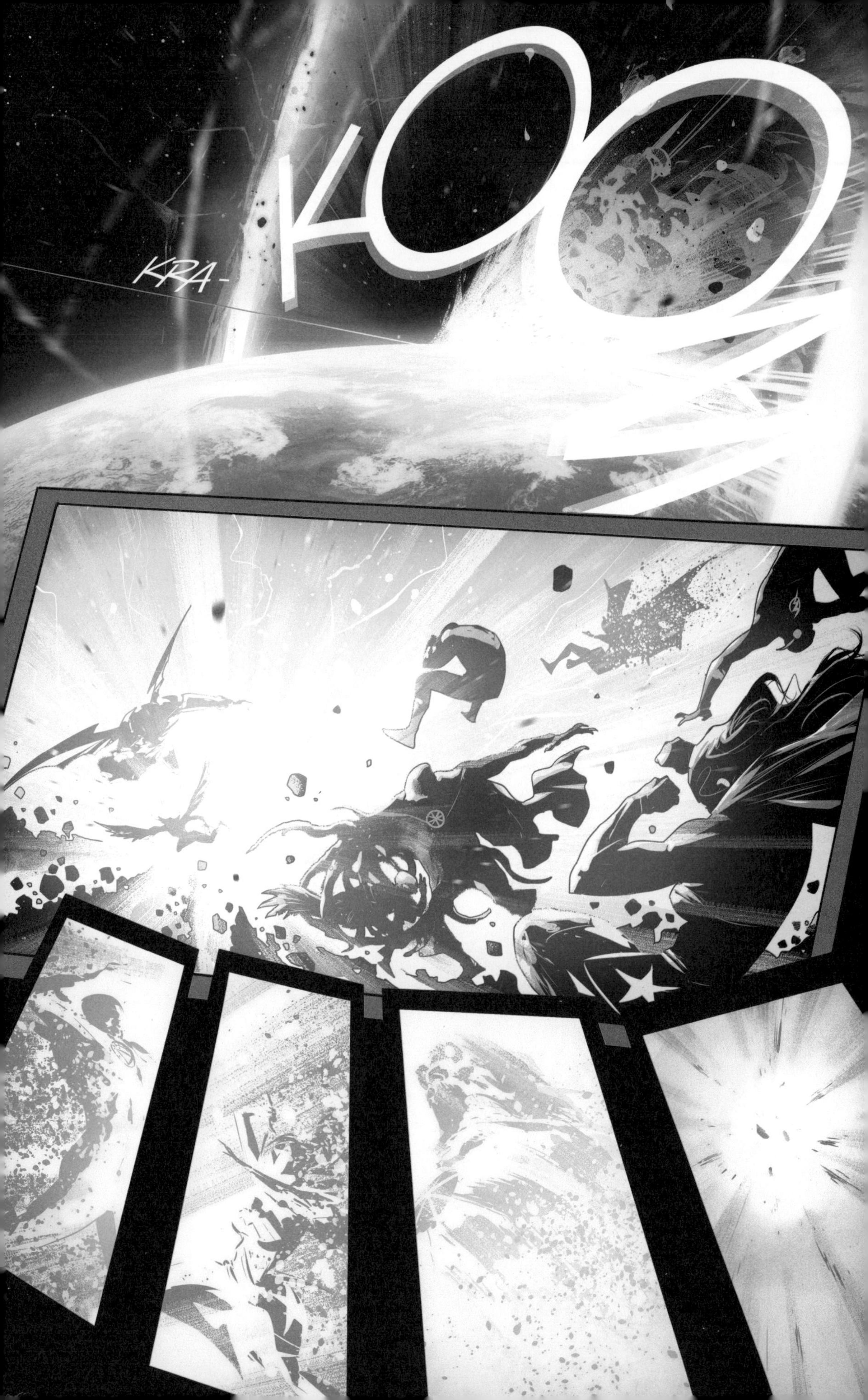
KRA-KOOM

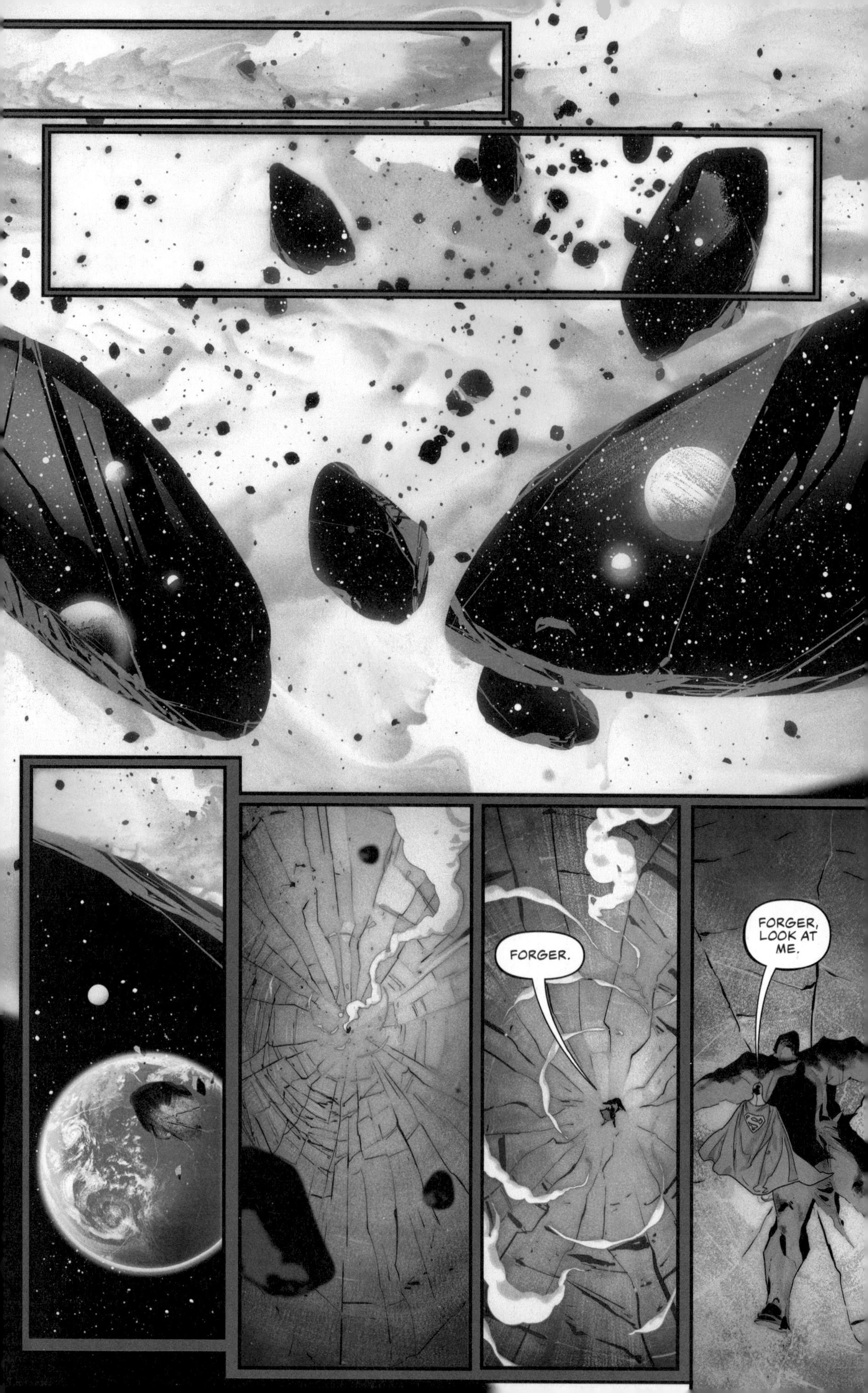
FORGER.
FORGER, LOOK AT ME.

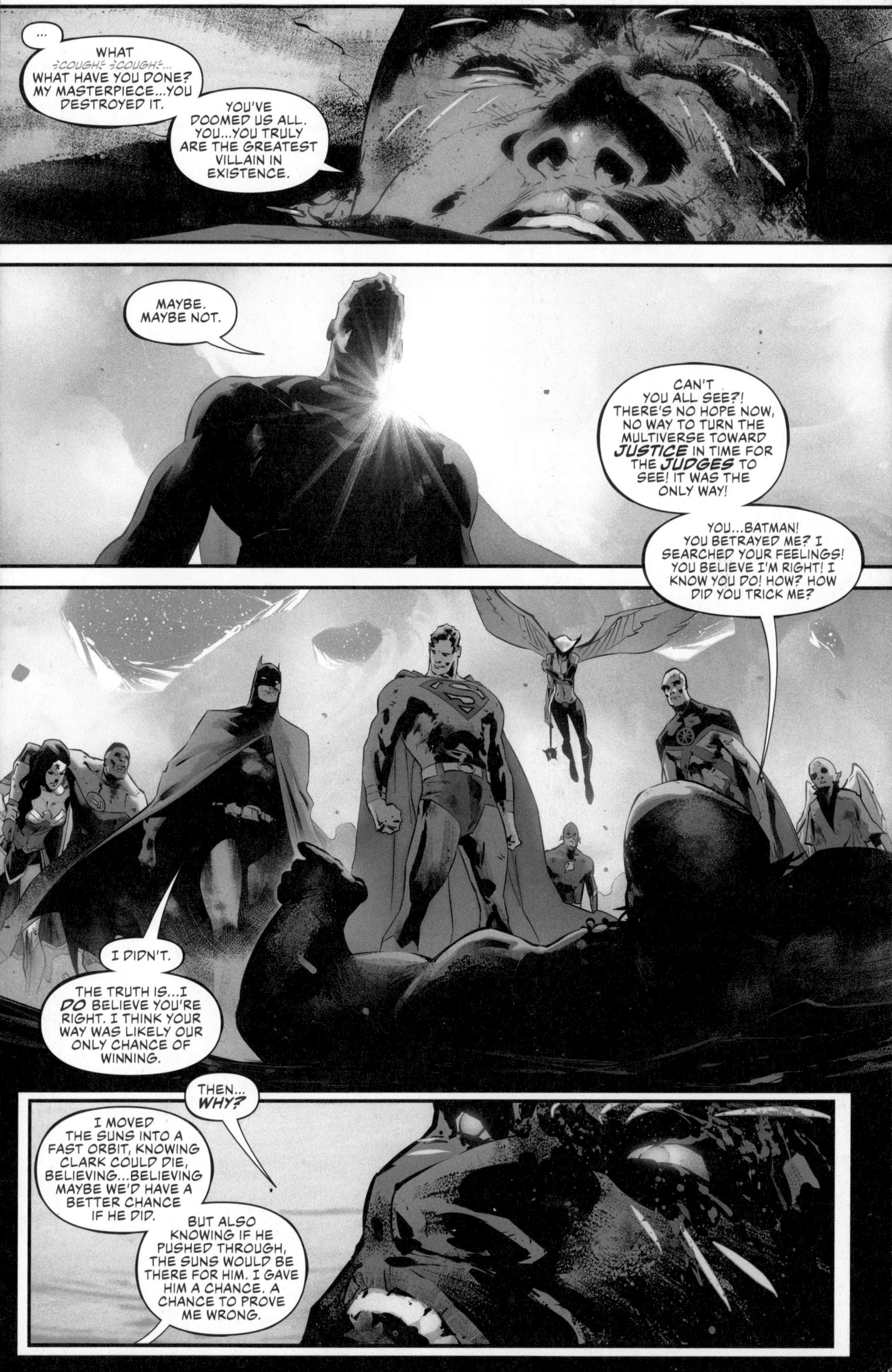

...
WHAT ~COUGH~ ~COUGH~... WHAT HAVE YOU DONE? MY MASTERPIECE...YOU DESTROYED IT.
YOU'VE DOOMED US ALL. YOU...YOU TRULY ARE THE GREATEST VILLAIN IN EXISTENCE.
MAYBE. MAYBE NOT.
CAN'T YOU ALL SEE?! THERE'S NO HOPE NOW, NO WAY TO TURN THE MULTIVERSE TOWARD JUSTICE IN TIME FOR THE JUDGES TO SEE! IT WAS THE ONLY WAY!
YOU...BATMAN! YOU BETRAYED ME? I SEARCHED YOUR FEELINGS! YOU BELIEVE I'M RIGHT! I KNOW YOU DO! HOW? HOW DID YOU TRICK ME?
I DIDN'T.
THE TRUTH IS...I DO BELIEVE YOU'RE RIGHT. I THINK YOUR WAY WAS LIKELY OUR ONLY CHANCE OF WINNING.
THEN... WHY?
I MOVED THE SUNS INTO A FAST ORBIT, KNOWING CLARK COULD DIE, BELIEVING...BELIEVING MAYBE WE'D HAVE A BETTER CHANCE IF HE DID.
BUT ALSO KNOWING IF HE PUSHED THROUGH, THE SUNS WOULD BE THERE FOR HIM. I GAVE HIM A CHANCE. A CHANCE TO PROVE ME WRONG.

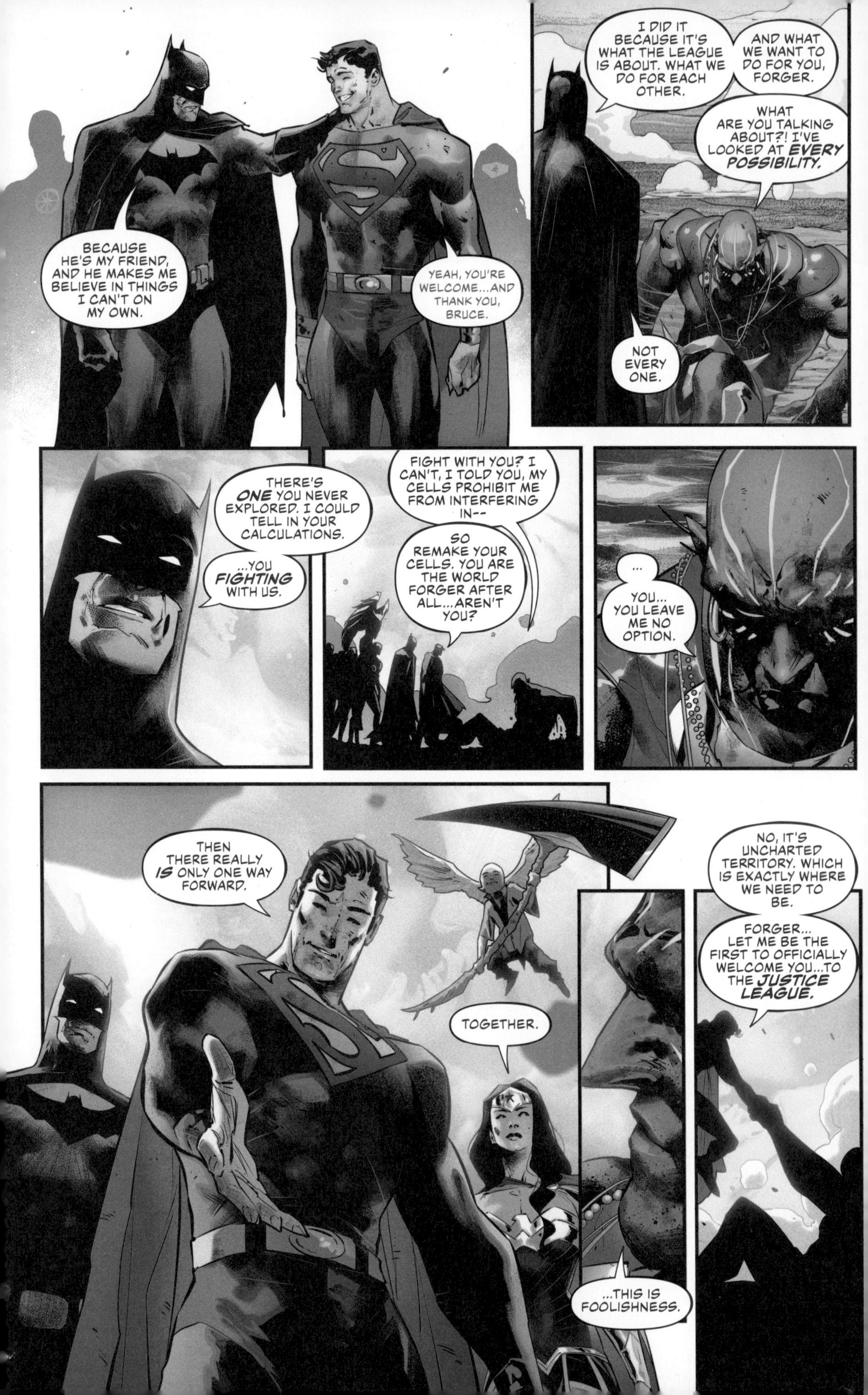
BECAUSE HE'S MY FRIEND, AND HE MAKES ME BELIEVE IN THINGS I CAN'T ON MY OWN.
YEAH, YOU'RE WELCOME...AND THANK YOU, BRUCE.
I DID IT BECAUSE IT'S WHAT THE LEAGUE IS ABOUT. WHAT WE DO FOR EACH OTHER.
AND WHAT WE WANT TO DO FOR YOU, FORGER.
WHAT ARE YOU TALKING ABOUT?! I'VE LOOKED AT EVERY POSSIBILITY.
NOT EVERY ONE.
THERE'S ONE YOU NEVER EXPLORED. I COULD TELL IN YOUR CALCULATIONS.
...YOU FIGHTING WITH US.
FIGHT WITH YOU? I CAN'T, I TOLD YOU, MY CELLS PROHIBIT ME FROM INTERFERING IN--
SO REMAKE YOUR CELLS. YOU ARE THE WORLD FORGER AFTER ALL...AREN'T YOU?
...
YOU... YOU LEAVE ME NO OPTION.
THEN THERE REALLY IS ONLY ONE WAY FORWARD.
TOGETHER.
...THIS IS FOOLISHNESS.
NO, IT'S UNCHARTED TERRITORY. WHICH IS EXACTLY WHERE WE NEED TO BE.
FORGER... LET ME BE THE FIRST TO OFFICIALLY WELCOME YOU...TO THE JUSTICE LEAGUE.

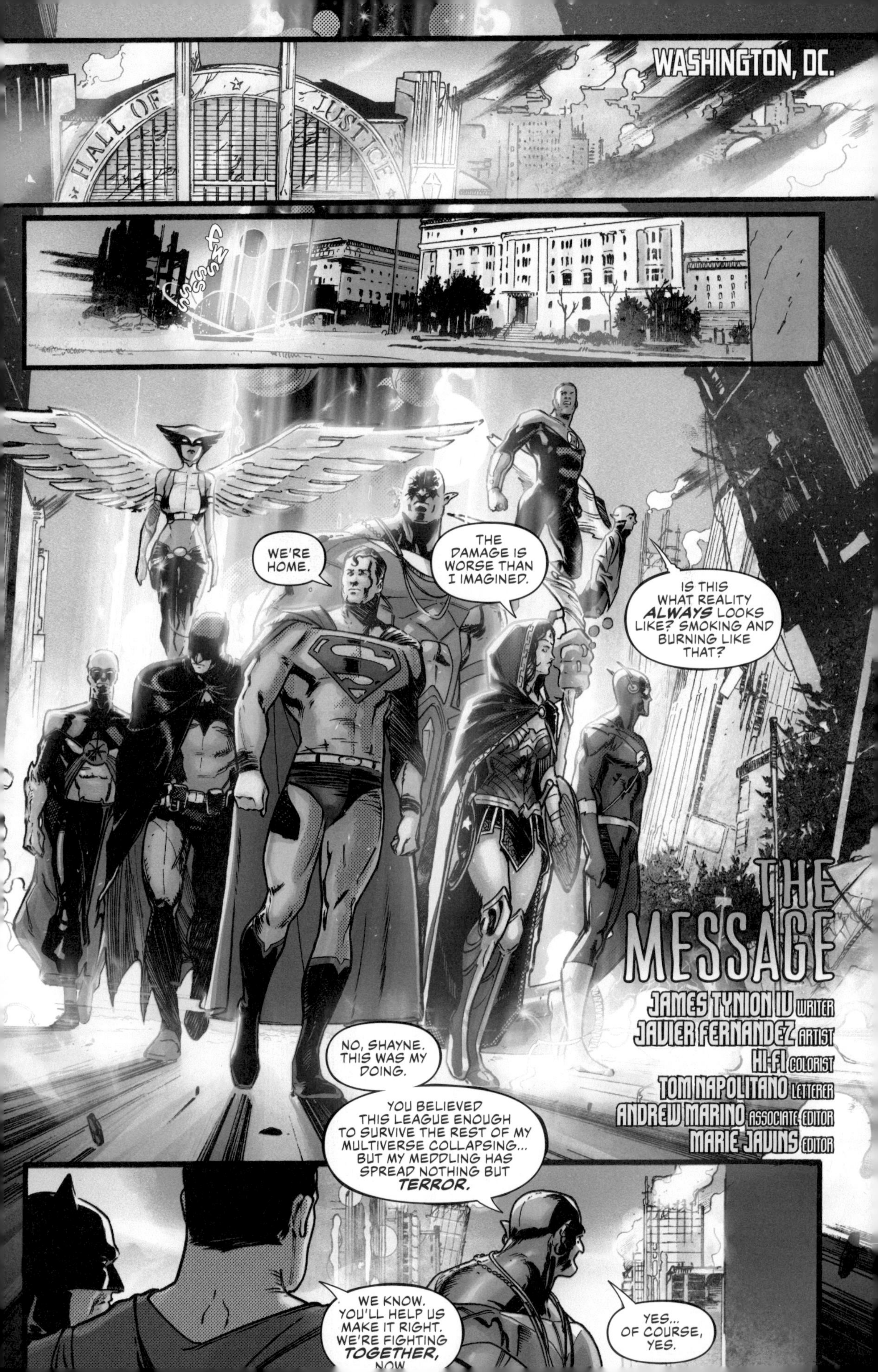
WASHINGTON, DC.
HALL OF JUSTICE
FWSSSSH
WE'RE HOME.
THE DAMAGE IS WORSE THAN I IMAGINED.
IS THIS WHAT REALITY ALWAYS LOOKS LIKE? SMOKING AND BURNING LIKE THAT?
THE MESSAGE
JAMES TYNION IV WRITER
JAVIER FERNANDEZ ARTIST
HI-FI COLORIST
TOM NAPOLITANO LETTERER
ANDREW MARINO ASSOCIATE EDITOR
MARIE JAVINS EDITOR
NO, SHAYNE. THIS WAS MY DOING.
YOU BELIEVED THIS LEAGUE ENOUGH TO SURVIVE THE REST OF MY MULTIVERSE COLLAPSING... BUT MY MEDDLING HAS SPREAD NOTHING BUT TERROR.
WE KNOW. YOU'LL HELP US MAKE IT RIGHT. WE'RE FIGHTING TOGETHER, NOW.
YES... OF COURSE, YES.

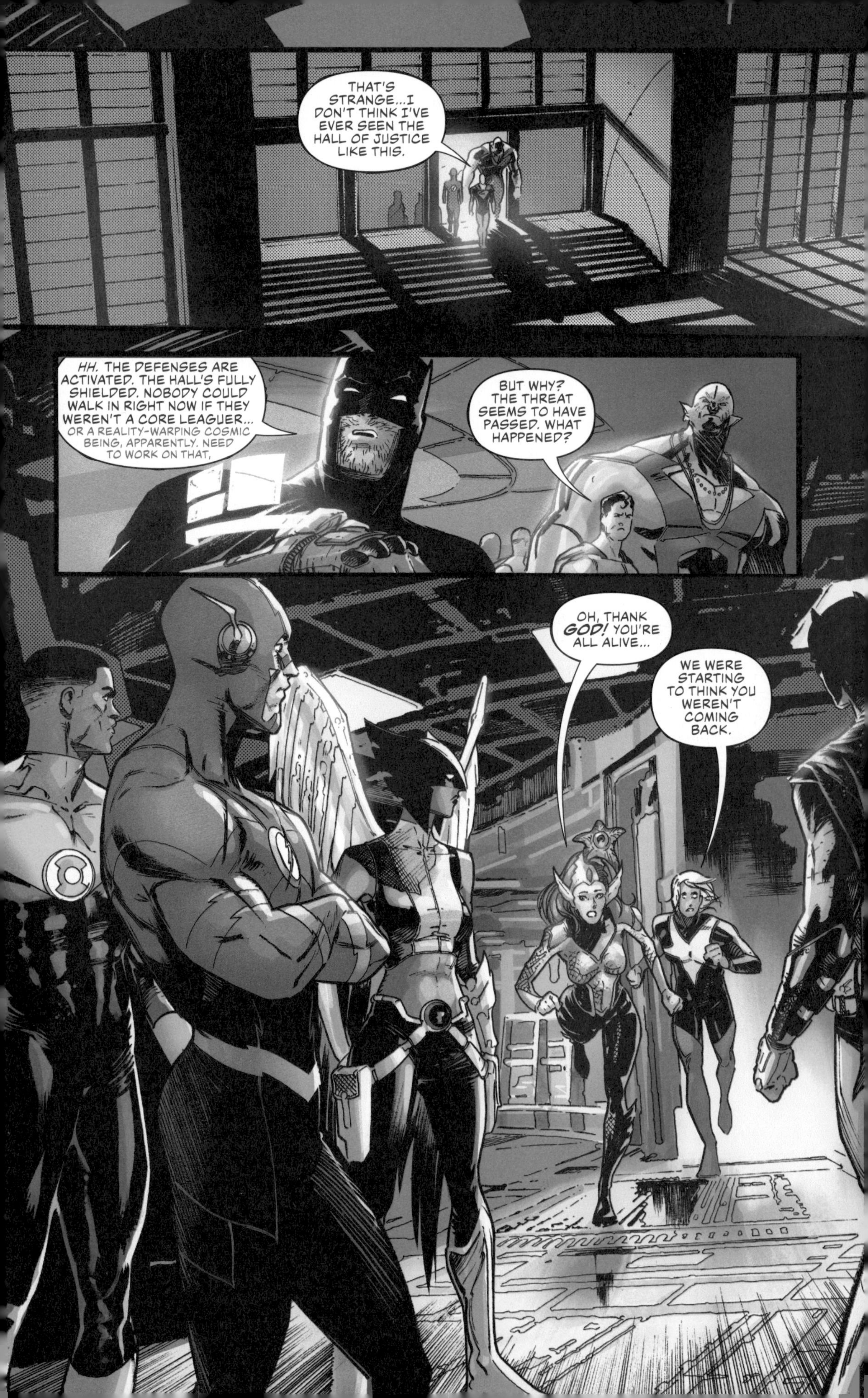
THAT'S STRANGE...I DON'T THINK I'VE EVER SEEN THE HALL OF JUSTICE LIKE THIS.
HH. THE DEFENSES ARE ACTIVATED. THE HALL'S FULLY SHIELDED. NOBODY COULD WALK IN RIGHT NOW IF THEY WEREN'T A CORE LEAGUER... OR A REALITY-WARPING COSMIC BEING, APPARENTLY. NEED TO WORK ON THAT,
BUT WHY? THE THREAT SEEMS TO HAVE PASSED. WHAT HAPPENED?
OH, THANK GOD! YOU'RE ALL ALIVE...
WE WERE STARTING TO THINK YOU WEREN'T COMING BACK.

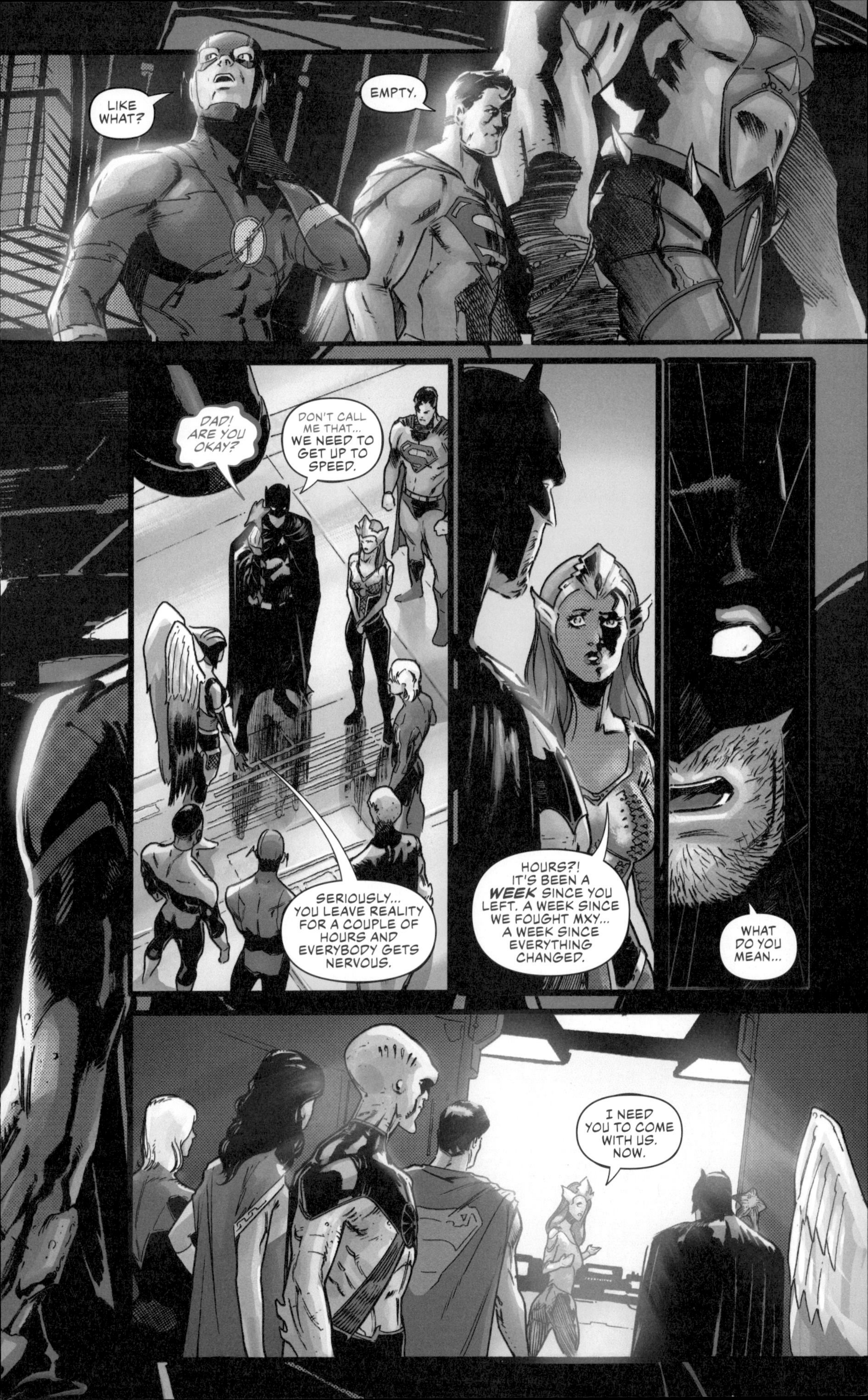
LIKE WHAT?
EMPTY.
DAD! ARE YOU OKAY?
DON'T CALL ME THAT... WE NEED TO GET UP TO SPEED.
SERIOUSLY... YOU LEAVE REALITY FOR A COUPLE OF HOURS AND EVERYBODY GETS NERVOUS.
HOURS?! IT'S BEEN A WEEK SINCE YOU LEFT. A WEEK SINCE WE FOUGHT MXY... A WEEK SINCE EVERYTHING CHANGED.
WHAT DO YOU MEAN...
I NEED YOU TO COME WITH US. NOW.

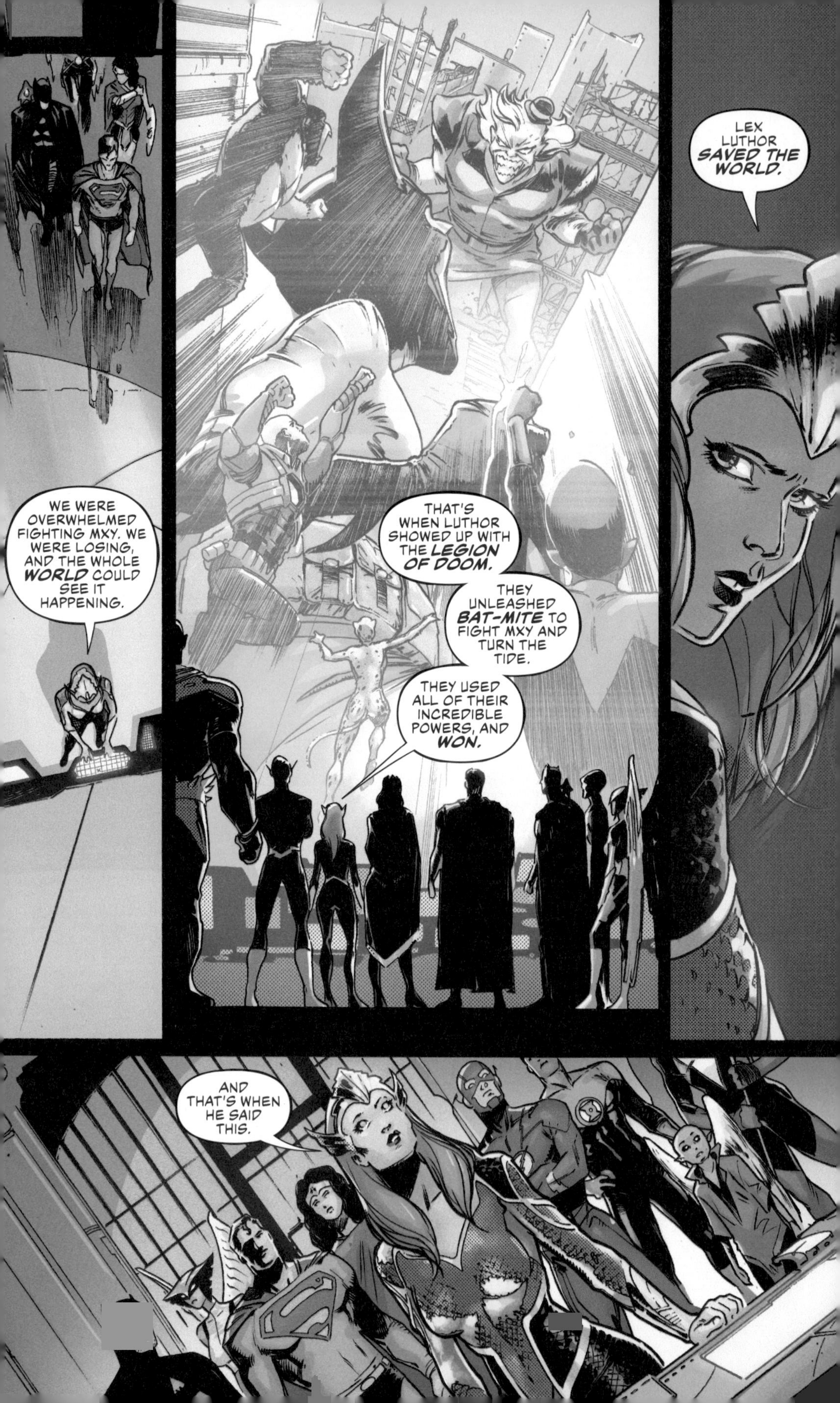

WE WERE OVERWHELMED FIGHTING MXY. WE WERE LOSING, AND THE WHOLE WORLD COULD SEE IT HAPPENING.
THAT'S WHEN LUTHOR SHOWED UP WITH THE LEGION OF DOOM.
THEY UNLEASHED BAT-MITE TO FIGHT MXY AND TURN THE TIDE.
THEY USED ALL OF THEIR INCREDIBLE POWERS, AND WON.
LEX LUTHOR SAVED THE WORLD.
AND THAT'S WHEN HE SAID THIS.

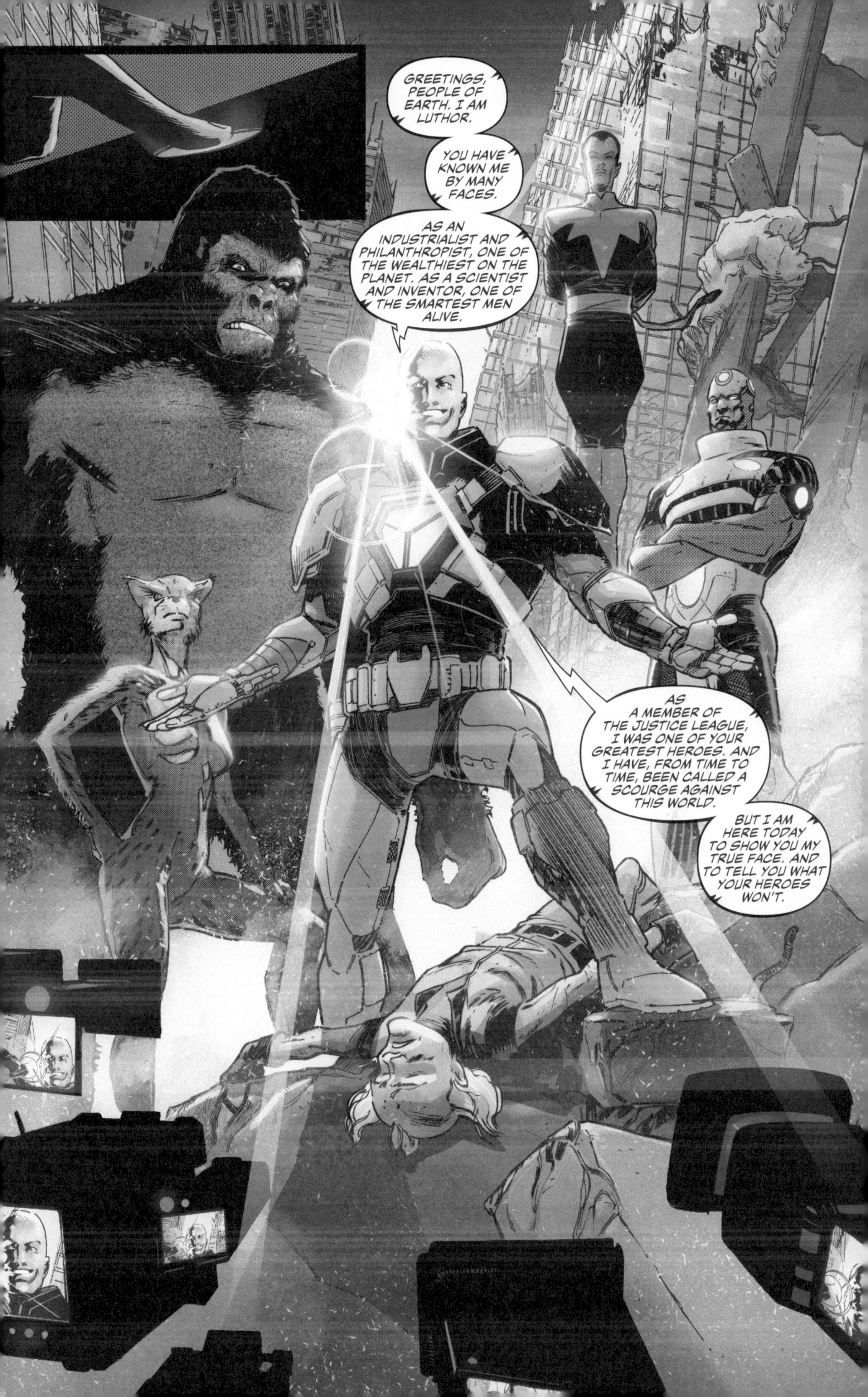
GREETINGS, PEOPLE OF EARTH. I AM LUTHOR.
YOU HAVE KNOWN ME BY MANY FACES.
AS AN INDUSTRIALIST AND PHILANTHROPIST, ONE OF THE WEALTHIEST ON THE PLANET. AS A SCIENTIST AND INVENTOR, ONE OF THE SMARTEST MEN ALIVE.
AS A MEMBER OF THE JUSTICE LEAGUE, I WAS ONE OF YOUR GREATEST HEROES. AND I HAVE, FROM TIME TO TIME, BEEN CALLED A SCOURGE AGAINST THIS WORLD.
BUT I AM HERE TODAY TO SHOW YOU MY TRUE FACE. AND TO TELL YOU WHAT YOUR HEROES WON'T.

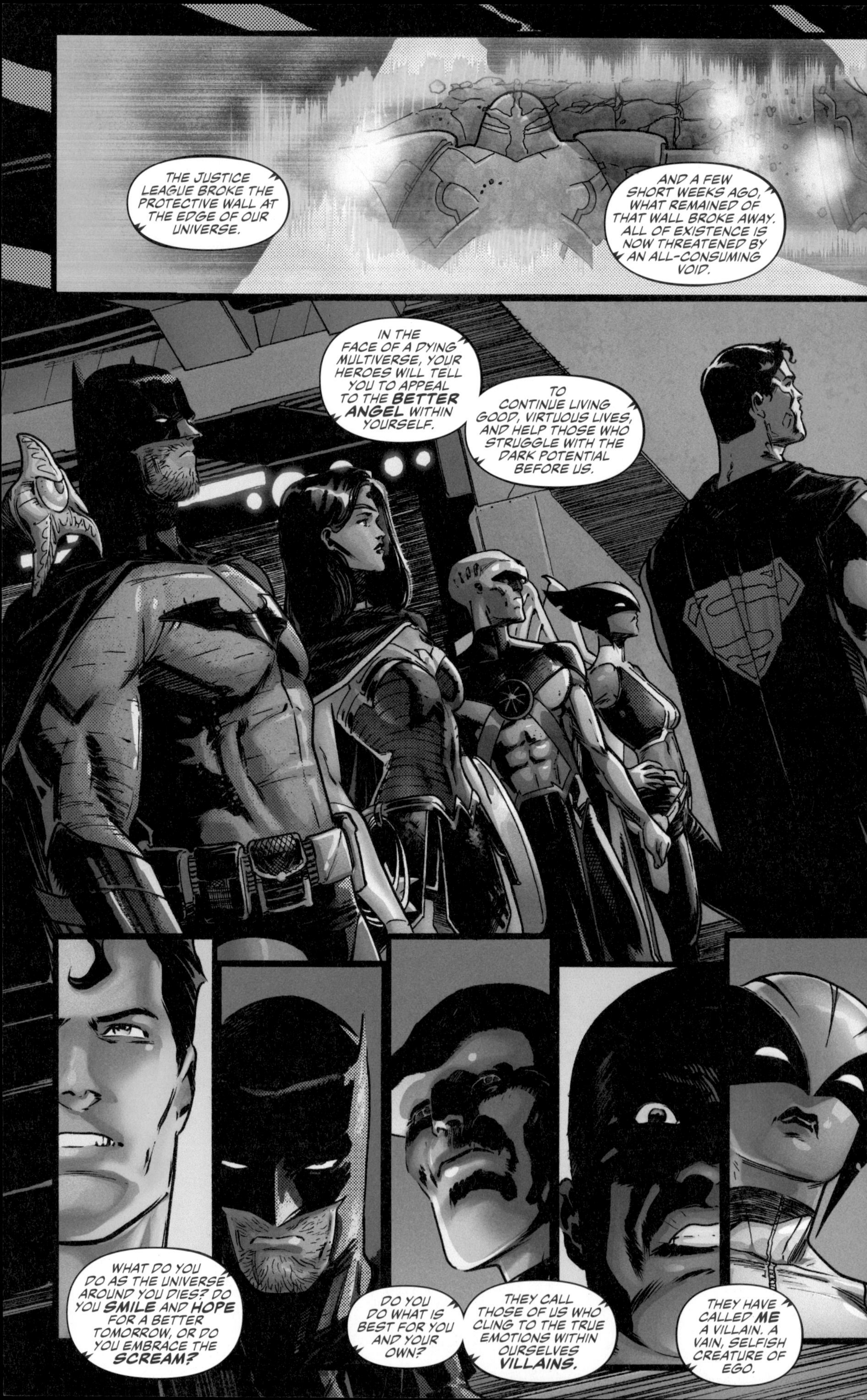
THE JUSTICE LEAGUE BROKE THE PROTECTIVE WALL AT THE EDGE OF OUR UNIVERSE.
AND A FEW SHORT WEEKS AGO, WHAT REMAINED OF THAT WALL BROKE AWAY. ALL OF EXISTENCE IS NOW THREATENED BY AN ALL-CONSUMING VOID.
IN THE FACE OF A DYING MULTIVERSE, YOUR HEROES WILL TELL YOU TO APPEAL TO THE **BETTER ANGEL** WITHIN YOURSELF.
TO CONTINUE LIVING GOOD, VIRTUOUS LIVES, AND HELP THOSE WHO STRUGGLE WITH THE DARK POTENTIAL BEFORE US.
WHAT DO YOU DO AS THE UNIVERSE AROUND YOU DIES? DO YOU **SMILE** AND **HOPE** FOR A BETTER TOMORROW, OR DO YOU EMBRACE THE **SCREAM?**
DO YOU DO WHAT IS BEST FOR YOU AND YOUR OWN?
THEY CALL THOSE OF US WHO CLING TO THE TRUE EMOTIONS WITHIN OURSELVES **VILLAINS.**
THEY HAVE CALLED **ME** A VILLAIN. A VAIN, SELFISH CREATURE OF EGO.

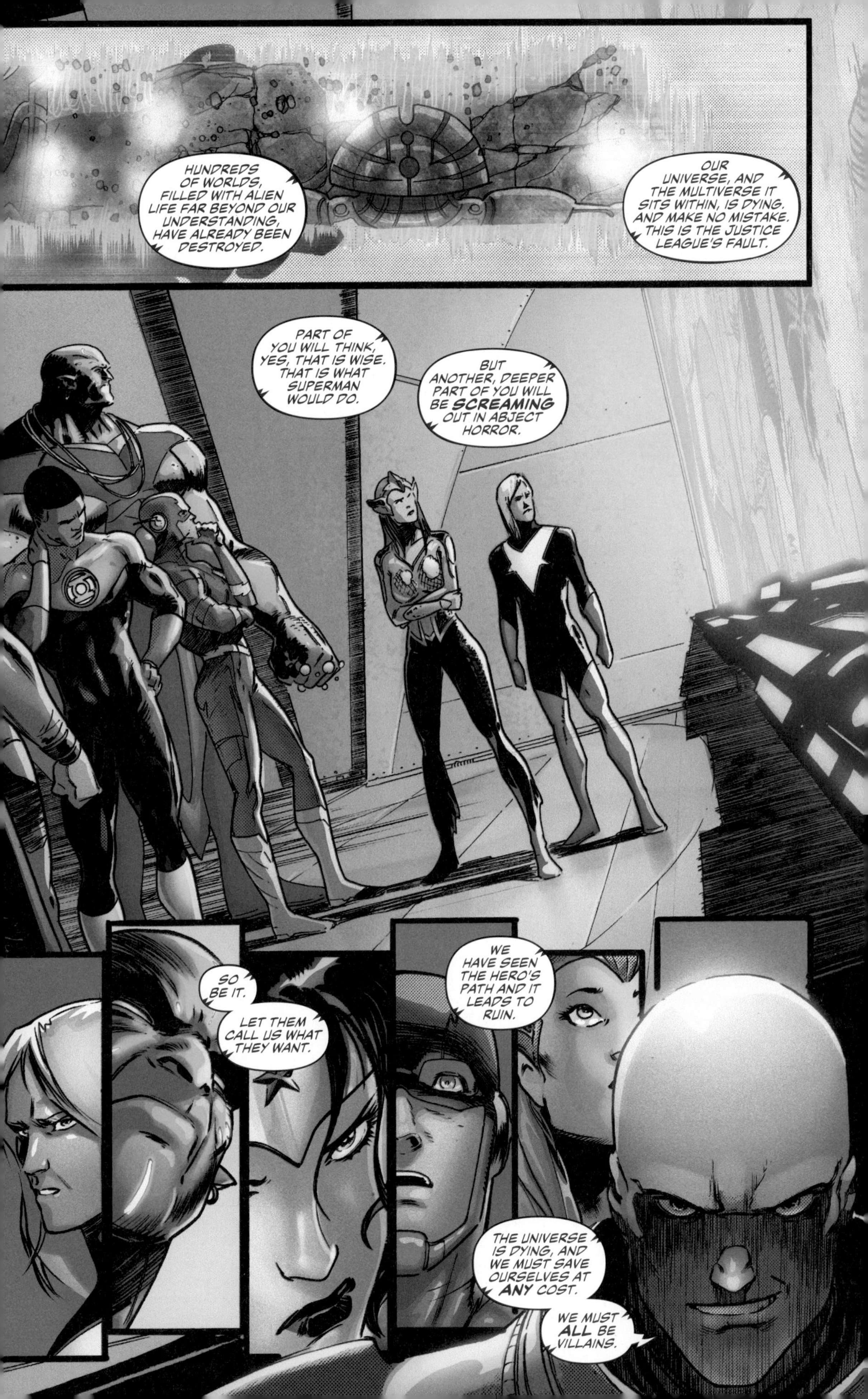
HUNDREDS OF WORLDS, FILLED WITH ALIEN LIFE FAR BEYOND OUR UNDERSTANDING, HAVE ALREADY BEEN DESTROYED.
OUR UNIVERSE, AND THE MULTIVERSE IT SITS WITHIN, IS DYING. AND MAKE NO MISTAKE. THIS IS THE JUSTICE LEAGUE'S FAULT.
PART OF YOU WILL THINK, YES, THAT IS WISE. THAT IS WHAT SUPERMAN WOULD DO.
BUT ANOTHER, DEEPER PART OF YOU WILL BE SCREAMING OUT IN ABJECT HORROR.
SO BE IT.
LET THEM CALL US WHAT THEY WANT.
WE HAVE SEEN THE HERO'S PATH AND IT LEADS TO RUIN.
THE UNIVERSE IS DYING, AND WE MUST SAVE OURSELVES AT ANY COST.
WE MUST ALL BE VILLAINS.

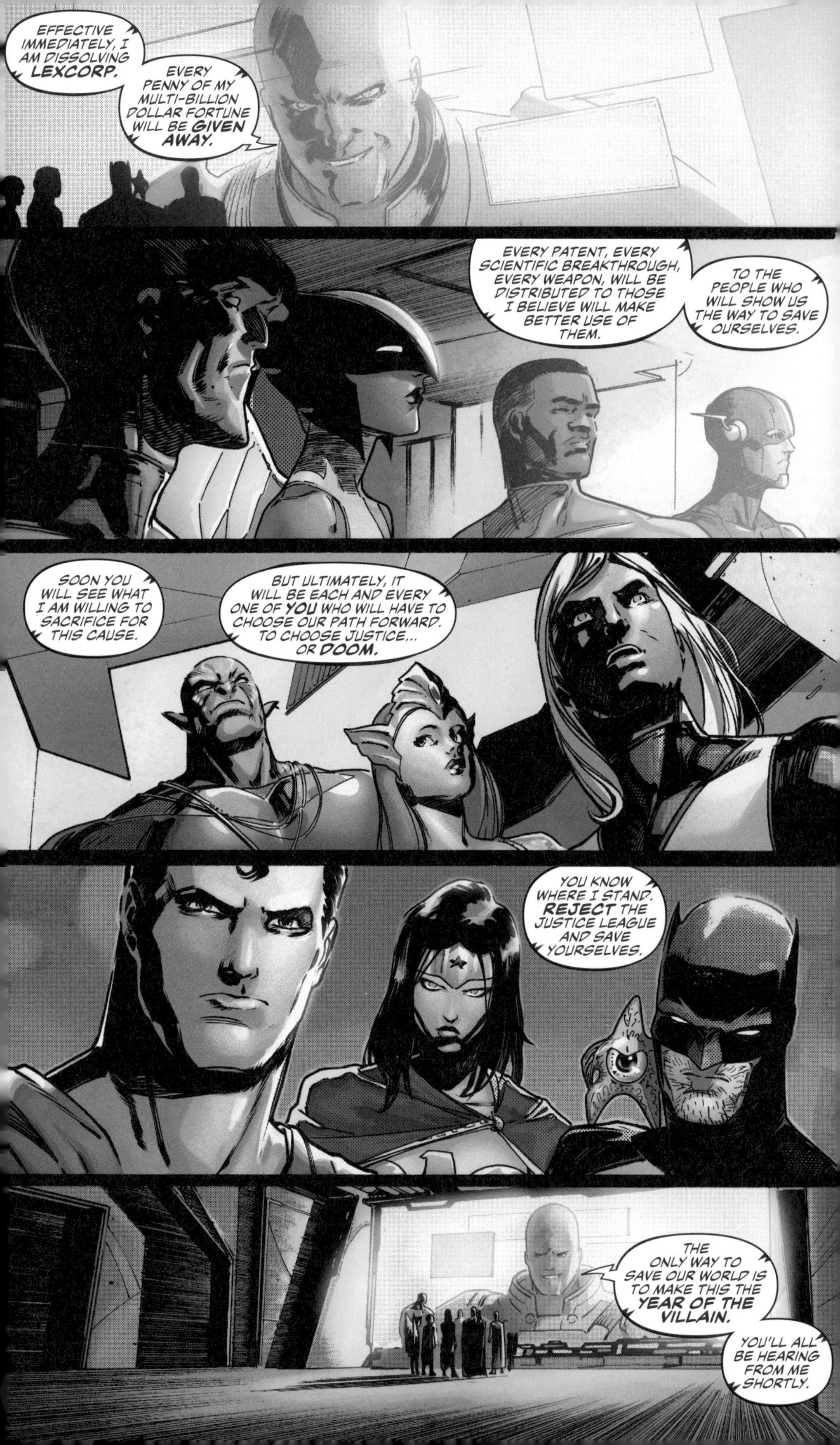
EFFECTIVE IMMEDIATELY, I AM DISSOLVING LEXCORP.
EVERY PENNY OF MY MULTI-BILLION DOLLAR FORTUNE WILL BE GIVEN AWAY.
EVERY PATENT, EVERY SCIENTIFIC BREAKTHROUGH, EVERY WEAPON, WILL BE DISTRIBUTED TO THOSE I BELIEVE WILL MAKE BETTER USE OF THEM.
TO THE PEOPLE WHO WILL SHOW US THE WAY TO SAVE OURSELVES.
SOON YOU WILL SEE WHAT I AM WILLING TO SACRIFICE FOR THIS CAUSE.
BUT ULTIMATELY, IT WILL BE EACH AND EVERY ONE OF YOU WHO WILL HAVE TO CHOOSE OUR PATH FORWARD. TO CHOOSE JUSTICE... OR DOOM.
YOU KNOW WHERE I STAND. REJECT THE JUSTICE LEAGUE AND SAVE YOURSELVES.
THE ONLY WAY TO SAVE OUR WORLD IS TO MAKE THIS THE YEAR OF THE VILLAIN.
YOU'LL ALL BE HEARING FROM ME SHORTLY.

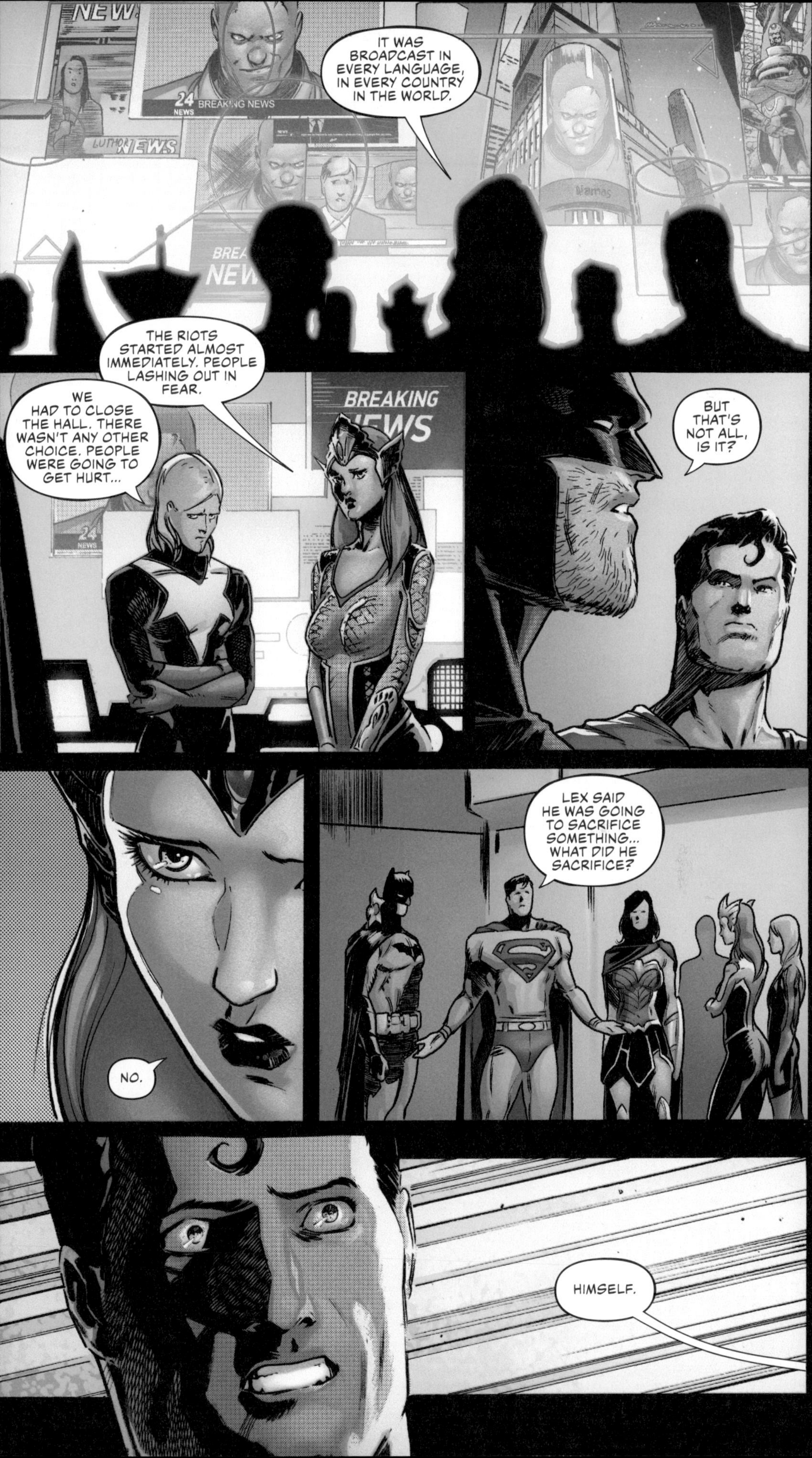
NEWS
24 BREAKING NEWS
LUTHOR NEWS
IT WAS BROADCAST IN EVERY LANGUAGE, IN EVERY COUNTRY IN THE WORLD.
BREAKING NEWS
THE RIOTS STARTED ALMOST IMMEDIATELY. PEOPLE LASHING OUT IN FEAR.
WE HAD TO CLOSE THE HALL. THERE WASN'T ANY OTHER CHOICE. PEOPLE WERE GOING TO GET HURT...
BREAKING NEWS
BUT THAT'S NOT ALL, IS IT?
NO.
LEX SAID HE WAS GOING TO SACRIFICE SOMETHING... WHAT DID HE SACRIFICE?
HIMSELF.

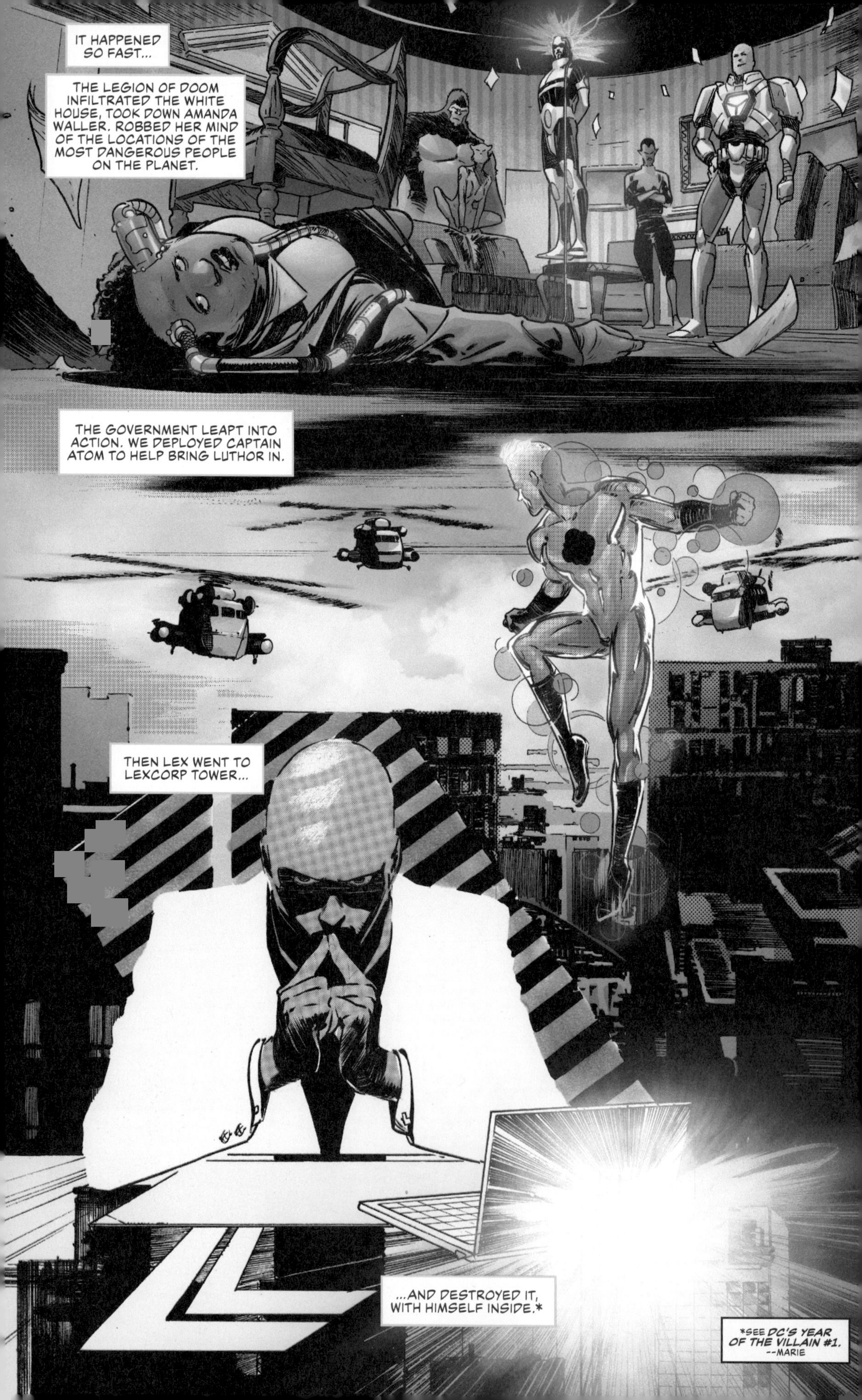
IT HAPPENED SO FAST...
THE LEGION OF DOOM INFILTRATED THE WHITE HOUSE, TOOK DOWN AMANDA WALLER. ROBBED HER MIND OF THE LOCATIONS OF THE MOST DANGEROUS PEOPLE ON THE PLANET.
THE GOVERNMENT LEAPT INTO ACTION. WE DEPLOYED CAPTAIN ATOM TO HELP BRING LUTHOR IN.
THEN LEX WENT TO LEXCORP TOWER...
...AND DESTROYED IT, WITH HIMSELF INSIDE.*
*SEE DC'S YEAR OF THE VILLAIN #1. --MARIE

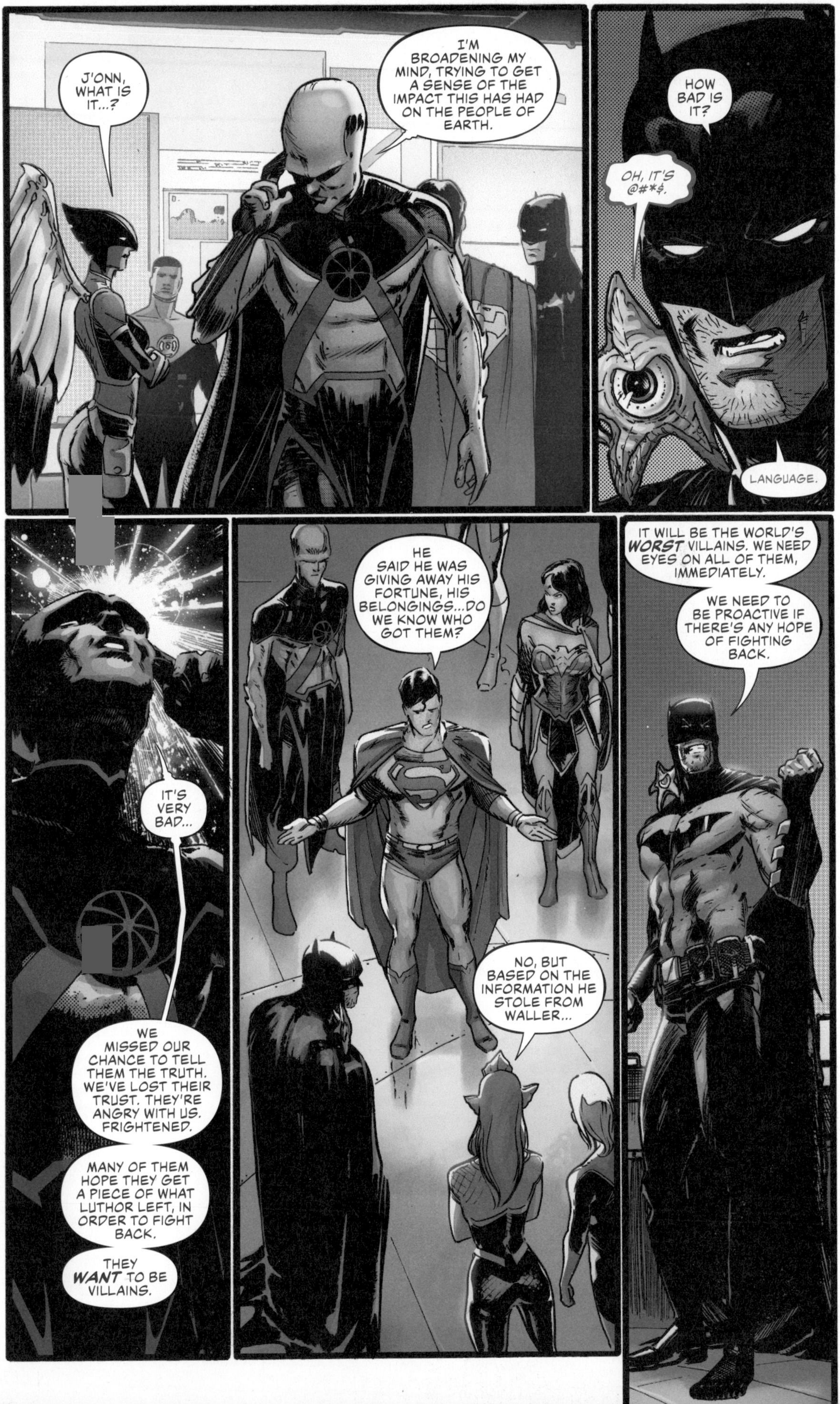
J'ONN, WHAT IS IT...?
I'M BROADENING MY MIND, TRYING TO GET A SENSE OF THE IMPACT THIS HAS HAD ON THE PEOPLE OF EARTH.
HOW BAD IS IT?
OH, IT'S @#*$.
LANGUAGE.
IT'S VERY BAD...
WE MISSED OUR CHANCE TO TELL THEM THE TRUTH. WE'VE LOST THEIR TRUST. THEY'RE ANGRY WITH US. FRIGHTENED.
MANY OF THEM HOPE THEY GET A PIECE OF WHAT LUTHOR LEFT, IN ORDER TO FIGHT BACK.
THEY WANT TO BE VILLAINS.
HE SAID HE WAS GIVING AWAY HIS FORTUNE, HIS BELONGINGS...DO WE KNOW WHO GOT THEM?
NO, BUT BASED ON THE INFORMATION HE STOLE FROM WALLER...
IT WILL BE THE WORLD'S WORST VILLAINS. WE NEED EYES ON ALL OF THEM, IMMEDIATELY.
WE NEED TO BE PROACTIVE IF THERE'S ANY HOPE OF FIGHTING BACK.

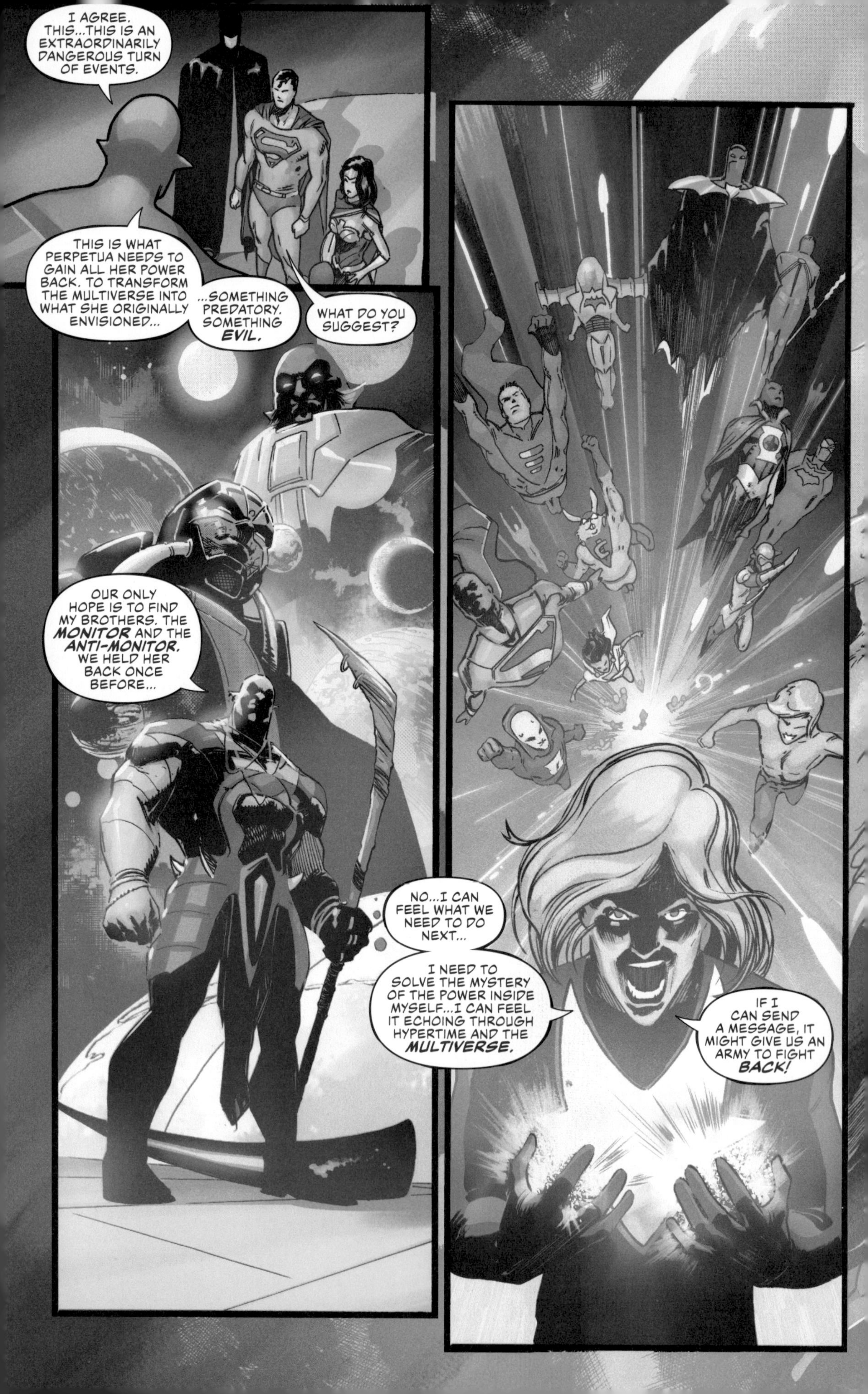
I AGREE. THIS...THIS IS AN EXTRAORDINARILY DANGEROUS TURN OF EVENTS.
THIS IS WHAT PERPETUA NEEDS TO GAIN ALL HER POWER BACK. TO TRANSFORM THE MULTIVERSE INTO WHAT SHE ORIGINALLY ENVISIONED...
...SOMETHING PREDATORY. SOMETHING **EVIL.**
WHAT DO YOU SUGGEST?
OUR ONLY HOPE IS TO FIND MY BROTHERS. THE **MONITOR** AND THE **ANTI-MONITOR.** WE HELD HER BACK ONCE BEFORE...
NO...I CAN FEEL WHAT WE NEED TO DO NEXT...
I NEED TO SOLVE THE MYSTERY OF THE POWER INSIDE MYSELF...I CAN FEEL IT ECHOING THROUGH HYPERTIME AND THE **MULTIVERSE.**
IF I CAN SEND A MESSAGE, IT MIGHT GIVE US AN ARMY TO FIGHT **BACK!**

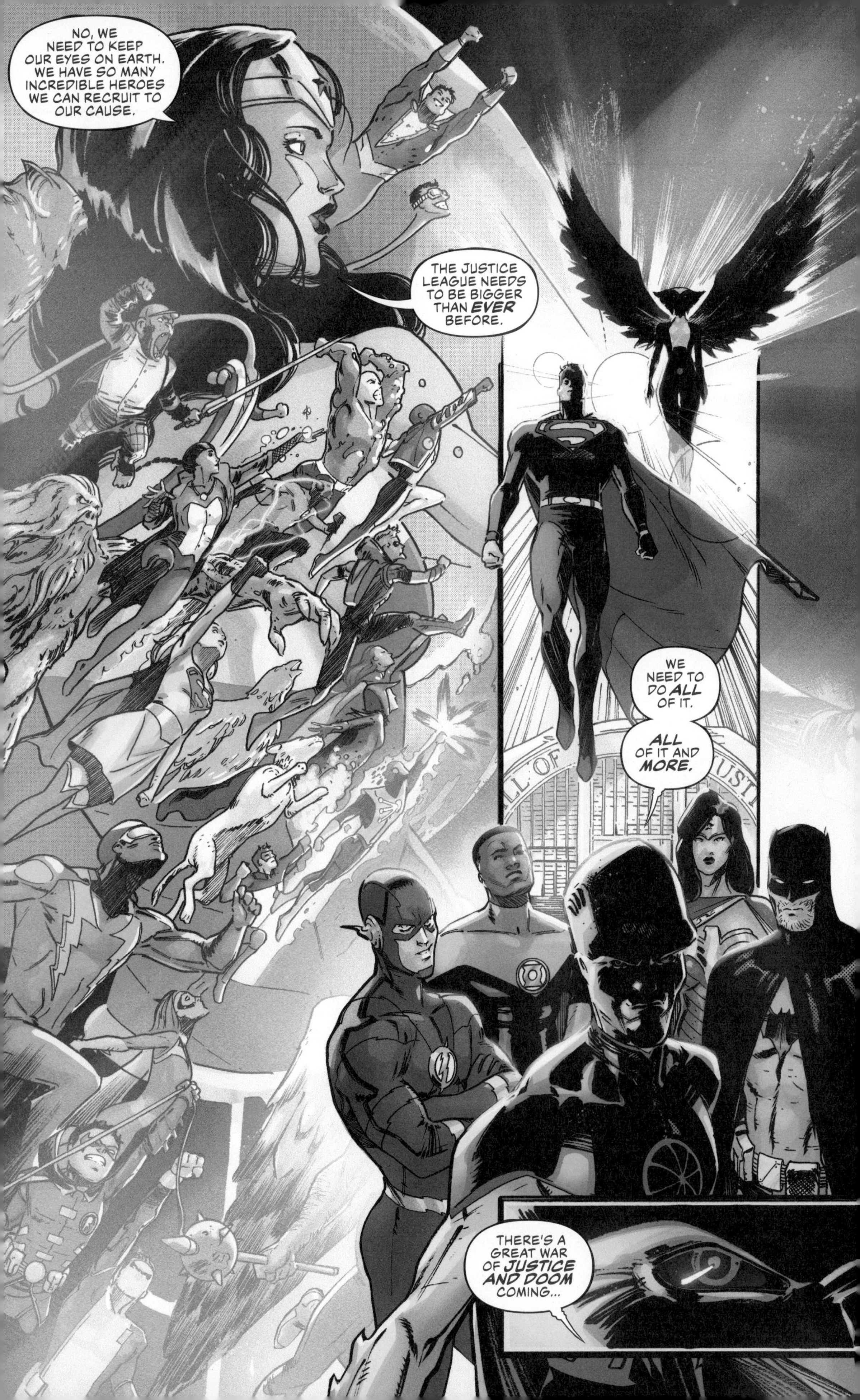
NO, WE NEED TO KEEP OUR EYES ON EARTH. WE HAVE SO MANY INCREDIBLE HEROES WE CAN RECRUIT TO OUR CAUSE.
THE JUSTICE LEAGUE NEEDS TO BE BIGGER THAN EVER BEFORE.
WE NEED TO DO ALL OF IT.
ALL OF IT AND MORE.
THERE'S A GREAT WAR OF JUSTICE AND DOOM COMING...

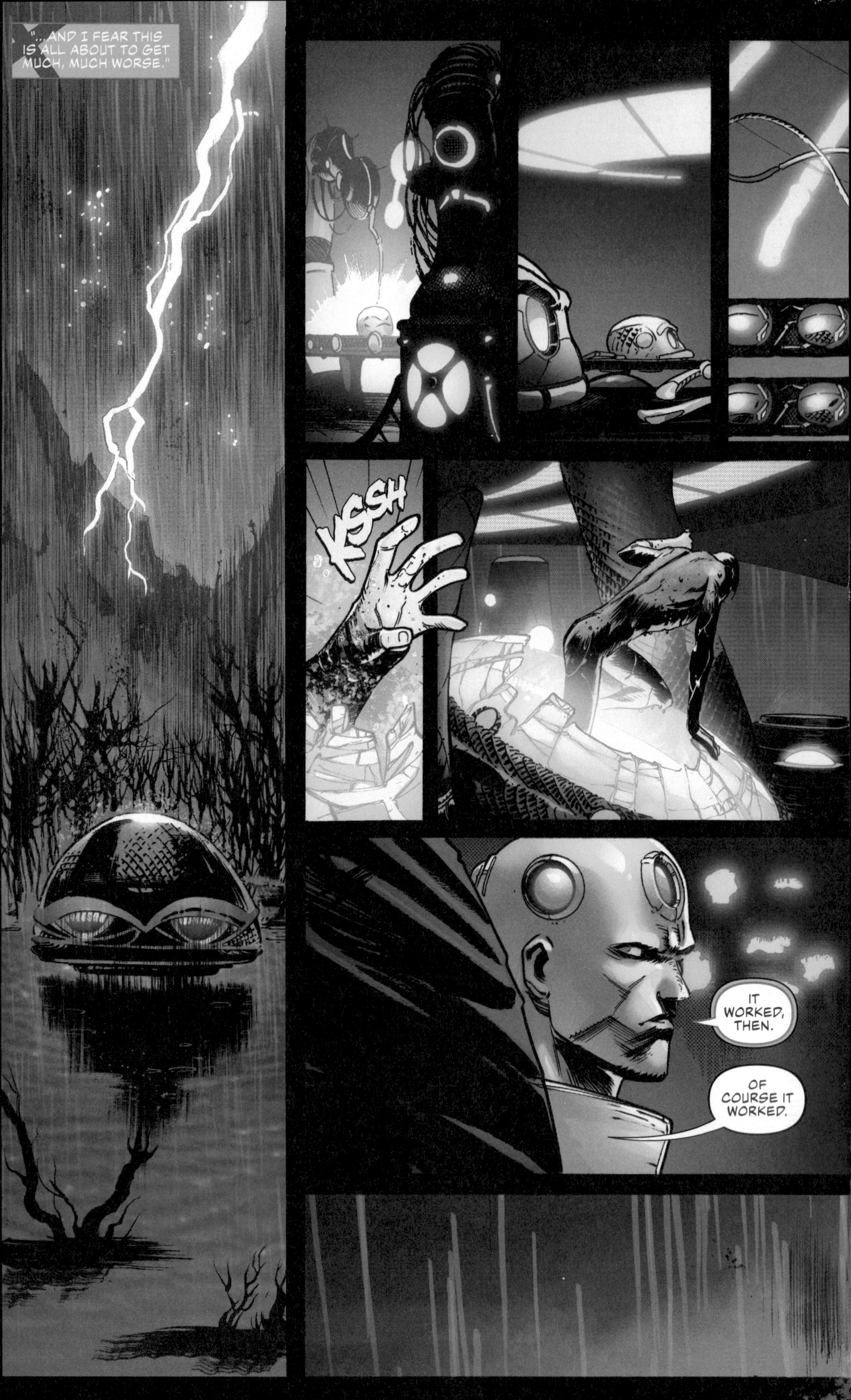
"...AND I FEAR THIS IS ALL ABOUT TO GET MUCH, MUCH WORSE."
KSSH
IT WORKED, THEN.
OF COURSE IT WORKED.

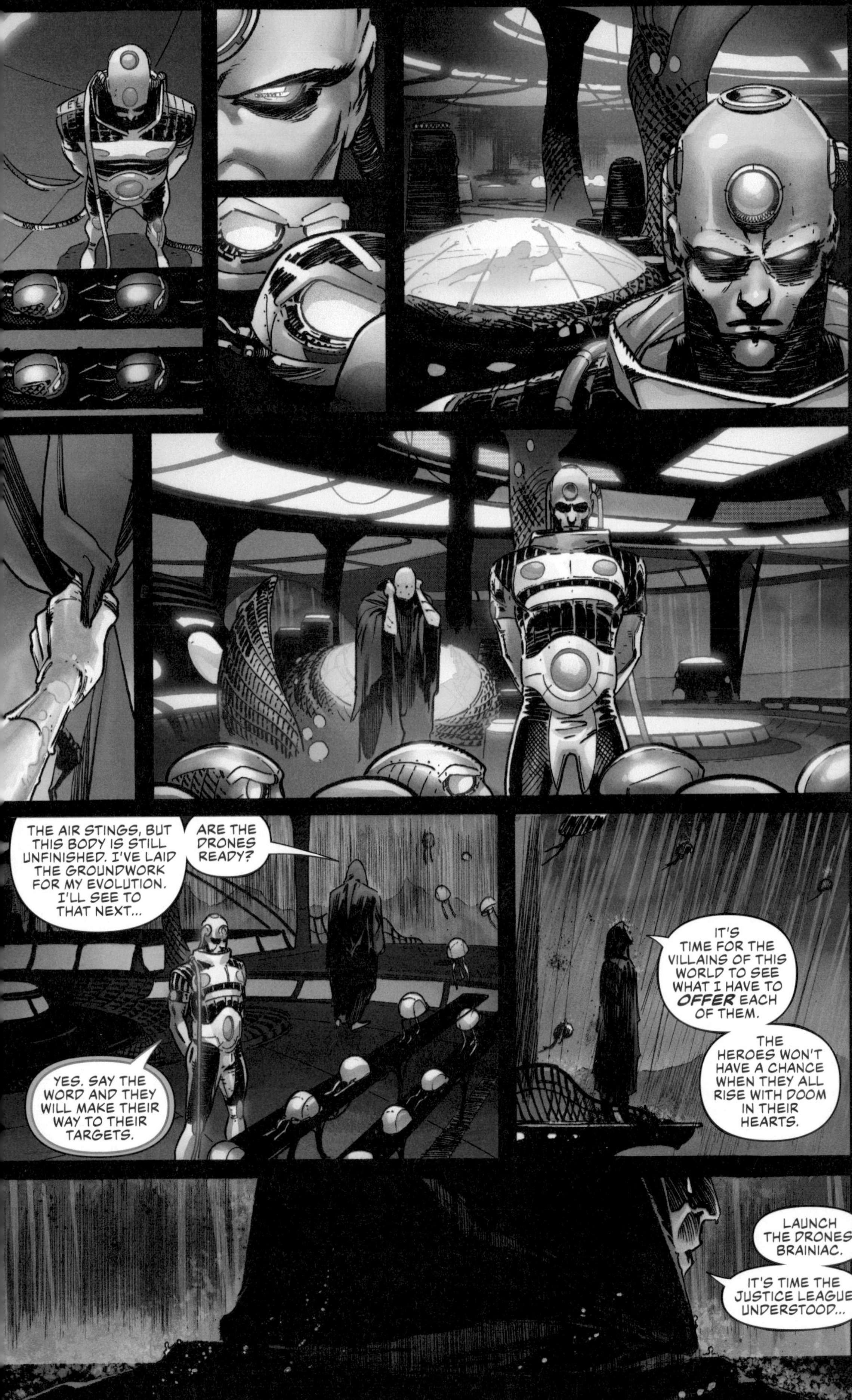
THE AIR STINGS, BUT THIS BODY IS STILL UNFINISHED. I'VE LAID THE GROUNDWORK FOR MY EVOLUTION. I'LL SEE TO THAT NEXT...
ARE THE DRONES READY?
YES. SAY THE WORD AND THEY WILL MAKE THEIR WAY TO THEIR TARGETS.
IT'S TIME FOR THE VILLAINS OF THIS WORLD TO SEE WHAT I HAVE TO OFFER EACH OF THEM.
THE HEROES WON'T HAVE A CHANCE WHEN THEY ALL RISE WITH DOOM IN THEIR HEARTS.
LAUNCH THE DRONES, BRAINIAC.
IT'S TIME THE JUSTICE LEAGUE UNDERSTOOD...

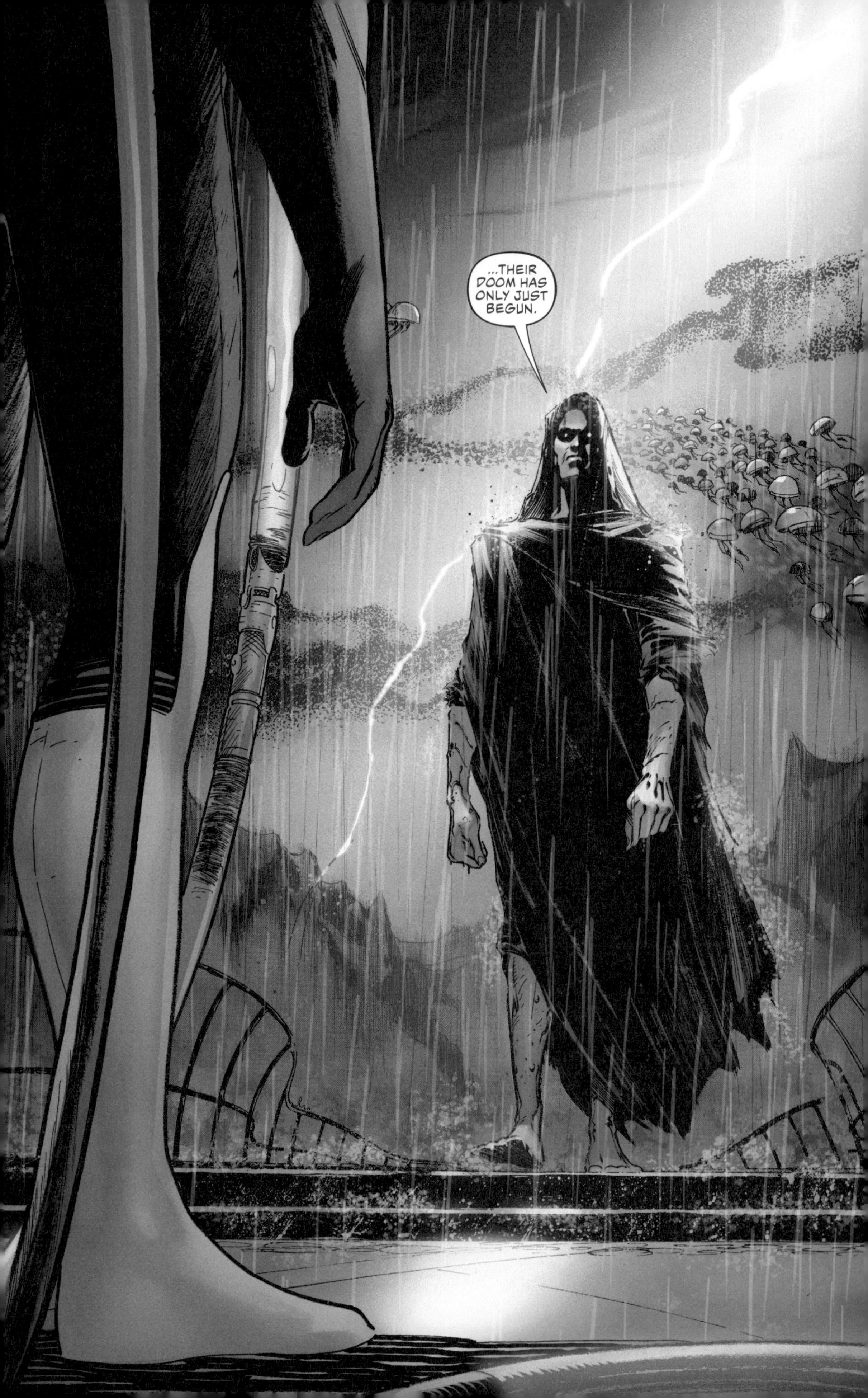
...THEIR DOOM HAS ONLY JUST BEGUN.

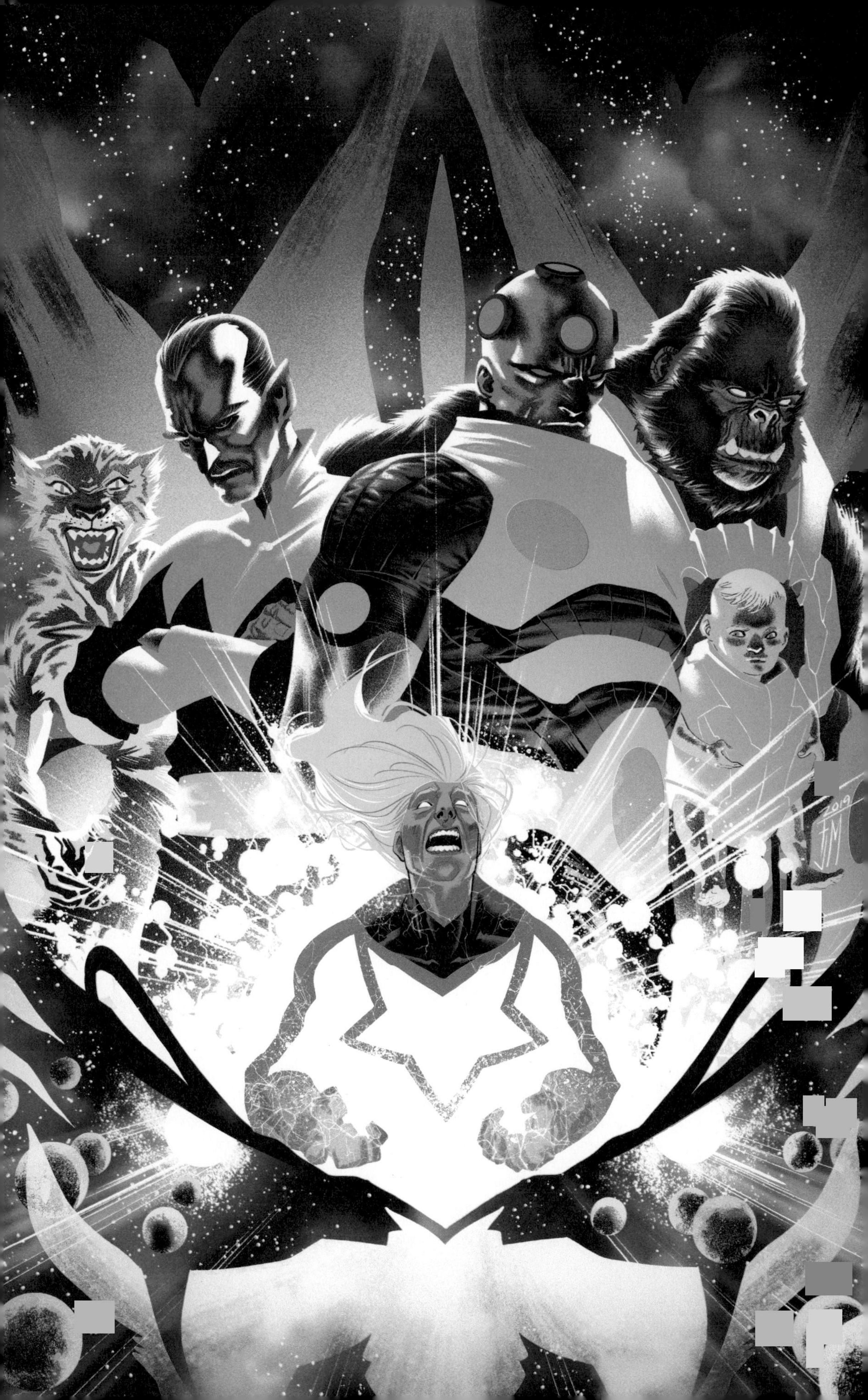

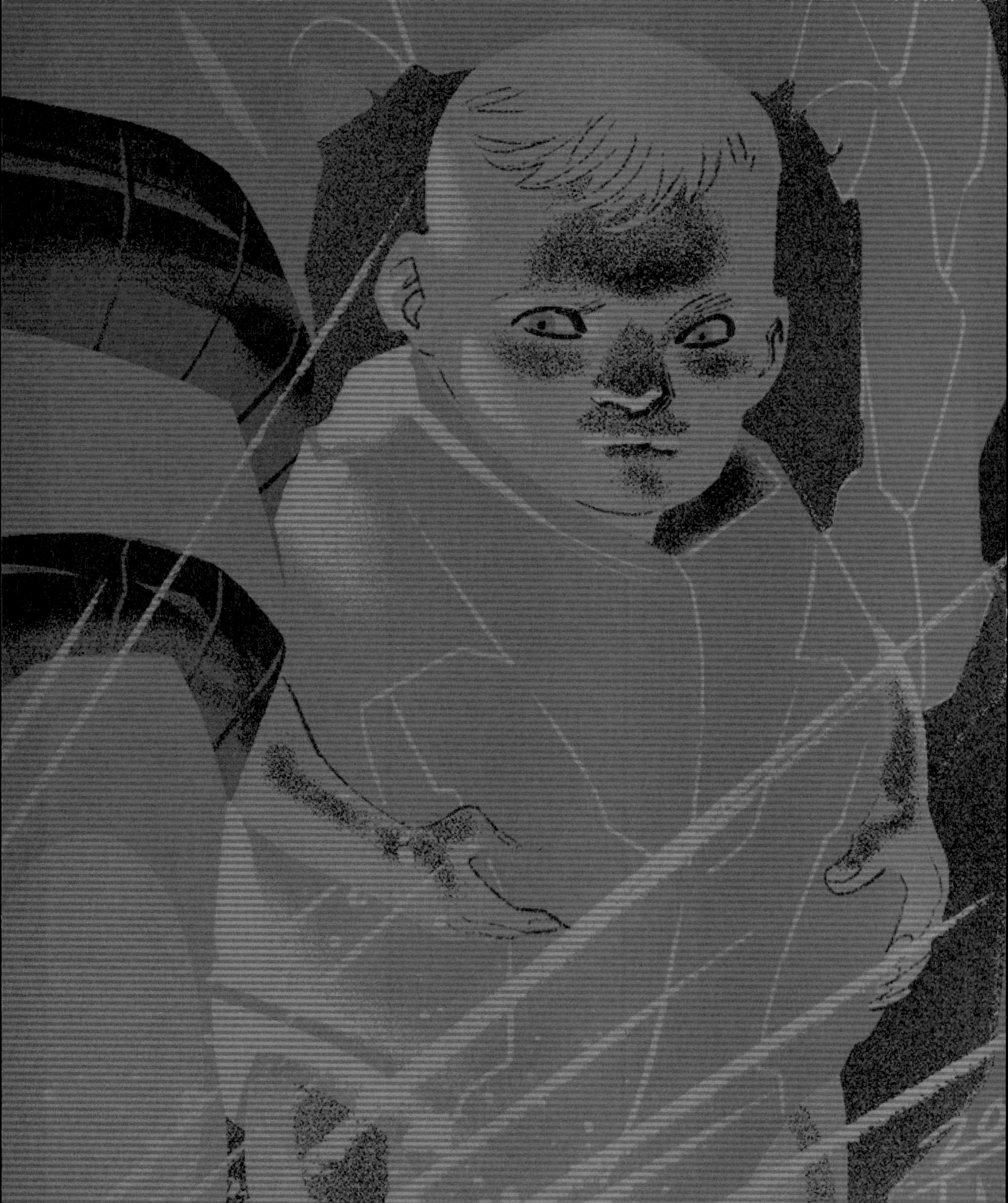

JUSTICE
LEAGUE
#26

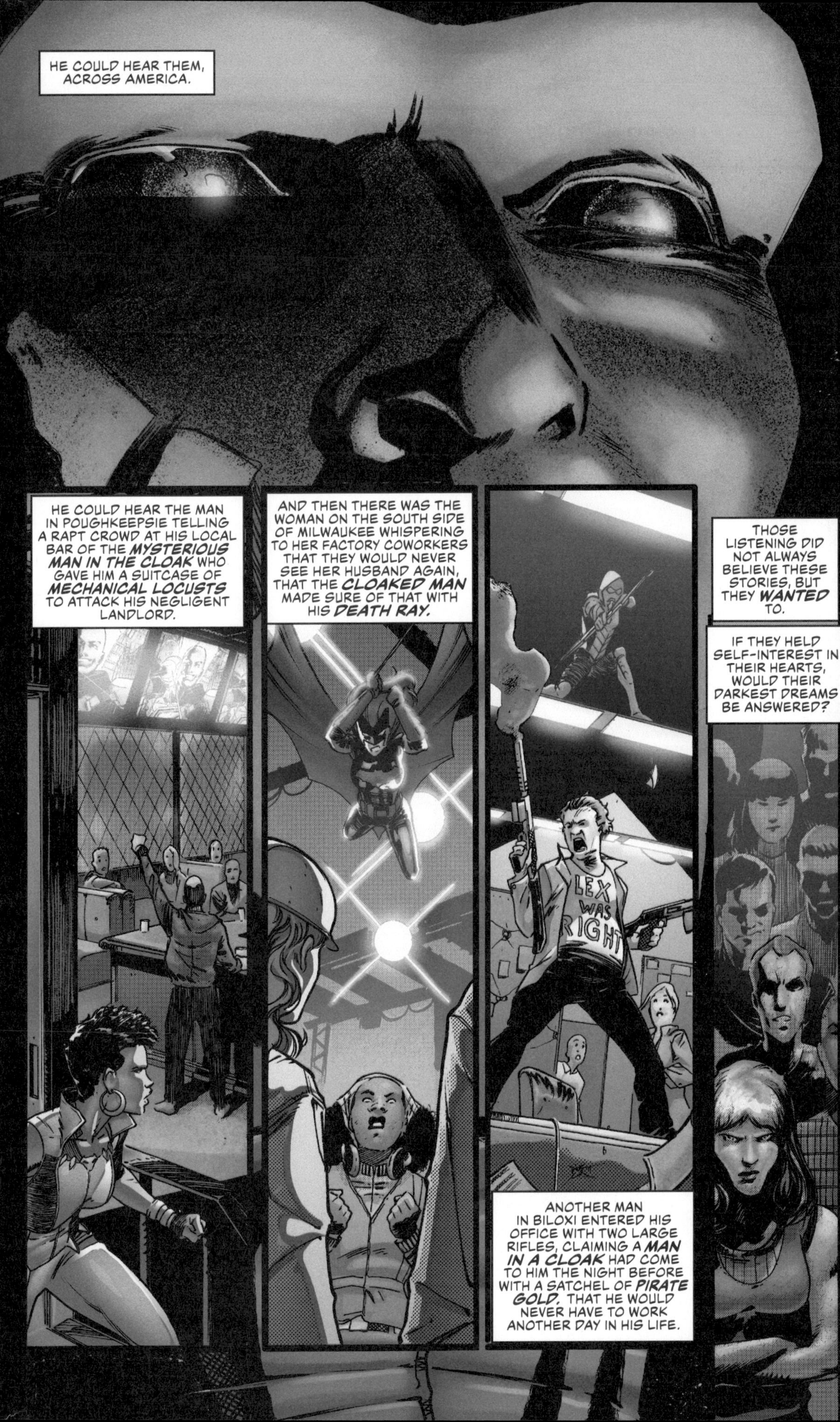

HE COULD HEAR THEM, ACROSS AMERICA.
HE COULD HEAR THE MAN IN POUGHKEEPSIE TELLING A RAPT CROWD AT HIS LOCAL BAR OF THE MYSTERIOUS MAN IN THE CLOAK WHO GAVE HIM A SUITCASE OF MECHANICAL LOCUSTS TO ATTACK HIS NEGLIGENT LANDLORD.
AND THEN THERE WAS THE WOMAN ON THE SOUTH SIDE OF MILWAUKEE WHISPERING TO HER FACTORY COWORKERS THAT THEY WOULD NEVER SEE HER HUSBAND AGAIN, THAT THE CLOAKED MAN MADE SURE OF THAT WITH HIS DEATH RAY.
LEX WAS RIGHT
ANOTHER MAN IN BILOXI ENTERED HIS OFFICE WITH TWO LARGE RIFLES, CLAIMING A MAN IN A CLOAK HAD COME TO HIM THE NIGHT BEFORE WITH A SATCHEL OF PIRATE GOLD. THAT HE WOULD NEVER HAVE TO WORK ANOTHER DAY IN HIS LIFE.
THOSE LISTENING DID NOT ALWAYS BELIEVE THESE STORIES, BUT THEY WANTED TO.
IF THEY HELD SELF-INTEREST IN THEIR HEARTS, WOULD THEIR DARKEST DREAMS BE ANSWERED?

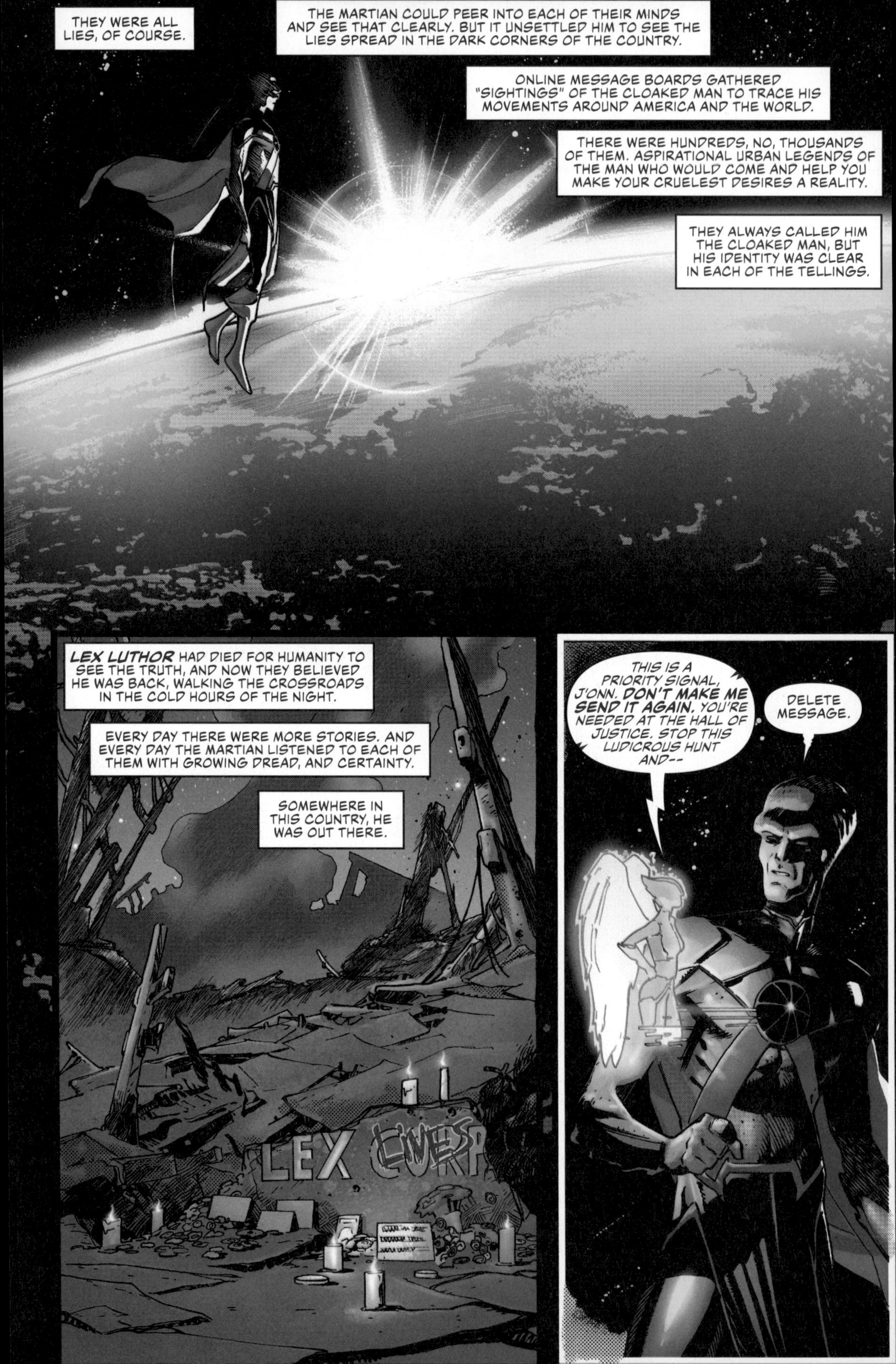
THEY WERE ALL LIES, OF COURSE.
THE MARTIAN COULD PEER INTO EACH OF THEIR MINDS AND SEE THAT CLEARLY. BUT IT UNSETTLED HIM TO SEE THE LIES SPREAD IN THE DARK CORNERS OF THE COUNTRY.
ONLINE MESSAGE BOARDS GATHERED "SIGHTINGS" OF THE CLOAKED MAN TO TRACE HIS MOVEMENTS AROUND AMERICA AND THE WORLD.
THERE WERE HUNDREDS, NO, THOUSANDS OF THEM. ASPIRATIONAL URBAN LEGENDS OF THE MAN WHO WOULD COME AND HELP YOU MAKE YOUR CRUELEST DESIRES A REALITY.
THEY ALWAYS CALLED HIM THE CLOAKED MAN, BUT HIS IDENTITY WAS CLEAR IN EACH OF THE TELLINGS.
LEX LUTHOR HAD DIED FOR HUMANITY TO SEE THE TRUTH, AND NOW THEY BELIEVED HE WAS BACK, WALKING THE CROSSROADS IN THE COLD HOURS OF THE NIGHT.
EVERY DAY THERE WERE MORE STORIES. AND EVERY DAY THE MARTIAN LISTENED TO EACH OF THEM WITH GROWING DREAD, AND CERTAINTY.
SOMEWHERE IN THIS COUNTRY, HE WAS OUT THERE.
LEX LIVES
THIS IS A PRIORITY SIGNAL, J'ONN. DON'T MAKE ME SEND IT AGAIN. YOU'RE NEEDED AT THE HALL OF JUSTICE. STOP THIS LUDICROUS HUNT AND--
DELETE MESSAGE.

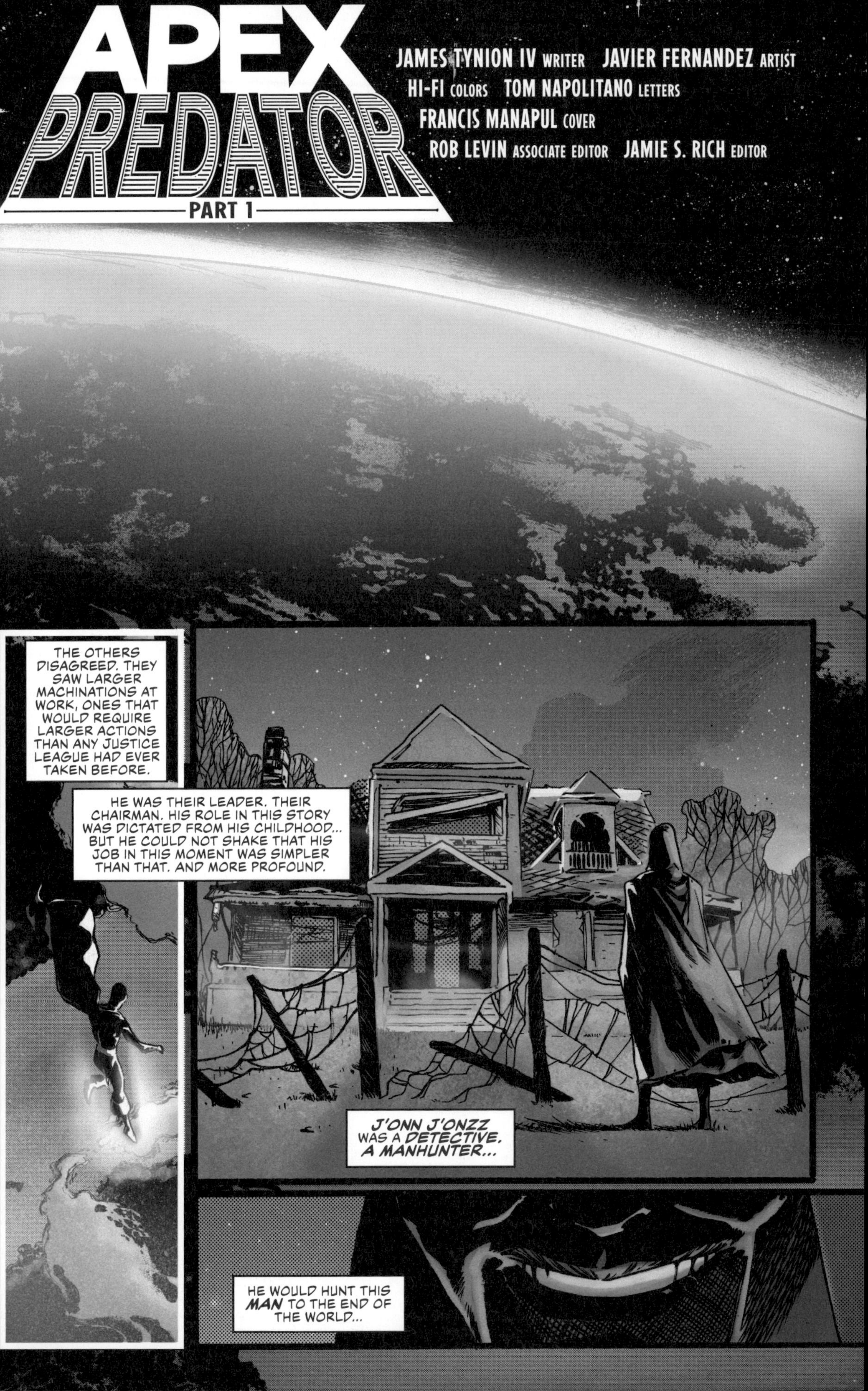
APEX PREDATOR
PART 1
JAMES TYNION IV WRITER JAVIER FERNANDEZ ARTIST
HI-FI COLORS TOM NAPOLITANO LETTERS
FRANCIS MANAPUL COVER
ROB LEVIN ASSOCIATE EDITOR JAMIE S. RICH EDITOR
THE OTHERS DISAGREED. THEY SAW LARGER MACHINATIONS AT WORK, ONES THAT WOULD REQUIRE LARGER ACTIONS THAN ANY JUSTICE LEAGUE HAD EVER TAKEN BEFORE.
HE WAS THEIR LEADER. THEIR CHAIRMAN. HIS ROLE IN THIS STORY WAS DICTATED FROM HIS CHILDHOOD... BUT HE COULD NOT SHAKE THAT HIS JOB IN THIS MOMENT WAS SIMPLER THAN THAT. AND MORE PROFOUND.
J'ONN J'ONZZ WAS A DETECTIVE. A MANHUNTER...
HE WOULD HUNT THIS MAN TO THE END OF THE WORLD...

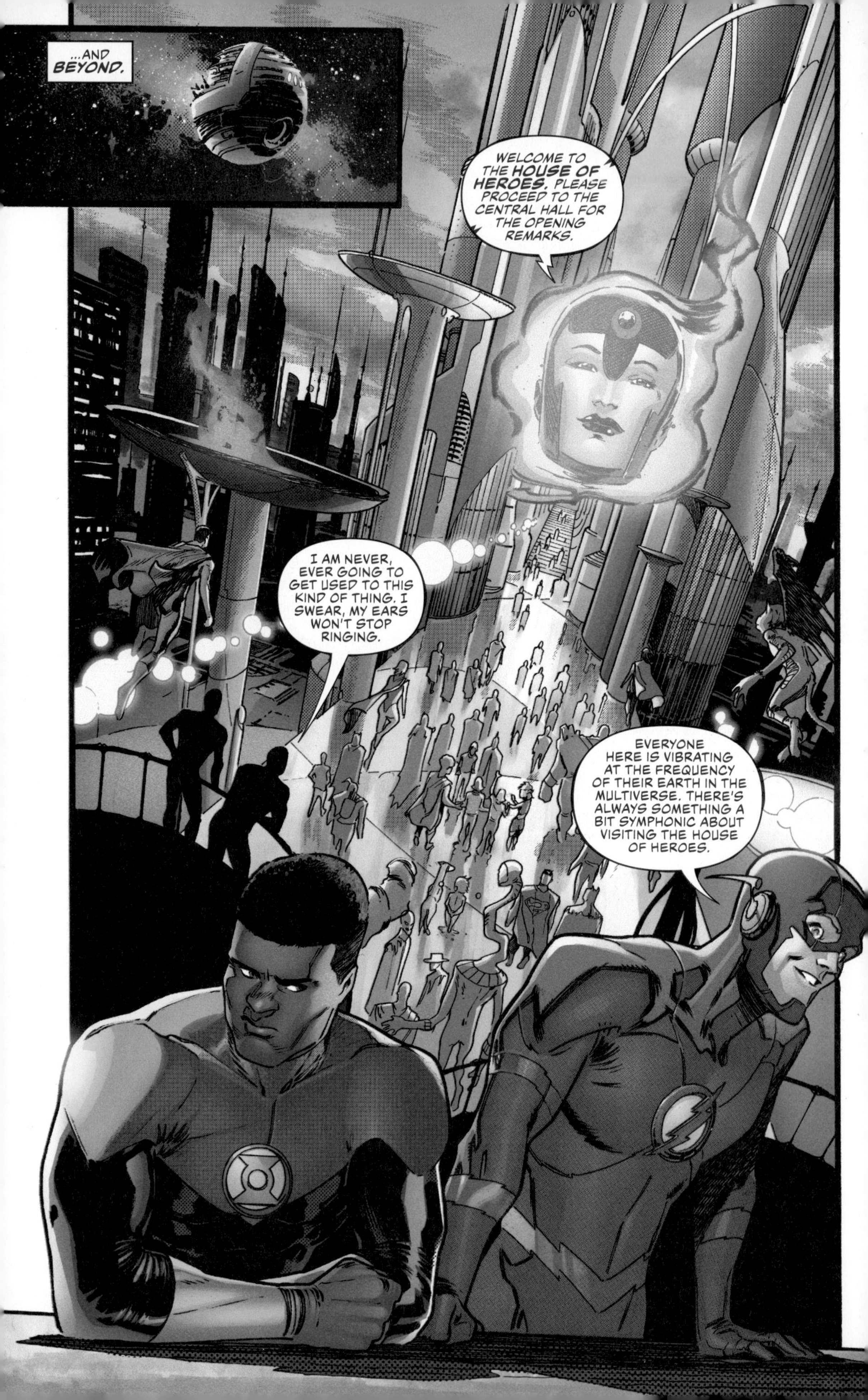

...AND BEYOND.
WELCOME TO THE HOUSE OF HEROES. PLEASE PROCEED TO THE CENTRAL HALL FOR THE OPENING REMARKS.
I AM NEVER, EVER GOING TO GET USED TO THIS KIND OF THING. I SWEAR, MY EARS WON'T STOP RINGING.
EVERYONE HERE IS VIBRATING AT THE FREQUENCY OF THEIR EARTH IN THE MULTIVERSE. THERE'S ALWAYS SOMETHING A BIT SYMPHONIC ABOUT VISITING THE HOUSE OF HEROES.

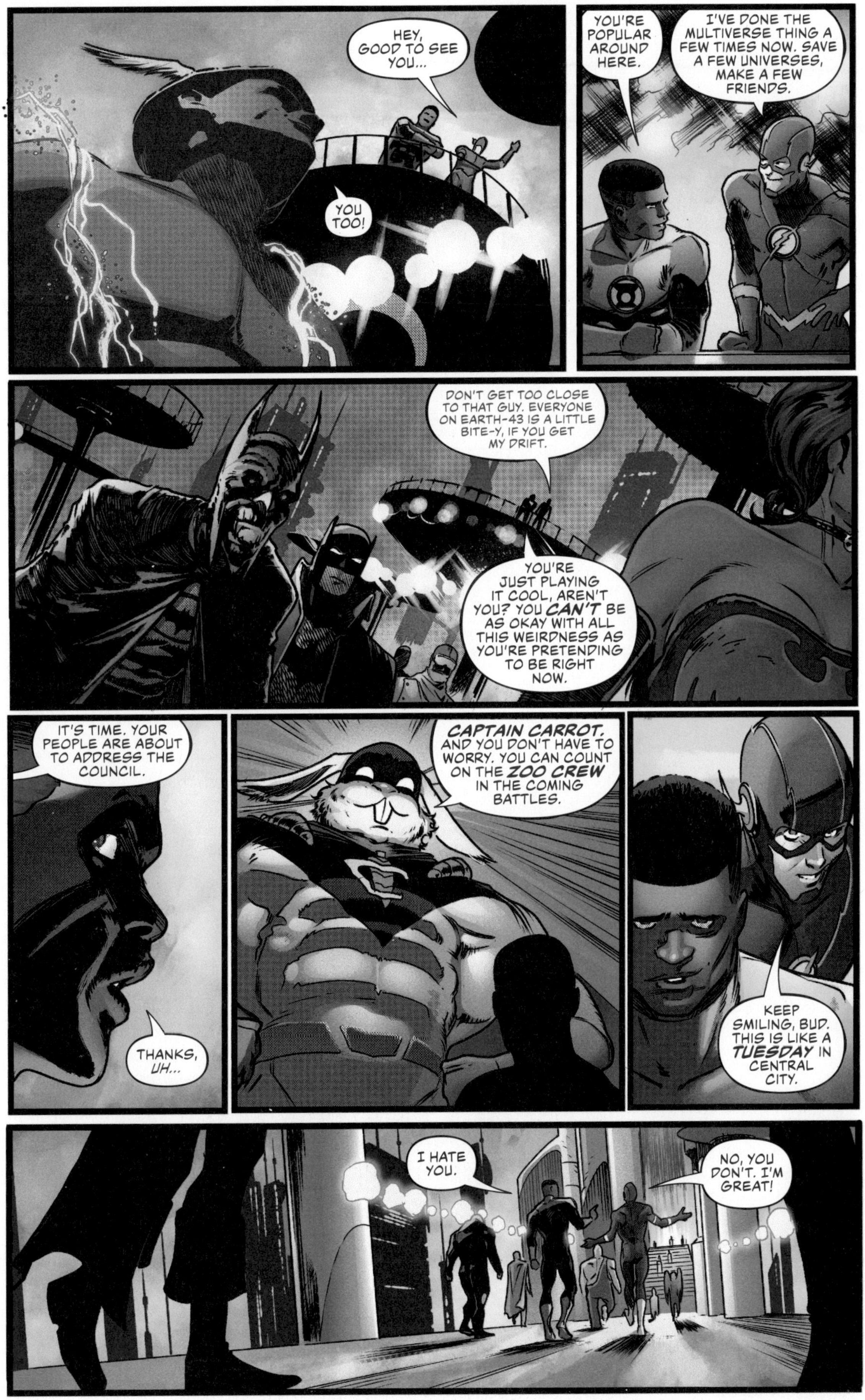
HEY, GOOD TO SEE YOU...
YOU TOO!
YOU'RE POPULAR AROUND HERE.
I'VE DONE THE MULTIVERSE THING A FEW TIMES NOW. SAVE A FEW UNIVERSES, MAKE A FEW FRIENDS.
DON'T GET TOO CLOSE TO THAT GUY. EVERYONE ON EARTH-43 IS A LITTLE BITE-Y, IF YOU GET MY DRIFT.
YOU'RE JUST PLAYING IT COOL, AREN'T YOU? YOU *CAN'T* BE AS OKAY WITH ALL THIS WEIRDNESS AS YOU'RE PRETENDING TO BE RIGHT NOW.
IT'S TIME. YOUR PEOPLE ARE ABOUT TO ADDRESS THE COUNCIL.
THANKS, *UH...*
CAPTAIN CARROT. AND YOU DON'T HAVE TO WORRY. YOU CAN COUNT ON THE *ZOO CREW* IN THE COMING BATTLES.
KEEP SMILING, BUD. THIS IS LIKE A *TUESDAY* IN CENTRAL CITY.
I HATE YOU.
NO, YOU DON'T. I'M GREAT!

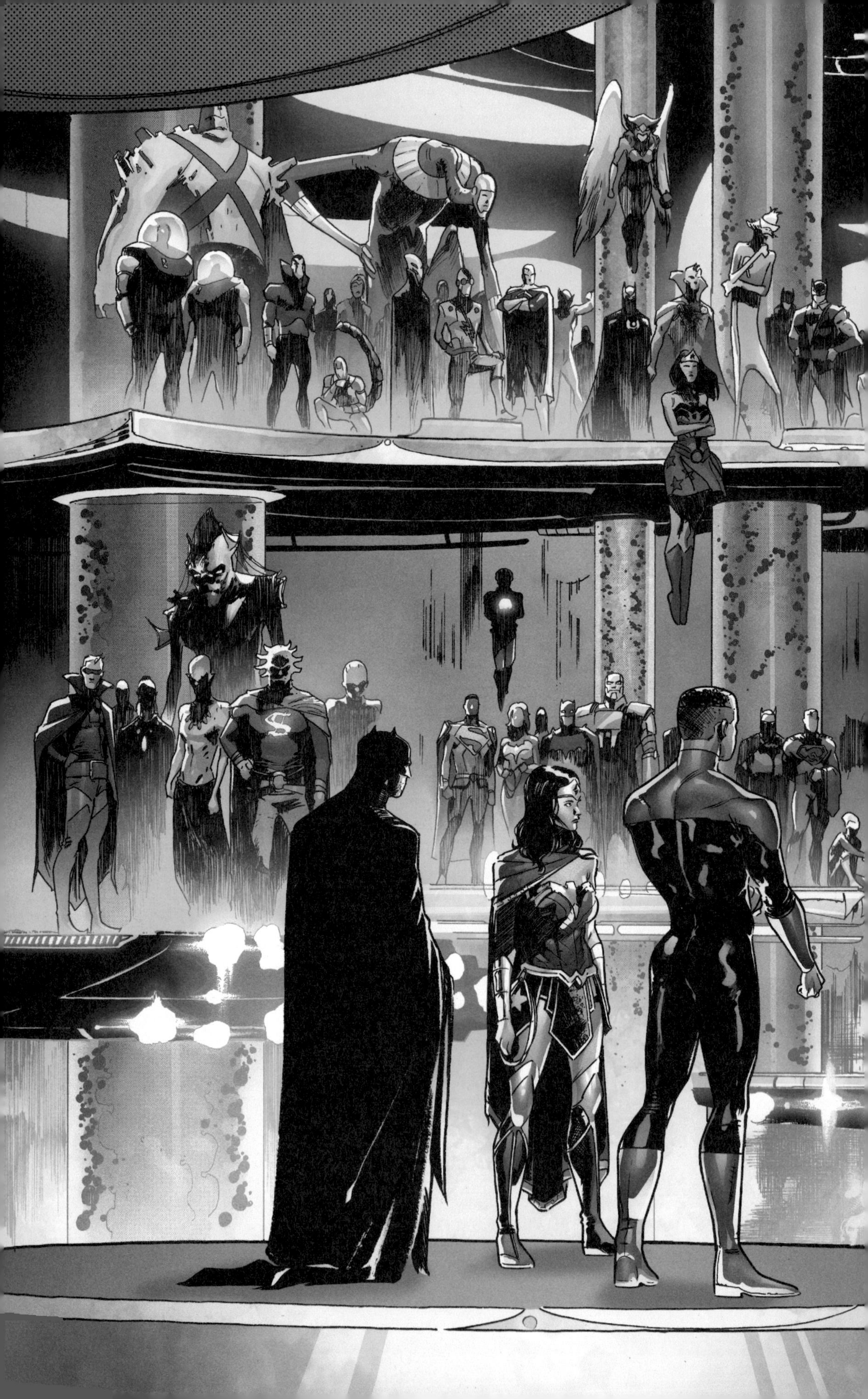

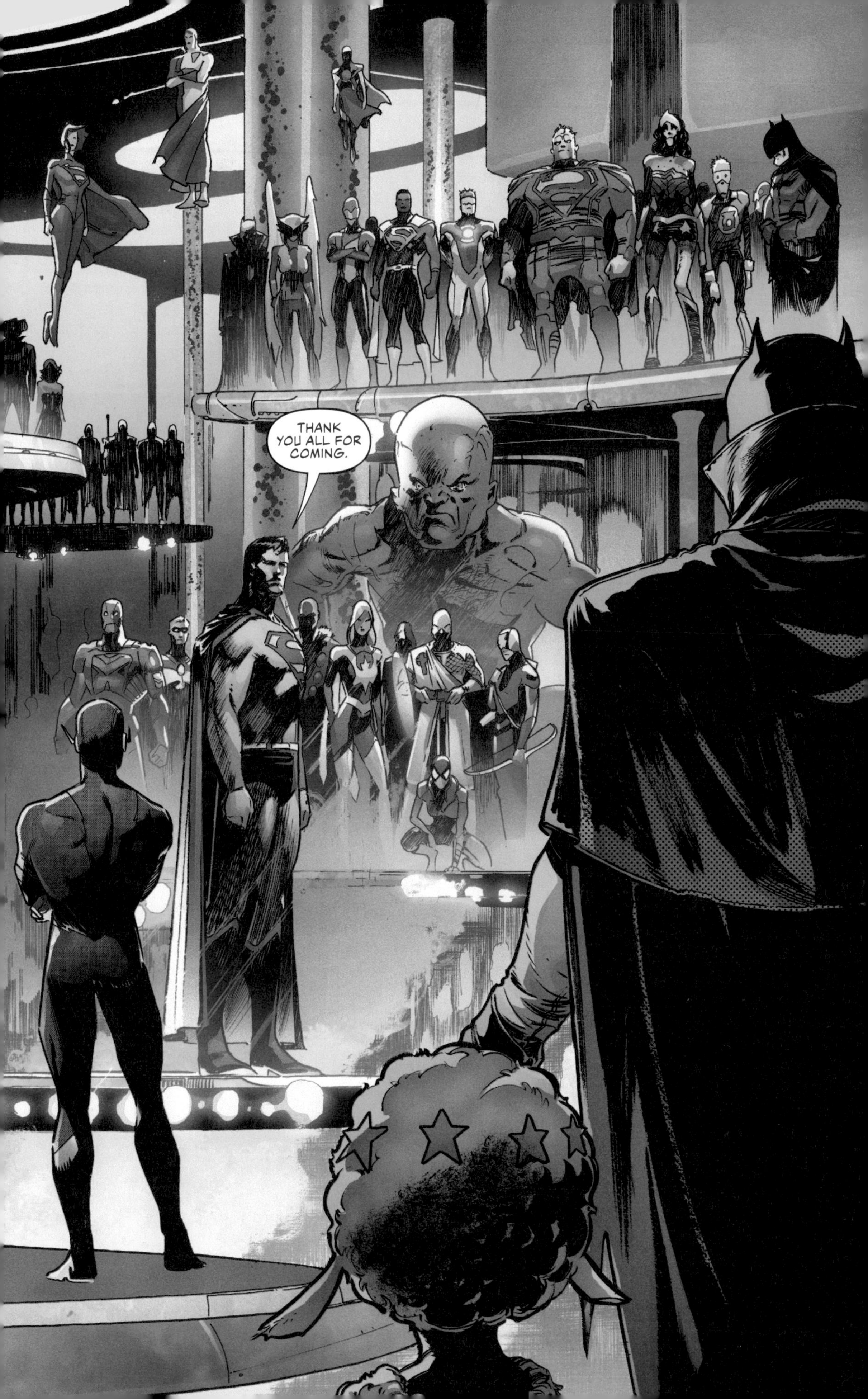
THANK YOU ALL FOR COMING.

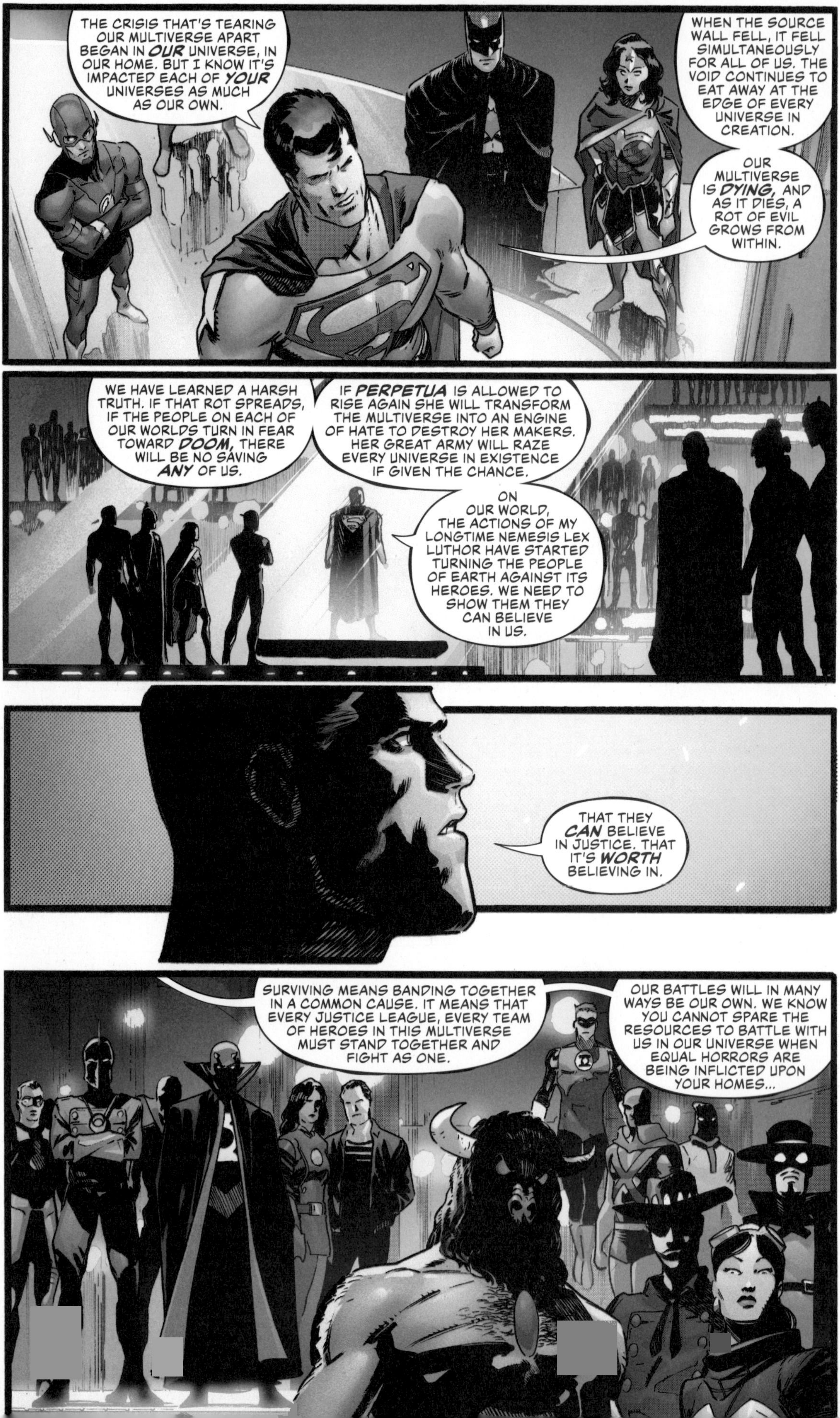
THE CRISIS THAT'S TEARING OUR MULTIVERSE APART BEGAN IN OUR UNIVERSE, IN OUR HOME. BUT I KNOW IT'S IMPACTED EACH OF YOUR UNIVERSES AS MUCH AS OUR OWN.
WHEN THE SOURCE WALL FELL, IT FELL SIMULTANEOUSLY FOR ALL OF US. THE VOID CONTINUES TO EAT AWAY AT THE EDGE OF EVERY UNIVERSE IN CREATION.
OUR MULTIVERSE IS DYING, AND AS IT DIES, A ROT OF EVIL GROWS FROM WITHIN.
WE HAVE LEARNED A HARSH TRUTH. IF THAT ROT SPREADS, IF THE PEOPLE ON EACH OF OUR WORLDS TURN IN FEAR TOWARD DOOM, THERE WILL BE NO SAVING ANY OF US.
IF PERPETUA IS ALLOWED TO RISE AGAIN SHE WILL TRANSFORM THE MULTIVERSE INTO AN ENGINE OF HATE TO DESTROY HER MAKERS. HER GREAT ARMY WILL RAZE EVERY UNIVERSE IN EXISTENCE IF GIVEN THE CHANCE.
ON OUR WORLD, THE ACTIONS OF MY LONGTIME NEMESIS LEX LUTHOR HAVE STARTED TURNING THE PEOPLE OF EARTH AGAINST ITS HEROES. WE NEED TO SHOW THEM THEY CAN BELIEVE IN US.
THAT THEY CAN BELIEVE IN JUSTICE. THAT IT'S WORTH BELIEVING IN.
SURVIVING MEANS BANDING TOGETHER IN A COMMON CAUSE. IT MEANS THAT EVERY JUSTICE LEAGUE, EVERY TEAM OF HEROES IN THIS MULTIVERSE MUST STAND TOGETHER AND FIGHT AS ONE.
OUR BATTLES WILL IN MANY WAYS BE OUR OWN. WE KNOW YOU CANNOT SPARE THE RESOURCES TO BATTLE WITH US IN OUR UNIVERSE WHEN EQUAL HORRORS ARE BEING INFLICTED UPON YOUR HOMES...

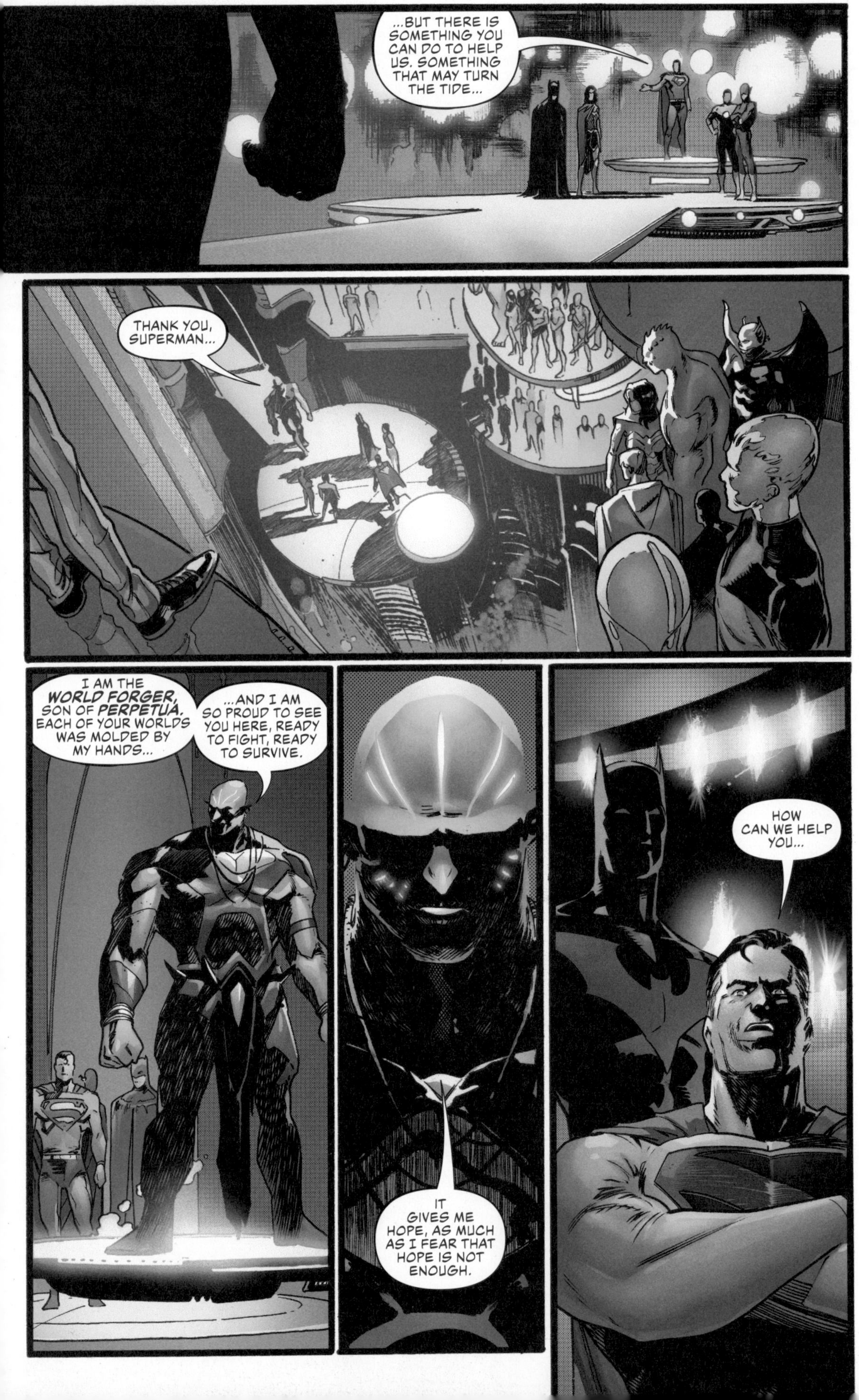
...BUT THERE IS SOMETHING YOU CAN DO TO HELP US. SOMETHING THAT MAY TURN THE TIDE...
THANK YOU, SUPERMAN...
I AM THE WORLD FORGER, SON OF PERPETUA. EACH OF YOUR WORLDS WAS MOLDED BY MY HANDS...
...AND I AM SO PROUD TO SEE YOU HERE, READY TO FIGHT, READY TO SURVIVE.
IT GIVES ME HOPE, AS MUCH AS I FEAR THAT HOPE IS NOT ENOUGH.
HOW CAN WE HELP YOU...

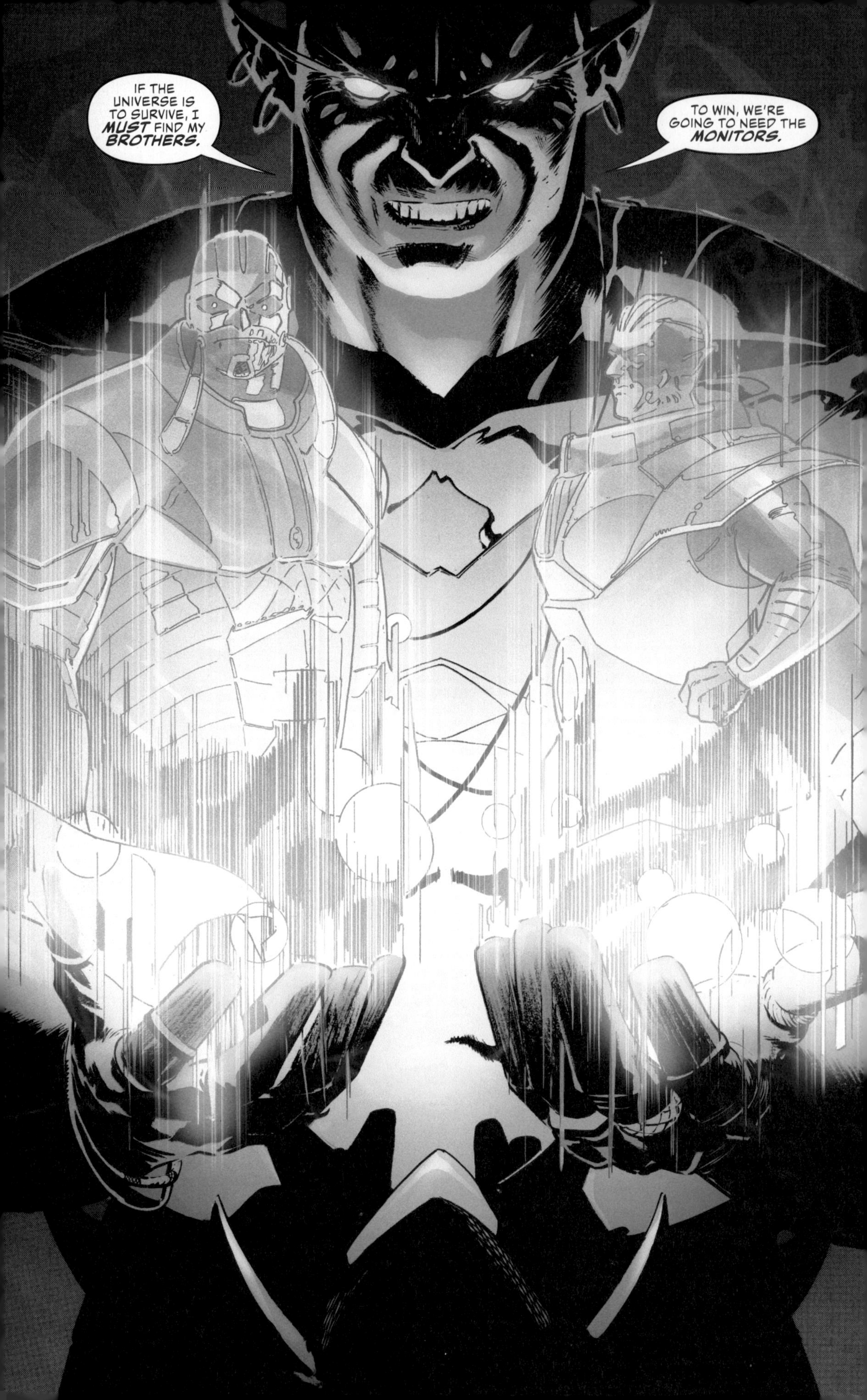
IF THE UNIVERSE IS TO SURVIVE, I MUST FIND MY BROTHERS.
TO WIN, WE'RE GOING TO NEED THE MONITORS.

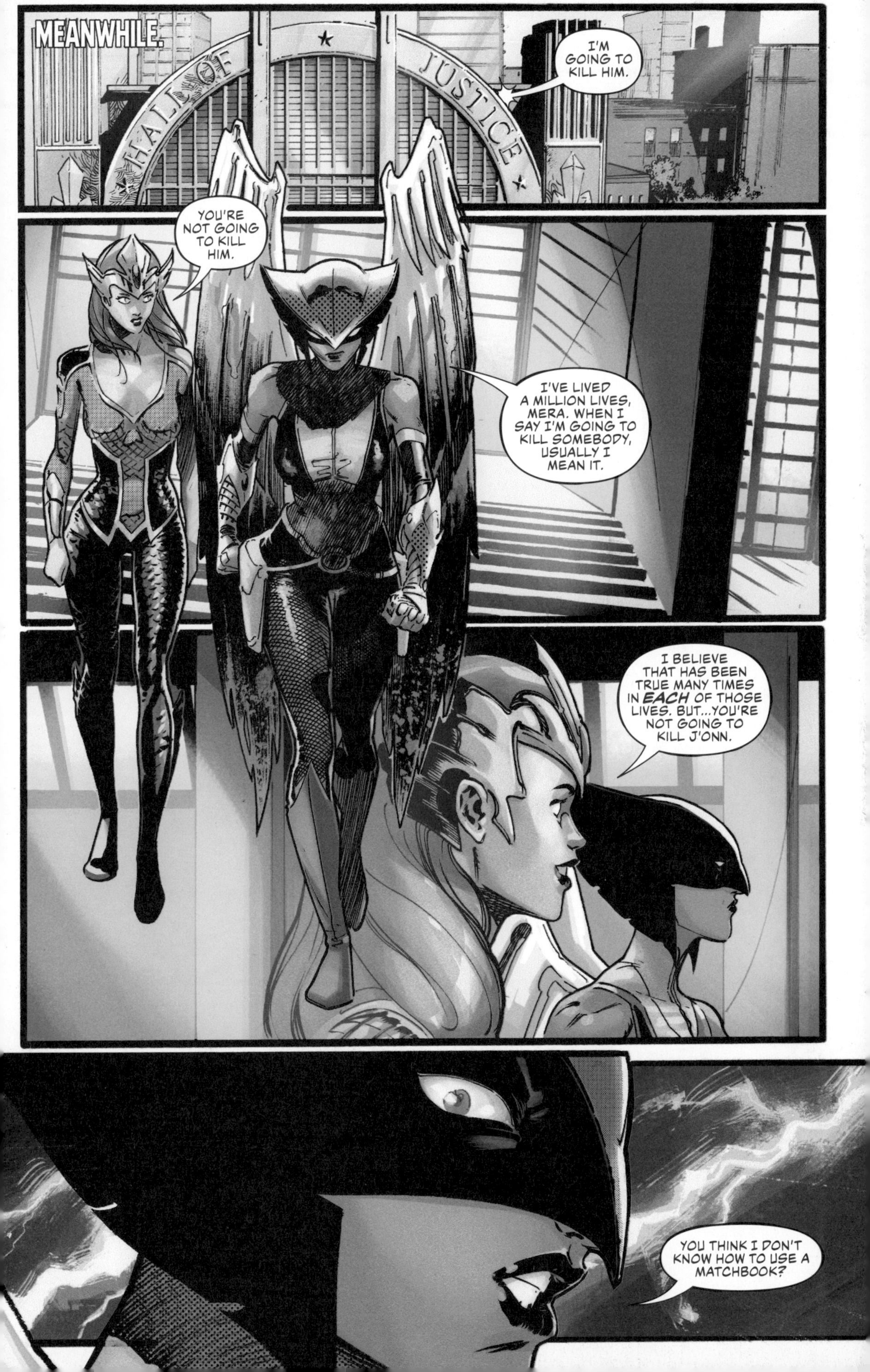
MEANWHILE.
HALL OF JUSTICE
I'M GOING TO KILL HIM.
YOU'RE NOT GOING TO KILL HIM.
I'VE LIVED A MILLION LIVES, MERA. WHEN I SAY I'M GOING SOMEBODY TO KILL SOMEBODY, USUALLY I MEAN IT.
I BELIEVE THAT HAS BEEN TRUE MANY TIMES IN EACH OF THOSE LIVES. BUT...YOU'RE NOT GOING TO KILL J'ONN.
YOU THINK I DON'T KNOW HOW TO USE A MATCHBOOK?

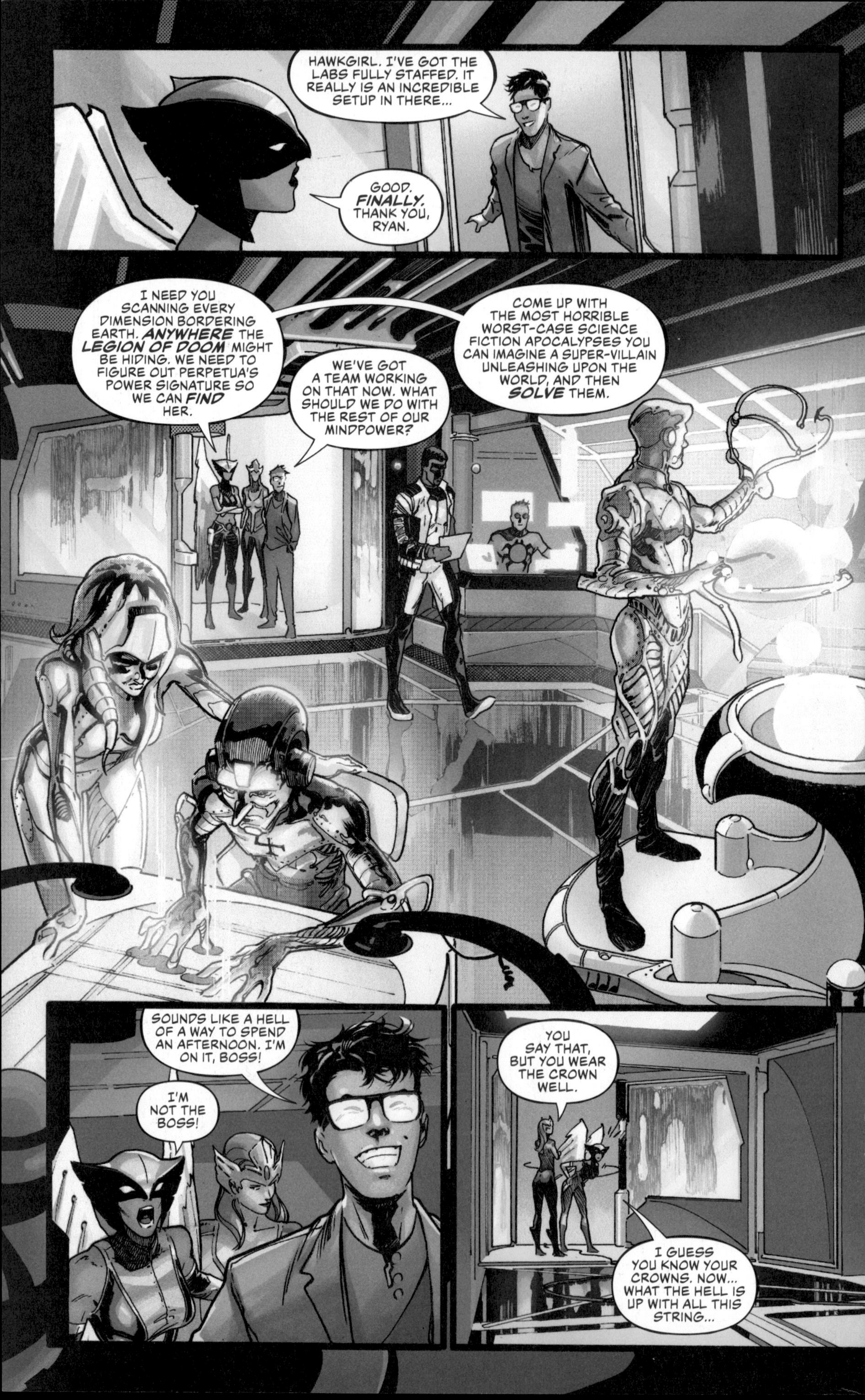
HAWKGIRL. I'VE GOT THE LABS FULLY STAFFED. IT REALLY IS AN INCREDIBLE SETUP IN THERE...
GOOD. FINALLY. THANK YOU, RYAN.
I NEED YOU SCANNING EVERY DIMENSION BORDERING EARTH. ANYWHERE THE LEGION OF DOOM MIGHT BE HIDING. WE NEED TO FIGURE OUT PERPETUA'S POWER SIGNATURE SO WE CAN FIND HER.
WE'VE GOT A TEAM WORKING ON THAT NOW. WHAT SHOULD WE DO WITH THE REST OF OUR MINDPOWER?
COME UP WITH THE MOST HORRIBLE WORST-CASE SCIENCE FICTION APOCALYPSES YOU CAN IMAGINE A SUPER-VILLAIN UNLEASHING UPON THE WORLD, AND THEN SOLVE THEM.
SOUNDS LIKE A HELL OF A WAY TO SPEND AN AFTERNOON. I'M ON IT, BOSS!
I'M NOT THE BOSS!
YOU SAY THAT, BUT YOU WEAR THE CROWN WELL.
I GUESS YOU KNOW YOUR CROWNS. NOW... WHAT THE HELL IS UP WITH ALL THIS STRING...

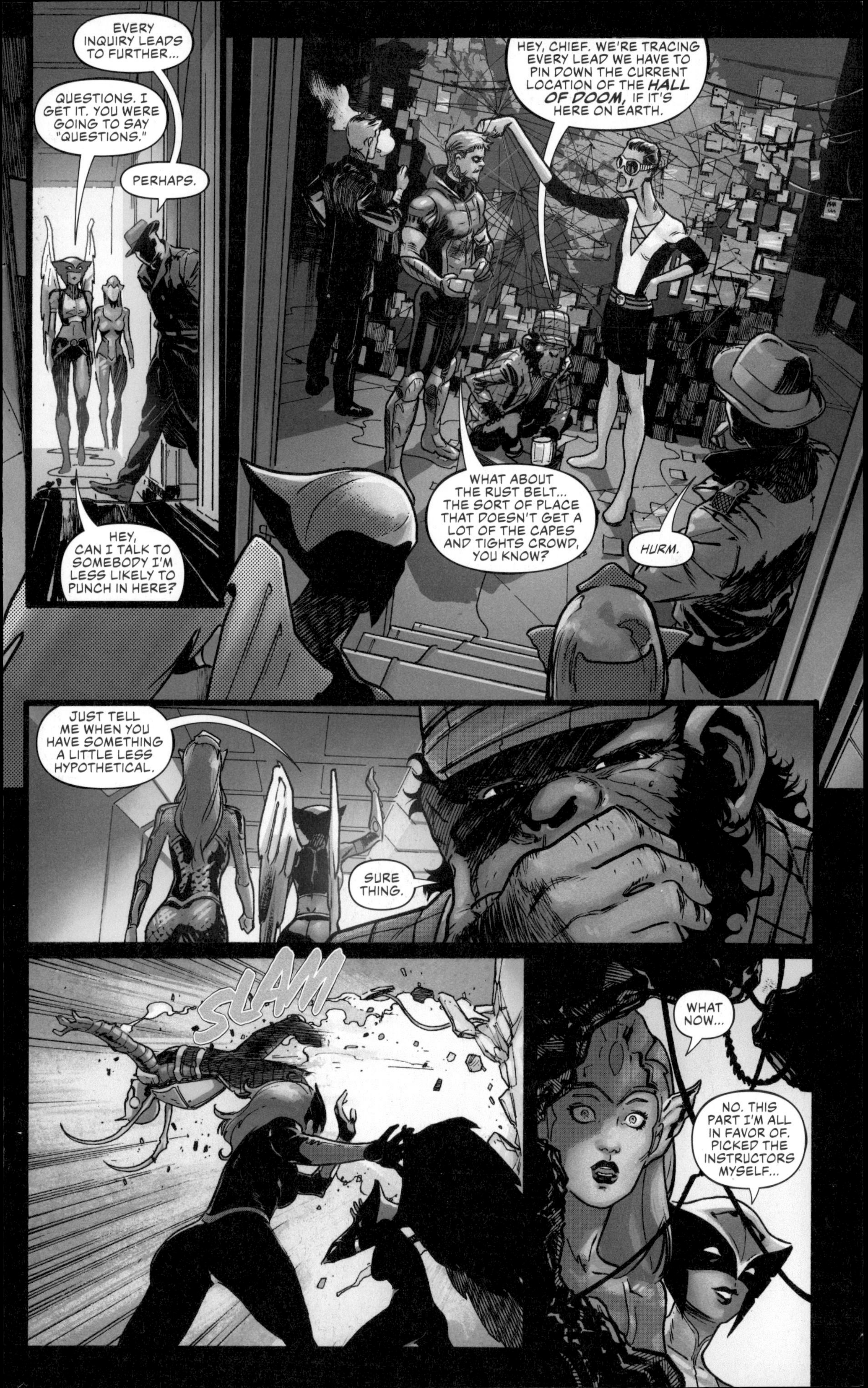
EVERY INQUIRY LEADS TO FURTHER...
QUESTIONS. I GET IT. YOU WERE GOING TO SAY "QUESTIONS."
PERHAPS.
HEY, CHIEF. WE'RE TRACING EVERY LEAD WE HAVE TO PIN DOWN THE CURRENT LOCATION OF THE HALL OF DOOM, IF IT'S HERE ON EARTH.
HEY, CAN I TALK TO SOMEBODY I'M LESS LIKELY TO PUNCH IN HERE?
WHAT ABOUT THE RUST BELT... THE SORT OF PLACE THAT DOESN'T GET A LOT OF THE CAPES AND TIGHTS CROWD, YOU KNOW?
HURM.
JUST TELL ME WHEN YOU HAVE SOMETHING A LITTLE LESS HYPOTHETICAL.
SURE THING.
SLAM
WHAT NOW...
NO. THIS PART I'M ALL IN FAVOR OF. PICKED THE INSTRUCTORS MYSELF...

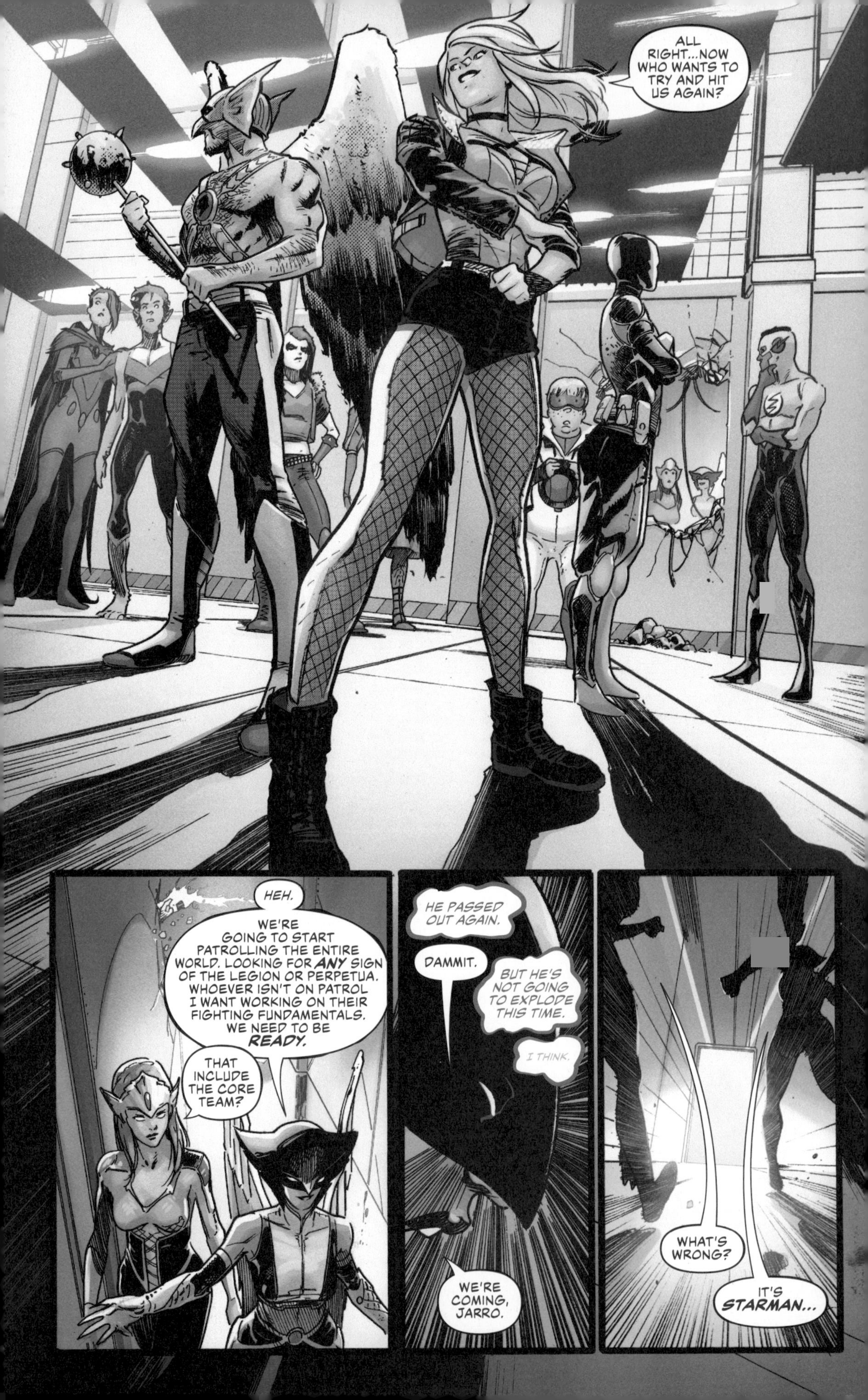
ALL RIGHT...NOW WHO WANTS TO TRY AND HIT US AGAIN?
HEH.
WE'RE GOING TO START PATROLLING THE ENTIRE WORLD. LOOKING FOR ANY SIGN OF THE LEGION OR PERPETUA. WHOEVER ISN'T ON PATROL I WANT WORKING ON THEIR FIGHTING FUNDAMENTALS. WE NEED TO BE READY.
THAT INCLUDE THE CORE TEAM?
HE PASSED OUT AGAIN.
DAMMIT.
BUT HE'S NOT GOING TO EXPLODE THIS TIME.
I THINK.
WE'RE COMING, JARRO.
WHAT'S WRONG?
IT'S STARMAN...

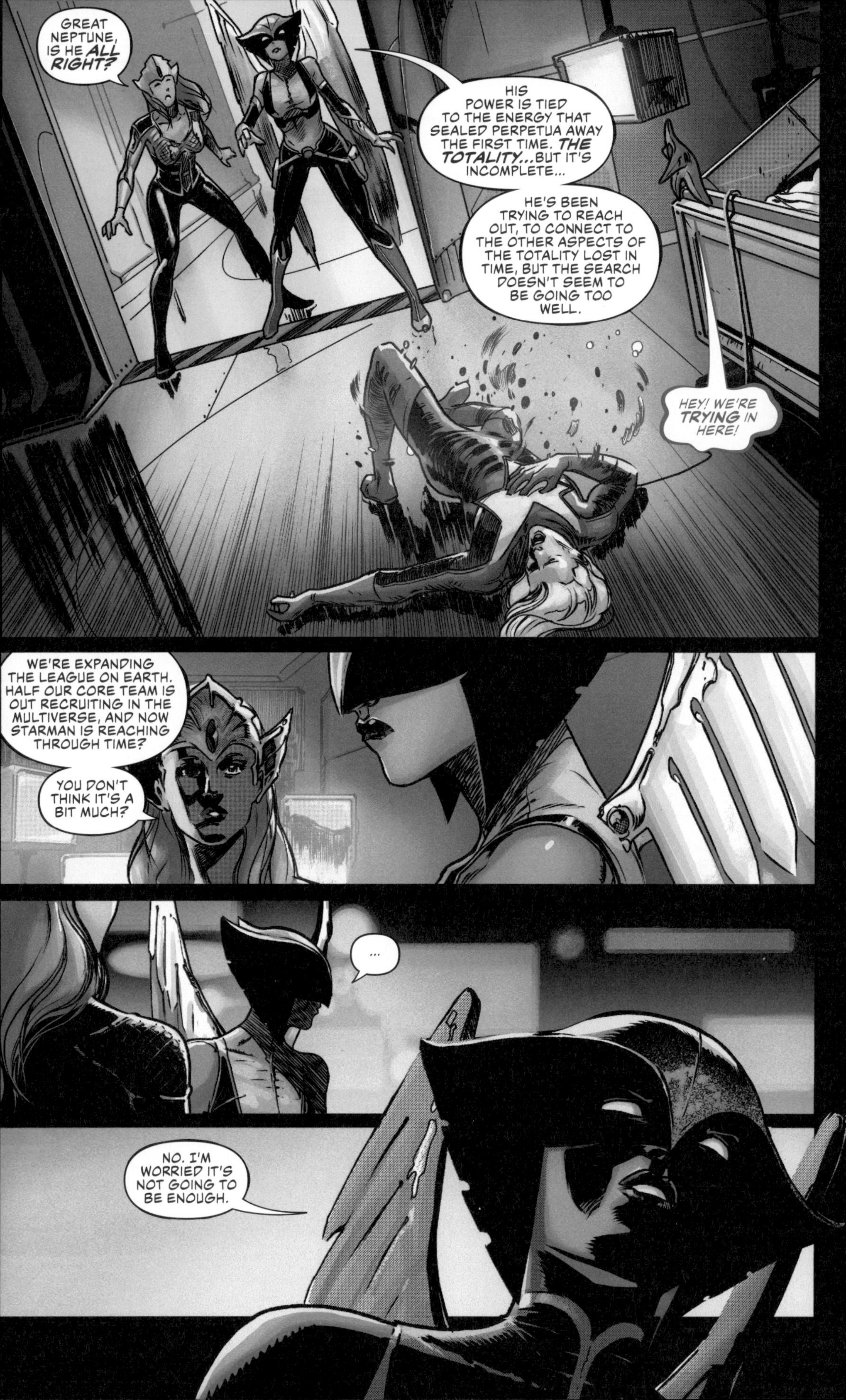
GREAT NEPTUNE, IS HE ALL RIGHT?
HIS POWER IS TIED TO THE ENERGY THAT SEALED PERPETUA AWAY THE FIRST TIME. THE TOTALITY... BUT IT'S INCOMPLETE...
HE'S BEEN TRYING TO REACH OUT, TO CONNECT TO THE OTHER ASPECTS OF THE TOTALITY LOST IN TIME, BUT THE SEARCH DOESN'T SEEM TO BE GOING TOO WELL.
HEY! WE'RE TRYING IN HERE!
WE'RE EXPANDING THE LEAGUE ON EARTH. HALF OUR CORE TEAM IS OUT RECRUITING IN THE MULTIVERSE, AND NOW STARMAN IS REACHING THROUGH TIME?
YOU DON'T THINK IT'S A BIT MUCH?
...
NO. I'M WORRIED IT'S NOT GOING TO BE ENOUGH.

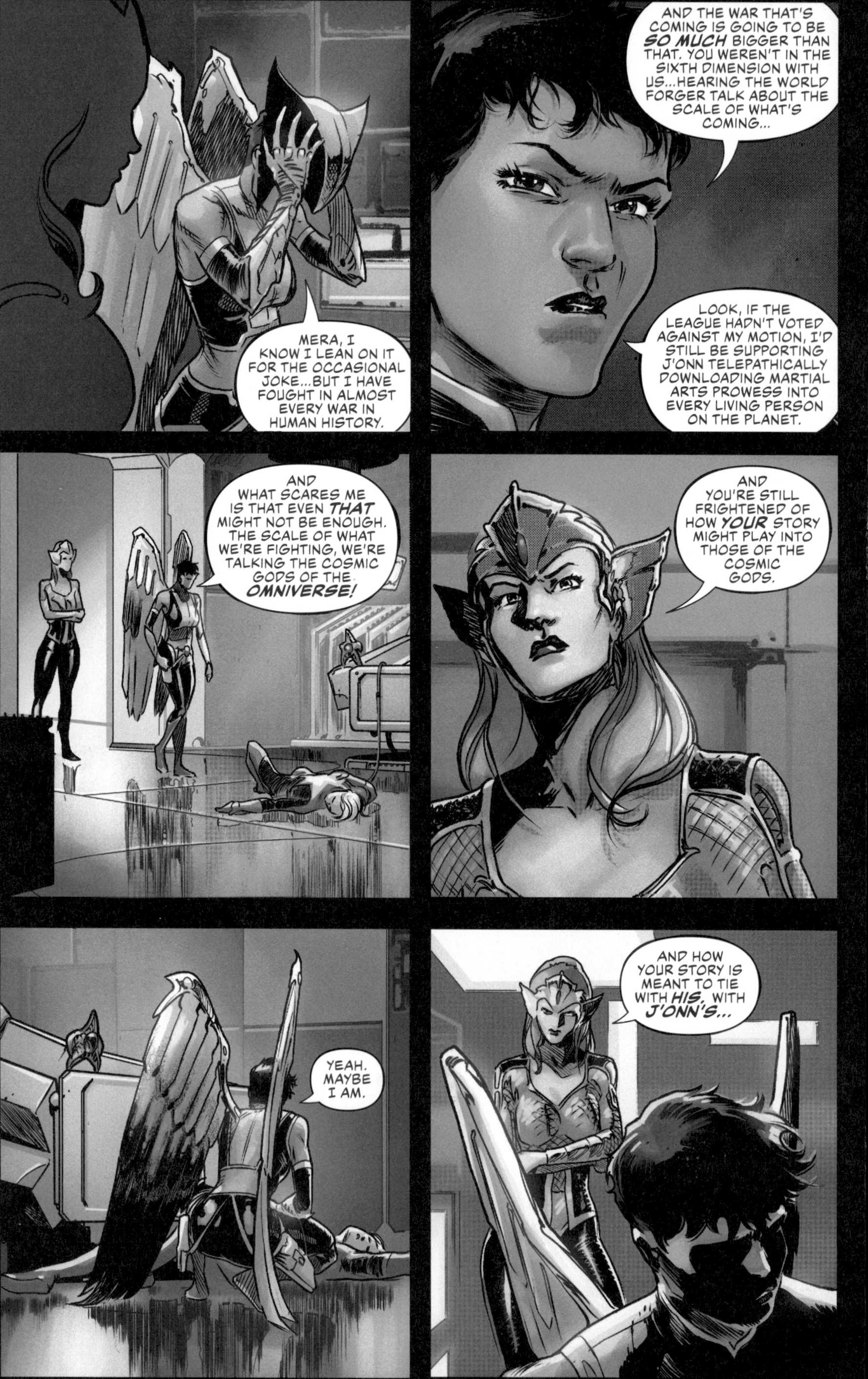
MERA, I KNOW I LEAN ON IT FOR THE OCCASIONAL JOKE...BUT I HAVE FOUGHT IN ALMOST EVERY WAR IN HUMAN HISTORY.
AND THE WAR THAT'S COMING IS GOING TO BE SO MUCH BIGGER THAN THAT. YOU WEREN'T IN THE SIXTH DIMENSION WITH US...HEARING THE WORLD FORGER TALK ABOUT THE SCALE OF WHAT'S COMING...
LOOK, IF THE LEAGUE HADN'T VOTED AGAINST MY MOTION, I'D STILL BE SUPPORTING J'ONN TELEPATHICALLY DOWNLOADING MARTIAL ARTS PROWESS INTO EVERY LIVING PERSON ON THE PLANET.
AND WHAT SCARES ME IS THAT EVEN THAT MIGHT NOT BE ENOUGH. THE SCALE OF WHAT WE'RE FIGHTING, WE'RE TALKING THE COSMIC GODS OF THE OMNIVERSE!
AND YOU'RE STILL FRIGHTENED OF HOW YOUR STORY MIGHT PLAY INTO THOSE OF THE COSMIC GODS.
YEAH. MAYBE I AM.
AND HOW YOUR STORY IS MEANT TO TIE WITH HIS. WITH J'ONN'S...

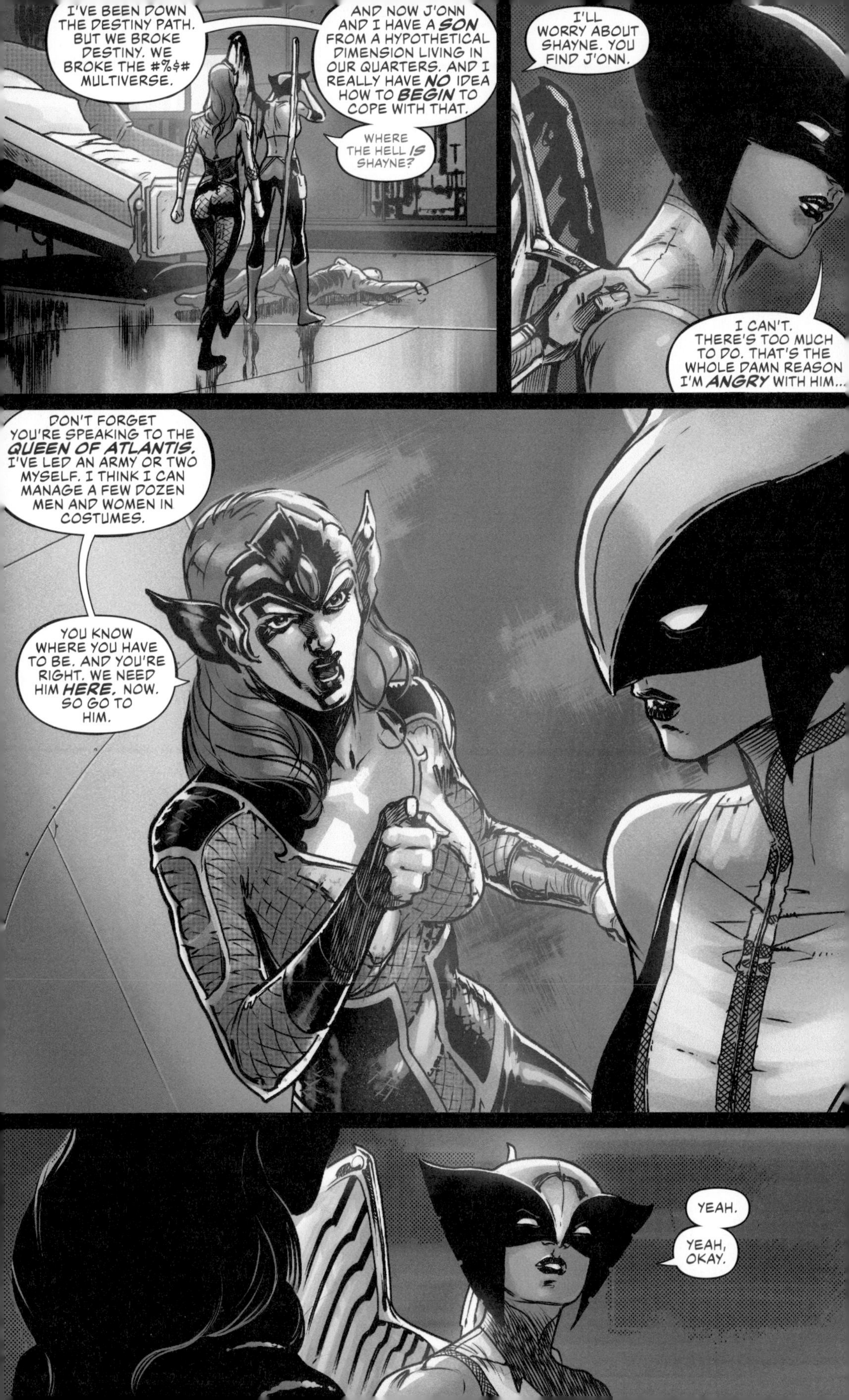
I'VE BEEN DOWN THE DESTINY PATH. BUT WE BROKE DESTINY. WE BROKE THE #%$# MULTIVERSE.
AND NOW J'ONN AND I HAVE A SON FROM A HYPOTHETICAL DIMENSION LIVING IN OUR QUARTERS. AND I REALLY HAVE NO IDEA HOW TO BEGIN TO COPE WITH THAT.
WHERE THE HELL IS SHAYNE?
I'LL WORRY ABOUT SHAYNE. YOU FIND J'ONN.
I CAN'T. THERE'S TOO MUCH TO DO. THAT'S THE WHOLE DAMN REASON I'M ANGRY WITH HIM...
DON'T FORGET YOU'RE SPEAKING TO THE QUEEN OF ATLANTIS. I'VE LED AN ARMY OR TWO MYSELF. I THINK I CAN MANAGE A FEW DOZEN MEN AND WOMEN IN COSTUMES.
YOU KNOW WHERE YOU HAVE TO BE. AND YOU'RE RIGHT. WE NEED HIM HERE. NOW. SO GO TO HIM.
YEAH.
YEAH, OKAY.

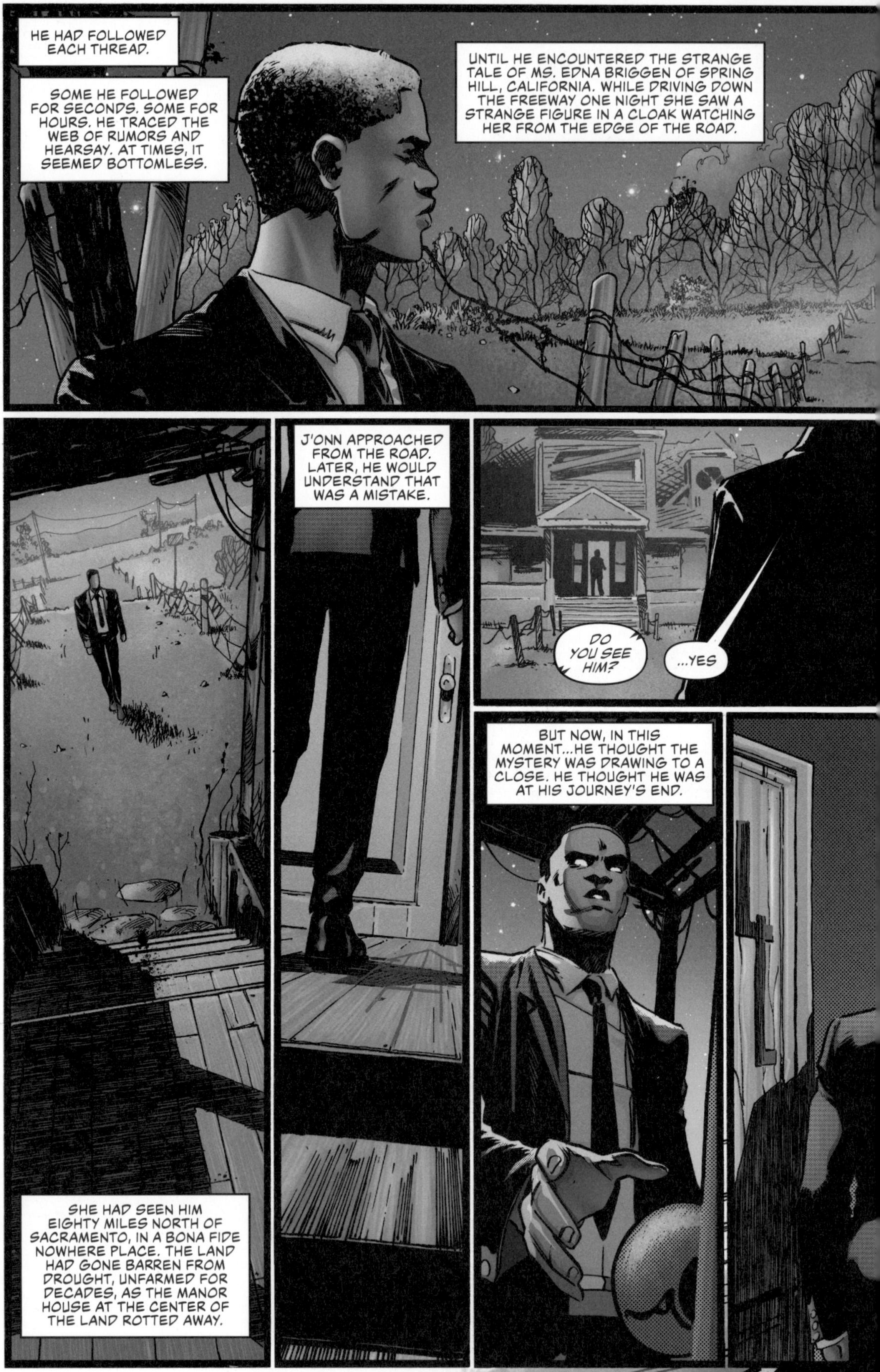
HE HAD FOLLOWED EACH THREAD.
SOME HE FOLLOWED FOR SECONDS. SOME FOR HOURS. HE TRACED THE WEB OF RUMORS AND HEARSAY. AT TIMES, IT SEEMED BOTTOMLESS.
UNTIL HE ENCOUNTERED THE STRANGE TALE OF MS. EDNA BRIGGEN OF SPRING HILL, CALIFORNIA. WHILE DRIVING DOWN THE FREEWAY ONE NIGHT SHE SAW A STRANGE FIGURE IN A CLOAK WATCHING HER FROM THE EDGE OF THE ROAD.
SHE HAD SEEN HIM EIGHTY MILES NORTH OF SACRAMENTO, IN A BONA FIDE NOWHERE PLACE. THE LAND HAD GONE BARREN FROM DROUGHT, UNFARMED FOR DECADES, AS THE MANOR HOUSE AT THE CENTER OF THE LAND ROTTED AWAY.
J'ONN APPROACHED FROM THE ROAD. LATER, HE WOULD UNDERSTAND THAT WAS A MISTAKE.
DO YOU SEE HIM?
...YES
BUT NOW, IN THIS MOMENT...HE THOUGHT THE MYSTERY WAS DRAWING TO A CLOSE. HE THOUGHT HE WAS AT HIS JOURNEY'S END.

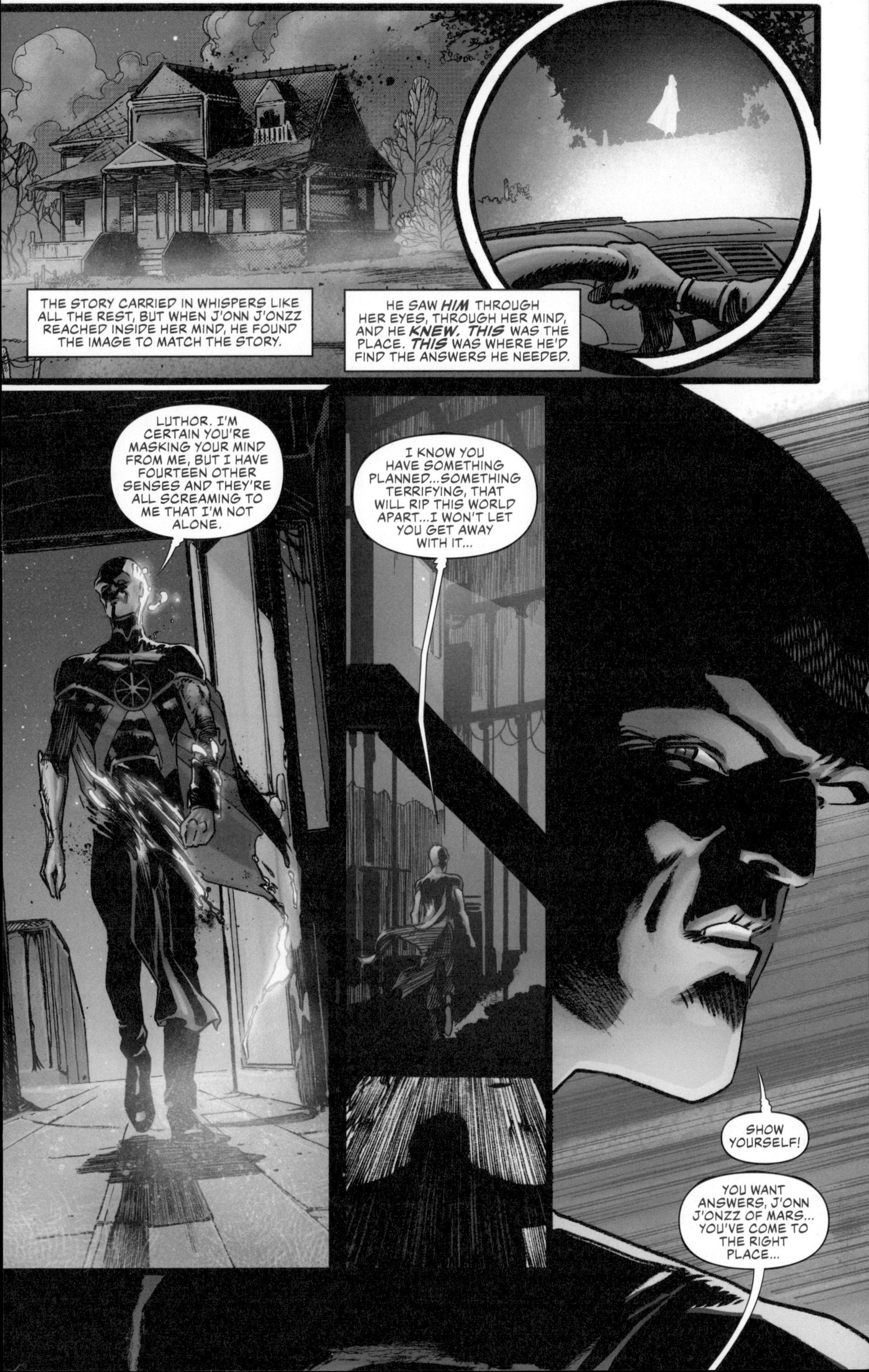
THE STORY CARRIED IN WHISPERS LIKE ALL THE REST, BUT WHEN J'ONN J'ONZZ REACHED INSIDE HER MIND, HE FOUND THE IMAGE TO MATCH THE STORY.
HE SAW ***HIM*** THROUGH HER EYES, THROUGH HER MIND, AND HE ***KNEW. THIS*** WAS THE PLACE. ***THIS*** WAS WHERE HE'D FIND THE ANSWERS HE NEEDED.
LUTHOR. I'M CERTAIN YOU'RE MASKING YOUR MIND FROM ME, BUT I HAVE FOURTEEN OTHER SENSES AND THEY'RE ALL SCREAMING TO ME THAT I'M NOT ALONE.
I KNOW YOU HAVE SOMETHING PLANNED...SOMETHING TERRIFYING, THAT WILL RIP THIS WORLD APART...I WON'T LET YOU GET AWAY WITH IT...
SHOW YOURSELF!
YOU WANT ANSWERS, J'ONN J'ONZZ OF MARS... YOU'VE COME TO THE RIGHT PLACE...

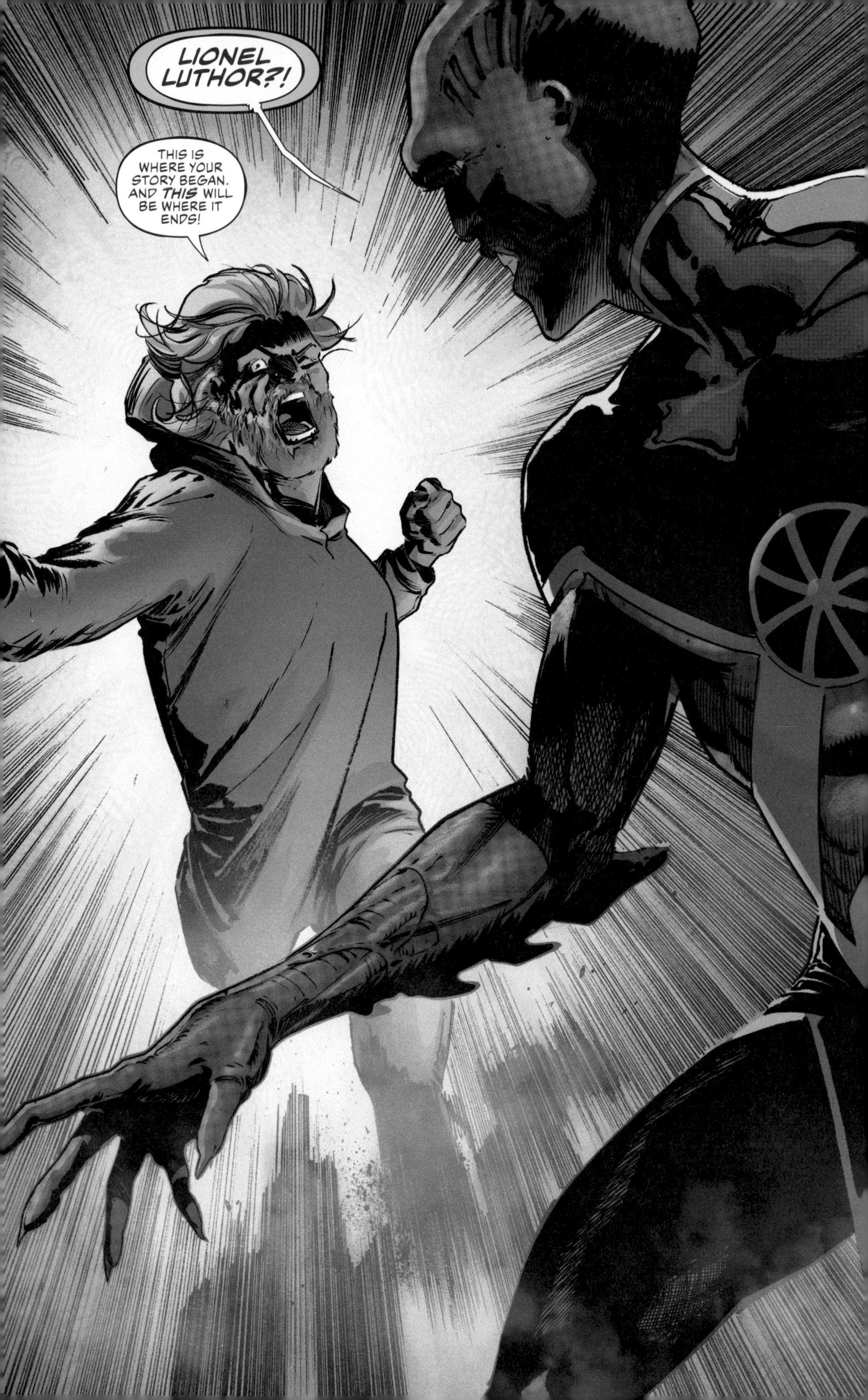
LIONEL LUTHOR?!
THIS IS WHERE YOUR STORY BEGAN. AND *THIS* WILL BE WHERE IT ENDS!

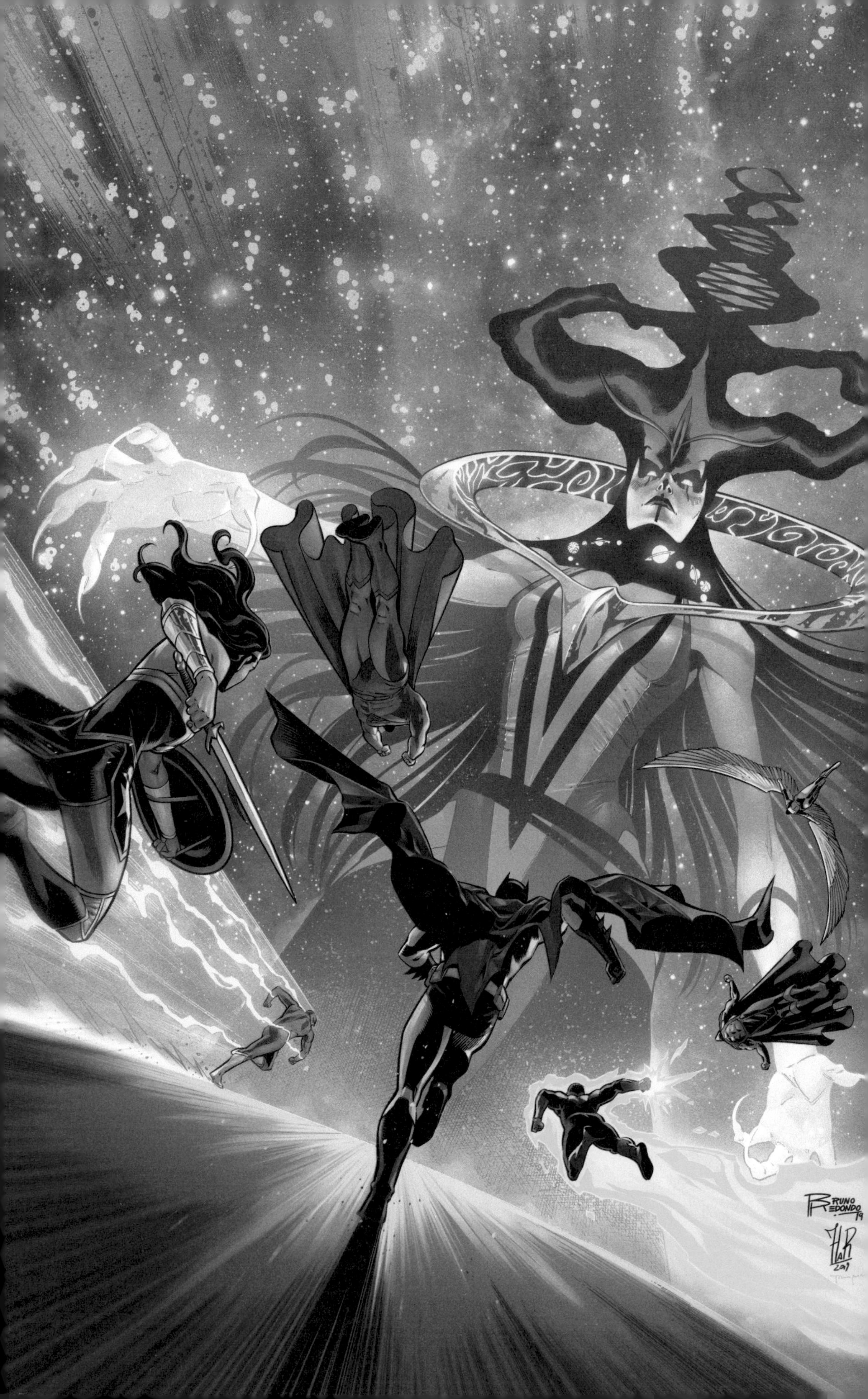

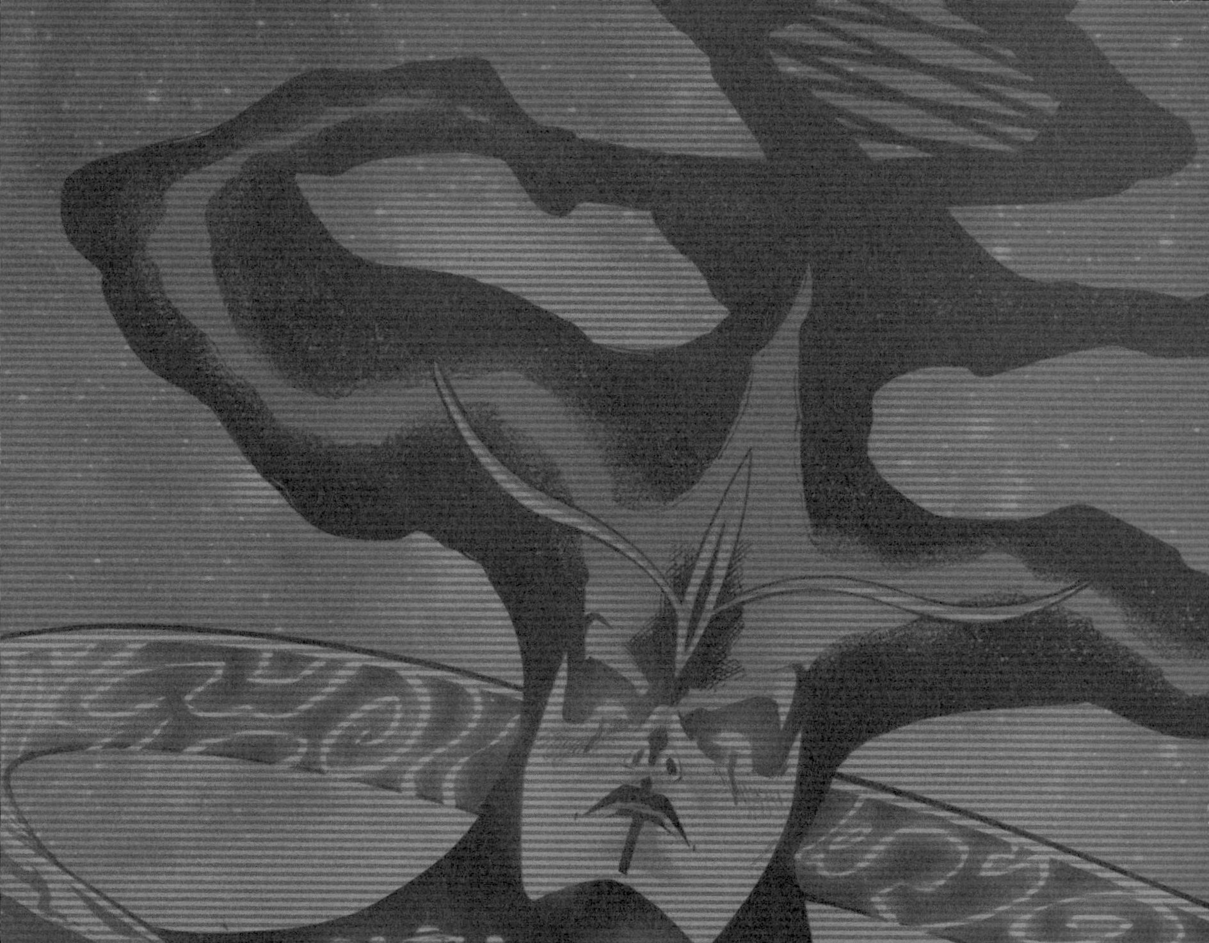

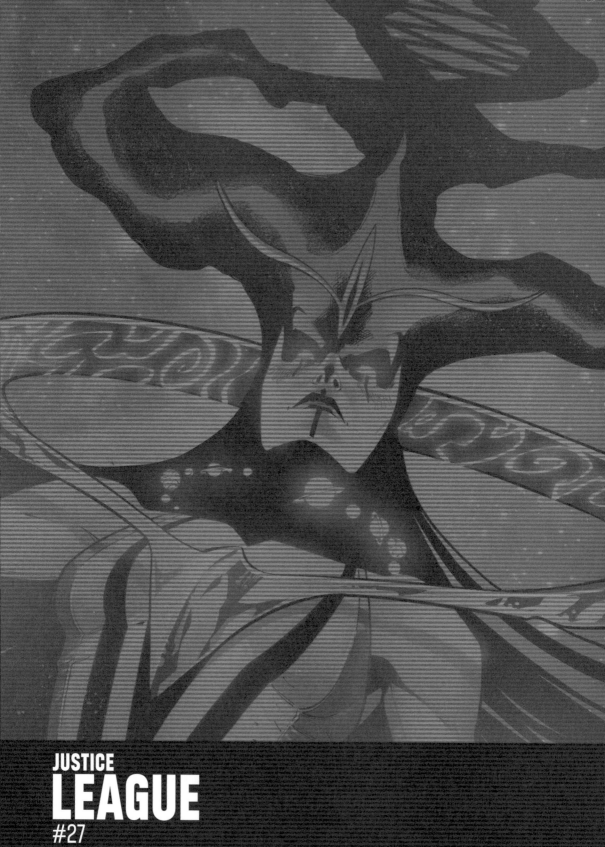

JUSTICE
LEAGUE
#27

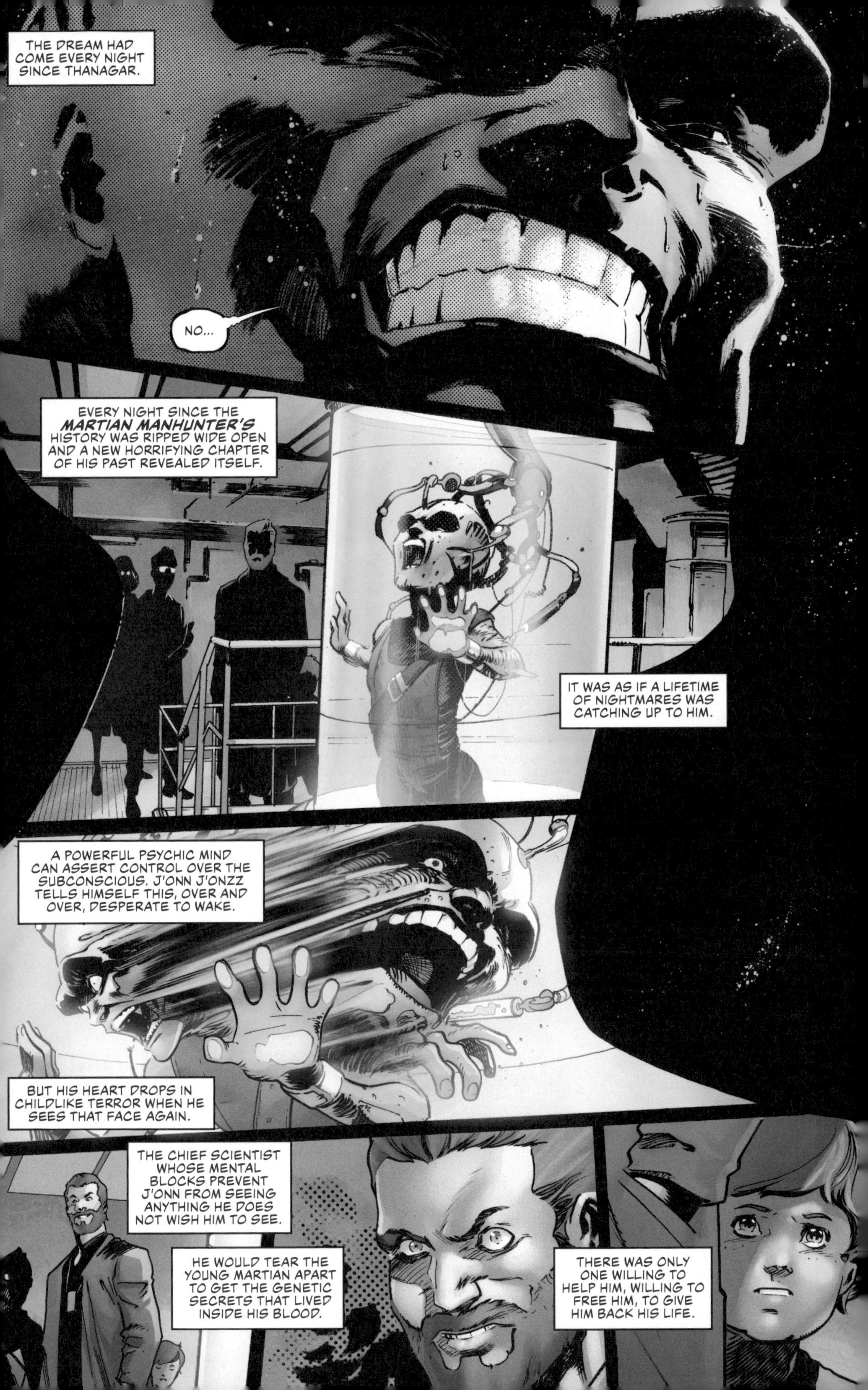
THE DREAM HAD COME EVERY NIGHT SINCE THANAGAR.
NO...
EVERY NIGHT SINCE THE *MARTIAN MANHUNTER'S* HISTORY WAS RIPPED WIDE OPEN AND A NEW HORRIFYING CHAPTER OF HIS PAST REVEALED ITSELF.
IT WAS AS IF A LIFETIME OF NIGHTMARES WAS CATCHING UP TO HIM.
A POWERFUL PSYCHIC MIND CAN ASSERT CONTROL OVER THE SUBCONSCIOUS. J'ONN J'ONZZ TELLS HIMSELF THIS, OVER AND OVER, DESPERATE TO WAKE.
BUT HIS HEART DROPS IN CHILDLIKE TERROR WHEN HE SEES THAT FACE AGAIN.
THE CHIEF SCIENTIST WHOSE MENTAL BLOCKS PREVENT J'ONN FROM SEEING ANYTHING HE DOES NOT WISH HIM TO SEE.
HE WOULD TEAR THE YOUNG MARTIAN APART TO GET THE GENETIC SECRETS THAT LIVED INSIDE HIS BLOOD.
THERE WAS ONLY ONE WILLING TO HELP HIM, WILLING TO FREE HIM, TO GIVE HIM BACK HIS LIFE.

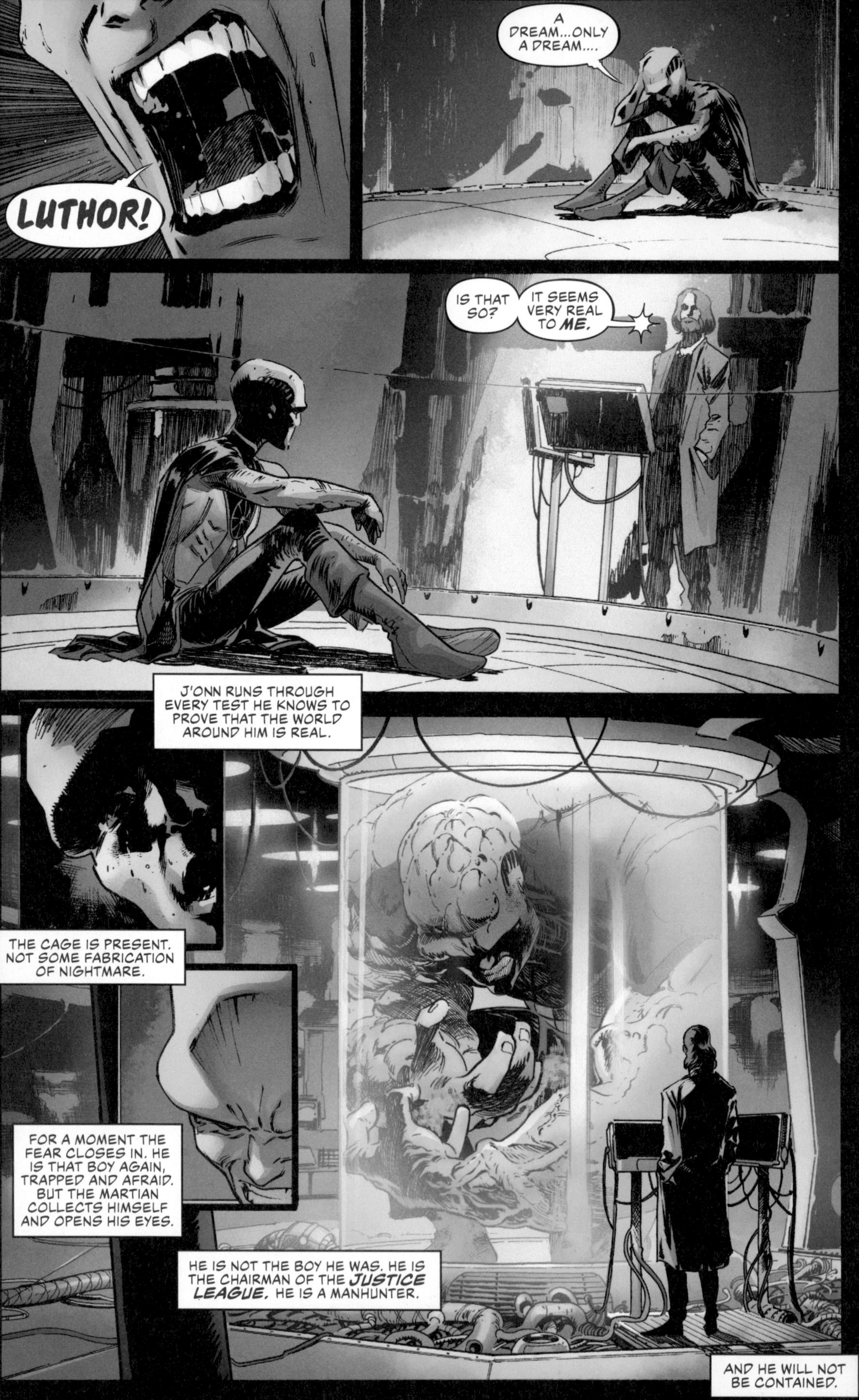
LUTHOR!
A DREAM...ONLY A DREAM....
IS THAT SO?
IT SEEMS VERY REAL TO ME.
J'ONN RUNS THROUGH EVERY TEST HE KNOWS TO PROVE THAT THE WORLD AROUND HIM IS REAL.
THE CAGE IS PRESENT. NOT SOME FABRICATION OF NIGHTMARE.
FOR A MOMENT THE FEAR CLOSES IN. HE IS THAT BOY AGAIN, TRAPPED AND AFRAID. BUT THE MARTIAN COLLECTS HIMSELF AND OPENS HIS EYES.
HE IS NOT THE BOY HE WAS. HE IS THE CHAIRMAN OF THE JUSTICE LEAGUE. HE IS A MANHUNTER.
AND HE WILL NOT BE CONTAINED.

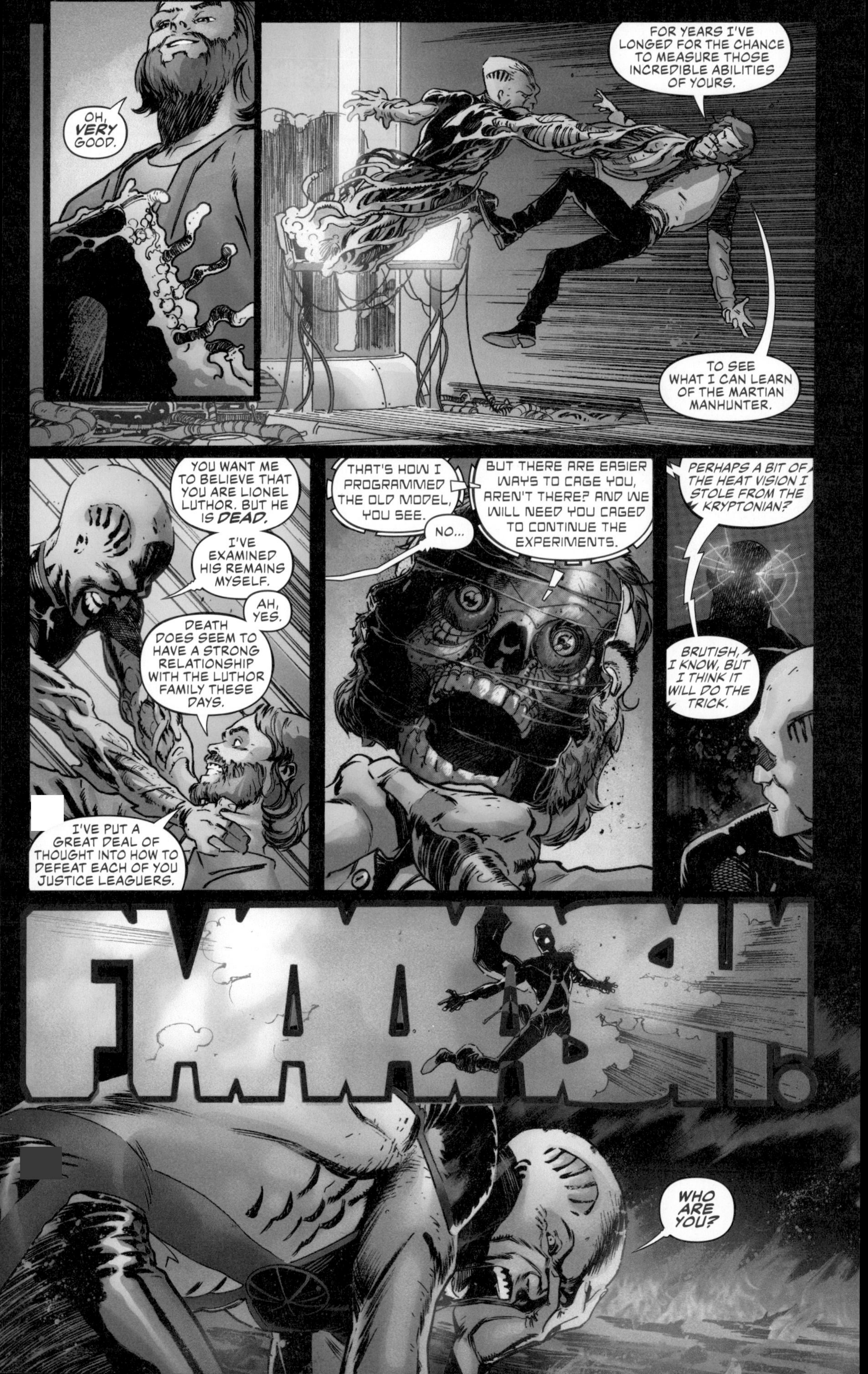
OH, VERY GOOD.
FOR YEARS I'VE LONGED FOR THE CHANCE TO MEASURE THOSE INCREDIBLE ABILITIES OF YOURS.
TO SEE WHAT I CAN LEARN OF THE MARTIAN MANHUNTER.
YOU WANT ME TO BELIEVE THAT YOU ARE LIONEL LUTHOR. BUT HE IS DEAD.
I'VE EXAMINED HIS REMAINS MYSELF.
AH, YES.
DEATH DOES SEEM TO HAVE A STRONG RELATIONSHIP WITH THE LUTHOR FAMILY THESE DAYS.
I'VE PUT A GREAT DEAL OF THOUGHT INTO HOW TO DEFEAT EACH OF YOU JUSTICE LEAGUERS.
THAT'S HOW I PROGRAMMED THE OLD MODEL, YOU SEE.
BUT THERE ARE EASIER WAYS TO CAGE YOU, AREN'T THERE? AND WE WILL NEED YOU CAGED TO CONTINUE THE EXPERIMENTS.
NO...
PERHAPS A BIT OF THE HEAT VISION I STOLE FROM THE KRYPTONIAN?
BRUTISH, I KNOW, BUT I THINK IT WILL DO THE TRICK.
WHO ARE YOU?

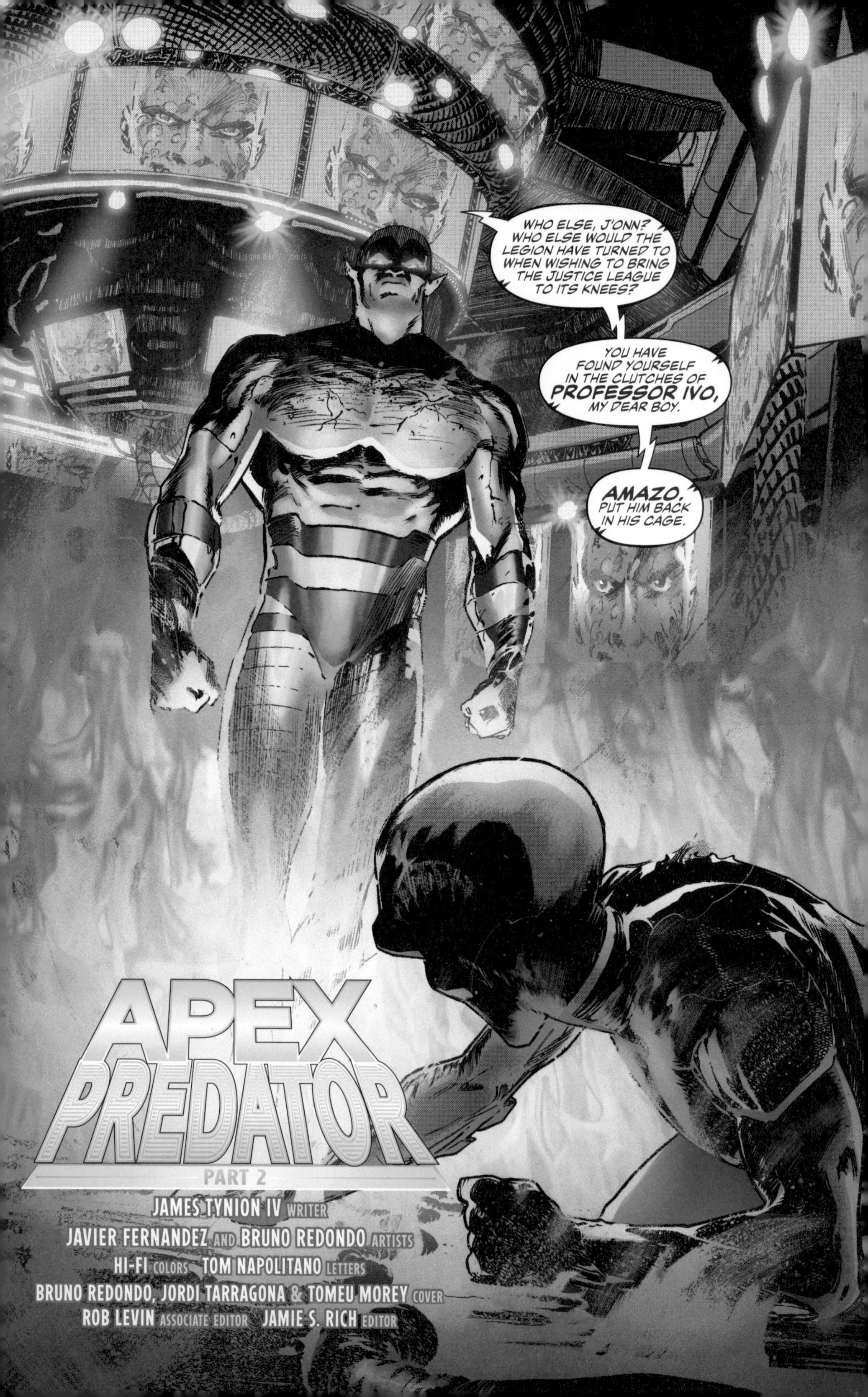
WHO ELSE, J'ONN? WHO ELSE WOULD THE LEGION HAVE TURNED TO WHEN WISHING TO BRING THE JUSTICE LEAGUE TO ITS KNEES?
YOU HAVE FOUND YOURSELF IN THE CLUTCHES OF PROFESSOR IVO, MY DEAR BOY.
AMAZO. PUT HIM BACK IN HIS CAGE.
APEX PREDATOR
PART 2
JAMES TYNION IV WRITER
JAVIER FERNANDEZ AND BRUNO REDONDO ARTISTS
HI-FI COLORS TOM NAPOLITANO LETTERS
BRUNO REDONDO, JORDI TARRAGONA & TOMEU MOREY COVER
ROB LEVIN ASSOCIATE EDITOR JAMIE S. RICH EDITOR

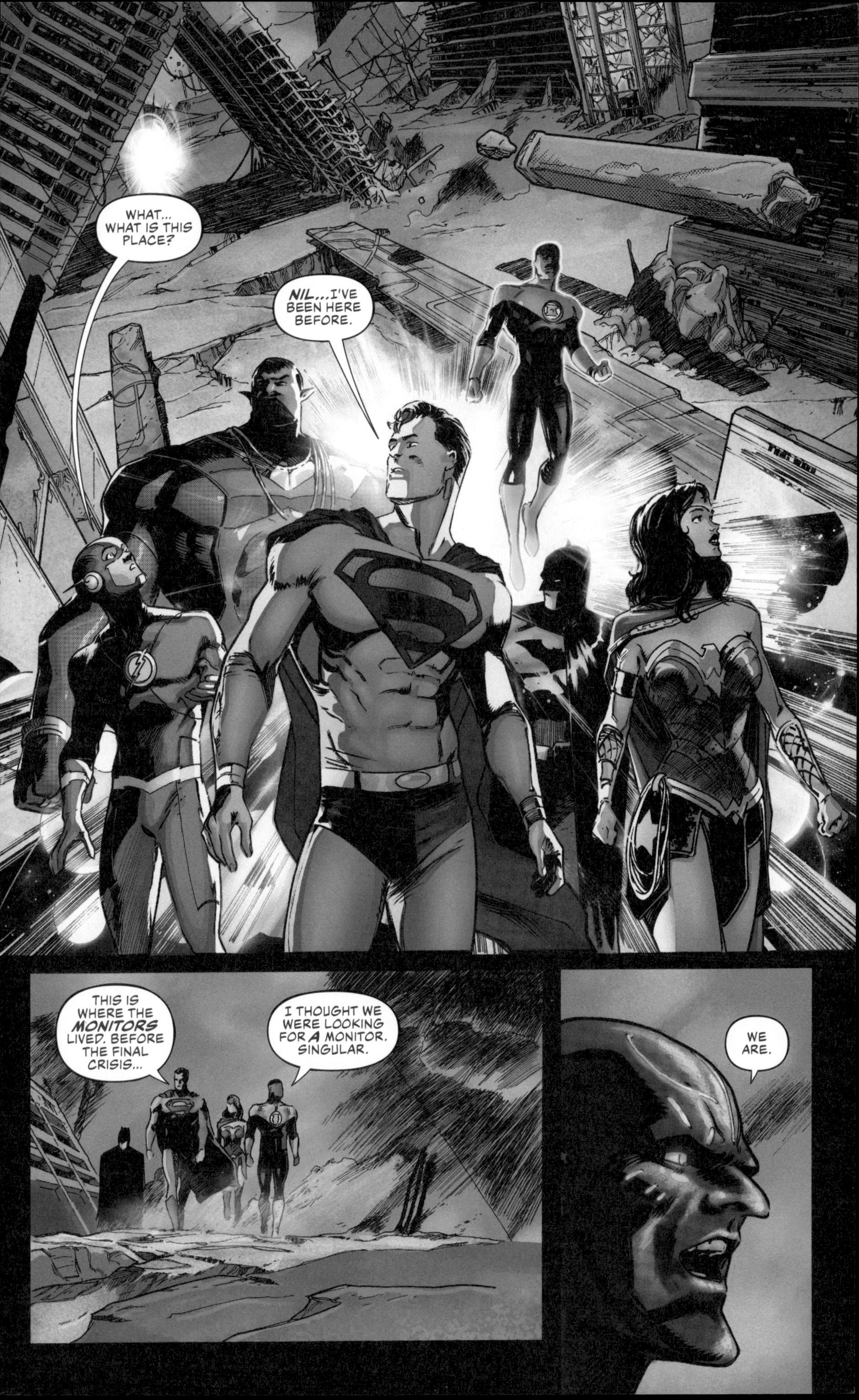
WHAT... WHAT IS THIS PLACE?
NIL...I'VE BEEN HERE BEFORE.
THIS IS WHERE THE MONITORS LIVED. BEFORE THE FINAL CRISIS...
I THOUGHT WE WERE LOOKING FOR A MONITOR. SINGULAR.
WE ARE.

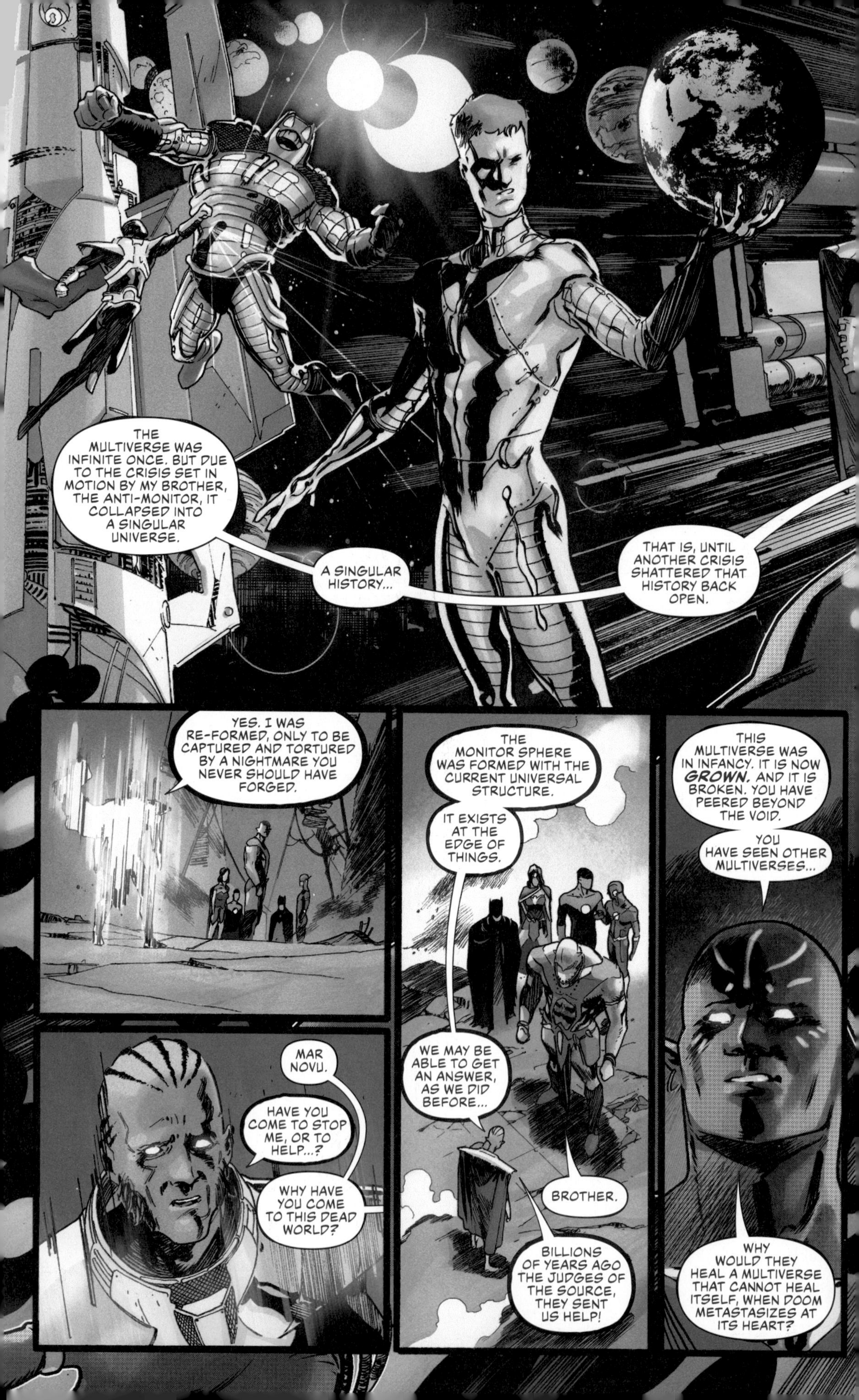
THE MULTIVERSE WAS INFINITE ONCE. BUT DUE TO THE CRISIS SET IN MOTION BY MY BROTHER, THE ANTI-MONITOR, IT COLLAPSED INTO A SINGULAR UNIVERSE.
A SINGULAR HISTORY...
THAT IS, UNTIL ANOTHER CRISIS SHATTERED THAT HISTORY BACK OPEN.
YES. I WAS RE-FORMED, ONLY TO BE CAPTURED AND TORTURED BY A NIGHTMARE YOU NEVER SHOULD HAVE FORGED.
MAR NOVU.
HAVE YOU COME TO STOP ME, OR TO HELP...?
WHY HAVE YOU COME TO THIS DEAD WORLD?
THE MONITOR SPHERE WAS FORMED WITH THE CURRENT UNIVERSAL STRUCTURE.
IT EXISTS AT THE EDGE OF THINGS.
WE MAY BE ABLE TO GET AN ANSWER, AS WE DID BEFORE...
BROTHER.
BILLIONS OF YEARS AGO THE JUDGES OF THE SOURCE, THEY SENT US HELP!
THIS MULTIVERSE WAS IN INFANCY. IT IS NOW GROWN. AND IT IS BROKEN. YOU HAVE PEERED BEYOND THE VOID.
YOU HAVE SEEN OTHER MULTIVERSES...
WHY WOULD THEY HEAL A MULTIVERSE THAT CANNOT HEAL ITSELF, WHEN DOOM METASTASIZES AT ITS HEART?

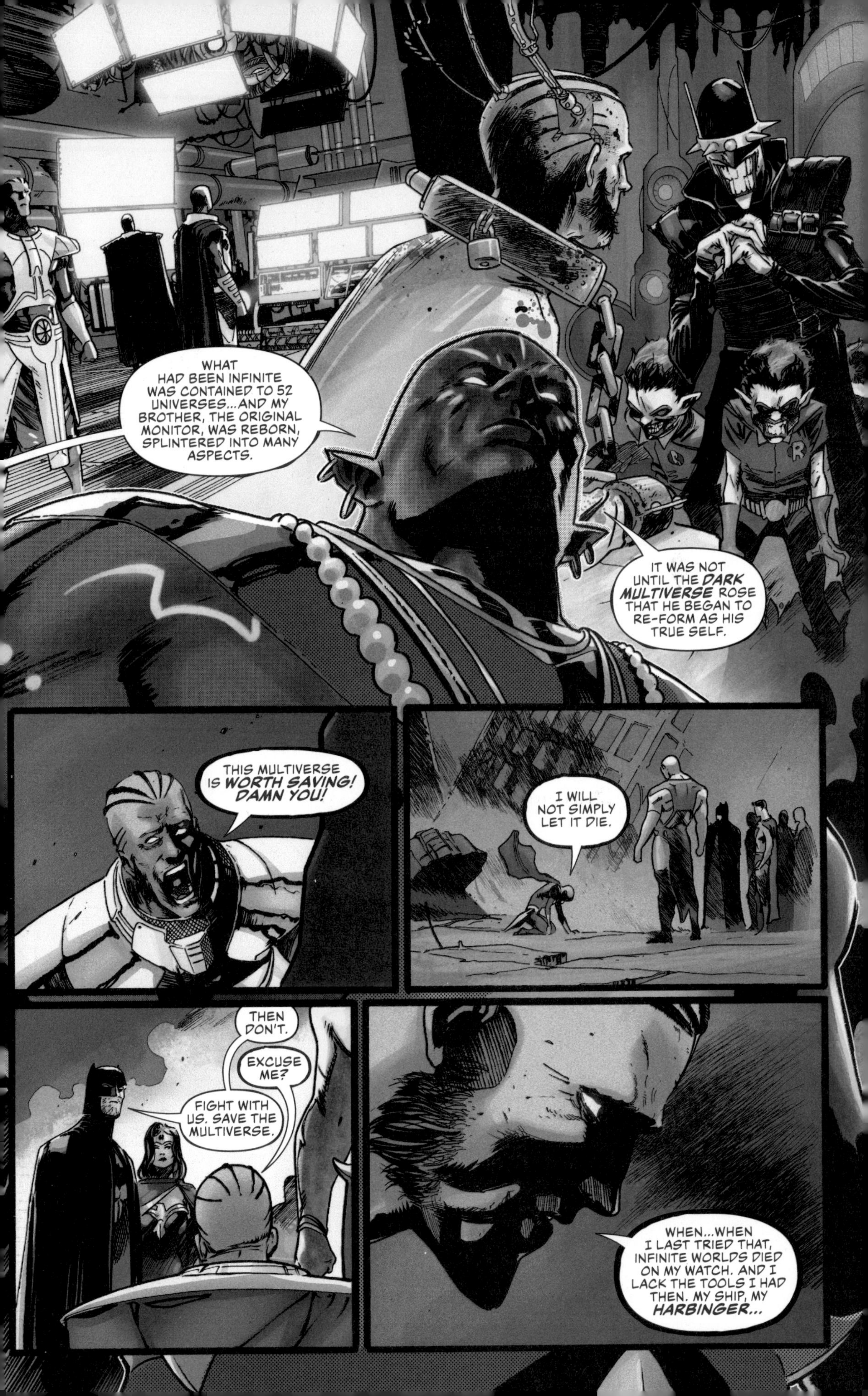
WHAT HAD BEEN INFINITE WAS CONTAINED TO 52 UNIVERSES...AND MY BROTHER, THE ORIGINAL MONITOR, WAS REBORN, SPLINTERED INTO MANY ASPECTS.
IT WAS NOT UNTIL THE *DARK MULTIVERSE* ROSE THAT HE BEGAN TO RE-FORM AS HIS TRUE SELF.
THIS MULTIVERSE IS *WORTH SAVING! DAMN YOU!*
I WILL NOT SIMPLY LET IT DIE.
THEN DON'T.
EXCUSE ME?
FIGHT WITH US. SAVE THE MULTIVERSE.
WHEN...WHEN I LAST TRIED THAT, INFINITE WORLDS DIED ON MY WATCH. AND I LACK THE TOOLS I HAD THEN. MY SHIP, MY *HARBINGER...*

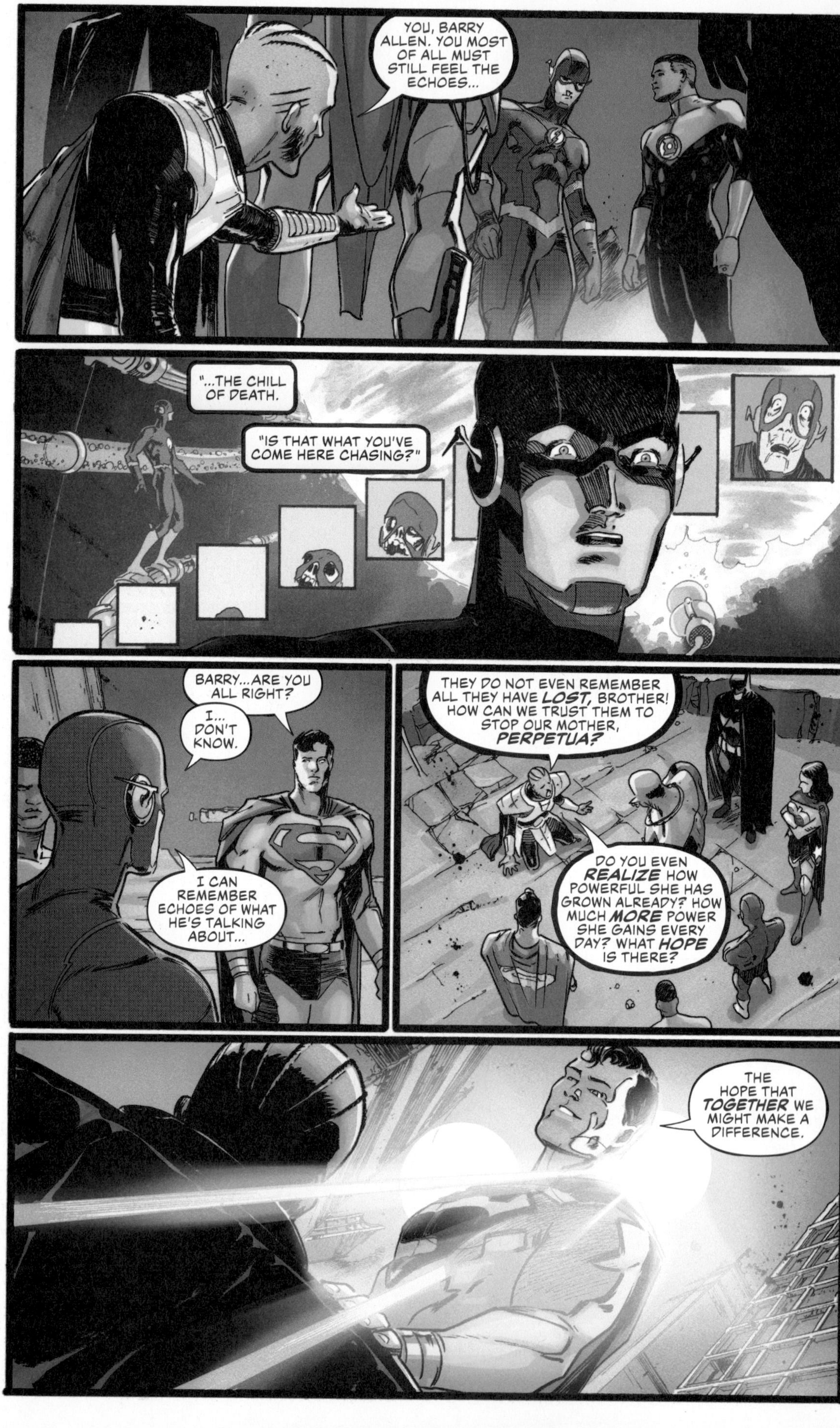
YOU, BARRY ALLEN. YOU MOST OF ALL MUST STILL FEEL THE ECHOES...
"...THE CHILL OF DEATH.
"IS THAT WHAT YOU'VE COME HERE CHASING?"
BARRY...ARE YOU ALL RIGHT?
I... DON'T KNOW.
I CAN REMEMBER ECHOES OF WHAT HE'S TALKING ABOUT...
THEY DO NOT EVEN REMEMBER ALL THEY HAVE LOST, BROTHER! HOW CAN WE TRUST THEM TO STOP OUR MOTHER, PERPETUA?
DO YOU EVEN REALIZE HOW POWERFUL SHE HAS GROWN ALREADY? HOW MUCH MORE POWER SHE GAINS EVERY DAY? WHAT HOPE IS THERE?
THE HOPE THAT TOGETHER WE MIGHT MAKE A DIFFERENCE.

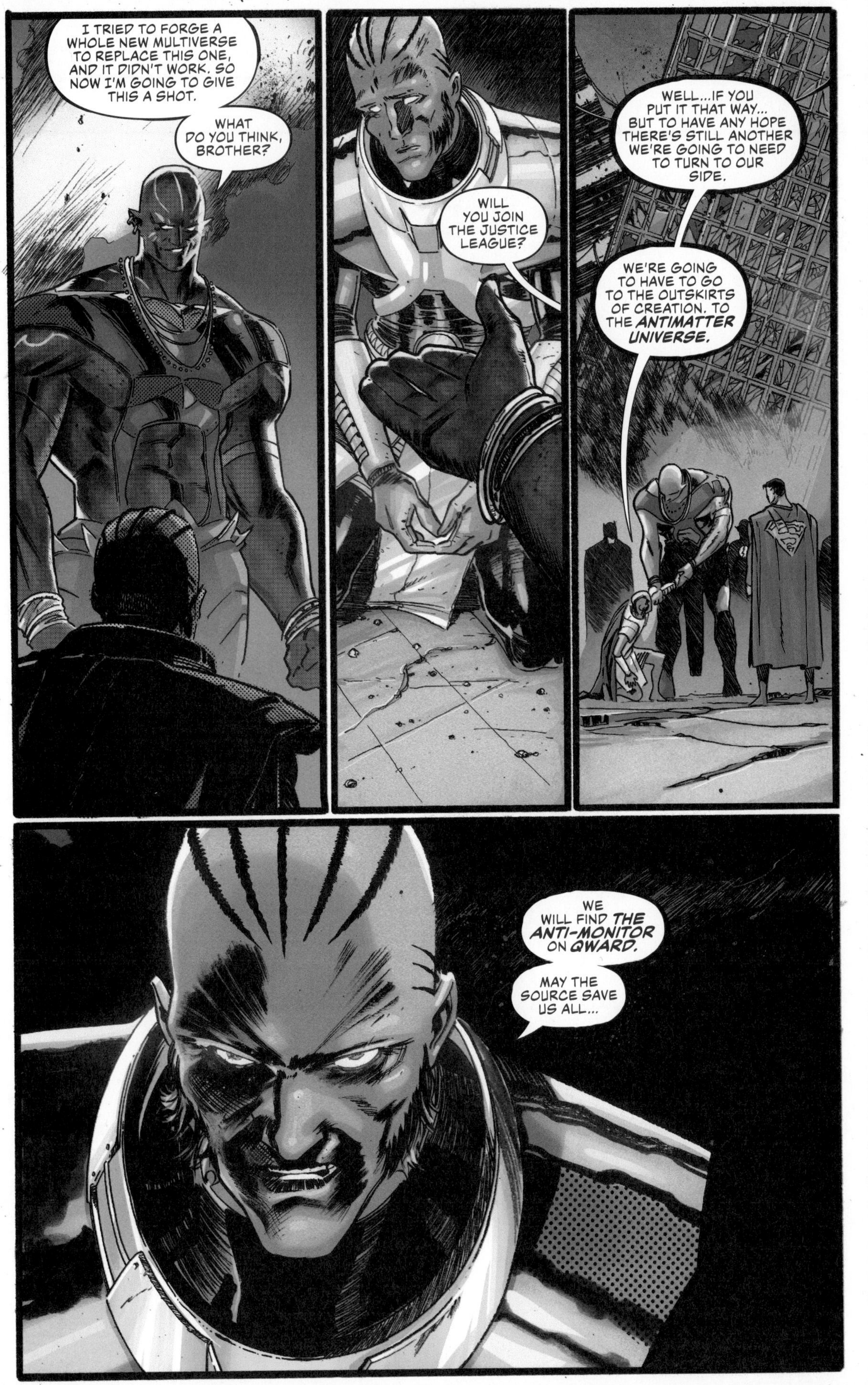
I TRIED TO FORGE A WHOLE NEW MULTIVERSE TO REPLACE THIS ONE, AND IT DIDN'T WORK. SO NOW I'M GOING TO GIVE THIS A SHOT.
WHAT DO YOU THINK, BROTHER?
WILL YOU JOIN THE JUSTICE LEAGUE?
WELL...IF YOU PUT IT THAT WAY... BUT TO HAVE ANY HOPE THERE'S STILL ANOTHER WE'RE GOING TO NEED TO TURN TO OUR SIDE.
WE'RE GOING TO HAVE TO GO TO THE OUTSKIRTS OF CREATION. TO THE ANTIMATTER UNIVERSE.
WE WILL FIND THE ANTI-MONITOR ON QWARD.
MAY THE SOURCE SAVE US ALL...

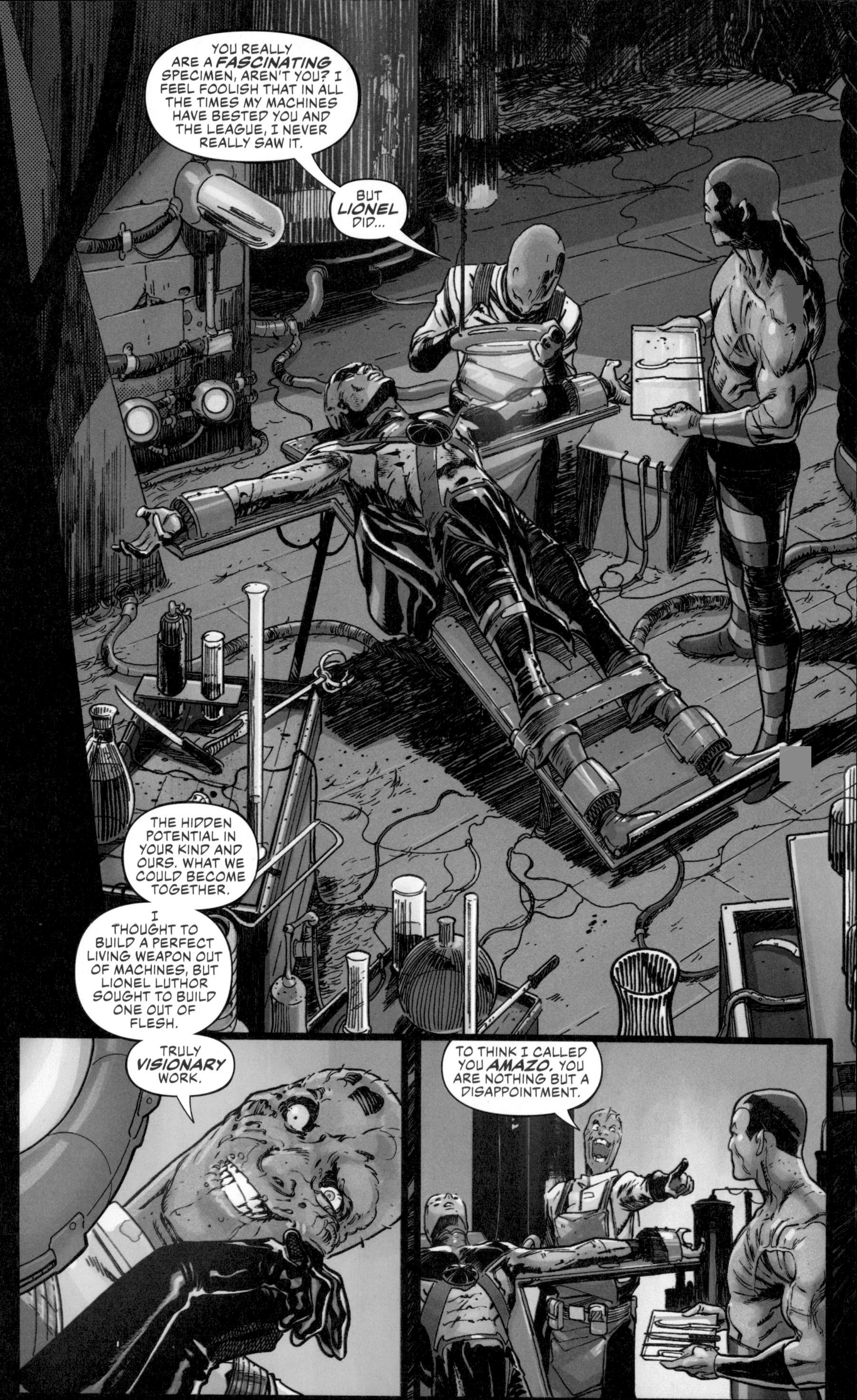
YOU REALLY ARE A FASCINATING SPECIMEN, AREN'T YOU? I FEEL FOOLISH THAT IN ALL THE TIMES MY MACHINES HAVE BESTED YOU AND THE LEAGUE, I NEVER REALLY SAW IT.
BUT LIONEL DID...
THE HIDDEN POTENTIAL IN YOUR KIND AND OURS. WHAT WE COULD BECOME TOGETHER.
I THOUGHT TO BUILD A PERFECT LIVING WEAPON OUT OF MACHINES, BUT LIONEL LUTHOR SOUGHT TO BUILD ONE OUT OF FLESH.
TRULY VISIONARY WORK.
TO THINK I CALLED YOU AMAZO. YOU ARE NOTHING BUT A DISAPPOINTMENT.

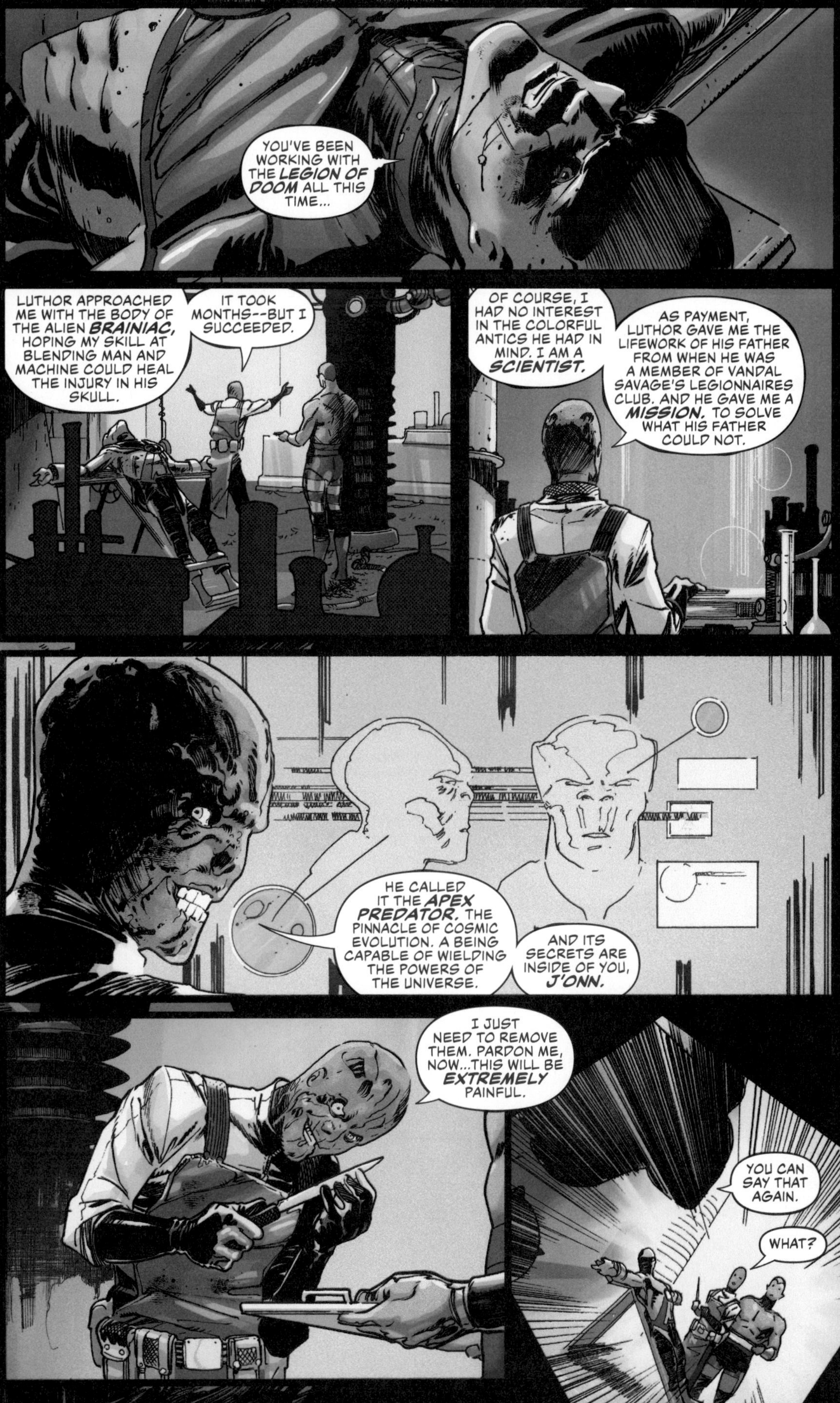
YOU'VE BEEN WORKING WITH THE LEGION OF DOOM ALL THIS TIME...
LUTHOR APPROACHED ME WITH THE BODY OF THE ALIEN BRAINIAC, HOPING MY SKILL AT BLENDING MAN AND MACHINE COULD HEAL THE INJURY IN HIS SKULL.
IT TOOK MONTHS--BUT I SUCCEEDED.
OF COURSE, I HAD NO INTEREST IN THE COLORFUL ANTICS HE HAD IN MIND. I AM A SCIENTIST.
AS PAYMENT, LUTHOR GAVE ME THE LIFEWORK OF HIS FATHER FROM WHEN HE WAS A MEMBER OF VANDAL SAVAGE'S LEGIONNAIRES CLUB. AND HE GAVE ME A MISSION. TO SOLVE WHAT HIS FATHER COULD NOT.
HE CALLED IT THE APEX PREDATOR. THE PINNACLE OF COSMIC EVOLUTION. A BEING CAPABLE OF WIELDING THE POWERS OF THE UNIVERSE.
AND ITS SECRETS ARE INSIDE OF YOU, J'ONN.
I JUST NEED TO REMOVE THEM. PARDON ME, NOW...THIS WILL BE EXTREMELY PAINFUL.
YOU CAN SAY THAT AGAIN.
WHAT?

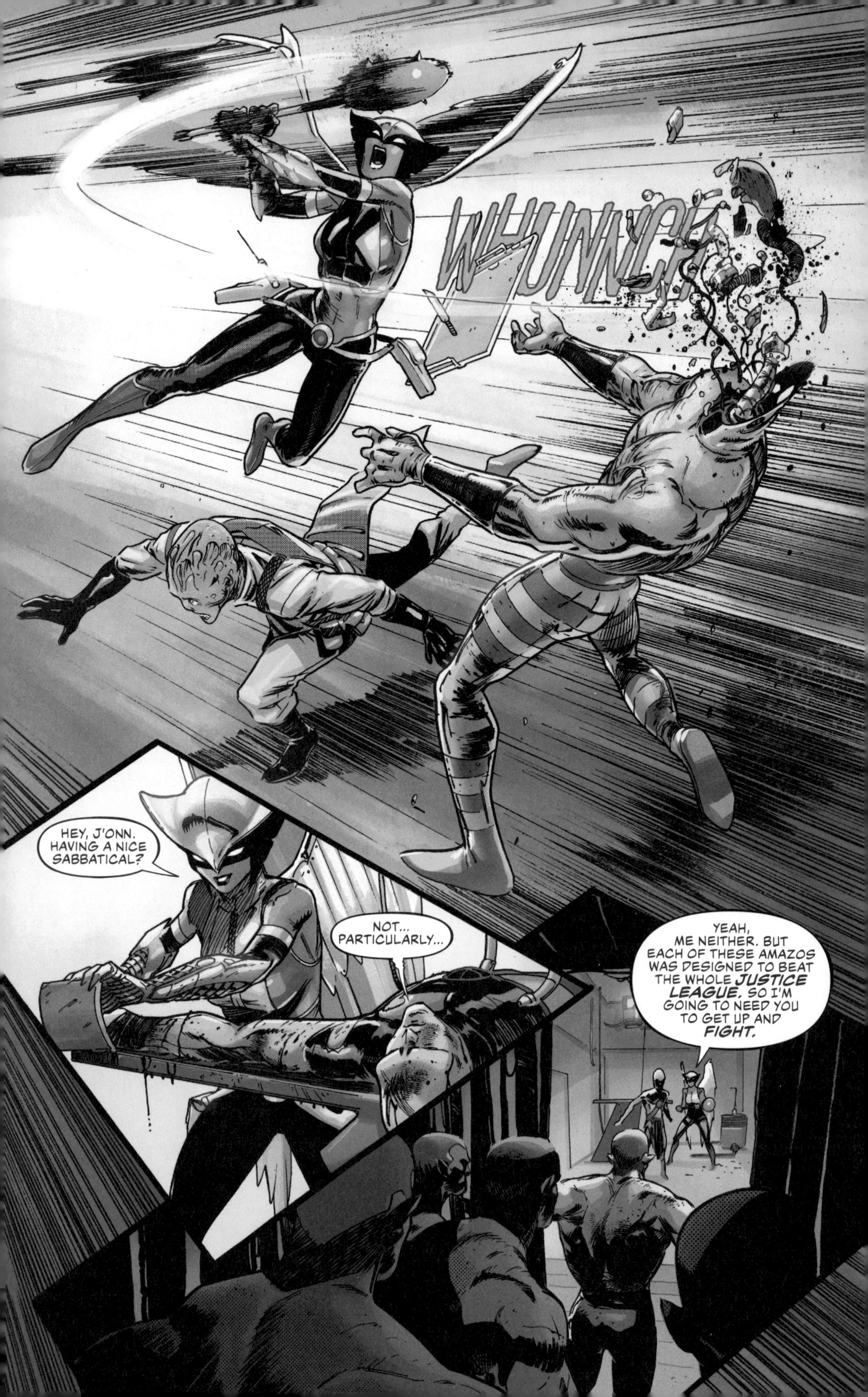
WHUNNCH
HEY, J'ONN. HAVING A NICE SABBATICAL?
NOT... PARTICULARLY...
YEAH, ME NEITHER. BUT EACH OF THESE AMAZOS WAS DESIGNED TO BEAT THE WHOLE JUSTICE LEAGUE. SO I'M GOING TO NEED YOU TO GET UP AND FIGHT.

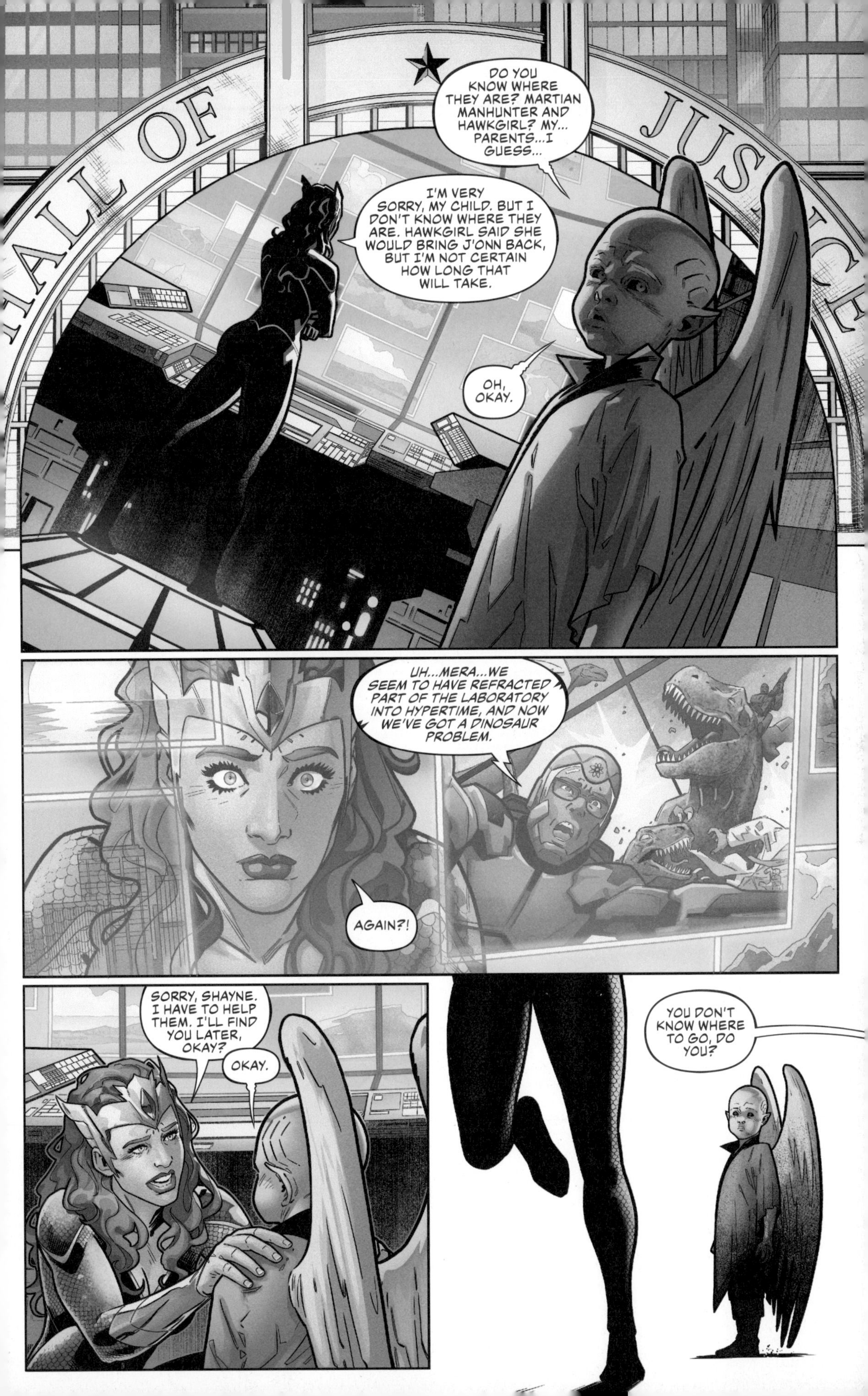
HALL OF JUSTICE
DO YOU KNOW WHERE THEY ARE? MARTIAN MANHUNTER AND HAWKGIRL? MY... PARENTS...I GUESS...
I'M VERY SORRY, MY CHILD. BUT I DON'T KNOW WHERE THEY ARE. HAWKGIRL SAID SHE WOULD BRING J'ONN BACK, BUT I'M NOT CERTAIN HOW LONG THAT WILL TAKE.
OH, OKAY.
UH...MERA...WE SEEM TO HAVE REFRACTED PART OF THE LABORATORY INTO HYPERTIME, AND NOW WE'VE GOT A DINOSAUR PROBLEM.
AGAIN?!
SORRY, SHAYNE. I HAVE TO HELP THEM. I'LL FIND YOU LATER, OKAY?
OKAY.
YOU DON'T KNOW WHERE TO GO, DO YOU?

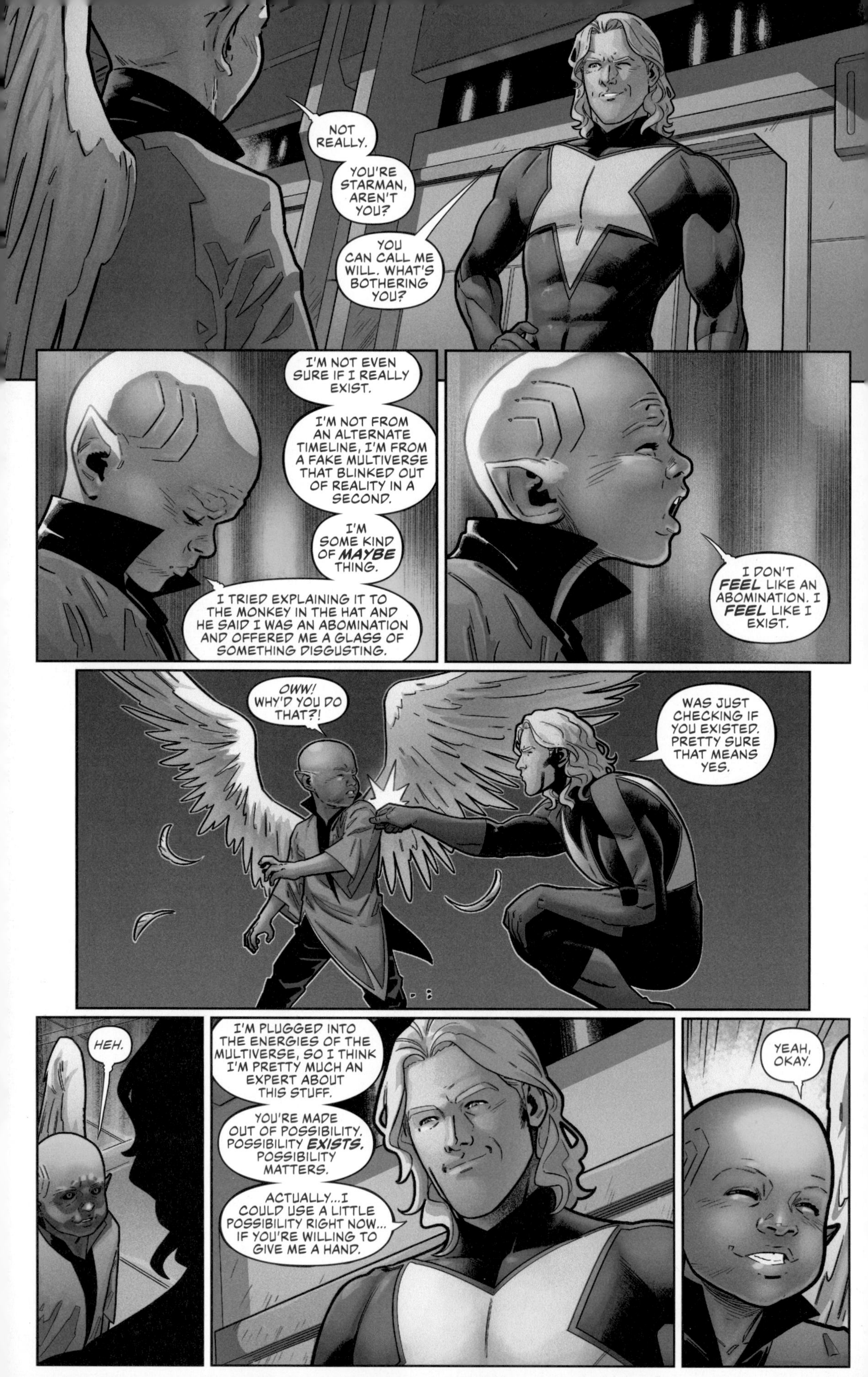

NOT REALLY.
YOU'RE STARMAN, AREN'T YOU?
YOU CAN CALL ME WILL. WHAT'S BOTHERING YOU?
I'M NOT EVEN SURE IF I REALLY EXIST.
I'M NOT FROM AN ALTERNATE TIMELINE, I'M FROM A FAKE MULTIVERSE THAT BLINKED OUT OF REALITY IN A SECOND.
I'M SOME KIND OF MAYBE THING.
I TRIED EXPLAINING IT TO THE MONKEY IN THE HAT AND HE SAID I WAS AN ABOMINATION AND OFFERED ME A GLASS OF SOMETHING DISGUSTING.
I DON'T FEEL LIKE AN ABOMINATION. I FEEL LIKE I EXIST.
OWW! WHY'D YOU DO THAT?!
WAS JUST CHECKING IF YOU EXISTED. PRETTY SURE THAT MEANS YES.
HEH.
I'M PLUGGED INTO THE ENERGIES OF THE MULTIVERSE, SO I THINK I'M PRETTY MUCH AN EXPERT ABOUT THIS STUFF.
YOU'RE MADE OUT OF POSSIBILITY. POSSIBILITY EXISTS. POSSIBILITY MATTERS.
ACTUALLY...I COULD USE A LITTLE POSSIBILITY RIGHT NOW... IF YOU'RE WILLING TO GIVE ME A HAND.
YEAH, OKAY.

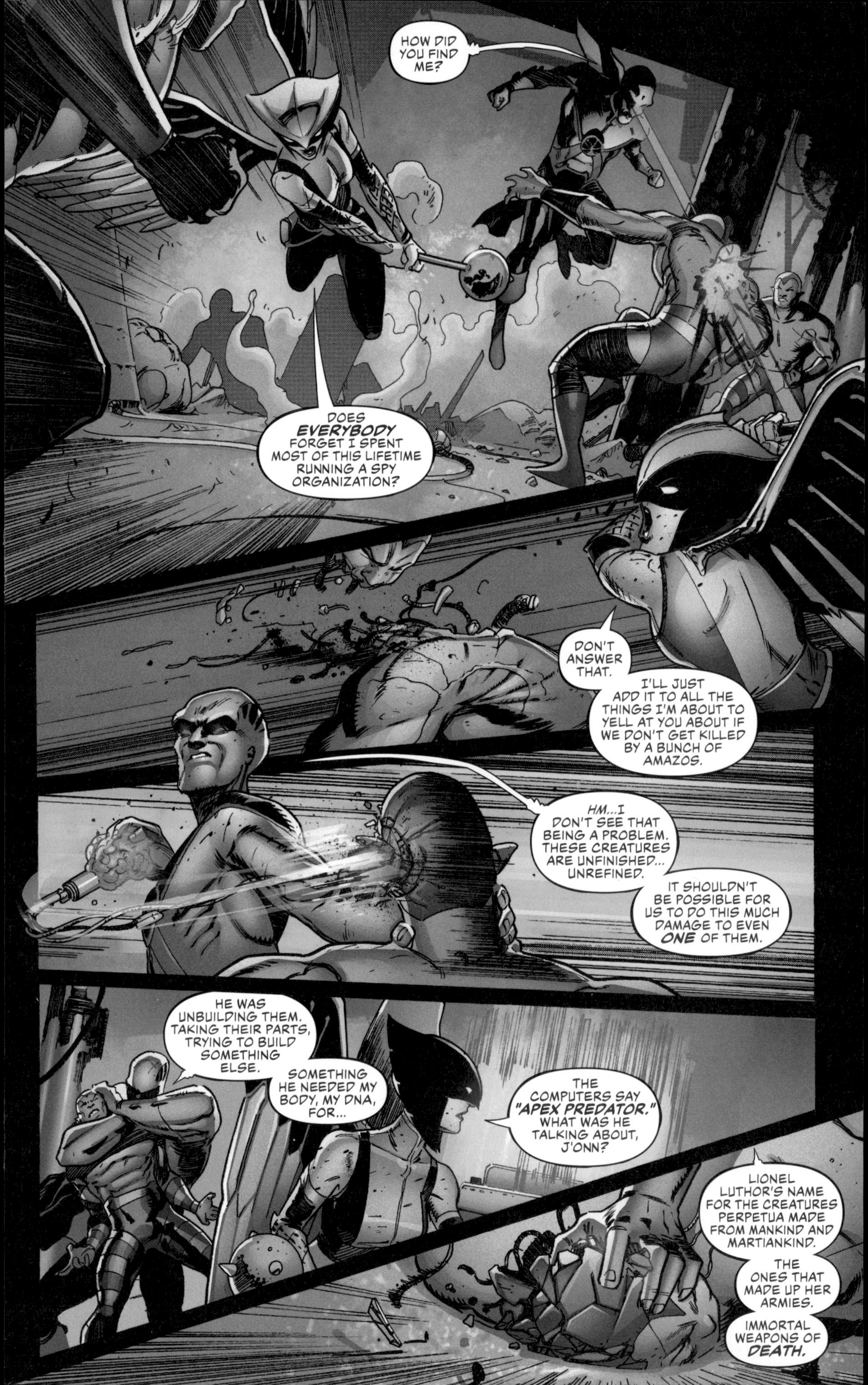
HOW DID YOU FIND ME?
DOES EVERYBODY FORGET I SPENT MOST OF THIS LIFETIME RUNNING A SPY ORGANIZATION?
DON'T ANSWER THAT.
I'LL JUST ADD IT TO ALL THE THINGS I'M ABOUT TO YELL AT YOU ABOUT IF WE DON'T GET KILLED BY A BUNCH OF AMAZOS.
HM...I DON'T SEE THAT BEING A PROBLEM. THESE CREATURES ARE UNFINISHED... UNREFINED.
IT SHOULDN'T BE POSSIBLE FOR US TO DO THIS MUCH DAMAGE TO EVEN ONE OF THEM.
HE WAS UNBUILDING THEM. TAKING THEIR PARTS, TRYING TO BUILD SOMETHING ELSE.
SOMETHING HE NEEDED MY BODY, MY DNA, FOR...
THE COMPUTERS SAY "APEX PREDATOR." WHAT WAS HE TALKING ABOUT, J'ONN?
LIONEL LUTHOR'S NAME FOR THE CREATURES PERPETUA MADE FROM MANKIND AND MARTIANKIND.
THE ONES THAT MADE UP HER ARMIES.
IMMORTAL WEAPONS OF DEATH.

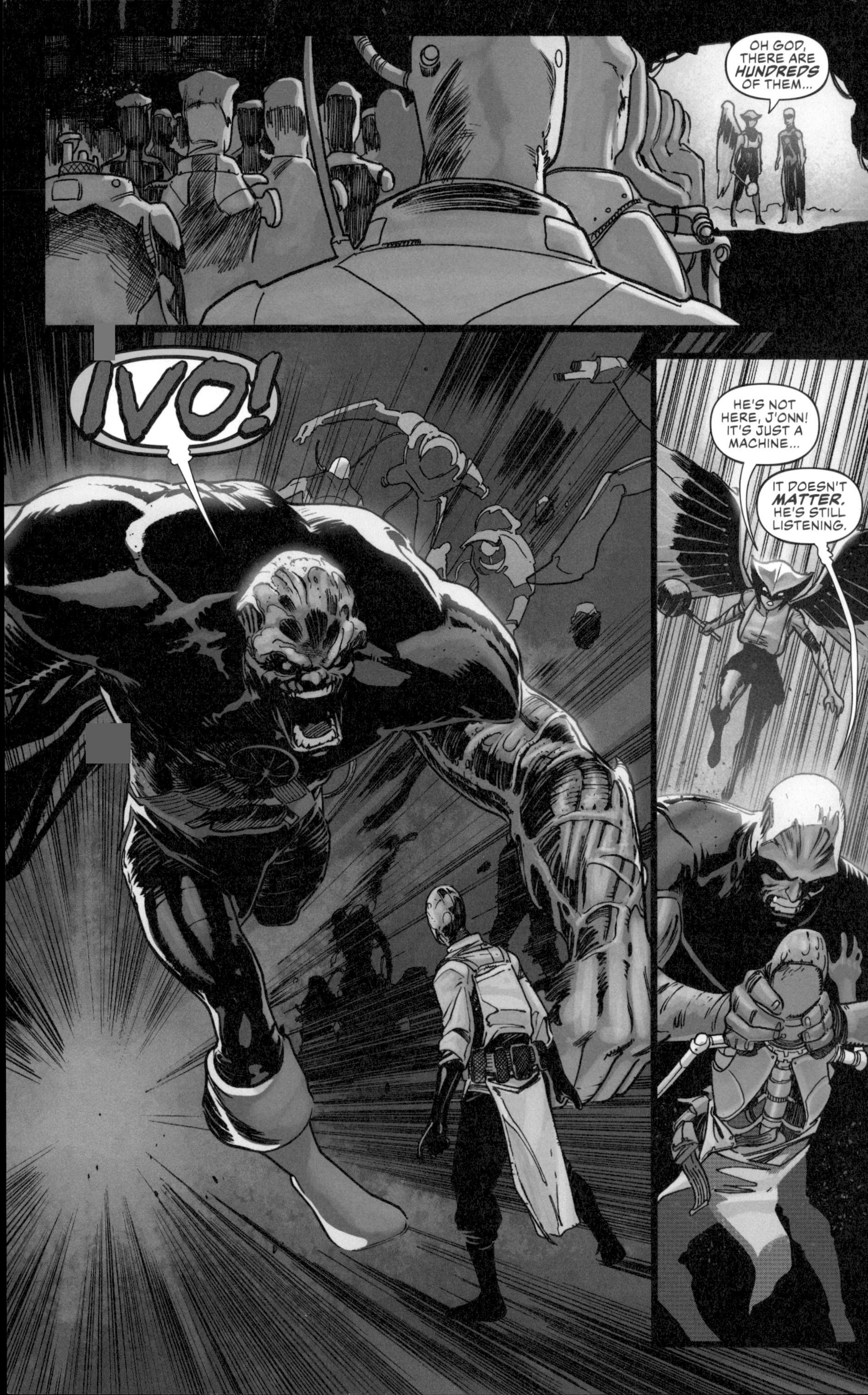

OH GOD, THERE ARE HUNDREDS OF THEM...
IVO!
HE'S NOT HERE, J'ONN! IT'S JUST A MACHINE...
IT DOESN'T MATTER. HE'S STILL LISTENING.

YES...BUT THEY ARE ALL INCOMPLETE, I FEAR.

HOW I WOULD HAVE LOVED TO SEE THEM RIP YOU ALL TO PIECES.

TELL ME, IVO!

TELL ME WHERE LUTHOR IS!

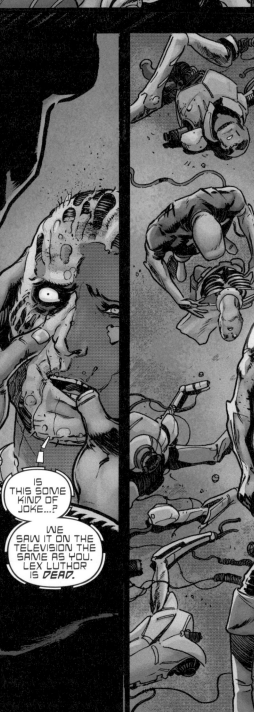

IS THIS SOME KIND OF JOKE...?

WE SAW IT ON THE TELEVISION THE SAME AS YOU. LEX LUTHOR IS DEAD.

COME ON, J'ONN.

I'VE CALLED REINFORCEMENTS. THEY'LL TAKE ALL OF THESE INTO JUSTICE LEAGUE CUSTODY.

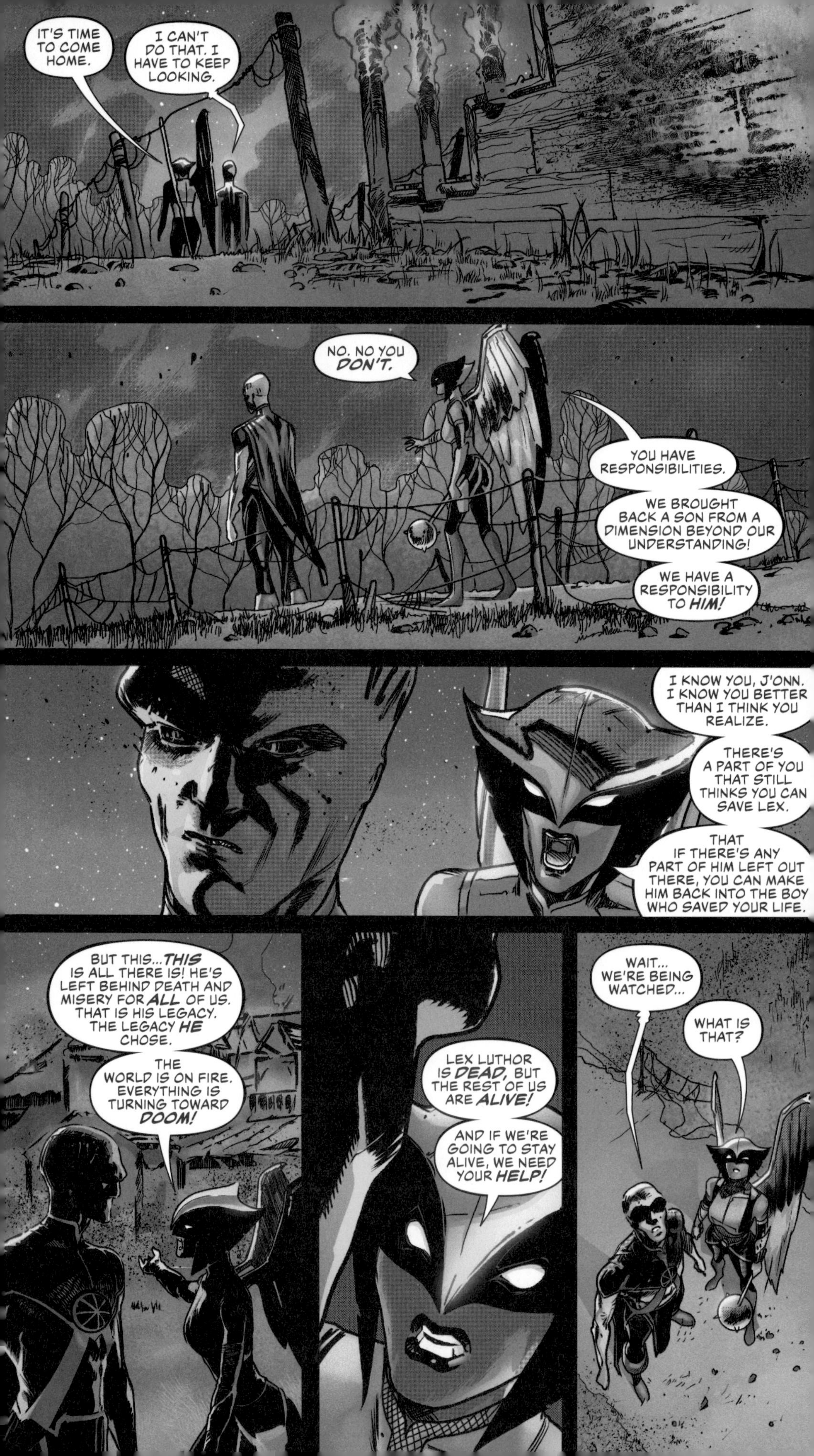

IT'S TIME TO COME HOME.
I CAN'T DO THAT. I HAVE TO KEEP LOOKING.
NO. NO YOU DON'T.
YOU HAVE RESPONSIBILITIES.
WE BROUGHT BACK A SON FROM A DIMENSION BEYOND OUR UNDERSTANDING!
WE HAVE A RESPONSIBILITY TO HIM!
I KNOW YOU, J'ONN. I KNOW YOU BETTER THAN I THINK YOU REALIZE.
THERE'S A PART OF YOU THAT STILL THINKS YOU CAN SAVE LEX.
THAT IF THERE'S ANY PART OF HIM LEFT OUT THERE, YOU CAN MAKE HIM BACK INTO THE BOY WHO SAVED YOUR LIFE.
BUT THIS...THIS IS ALL THERE IS! HE'S LEFT BEHIND DEATH AND MISERY FOR ALL OF US. THAT IS HIS LEGACY. THE LEGACY HE CHOSE.
THE WORLD IS ON FIRE. EVERYTHING IS TURNING TOWARD DOOM!
LEX LUTHOR IS DEAD, BUT THE REST OF US ARE ALIVE!
AND IF WE'RE GOING TO STAY ALIVE, WE NEED YOUR HELP!
WAIT... WE'RE BEING WATCHED...
WHAT IS THAT?

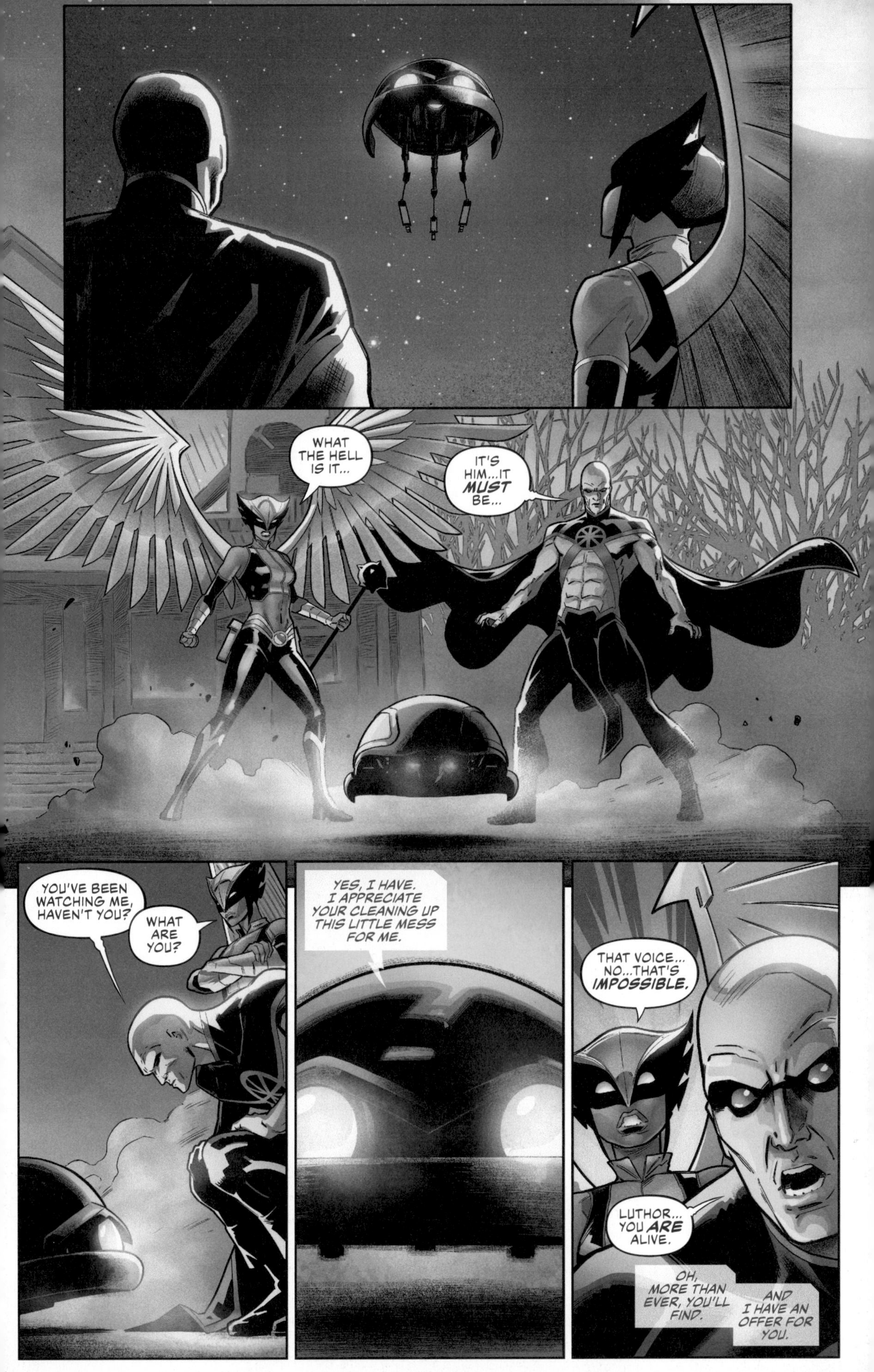
WHAT THE HELL IS IT...
IT'S HIM...IT MUST BE...
YOU'VE BEEN WATCHING ME, HAVEN'T YOU?
WHAT ARE YOU?
YES, I HAVE. I APPRECIATE YOUR CLEANING UP THIS LITTLE MESS FOR ME.
THAT VOICE... NO...THAT'S IMPOSSIBLE.
LUTHOR... YOU ARE ALIVE.
OH, MORE THAN EVER, YOU'LL FIND.
AND I HAVE AN OFFER FOR YOU.

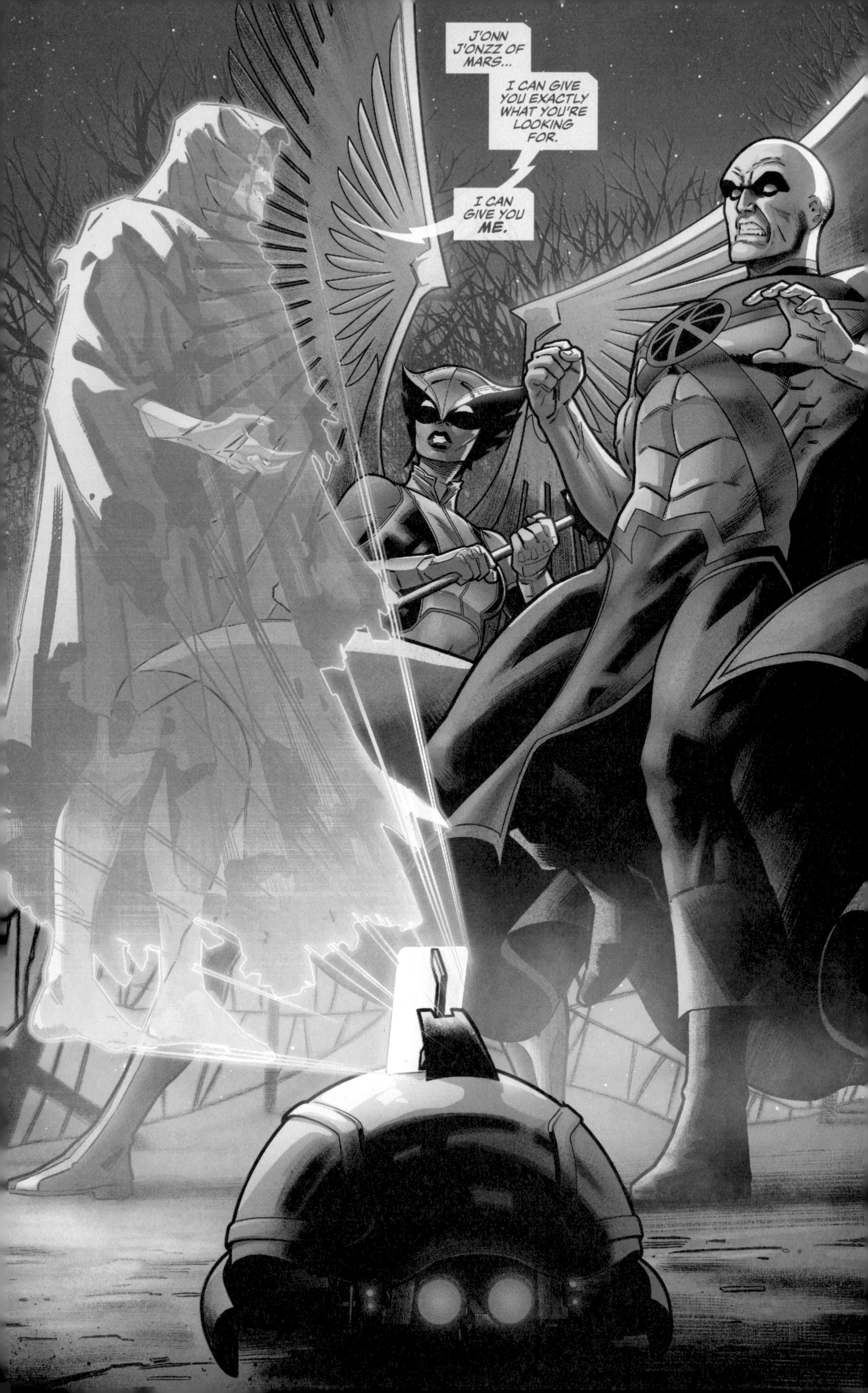
J'ONN J'ONZZ OF MARS...
I CAN GIVE YOU EXACTLY WHAT YOU'RE LOOKING FOR.
I CAN GIVE YOU ME.

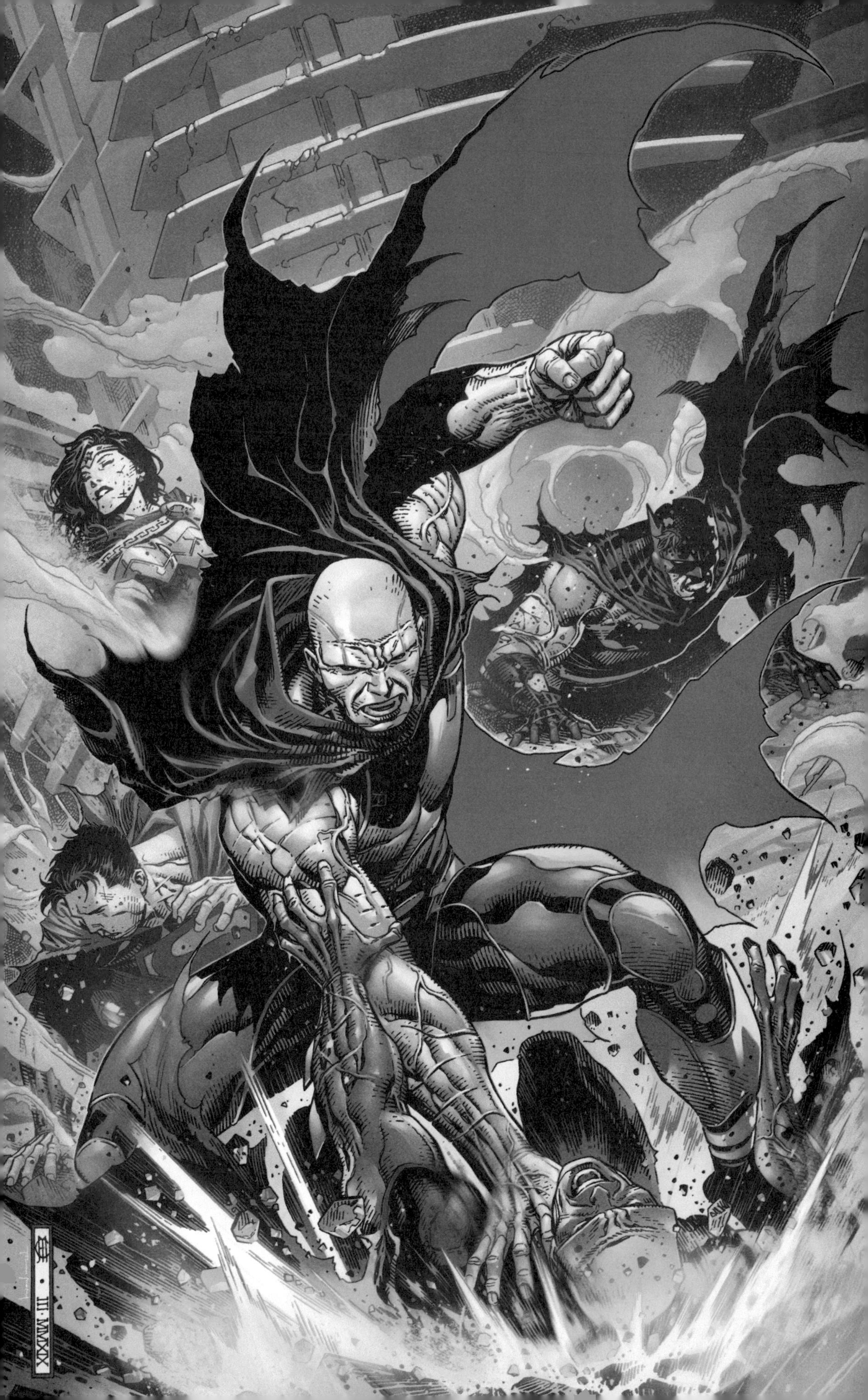
III · MMXX

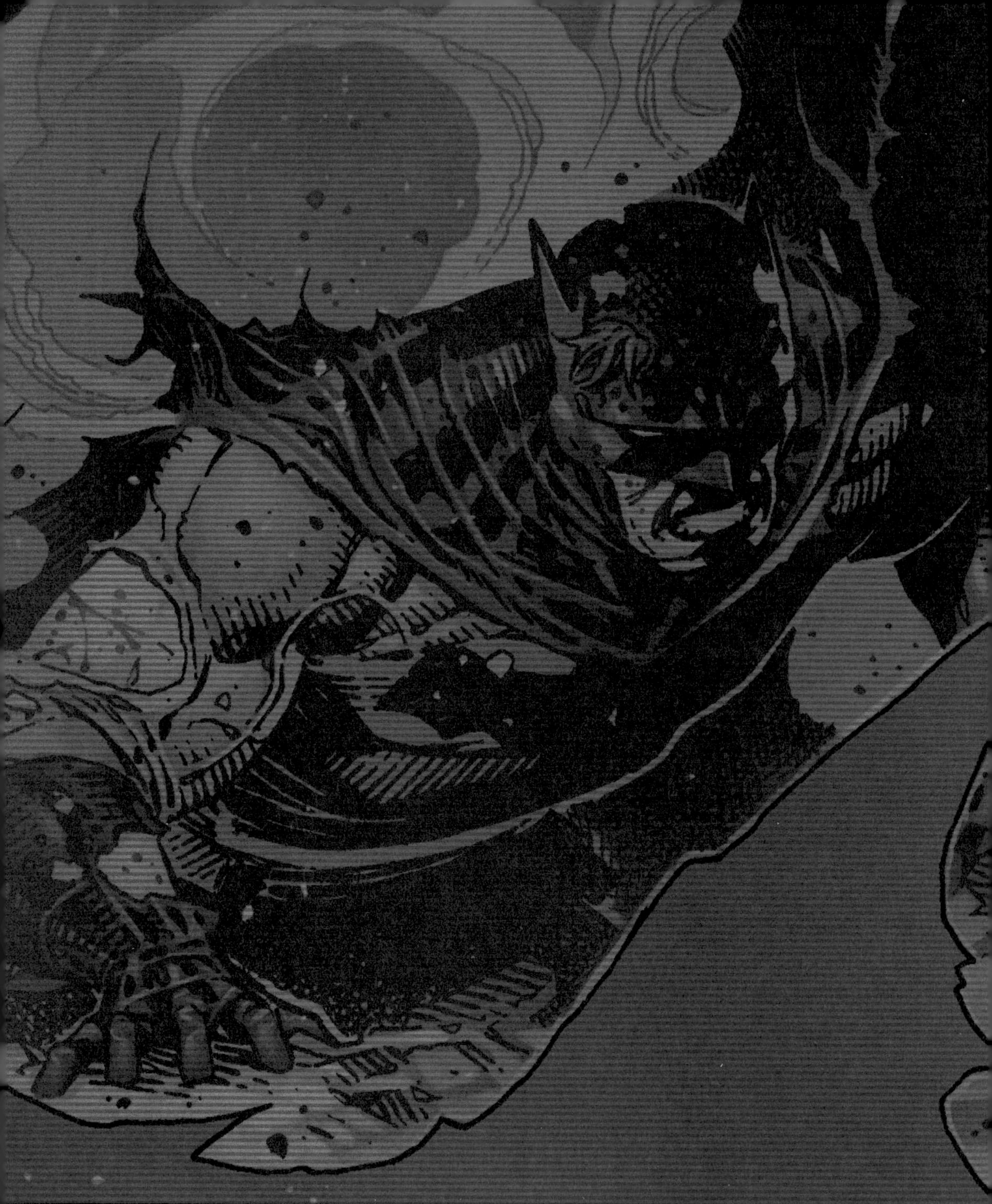

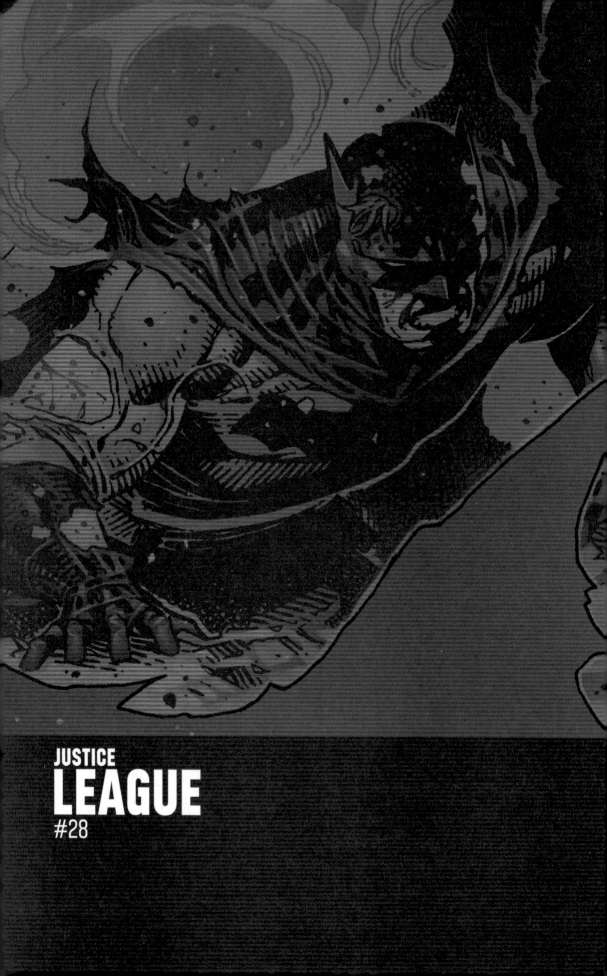

JUSTICE LEAGUE
#28

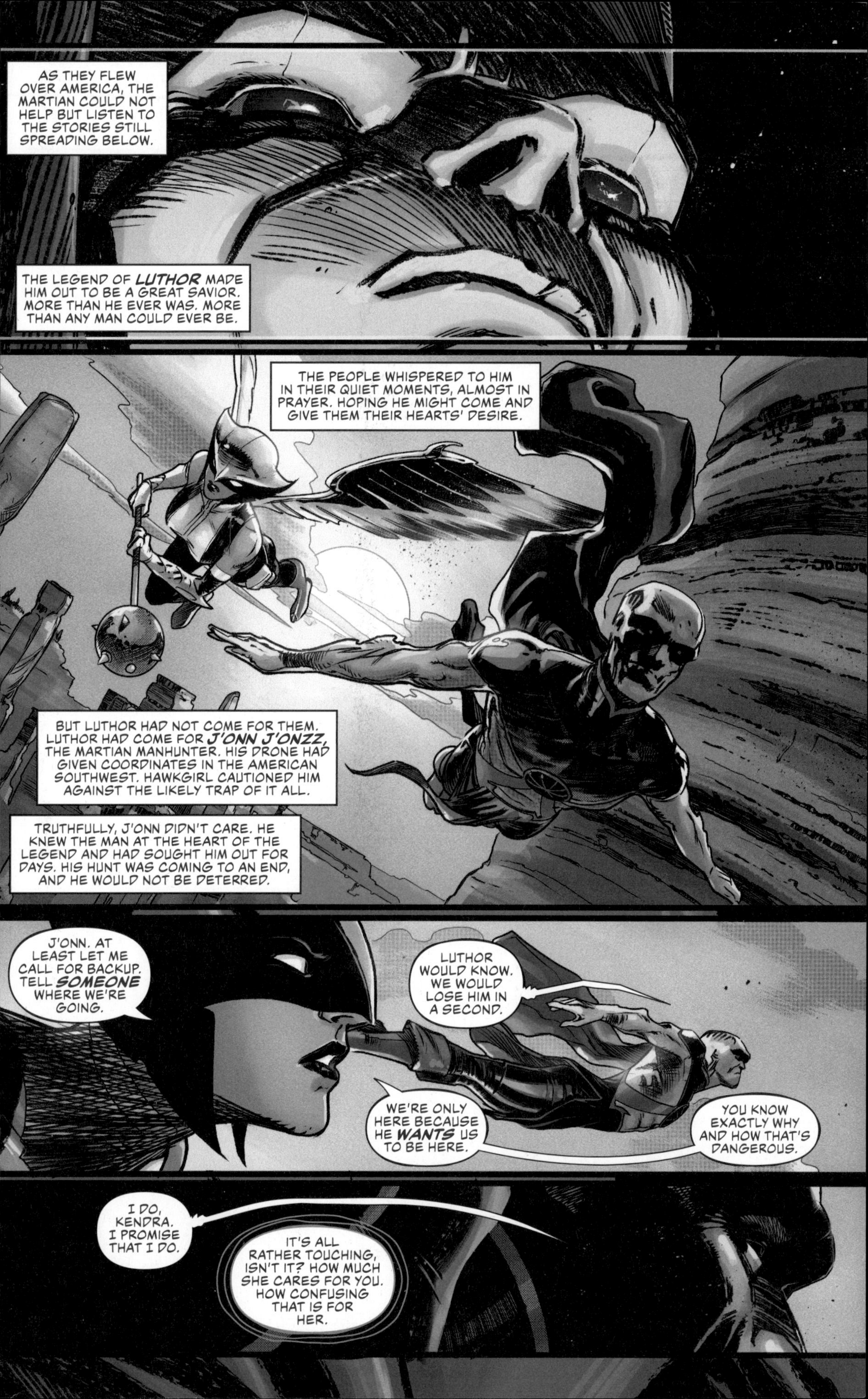
AS THEY FLEW OVER AMERICA, THE MARTIAN COULD NOT HELP BUT LISTEN TO THE STORIES STILL SPREADING BELOW.
THE LEGEND OF LUTHOR MADE HIM OUT TO BE A GREAT SAVIOR. MORE THAN HE EVER WAS. MORE THAN ANY MAN COULD EVER BE.
THE PEOPLE WHISPERED TO HIM IN THEIR QUIET MOMENTS, ALMOST IN PRAYER. HOPING HE MIGHT COME AND GIVE THEM THEIR HEARTS' DESIRE.
BUT LUTHOR HAD NOT COME FOR THEM. LUTHOR HAD COME FOR J'ONN J'ONZZ, THE MARTIAN MANHUNTER. HIS DRONE HAD GIVEN COORDINATES IN THE AMERICAN SOUTHWEST. HAWKGIRL CAUTIONED HIM AGAINST THE LIKELY TRAP OF IT ALL.
TRUTHFULLY, J'ONN DIDN'T CARE. HE KNEW THE MAN AT THE HEART OF THE LEGEND AND HAD SOUGHT HIM OUT FOR DAYS. HIS HUNT WAS COMING TO AN END, AND HE WOULD NOT BE DETERRED.
J'ONN. AT LEAST LET ME CALL FOR BACKUP. TELL SOMEONE WHERE WE'RE GOING.
LUTHOR WOULD KNOW. WE WOULD LOSE HIM IN A SECOND.
WE'RE ONLY HERE BECAUSE HE WANTS US TO BE HERE.
YOU KNOW EXACTLY WHY AND HOW THAT'S DANGEROUS.
I DO, KENDRA. I PROMISE THAT I DO.
IT'S ALL RATHER TOUCHING, ISN'T IT? HOW MUCH SHE CARES FOR YOU. HOW CONFUSING THAT IS FOR HER.

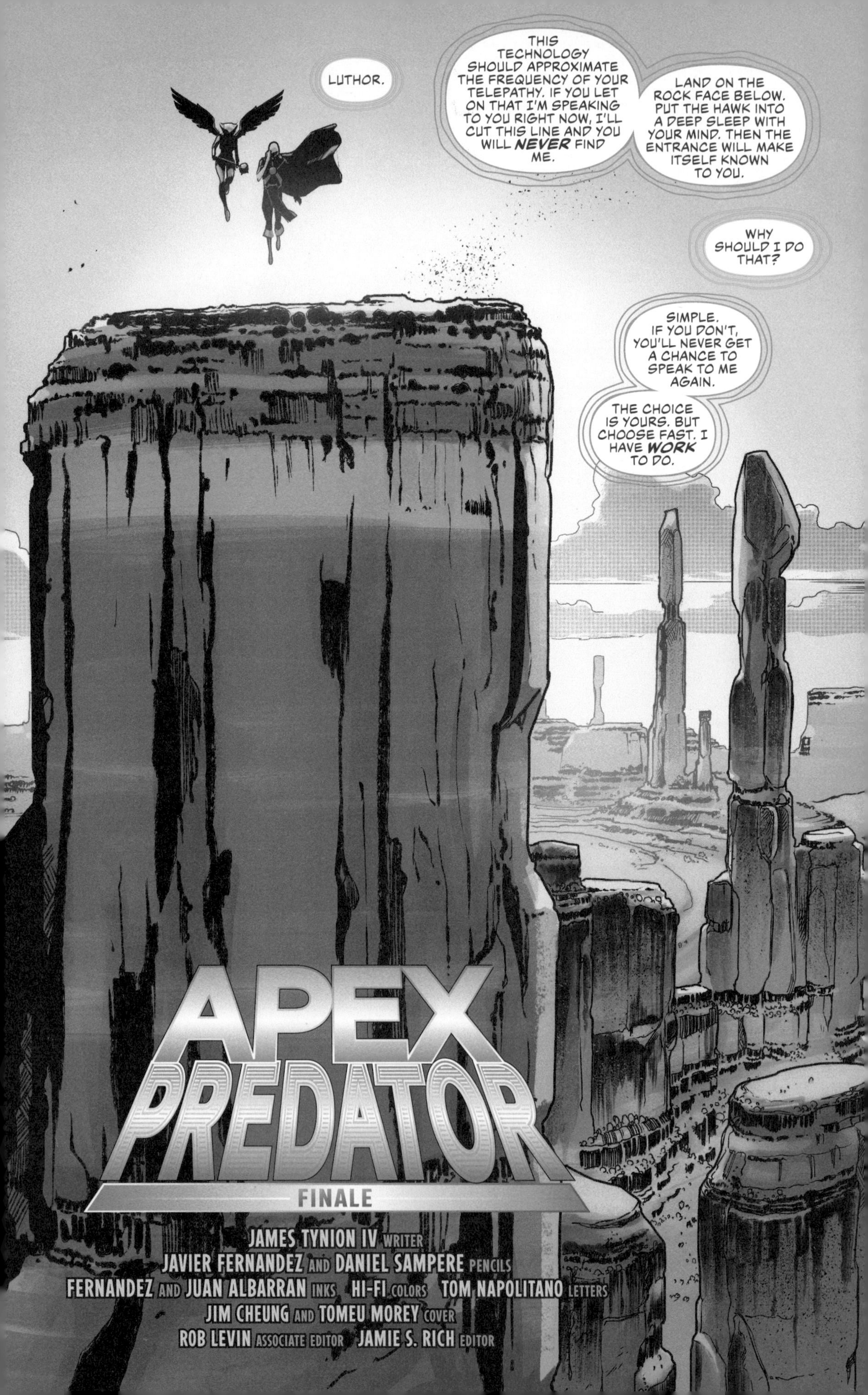
LUTHOR.
THIS TECHNOLOGY SHOULD APPROXIMATE THE FREQUENCY OF YOUR TELEPATHY. IF YOU LET ON THAT I'M SPEAKING TO YOU RIGHT NOW, I'LL CUT THIS LINE AND YOU WILL **NEVER** FIND ME.
LAND ON THE ROCK FACE BELOW. PUT THE HAWK INTO A DEEP SLEEP WITH YOUR MIND. THEN THE ENTRANCE WILL MAKE ITSELF KNOWN TO YOU.
WHY SHOULD I DO THAT?
SIMPLE. IF YOU DON'T, YOU'LL NEVER GET A CHANCE TO SPEAK TO ME AGAIN.
THE CHOICE IS YOURS. BUT CHOOSE FAST. I HAVE **WORK** TO DO.
APEX PREDATOR
FINALE
JAMES TYNION IV WRITER
JAVIER FERNANDEZ AND DANIEL SAMPERE PENCILS
FERNANDEZ AND JUAN ALBARRAN INKS HI-FI COLORS TOM NAPOLITANO LETTERS
JIM CHEUNG AND TOMEU MOREY COVER
ROB LEVIN ASSOCIATE EDITOR JAMIE S. RICH EDITOR

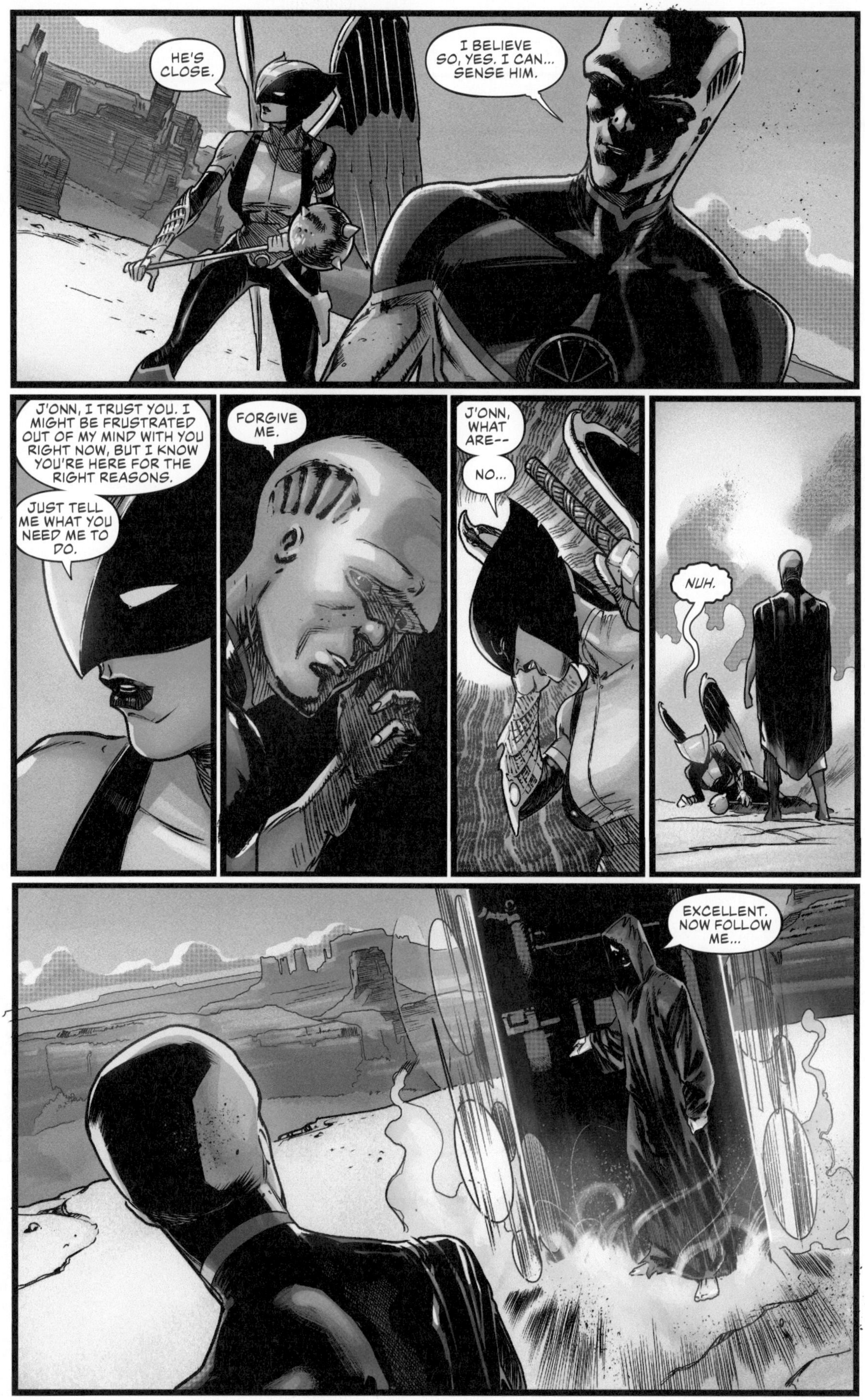
HE'S CLOSE.
I BELIEVE SO, YES. I CAN... SENSE HIM.
J'ONN, I TRUST YOU. I MIGHT BE FRUSTRATED OUT OF MY MIND WITH YOU RIGHT NOW, BUT I KNOW YOU'RE HERE FOR THE RIGHT REASONS.
JUST TELL ME WHAT YOU NEED ME TO DO.
FORGIVE ME.
J'ONN, WHAT ARE--
NO...
NUH.
EXCELLENT. NOW FOLLOW ME...

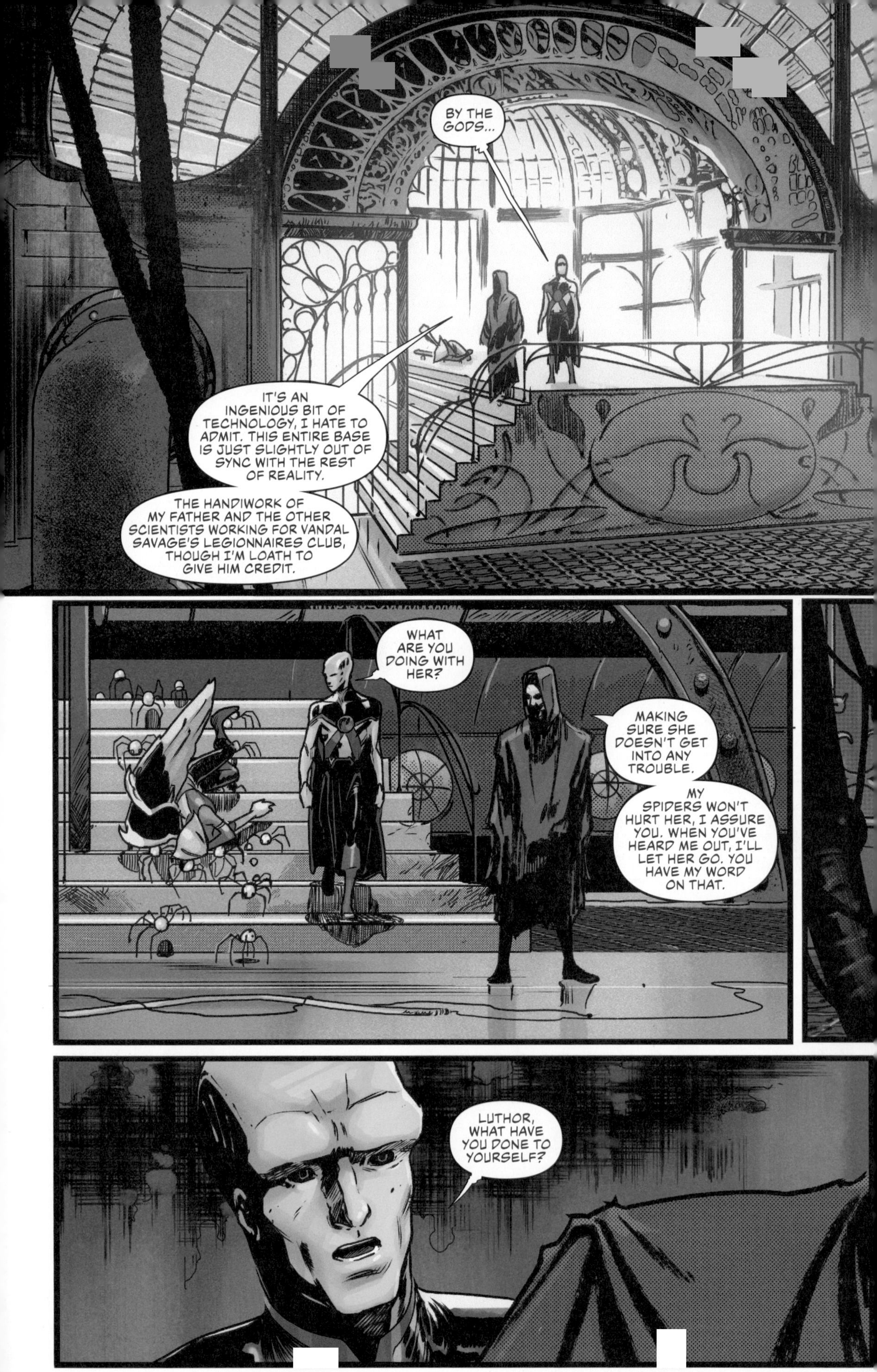
BY THE GODS...
IT'S AN INGENIOUS BIT OF TECHNOLOGY, I HATE TO ADMIT. THIS ENTIRE BASE IS JUST SLIGHTLY OUT OF SYNC WITH THE REST OF REALITY.
THE HANDIWORK OF MY FATHER AND THE OTHER SCIENTISTS WORKING FOR VANDAL SAVAGE'S LEGIONNAIRES CLUB, THOUGH I'M LOATH TO GIVE HIM CREDIT.
WHAT ARE YOU DOING WITH HER?
MAKING SURE SHE DOESN'T GET INTO ANY TROUBLE.
MY SPIDERS WON'T HURT HER, I ASSURE YOU. WHEN YOU'VE HEARD ME OUT, I'LL LET HER GO. YOU HAVE MY WORD ON THAT.
LUTHOR, WHAT HAVE YOU DONE TO YOURSELF?

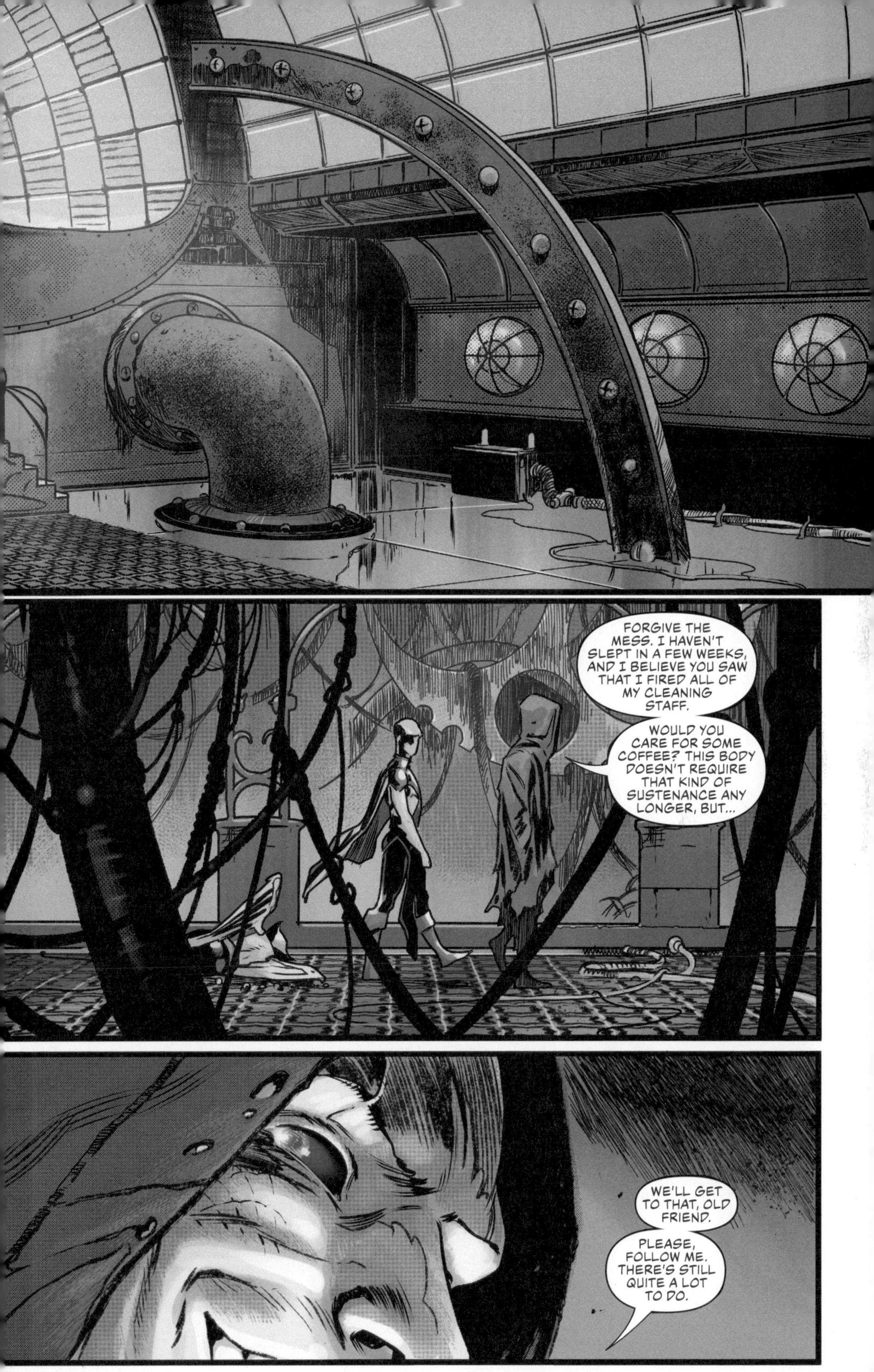
FORGIVE THE MESS. I HAVEN'T SLEPT IN A FEW WEEKS, AND I BELIEVE YOU SAW THAT I FIRED ALL OF MY CLEANING STAFF.
WOULD YOU CARE FOR SOME COFFEE? THIS BODY DOESN'T REQUIRE THAT KIND OF SUSTENANCE ANY LONGER, BUT...
WE'LL GET TO THAT, OLD FRIEND.
PLEASE, FOLLOW ME. THERE'S STILL QUITE A LOT TO DO.

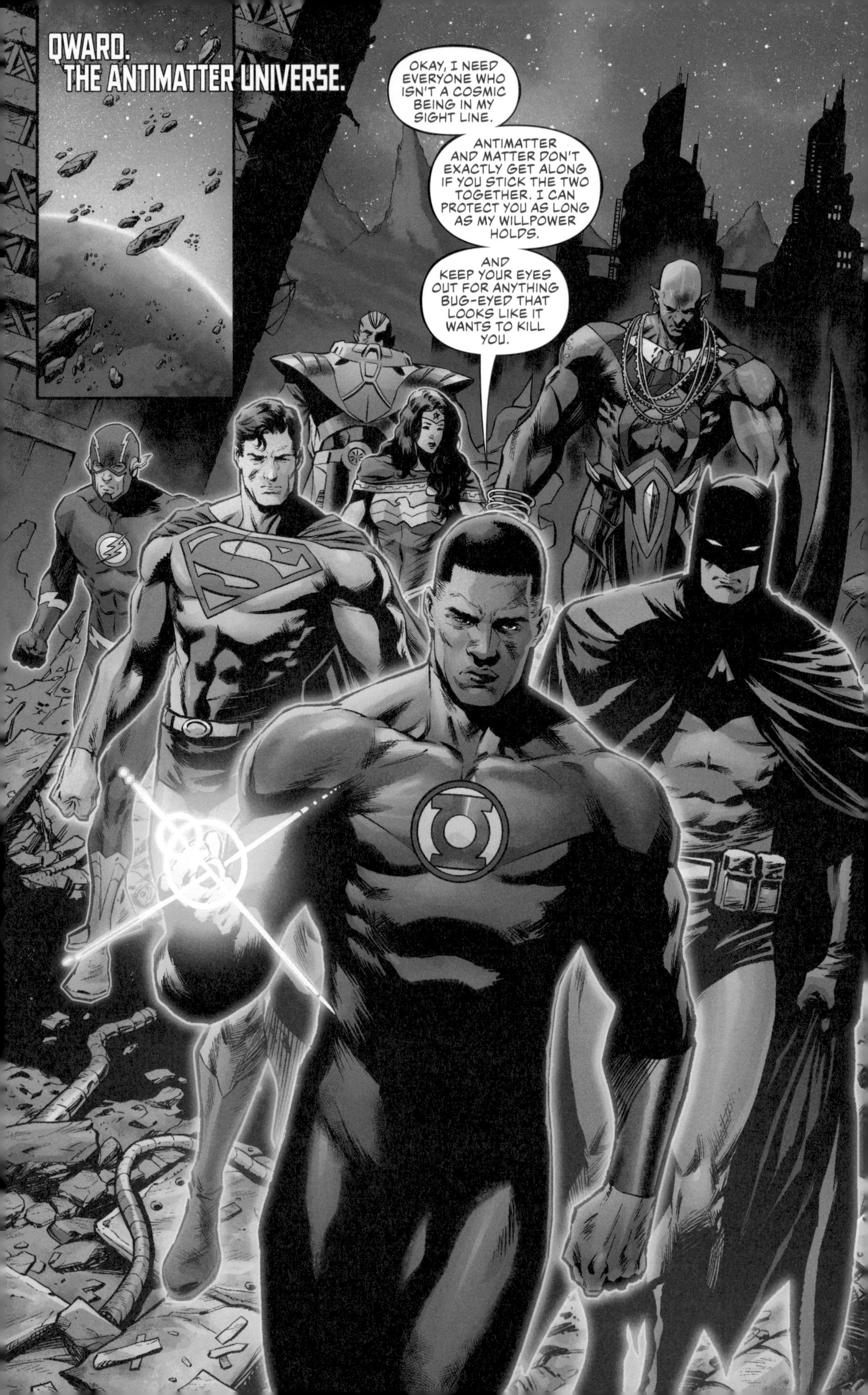
QWARD. THE ANTIMATTER UNIVERSE.
OKAY, I NEED EVERYONE WHO ISN'T A COSMIC BEING IN MY SIGHT LINE.
ANTIMATTER AND MATTER DON'T EXACTLY GET ALONG IF YOU STICK THE TWO TOGETHER. I CAN PROTECT YOU AS LONG AS MY WILLPOWER HOLDS.
AND KEEP YOUR EYES OUT FOR ANYTHING BUG-EYED THAT LOOKS LIKE IT WANTS TO KILL YOU.

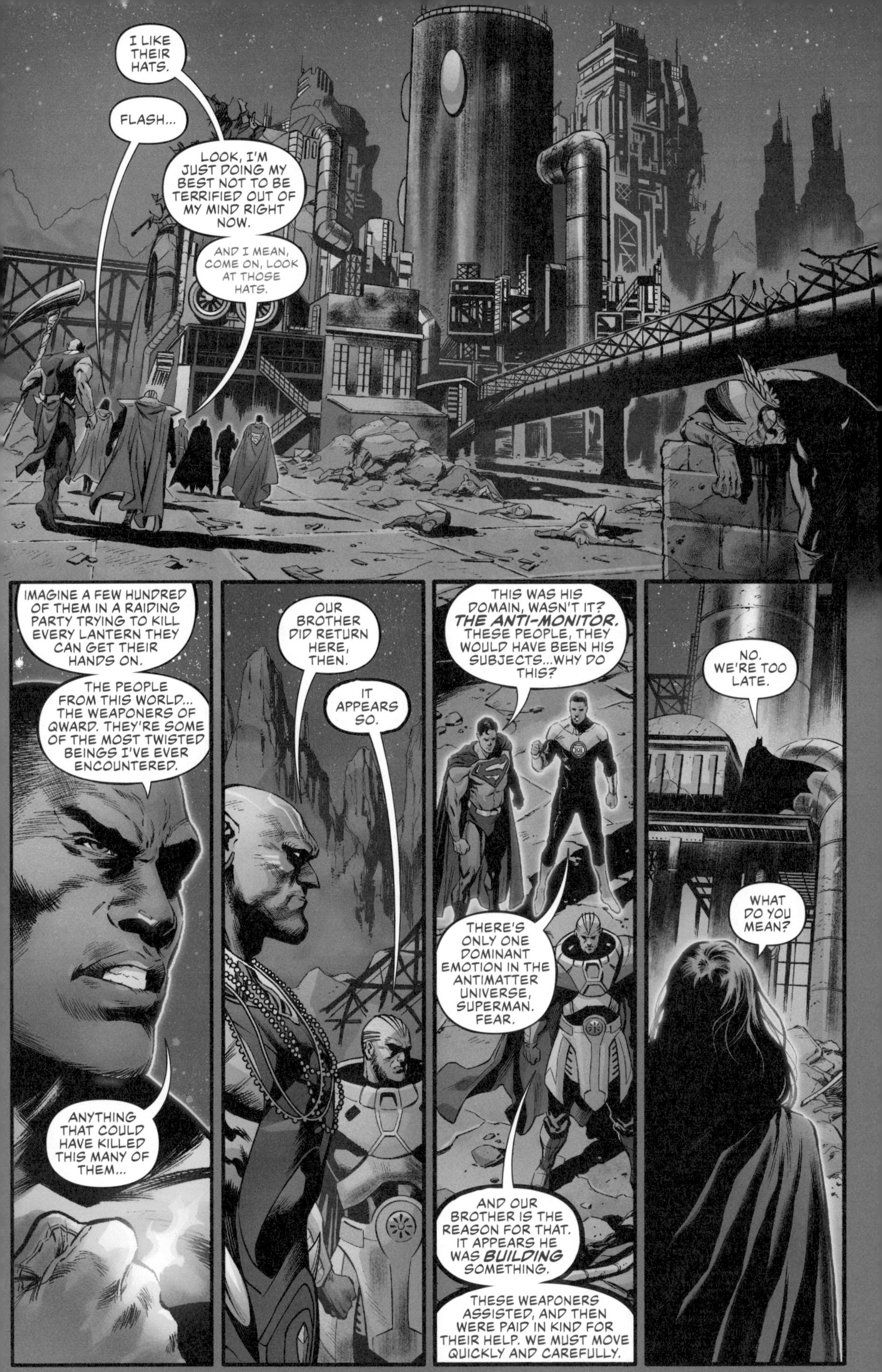
I LIKE THEIR HATS.
FLASH...
LOOK, I'M JUST DOING MY BEST NOT TO BE TERRIFIED OUT OF MY MIND RIGHT NOW.
AND I MEAN, COME ON, LOOK AT THOSE HATS.
IMAGINE A FEW HUNDRED OF THEM IN A RAIDING PARTY TRYING TO KILL EVERY LANTERN THEY CAN GET THEIR HANDS ON.
THE PEOPLE FROM THIS WORLD... THE WEAPONERS OF QWARD. THEY'RE SOME OF THE MOST TWISTED BEINGS I'VE EVER ENCOUNTERED.
ANYTHING THAT COULD HAVE KILLED THIS MANY OF THEM...
OUR BROTHER DID RETURN HERE, THEN.
IT APPEARS SO.
THIS WAS HIS DOMAIN, WASN'T IT? *THE ANTI-MONITOR.* THESE PEOPLE, THEY WOULD HAVE BEEN HIS SUBJECTS...WHY DO THIS?
THERE'S ONLY ONE DOMINANT EMOTION IN THE ANTIMATTER UNIVERSE, SUPERMAN. FEAR.
AND OUR BROTHER IS THE REASON FOR THAT. IT APPEARS HE WAS *BUILDING* SOMETHING.
THESE WEAPONERS ASSISTED, AND THEN WERE PAID IN KIND FOR THEIR HELP. WE MUST MOVE QUICKLY AND CAREFULLY.
NO. WE'RE TOO LATE.
WHAT DO YOU MEAN?

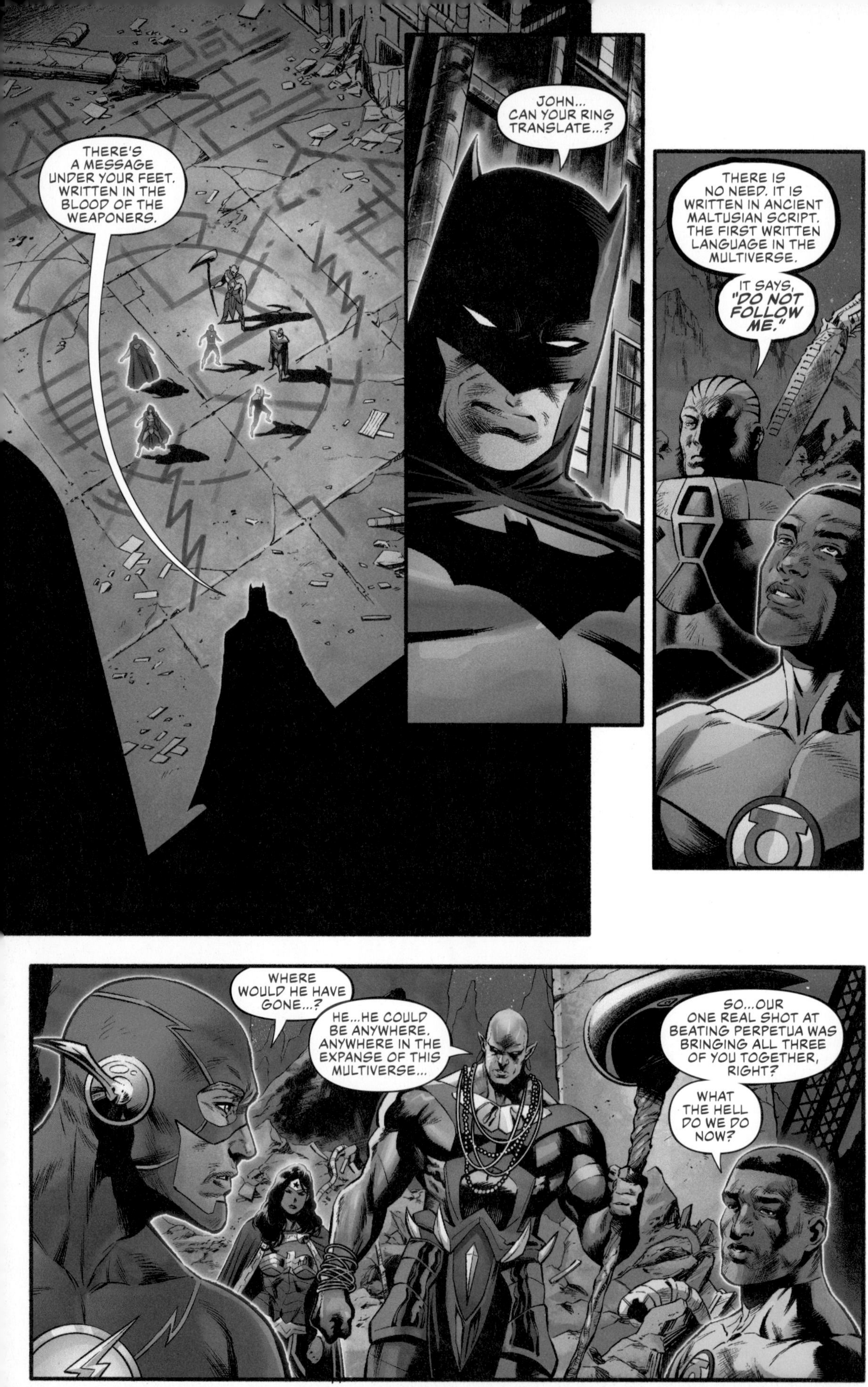
THERE'S A MESSAGE UNDER YOUR FEET. WRITTEN IN THE BLOOD OF THE WEAPONERS.
JOHN... CAN YOUR RING TRANSLATE...?
THERE IS NO NEED. IT IS WRITTEN IN ANCIENT MALTUSIAN SCRIPT. THE FIRST WRITTEN LANGUAGE IN THE MULTIVERSE.
IT SAYS, "DO NOT FOLLOW ME."
WHERE WOULD HE HAVE GONE...?
HE...HE COULD BE ANYWHERE. ANYWHERE IN THE EXPANSE OF THIS MULTIVERSE...
SO...OUR ONE REAL SHOT AT BEATING PERPETUA WAS BRINGING ALL THREE OF YOU TOGETHER, RIGHT?
WHAT THE HELL DO WE DO NOW?

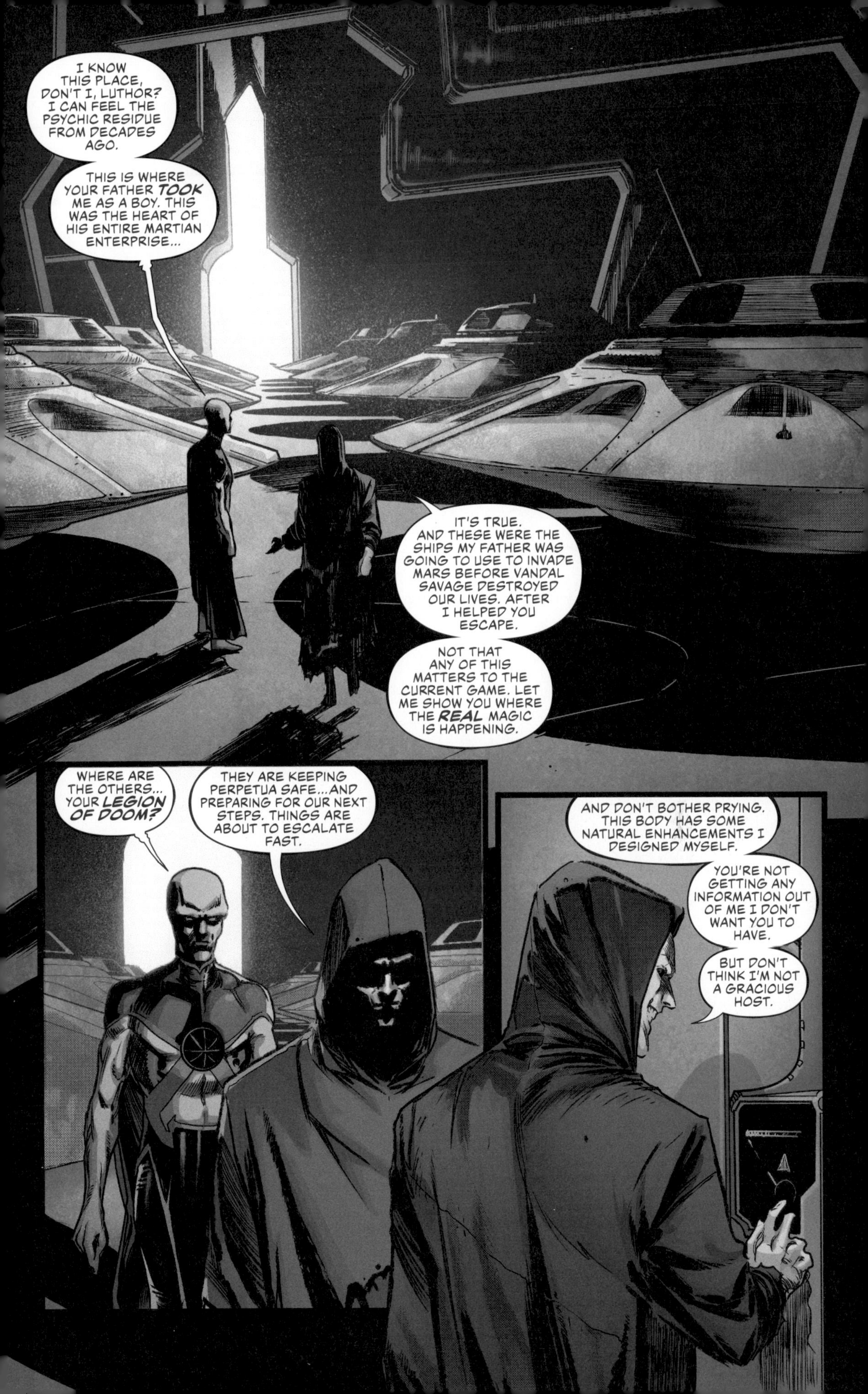
I KNOW THIS PLACE, DON'T I, LUTHOR? I CAN FEEL THE PSYCHIC RESIDUE FROM DECADES AGO.
THIS IS WHERE YOUR FATHER TOOK ME AS A BOY. THIS WAS THE HEART OF HIS ENTIRE MARTIAN ENTERPRISE...
IT'S TRUE. AND THESE WERE THE SHIPS MY FATHER WAS GOING TO USE TO INVADE MARS BEFORE VANDAL SAVAGE DESTROYED OUR LIVES. AFTER I HELPED YOU ESCAPE.
NOT THAT ANY OF THIS MATTERS TO THE CURRENT GAME. LET ME SHOW YOU WHERE THE REAL MAGIC IS HAPPENING.
WHERE ARE THE OTHERS... YOUR LEGION OF DOOM?
THEY ARE KEEPING PERPETUA SAFE...AND PREPARING FOR OUR NEXT STEPS. THINGS ARE ABOUT TO ESCALATE FAST.
AND DON'T BOTHER PRYING. THIS BODY HAS SOME NATURAL ENHANCEMENTS I DESIGNED MYSELF.
YOU'RE NOT GETTING ANY INFORMATION OUT OF ME I DON'T WANT YOU TO HAVE.
BUT DON'T THINK I'M NOT A GRACIOUS HOST.

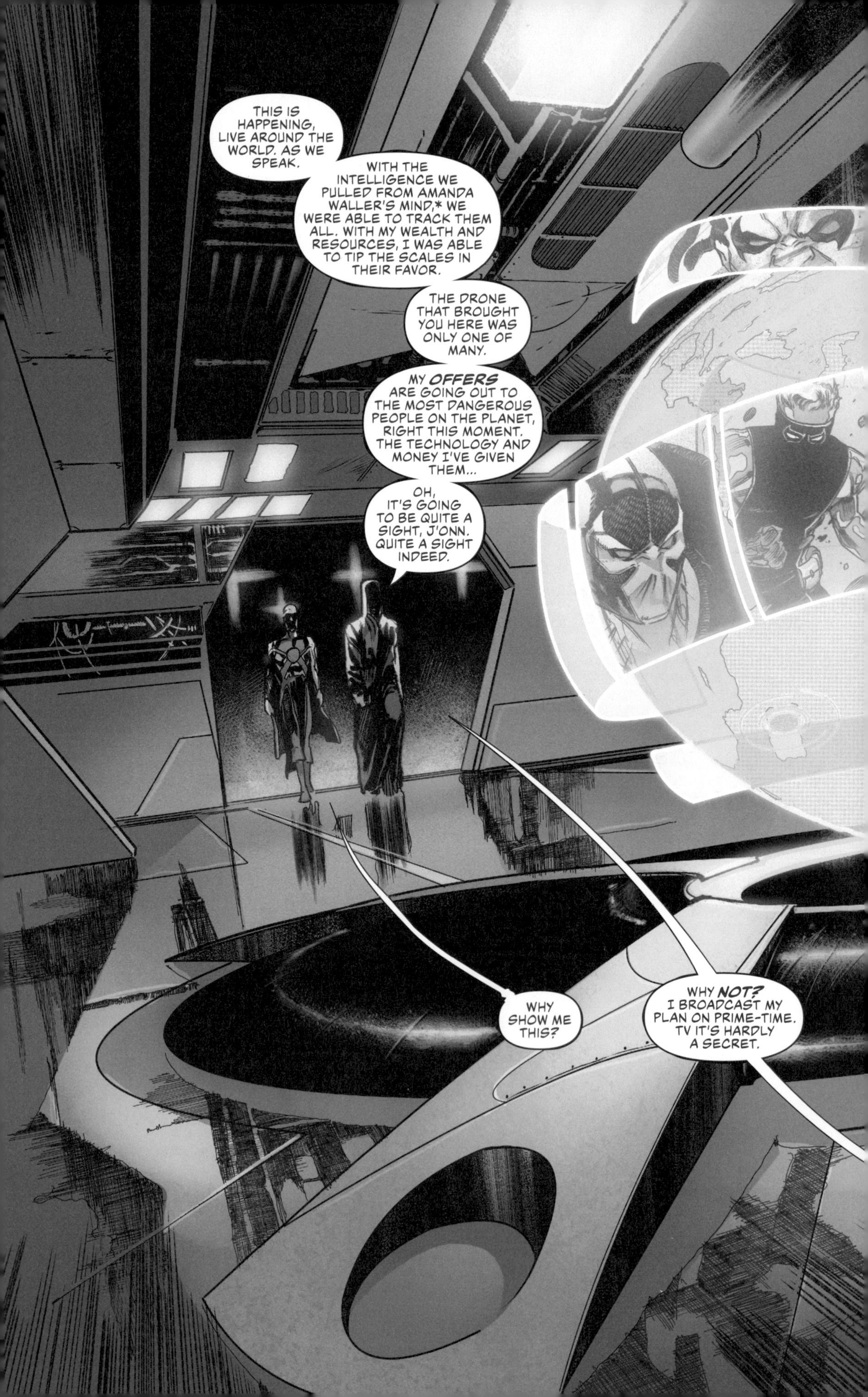
THIS IS HAPPENING, LIVE AROUND THE WORLD. AS WE SPEAK.
WITH THE INTELLIGENCE WE PULLED FROM AMANDA WALLER'S MIND,* WE WERE ABLE TO TRACK THEM ALL. WITH MY WEALTH AND RESOURCES, I WAS ABLE TO TIP THE SCALES IN THEIR FAVOR.
THE DRONE THAT BROUGHT YOU HERE WAS ONLY ONE OF MANY.
MY **OFFERS** ARE GOING OUT TO THE MOST DANGEROUS PEOPLE ON THE PLANET, RIGHT THIS MOMENT. THE TECHNOLOGY AND MONEY I'VE GIVEN THEM...
OH, IT'S GOING TO BE QUITE A SIGHT, J'ONN. QUITE A SIGHT INDEED.
WHY SHOW ME THIS?
WHY **NOT?** I BROADCAST MY PLAN ON PRIME-TIME. TV IT'S HARDLY A SECRET.

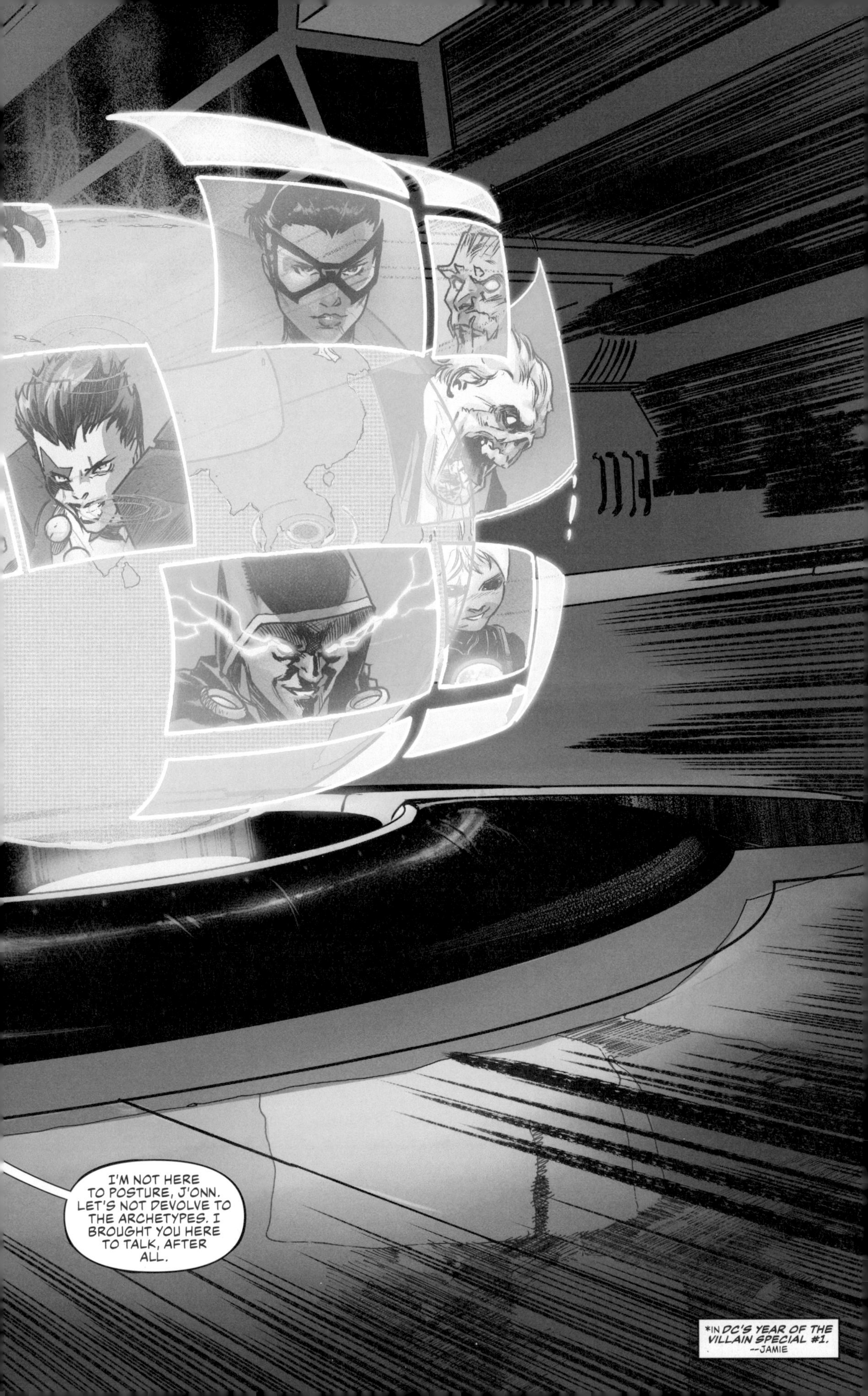
I'M NOT HERE TO POSTURE, J'ONN. LET'S NOT DEVOLVE TO THE ARCHETYPES. I BROUGHT YOU HERE TO TALK, AFTER ALL.
*IN DC'S YEAR OF THE VILLAIN SPECIAL #1. --JAMIE

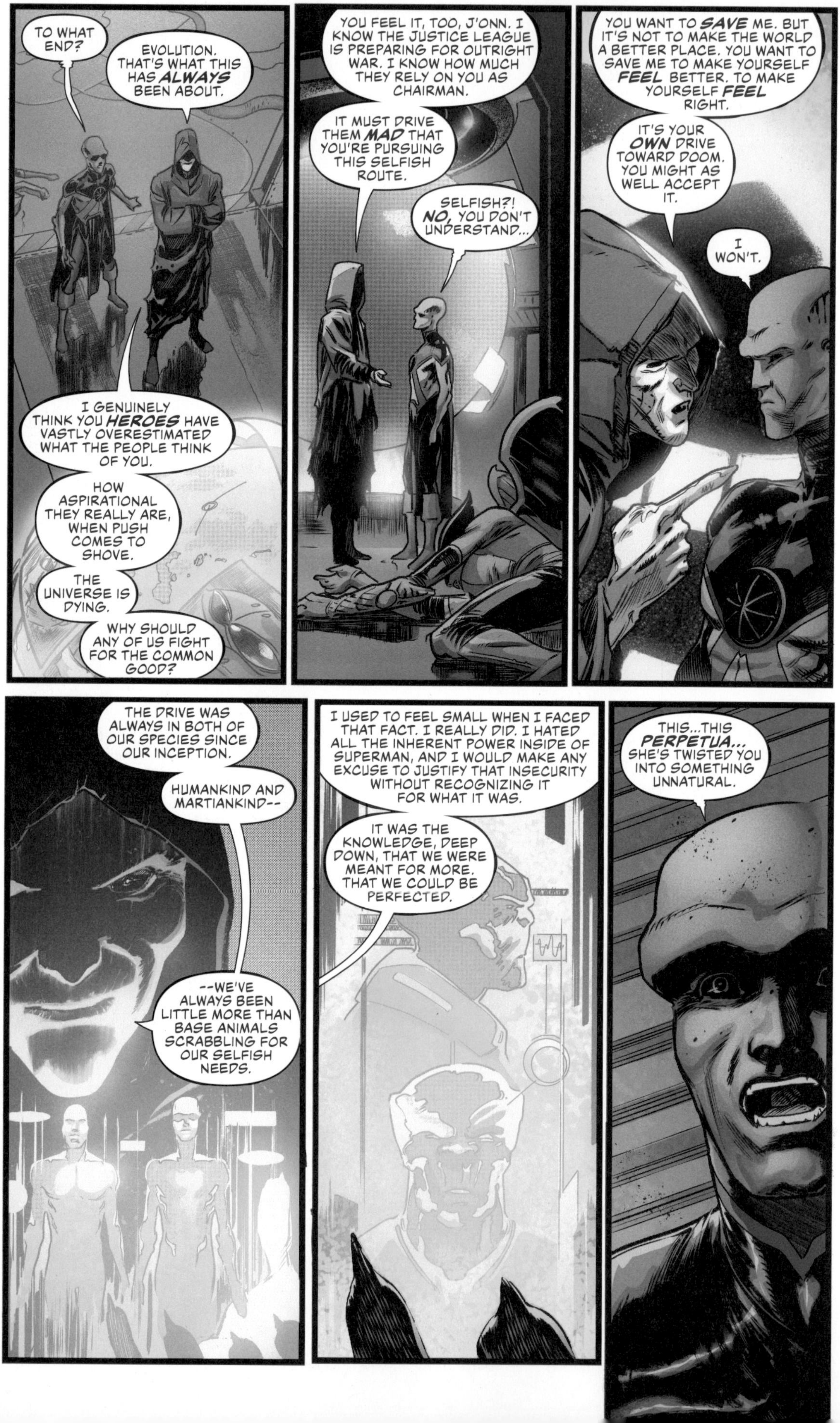
TO WHAT END?
EVOLUTION. THAT'S WHAT THIS HAS ALWAYS BEEN ABOUT.
I GENUINELY THINK YOU HEROES HAVE VASTLY OVERESTIMATED WHAT THE PEOPLE THINK OF YOU.
HOW ASPIRATIONAL THEY REALLY ARE, WHEN PUSH COMES TO SHOVE.
THE UNIVERSE IS DYING.
WHY SHOULD ANY OF US FIGHT FOR THE COMMON GOOD?
YOU FEEL IT, TOO, J'ONN. I KNOW THE JUSTICE LEAGUE IS PREPARING FOR OUTRIGHT WAR. I KNOW HOW MUCH THEY RELY ON YOU AS CHAIRMAN.
IT MUST DRIVE THEM MAD THAT YOU'RE PURSUING THIS SELFISH ROUTE.
SELFISH?! NO, YOU DON'T UNDERSTAND...
YOU WANT TO SAVE ME. BUT IT'S NOT TO MAKE THE WORLD A BETTER PLACE. YOU WANT TO SAVE ME TO MAKE YOURSELF FEEL BETTER. TO MAKE YOURSELF FEEL RIGHT.
IT'S YOUR OWN DRIVE TOWARD DOOM. YOU MIGHT AS WELL ACCEPT IT.
I WON'T.
THE DRIVE WAS ALWAYS IN BOTH OF OUR SPECIES SINCE OUR INCEPTION.
HUMANKIND AND MARTIANKIND--
--WE'VE ALWAYS BEEN LITTLE MORE THAN BASE ANIMALS SCRABBLING FOR OUR SELFISH NEEDS.
I USED TO FEEL SMALL WHEN I FACED THAT FACT. I REALLY DID. I HATED ALL THE INHERENT POWER INSIDE OF SUPERMAN, AND I WOULD MAKE ANY EXCUSE TO JUSTIFY THAT INSECURITY WITHOUT RECOGNIZING IT FOR WHAT IT WAS.
IT WAS THE KNOWLEDGE, DEEP DOWN, THAT WE WERE MEANT FOR MORE. THAT WE COULD BE PERFECTED.
THIS...THIS PERPETUA... SHE'S TWISTED YOU INTO SOMETHING UNNATURAL.

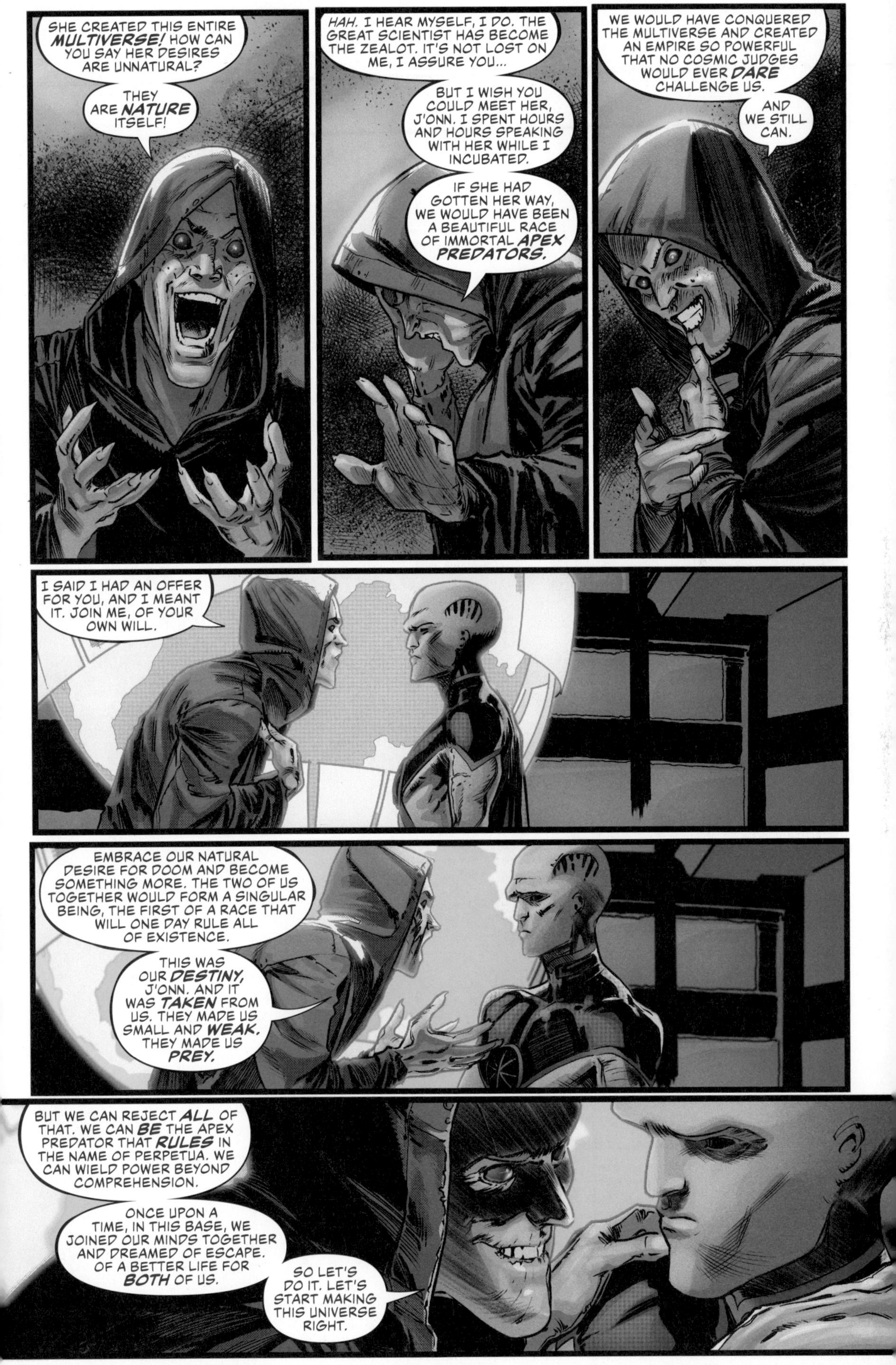
SHE CREATED THIS ENTIRE MULTIVERSE! HOW CAN YOU SAY HER DESIRES ARE UNNATURAL?
THEY ARE NATURE ITSELF!
HAH. I HEAR MYSELF, I DO. THE GREAT SCIENTIST HAS BECOME THE ZEALOT. IT'S NOT LOST ON ME, I ASSURE YOU...
BUT I WISH YOU COULD MEET HER, J'ONN. I SPENT HOURS AND HOURS SPEAKING WITH HER WHILE I INCUBATED.
IF SHE HAD GOTTEN HER WAY, WE WOULD HAVE BEEN A BEAUTIFUL RACE OF IMMORTAL APEX PREDATORS.
WE WOULD HAVE CONQUERED THE MULTIVERSE AND CREATED AN EMPIRE SO POWERFUL THAT NO COSMIC JUDGES WOULD EVER DARE CHALLENGE US.
AND WE STILL CAN.
I SAID I HAD AN OFFER FOR YOU, AND I MEANT IT. JOIN ME, OF YOUR OWN WILL.
EMBRACE OUR NATURAL DESIRE FOR DOOM AND BECOME SOMETHING MORE. THE TWO OF US TOGETHER WOULD FORM A SINGULAR BEING, THE FIRST OF A RACE THAT WILL ONE DAY RULE ALL OF EXISTENCE.
THIS WAS OUR DESTINY, J'ONN. AND IT WAS TAKEN FROM US. THEY MADE US SMALL AND WEAK. THEY MADE US PREY.
BUT WE CAN REJECT ALL OF THAT. WE CAN BE THE APEX PREDATOR THAT RULES IN THE NAME OF PERPETUA. WE CAN WIELD POWER BEYOND COMPREHENSION.
ONCE UPON A TIME, IN THIS BASE, WE JOINED OUR MINDS TOGETHER AND DREAMED OF ESCAPE. OF A BETTER LIFE FOR BOTH OF US.
SO LET'S DO IT. LET'S START MAKING THIS UNIVERSE RIGHT.

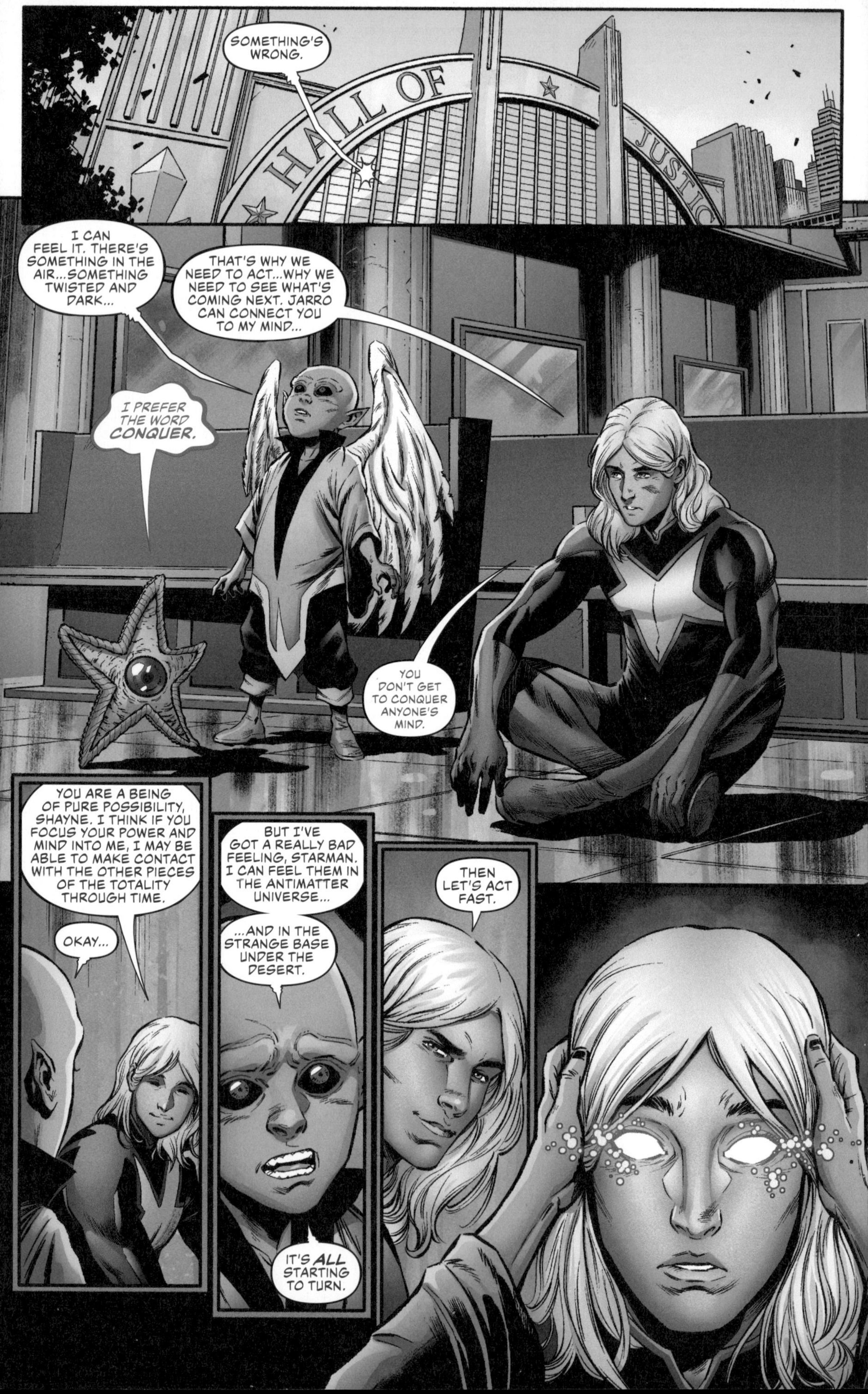
SOMETHING'S WRONG.
HALL OF JUSTIC
I CAN FEEL IT. THERE'S SOMETHING IN THE AIR...SOMETHING TWISTED AND DARK...
THAT'S WHY WE NEED TO ACT...WHY WE NEED TO SEE WHAT'S COMING NEXT. JARRO CAN CONNECT YOU TO MY MIND...
I PREFER THE WORD CONQUER.
YOU DON'T GET TO CONQUER ANYONE'S MIND.
YOU ARE A BEING OF PURE POSSIBILITY, SHAYNE. I THINK IF YOU FOCUS YOUR POWER AND MIND INTO ME, I MAY BE ABLE TO MAKE CONTACT WITH THE OTHER PIECES OF THE TOTALITY THROUGH TIME.
OKAY...
BUT I'VE GOT A REALLY BAD FEELING, STARMAN. I CAN FEEL THEM IN THE ANTIMATTER UNIVERSE...
...AND IN THE STRANGE BASE UNDER THE DESERT.
IT'S ALL STARTING TO TURN.
THEN LET'S ACT FAST.

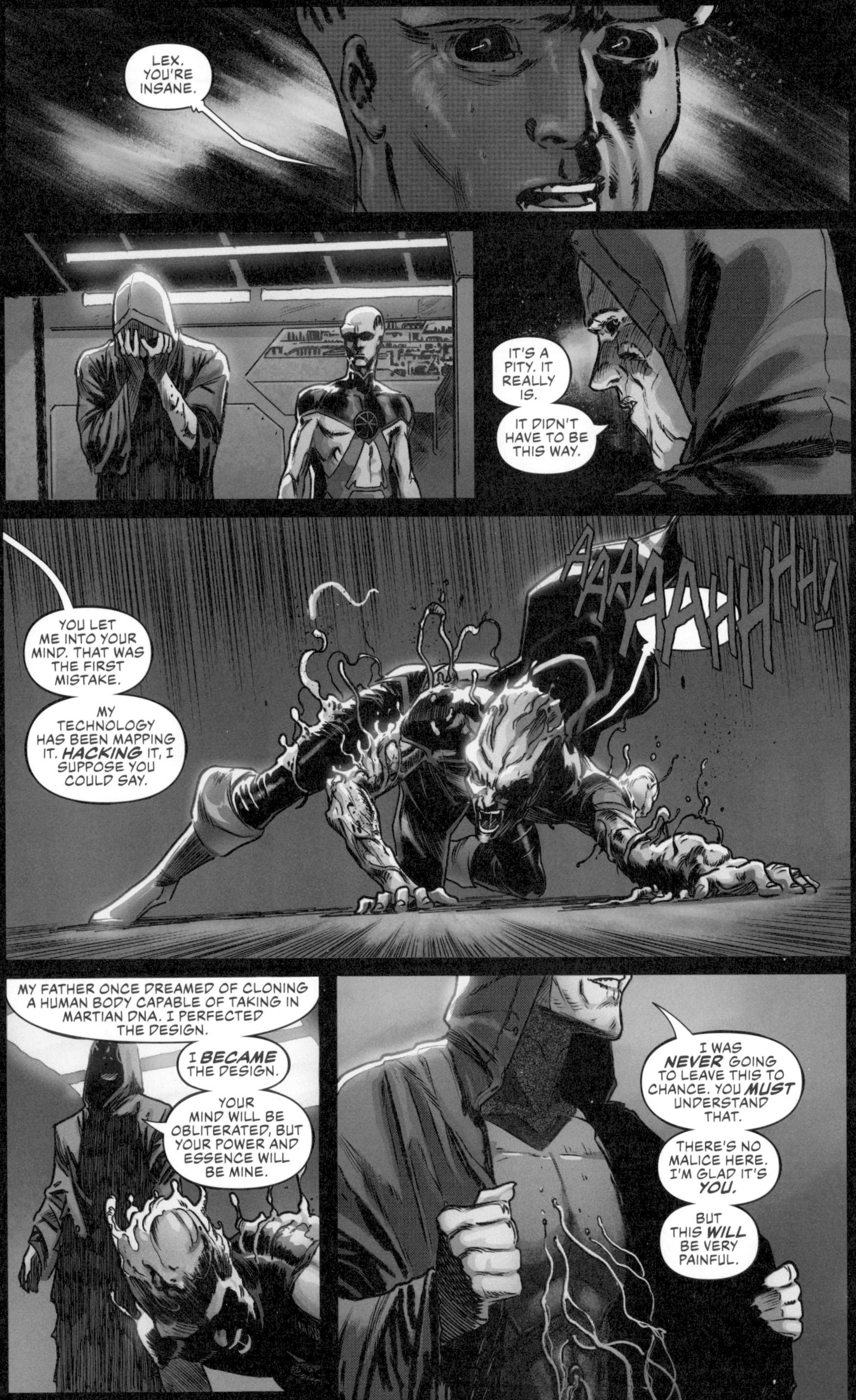

LEX. YOU'RE INSANE.
IT'S A PITY. IT REALLY IS.
IT DIDN'T HAVE TO BE THIS WAY.
AAAAAAHHHH!
YOU LET ME INTO YOUR MIND. THAT WAS THE FIRST MISTAKE.
MY TECHNOLOGY HAS BEEN MAPPING IT. HACKING IT, I SUPPOSE YOU COULD SAY.
MY FATHER ONCE DREAMED OF CLONING A HUMAN BODY CAPABLE OF TAKING IN MARTIAN DNA. I PERFECTED THE DESIGN.
I BECAME THE DESIGN.
YOUR MIND WILL BE OBLITERATED, BUT YOUR POWER AND ESSENCE WILL BE MINE.
I WAS NEVER GOING TO LEAVE THIS TO CHANCE. YOU MUST UNDERSTAND THAT.
THERE'S NO MALICE HERE. I'M GLAD IT'S YOU.
BUT THIS WILL BE VERY PAINFUL.

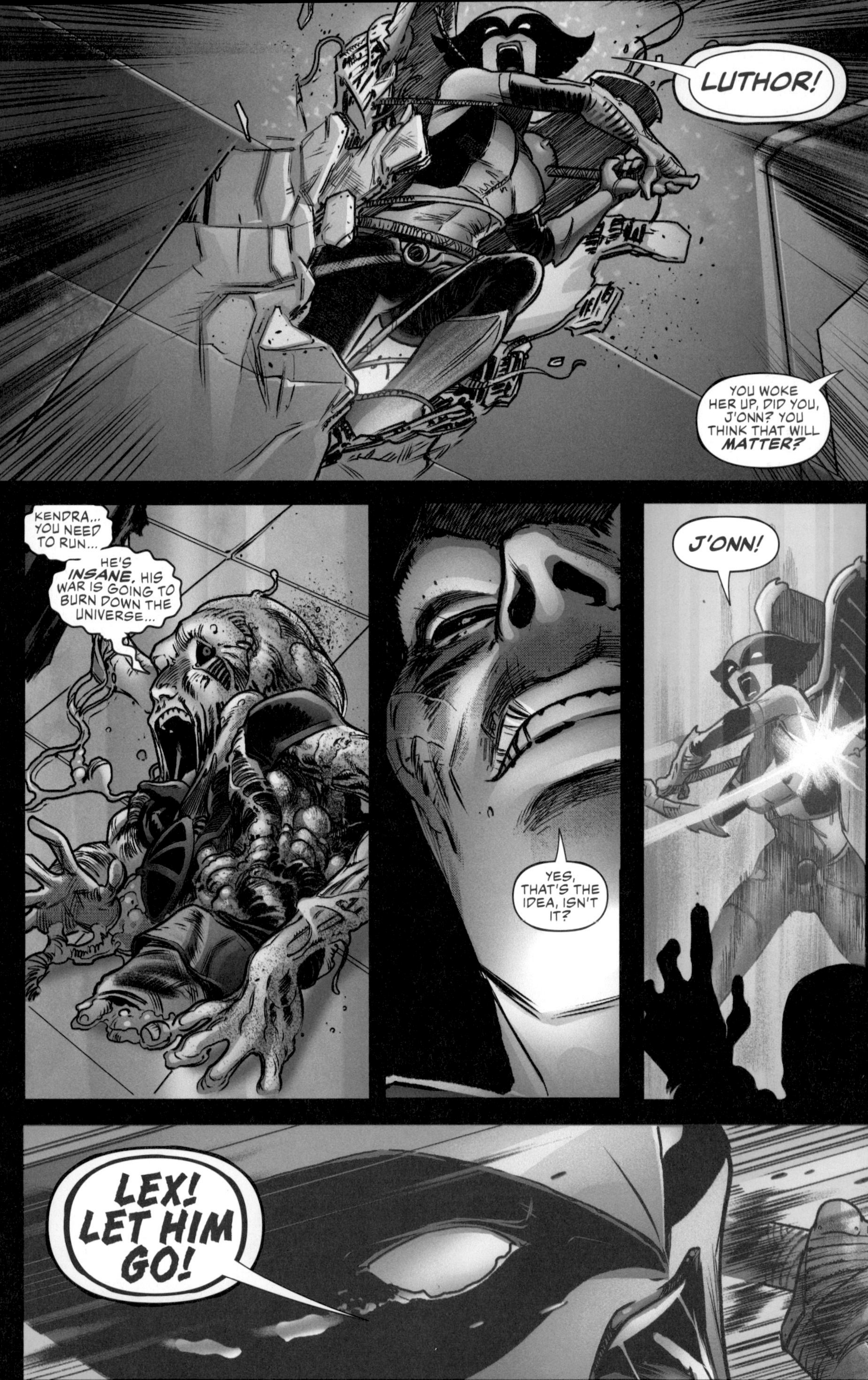
LUTHOR!
YOU WOKE HER UP, DID YOU, J'ONN? YOU THINK THAT WILL MATTER?
KENDRA... YOU NEED TO RUN...
HE'S INSANE. HIS WAR IS GOING TO BURN DOWN THE UNIVERSE...
YES, THAT'S THE IDEA, ISN'T IT?
J'ONN!
LEX! LET HIM GO!

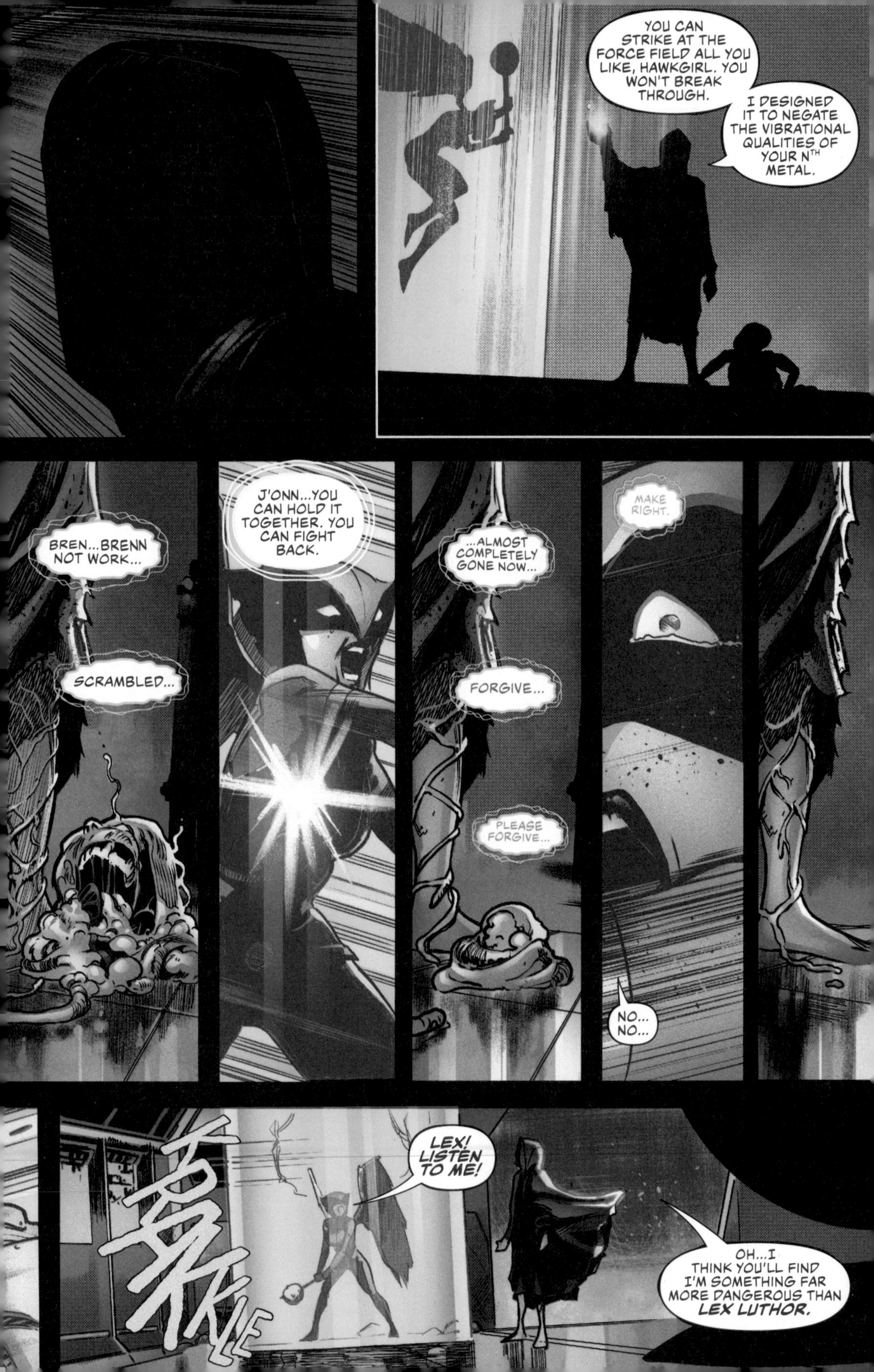
YOU CAN STRIKE AT THE FORCE FIELD ALL YOU LIKE, HAWKGIRL. YOU WON'T BREAK THROUGH.
I DESIGNED IT TO NEGATE THE VIBRATIONAL QUALITIES OF YOUR Nth METAL.
BREN...BRENN NOT WORK...
SCRAMBLED...
J'ONN...YOU CAN HOLD IT TOGETHER. YOU CAN FIGHT BACK.
...ALMOST COMPLETELY GONE NOW...
FORGIVE...
PLEASE FORGIVE...
MAKE RIGHT.
NO... NO...
KRKKLE
LEX! LISTEN TO ME!
OH...I THINK YOU'LL FIND I'M SOMETHING FAR MORE DANGEROUS THAN LEX LUTHOR.

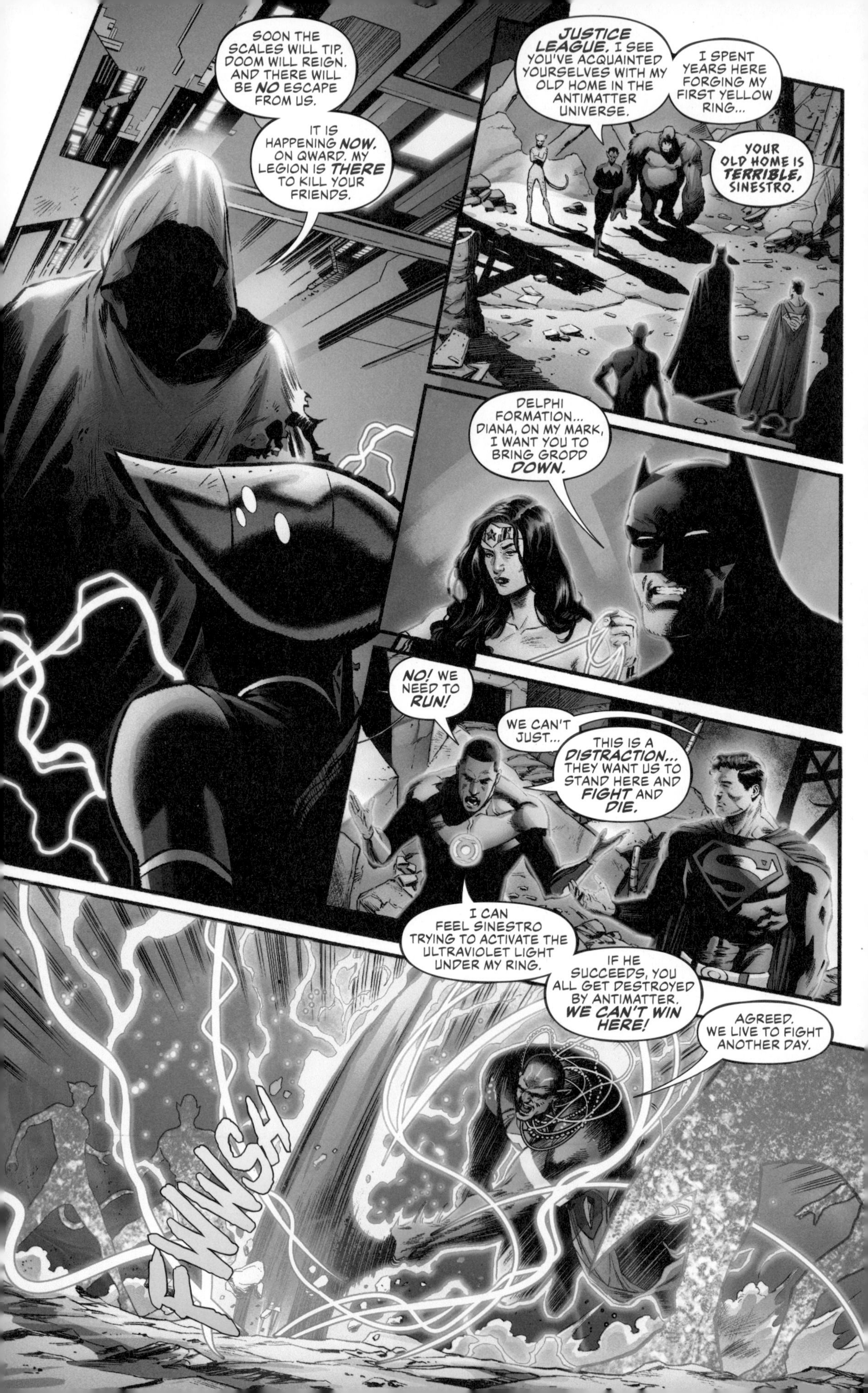
SOON THE SCALES WILL TIP. DOOM WILL REIGN. AND THERE WILL BE NO ESCAPE FROM US.
IT IS HAPPENING NOW. ON QWARD. MY LEGION IS THERE TO KILL YOUR FRIENDS.
JUSTICE LEAGUE. I SEE YOU'VE ACQUAINTED YOURSELVES WITH MY OLD HOME IN THE ANTIMATTER UNIVERSE.
I SPENT YEARS HERE FORGING MY FIRST YELLOW RING...
YOUR OLD HOME IS TERRIBLE, SINESTRO.
DELPHI FORMATION... DIANA, ON MY MARK, I WANT YOU TO BRING GRODD DOWN.
NO! WE NEED TO RUN!
WE CAN'T JUST...
THIS IS A DISTRACTION... THEY WANT US TO STAND HERE AND FIGHT AND DIE.
I CAN FEEL SINESTRO TRYING TO ACTIVATE THE ULTRAVIOLET LIGHT UNDER MY RING.
IF HE SUCCEEDS, YOU ALL GET DESTROYED BY ANTIMATTER. WE CAN'T WIN HERE!
AGREED. WE LIVE TO FIGHT ANOTHER DAY.
FWWSH

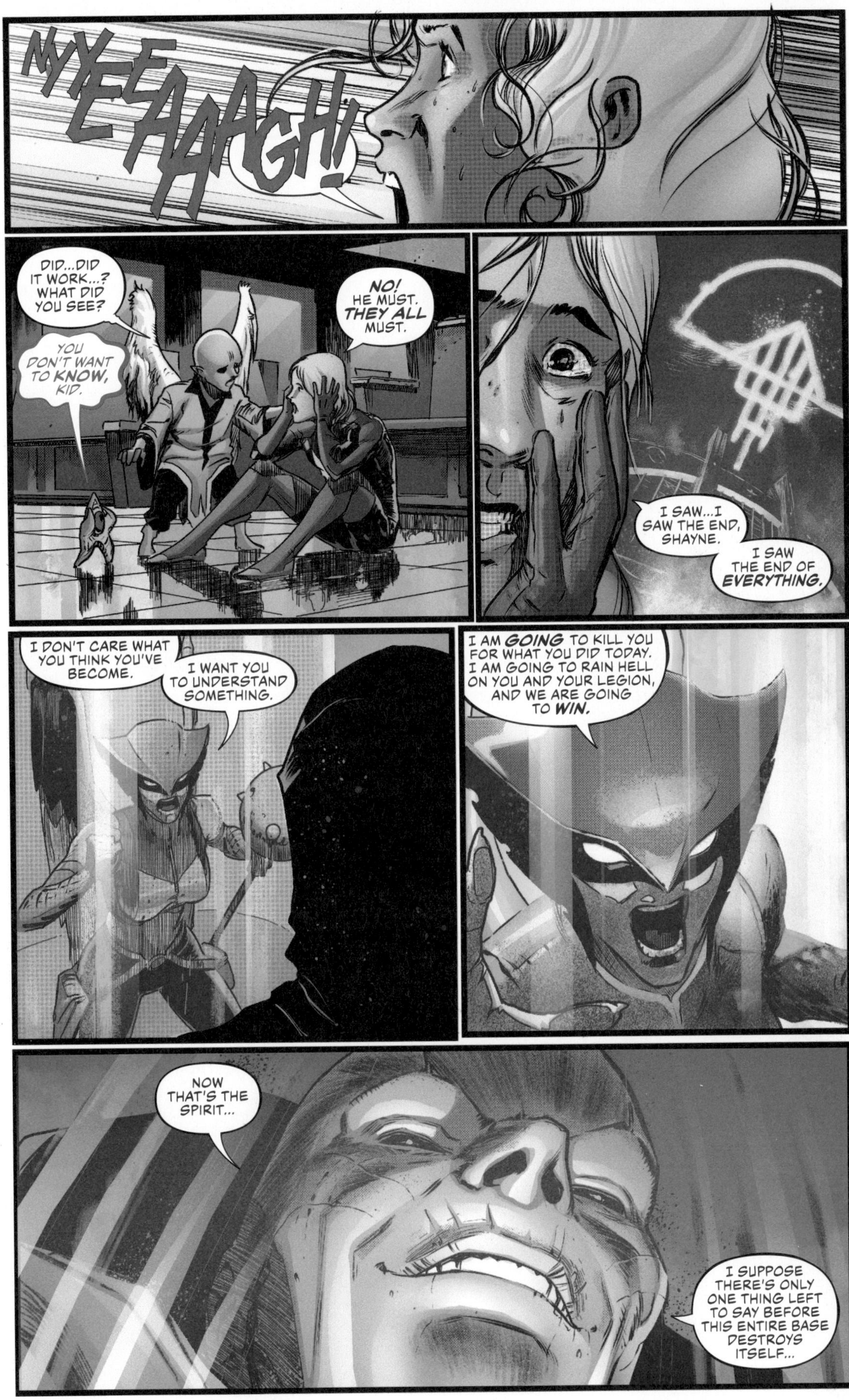
NYYEEAAAGH!!
DID...DID IT WORK...? WHAT DID YOU SEE?
YOU DON'T WANT TO KNOW, KID.
NO! HE MUST. THEY ALL MUST.
I SAW...I SAW THE END, SHAYNE.
I SAW THE END OF EVERYTHING.
I DON'T CARE WHAT YOU THINK YOU'VE BECOME.
I WANT YOU TO UNDERSTAND SOMETHING.
I AM GOING TO KILL YOU FOR WHAT YOU DID TODAY. I AM GOING TO RAIN HELL ON YOU AND YOUR LEGION, AND WE ARE GOING TO WIN.
NOW THAT'S THE SPIRIT...
I SUPPOSE THERE'S ONLY ONE THING LEFT TO SAY BEFORE THIS ENTIRE BASE DESTROYS ITSELF...

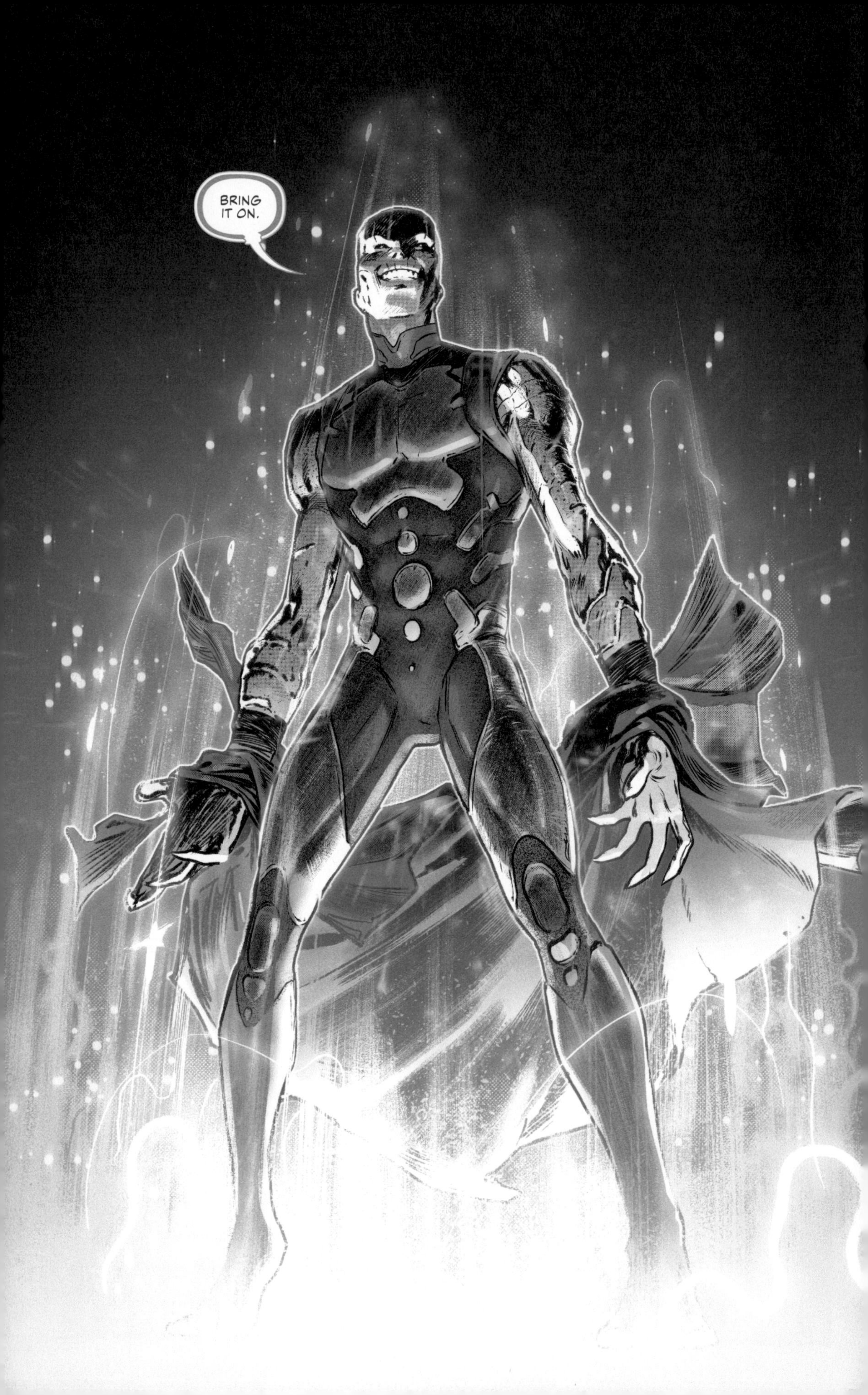
BRING IT ON.

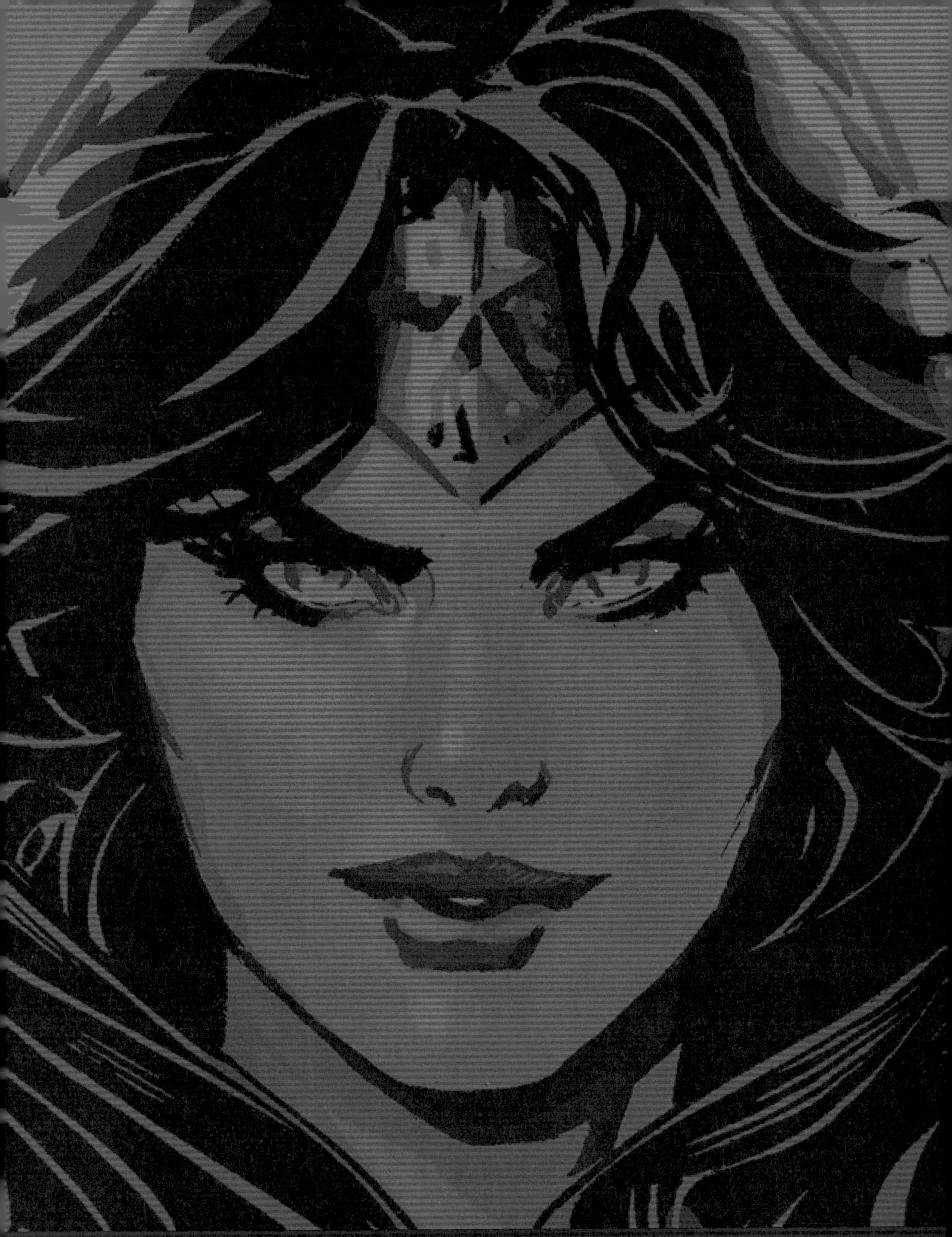

VARIANT COVER GALLERY

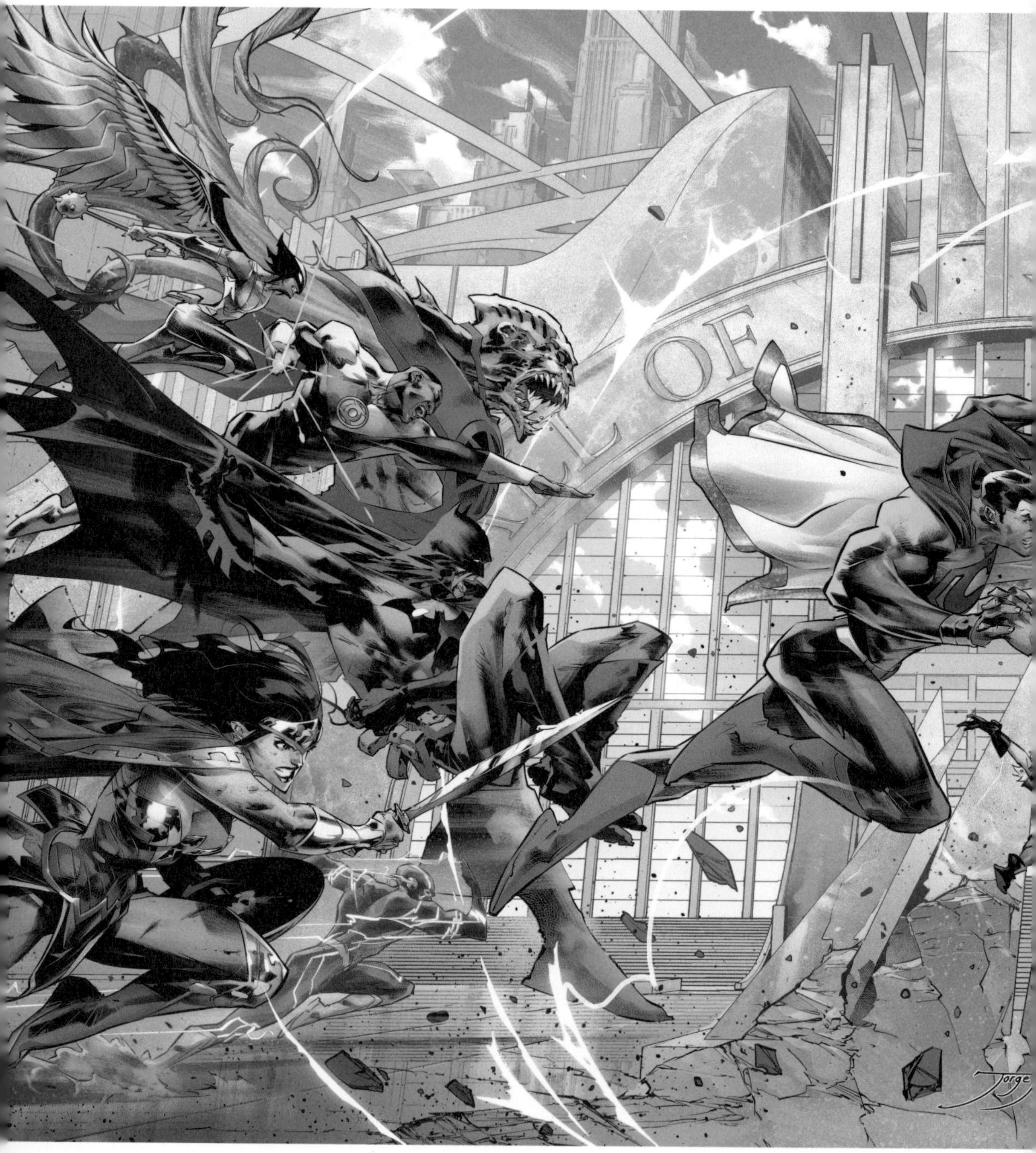

JUSTICE LEAGUE #20 variant cover triptych
by JORGE JIMENEZ and ALEJANDRO SANCHEZ

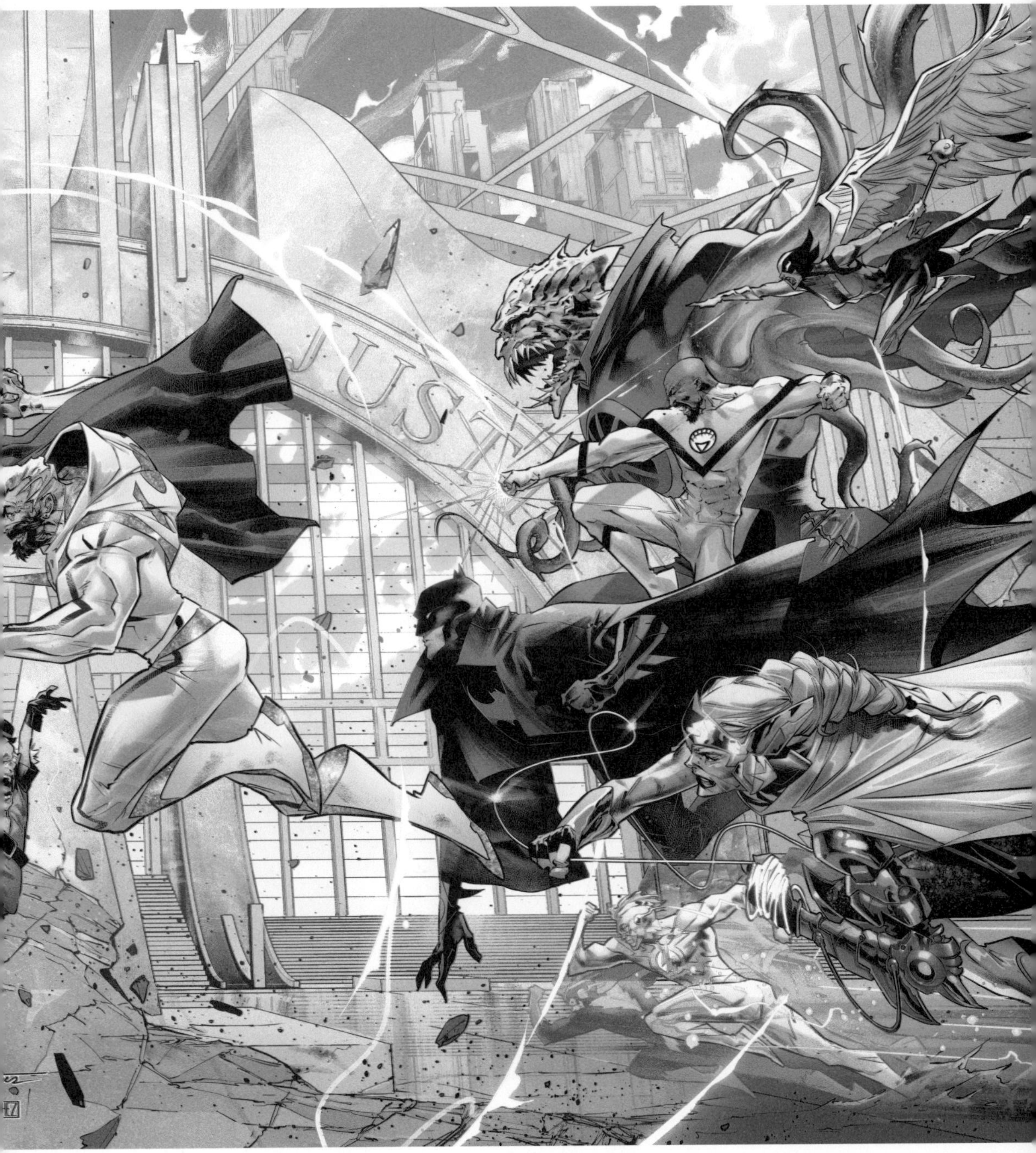
JUST

JUSTICE LEAGUE #19 variant cover
by ROB LIEFELD

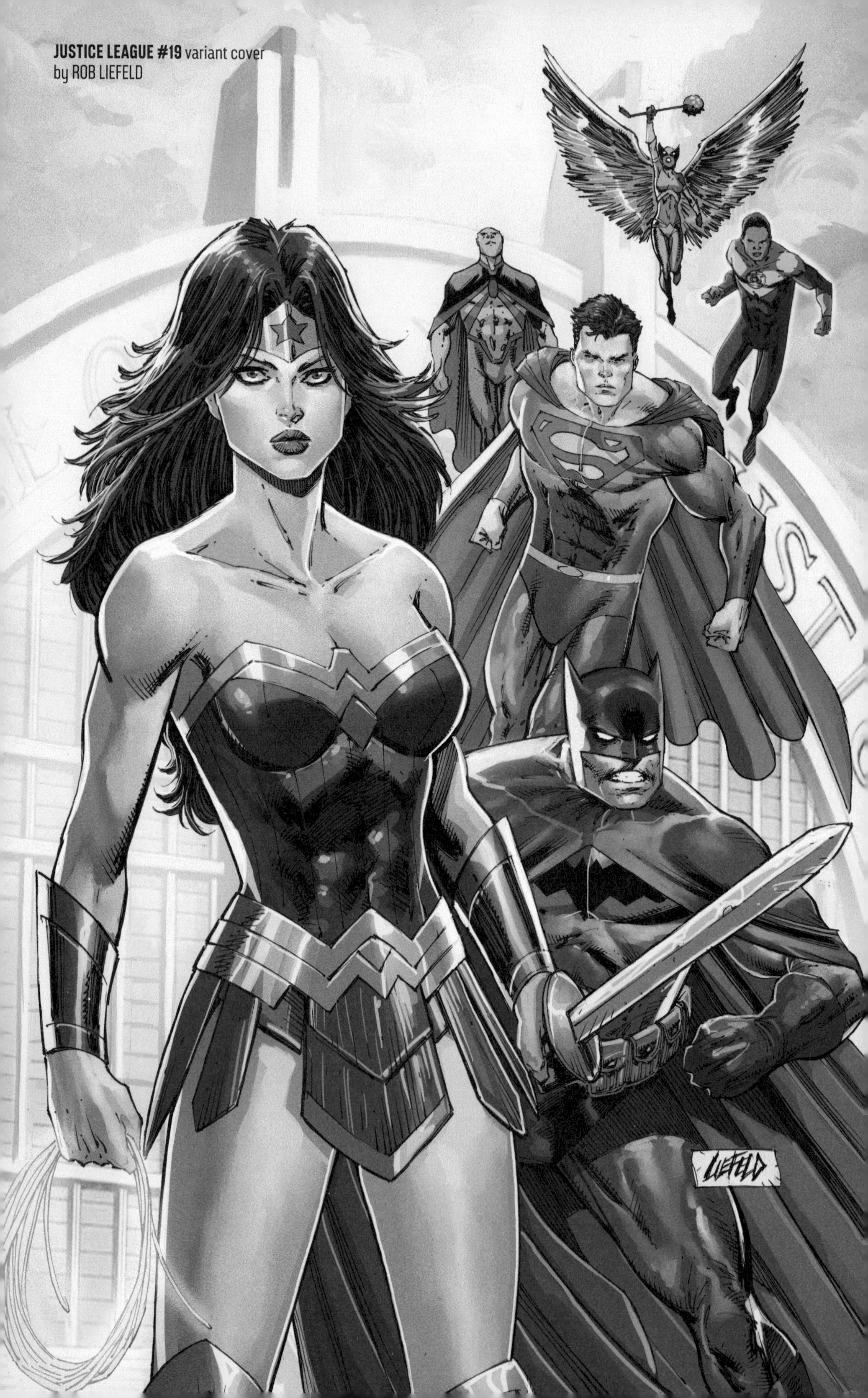
LIEFELD

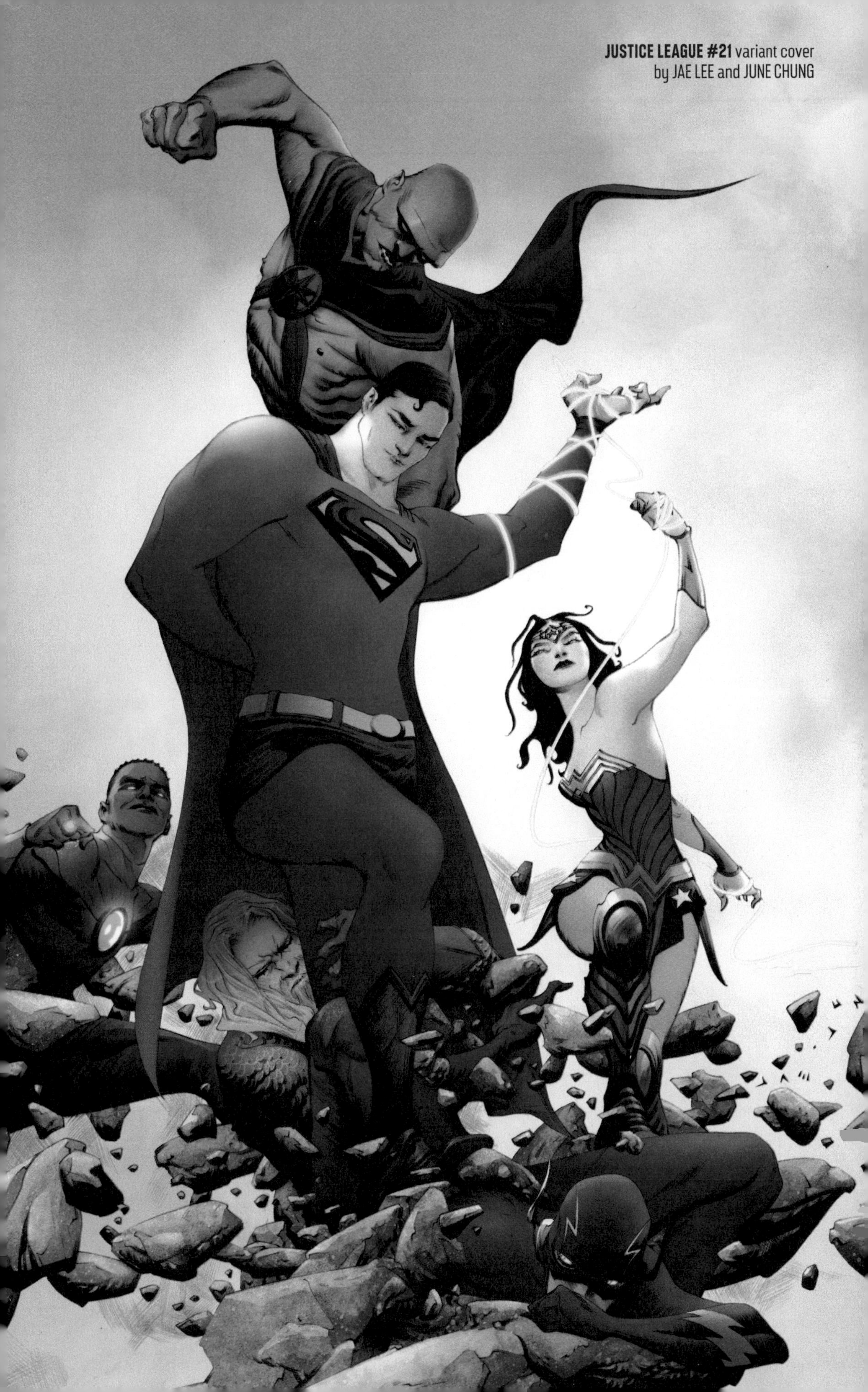

JUSTICE LEAGUE #21 variant cover
by JAE LEE and JUNE CHUNG

JUSTICE LEAGUE #22 variant cover
by LEINIL FRANCIS YU and ROMULO FAJARDO JR.

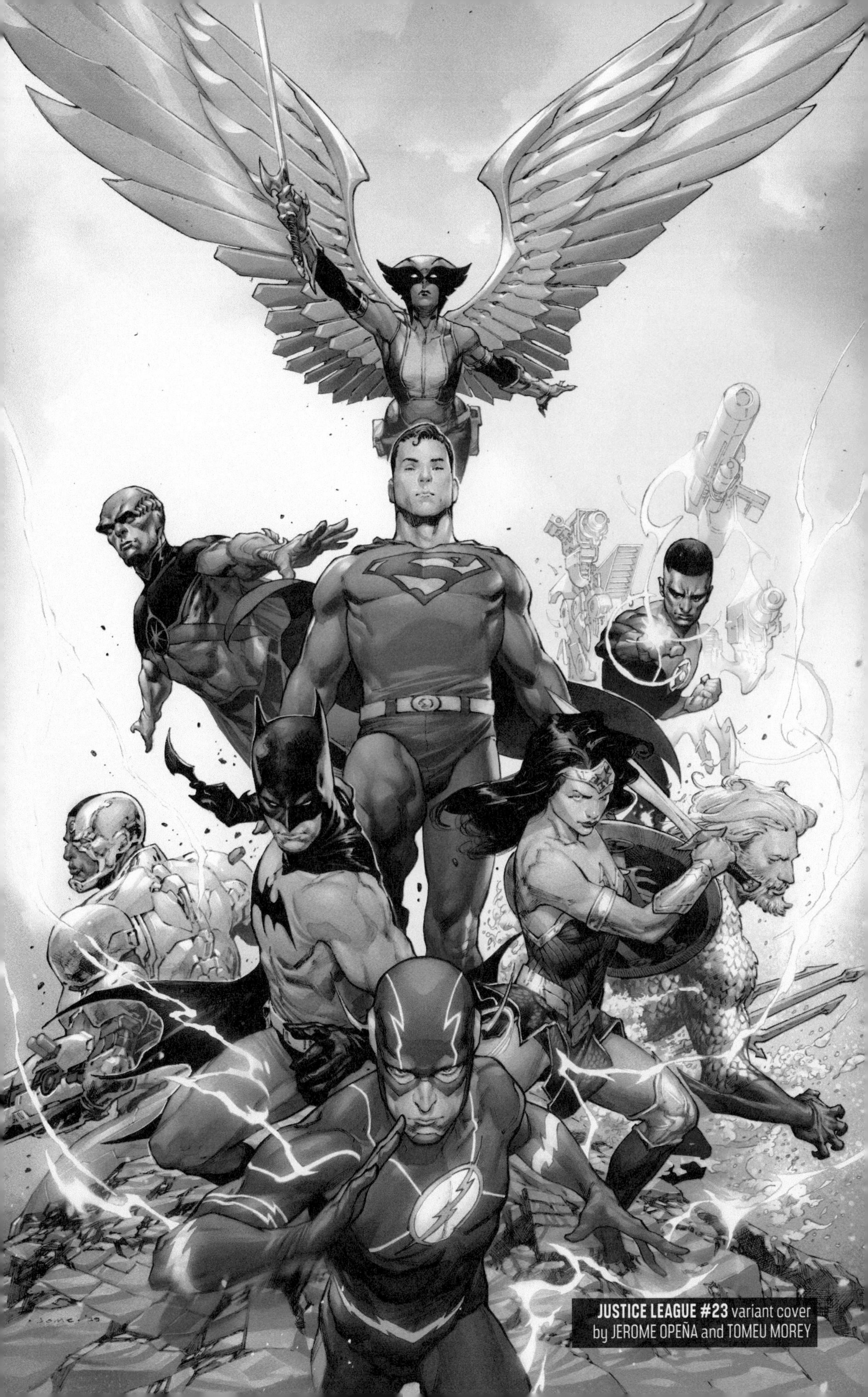

JUSTICE LEAGUE #23 variant cover
by JEROME OPEÑA and TOMEU MOREY

JUSTICE LEAGUE #24 variant cover
by JEROME OPEÑA and TOMEU MOREY

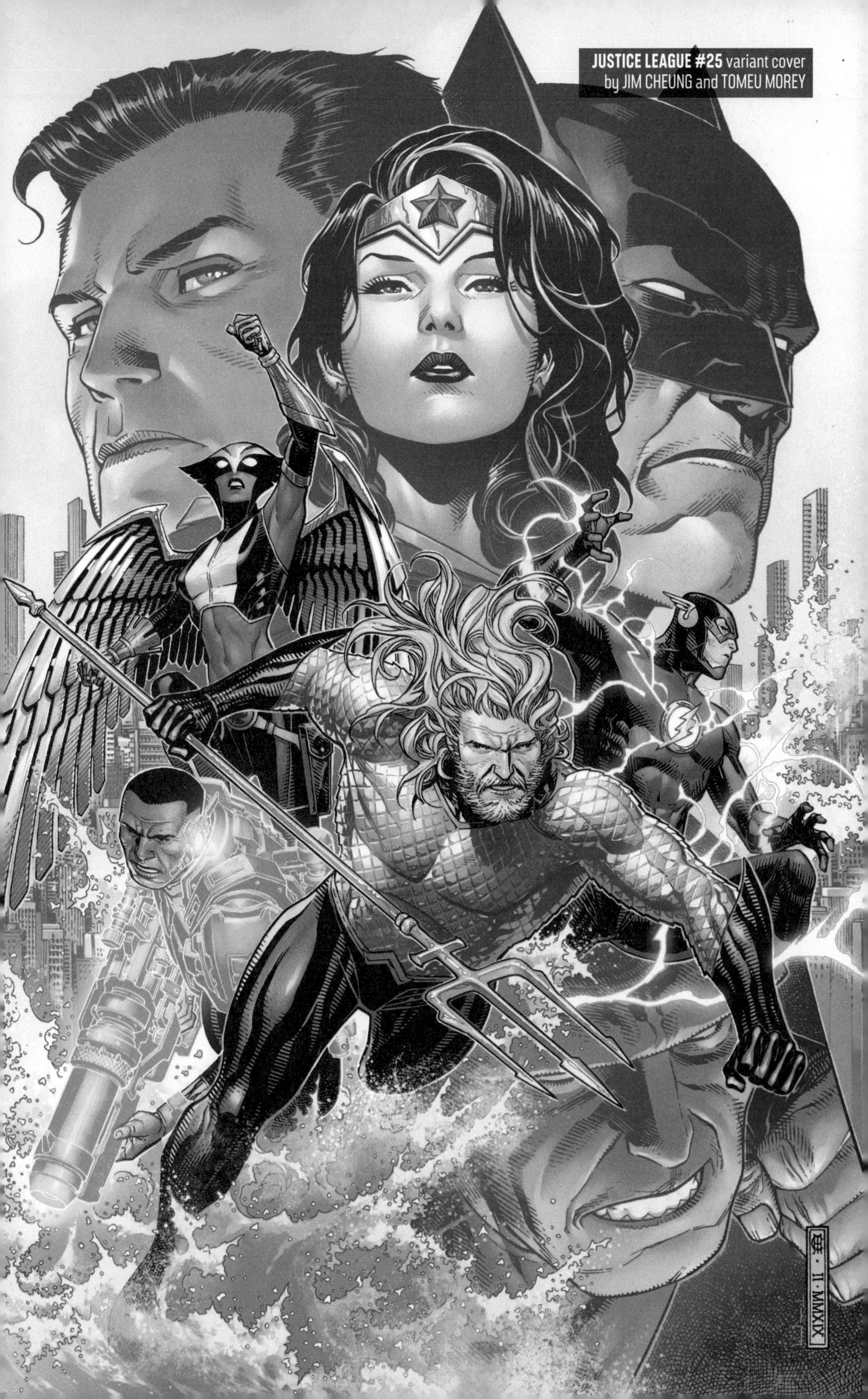
11 · MMXIX

JUSTICE LEAGUE #25 variant cover
by JIM CHEUNG and TOMEU MOREY

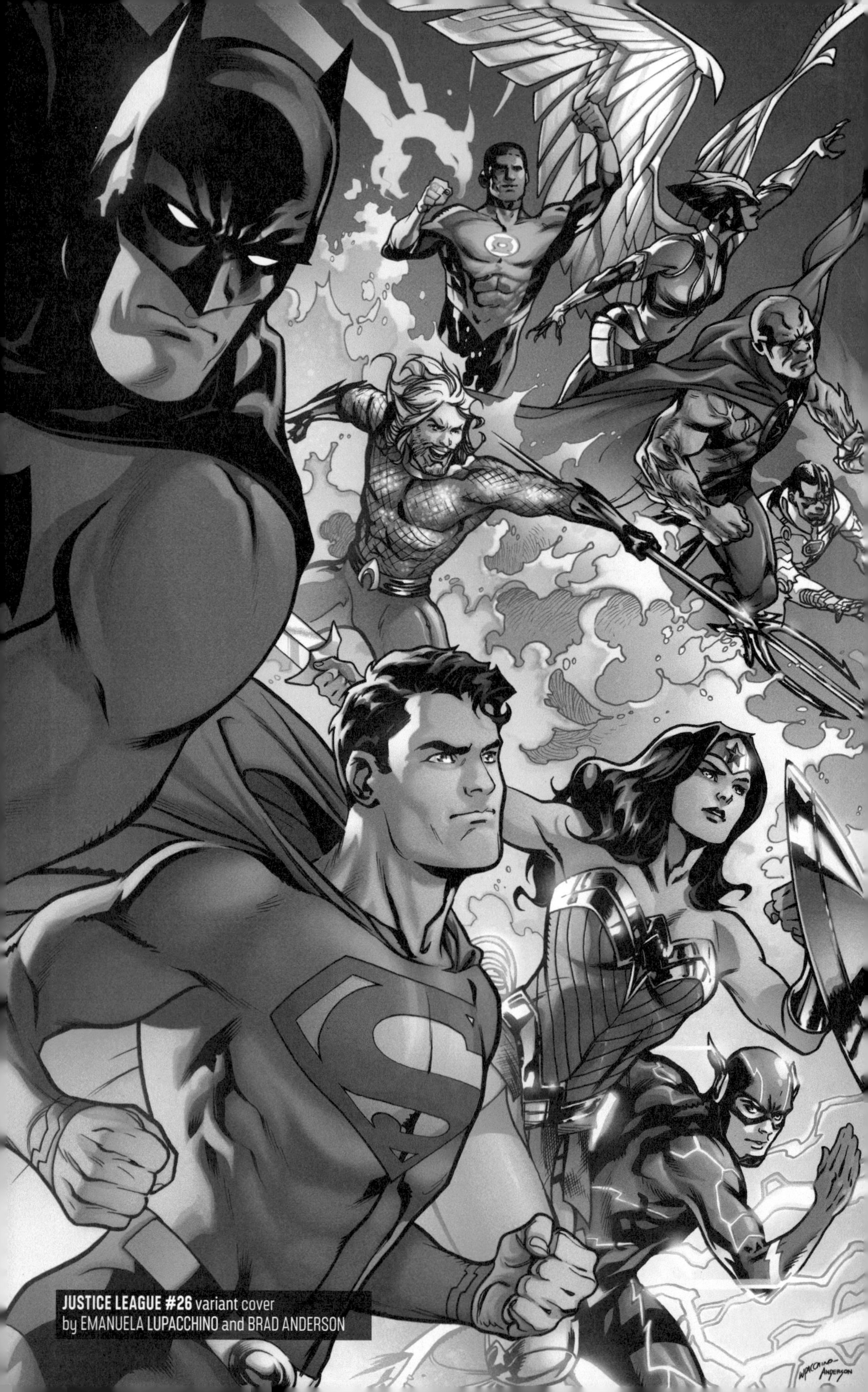

JUSTICE LEAGUE #26 variant cover
by EMANUELA LUPACCHINO and BRAD ANDERSON

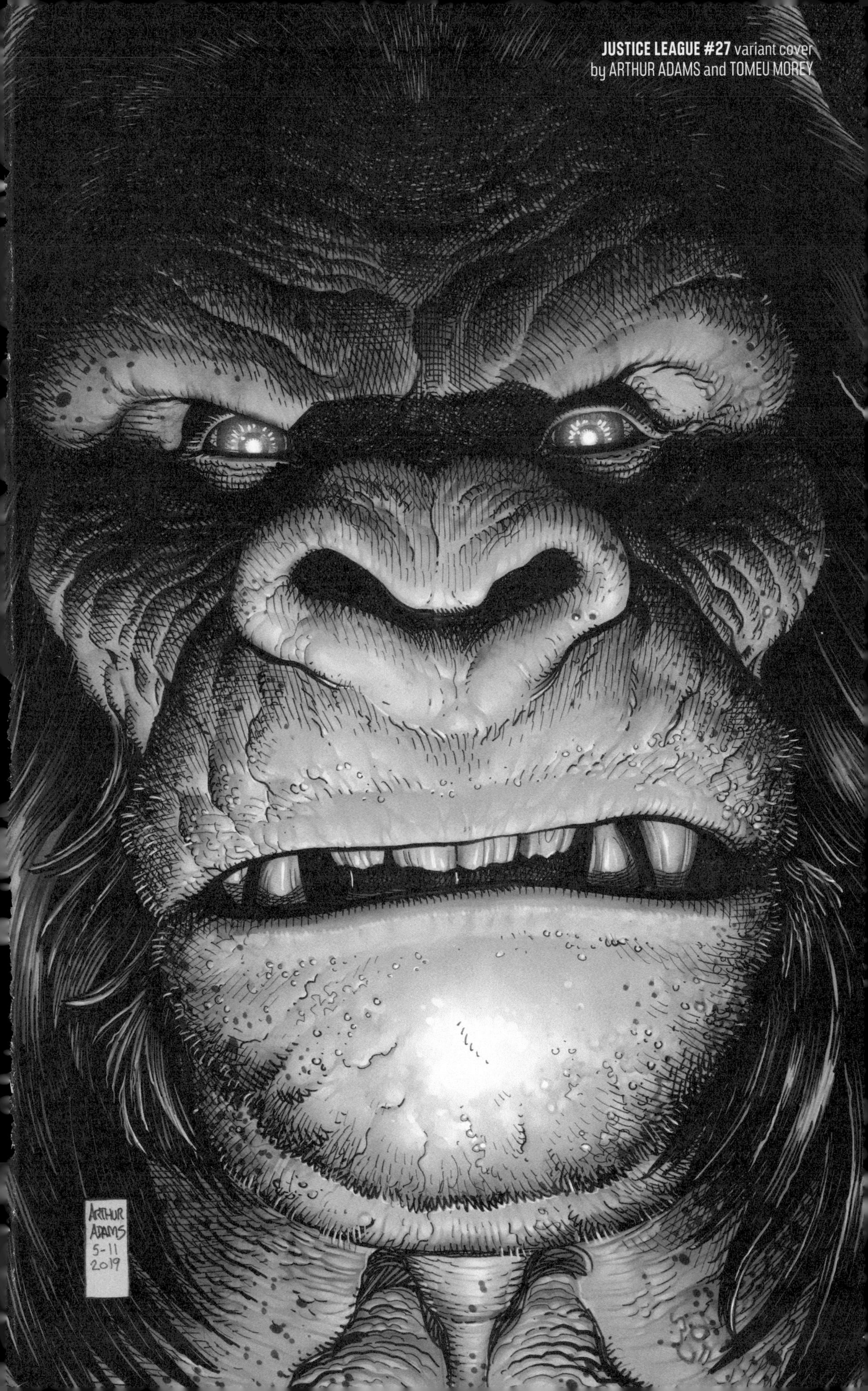
ARTHUR ADAMS 5-11 2019
JUSTICE LEAGUE #27 variant cover
by ARTHUR ADAMS and TOMEU MOREY

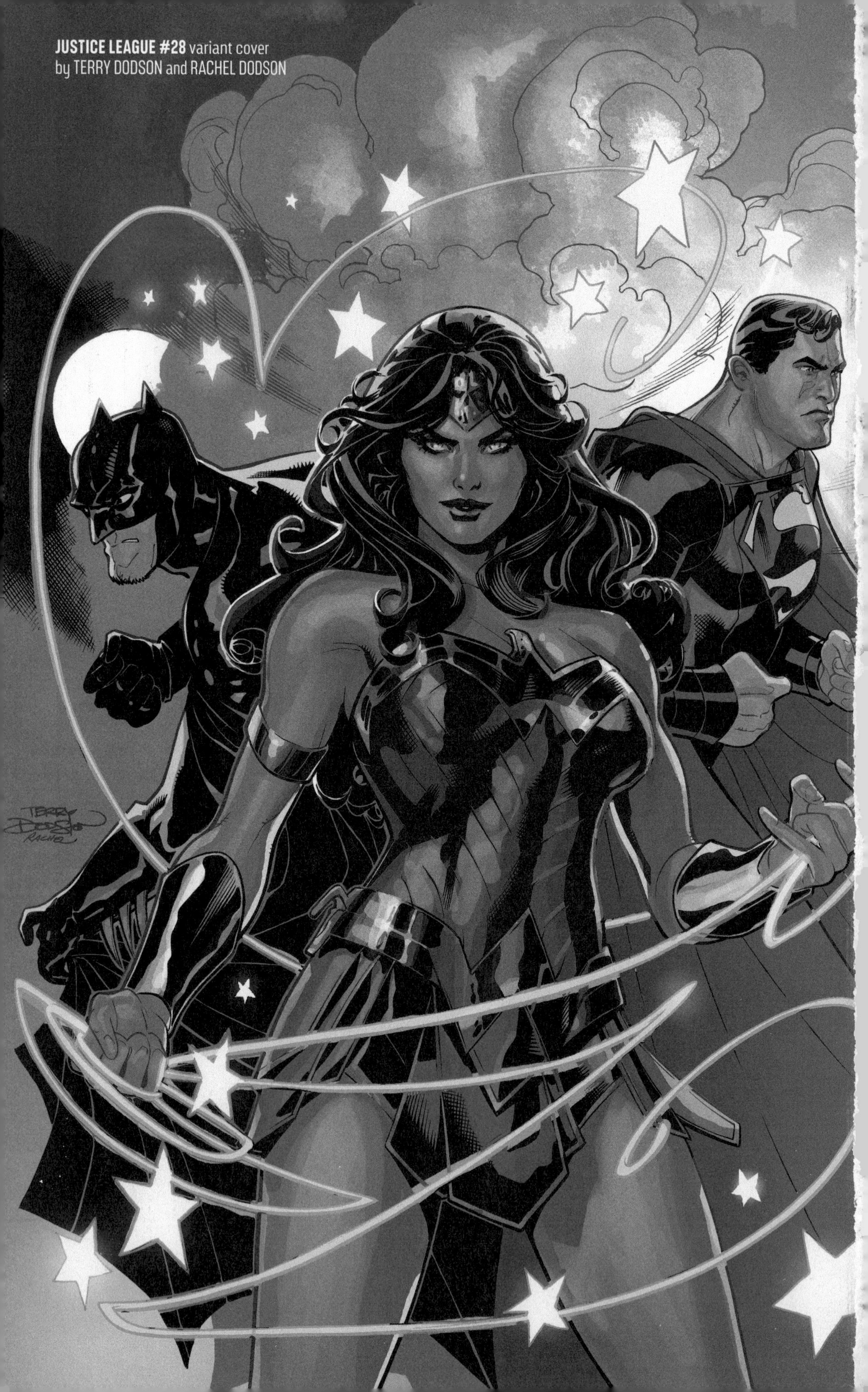

JUSTICE LEAGUE #28 variant cover
by TERRY DODSON and RACHEL DODSON